Cambridge Studies in Music

General Editors: John Stevens and Peter le Huray

The Music of the English Parish Church, Volume 1

The Music
of the
English Parish Church

NICHOLAS TEMPERLEY
PROFESSOR OF MUSIC, UNIVERSITY OF ILLINOIS

Volume 1

CAMBRIDGE UNIVERSITY PRESS

CAMBRIDGE

LONDON   NEW YORK   MELBOURNE

Published by the Syndics of the Cambridge University Press
The Pitt Building, Trumpington Street, Cambridge CB2 1RP
Bentley House, 200 Euston Road, London NW1 2DB
32 East 57th Street, New York, NY 10022, USA
296 Beaconsfield Parade, Middle Park, Melbourne 3206, Australia

First published 1979

Printed in Great Britain at the
University Press, Cambridge

Library of Congress Cataloguing in Publication Data
Temperley, Nicholas.
The music of the English parish church.
(Cambridge studies in music)
Bibliography: p.
Includes index.
1. Church music – England – History and criticism.
2. Church music – Church of England – History and
criticism. I. Title. II. Series.
ML3131.T44   783'.026'342   77–84811

ISBN 0 521 22045 9 volume 1
ISBN 0 521 22046 7 volume 2

Contents

Contents

Tables

Plates

(between pages 168 and 169)

1   Fifteenth-century rood-loft at South Warnborough (Hants)

The loft, surmounting the screen dividing the nave from the chancel, would have supported an organ and housed the lay singers. The rood-screen with its painting of the crucifixion was removed at the Reformation.
> Photo: Ray and Gillian Harris, 1977.

2   Fifteenth-century chancel stalls at Fressingfield (Suffolk)

Minor orders of clergy, including chantry priests and parish clerks, occupied these stalls, possibly with boy choristers in the front rows. On the patronal festival and other great occasions, polyphony was sung with the help of a portative organ.
> Photo: Ray and Gillian Harris, 1977.

3   Carmelite friars at mass in about 1395

A choir of four monks is shown singing as the priest begins to celebrate Holy Saturday Mass. (This is not a parochial service; no representation of parish church worship in England before the Reformation has been identified.)
> For discussion see Mc Kinnon: 30–1.
> Source: A missal from Whitefriars, London (British Library Add. 29704): fol. 6v. Original size.

4   The Puritan concept of baptism and communion, 1578

In baptism the minister wears a Geneva gown and reads from a book. At communion the people gather round a plain table rather than an altar, and the minister distributes bread to them standing.
> Source: [Richard Day], *A booke of Christian prayers*, [2nd edn], London, 1578 (STC 6429): fol. R1v(61v), R2r(62r). Original size.

5   A high-church ideal of communion in Queen Anne's time

The congregation once more kneels in front of an altar, enclosed by communion rails in a sanctuary, where the surpliced priest is blessing the elements. The apparition of Christ above, and the biblical texts cited, tend to support the doctrine of the real presence of Christ in the communion elements. But the tablet containing the ten commandments on the east wall serves as a reminder that this is a reformed protestant church.
> Source: Wheatly: frontispiece. Original size.

6   Communion at an Oxford church in late Georgian times

Another high-church representation, this time of an actual scene at St Peter-in-the-East, Oxford. The surpliced priest is reading the communion service to the small congregation kneeling at the rails, while the parish clerk, who has probably read the Epistle from the north side of the altar, enunciates the responses and amens, with little support from the people. A communion hymn may have been sung during the ceremony.

Source: John P. Neale & John Le Keux, *Views of the most interesting ... churches in Great Britain*, II, London, 1825: St Peter-in-the-East, Oxford, plate 2. (Original: 121 × 93 mm.)

7   John Day (1522–84), aged 39–40

Source: *The worckes of Thomas Becon*, III, London, 1563 (STC 1710): colophon. (Original: 180 × 131 mm.)

8   John Playford (1623–86/7), aged 40

Source: PC 23/4: frontispiece. (Original: 110 × 78 mm.)

9   William Tans'ur (*c*. 1700–83), aged 72

Source: PC 210: frontispiece. (Original: 75 × 90 mm.)

10   Dr Edward Miller (1735–1807), aged about 59

Source: Portrait painted and engraved by Thomas Hardy, from a copy at Doncaster parish church, undated, reproduced by kind permission of the vicar and churchwardens. The painting, which has not been heard of since 1855, may have been exhibited at the Royal Academy in 1794 as 'Portrait of a gentleman'. (Original: 168 × 138 mm.)

11   St James's square and church, Westminster, about 1720

Built in the 1680s to provide suburban dwellings for the nobility and wealthy gentry, the square was a planned community with the church as its centrepiece. The double row of houses behind the church is Piccadilly.

Source: Engraving by Sutton Nicholls, London, [*c*. 1720]. Original 178 × 128 mm.

12   St James's church, Westminster, looking west

The church, built in 1684, is shown before its partial destruction by bombing in 1940. It appears much as it was after erection of the organ presented by Queen Mary II in 1691, though the sides of the pews in the galleries were originally higher. The charity children sat on either side of the organ in the upper level of the west gallery.

Source: Print from a drawing by Leslie Wilkinson, 1904, reproduced in *The Builder*, 24 December 1904 (Greater London Council Print Collection: Westminster DD25488, here reduced to about half size).

13   The charity school of St John, Wapping

The school was founded in 1695 for 60 boys and 60 girls. This building, which is still standing, was erected in 1760 with separate entrances for girls and boys, each surmounted by a statue of a child in charity uniform.

Source: J. Burford & J. D. M. Harvey, *Some lesser known architecture of London*, New York, 1926: plate 20.

14   A service at St Martin-in-the-Fields in 1747

The church was rebuilt in 1724. Hogarth's print shows it in reverse, with the three-decker pulpit on the south side of the nave instead of the north, as it really was. A metrical psalm before or after sermon is in progress, with the preacher in the pulpit, the rector or curate in the middle-level reading desk, and the parish clerk at least nominally leading the psalm singing from the lower level. The figures in the west gallery are probably charity children.

Source: Engraving by William Hogarth, *The Industrious 'Prentice performing the duty of a Christian,* [London], 30 September 1747. (Original: 113 × 155 mm.)

15 A northern parish choir in 1700

A choir of about ten singers, including two women, sing a metrical psalm under the direction of the parish clerk, while the sexually segregated congregation sits on facing benches. The parson is not to be seen, probably because he is changing vestments. (For further discussion see p. 154.)

Source: Engraving by F. H. van Hove, PC 47: frontispiece. Original size.

16 A village choir in about 1770

In this satirical picture, eight men and youths sing from a single book in a singers' pew or gallery, the leader holding a pitchpipe. The man with a white wig is possibly the parish clerk or singing teacher. The mouths are distorted to suggest uncouth singing.

Source: Print by Samuel H. Grimm; London, [*c.* 1770]. (Original: 178 × d136 mm.)

17 Sunday matins in a village church in 1790

The chaotic scene, including the cleaner's ladder and mop, may be a product of satirical exaggeration. It shows the parson standing inert in his reading desk while the clerk just below him leads a metrical psalm. A few members of the congregation are singing, but the music is evidently dominated by the singers in the gallery to the accompaniment of a flute, violin and bassoon.

Source: Print by J. Wright, 1790. (Original: 101 × 161 mm.)

18 A country choir in 1823

The choir, made up of young men and girls and a row of Sunday school children, is under observation by Mrs Read (at left), who notes some flirtation and a tendency for the choir director to use his baton to discipline the children.

Source: Cameron: frontispiece. (Original: 49 × 73 mm.)

19 The church at Puddletown (Dorset), looking down from the west gallery

The combined pulpit and reading desk, pews, and west gallery were built in 1635, probably under pressure from Archbishop Laud. Later the gallery was used by the choir and band, including Thomas Hardy's grandfather who played the cello (Puddletown is the 'Weatherbury' of Hardy's Wessex novels). The music desks can be seen. In 1845 the band, consisting of piccolo, 2 clarinets, bassoon, and 2 'bass viols' (cellos), was replaced by a barrel organ.

Photo: Ray and Gillian Harris, 1977.

20 Morning service at St John the Evangelist, Westminster, about 1830

The church, now known as St John the Evangelist, Smith Square, was built in 1728 for a new parish carved out of St Margaret's, Westminster. It had no organ until 1750. In this undated engraving it is probable that the sermon is in progress, while a gowned verger shows a latecomer to her seat. Charity children fill the organ gallery under the watchful eyes of male and female governors.

> Source: Engraving by E. Page, Holborn, [*c.* 1830] (Westminster City Library, Box 51, no. 41B). (Original width 241 mm.)

21 Charity children going to St Paul's cathedral, about 1840

Escorted by beadles the children are walking westward along Cheapside towards the cathedral, where five or six thousand children from the city parishes met on a day in June each year from 1801 to 1877 to sing and chant the music of a special service. The church of St Mary-le-Bow, rebuilt by Wren, is prominent.

> Source: Wood engraving, [*c.* 1840] (Guildhall Library, London: Noble C.49). Original size.

22 The choir at Bow Brickhill (Bucks), about 1840

The parish choirmaster conducts from a large book, while the children sing the metrical psalm or hymn, probably from the backs of their prayer books. Men and women singers are supported by a clarinet, bassoon and 'bass viol'. The painting, 'A village choir' by Thomas Webster, was exhibited at the Royal Academy in 1847.

> Source: Photographic reproduction in Macdermott (1948): facing p. 7.

23 A village choir rehearsal in 1863

The choir is rehearsing the Christmas anthem in the imaginary village church of 'Layndon'. There are five instruments (flute, clarinet, bassoon, violin and cello), all played by men; the church has no organ or harmonium. The anthem is rehearsed for three weeks by Mr Screebes, the parish clerk. The curate, with top hat in hand, is taking part; the seated figure in the foreground is the local doctor.

> Source: Drawing by A. Hunt, *Illustrated London News*, 19 December 1863.

24 Singing galleries and barrel organ at Wissington (Suffolk)

The organ, made by John Gray of London in 1839, was acquired by subscription and placed between two small musicians' galleries. It had 4 stops, 27 notes, and 3 barrels with ten tunes on each, and was hand blown by a separate mechanism.

> Source: Boston & Langwill: Plate 4. Reproduced by kind permission of Mr Langwill.

25 Barrel organ at Shelland (Suffolk)

The player is Robert Armstrong, who was parish clerk at Shelland from 1885 to 1935, and was succeeded by his son; the barrel organ is still used for church services, after restoration in 1956 by Noel Mander. It has 6 stops, 31 notes, and 3 barrels with twelve tunes on each.

> Source: Boston & Langwill: Plate 11. Reproduced by kind permission of Mr Langwill.

26 Halifax parish church looking west, 1840

The medieval church was provided with galleries early in the seventeenth century to accommodate the growing population. The gallery between the nave and the long chancel housed first the singers and then the organ, erected in 1764 by public subscription, at the instigation of Henry and Joah Bates, sons of Henry Bates, parish clerk of Halifax. It is seen here in 1840, with the three-decker pulpit also still in place; the organ was not moved to the chancel until 1878.

Source: Engraving by P. Ganci after William Moore jun. of York, Halifax, 1840. Reproduced by permission of Calderdale Central Library. Original size.

27 A choral procession in a London suburban church, 1865

The church of St Peter, Vauxhall was newly built when this engraving was prepared; this is one of the very few representations of a surpliced choir from the first half of Victoria's reign. A choir of 30 men and boys sang fully choral services with Gregorian chants in 1867 (Mackeson, 1866–95: 1867) but no organ was installed until 1870 (:1873, p. 90). It is probable that a processional hymn was sung as the choir entered the chancel. The church is a typical Victorian modification of the medieval plan, with a chancel wide enough to accommodate choir stalls without lessening the visibility of the altar.

Source: *The Builder* 23 (1865): 627. Original size.

28 Opposition to Tractarian innovations, 1866

The engraving, 'Parishioners astonished at the appearance of their restored parish church', is from a scarce book of anti-Tractarian propaganda. The design of the altar resembles that of Plate 27. It is difficult to say what liturgical moment is represented: the priest and his assistant have turned eastward, but the choir, apparently of young men in surplices and bands, is singing and facing inwards.

Source: *St Dorothy's home: A tale for the times,* London: English Protestant Printing & Publishing Society, 1866. Reproduced by kind permission of Dr Bernarr Rainbow, Richmond, Surrey. Original size.

29 The Reverend Thomas Helmore (1811–70)

Source: Oil portrait by an unknown artist, at the College of S. Mark and S. John, Plymouth. Copied here from Rainbow, 1970, by kind permission of Dr Rainbow.

30 The Reverend Dr John Bacchus Dykes (1823–76)

Source: Fowler: frontispiece.

31 The Reverend Percy Dearmer (1867–1936)

The photograph was taken while he was incumbent of St Mary-the-Virgin, Primrose Hill, Hampstead.

Source: A photograph in the archives of St Mary-the-Virgin, Primrose Hill, reproduced by kind permission of the vicar and churchwardens.

32 Sir Sydney H. Nicholson (1875–1947)

Source: A photograph in the possession of the Royal School of Church Music, reproduced by kind permission.

33 The church of St Mary Summerstown, Wandsworth, in about 1910

The church was built in 1903–4 to an open modern design by Godfrey Pinderton (architect), and is a typical low-church interior of its date. The east wall still has boards on which the Lord's prayer and commandments are inscribed, and there is little ornament of any sort. Nevertheless, there are choir stalls in the chancel, communion rails, and an organ in the south chancel which (in this case) is also the base of the church tower.

Source: Sir C. Nicholson & C. Spooner, *Recent ecclesiastical architecture*, London, [1910/11]: 232.

34 The church of St Mary-the-Virgin, Primrose Hill, Hampstead, in 1937

This church has been Anglo-Catholic throughout its history. It was built in 1872 as a chapel of ease in the parish of St Saviour, Eton Road, and consecrated as a parish church in 1885. Percy Dearmer, vicar from 1901 to 1915, made a number of alterations, including the whitening of the interior walls and the erection of the reredos (1914). When this photograph was taken, on Easter Day (March 28) 1937, Dearmer's alterations and ceremonial innovations were intact. It depicts the censing of oblations while a deacon steadies the stem of the chalice. Easter hymns indicated on the hymn board are from *The English hymnal*, which grew from the practice at this church.

Photo: J. & A. Ducrow, Hampstead, reproduced by kind permission of the Reverend Francis Stephens.

35 Chalfont St Giles and District Choirs Festival meeting at Amersham (Bucks), 1934

The representatives of thirteen choirs are shown here in front of Amersham parish church on 2 June 1934. About 150 are present, including clergy, men and boys (all surpliced), and women (some surpliced, others in day dress). It was the 4th annual gathering of the association, which was formed under the auspices of the Society for English Church Music. The music sung on this occasion was that of the S.E.C.M. Choirbook no. 2.

Source: *English Church Music* IV (1934): facing p. 79; reproduced by kind permission of the Royal School of Church Music.

36 The choir of Badwell Ash (Suffolk) in 1972

Photo: West Suffolk Newspapers Ltd., reproduced by permission.

37 A service at St Luke, Brighton in 1978

A group of instruments is regularly used to accompany the hymns at this church: shown here are an electric guitar (with speakers on a shelf above), piano, cornet, trumpet, trombone, two flutes, and electronic organ.

Photo: Ray and Gillian Harris, 1978.

38 The church of Holy Trinity, Twydall (Kent)

The church was built in 1964 in a suburb of Gillingham. It seats just over 300 including 30 choir members, who sit in the front rows of the four bays of seats. The congregation is brought close to the altar, pulpit, reading desk and organ, which are all in one corner of the square-shaped building. A small 'lady chapel' is behind the altar, and at times when the church is full the congregation completely surrounds the altar.

Photo: Ray and Gillian Harris, 1978.

Figures

Preface

In 1967 Andrew Porter asked me to review Ralph Daniel's book, *The anthem in New England before 1800*, for *The Musical Times*. I was astonished to learn that the early American music of the Billings school was founded on a flourishing tradition in English parish churches whose very existence I had never suspected, and could never suspect from reading any book on English music then in print. The more I looked, the more surprised and fascinated I became. One thing led to another; I could not resist exploring parish church music further, following the trail back to the middle ages, and forward to the present age.

This book is the outcome. It is offered not as an apologia for neglected gems of English art, still less as a plea for their revival, but simply as a work of musical history. It tells what the music was like in English parish churches of different kinds at each period; traces the many changes in this music; and tries to explain why they occurred. The reader is likely to find that large parts of the book describe music and musical practices that are entirely unfamiliar: they have long ago disappeared, and have not been described in any recent writing. Indeed, by far the greatest part of my research has been concerned with establishing facts. Because these facts may excite surprise and even doubt, I have provided full documentation for them; to support generalisations I have given statistical information in tables and appendices. In addition, the music volume provides complete pieces or movements to illustrate the practice of each period. But I do not pretend to discuss, evaluate, or represent the contributions of the individual composers who, particularly during the last hundred and fifty years, have provided original music for parish church use. Some pieces in the music volume may be found suitable for revival; I hope they will; but this is incidental to their purpose. Others are already well known.

Perhaps it is surprising that the music of the English parish church has never been fully chronicled, when we recall that until recently it was the only regular, formal musical experience for perhaps half the population of England. But most books on music, especially those published in England, are about great works of art; the history of music is presented only as a setting for these. So we find that cathedral music has been treated extensively by many authors over the last century, while parish church music, which has a low output of musical masterpieces, has attracted few writers. No general history of English music gives more than passing attention to the parish church; only one history of English church music, Kenneth Long's, does so; only one general history of English worship, Horton Davies's, gives more than passing attention to music. For scholars who are not English, the Anglican Church is an insular aberration, deserving little notice. It found no place in the standard general history of protestant church music, by Friedrich Blume, until this was translated into English, when a short chapter was allotted to Anglican cathedral and parochial music combined: even then, nothing like Blume's comprehensive and detailed treatment of Lutheran music could be provided in the space available. Some recent books devoted to particular periods (le Huray; Dearnley) have looked into parish church music in some detail, and one book-length study of the music in one period has been published (Rainbow), written from the point of view of a particular party in the Church. Much attention has been lavished on the English hymn and hymn tune, but its purpose has been either to trace the origin of particular texts and tunes (Frere & Frost), to provide the bibliographical tools for such a task (Julian; Frost), or to make a critical assessment of hymns and their tunes (L. Benson; Routley, 1957). Such studies have generally concentrated on the printed sources of hymn texts and tunes, rarely going beyond them for evidence of how, where, and when hymns were sung.

The choice of the *parish* church may seem arbitrary: there was of course no absolute musical barrier separating parish churches from other Anglican churches on one side, or from nonconformist churches on the other. But the field had to be limited in some way. I soon found that the music of parish churches alone was vast enough, and varied enough, to tax my powers of organisation and description to their limits. And the distinction is convenient. It is at least relatively easy to decide what is and what is not a parish church, even though it is not always easy to decide what is or is not parish church music. Parish churches have had a certain function, well defined by law and custom, from time immemorial; this is not true of nonconformist chapels. Cathedral music has already been thoroughly investigated and described. I have therefore considered the music of cathedrals, private chapels, and nonconformist chapels only when it has a bearing on the main subject, though I have treated chapels of ease and other subordinate Anglican churches within a parish as if they were parish churches.

The heart of this book deals with the period from 1549 to 1965, when (with two interruptions) the law required the celebration in parish churches of the services set forth in the Book of Common Prayer. For the period before the Reformation, the evidence is very limited, and cannot easily be extended: Frank Harrison has said about all that can be said on the subject in seven pages. As for the present time, it would be impractical to attempt to judge or even summarise the use of experimental liturgies. It may be thought that the history of parish church music offers valuable hints about what is advisable today. But such conclusions are not for me to draw.

Although I hoped to discover every important or widespread phenomenon in the history of parish church music, I could not investigate the musical history of every parish church. For archival work I chose four contrasting regions: the West Riding of Yorkshire, which was hit by early industrialisation and changed rapidly from the eighteenth century onwards; the county of Dorset, which has changed relatively little over the centuries; central London, which has had its own unique history; and the cathedral city of York. In these areas I tried to build a complete picture by consulting as many original documents as possible. For Sussex I was able to benefit from the archival work of Canon K. H. Macdermott, and for Norfolk from that of Dr A. H. Mann and Canon Noel Boston. Many other areas await further researches, which may, for all I know, uncover local movements in parish church music that differ from anything described in this book. However, I have been able to use a fair sample of published transcriptions of archives from parishes all over the country; and the printed collections of church music, especially in the eighteenth century, come from many localities.

In dealing with the large quantity of parish church music between the Reformation and 1800 I have made use of two thematic indexes now in progress at the University of Illinois, one of psalm tunes, the other of parochial anthems. It is hoped eventually to make these indexes complete for English parish church music up to 1800, then to incorporate American sources.

In a book which is mainly designed to establish a factual record, there is a danger of clogging the narrative with so many facts and references that it becomes unreadable. I have tried to keep up the flow of the text with as few interruptions as possible, while still giving the reader easy access to the sources. Footnotes have been kept to a minimum. All source citations are given in parentheses in the text; I should explain that (:88) indicates a page number in a source just referred to, or in the only listed work by an author just mentioned. Readers who do not want to refer to the sources should quickly form the habit of skipping over these references. The bibliography is in three sections: (1) manuscript sources (MS); (2) printed collections of music (PC); (3) other sources, including dissertations and gramophone records.

To avoid cluttering the text with the dates of birth and death of persons mentioned, I have supplied these in the index, with a brief identification of each person. All printed collections of music listed chronologically in the 'PC' section of the bibliography are listed under the compiler's name in the index, which also gives the counties (pre-1972) of all English places listed, other than large cities. In addition, it includes a glossary of technical terms. Because some readers may be more familiar with musical terms than with ecclesiastical ones, and others *vice versa*, I have thought it best in general not to define ordinary technical terms in the text, but to provide definitions in the index.

In quoting from sources I have modernised spelling and capitalisation everywhere, but have usually left punctuation intact: where the punctuation has been altered (for the sake of clarity), the fact is noted. Italics and other differentiated types have been retained unless they appear to have been purely decorative in the source. The spelling of surnames has been consistently modernised (Marbeck, East, Beacon rather than Merbecke, Est(e), Becon). But in the titles of books, both in the text and the bibliography, original spellings and abbreviation marks (but not capitalisation or letter forms) have been retained. No distinctions of churchmanship are implied by the use of the words 'priest', 'clergyman', 'minister', or 'parson'. The English canticles (Te deum, Magnificat) are distinguished by type from their Latin equivalents (*Te deum*, *Magnificat*).

It is a pleasure to record the generous co-operation and advice I have had from colleagues and from scholars working in related fields. In particular I should like to thank Dr Hugh Baillie, Professor Ian Bent, Mrs Betty Birkby, Dr Magnus Black, Dr Bertrand Bronson, Dr Alan Buechner, Dr Bunker Clark, Dr Richard Crawford, Mr Brian Crosby, the late Dr Charles Cudworth, Dr Ralph Daniel, Dr Yvonne Davies, Miss Margaret Dean-Smith, Dr Robert Illing, Dr Harry Diack Johnstone, Dr Gerald Knight, Dr Karl Kroeger, Dr Donald Krummel, Mr Lyndesay G. Langwill, Dr Peter le Huray, Mr Irving Lowens, Dr James Mc Kinnon, Mr Mason Martens, Mr Oliver Neighbour, Dr Bernarr Rainbow, Mr Derek Shute, Dr Alan Smith, Dr Watkins Shaw, Mr William Tallmadge, Mr Norman Tildesley, Professor Michael Tilmouth, Dr Tom Ward, Mr Roger Wilkes, Mrs Ruth Wilson, and Mr Paul Yeats-Edwards. Of the many books on which I have relied for ideas and opinions as well as information, Dr Horton Davies's masterly five-volume survey, *Worship and theology in England*, is second to none. I have also, as the reader will discover, made heavy use of Peter le Huray's *Music and the Reformation in England*, the late Louis F. Benson's *The English hymn*, and the works of the Reverend Erik Routley; while several bibliographical works have been virtually indispensable, especially A. W. Pollard and G. R. Redgrave's *Short title catalogue*, Maurice Frost's *English and Scottish psalm and hymn tunes* and his revision of Bishop Frere's *Historical edition of Hymns ancient and modern*, and Edith Schnapper's *British union-catalogue of early music*. Paul Yeats-Edwards's *English church music: a bibliography*, though it appeared too late for me to make the fullest use of it, is invaluable as the first comprehensive bibliography of this subject.

I cannot hope to thank individually the countless members of library staffs who have patiently dealt with my demanding enquiries, but the following must be singled out for help beyond the call of duty: Canon Ashworth, Ripon Minster Library; Mr Bernard Barr, York Minster Library; Mr R. M. Beaumont, Southwell Minster Library; Mr A. Betteridge, Halifax Central Library; Mr Carey S. Bliss, Henry E. Huntington Library, San Marino (California); Miss G. E. Coldham, British and Foreign Bible Society; Miss V. H. Cummings, British Library; Miss Cole, New York Public Library; Mr Donovan Dawe, Guildhall Library, London; Mr Roger Duce, National Library of Scotland; Mr A. R. B. Fuller, St Paul's Cathedral Library; Miss Jean Geil, University of Illinois Music Library; Miss M. E. Holmes, Dorset Record Office; Mr Trevor Kaye, Wren Library, Trinity College, Cambridge; Mr Alfred Kuhn, Yale University Music Library; Mr William McClellan, University of Illinois Music Library; Miss Dorothy McCulla, Birmingham Public Library; Mr D. J. McKitterick, Cambridge University Library; Mr W. R. Macdonald, Aberdeen University Library; Mr Frederick Nash, and his assistants, Mrs Mary Ceibert and Miss Louise Fitton, University of Illinois Rare Book Room; Mr Oliver Neighbour, British Library; Dr Watkins

Shaw, Parry Library, Royal College of Music; Dr D. M. Smith, Borthwick Institute, York; Mr W. J. Smith, Greater London Record Office; Mr N. V. Tilley, Bradford Central Library; Mr Malcolm Turner, British Library; Mr Peter A. Ward-Jones, Bodleian Library, Oxford; Mr H. J. R. Wing, Christ Church, Oxford; Mr Thomas Wright, Clark Memorial Library, University of California at Los Angeles.

With one exception I have received courteous co-operation from private collectors of books and music. Mr Theodore Finney and Mr James J. Fuld have been especially helpful. I much appreciated the facilities offered me to work in the private archives or collections of the Dorset County Museum, the Royal School of Church Music, the Sussex Archaeological Society, and the Worshipful Company of Stationers and Newspaper Makers. For the study of church records I feel particularly grateful for assistance, since parish clergy and officials are burdened with many responsibilities more immediate than the satisfying of antiquarian researchers. In this connection I would mention especially the Reverend Donald Collins, rector of Middleham; the Reverend W. H. Gibb, vicar of Winterbourne Abbas; the Reverend Canon Livermore, rector of Poole; the Reverend James Richardson, assistant curate of St Peter's collegiate church, Wolverhampton; the Reverend Francis Stephens, curate of St Mary-the-Virgin, Primrose Hill; the Reverend Charles Williams, vicar of Ifield; Mr J. E. Dunhill, verger of Leeds Parish Church; Mr Roger Job, precentor of Manchester Cathedral; Mr A. J. Roberts, churchwarden of St Dunstan, Stepney. Special thanks go to some twenty incumbents of churches in Sussex, whose replies to my questionnaire are the basis of the tables in Appendix 2, and one of whom, the Reverend G. H. Paton, rector of Ripe and Chalvington, helped me further in correspondence; and to Mrs S. E. Graney, who undertook the distribution of the questionnaires from the diocesan church office.

I have twice enjoyed the hospitality of the Royal School of Church Music, and the kind assistance of its successive directors, Dr Gerald Knight and Dr Lionel Dakers. I owe a special debt to Miss Katharine Pantzer, who generously placed her notes on the early Sternhold and Hopkins editions at my disposal, thus allowing me an advance look at her meticulous revision of the *Short title catalogue*, and also helped me with several thorny bibliographical problems. Mr Neely Bruce, by his enthusiastic and inspiring performances of some of the examples in the music supplement, first with the American Music Group and then with the Wesleyan Singers, has brought dead traditions to life and revealed unsuspected qualities in early English psalmody. Dr Wendell Williams brought his expertise as an engineer to bear on the problem of recovering the music of barrel organs from tune barrels detached from their organs, and made valiant efforts to transfer such information on to graph paper. Mr and Mrs Tucker, of Winterbourne Abbas, talked to me for many hours of their memories of Mrs Tucker's father, John Dunford, last survivor of the last of the Dorset church bands. The Reverend Jonathan Boston, vicar of Horsford (Norfolk), allowed me to play barrel organs in his father's collection and to make tape recordings. The Reverend William Oswald helped me to understand the nature of eighteenth-century parochial worship. Mr Denys

Parsons was good enough to spend many hours looking things up for me at the British Library, and Dr Hugh Macdonald did the same at the Bodleian Library. Ray and Gillian Harris travelled to many remote parishes to photograph churches for me, and are responsible for five of the plates used in this book (Pl. 1, 2, 19, 37 and 38).

I owe a great deal to the help of my successive research assistants at the University of Illinois: James Smith, Lynn Trowbridge, Richard Green, Dale Cockrell, Rodney Patterson, Dalyne Shinneman, Thomas McGeary, and Carl Manns; to Mrs Ruth Burnham, who typed out the manuscript with uncanny accuracy and unfailing patience; and to Mrs Pat Madsen, Mrs Vera Vogel, and Miss Valerie Woodring, who also helped with the preparation of the book and with correspondence relating to it.

The following have generously made materials available for photographic reproduction: The Trustees of the British Library (Pl. 3, 15, 18, 23, 30, 35, Figs. 4, 7); Calderdale Public Library (Pl. 26); Cambridge University Library (Fig. 1); The College of S. Mark and S. John, Plymouth (Pl. 29); the vicar and churchwardens of Doncaster parish church (Pl. 10); Greater London Council (Pl. 12); Guildhall Library, London (Pl. 21); Mr Lyndesay G. Langwill (Pl. 24, 25); the vicar and churchwardens of St Mary-the-Virgin, Primrose Hill, Hampstead (Pl. 31, 34,); Dr Bernarr Rainbow (Pl. 28); the Royal School of Church Music (Pl. 32); the University of Illinois (Pl. 4, 5, 7, 8, 9, 27, 33, Figs. 2, 3, 5, 6, 8); Westminster Public Libraries (Pl. 20).

Lastly, I am deeply indebted for financial assistance in this project to the National Endowment for the Humanities, to the University of Illinois Research Board and Center of Advanced Studies, and to the President and Fellows of Clare Hall, Cambridge. The University of Illinois Library greatly assisted my work by acquiring large numbers of microfilms of materials in other libraries.

NICHOLAS TEMPERLEY
Urbana, Illinois
September, 1978

Abbreviations

A	alto; anthems	MSS.	manuscripts
a, **a**	alto	O	independent organ part (see p. 365)
B	bass		
b, **b**	bass	O	independent organ part (see p. 365)
BO	barrel organ		
C	chants	o.	organist of
c	congregational part (see p. 365); crotchet; common time	P, **P**	psalms, psalm tunes (see p. 365)
c.	dotted crotchet	PC	printed collection of church music (see pp. 364–90)
C.M., CM	common metre (see p. 60)		
DCM	double common metre (see p. 60)	p.c.m.	parish church music
		pst	psalmodist
DLM	double long metre (see p. 60)	q	quaver
		q.	dotted quaver
DNB	*Dictionary of National Biography* (see p. 398)	R	responses to the ten commandments
		r.	rector of
DSM	double short metre (see p. 60)	R.S.C.M.	Royal School of Church Music
F.	Frost (M. Frost, *English and Scottish psalm tunes*: see p. 400)	S	soprano; service settings
		s	semibreve; soprano
		s	soprano
g, **g**	part in the G clef (see p. 365)	s.	dotted semibreve
		S.E.C.M.	School of English Church Music
H	hymn tunes (see p. 365)		
		S.M., SM	short metre (see p. 60)
I	independent instrumental part (see p. 365)	S.P.C.K.	Society for Promoting Christian Knowledge
		sq	semiquaver
i	optional instrumental part (see p. 365)	sq.	dotted semiquaver
		STC	*Short Title Catalogue* number (see p. 410)
L	liturgical settings (see p. 365)	T	tenor; set pieces (see p. 365)
L.M., LM	long metre (see p. 60)	t, **t**	tenor
m	minim	v.	verse; vicar of
m.	dotted minim	X	10 (see p. 60)
MS	manuscript source (see pp. 359–63)	Y	11 (see p. 60)
		Z	12 (see p. 60)
MS.	manuscript		

Abbreviations

Currency

Sums of money mentioned in the text are in terms of pounds, shillings, and pence

12 old pence (12d.) = 1 shilling (1s.)
20 shillings (20s.) = 1 pound (£1)
21 shillings (21s.) = 1 guinea (£1 1s.)
half-a-crown = 2s 6d

Counties

Beds	Bedfordshire	Middx	Middlesex
Berks	Berkshire	Norf.	Norfolk
Bucks	Buckinghamshire	Northants	Northamptonshire
Cambs	Cambridgeshire	Northumb.	Northumberland
Ches.	Cheshire	Notts	Nottinghamshire
Corn.	Cornwall	Oxon	Oxfordshire
Cumb.	Cumberland	Rut.	Rutland
Derbys.	Derbyshire	Salop	Shropshire
Devon	Devonshire	Som.	Somerset
Dorset		Staffs	Staffordshire
Durham		Suff.	Suffolk
Essex		Surrey	
Glos	Gloucestershire	Sussex	
Hants	Hampshire	Warks	Warwickshire
Here.	Herefordshire	Westm.	Westmorland
Herts	Hertfordshire	Wilts	Wiltshire
Hunts	Huntingdonshire	Worcs	Worcestershire
Kent		Yorks	Yorkshire
Lancs	Lancashire	E.R.	East Riding
Leics	Leicestershire	N.R.	North Riding
Lincs	Lincolnshire	W.R.	West Riding

1 The significance of parish church music

The higher developments of Christian art have generally been associated with great cathedrals, abbeys and royal chapels, rather than with the humbler churches of ordinary people. For this reason it is the former that have received the chief attention of critics and historians of the arts. But to the enquirer who is interested in religious art as a reflection of society, the local church, serving a small self-contained community, may be a more rewarding field of study.

Local churches, whether in town or village, are sensitive to social and economic changes and to movements of popular opinion; whereas they are remote from the influence of theological, aesthetic or political ideas that thrive in seats of government, learning, fashion, and commerce. Church authorities have usually failed to impose on local churches, for any length of time, the uniformity of worship that has often seemed to them desirable. Local customs have crept in, to provide forms of expression more spontaneous than those devised by a remote authority. For instance the rules for liturgical uniformity laid down by the Council of Trent, though strongly supported by powerful ecclesiastical and civil authorities, were widely ignored and departed from in many parts of the Catholic world. In France during the eighteenth century many dioceses published and used their own breviaries in open defiance of papal edict. Similarly, in Lutheran Germany at the same period a wide variety of local forms of worship was found. Some bodies, such as the Independents in England and New England, recognised this reality by making each congregation the supreme arbiter of its own practice.

The Church of England has often been contrasted with other protestant churches as a hierarchical and authoritarian body, with a fixed liturgy enforced by law. It is true that the form of worship has been laid down in minute detail by parliament ever since the Reformation; that this liturgy can be changed only by act of parliament, and in fact remained substantially the same for more than four hundred years apart from the interregnum of civil war and Commonwealth; and that any priest who departs significantly from the rubric can be, and has been, brought into line by episcopal reprimand, by court injunction, or in the case of persistent disobedience by deprivation of his office.

But closer study shows many cracks and holes in the monolith. The cathedrals, it is true, have preserved considerable continuity, though even there changes have not been unknown. But the cathedrals have been essentially aristocratic institutions, together with the royal and collegiate foundations which have shared their form of worship. Forming rather less than one per cent of the total number of Anglican places of worship, they have been insulated from the public, and indeed have had no clear social

1

function since the Reformation severed them from foundations of learning and education. In periods of religious zeal they have been maintained for the greater glory of God, and their rich endowments have been used in part to develop a school of musical composition and performance whose excellence needs no emphasis here. At other times the cathedrals and their endowments have been used chiefly for the comfort of the aristocratic dignitaries who controlled them. But at no time have they been in any immediate way responsive to public opinion: except indeed during the Puritan ascendancy, when public opinion stopped the choral services in cathedrals altogether.

When we turn from the cathedrals to the parish churches, where the great majority of Anglicans have performed their daily, weekly or yearly devotions, we find a very different story. The variety of forms of worship and of their manner of performance has been enormous. If the same observer could have attended a Sunday morning service at St Olave, Hart Street (Samuel Pepys's church) in 1670 and at St Alban, Holborn in 1870, to mention only London churches, he would have found it hard to see much in common between the two experiences, so totally would they have differed in character, atmosphere, and apparent meaning. And yet both would have been subject to substantially the same laws and the same liturgy. How can this be explained?

First it must be said that legal control over Anglican worship is really much weaker than it appears. Difficult as it has been to effect any legal changes in the liturgy, it has been equally difficult to discipline illegal departures from it. The machinery of the ecclesiastical courts was cumbersome and expensive, and their power to enforce judgments was weak. Parish priests were secure in the lifetime enjoyment of their livings, which could only be taken from them for extreme cases of neglect or immorality. The bolder spirits among the clergy often found that they could get away with open disregard of the law: the authorised service was widely ignored by Puritans in the sixteenth century, by ritualists in the nineteenth, and by reformers in the twentieth. If the congregation approved or acquiesced, prosecution was unlikely. If public clamour was loud enough to lead to legal prosecution of the offender, he might still escape through ingenious argument before the court. Rarely has an incumbent been actually deprived of his living on grounds of illegal deviations from the liturgy. Many rubrics were so widely disregarded, over so long a period, that any attempt to enforce them would have been futile: the rubric directing the use of the Athanasian creed is but one example. Others have been open to varying interpretation, so that it has been possible to change their practical effect in response to movements in public opinion, conveniently avoiding any upheaval. This process is found to some degree in all legal systems, but it is specially characteristic of England, with its unwritten constitution, its common law, and its judge-made law which often modifies the effect of statutes in a way which was not intended by the legislators, but which reflects the prevailing ideas of the moment. An excellent example was the introduction of hymn singing into Anglican services. It was never authorised by parliament, and until the end of the eighteenth century was generally regarded as illegal. But as more and more

Evangelical clergy introduced hymns with the approval of their congregations, the practice became respectable; and when in 1820 proceedings were actually taken against a clergyman for introducing hymns, the court declined to interfere. Since that time hymn singing has been an unquestioned part of Anglican worship, but it has never been thought necessary to authorise it by statute.

The reality would seem to be that the law protects the church from flagrant or eccentric deviations from the liturgy, but has only a mildly delaying effect on changes that are sanctioned by public opinion. And, if it has been hard to enforce the law against an unconventional parson, it has been next to impossible to control a wilful congregation, at least since the decline of royal power. In Elizabeth I's reign the archbishop's inspectors might succeed in intimidating a congregation, but after the Commonwealth a sturdy democratic spirit often asserted itself in public worship. It is difficult to stop a churchful of people from singing, and there are many instances of a congregation or even a small group of singers carrying the day against the wishes of their parson.

Thus actual departures from the liturgy, in the form of omissions and additions, have been frequent. But a far more significant kind of variety has been in those aspects of worship about which the rubric is silent or indeterminate. Chiefly this means the background against which the words of the liturgy are heard. There is immense scope for variety of expression in the visual background: the architecture of churches, their decoration, furnishing and lighting, the position and movements of the clergy and others taking part, their vestments, their gestures, the position of each member of the congregation with respect to the building and its other occupants – all these and other elements have their effect upon the total visual impression received by those taking part, and none of them is so closely defined by rubric that wide variation has not in practice been possible.

But an even greater source of variation is in the auditory context of the liturgy. Though the words themselves are laid down, it is not always certain whether they are to be said or sung and by whom. If they are said by the minister, his personal manner and emphasis will of course have its effect. If they are sung, the full resources of music, with all its power over the emotions of men, are admitted to the service. On the use and selection of music the rubric is silent. Nor does it either authorise or forbid the introduction of instrumental music before, after, or during the service.

Of all the factors in worship that are subject to any kind of control, music is the one that has had the greatest freedom and scope in the Church of England, and so music has been the leading element in the vast variety of character that Anglican services have assumed through the ages. It was said in 1824 that music is 'the characteristic difference between cathedrals and other churches' (*Quarterly* VI, 1824: 326), and the same might often be said in comparing one parochial service with another. Music, being almost entirely untrammeled by legal restrictions, has been in parish churches highly sensitive to popular opinion. In the seventeenth century, for instance, a characteristic style of singing developed entirely spontaneously by oral transmission from generation to generation, without effective

3

interference by church authorities or professional musicians. In the eighteenth century parish choirs arose, at first in response to the wishes of church leaders, but they soon became more or less free of clerical control and developed a musical life of their own. In the nineteenth century, on the other hand, a strong impetus for reform gripped the nation, and the practices of the Church were overhauled along with almost everything else: musical changes were often carried through in this period against the wishes of local congregations. Once the people had become accustomed to the new Victorian tradition, however, they clung to it tenaciously, and we will find that it has survived even the radical reforms of recent times.

These conflicting currents can be linked to three distinct attitudes to the place of music in worship, which can be traced throughout the history of Christianity, and which vary with the theological principles held by different sects and parties. There have always been those who recognise the great emotional power of music to move men's spirits. Some have as a consequence come to mistrust this mysterious power and to exclude it altogether from worship, in spite of clear biblical injunctions to praise God with psalms, and hymns, and spiritual songs, and with instruments of music (e.g. Psalm 150:3–5; Colossians 3:16). This was the attitude of the Quakers, and, for a time, of the General Baptists, but it has never found appreciable support in the Church of England, except perhaps from the unmusical. Others, also acknowledging the emotional power of music, have been concerned to harness it for the good of men's souls. This view has been held by Lutherans, Puritans, Evangelicals, and Tractarians; it has led to a concern that music should be sung earnestly and spontaneously by the entire congregation, and that both the text sung and the music itself should be appropriate to the purpose – but of course, opinions have varied widely as to what music is appropriate. A third body of opinion denies the role of music as an actual vehicle of religious expression, but values it as an ornament in the offering to God, as a part of the 'beauty of holiness'. This was the prevailing view in the eighteenth and nineteenth centuries; it has often gained the support of the moderate churchman of no particular zeal or party, of those more or less agnostic or apathetic church members who value church as a political or social institution, and of those who want to relieve the tedium of the service with pleasant music. It has encouraged professionalism and has often led to the virtual silencing of the congregation. It produced both the tradition of the 'charity children' singing in the gallery of London churches in the Georgian era, and the surpliced choir of late Victorian times.

In the English parish church, the conflict between the second and third of these views remains unresolved. There has never been full agreement as to whether the primary goal is for the people to sing as well as they can, or for the music to be as good as possible. It will be found that this issue lies at the back of most of the conflicts and difficulties that have punctuated the history of parish church music. For the musical historian the resulting interactions between 'folk' and 'art' music make a fascinating study, which runs through the length of this book. At times the conflict has led to a compromise that satisfied nobody, but at other times it.has led to a creative synthesis of lasting value, such as, for example, the Victorian hymn tune.

One of the main tasks of this book will be to recover the folk traditions of English psalmody from the obscurity into which they have fallen. Some of the evidence about psalmody comes from those who have attacked or ridiculed it, but we will extract only the factual information such writings afford, declining to adopt the value judgments of those who have criticised one musical culture from the standpoint of another. But a richer source of information is the store of music that has survived from all periods, some of it in manuscript but a much greater proportion in print. Although the existence of this music has always been known, it has never been systematically studied for evidence of the processes of oral transmission of music. Most students of English folk music have concentrated their attention on the folk ballad. They have had to deal with a very large body of material, most of which is quite evidently of considerable antiquity; and yet they have found a relative dearth of early sources, and have had to rely largely on recently collected materials for the music of the ballads. In some cases hundreds of variant versions of a folk song have been gathered from different parts of the world, but the process by which the different versions have evolved from some unknown original has had to be filled in largely by speculation. In the case of psalm tunes the situation is quite otherwise. We have a body of musical material comparable in size, in popularity, and in importance to the ballads; the oral tradition is now practically dead, but we can study an enormous collection of historical sources, most of them precisely dated, extending over three and a half centuries. If we examine the sources with the understanding gained from the relevant external information, we can discover in them all the processes of evolution and transformation that have been observed in folk songs and ballads, and can moreover chart their historical course with some accuracy.

But we shall be equally concerned with the motives, the methods, and the achievements of those who have been concerned throughout history to 'improve' parish church music, by interfering with the tradition of popular psalmody. Their motives have been religious or aesthetic, or a combination of the two. The most effective weapon against any tradition of folk psalmody was an organ, as was fully realised by those who wished to reform church music: Dr Busby in 1820 said 'an instrument powerful enough to drown the voices of parish clerk, charity children, and congregation, is an inestimable blessing'. With an organ came an organist, whose training was inevitably based on the conventional art music of the time. It was an easy matter for him to impose his style on the singing of the congregation, to the satisfaction of the clergy and educated classes. In the Protestant churches of Germany, Holland and France, organs to accompany congregational singing were usual after about 1600, and hence no folk psalmody had a chance to evolve. But for long years most English parish churches lacked organs. They were discouraged in Elizabeth I's reign, destroyed in the civil war; and the process of regaining them after the Restoration took a full two centuries in country churches.

During all this time folk psalmody flourished in England – and also in Scotland and America, where the prejudice against organs was stronger still. This older form of Anglican folk psalmody may be said to have expired in about 1900, when the last surviving church bands were replaced by organs or harmoniums. It has probably not been heard by anyone now living, though some of its practices have survived in parts of the United States and Canada. Efforts to reform or eliminate popular kinds of church music can be traced from the very time at which congregational music was first introduced in the English church. They gained strong momentum as middle-class prosperity increased in the later eighteenth century, and were thoroughly successful by Victorian times, when many parish churches were virtually converted into cathedrals.

But of course 'folk' music need not be antiquated or rustic. As long as people base their singing on what they have heard as part of their cultural inheritance, not on what they consciously learn or read from notes, there is a folk music in existence; and this process must always be present to some extent in congregational singing. Victorian hymn tunes in their turn entered the folk domain. When, in recent times, 'pop' music was introduced into the Church, it was not an expression of popular culture but an interference with popular culture.

We find, then, in the musical history of the parish church, a constant interplay of forces, which in turn depended on larger movements in English society. The Anglican tradition itself has probably never held the affections of more than half the English people: from 1559 to 1689 (with one interruption) outward conformity to it was more or less imposed by law, but since that time toleration of dissent has permitted the growth of other churches. The Baptists, Congregationalists, Methodists, Salvation Army, and many other dissenting bodies have harboured strong musical traditions of their own, any of which would be an interesting object of study. But they lack the interaction of authority and popular assertion, of landed aristocrat and rural labourer, of cultivated artist and untrained enthusiast, that is the special heritage of the Anglican parish church.

2 The Reformation era (1534–59)

Parish church music before the Reformation

Little is on record of the music at ordinary parish churches before the fifteenth century. The earliest country churches in England were minsters, from the time of conversion until the early tenth century. They were staffed by a community of parish clergy – priests, deacons, subdeacons, and clerks in minor orders. The head of the community was often called abbot (or abbess), or provost; but the priests were not monks, and lived according to the rules of the Council of Aachen (816–17). Mass was sung, and two only of the offices – matins and vespers (Addleshaw: 5–13). Many of these minster churches survived until the Reformation.

Later parish churches had one priest only, who had to say mass and all eight offices – publicly if possible, as stated in the Canons of Edgar (1006–8). But matins and vespers remained the chief services, with the mass. In the absence of any endowments for music or any staff to assist the priest, there was no way for parish churches to share in the medieval development of sacred polyphony. As early as the fourth century, the Council of Laodicea had ruled that only the canonical singers were entitled to chant (Landon). Though parts of the chant had originally been sung by the people at large, the various accretions had placed it beyond the reach of any but skilled singers, while the Latin language made the congregational chanting of psalms and other non-recurrent texts impossible. The parish clerk chanted alternate verses of the psalms and responses, and read the epistle at mass (Atchley). The hymns at the daily offices were musically simpler and could possibly have been sung by the people: many of them were cast in the metres of popular song. But the office was not generally congregational. In all probability, the priest and clerk alone would read or chant the liturgy of mass and office in most churches before the later fifteenth century, and in smaller ones until the Reformation. Such pictorial evidence of choral singing as exists comes from royal, cathedral and monastic sources (Pl. 3; see Mc Kinnon).

During the hundred or so years before the Reformation, there was a general tendency throughout Europe for ever greater elaboration of liturgical music. Naturally, this was at its height in the great choral foundations, for which the most ambitious music was written, but it was also clearly evident in parish churches (Harrison: 197–201). A growing number of English churches, even quite small ones, were endowed with organs and chantries by devout and wealthy parishioners, especially in the more prosperous parts of the country, such as London, Kent, and East Anglia. The building of a rood-loft between the nave and chancel of a church (Pl. 1), which commonly took place during the fifteenth or early sixteenth century, had as its practical purpose the support of a great organ, which was used to accompany plainsong at the unison, and required much physical exertion to play. A secondary or portative organ was often placed in the lady chapel or other side chapel, with mechanical action and chromatic compass, capable of accompanying polyphony. In the 1540s small portable reed-organs (regals) also became popular. Some idea of the spread of parish church organs by the end of Henry VIII's reign can be gathered from the inventories that were made in the following reign as a prelude (in most cases) to the dismantling of the organs. In Kent, 16 parishes out of 136 for which inventories survive had organs: of these, six were in the cathedral cities of Canterbury and Rochester. In the East Riding of Yorkshire the proportion was 19 out of 207; in the city of Exeter, 5 out of 21 (Wallcott *et al.*; Page; Cresswell), Cox (:197–204) gives extensive extracts concerning organs from churchwardens' accounts of the first half of the sixteenth century.)

A growing source of support for music in parish churches was the endowment of chantries. Aristocrats and wealthy merchants would frequently make provision for masses to be sung for them after death. The chantry priests thus provided for, and other minor clergy attached to a parish church, would then augment their income by singing also in the general services of the church – and also playing the organ, copying music, teaching schoolchildren, and so on. In some parishes several chantry priests would be formed into a 'college'; several dozen of these collegiate parish churches existed at the time of the Reformation (Cook: 221–2 and *passim*). A few very large and wealthy foundations, such as that at Fotheringhay founded by the Dukes of York, were able to afford a fully-fledged choir. More often there were two or three chantry priests, who were able to sing some polyphony with the assistance of the parish clerk. Some parishes had song schools: at St Mary, Warwick, the master of the song school was expected to be present at Lady mass every day with two of his pupils (A. H. Thompson, 1942:22). At the little village of Cotterstock a fourteenth-century foundation provided for two clerks with competent skill in reading and singing, and 'matins, vespers and the other hours' were to be 'solemnly sung in choir daily, with mass of the day and mass of our Lady at the high altar, and this distinctly and audibly with good psalmody and suitable pauses in the middle of each verse of the psalms' (:24).

In many places it was the chantry priests alone who made polyphony a possibility. The people of Doncaster told the church commissioners in Edward VI's reign that by reason of the chantry priests 'there is at daily matins, mass, and evensong [singing] by note' (Wood-Legh: 293) – that is, 'pricksong' or polyphony sung from part-books as distinct from improvised faburden.

In addition, vestries were beginning to be willing to pay for music out of the parish rates. Many church accounts show payments for music during this period. By about 1500 the richer churches were beginning to acquire a staff of full-time musicians, variously called 'clerks' or 'conducts', who worked under the parish clerk (Baillie, 1957: 45–51; Harrison: 197–201; Wood-Legh: 276). Thus a male choir could be formed, and in some churches there were also choirboys available, especially for Lady mass. In the larger churches, the chancel was extended and fitted with choir stalls (Pl. 2). Parish churches hired choirboys from cathedrals or other choral foundations to celebrate their patronal festivals and other special occasions. For processions outside the church, waits and minstrels were often added. But there is little likelihood that instruments other than organs accompanied singing in church, at least as a normal rule (Mc Kinnon). No musical manuscript positively identified with a parish church from this period appears to have survived,* though some of the music in the manuscript Trent Codex 90 by English composers of the mid and later fifteenth century might well have been designed for parochial use (see ex. 1†).

Hugh Baillie has made a comprehensive study of the music at London churches before and after the Reformation. He has found records of elaborate polyphonic music (pricksong) on Sundays at some half-dozen parish churches which had musical establishments. The most ambitious of all, St Mary-at-Hill, had its own choir school, established in 1523 and possibly the first ever founded for a parish church: in Baillie's opinion there may have been daily polyphonic services at this church. Musicians connected with it included Thomas Tallis, William Mundy, Robert Okeland, Richard Winslate, and Philip ap Rhys (Baillie, 1957: 199–201; Baillie, 1955). At a further twenty churches there is some documentary evidence suggesting that polyphony was heard, at any rate on major feasts: Baillie estimates that nine out of ten London churches had polyphony on such occasions (1957: 206–20). As he points out, 'most of the surviving sacred music of the late fifteenth and early sixteenth centuries . . . was either written for a special occasion or else for special services recurring throughout the year' (223–4). (For an anonymous *Salve festa dies* probably used for processions on major feasts at a parish church, see MS 25, fol. 120, partly transcribed Harrison: 405.)

What was the music like in more ordinary circumstances? In small country churches there may have been no music, or unadorned plainsong, but where any trained musicians at all were available, faburden was practised. This was a method of harmonising the simpler kinds of chant, especially psalm chants, by improvisation governed by certain rules. The basic pattern was for the chant (usually in the cantus or upper voice) to be followed a 6th below by the tenor, with a 7–6 suspension just before the cadence and an octave for the last note. In the fifteenth century a third (altus) part sang largely in strict parallel 4ths below the cantus. By the sixteenth century a free bass was usually added, and the altus, if present, also moved freely so as to amplify the harmony (Trumble: 41–65). Because faburden was improvised, few written examples have survived. In one *Magnificat* by the English composer, Christopher Anthony (ex. 1), the setting is mostly in simple three-part polyphony on the plainsong, such as might well have been sung at a parish church at vespers on one of the major feasts of the Virgin. Many of the verses are close to faburden in style. One

---

* A possible exception is the Pepys manuscript (MS 2a), emanating apparently from Kent and dating from the mid-fifteenth century. Charles, however (:70), considers that it was for the use of a school in which boys were taught by monks.
† For music examples see Volume 2.

(verse 8) has a *contra* part in strict faburden. Instead of writing it out in full the scribe merely wrote '*per* faulxbourdon' (cited Harrison: 347).

Evidently the faburden was sung by the parish clerks, as the most skilled musicians available, while the rest of the choir sang the plainsong, supported at the unison by the organ when there was one. At Faversham in 1506, the clerks were required to 'set the choir' on an appropriate pitch for beginning the plainsong, then each was to sing his part in the faburden: 'and where plain song faileth one of them shall leave faburden and keep the plain song unto the time the choir be set again' (Legg, 1903: 76). The question that naturally arises is: who sang in this choir? Not, presumably, trained musicians, since these would not have needed the help of the clerks and would, indeed, have been doing something more difficult than singing plainsong. There is reason to believe that such parish choirs consisted at least partly of volunteers. Bishop Brooks's Injunctions to the clergy of Gloucester diocese in 1556 required 'that the churchwardens of every parish, where service was accustomed to be sung, shall exhort all such as can sing and have been accustomed to sing in the time of the schism, or before, and now withdraw themselves from the choir, to exercise themselves in singing and serving God there' (Frere & Kennedy: II, 405). Doubtless these voluntary choirs sang plainsong, with the clerks providing faburden (as at Faversham) where this was feasible. It is likely that the chancel stalls were reserved for minor clergy, including chantry priests and parish clerks, while lay singers occupied the rood-loft (Gasquet: 45; Addleshaw & Etchells: 16–17).

The formation of choirs in smaller parish churches created a demand for many copies of the liturgical music. A considerable number of liturgical books of the Sarum use were printed, both in England and abroad, between 1480 and 1547 (STC; Steele). Some were for monastic, but others no doubt for parochial use. The responses of the priest's chant were designated for choir, and printed monophonically; where skilled musicians were available they were sung in faburden (Fig. 1).

Participation by ordinary parishioners in the service of the church may well have been on the increase during the latter part of Henry VIII's reign, under the influence of Lutheran ideas which were fitfully encouraged by the king but were steadily gaining ground with the intellectual leaders of the time. Elaboration of choral polyphony had reached an extreme in the florid music sung during the first quarter of the sixteenth century. Shortly after visiting Cambridge, in 1516, Erasmus wrote in his commentary on the New Testament: 'Modern church music is so constructed that the congregation cannot hear one distinct word. The choristers themselves do not understand what they are singing, yet according to priests and monks it constitutes the whole of religion' (Froude: 115, quoted Doe: 85).

Such music was three times removed from the people: by the foreign language, by the elaboration that disguised the text, and by their own non-participation. Reformers wanted to remedy all these faults, with varying degrees of extremism. Luther, always a moderate, retained many features of the Latin service, including some of the popular office hymns, but he introduced German hymns alongside them. While retaining the polyphony of trained choirs, he encouraged at the same time a more homely type of

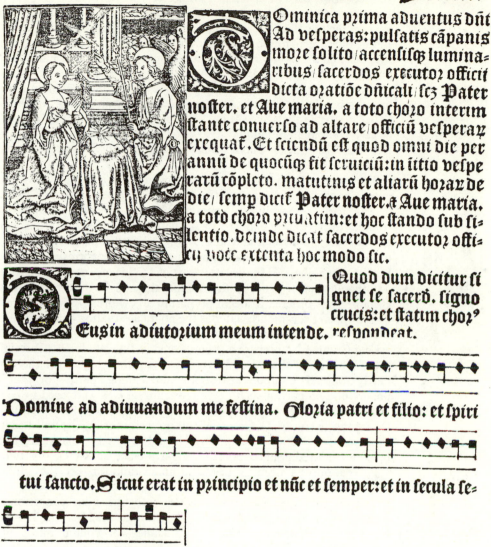

Fig. 1 Responses at vespers of the First Sunday in Advent (Sarum Antiphonal, STC 15790, [London], 1519, fol. a4r)

choral music, in which amateurs could join in four-part harmony in the singing of both Latin and German hymns: this was partly to wean the youth away from their 'carnal and lascivious songs', and he expected the singers to feel in their hearts what they sang with their lips (Buszin: 88).

Henry VIII himself had little taste for liturgical reform (DeVos: 9–21), and although he ordered Cranmer to prepare vernacular liturgies, he never authorised them for public use. But Paul Doe has argued convincingly that the Latin polyphony of the latter part of Henry's reign shows a distinct simplification of style as well as other features probably derived from Lutheran influences. The three English masses based on the 'Western Wynde' melody, by Taverner, Tye and Shepherd, may well date from the 1540s: they are all found in a single source, the Gyffard part-books, which suggests that they were composed in response to a specific demand. As Doe points out, there was no English precedent for the use of a popular melody as the basis for a mass, and Taverner placed the tune prominently in the tenor, much in the manner of many German hymn settings of the time. Other masses in the same source are not based on plainsong, but are in a largely syllabic, homophonic style closely allied to improvised faburden: Doe cites Taverner's 'Playn Song' mass and Tallis's four-part mass as examples (:88–93).

Thomas Cranmer, who became Archbishop of Canterbury in 1533, was given a good deal of freedom in the details of church government. Probably he was largely responsible for encouraging these developments. He himself is likely to have been exposed to Lutheran influences during his time at Cambridge, as student and teacher, in the 1520s. From the time of his visit to Germany in 1531 he maintained a considerable correspondence with Lutheran theologians. In the latter part of 1537 Henry considered forming a Lutheran alliance to deal with a military threat from the Catholic powers. Cranmer was ordered to begin preparing a new liturgy, but the pressure was dropped a few months later as the political situation again shifted.

In 1544 the king made another move in the direction of protestantism by asking Cranmer to prepare a processional in English, for use throughout the realm in time of need or distress, 'forasmuch as heretofore the people, partly for lack of good instruction and calling, partly for that they understood no part of such prayers or suffrages, as were used to be sung and said, have used to come very slackly to the procession' (Brightman: I, lix; quoted le Huray: 5). Cranmer's litany was accordingly published in the same year (PC 1). It was accompanied by music based on plainsong, printed in a new and simplified notation. The preface shows clearly that the congregation was meant to hear and understand the text, though not to sing it audibly (Hunt: 17, 86).

During subsequent correspondence with the king concerning the translation of other Latin processionals, Cranmer on 7 October 1544 wrote his well-known letter stating his principles for church music in the vernacular:

In mine opinion, the song that shall be made thereunto would not be full of notes, but, as near as may be, for every syllable a note; so that it may be sung distinctly and devoutly, as be in matins and evensong *Venite*, the hymns *Te deum*, *Benedictus*, *Magnificat*, *Nunc dimittis*, and all the psalms and versicles; and in the mass *Gloria in excelsis*, *Gloria patri*, the creed, the preface, the *Pater noster* and some of the *Sanctus* and *Agnus*. As concerning the *Salva festa dies*, the Latin note, as I think, is sober and distinct enough; wherefore I have travailed to make the verses in English, and have put the Latin note unto the same. Nevertheless, they that be cunning in singing can make a much more solemn note thereto. I made them only for a proof, to see how English would do in song. (Brightman: I, lxi; quoted le Huray: 7)

As Cranmer's settings, referred to in this letter, have not survived, his exact meaning is matter for speculation. Possibly he was advocating homophony of the faburden type, by contrast with elaborate polyphony such as 'they that be cunning in singing' could make. Or he may have been thinking of a monophonic setting adapted from plainsong, to which 'they that be cunning in singing can make a much more solemn note' by adding homophonic or polyphonic parts. Several faburden settings of Cranmer's litany have survived (see ex. 2).

Such trends in the last two decades of Henry VIII's reign represented the moderate reforming position. Cranmer brought the music of the service closer to the people in several ways: by substituting the vernacular for the Latin language in the case of the processional of 1544, and by publishing English forms of the Latin texts in primers for private use; by trimming the more florid forms of polyphony, and bringing in a simpler musical style that allowed the text to be clearly heard; and by allowing ordinary parishioners to join in choirs with trained musicians, at least in the singing of the chant. But he stopped short of the ultimate step, which would allow the whole congregation to sing its own music in worship. The enormous popularity of hymn singing among the Lutherans could not have failed to come to the notice of English authorities. But, as long as Henry VIII lived, it was not permitted to spread to his domain.

Parish church music under Edward VI

One of the first acts of reform in the new reign was the suppression of chantries, by an act of parliament passed in 1547. It brought to an abrupt end the careers of many professional musicians, and thus placed severe restrictions on the capabilities of a parish choir. In 24 London churches named in the chantry certificates submitted to the authorities, there had been, in all, 74 conducts, all of whom were now disendowed (Baillie, 1957: 86). Organs in most churches were dismantled or sold during Edward's reign (:124). The parish clerks remained, although they too were greatly impoverished when the property of their guild, the Fraternity of St Nicholas, passed to the Crown. After prolonged legal wrangles the hall of the Company of Parish Clerks was surrendered on 14 May 1551 (Christie: 90–7).

Some of the richer churches managed to retain a small choir of trained men; in some parishes, particularly in the west of England, musicians were paid out of parish funds (le Huray: 18). But many churches were now reduced to a state that made polyphony impossible. They had only the parish clerk, with whatever inexpert assistance could be obtained from parishioners. The existence of voluntary choirs in some churches at this period is attested by the quotations already given. Elsewhere the clerks were left to carry on the music entirely alone. An imperfect passage in Henry Machyn's diary, dated July 1552, may refer to the funeral of Sir Robert Dormer at a London church: 'the morning without singing but . . . the clerk, and without any more service done' (Machyn: 22). At many other funerals of great persons, however, money was found – presumably from the estate of the deceased – to pay for the traditional elaborate ceremony, often including both priests and clerks singing polyphony. At Lord

Wentworth's funeral at Westminster Abbey on 7 March 1551 – with a sermon by none other than Miles Coverdale, the Puritan reformer – there was a procession with a hundred choirboys, priests and clerks in surplices (Machyn: 3–4). It would seem therefore that economic stringency, quite as much as doctrinal rigour, stood in the way of elaborate music in the ordinary services of the parish church.

Of course, the other great source of change at this time was the introduction of a new liturgy in English. This, too, came about by gradual stages, but the momentum of the reform was not to be stopped, and it soon had the force of law. The English litany had already been introduced, and lessons read in English. The accession of Edward, and the appointment of the Duke of Somerset as lord protector, were followed by a period in which cathedrals and the universities were encouraged to experiment with English translations of the services, and fragments of these experimental translations have survived – in some cases with music (Frere, 1899–1900). At the same time, parish clergy were enjoined to teach their flock to say the Lord's prayer, creed, and ten commandments in English by heart (Injunctions, 1547: clauses 4, 9; cited Frere & Kennedy: I, 116, 119). At the chapel royal, St Paul's and Westminster Abbey, the mass ordinary was sung in English late in 1547 and early in 1548, and an official English *Order of communion* was proclaimed in March 1548. This was not a complete communion service, but was 'merely supplementary to the Latin mass, which was to be celebrated as formerly up to and inclusive of the priest's communion' (E. C. S. Gibson: ix-x). It was a temporary expedient, for use 'until other order shall be provided'. Eventually, on 21 January 1549, parliament passed the first Act of Uniformity, which required that on or before the feast of Pentecost (9 June) in that year, all existing Latin services should be replaced by the English services appointed in the newly published *Book of common prayer*. This incorporated much matter from the primers of Henry VIII's time, and was largely a translation and amalgamation of the familiar Latin services. The new matins and evensong were compressions of several of the old office hours; the communion, 'commonly called the mass', and the services of baptism, marriage, purification and burial were closely modelled on their originals, while the litany was Cranmer's of 1544 (le Huray: 18–22). Apart from the fact that it was in English, the greatest novelty in the new liturgy was its uniformity, superseding both local variants ('now from henceforth, all the realm shall have but one use') and the intricate structure of specialised liturgies that had been associated with the major and minor feasts of the church year (*Book of common prayer*: preface). Another innovation, peculiar to the English church, was the order to read through the entire psalter every month, and its division into thirty parts for this purpose. The psalms were not, however, printed with the prayer book (Burges: fol. C4v; A. J. Stephens: 4, 50); they were to be found in the translated bibles already by law present in every parish church. The translated liturgy was completed by the publication of an English ordinal in March 1550 (E. C. S. Gibson: xii).

Most of the Latin texts which the prayer book replaced had had traditional music associated with them: by contrast, most of the new liturgy had never been set to music at all. Church musicians were thus confronted with the task of providing new music for singing, just at a time when the musical resources of the church were being drastically weakened. It is not surprising that in many cases they simply adapted the old music to the new words, with as little change as possible. The music printed with Cranmer's litany had shown how this might be done. Examples of early experiments in monophonic settings of the English liturgy, based on plainsong, have survived in a manuscript that dates from Edward's reign (MS 28; see Frere, 1899–1900: 232–3, and Hunt: 23–5, 52–63). The most comprehensive attempt to cater for the new needs was John Marbeck's *Booke of common praier noted*, which appeared in 1550 (PC 3). According to the preface it contained 'so much of the order of common prayer as is to be sung in churches', but omitting the litany, presumably because this was already available in a musical setting. As well as matins and evensong and the communion service there was a setting of the Athanasian creed, appointed for the six major festivals at morning prayer. Of the occasional services Marbeck provided music only for burial and for 'communion when there is a burial'. Three copies of his book were purchased by the parish church of St Mary Magdalen, Milk Street, and probably many other London churches acquired copies (DeVos: 66).

Marbeck's music was partly adapted plainsong, partly original melody in a similar style (ex. 3). Since its revival in the nineteenth century, it has often been treated with success as congregational music. It is extremely doubtful, however, that it was ever intended for such use. The 1549 prayer book gives many indications of the 'clerks' answering the priest in responses, but very few of any part being taken by the people. After the naming of the gospel in the communion service 'the clerks and people shall answer, *Glory be to thee, O Lord*'; and after each of the curses in the Ash Wednesday service, 'the people shall answer, and say, *Amen*'. Otherwise there is no suggestion of the people taking any vocal part whatever, let alone singing. At the burial service, for example, the direction for the opening sentences is 'the priest shall say, or else the priest and clerks shall sing' (E. C. S. Gibson: 214, 269, 280). Moreover a psalter published in August 1549, designed for the use of parish clerks, has a unique appendix entitled 'All that shall appertain to the clerks to say or sing' at the communion, and at the occasional services for marriage, burial, purification of women, visitation of the sick, and Ash Wednesday. It is clear from this that the clerks were intended to say or sing those parts of the liturgy not assigned to the priest, including the creed, Lord's prayer, Agnus dei, responses, alternate verses of psalms, and even, probably, the word 'Amen' (Legg, 1903: 34–55). Marbeck indicates singing by 'the choir with the priest' for the Lord's prayer and creed, 'priest' and 'answer' for versicles and responses; he gives no direction elsewhere.

This music, then, was evidently for the use of parish churches that had enough clerks or voluntary choir members to sing a simple monophonic setting of the liturgy. It could easily have been harmonised in two or more parts in faburden style, without the need for additional written-out parts; for the clerks of some parish churches had long been in the habit of singing plainsong in this manner. For anthems and canticles some churches no doubt sang in simple polyphony, of which a substantial amount has survived from this period (see exx. 4, 6a; le Huray: 172ff). The smaller churches may have had little or no music of any kind, and this possibility is recognised by the alternative direction for canticles and psalms to be 'said or sung' which is found at many points in the 1549 prayer book. There is evidence that, so far from congregations being allowed to participate in the new service, they were often given little chance even to understand the English words. John Hooper wrote to Heinrich Bullinger on 27 December 1549:

The public celebration of the Lord's supper is very far from the order and institution of the Lord ... They still retain their vestments and the candles before the altars; in the churches they always chant the hours [at matins and evensong] and other hymns relating to the Lord's supper [the Gloria in excelsis, Agnus dei etc. in the communion service], but in our own language. And that popery may not be lost, the mass priests, although they are compelled to discontinue the use of the Latin language, yet most carefully observe the same tone and manner of chanting to which they were heretofore accustomed under the papacy. (Robinson, 1846–7: I, 72)

During the course of Edward's reign, the pace of reform steadily increased. Cranmer had invited protestant theologians from all Europe to take refuge in England, and this had meant not only the return of English exiles such as Coverdale and Hooper, but the arrival of such influential foreign reformers as Martin Bucer, Pietro Martire Vermigli (known in England as 'Peter Martyr'), Jan Laski (known as John à Lasco), and the Scotsman John Knox (Knappen: 72–80). A strong Puritan party took shape, and agitated for further reforms with which the majority of Englishmen had little sympathy. They gained, in the end, the support of the young king and swept the vacillating Cranmer along with them. The chief measure of their success was the revised *Book of common prayer*, authorised by the second Act of Uniformity (1552) which prescribed its adoption not later than All Saints' day (1 November) in that year. Some of the most significant changes in the new book concerned the communion service, and the famous 'black rubric' was introduced to rule out a Catholic interpretation of the sacrament. Also noticeable, however, was a marked increase in congregational participation in the services. Before morning and evening prayer (as matins and evensong were now renamed) was added 'a general confession, to be said of the whole congregation after the minister, kneeling', followed by the absolution by the 'minister alone'; the creed was now to be 'said ... by the minister and the people, standing'; and 'the minister, clerks and people' were to 'say the Lord's prayer in English, with a loud voice'. In the communion service the old ninefold *Kyrie eleison* was replaced by a new feature, the recital of the ten commandments by the priest: 'and the people kneeling, shall after every commandment ask God's mercy for their transgression of the same, after this sort'. The response, reminiscent of the old *Kyrie*, was specifically assigned to the 'people', and read: 'Lord, have mercy upon us, and incline our hearts to keep this law', with a variant after the tenth commandment (E. C. S. Gibson: 348, 354, 371).

Of the various influences that played a part in this pronounced change, one, which has not been widely recognised, is of particular interest for our purpose. This was the establishment in London in July 1550 of a church for foreign protestant communities, in which Reformed services were conducted in French, Dutch, German, and Italian under the general supervision of John à Lasco, a former Polish bishop (Lindeboom). The privy council made over to the French and Dutch refugees the abandoned Augustinian church of Austin Friars, and allowed them 'freely and peacefully to enjoy, use, and exercise their own rites and ceremonies and their own peculiar ecclesiastical discipline, notwithstanding that they do not agree with the rites and ceremonies customary in our kingdom, without impeachment, molestation, or disturbance' (Knappen: 90). This was the first time that a fully Reformed service had been legally permitted on English soil, and the example in practice must have won over many more converts than the unproved arguments of theologians. The more moderate party, led by Nicholas Ridley, bishop of London, perceived this danger, and did all it could to block the move: the right to administer the sacrament was withheld until late in 1551, and in 1552 the ecclesiastical authorities arrested some of the foreigners for not attending their parish churches. Nevertheless, the church flourished, and by the end of Edward's reign its position was secure. A second building was converted for the Flemish–German community – the chapel of St Anthony's hospital, Threadneedle Street; in 1551 an Italian congregation was included in the organisation. A similar body was also founded at Glastonbury to cater for the French and Walloon linen workers there, under Valérand Poullain as minister (Knappen: 90–1). The orders of worship in the two churches were printed, Poullain's at London in 1552 (in French), à Lasco's at Frankfurt in 1555 (in Latin).

According to à Lasco's account the king and council allowed these services in order to set an example of further reform to the English people (à Lasco: II, 10). At Austin Friars there was a Sunday morning service, including a celebration of communion in which the participants sat round a table; an exposition of the catechism on Sunday afternoons; and two other gatherings for spiritual edification during the week, called 'prophesyings'. The Sunday morning service took the following form:

1 Confession of sins
2 Absolution by the minister
3 Lord's prayer
4 Psalm
5 Lesson
6 Sermon (not more than an hour)
7 Prayer
8 Ten commandments (with responses)
9 Prayers
10 Creed (said by all present)
11 Prayers
12 Lord's supper (if any wish to take it)
13 Psalm
14 Dismissal

The general influence of this form of worship, with its emphasis on congregational participation, on the 1552 prayer book is obvious. Brightman has pointed out some close parallels of wording, notably in the general confession and the response to the tenth commandment (Brightman: I, cxlvi, clvi–clxv). A Lasco's directions for the singing of psalms are worth quoting in full:

After the Lord's prayer is finished, by order of the minister a psalm is begun by persons specifically appointed for this purpose with a view to avoiding confusion in the singing, the whole congregation soon joining the singing with the utmost propriety and dignity.

And for the psalm at the end of the service:

Then those who are specially appointed may begin with all dignity a psalm in the common tongue, in which the whole congregation soon joins with equal dignity; and it must be sung with such moderation, even by the whole congregation together, that all who know the language at all can easily understand everything that is to be sung.*

There can be little doubt that metrical psalms were meant – otherwise this last object would have been unattainable. The description also suggests unaccompanied singing. It appears that the music used at these services was taken from the *Souter Liedekens* of Clemens non Papa, which were Dutch popular songs adapted to the psalm verses (DeVos: 77–8).

Poullain's order of service for the small French community at Glastonbury was similar in general outline; it was closely modelled on the practice of Calvin at Strasbourg. It included metrical psalms, and also the ten commandments sung in metre (Brightman: II, clvi–clxi).

These are the earliest records of congregational singing of metrical psalms at an authorised service in England. This form of music, the hallmark of the Reformation, was to become, and to remain for a hundred and fifty years, almost the only kind of song heard in an English parish church. The question that naturally arises is whether it was tried out in English churches, in imitation of Austin Friars, during the closing months of Edward's reign. It may have been so, though no positive evidence has ever been found: Strype's claim that metrical psalms were authorised by the 1549 Act of Uniformity (Strype: II, i, 135–6) is unfounded (Huttar: 34, n. 20), and the musical settings of metrical psalms that have survived from the Edwardian period (to be described later) all seem to be designed for choral rather than congregational singing.

If any experiments in congregational psalm singing were made at this time, they were not extensive. For when the Frankfurt exiles in 1554 decided on an order of service for their community, they required 'the

---

* Post absolutam vero dominicam precationem iussu ministri ordiuntur psalmum aliquem, qui ad id peculiariter propter vitandam cantus confusionem destinati sunt, succinent protinus tota ecclesia cum summa modestia et gravitate.

Tum qui ad id sunt peculiariter ordinati, auspicantur magna gravitate psalmum aliquem lingua vulgari, quibus mox pari gravitate succinit tota ecclesia, tantaque moderatione canitur quidquid omnino canitur a tota ecclesia, ut omnia quae canuntur intelligi ab omnibus, qui linguam modo norunt, facile [p]ossint. (à Lasco: II, 83, 90)

people to sing a psalm in metre in a plain tune; as was, and is accustomed in the French, Dutch, Italian, Spanish and Scottish, churches' (Whittingham: 25). Such wording would hardly have been used if the practice had already been common in English churches. It was the exiles themselves, during the Catholic reaction of the reign of Mary I (1553–8), who first adapted the practice to regular English use, and who produced the first English psalm tunes. Before we study their music it will be necessary to trace the growth of continental hymnody and psalmody which was the model for their work.

Popular song of the Reformation

One of the strongest weapons in the hands of the reformers was popular song. Religious polemics, theological reasoning, and attacks on superstition could make little appeal to the ordinary people, but they could and did respond warmly to the opportunity to take part in the music of worship. The way was first shown by the followers of John Hus in Bohemia, who in the fifteenth century sang hymns at their open-air gatherings. The printing press made possible the circulation of hymn texts, so that from early in the sixteenth century the new religion could be put into the very mouths of the people by allying it to popular song (L. F. Benson: 21; Blankenburg: 593).

The leaders of the movement had little choice in the selection of music for such occasions. They must choose folk songs – the only kind of music that the congregation knew how to sing. By providing texts that fitted the popular tunes, they could immediately create a new body of hymns, to be sung at sight by those who could read the printed hymn sheets, and to be easily committed to memory by the illiterate. Inevitably, therefore, the earliest protestant hymns are in the form of popular songs – metrical, rhyming, strophic, and in one of a small number of simple metres, chiefly made up of four-foot and three-foot lines.

Luther realised the potency of this weapon, and was quick to seize hold of it. He himself was steeped in the tradition of popular hymnody, which in Germany had already a long history, having developed quite apart from the Latin hymnody of the church (Julian: 413–15; Blume: 17–34). In his great hymn collections from 1524 onwards he printed tunes, some of them already existing as folk hymns or as secular folk songs. Any good tune was acceptable, even if its original words were irreligious or bawdy: indeed an important secondary motive in the creation of hymns was to provide a substitute for lascivious folk songs which were felt to be an evil influence. By using the tunes with new texts Luther was following an age-old principle of the Jewish and Christian churches, that the best way to beat a pagan culture was to take it over as fully as possible.

With the hymn-singing tradition established, new tunes could also be introduced, if they were not too different in style from popular song. Luther, or the musicians in his circle, adapted plainsong hymns of the old Church, and composed new ones as well – often so closely modelled on the old that whole phrases of older tunes were incorporated into them. The great organs which had been used to play the chant were equally well adapted to accompany the hymn tunes in unison. With the improvements in organ design that rapidly transformed the instrument in the sixteenth century, more elaborate accompaniments were possible. Luther also encouraged four-part singing of the hymns in a largely homophonic style, in which untrained musicians could readily join. So the takeover of popular singing into the Lutheran church was an almost effortless process, and was entirely successful. It was the beginning of a musical tradition that was to prove both fruitful and popular for more than two hundred years.

For the more radical protestant reformers, the attitude to popular song was less simple. Lacking Luther's affection for the old rites, they were inclined to root out everything connected with them, including organs, choirs, and the hymns of the Roman breviary. In the new order of worship they would include nothing that did not have the express authority of the bible. Zwingli sought to ban music altogether from the service, though he was himself an accomplished musician. He ordered organs to be destroyed and choirs disbanded at Zurich in 1525 – an act which was to be a model of destruction for many years to come. The early German Reformed sect, which was centred at Strasbourg with Martin Bucer as one of its leading figures, looked for a compromise between the Lutheran and Zwinglian positions, which they found in the singing of metrical psalms. Their *Kirchenampt*, published at Strasbourg about 1524, included 22 psalms among its 30 texts, and by 1538 they had produced a complete metrical psalter, the first of its kind designed for public worship (Huttar: 35; Julian: 1543). Luther also included metrical psalms in his collections, but no complete psalter was officially adopted by the Lutheran church until 1569.

The compromise of metrical psalms appealed also to Jean Calvin. He did not, with Zwingli, dismiss the possibilities of congregational song in worship. He saw its great advantages. But there was nothing in French-speaking Europe analogous to the solid German tradition of *geistliche Gesänge* which could be taken over for religious purposes. French popular song was secular, largely erotic, and often obscene or superstitious. Nor did Calvin feel any special liking for the Latin liturgical hymns, which, to him, showed only how easily errors of doctrine can arise if texts of human composition are allowed into the service. He therefore came down strongly in favour of using only the words of God – that is, the songs of biblical origin, consisting of the psalms and a few lyrical passages from other parts of the Scripture. His mature conclusion on the point is carefully expressed in the preface to a work he published in 1542:

Look where we may, we will never find songs better, nor more suited to the purpose, than the Psalms of David; which the Holy Ghost himself composed. And so, when we sing them, we are certain that God puts the words in our mouth, as if he himself sang in us to magnify his praise. (Calvin: fol. A7r, A7v)

Calvin did not, we may notice, expressly forbid the singing of non-scriptural hymns. But he used his increasing influence to encourage the use of psalms, and psalms alone, and it was this influence that ultimately prevailed in the non-Lutheran portions of the protestant Reformation, including the Anglican.

Calvin's wish to adhere strictly to biblical texts came up against the awkward fact that the psalms were in prose. No one knew how they had been sung in biblical times: certainly they could not be sung in prose by an untutored congregation. The only kind of song the people could sing was the kind they knew already. So Calvin followed the German Reformed churches in adopting *metrical* psalms as the basis of church song, accepting the unavoidable deviation from literal translation in the interest of having all join in the singing. It was at Strasbourg that he began to take steps towards the compilation of a French metrical psalter. Expelled by the council of Geneva in 1537 for his efforts to ban non-biblical hymns, he settled the following year in Strasbourg as pastor of the French congregation. There he encountered the psalm versions of Clément Marot, a court poet who had turned in about 1532 to the versification of some of the psalms. Marot's motives are obscure, but they certainly had little to do with the protestant movement. (Religious and courtly poetry were not thought incompatible in the Renaissance; many poets wrote both.) The verses were widely circulated and became enormously popular – so much so that Marot in 1542 had to leave France to escape prosecution for translating the Scriptures into the vernacular; he settled in Geneva. By that time Calvin, who shrewdly recognised the high quality of Marot's verse, had already made use of 13 of his psalms in a collection published at Strasbourg in 1539. He had returned to Geneva in 1541 and had been authorised by the town council to introduce the Strasbourg psalms into regular use. On Marot's arrival in Geneva in 1542 Calvin was able to use 17 additional versions already written by him, and to induce him to complete 19 more, as well as renderings of the Nunc dimittis and the ten commandments. After Marot's departure from Geneva and death in 1544, Calvin commissioned Theodore Beza (de Bèze) to finish the task. The complete psalter did not appear until 1562 (Douen; W. Pratt: 11–17).

Folk song played a smaller part in the music of the French psalter than in that of the Lutheran hymn books. For the Strasbourg edition of 1539 some German melodies were adapted; the tunes for the Geneva edition completed in 1562 were probably compiled successively by Guillaume Franc, Louis Bourgeois and Pierre Dagues, all working directly under Calvin's supervision (Blankenburg: 520). As in the case of Lutheran tunes, few of these melodies are likely to have been freshly composed: such a notion was foreign to sixteenth-century musical practice, and much of the fulsome praise that has been heaped on Bourgeois as the 'composer' of the tunes is exaggerated or misplaced. Many of them were adapted or built up from fragments of Gregorian melodies. Five were closely modelled on secular chansons; one (Psalm 36) is from a Lutheran source. Douen, once the leading authority on the French metrical psalter, stated that no less than 34 of the 124 tunes took their first line from a secular chanson, but did not follow it for the rest of the melody (Douen: I, 718–23). Such a practice would seem to defy common sense. If the French reformers had wished to encourage their congregations by using a well-known tune, they would have used the whole of it; if they had wished to avoid its secular associations, they would have used none of it. And Douen's theory has, indeed, been discredited (Blankenburg: 521), though it is more than likely that parts of chansons were among the melodic fragments which went into the making of the tunes.

At any rate, the resulting body of melodies is an extraordinarily successful one, and is the most important musical achievement of the Reformation. The tunes were almost instantly adopted throughout the French-speaking Reformed community, and were soon taken over wholesale by the Dutch Reformed church, and in great part by the German, Scottish and other Reformed bodies. Waldo Selden Pratt has thoroughly analysed the melodies, pointing out their astonishing variety of rhythm, phrase structure, and melodic pattern (:32–56). Each is distinctive, and this, perhaps, chiefly accounts for their success. Above all it is their rhythmic structure that distinguishes them from each other, and, as a body, from other psalm and hymn tunes of the time. The rhythms are formed largely by arrangement of two note values, the semibreve and the minim, and in most tunes a certain pattern is used consistently. As there is immense variety of metre among the psalm versions, such consistency within each tune naturally produces sharp differences between tunes, and undoubtedly was of great assistance in teaching them to the people and spreading them rapidly over Europe.

Calvin did not allow harmonised versions of the tunes in church, but these nevertheless appeared with great frequency for domestic use, the first being Bourgeois's setting of 1547, the most popular those of Goudimel and Le Jeune. Calvin did not allow the use of the organ, but in Dutch and German Reformed churches the psalm tunes were accompanied on the organ, and were used as the basis of elaborate polyphonic settings, both vocal and instrumental: notable examples are those of Lassus (Munich, 1575–8) and Sweelinck (Amsterdam, 1612–14). There can be little question that the genius of the French psalm tunes contributed much to the popularity of the Reformed religion.

Metrical psalms in England up to 1553

In England as in France, the metrical psalm first became popular as a variant of courtly verse, which was later converted to use by protestant reformers. The fashion for metrical psalms in Paris stimulated by Marot's versions was probably the direct impetus for such poets as Sir Thomas Wyatt, Sir Thomas Smith and the Earl of Surrey, who brought a similar fashion to England in the 1540s (H. Smith: 262–3; Huttar: 118–22). These versions were primarily a poetical exercise, stimulated only indirectly by the Reformation through the discovery of the bible as a work of literature. John Croke in about 1547 translated 13 psalms and dedicated them to his wife with these words:

> To turn these psalms to English verse, enjoined
> By my much valued wife, Prudentia hight,
> Love, stationed in the virtues of her mind,
> My pen directed, and the task was light.

No trace of any reforming motive is to be found in these Henrician versions, with one notable exception – Miles Coverdale's *Goostly psalmes and spirituall songes*, which probably dates from the time of Henry's brief flirtation with Lutheranism, as it is heavily dependent on Lutheran sources for both words and music (see Frost: 293–339). The book had a short life and was ceremonially burnt in 1546. There is no reason to think that it was ever used in church.

Thomas Sternhold belongs to the courtly tradition. He was himself a courtier – groom of the robes to Henry VIII and Edward VI. George Puttenham in about 1570 said that Henry actually 'made him groom of his privy chamber and gave him many other good gifts' as a direct reward 'for a few psalms of David turned into English metre' (G. G. Smith: II, 17; Huttar: 292, 294 n. 7). Sternhold was certainly in the king's service, as we know from court records, and was given a grant of 100 marks in Henry's will. Other traditional details about Sternhold and his psalms are of more doubtful authenticity. We may or may not believe Anthony à Wood's statement that he wrote his versions with a view to persuading his fellow courtiers to give up their 'amorous and obscene songs' (à Wood: cols. 62–3, art. 82, quoted H. Smith: 250–1); nor are we bound to accept Strype's picture of him singing his psalms to a familiar tune while he accompanied himself at the organ (Strype: II, ii, 115). But Sternhold's own words show his motives, which had nothing to do with the congregational uses to which his versions would ultimately be put. When he published *Certayne psalmes drawen into Englishe metre* (STC 2422) early in Edward's reign (probably in 1549), he dedicated them to the young king in the following terms:

Seeing further that your tender and godly zeal doth more delight in the holy songs of verity than in any feigned rhymes of vanity, I am encouraged to travail further in the said book of psalms, trusting that as your grace taketh pleasure to hear them sung sometimes of me, so ye will also delight not only to see and read them yourself, but also to command them to be sung to you of others. (Sternhold: preface)

As poetry, Sternhold's versions were decidedly inferior to others of his time. Because their purpose was moral edification, rather than enjoyment, he frequently omitted much of the vivid imagery in the original psalms, presenting their meaning in a flat and plain manner. A well-known example is his treatment of Psalm 34, verses 8–10. The Great Bible translation, which was very probably Sternhold's source, has the following:

> O taste and see how gracious the Lord is: blessed is the
> man that trusteth in him.
> O fear the Lord, ye that are his saints: for they that
> fear him lack nothing.
> The lions do lack, and suffer hunger: but they who seek
> the Lord shall want no manner of thing that is good.

Sternhold has:

> See and consider well, therefore, that God is good and just:
> O happy man that maketh him his only stay and trust.
> Fear ye the Lord, ye holy ones, above all earthly thing:
> For they that fear the living Lord are sure to lack nothing.
> The mighty and the rich shall want, yea thirst and hunger much:
> But as for them that fear the Lord, no lack shall be to such.

Sternhold's didactic purpose is further emphasised by the extra couplet which he added at the beginning of each psalm, driving home its moral significance. That for Psalm 1 reads as follows:

> How happy be the righteous men, this psalm declareth plain:
> And how the ways of wicked men be damnable and vain.

Of the 19 psalms in Sternhold's first collection, 17 are in the simple metre later known as 'ballad metre' or 'common metre' (8686).*

However fashionable metrical psalms may have been at court, their publication was hardly encouraged so long as Henry VIII lived (with the temporary exception of Coverdale's book). But after his death in 1547 a number of versions appeared, including Wyatt's (1549), Sternhold's (1549?), Francis Seager's (1553), and the first complete metrical psalter in English, Robert Crowley's (1549). Not only the psalms but other parts of the bible were versified, a well-known example being Christopher Tye's *Actes of the Apostles*, also dedicated to the king and published in 1553. Sternhold died in 1549, and on 24 December in that year appeared *Al such psalmes of David as Thomas Sterneholde ... did in his lyfe tyme drawe into English metre*, with 18 psalms (all common metre) added to the original 19, and a further 7 psalms supplied by John Hopkins, a country clergyman. Hopkins, who apparently saw the book through the press, modestly disclaimed any wish to have his verses 'fathered on the dead man' or even 'compared with his exquisite doings'. His versions were also in common metre: they were similar in style and character to Sternhold's, except that Hopkins rhymed the 8-syllable lines as well as the 6-syllable ones. The book proved popular and appeared in at least nine more editions during Edward's reign, and even in one dated 1554 (STC 2422–6.5).

Poetry in those days was primarily meant to be sung, and it seems likely that these psalms were widely sung in cultivated domestic circles in the same way as courtly songs, such as those in Musica Britannica XVIII (Stevens, 1962). Edward VI in 1549 was commended for having Sternhold's psalms 'sung openly before your grace in the hearing of all your subjects' (Baldwin: dedication; cited DeVos: 89). The question of tunes will be discussed later. Metrical psalms were also used in church – not for congregational singing, but as the texts of simple polyphonic pieces, perhaps replacing chanted psalms in festal use. The Wanley partbooks (MS 85), which undoubtedly date from Edward VI's reign, contain a number of prose anthems (ex. 6a) and settings of the liturgy from the 1549 prayer book, indicating that they were used by a church choir. They also have two settings of metrical psalms from Sternhold's first collection – one strophic (ex. 4), the other through-composed. These do not quite amount to 'tunes', for they are not entirely homophonic, but their rhythms are strongly conditioned by the metrical texts. A very similar kind of simple polyphony, with texts in common metre, is to be found in Tye's *Actes* (see Frost: 343–73), and in one of the two musical settings provided with Seager's

---

* For a note on metres see page 60. Common-metre verses were often printed, as here, in long lines of 14 syllables, or 'fourteeners'.

Certayne Psalmes (Frost: 340, tune 293). It is quite close in style both to the Latin polyphony of the 1540s (Taverner's and Tallis's masses have already been cited) and to the mid-century style of secular polyphony (such pieces as Edwardes's 'In going to my naked bed' and Shepherd's 'O happy dames', both in common metre, are representative: see Stevens, 1951, nos. 81, 111). In the Lumley part-books (MS 37), there are several settings of metrical psalms, and also of a metrical Benedictus and Jubilate, in a very similar style. In this case the translator of the versions has not been identified. Some similar settings in later manuscripts have been identified as Edwardian by close study of their texts (DeVos: 91–3).

A more distinctly liturgical type of setting also dates from this period. It is to be found in Crowley's *Psalter* of 1549. Robert Crowley was a poet of some repute, a Puritan (he joined the Marian exiles in 1555), and a printer; he printed his own metrical version of the psalms and published it on 20 September 1549 (PC 2: title page). The date is possibly significant, when we recall that the *Book of common prayer* had been published on 8 March in the same year, containing 'A table for the order of the psalms to be said at Matins and evensong', but nowhere specifying what translation of the psalms was to be used. The prose psalter had been published separately from August 1548 onwards, and copies are known to have been purchased by a number of parish churches (Legg, 1903: xv–xvi). But there seems to have been no legal bar to the use of metrical psalms at the daily services; and, as Wickham Legg suggests, it may have been precisely to take advantage of this possibility that Crowley hurriedly printed his *Psalter*. Its full title was *The psalter of David newely translated into Englysh metre in such sort that it maye the more decently, and wyth more delyte of the mynde, be read and songe of al men. Whereunto is added a note of four partes, with other thynges, as shall appeare in the epistle to the reader*. There is nothing in this wording, or in the epistle, to suggest a liturgical use for the metrical psalms: perhaps this would have been forcing the pace of reformation too fast for the authorities. But the music printed with them is very different from the measured polyphony of the settings so far described. It is nothing other than the 7th psalm tone (marked 'plain song' in the tenor part) harmonised in four parts, faburden style (ex. 5). The obvious inference is that these metrical psalms were to be sung in exactly the way the Latin prose psalms had been sung under the old rite. Crowley calls the music 'a note of song of 4 parts, which agreeth with the metre of this psalter in such sort, that it serveth for all the psalms thereof, containing so many notes in one part as be syllables in one metre, as appeareth by the ditty that is printed with the same'. The underlaid 'ditty' is the first verse of Psalm 1. Since the texts are metrical, and moreover all in the same metre (Crowley used common metre throughout all 150 psalms), a specific note can be printed for every syllable, according to Cranmer's principle, instead of a reciting note such as might be used for prose psalms. Even though only one psalm tone is printed – again suggesting that the book was brought out in a hurry – it is obvious that church choirs would have had little difficulty in applying the familiar faburden technique to the metrical psalms using any other of the traditional tones. As a matter of fact, one other adaptation of a psalm tone to metrical texts has survived. Seager, in his collection of 19 psalm versions printed in 1553, provided two musical settings in four-part harmony, repeating them as required for all the psalms in the book. One of them, as already mentioned, is in the polyphonic style of the Wanley books. The other is a harmonisation in faburden style of the 6th psalm tone (Frost: 341, tune 294). Like all the Edwardian settings, these faburdens were so pitched that they could be sung by a choir of men including altos (or counter-tenors), such as existed in many parish churches of modest resources. No doubt they were sung in some churches, though there is nothing to prove it.

The ultimate popularity of Sternhold's psalms may be put down to their direct and simple language, avoiding all flowery conceits and learned vocabulary. Still more important was their uniformity and simplicity of metre. All but two of the versions in Sternhold's first collections are in common metre. This was not only a departure from continental precedents; it was also unusual in English verse of the time. It used to be said that Sternhold chose this metre because it was the metre of the popular ballad (H. Smith: 254). It is true that the majority of the ballads in Child's collection, for example, are in this metre, as are hundreds of broadside ballads. But this metre was neither common nor particularly to be associated with popular ballads before the 1540s. Doughtie has suggested, on the contrary, that Sternhold, 'adapting a metre from Surrey and the courtly makers, *made* the metre popular through his translations of the psalms', and has pointed out that the type was known as 'Sternhold's metre' before it was called 'ballad metre' (:17).

The tendency to iron out the metres of secular poetry, restricting them to common metre and a few other simple forms, and reducing equal lines to the same number of syllables, began only with Richard Tottel's *Songes and sonettes* (1557) (Doughtie: 13). Perhaps the process originated in the metrical psalm collections. For if psalms were to be sung in church, there were solid reasons for standardising their metre. Not only was it a clear principle of Calvinist reform that the words must be clearly audible, but Cranmer's guideline ('for every syllable a note') had been echoed in several official injunctions about the kind of music to be used in church (le Huray: 9, 25). Moreover if all the psalms were in one of a small number of metres, they could be sung to a few familar tunes, so that it would be all the easier for the people to join in the singing. What these tunes may have been is a matter to be considered later.

The Marian exiles

The departure of several hundred protestants to the continent after the accession of Mary I was not, as has sometimes been suggested, a hurried flight from persecution, but rather a planned and orderly establishment of an English protestant colony (Garrett: 38–59). At first some hoped that Mary, though well known to be a Roman Catholic, would maintain the Church of England as established by law. She did indeed move cautiously, respecting the law. She waited for parliament to repeal the Edwardian Act of Uniformity, and to restore the Roman form of worship as it existed in the last year of Henry VIII's reign.* She married Prince Philip of Spain on 25 July 1554. The formal reconciliation with Rome and the restoration of papal supremacy were not accomplished until 30 November 1554. But the large amounts of wealth and property confiscated from the Church in the two previous reigns were never returned: even the older Catholic noblemen were not eager to give up their recently acquired possessions.

Then, indeed, Queen Mary brought about a full return to the old Latin services in all their elaboration, and with as much splendour as the time and the situation permitted (Doe: 94). In parish churches it was hardly possible to restore the music as it had been before the disendowment of chantries. But organs were put in order in many churches, for instance at Wing (Ouvry: 233); rood-lofts were built, as at Hubberholme (Pevsner: 33); pricksong books (i.e., manuscript partbooks of vocal polyphony) were brought back into use, as at St Dunstan-in-the-West, London (Baillie, 1957: 212) or acquired, as at St Mary Woolnoth, London (:204). No Latin liturgical books with music had been printed in England since 1520; at least thirteen appeared between 1554 and 1557 (Steele: nos. 22–34). The authorities put some pressure on parish priests to maintain voluntary choirs to assist the parish clerks (Frere & Kennedy: II, 351–2, 405; quoted above, p.10).

At the same time, and in the face of growing evidence of plots against her rule, the queen set about the legal prosecution of those protestant leaders who refused to conform. Parliament revived the old heresy laws, and the first martyrdoms took place in February 1555. So there was a period of more than eighteen months at the beginning of Mary's reign in which it was possible to conduct worship according to the 1552 prayer book, and even to hope for some compromise in the future. Therefore the groups who chose to go into exile during this period of truce were radical protestants – the Puritans, who saw no hope of a fully reformed church under Mary and were bent on setting one up abroad. They were joined later by the more moderate reformers, soon to form the nucleus of the Anglican church, who had stayed at home so long as they felt there was any hope of a compromise or of freedom to worship as they saw fit.

Not more than a few thousand people went into exile. Settlements were made in several cities: first at Strasbourg, Frankfurt, Zurich, Emden, and Wesel; later at Basle, Geneva, and Aarau. In each case permission had to be obtained from the local authorities, who exercised a nominal sovereignty over the exiles, but in practice they were free to pursue their religious plans almost without restraint. Their situation was thus totally different from what it had been in England. Then, laws enacted by the state had closely regulated the details of worship, and had been enforced by ecclesiastical and civil authority. Now, everything could be settled by majority vote of the (adult male) church members. Their position was like that of the foreign refugees in London in 1550–3.

The only detailed contemporary witness of their proceedings is *A brieff discours off the troubles begonne at Franckford*, a tendentious account

* This included the use of the English bible and Cranmer's English litany. One edition of the English litany, indeed, was actually printed in Mary's reign, including a prayer for Philip and Mary (STC 16453).

published at London in 1575 and believed to be the work of William Whittingham, a Puritan leader, translator of the 'Geneva' bible and of several metrical psalm versions, and later Dean of Durham.* The Frankfurt story was briefly as follows (details from Arber, 1907: xiii–xvi): The first group of exiles, led by Whittingham, arrived at Frankfurt on 27 June 1554. The magistrates had already granted the Church of the White Ladies to the use of the Walloon protestants previously at Glastonbury. Poullain, who was still the leader of this community, eagerly welcomed the English refugees, offered to share his church with them, and urged them to seek permission from the Frankfurt magistracy. They did so, and the magistrates on 14 July allowed them to use the church – but with the significant stipulation that 'the English should not dissent from the Frenchmen in doctrine or ceremonies'. The exiles then formed themselves into a church with about fifty members, on 29 July. They began to consider the organisation of their church and the form of their worship. The prayer book of 1552 was considered, and the following decisions reached:

That the answering aloud after the minister should not be used: the litany, surplice, and many other things also omitted . . . That the minister, in place of the English confession, should use another . . . And the same ended; the people to sing a psalm in metre in a plain tune; as was, and as is accustomed in the French, Dutch, Italian, Spanish, and Scottish, churches. . . . After the sermon, a general prayer . . . the Lord's prayer, and a rehearsal of the articles of our belief. Which ended, the people to sing another psalm as afore. Then the minister pronouncing his blessing . . . the people to depart. (Arber, 1907: 24–5)

A minority of members wanted to use the prayer book without modification, but they were outvoted. The English translation of the form of worship used by Calvin at Geneva was also rejected. On 2 August the church promulgated an invitation to all English exiles anywhere in Europe to join them, and on 24 September John Knox was elected pastor. A month later a new party from England arrived, led by David Whitehead, strengthening the Anglican minority; disputes between the two parties followed. Knox, supported by Whittingham, wrote to Calvin and tried to get him to condemn the prayer book, but Calvin declined, though offering some objections to it. With the martyrdoms beginning in England, a fresh wave of exiles arrived on 4 March 1555 led by Richard Cox. The newcomers wanted to use the prayer book, including the oral responses that were so much disliked by the Puritan party. On 19 March Cox asked that his party be admitted to the church without subscribing to its discipline. Knox pleaded for them, and the church admitted them. The new Anglican majority promptly turned Knox out, and asked and obtained permission from the Frankfurt magistracy to use a revised form of the prayer book. Knox returned to Geneva, soon to be followed by Whittingham, who succeeded him as pastor of the English church there, and by many of the other Puritan members of the Frankfurt community. The Frankfurt church continued to use the prayer book. As we shall see, it is likely that they also continued to sing metrical psalms.

At Geneva Whittingham came into close relationship with Calvin, whose

* Whittingham's authorship has been questioned, however (Collinson).

sister he married. In 1556 he published the chief literary monument of the exile, *The forme of prayers and ministration of the sacraments, &c. used in the Englishe congregation at Geneva: and approved, by the famous and godly learned man John Calvin* (STC 16561). Attached to the book are a collection of metrical psalms (PC 701) and a catechism. The imprint on the title page is 1556, and the colophon and preface are dated 10 February 1556.

In the preface Whittingham justified the use of singing in worship, with biblical texts and *a priori* arguments, but claimed that Satan, 'chiefly by the papists his ministers', had 'abused this notable gift of singing', by means of unintelligible language, and 'by a curious wanton sort, hiring men to tickle the ears, and flatter the fantasies'. He echoed Calvin in holding that the psalms were the most suitable songs for public worship; and he justified the use of metre not on practical grounds, but on the theory that the Hebrew psalms had been metrical. After paying tribute to the excellence of Sternhold's version, he explained that he had considerably revised them for the sake of approaching more closely to the original Hebrew.

The order of prayers fills out in greater detail the decisions reached at Frankfurt in 1554. It was to become the prototype for Presbyterian worship. Daily prayers begin with a confession; 'this done, the people sing a psalm all together, in a plain tune, which ended, the minister prayeth'. After the sermon, more prayers and the creed follow. 'Then the people sing a psalm, which ended, the minister pronounceth one of these blessings, and so the congregation departeth.' There is also an order of communion, after which 'the people sing the 103 psal[m] My soul give laud &c. or some other of thanks giving, which ended, one of the blessings before mentioned is recited, and so they rise from the table and depart': an indication that psalms were sung sitting down. Occasional services are also included. At the end of the marriage service 'is sung the 128. psalm, Blessed are they that fear the Lord, &c. or some other appertaining to the same purpose'.

This order bears a general resemblance to earlier Reformed liturgies, especially those of Calvin. It borrows several features from the Edwardian rites of Poullain and à Lasco, especially in the rubrics relating to psalm singing. For instance the post-communion psalm is not found in Calvin's liturgy (Maxwell: 182, n. 12), but à Lasco designated a psalm at this point: the particular psalm chosen in the Geneva book (103) was used by Luther during his German Mass. A Lasco had specified Psalm 127 or 128 for use after the marriage service (:267).

The psalms printed with the Geneva service book had a separate title page: *One and fiftie psalmes of David in Englishe metre, whereof .37. were made by Thomas Sterneholde: ād the rest by others. Cōferred with the hebrewe, and in certyn places corrected as the text and sens of the prophets required.* The psalms consisted of the 44 already published by Sternhold and Hopkins, with seven new ones and a metrical version of the ten commandments all contributed by Whittingham. The revision of the older versions was considerable (Livingston: 29), as can be seen by comparing Sternhold's rendering of Psalm 1, verse 1:

> The man is blest that hath not gone by wicked rede astray:
> Ne sat in chair of pestilence, nor walked in sinner's way.

with Whittingham's revision:

> The man is blest that hath not bent to wicked rede his ear:
> Nor led his life as sinners do, nor sat in scorner's chair.

Of the eight new versions, four in common metre and one in short metre may have been written at Frankfurt when the Sternhold–Hopkins influence was predominant. The greater metrical variety of the French versions had its effect after Whittingham reached Geneva, and his versions of Psalm 130 and the ten commandments are directly based on those in the French psalter and set to the French tunes (though the commandments tune is adapted from 9898 to 8888, or LM. See Frost: 207–8). One other French tune was taken over, that to Psalm 128: being nearly in common metre (7676) it could be fitted to Sternhold's version of the same psalm with only slight modification. The remaining 49 tunes were new (Frost: 3).

A second edition of the service book appeared in 1558. It showed a far more pronounced debt to the French psalter by its additions. Whittingham added nine psalms, including the immense Psalm 119, and the Nunc dimittis; seven of these ten pieces were adapted to French psalm tunes, and were consequently in unusual metres hitherto foreign to the English tradition. The double common-metre tune for Psalm 119 (F. 132) was based on Walther's tune for the Lutheran creed (Zahn 7971; see Frost: F. 258). Two other new psalms were contributed by John Pullain (not connected, as far as is known, with Valérand Poullain), both in unusual metres though not directly taken from French sources. As well as the twelve tunes for these new versions, five more were added to replace tunes from the 1556 edition: one of these was from the French psalter. Of the 1556 tunes, 25 were retained, but 27 were omitted. In this edition some psalms were printed without proper tunes; instead they were provided with a cross-reference to the tune of another psalm.

The Anglo-Genevan series continued after Elizabeth's accession in 1558, when Whittingham stayed on at Geneva, with others in his community, to complete the translation of the Bible. It led ultimately to the Scottish psalter (see Livingston; Frost), but this plays no direct part in our story. The Geneva editions of 1556 and 1558 also formed the nucleus of the permanent English psalm book from 1562 onwards, as to both words and tunes.

The Geneva Puritans were not, however, the only English exiles who practised congregational singing, nor were they the only ones whose songs were perpetuated in the Elizabethan psalm book. The Anglican party, centred at Strasbourg and dominant at Frankfurt after March 1555, also sang metrical psalms, to which they added metrical canticles and hymns of various kinds.

Richard Cox, who had helped to draw up both the 1549 and the 1552 prayer book, took the lead in making a further revision of the book at Frankfurt in an effort to appease the Puritan party. He met with Lever, Whittingham, and Knox at Poullain's house late in March 1555, in an attempt to secure agreement. Writing to Calvin on 5 April 1555, he said that he had given up private baptisms, confirmation of children, saints' days, kneeling at communion, surplices, crosses 'and other things of the like character. We retain however the remainder of the form of prayer and of the administration of the sacraments, which is prescribed in our book' (Robinson, 1846–7: II, 754). The letter was signed by Cox and nine other Anglican leaders, including Edmund Grindal (later archbishop of York and then of Canterbury), Thomas Beacon, Thomas Sampson, Edwin Sandys, and David Whitehead.

Garrett has pointed out (:135) that this liturgy has survived in a manuscript found among Sampson's papers in 1871 (MS 34). The manuscript appears to be a draft, for although it refers to those 'whose names are subscribed', no signatures appear. Knox, we read, broke up the conference on the third day when he found that non-scriptural passages were to be retained (Maxwell: 46). The order is similar to that of the 1552 prayer book, but with the lessons and canticles reduced to one at morning and evening prayer, and greatly shortened services of communion, baptism, matrimony, and visitation of the sick. At the beginning of morning and evening prayer are the words 'First a psalm sung by the whole congregation'.

It is likely that this liturgy, or the 1552 prayer book itself, was used throughout the rest of the exile period by the Anglican communities. Fortunately our knowledge of their musical practice is greatly assisted by an edition of Sternhold and Hopkins's psalms which has recently come to light at Harvard University Library (Sternhold *et al.*). This small book is without imprint or date, and contains no music. Bibliographical considerations have led to the conclusion that it was printed by Hugh Singleton, using a German type, possibly at Wesel, where there was a colony of English exiles from 1555 until the spring of 1557.

It contains all the Sternhold and Hopkins psalms from the Edwardian editions, but in their original forms, not in Whittingham's revisions, and retaining the prefatory 4-line stanzas giving a summary of the contents of each, which Whittingham had replaced by prose summaries. On the other hand it also contains all seven of the new versions added by Whittingham in 1556, with prose summaries. These are signed 'Ge.' (in one case 'Gene.'). The implication is clear. The compiler had a copy of the 1556 Geneva book, but instead of copying from it throughout, he retained the original versions of the old psalms because these were already well known to the congregation that would use his book. He added the new versions, acknowledging their source in the Geneva psalm book, but not knowing that Whittingham was their author (there is no indication of this in the 1556 edition). He also added prayers and catechisms from the 1556 book.

Most significant are the new items found in this book. Here for the first time we find Cox's version of the Lord's prayer, written in a metre (888888) that allowed it to be sung to the Lutheran 'Vater unser' – with which tune it was printed in all later English editions. This alone suggests a strong link with Strasbourg, and with the Prayer Book party of which Cox was a leader. There is also a group of five hymns and canticles – Benedictus, Magnificat, Nunc dimittis, Lord's prayer (another version), and creed – all in common metre ('Master Sternhold's metre', as the title of one of them calls it) and in evident imitation of Sternhold's style and rhyming scheme, with prefatory stanzas. These suggest Anglican influence, too; perhaps they were used in place of the prose canticles of the 1552 prayer book and Cox's Liturgy. The one new psalm version is in similar style, and it is Psalm 95 (misnumbered 94 – perhaps from the Vulgate numbering). This is the Venite, which the prayer book selects for daily singing along with the canticles. All these versions except the duplicate Lord's prayer were to become a part of the permanent selection. The Venite was later placed among the hymns and marked to be sung to the tune of Benedictus. The Benedictus, Magnificat, Nunc dimittis and creed have tunes of their own from 1560 onwards, and these were no doubt the ones sung at Strasbourg or elsewhere by the English exiles. The one for the Nunc dimittis (ex. 7a) is a particularly interesting link. It is identical with one of the tunes in the 1556 Geneva book – the one for Psalm 19 (F. 37). It was rejected from the 1558 edition, but turns up again in 1560 (PC 6) as the tune for the Nunc dimittis (ex. 7b). It seems reasonable to infer that this tune was known in the early days of the exile, and was continued in use by the Anglican party after its abandonment by the Geneva group. The 1560 edition, which is the first surviving one dating from after Elizabeth's accession, was clearly influenced by the 'Wesel' book as well as by the Geneva editions. It contained the metrical canticles with their prefatory stanzas still intact.

To return to the 'Wesel' book, there is another interesting group of six hymns, all in common metre, and all signed 'W. S.'. The author's identity can be established. He was William Samuel, poet and divine, who was in exile in Geneva in 1557.* There are two settings of the ten commandments: one ends with stanzas clearly derived from the responses to the commandments that are a distinctive feature of the 1552 prayer book:

> O Lord, of us have thou mercy,
>   And make thy flock incline
> To will in heart and do in deed
>   Those biddings that are thine.
> And write these laws within our hearts:
>   Thus unto thee we pray
> That we may think of all thy hests
>   Both night and eke by day.

Another of Samuel's hymns, hitherto treated as anonymous, is the Thanksgiving after the Lord's supper which found its way into the permanent psalm book, and which in Julian's opinion is 'historically of the most importance' among the 24 hymns in that collection (:1541). It never acquired a tune of its own. The book was completed by 18 prayers, three catechisms, the Athanasian creed in prose (as in the prayer book), and an anonymous penitential hymn, 'O Lord my God, thou dost well know', written for a woman's use, as it contains the line: 'And with thy handmaid be not wroth'. This may remind us that any book of this sort was probably designed for private domestic as well as congregational use.

---

* Robert Crowley identified Samuel as the author of 'A prayer to God for his afflicted church in England', which was also signed 'W. S.' in the 'Wesel' book (Crowley: 2). Samuel was an inveterate versifier: he had published the Pentateuch in 1551 and completed the Old Testament by 1569 (*DNB*).

The evidence about the singing of the 'Anglican' exiles is slender, but it seems sufficient to justify certain tentative inferences. They used Sternhold and Hopkins's psalms, probably with some tunes brought from England. To these they added a few more versions in the same style and metre. In their use of the prayer book services, they probably substituted metrical versions of the canticles for the prose versions officially authorised, perhaps finding that the prose versions could not be effectively sung in the absence of a trained choir. (This practice was tried later in England, where, however, it was illegal, and eventually dropped out of use.) In Strasbourg they may have adapted some of the German tunes to their psalms, or (as in Robert Wisdom's case) written special versions to fit the German tunes.

The early psalm tunes

The tunes of the 1556 and 1558 psalm books printed at Geneva (see ex. 9) are quite unlike any of the music associated with metrical psalms from the Edwardian period, and the context of the books leaves no doubt that they were meant for singing in worship, by the congregation without any accompaniment. Although this practice itself was obviously imitated from continental protestant churches, or from à Lasco's church in London, the amount of musical borrowing from continental sources is insignificant, especially in the 1556 edition. The tunes, then, have no obvious source. They are either from an English tradition that survives in no other written form, or else they are the product of the Protestant exiles themselves.

We know that the psalms were sung at Frankfurt, 'in a plain tune', and we may infer that printed copies of the Sternhold and Hopkins texts had been brought from England. It must also be assumed that the 49 new tunes in the 1556 edition are largely those that had been sung at Frankfurt. How much musical talent could the small community provide? Several members had been chantry priests in earlier times, and so would have had some musical training. One of them must have prepared the Geneva book for the printer. A likely candidate is John Staunton (Stanton), who had been a chantry priest at Hereford in the 1540s, was a founding member of the church at Frankfurt in 1554, and went with Whittingham to Geneva in 1555. He became a deacon of the congregation there in December 1555, and was thus presumably close to Whittingham, who is said to have possessed musical ability himself (Garrett: 297). But it would be surprising if Staunton, or any of the other protestant exiles, actually created a body of tunes of an entirely new type. The more likely supposition is that they were already known to the exiles when they left England.

One might expect the tunes to have been 'popular', in character if not in actual origin. Not only had this been the case with the German and French reformers, and with the Dutch Reformed church at Austin Friars, but the uniformity of metre in the English psalms strongly suggests that they were meant to be communally sung. The tunes of 1556, however, bear little resemblance to most people's idea of a popular ballad or folk song.

Tunes such as 'Rowland' (ex. 8a) or 'Guy of Warwick' (ex. 8b), associated with ballad verse of the sixteenth century, are strongly rhythmical, with definite underlying beats, and frequently include sequential repetition (ex. 8a), or are built up from small melodic germs (ex. 8b). Many have a whole line repeated. These features give the tunes structure, predictability, and memorability. They are only weakly present or wholly lacking in the tunes of the English psalm book of 1556. Some elements of structure can be found in 10 of the 49 tunes,* and these may seem to us more 'catchy', singable, or popular than the others. One tune, that for Psalm 44 (F. 63, ex. 9a), is comparable to 'Rowland' in structural strength; another, that for Psalm 137 (F. 157), was commended for its 'exceptional beauty' by Robert Bridges, who had an extremely low opinion of the rest (1899–1900: 55–6). Most of the remaining tunes are a dreary waste. Some have an occasional shapely phrase or cadence figure, often seeming to be there almost by accident (ex. 9b). Others seem almost wholly lacking in melodic, rhythmic, or structural vitality, and in addition are strictly set in modes that were fast becoming obsolete (ex. 9c), so that they avoided the popular cadences of the modern major and minor scales, already normal in art music. Above all, these tunes lack the strong rhythmical framework of those in ex. 8, and refuse to fit into any regular measure. None of them has ever been identified with any secular melody (though, to be sure, some were later adopted for use with secular verses: Ward, 1957: 165, n. 46; C. Simpson: 584–5).

But a closer study of the evidence reveals that we have very little reliable data about popular ballad tunes of the mid-sixteenth century, if indeed any such existed. Our own notion of the character of ballad tunes is derived from sources that are later in date – many of them centuries later. For example, the source for the music of ex. 8a is a German book of 1613, while that of ex. 8b dates from 1730, though both are named as ballad tunes in sixteenth-century English sources. Claude Simpson, in his authoritative study of the music of the broadside ballad, found only a handful of actual musical sources of ballad tunes dating from before 1600, and most of these were in the form of lute or keyboard arrangements. Tunes are mentioned by name in Tottel's *Songes and sonettes* and on Elizabethan broadsides, but in every case one has to turn to a much later source to find a tune of the same name in musical notation. One may reasonably ask, then, whether popular ballads were really sung to tunes of this type in the sixteenth century.

John Ward has concluded that the *popular* singing of ballads began only in the mid-sixteenth century, and was inspired by courtly singing. 'Not until the mid-century do ballad tunes begin to be mentioned; most of the early examples are associated with poems of high quality, like those of Tottel's *Songes and sonettes*, and seem to be products of a court fashion for singing lyric poetry to the lute' (1957: 179). Perhaps, then, the oldest ballad tunes that have come down to us in written sources and in oral tradition originated in the art music of Henry VIII's time. Here, indeed, we can find tunes of the same general character (ex. 10).

What, then, could *popular* singing have been like before this influence affected it? Turning to the nearest available source in time, we may consider

* F. 17, 37 (ex. 7a), 52, 53, 63 (ex. 9a), 71, 84, 101, 157, 171.

A newe ballade of a lover extollinge his ladye. To the tune of Damon and Pithias (London, 1568), which is apparently the only Elizabethan broadside ballad with music (C. Simpson: 158). The tune (ex. 11)* has baffled scholars of the popular ballad. To Chappell it was 'worthless as music, and, I suspect, very incorrectly printed. It seems a mere claptrap jumble to take in the countryman' (Lilly: 278). To Simpson it was 'quite unlike the usual Elizabethan ballad tune' and suggested plainsong (:158, and n. 1): Ward found it 'recitation-like' and thought it 'may be a remnant of a popular style hitherto unnoted' (1957: 168–9). But to anyone who has worked with Sternhold and Hopkins the resemblance to psalm tunes is immediately obvious (cf. ex. 9). It is in one of the psalm metres (DSM); it seems to ramble with little purpose, but has characteristic 'psalm tune' cadences after its fourth, sixth and eighth phrases; it is largely in semibreves and minims (crotchets and quavers in the transcription), but these cannot be fitted into regular measures. Several of its phrases, indeed, have a direct resemblance to those of ex. 9b.

It turns out, however, that this tune is not as amorphous as it appears, and that it, too, has an origin in art music. It is a parody of a theatre song. Andrew Sabol discovered the melody in a manuscript source (MS 26a) with lute accompaniment, with the original words of the lament 'Awake ye woeful wights' from Richard Edwards's play *Damon and Pithias*, performed in 1564 (Sabol: 224, n. 7). In this source (transcribed in ex. 11b) the pitches and durations of the melody are largely the same as those in the broadside, though it is transposed to a different register. (The last phrase is slightly extended.) But the rests between lines differ from those in the broadside version, allowing the tune to be fitted into a clear triple time, which is definitely established by the accompaniment: it is varied by characteristic hemiola rhythm. Thus the broadside version could be sung in the proper rhythm by someone who already knew the tune (and most broadsides, of course, were based on that assumption). For a person who could read music but did not know the tune, it would be of little assistance.

A third source of the same melody appears in an Elizabethan manuscript associated with Durham cathedral (MS 34b: fol. 89r–91v). Here it is fitted to a 9-verse hymn which is a sacred parody of the original words, beginning 'I woeful wretched wight/ With cruel tears distraught/ In thee do put my whole delight/ That made all things of naught.' The tune is set an octave lower than in ex. 11b, and headed 'Tenor *part* for iii men'. In this source there are no rests between lines, but only barlines, perhaps representing the lute interludes. The same manuscript has tenor parts of various sacred and secular pieces, and the treble part of four of Shepherd's settings of Sternhold's metrical psalms also found in MS 26. So it provides a tenuous link between this ballad tune and the psalm tunes.

An inference about the psalm tunes may be drawn from this slender evidence. Perhaps they too were originally sung with lute or other instrumental accompaniment (and one recalls their origin as an offshoot of

---

* Ward (1957: 167) and Simpson emend the tune by adding flats to 12 notes, but a more likely emendation is to shift the clef (as in ex. 11a) to make the tune Dorian. Moreover this brings the tune into conformity with the other sources (see ex. 11b).

courtly verse, sung by the courtier Sternhold to the young king Edward). Perhaps they too were conceived in a clear rhythm which is not apparent from the printed sources, where the rests are carelessly recorded or merely indicate brief instrumental interludes. The music in the Geneva editions may have been designed for people who already knew the tunes in accompanied form, but who followed Zwingli and Calvin in disapproving the use of instruments in church on theological grounds. There were indeed, among the leaders of the Puritan exiles, people who had been closely attached to the court; who may have been present when Edward VI had Sternhold's psalms 'sung openly'; and who would have sung them privately in their own families or social gatherings, where instruments were unobjectionable.

Unaccompanied tunes, with the same rhythmic vagueness and general character as the psalm tunes, are found in John Hall's *Court of Virtue* (London, 1565), but rather than being 'obviously inspired by Calvinist psalmody' (Ward, 1957: 16a), they may have been the very tunes, or types of tune, used with the verses of *The Court of Venus* of which Hall's book was a moralistic parody.* Their resemblance to the psalm tunes may be due to their common origin in a type of art song.

There is some evidence to confirm this view of the origin of the early psalm tunes, though it is late in date. Edmund Howes, in the 'Historical preface' which he added to John Stow's *Annales* for an edition of 1615, summed up the English Reformation in this way:

In the first and second year of his [Edward VI's] reign, the mass was wholly suppressed, and part of King David's psalms were turned into English verse, by Hopkins and Sternhold, grooms of the king's chamber, and set them to several tunes, consisting of galliards and measures: the rest of the psalms were turned into verse in the reign of Queen Elizabeth, and for divers years were called Geneva psalms. (Stow & Howes, 1615: fol. 6v)

Exactly what Howes meant by 'measures' it is hard to say, but 'galliards' were dances, and dances imply instruments and clear rhythm, neither of which can be found in the printed psalm books. It is interesting to note that in the 1631 edition of Stow, perhaps under pressure from Laud or his subordinates, this passage was printed with the words 'consisting of galliards and measures' omitted.

To the protestant exiles there was nothing undesirable about using the style of courtly songs and dances for singing the psalms. Indeed it suited their purpose of replacing 'amorous and obscene songs' in the affections of the people. We need not be surprised at their choice of a style that was austere and sophisticated rather than popular. They were, for the time being, concerned only with a small and dedicated group, who did not need to be won over to the cause. If the tunes seem to us bleak and unappealing, this may be because some of their character was lost when they were deprived of accompaniment. Such a hypothesis must remain tentative in the absence of any early source of the psalm tunes with accompaniments.

---

* It is suggestive that the music type-face of Hall's book was also used in *A newe ballade* and the 1560 psalm book (PC 6), but in no other known English publication (Krummel: 43).

But it is worth recalling that the title page of John Day's harmonised psalm book of 1563 said the psalms might be 'sung to all musical instruments . . . for the increase of virtue: and abolishing of other vain and trifling ballads'. One looks with new interest at Allison's book of 1599, which sets out the common psalm tunes with accompaniments for 'the lute, orpharion, cittern or bass viol', and at the other harmonised versions for domestic use. In most of them the tunes take on a clear rhythmic structure in common or triple time.

Summary and evaluation

The period before the Reformation saw a development of parish church choirs that would be equalled only in the later nineteenth century. These choirs were made up of paid professional musicians, including chantry priests, supplemented in some churches by trained choirboys and by volunteers. Despite the suppression of chantries in 1547, some choirs continued to function through the reigns of Edward and Mary and into the early years of Elizabeth. In smaller churches, only the priest and parish clerk contributed to the singing; there is no evidence of congregational participation in church music before 1559.

Parish churches dealt with the uncertainty and radical changes of this period by making the smallest alterations in their musical practice that would meet the successive changes in the liturgy, laws, and available endowments. For the Roman service, the choirs sang plainsong, including psalm tones, harmonised in faburden style, and, on festal occasions, simple settings of hymns, motets, antiphons, and sections of the mass. In the absence of choirs the priest and parish clerk probably sang plainsong alternately. Between 1549 and 1554 the English liturgy was sung to adapted plainsong, exemplified by Cranmer's Litany and Marbeck's *Booke of common praier noted*, while the psalms (metrical or prose) were sung to the psalm tones in faburden as before. Simple, mildly polyphonic canticles, anthems and hymns were sung where the musical resources allowed.

The faburden practice, which supplied sonorous harmony to a chant with the minimum of technical difficulty, proved well adapted to the times, and provided some continuity to smooth over the stark contrast between old and new liturgies. To the radical reformers, indeed, it seemed that the musicians were making the English words sound too much like the Latin. For extended settings, a simple, mainly homophonic style was adopted, and was found equally suited to Latin or English, prose or verse, sacred or secular. As one might expect, there is little creative innovation in these early Anglican hymns and anthems. They are dignified, technically competent, and restrained: well suited to their limited purpose of preserving musical decency in difficult times.

The protestant exiles developed a new form of worship, influenced by continental Reformed practice, in which all present, probably including women and children, were to take part in the singing. The whole structure of antiphonal and responsorial singing by priests and choirs was abolished. Metrical psalms were to be sung, strophically and in unison, without accompaniment or choral leadership. A few of the tunes provided were borrowed from the French psalm book, but most were unrelated to any continental source, and are lacking in rhythmic regularity and any sense of harmonic direction. They may represent a current style of accompanied secular song divested of its accompaniment.

3 The establishment of Anglicanism (1559–1644)

Parish church music under Elizabeth I

Queen Mary's death on 17 November 1558 and the accession of her half-sister brought another period of uncertainty as to the future of the Church in England. Like her predecessor, Elizabeth awaited the action of parliament on religious matters, and at first she was reluctant to give any indication of her intentions. Intense speculation and dissension took place between the rival parties – Catholic against Protestant, and, within the Protestant section, Puritan against Anglican, 'some declaring for Geneva, and some for Frankfurt' (Robinson, 1842–5: I, 17). To silence disputes the queen issued a proclamation on 27 December 1558 ordering the Latin services to be continued as established by law, allowing only the litany, gospels and epistles, ten commandments, Lord's prayer and creed to be said in English (Clay: xi). Her own coronation in January was performed according to the traditional Roman rite. Some of the more zealous reformers did not wait for a change in the law, but 'preached the gospel in certain parish churches', or introduced services according to the 1552 Prayer Book (Clay: xi).

The new Act of Uniformity was passed by parliament on 28 April 1559, and set forth a prayer book which in most respects was modelled on that of 1552, but on the question of vestments returned to the more catholic book of 1549. The new services were not to begin until 24 June, but Elizabeth began to use the English service in the chapel royal on 12 May (Machyn: 197). During the summer a royal visitation took place to ensure the general use of the prayer book, and a set of royal injunctions was issued to deal with matters not covered by the Act. Based on the Edwardian injunctions of 1547, they had a number of additional clauses, including a passage specially devoted to music. After ordering that all foundations in support of church music be maintained, including those still existing in parish churches, the Queen permitted non-liturgical music in this carefully worded passage:

And that there be a modest distinct song, so used in all parts of the common prayers in the church, that the same may be as plainly understood, as if it were read without singing, and yet nevertheless, for the comforting of such that delight in music, it may be permitted that in the beginning, or in the end of common prayers, either at morning or evening, there may be sung an hymn, or such like song, to the praise of Almighty God, in the best sort of melody and music that may be conveniently devised, having respect that the sentence of the hymn may be understood and perceived. (Frere & Kennedy: III, 8)

This pronouncement had important long-term effects on both cathedral and parish church music, and would be repeatedly cited as authority for action or reaction by both conservative and reforming parties in the Church. It was, indeed, a prime example of the spirit of compromise that informed all the queen's policies. The Puritans were clearly given the right to sing metrical psalms, but not in such a way as to disturb the liturgy. On the other hand, the traditionalists were explicitly permitted to continue to chant the service, but the text must be clearly intelligible. The provision for the maintenance of foundations and endowments for music allowed professional choirs to continue in a small number of parish churches, as well as in cathedrals, for hundreds of years after the Reformation.* The sentence quoted was held to justify the singing both of anthems in cathedrals and of metrical psalms in parish churches: it will be referred to at various points in our narrative.

But act, injunctions, visitations, and royal example were not enough to establish the English service all over the country. The majority of the people were Roman Catholic in sympathy: it was said that only London and Kent had Protestant majorities (Benham: viii). The new services were cold and austere by comparison with the colourful Roman rites that had been fully restored under Mary. The authorities well knew this, as a passage from the official book of homilies issued in 1563 vividly illustrates:

A woman said to her neighbour: Alas gossip, what shall we now do at church, since all the saints are taken away, since all the goodly sights we were wont to have, are gone, since we cannot hear the like piping, singing, chanting, and playing upon organs that we could have before. But (dearly beloved) we ought greatly to rejoice and give thanks, that our churches are delivered out of all those things which displeased God so sore, and filthily defiled his holy house and his place of prayer. (Homilies, 1563: 131)

Roman Catholic worship continued in secret hiding places throughout Elizabeth's reign, and in the private chapels of Catholic noblemen. But this was for the minority, those whose devotion to the traditional Church was inflexible. Ordinary people's feelings were more probably those expressed by the woman in the homily – a simple sense of loss and regret at the passing of treasured experience. Elements of Catholic religion persisted in parish church worship here and there. At Ludlow, Latin motets were still being sung near the end of the century (A. Smith: 458): at Bramley the rood painting illegally remained in place until 1573 (Mildon: 61, 74). In church architecture, the gothic style was maintained, in marked contrast to the use of renaissance architecture for Reformed churches on the continent (Davies: I, 357–9), though the interior decoration of the churches was much altered, saints and images giving way to the royal arms and boards inscribed with the Lord's prayer and the ten commandments. As far as music was concerned, many churches retained for a while a small choir of four to six men, led by the parish clerk, and accompanied by an organ. These choirs certainly sang simple polyphonic music of the kind found in the Edwardian part-books. They also no doubt chanted the English liturgy and prose psalms, in plainsong with faburden, in a way that sounded very much like the chanting of the Latin mass and offices.

* Since the music in these churches occupied a distinct place, and had little in common with that in the ordinary parish churches, it is dealt with separately in Appendix 1.

This emphasis on continuity with the medieval Church, expressed both in the Anglican liturgy and in the queen's religious policies, was probably welcomed by the majority of English people. For the determined reformers the pace of change was far too slow. The Puritan party, small though it might be in numbers, was vocal, articulate, determined, and influential, especially in towns and among the educated upper middle class in general. The 1559 Act was followed by a period of Puritan agitation, dissension, and in some cases defiance of the law, culminating in the vestiarian controversy of 1563–8. The disputes were not about fundamental differences of theology among the parties, but about forms of worship which the authorities sought to impose on the clergy.

Music was a lively issue in this controversy. There was much variation within the Puritan party as to the exact position that music should have in Reformed worship. Thomas Beacon, who had been Cranmer's chaplain under Edward VI and who contributed two metrical psalms to the Sternhold and Hopkins psalm book, expressed the more extreme view (Beacon, fol. xiii; cited Davies, I: 382). Few Puritans went so far as to condemn singing in church altogether; for they recognised that it was clearly enjoined in several passages of Scripture. But they considered it an inessential part of worship, useful only as a means of bringing the word of God home to the weak-minded; and they looked with deep suspicion on any tendency towards elaboration, as also on anything that was associated with Romanism. Thus John Northbrooke in 1577:

First we must take heed that in music be not put the whole sum and effect of godliness and of the worshipping of God, which among the papists they do almost ... think that they have fully worshipped when they have long and much sung and piped. Further, we must take heed that in it be not put merit or remission of sins. Thirdly, that singing be not so much used and occupied in the church that there be no time, in a manner, left to preach the word of God and holy doctrine ... Fourthly, that rich and large stipends be not so appointed for musicians that either very little, or, in a manner, nothing is provided for the ministers which labour in the word of God. Fifthly, neither may that broken and quavering music be used wherewith the standers-by are so letted that they cannot understand the words, not though they would never so fain. Lastly, we must take heed that in the church nothing be sung without choice, but only those things which are contained in the holy scriptures, or which are by just reason gathered out of them, and do exactly agree with the word of God. (Northbrooke: 113–14)

An influential summing-up of the Calvinist position was that of Heinrich Bullinger, whose *Decades*, published in German in 1569, were widely circulated in English, and were commended in 1586 by Archbishop Whitgift as a course of study for clergymen (Bullinger: v, 190–1).

The opposing case was most fully expounded by an Anglican clergyman, John Case, fellow of St John's College, Oxford, who was an enthusiast for music in general and saw it as an essential part of worship. He began by quoting scriptural authority for the use of music in church, and established his Calvinist credentials by admitting that nothing but the word of God should be sung: he abhorred 'rotten rythmes of popery, and superstition, invocation or praying unto saints'. Thus far he agreed with 'the greatest adversaries of our profession'.

Only herein we differ, that they would have no great exquisite art or cunning thereunto, neither the noise of dumb instruments, to fill up the measure of the praises of God: & I allow of both. Wherein if I be not too much affectioned, methinks they do great injury to the word of God, in that they can contentedly permit it to be sung plainly, denying the outward helps and ornaments of art, to add more grace and dignity thereunto. . . . Therefore in our English church, the psalms may be sung, and sung most cunningly, and with diverse artificial instruments of music, and sung with sundry several and most excellent notes. (Case: 136)

Case went on to refute Puritan objections in detail. Some, he said, object only to hired singers with their 'cunning and exquisite music, wherein the bass and contratenors, & other parts sing with full choir', causing vain repetition and obscuring the text. In reply Case asked 'why the people may not take as good edification by the singing which others sing, as by the prayers that others read', and said that since only familiar words were sung their comprehension was not affected by textual overlap, and was actually assisted by repetition (:140–1).

The issue of music's proper place in worship has never been fully resolved in the Church of England; both points of view are still represented in the Church to-day. The negative attitude to music, being based chiefly on intellectual arguments, has probably never had wide popular support, but it has been expounded by influential minorities. In early Elizabethan times vigorous efforts were made to have elaborate music banished by authority. The Puritan party was strong in the lower house of Convocation of the province of Canterbury, and a motion was introduced there in 1562 to abolish 'all curious singing and playing of the organs'. It was easily defeated, but a less radical programme of reform, including the proposal that 'the use of the organ be removed', almost succeeded (the voting was 59 to 58 against) (le Huray: 35; Knappen: 184). In some parts of the country a Puritan bishop would encourage departures from the authorised liturgy: 'prophesyings' were introduced at Norwich in 1564, and at Northampton in 1571, in which metrical psalms were the only form of singing (Strype: II, i, 133; Knappen: 253–5). Archbishop Parker's inspectors reported in 1565 that 'while some keep precisely to the order of the book, others intermeddle psalms in metre' (Frere, 1904: 115). Bishop Horne of Winchester banned organs throughout his diocese, and forbade singing that drowned, lengthened or shortened any word or syllable, or repeated words or sentences (Mildon: 314; Frere & Kennedy: III, 319).

By the 1570s, though controversy was never completely stilled, a fairly stable position had been reached. It was simply this. As far as music was concerned, the Anglican ideal prevailed in cathedrals, while in parish churches the Puritan pattern of congregational metrical psalm singing was allowed to establish itself.

From the beginning there was opposition to metrical psalms in cathedrals and colleges. At Exeter Cathedral in 1559 the congregation sang a metrical psalm, during choral service: the dean and chapter forbade the practice, to be overruled, however, by Archbishop Parker (Frere, 1904: 44; le Huray: 375–6). At Merton College, Oxford in 1562, a Fellow snatched the psalm book out of the hands of one of his colleagues who was singing a metrical psalm at a college feast (Thompson & Frere: II, 696–715).

It is true that metrical psalms were sung at most cathedrals. There was a clear separation, however, between the choral service sung and intoned in the choir with organ accompaniment, and the sermon that followed, usually in the nave or (at Canterbury) in the chapter-house. In many cathedral cities it became customary for people to attend morning service in their parish churches, then gather in the cathedral nave to hear the sermon. It was on these occasions that metrical psalms were sung, sometimes before and usually after the sermon (A. Smith: 238–45). It is doubtful whether the organ took part in this proceeding. The only reference to an organ accompanying a metrical psalm from any period in Elizabeth's reign is in Machyn's diary for 17 March 1560, and it refers to a parish church where a well-known Puritan divine had been installed vicar (Machyn: 152, cited A. Smith: 637). No organ settings of psalm tunes have survived in print or in manuscript, other than two in the Mulliner Book (MS 27) which may be pre-Elizabethan.

The first recorded congregational singing in an English church was at St Antholin, London, on 21 September 1559, when 'began the new morning prayer..., after Geneva fashion – begin to ring at 5 in the morning; men and women all do sing, and boys', as Machyn put it (:212), duly noting the most striking feature of the new order. John Jewel, who had been a member of Cox's 'Anglican' group at Frankfurt, thus described the innovation in a letter to Peter Martyr:

Religion is somewhat more established now than it was. The people are everywhere exceedingly inclined to the better part. Church music for the people [*ecclesiastica et popularis musica*] has very much conduced to this. For as soon as they had once commenced singing publicly in only one little church in London, immediately not only the churches in the neighbourhood, but even distant towns, began to vie with one another in the same practice. You may now sometimes see at Paul's Cross, after the service, six thousand persons, old and young, of both sexes, all singing together and praising God. (Robinson, 1846–7: II, 40–1; translation, here modified, I, 71)

Now, for the first time, the potent weapon of popular song, found so effective by reformers everywhere on the continent, had been unleashed in England. It soon carried the day, encouraged by the Puritan leaders, who 'did persuade the people from the reverent use of service in song... So as the estimation & reputation of song in churches (except *Geneva* psalms) was in short time in no regard (nay in detestation) with the common people' (MS 36, fol. 5v).

In many parish churches in the early years of Elizabeth, there was still a small choir accompanied by an organ. Alan Smith has made an exhaustive examination of the surviving church and municipal records of the period. He finds that many London church organs were kept in repair until about 1571 and were then allowed to fall into disuse; he attributes the change to the death in that year of John Howe, who had taken care of most of the organs until that time (A. Smith: 288). But payments to choir members also seem to have ceased in many London churches in or shortly after 1570 (:293–6), and the same was also true of parish churches in many other cities, including Exeter, Oxford, and York (:265–7). Throughout the country many churches ceased to use their organs between 1570 and 1585.

Most of the organs still in use had survived from earlier in the century. Few detailed specifications have survived from this period. Anthony Duddington's organ for All Hallows, Barking, was built in 1519 at a cost of £54. It had one manual with 27 'plain keys', that is a compass of over 3 octaves, or of 4 octaves with some notes missing in the lowest octave, as was customary. It had several ranks of pipes, but the details are disputed. John Howe's organ at Holy Trinity, Coventry (1522) also had one manual with 27 'plain keys', and 7 stops. Regals were still popular, and were sometimes used together with a larger pipe organ, as at St Martin-in-the-Fields (Clutton & Niland: 48–9, 52).

Smith found references to 84 parish church choirs in Elizabeth's reign, of which at least 36 (26 of them in London) were disbanded, mostly before 1580 (:370; Table 8). Only 24 parish church organists are mentioned; 101 parish churches are known to have had organs, but 48 of them were destroyed, sold, or allowed to fall into disrepair, and many of the other 53 may have suffered the same fate unrecorded; only 6 new organs are known to have been built for parish churches in the entire reign (:427ff). One writer said that over 100 organs were pulled down (MS 36: fol. 5v). At Bristol, there was an unusual custom whereby the singing men from the cathedral toured the city churches at certain times (A. Smith: 282–4). But the following description of Sunday worship in a parish church about the middle of Elizabeth's reign must be regarded as typical:

After a certain number of psalms read, which are limited according to the dates of the month, for morning and evening prayer, we have two lessons, whereof the first is taken out of the old testament, the second out of the new ... After morning prayer we have the litany and suffrages ... This being done, we proceed unto the communion, if any communicants be to receive the eucharist; if not we read the decalogue, epistle and gospel, with the Nicene creed (of some in derision called the dry communion), and then proceed unto an homily or sermon, which hath a psalm before and after it, and finally unto the baptism of such infants as on every sabbath day (if occasion so require) are brought unto the churches; and thus is the forenoon bestowed. In the afternoon likewise we meet again, and after the psalms and lessons ended, we have commonly a sermon, or at the leastwise our youth catechised by the space of an hour. And thus do we spend the sabbath day in good and godly exercises, all done in the vulgar tongue, that each one present may hear and understand the same. (Holinshed: I, 232)

This precisely follows the order of worship laid down in the *Book of common prayer*, with the addition of (metrical) psalms sung before and after sermon – going rather beyond the royal injunctions of 1559. And these are the only musical feature mentioned. The psalms in morning and evening prayer were the prose psalms, and they were 'read' – the only way they could be performed in a church with neither choir nor organ.

Even the parish clerk, sole survivor of the musical staff of earlier times, was hardly expected to sing any more. Early in the reign the following questions had been posed 'for clerks and their duty':

I. Whether that the song in the church be modest and distinct, so devised and used, that the ditty may plainly be understood, or no?

II. Whether they use to sing any number of psalms, dirige-like, at the burial of the dead, or do any other thing otherwise than it is appointed by the common order of the service-book, or no? (Strype: I, ii, 498)

In striking contrast the Puritan Edmund Grindal, when Archbishop of York, issued injunctions on the appointment of a parish clerk, saying that he must obey the parson and 'be able to read the first lesson, the epistle and the psalms, with answer to the suffrages as is used, and that he keep the books and ornaments of the church fair and clean... and also that he endeavour himself to teach young children to read if he be able to do so' (Purvis: 189). Nothing here about singing or music. Already the office had taken on the character it was to have in the seventeenth and eighteenth centuries. Various complaints against parish clerks were recorded in the diocese of York. The only one that had anything to do with music was against William Stead, clerk of Holy Trinity, Kingston-upon-Hull, dated 1 December 1570. He was accused of neglect of duty, collusion with papists, drunkenness and various other faults, including too much playing and singing, which took up the time that might have been used for the sermon. Stead in reply claimed that he never played in service time, 'but the preacher hath always two hours at the least to make his sermon in.... Commonly of Sundays and holy days he doth play four times at the morning prayer and four times at the evening prayer of the organs which playing doth not continue long, neither is hurtful nor hindrance to divine service' (Purvis: 227). Presumably he played short voluntaries at intervals in the spoken liturgy (see p. 135). At any rate the only recorded complaint about the music provided by a parish clerk was that he made too much, not too little. Under the canons of 1603, the incumbent was required to appoint a parish clerk who was honest and literate and also 'for his competent skill in singing (if it may be)' (Canons, 1603: Canon 91, cited E. Gibson, 1713: 241). So a parish church was lucky if it had even one professional singer to hand.

Already we see well established the striking dichotomy between cathedral and parochial music that has been a permanent characteristic of Anglican worship. It existed in spite of the fact that cathedrals and parish churches were governed by the same sovereign and bishops, and had to use the same liturgy. At first sight it would appear that the Anglican and Puritan parties had divided the victory. But if the Puritans succeeded in imposing their ideas so completely on the music of parish churches, why did they not succeed equally in other adjuncts of worship such as vestments, and why did they fail to secure the slightest change in the liturgy and rubrics?

The answer must be that the disappearance of all music except metrical psalms from most parish churches was not primarily due to Puritan propaganda, but to other factors that had little to do with religious controversy. In the first place, there was very little money to support any kind of professional music. Though the queen herself liked elaborate music and ceremony, and had ordained in her injunctions that choral foundations were to be maintained, in fact almost all musical endowments for parish churches had already been appropriated by the crown, or were too insignificant to maintain a choir or even to keep an organ in repair. The inevitable decline in parish choirs was greatly accelerated by the severe inflation of the first part of Elizabeth's reign. In most cases, parishioners were probably quite willing to let the choirs go, and certainly were in no mood to tax themselves in support of choir music. This was not so much because of religious objections to choirs, but because metrical psalm singing, like ballad singing, was becoming a popular activity. The descriptions of its reception when first introduced in London churches show how quickly it caught hold. People welcomed with delight a verse form and a musical form which they could understand and enjoy, and which let them express hearty feelings instead of listening passively while priests and choirs performed mysterious ceremonies. They sang not because they were Puritans, but because they were singers. They were permitted, and by some encouraged, to sing in church as well as in cottage, field, tavern and street. They grasped the new privilege and clung to it tenaciously. Some of the texts and tunes of the psalms entered the folk repertory alongside secular songs, ballads and dances. In the eighteenth century, when choirs began to reappear, they met fierce resistance to any attempt to deprive people of the pleasure of singing psalms. For the psalms were the church music of the common people.

At the same time, the aristocratic and learned classes recoiled from the congregational singing of metrical psalms. It was not only that Calvinism preached doctrines dangerous to the existing orders of society. Sternhold and Hopkins had couched the psalms in language that was crude and for the most part distasteful to any sophisticated person, and the lower orders had seized the opportunity to take over the music of the service. Most of the gentry, including many of the clergy, would have nothing to do with the practice; and as we shall see, this remained true for two centuries and more. The psalm before sermon was sung while the minister retired to the vestry to change from a surplice to a gown. (In the eighteenth century William Grimshaw would use the 'psalm time' to storm round the parish, hunting up his flock and bringing them back to church to hear the sermon (Balleine: 53).) Queen Elizabeth had shown her distaste by pointedly leaving when a psalm was sung at the state opening of parliament in 1562 (Nicholas: I, 197, cited A. Smith: 170).

An important question concerns the legality of metrical psalms, first as a substitute for prose psalms; secondly as an addition before or after the liturgical service; thirdly as an interpolation in the middle of the service. The prose psalms are *now* an integral part of the prayer book, but they were not, strictly speaking, part of the book whose use was enjoined by the Acts of Uniformity in 1549, 1552 or 1559. At the appropriate point in morning and evening prayer these books merely say 'Then shall follow certain psalm was sung at the state opening of parliament in 1562 (Nicholas: I, 197, words to the same effect)'; the table, attached to the book, is headed 'The order how the psalter is appointed to be read', and allots psalms by number to each day of the month. While there is little doubt that the *intention* was to have the prose psalms read or chanted, a strict interpretation might have allowed metrical psalms instead. No legal judgment on this point has been discovered. As already pointed out, Crowley's metrical psalter of 1549 may have been issued with this object in view, and it is quite likely that metrical psalms were used instead of prose psalms in some churches in Elizabeth's time. Machyn's description of 1559 ('began the new morning prayer at St. Antholin's in Boge-row, after Geneva fashion') seems to suggest this, as there was nothing in the order of morning prayer itself that derived from Geneva. Whether such a practice was legal is a matter of opinion, but it is certain that in some churches innovation went beyond the bounds of legality by the use of metrical substitutes for the canticles, which were printed in prose form in the prayer book: 'in very little time they [the Puritan party] prevailed so far in most parish churches, as to thrust the Te deum, the Benedictus, the Magnificat, and the Nunc dimittis quite out of the Church' (Heylyn: I, 119–20; see also Addy: 13; Nicholls: fol. Fffflr).

It has been pointed out by Heylyn, and by many others since, that Elizabeth in her Injunctions of 1559 merely tolerated metrical singing, without explicitly enjoining it or admitting it as an integral part of the service. But it is not so well known that later in her reign she gave a more positive sanction. She did this in certain special services, which she enjoined for public use by the authority conferred upon her by the Act of Uniformity; they thus had the full force of law. Many of these services contained lists of 'psalms which may be sung or said before the beginning, or after the ending of public prayer', referring back to the wording of the Injunctions. In the earliest examples the psalms were then listed by number, so that either prose or metrical psalms could be intended. A form of prayer issued by Archbishop Parker in 1566 (STC 16510) evidently favoured prose psalms. But in 1576 there was printed the first Accession service, entitled *A fourme of praier with thankes giving, to be used every yeere, the 17 of November, beying the day of the queenes maiesties entrie to her raigne* (STC 16479). The service set out in this publication includes 'The xxi. psalm in metre before the sermon, unto the end of the vii. verse. And the c. psalm after the sermon.' A revised version of this, printed in 1578 (STC 16480), has instead of the psalms three metrical hymns. One is 'A thanksgiving, to be sung as the 81. psalm', beginning 'Be light and glad, in God rejoice', and in common metre like Hopkins's Psalm 81; the next 'An anthem or prayer for the preservation of the Church, the queen's majesty, and the realm, to be sung after evening prayer at all times', and thus intended for regular use, not simply on Accession day. This is a remarkable hymn in long metre, beginning 'Save, Lord, and bless with good increase', with a two-line refrain after each six-line stanza. Finally there is 'A song of rejoicing for the prosperous reign of our most gracious sovereign lady Queen Elizabeth. Made to the tune of the 25. psalm.' This piece, beginning 'Give laud unto the Lord', is an acrostic, the initial letters of the 16 lines spelling 'GOD SAVE THE QUEENE'; it is signed 'I. C.'. In 1580 appeared *The order of prayer, and other exercises upon Wednesdayes and Frydayes, to be used throughout the realme by order aforesaide, to avert Gods wrath from us, threatned by the late terrible earthquake* (STC 16513). It directed the singing of Hopkins's Psalm 46 'after the sermon, or homily', and this time the metrical psalm was printed with a tune (not the one found in *The whole book of psalms*, PC 12).

It will be noticed that the Accession service included a psalm before as well as after sermon. The psalm after the sermon was to all intents and purposes covered by the Injunctions, for when there was no sacrament the Sunday morning service ended with the alms collection and final prayer immediately after the sermon. A psalm sung before the sermon, however, was distinctly an interpolation in the liturgy for the communion service. (Sermons could not legally be delivered except as part of the ante-communion service, until the passing of the Act of Uniformity Amendment Act, 1872.) The queen had authorised it in the special Accession service, but there seems to have been no authority for the practice in an ordinary service, although Holinshed mentioned it as apparently normal in 1577. *The whole booke of psalms* from 1566 onwards described the psalms as 'allowed to be sung in all churches, of all the people together, before and after morning and evening prayer, as also before and after sermons', and this may have been taken as authority. But there is no trace of the last phrase in the Injunctions, and in any case a change *within* the liturgy would have required the authority of an act of parliament. Nevertheless, as already stated, a metrical psalm in this position became a well established custom. Indeed it was probably more common than a psalm before the beginning of the service, which is not specifically mentioned as a practice until about 1700 (Tate: 7).

Elizabeth's injunctions made no distinction between metrical psalms and hymns. A metrical hymn before or after service, therefore, would have been just as legal as a psalm. The continuing presence of nine original hymns in *The whole book of psalms* suggests that they were sometimes used, despite the Calvinist preference for scriptural texts. Most of them were set as anthems, probably for cathedral use. These were the most popular:

The humble suit of a sinner ('O Lord, of whom I do depend') (John   set 10 times
    Markant)
The lamentation ('O Lord, in thee is all my trust') (Anonymous)   set 10 times
The lamentation of a sinner ('O Lord, turn not away thy face') (John   set 8 times
    Markant)

(Daniel & le Huray: 57)

The psalm-book tune of *The lamentation of a sinner* (F. 10) won a good deal of popularity, and was used with other texts.

There remains to be noticed an important liturgical use of metrical hymns, which, although never authorised, persisted by custom at least into the eighteenth century. This was the singing of a hymn during the period in the communion service when the members of the congregation received the sacrament. The Reformation had changed the character of the eucharist more than any other part of worship (see Pl. 3, 4), especially where Puritan ideas prevailed. Nevertheless the idea of music to accompany communion was never wholly lost. In the 1549 prayer book, it had been laid down that 'In the communion time the clerks shall sing "O lamb of God..." [the Agnus Dei] beginning so soon as the priest doth receive the holy communion; and when the communion is ended, then shall the clerks sing the post communion [one of a number of scriptural sentences]'. Although this passage was deleted in 1552, it is evident that the custom of singing at this point was maintained, and one of the hymns in *The whole book of psalms* specifically catered to it. This was William Samuel's hymn, 'The

Lord be thanked for his gifts', mentioned in the last chapter. It was headed *A thanksgiving after the receiving of the Lord's supper*, and its great length (124 lines) perhaps fitted it for the long period of waiting when the congregation of communicants was a large one. It had no tune to itself, but was generally referred to the tune of Psalm 137 (F. 157). Daman provided a new tune for it in 1579 (F. 191); East set it to 'Oxford' and Ravenscroft to 'Martyrs'. Daman also provided a new hymn for the same purpose, and gave both the same title: *A thanksgiving to be sung at the ministering of the Lord's supper* (F. 227). This suggests that the hymn was now definitely sung during, not after, the administration of the sacrament, and there is confirmation of this from George Wither, who provided his own 200-line hymn to meet 'the custom among us that during the time of administering the blessed sacrament of the Lord's supper there is some psalm or hymn sung, the better to keep the thoughts of the communicants from wandering' (PC 18). Further communion hymns were provided by Playford in 1677 (PC 29; F. 199) and by Tate and Brady in 1700 (PC 48). The custom was acknowledged in the prayer book of the Protestant Episcopal Church of America (1789) by the insertion of a rubric at this point, 'Here shall be sung a hymn or part of a hymn.' (Further evidence in *Read & Others v. The Bishop of Lincoln*, *The Law Times* LXIV n.s. (1891): 170–3.) It would be difficult to find a clearer example of the victory of tradition over authority.

In general, the legal status of metrical psalms and hymns was comparable to that of anthems. In the chapel royal, in cathedrals, and in some college chapels, where aristocratic and cultivated opinions prevailed, choral music, including chanting and polyphonic settings of the canticles, was encouraged, and the means of its support was provided out of the endowments of the institution. The extra-liturgical music permitted by the injunctions took the form of an anthem performed after morning or evening service, which in the 1559 prayer book ended with the third collect. This became a traditional place for the anthem. When, in 1662, additional prayers were affixed to the end of morning and evening prayer, it became necessary to insert before them a special rubric which has become famous: 'In quires and places where they sing, here followeth the anthem.' It was the first time that any difference between cathedral and parochial service had been recognised in the liturgy. Before that date, anthems and metrical psalms had the same legal standing: they were not part of the liturgy, but they were permitted to be sung before or after a service. Metrical psalms were as much the mark of a parochial as anthems were of a cathedral service.

Parish church music under the first two Stuarts

The Puritan wing of the Church looked forward optimistically to the accession of James VI of Scotland to the English throne, when they hoped that the Reformation would be completed. But on Elizabeth's death in 1603 they were soon disappointed, for the new king had no intention of disturbing the relative tranquillity of the Church. At a conference at Hampton Court in 1604 the Puritans' requests for reforms of liturgy and

Church government were listened to, and turned down. Minor revisions of the prayer book were made, but the canons of 1604 tended to entrench the Anglican position more firmly than ever (Knappen: 317–29). There is no reason to suspect any sudden change in parish church practice at this time.

Indeed a new impetus in the 'high church' direction, as it would later be termed, had already made headway, at least among the upper clergy. Whereas in the earlier part of Elizabeth's reign the Puritans and Catholics had an almost complete monopoly of the serious-minded, now such theologians as Andrewes and Hooker were developing a positive and closely reasoned defence of the Anglican position. The rebellion against Calvinism, begun at Cambridge in the 1590s, spread rapidly after James I's accession. Hooker's famous *Ecclesiastical polity* (published 1594–7), the most important apologia for Anglicanism in this period, contains a memorable passage in praise of church music:

a thing for all occasions . . . as seasonable in grief as in joy; as decent, being added unto actions of the greatest weight and solemnity, as being used when men most sequester themselves for action . . . a thing which all Christian churches of the world have received, a thing which so many ages have held, . . . a thing which always heretofore the best men and wisest governors of God's people did think they never could command enough. (Hooker: v, section 38)

The growing appreciation of beauty as an ornament to worship, and the deepening reverence for the Anglican liturgy, by now as old as its oldest practitioners, combined to favour the cathedral style of service, which flourished in the first forty years of the seventeenth century. The movement reached its height during the reign of Charles I, and its most powerful spokesman was William Laud, Bishop of London (1628–33) and Archbishop of Canterbury (1633–44). Laud expressed with great clarity his own reasons for cherishing the ceremonies of the church:

It is true, the inward worship of the heart is the true service of God, and no service acceptable without it; but the external worship of God in his Church is the great witness to the world that our heart stands right in that service of God . . . These thoughts are they, and no other, which have made me labour so much as I have done for decency and an orderly settlement of the external worship of God in the Church; for of that which is inward there can be not witness among men nor no example for men. Now, no external action in the world can be uniform without some ceremonies; and these in religion, the ancienter they be the better, so they may fit time and place. Too many overburden the service of God, and too few leave it naked. And scarce anything hath hurt religion more in these broken times than an opinion in too many men, that because Rome hath thrust some unnecessary and many superstitious ceremonies upon the Church, therefore the Reformation must have none at all. (Hutton: 53)

It is not surprising that the chief object of Laud's attention was the cathedral service, where the ceremonies he loved could be found in their most splendid form. In his administration of the Church, and above all in his metropolitical visitation of 1634 (the first since the Reformation), he enquired with minute detail into the obligations of cathedral chapters in carrying out the rubrics in their services. Many parishes were compelled to repair and improve their churches (Pl. 19), but there was less interference with their conduct of worship (Hutton: 66). A number of Puritan ministers were ejected from their livings, and many went into exile in Holland or New England.

The liturgical innovations of John Cosin, prebendary of Durham cathedral, caused first a local and then a national scandal, leading ultimately to Cosin's deprivation by the Long Parliament in 1642. As far as music was concerned Cosin greatly increased the amount of intoning, chanting and choral polyphony, and in 1628 or before he 'banished the singing of psalms in the vulgar tunes' (Buttrey: 249; Hierurgia: II, 225–6). Shortly afterwards his innovations were reversed by Bishop Howson, who wrote to Laud in 1630 that he had reduced the length of the cathedral service by cutting much of the choral music, and that this 'gave general content; the people, after their own parochial services, which were early, coming by troops to the cathedral, there being no set sermon in the morning in the whole city' (Hutton: 33). The metrical psalm that followed the sermon in some cathedrals was now accompanied on the organ, as for example at York (Mace: 19), and at Worcester (Atkins: 57). The custom was resumed after the Restoration, and at Ely it lasted until 1843 (Dickson, 1895: 58). Some of the organ settings of psalm tunes used by Thomas Tomkins, organist of Worcester from 1596 to 1646, were printed in his *Musica deo sacra* (1668) (ex. 19a).

As for the parishes, most of them no longer had means of supporting organs or choirs, and had learned to manage without either. The few references to organs or choirs performing in this period come mostly from two parts of England remote from London, focus of the Puritan movement: the north, and more particularly, the south-west. The following references have been found:

Aldborough (Yorks)	Contract for upkeep of organ signed in 1617	Leadman: 192
Houghton-le-Spring (Durham)	Organ played until 1626 Parish clerk until 1608 was a vicar–choral of Durham cathedral	Barmby: 289, 297
St Oswald, Durham	Organ pipes sold 1622 Vicar–choral sang in the church	Barmby: 149, 177
Sheffield (Yorks)	Organ maintained until 1620	*The Organ* 15, 1924: 130
Launceston (Corn.)	Organ repaired in 1621–2	Peter & Peter: 318
Cheddar (Som.)	Organ repaired in the 1630s	Riley: 329–30
St Giles-in-the-Fields (Middx)	New organ presented in 1631	*Survey of London* v, 1914: 129
St Ives (Corn.)	Organ repaired until 1640	Matthews
Hartland (Devon)	Singing boys paid until 1608; part-books bought in 1598–9; organ repaired until 1637	H. Riley: 573–4

Sidbury (Devon)	Organ repaired in 1639	Cox: 204
St Martin, Salisbury	Organ repaired until about 1640	Pearce, 1911: 149-51
Basingstoke (Hants)	Inventory lists organ until 1645	Baigent: 510
Bristol	Several churches had organs in use in 1634; two acquired new ones in 1626, 1629	MS 35: 315; Hooper: 213 ff, 252, 255
Bruton (Som.)	New organ opened in 1637	H. Sydenham: title

Laud or his subordinates did make efforts to compel parish churches to restore their organs, at least in London. Sir John Lambe, a member of the court of high commission, ordered the parishioners of several city churches to have their organs repaired in 1637. At St Michael, Crooked Lane, the vestry drew up a list of 'Reasons against the organ'. They said the organ had been taken down with the rood-loft and had been disused since Queen Mary's time, that it was beyond repair, and that the parish was too poor to maintain an organ: 'whereas the inhabitants heretofore have been merchants, stockfishmongers and men of great estates, now for the most part they are poor handicraft tradesmen'; and they were burdened with other taxes (State Papers, Domestic, Car. I, vol. 351, no. 102; cited *The Organ* 5, 1925: 7). The protest appears to have prevailed. Very few London churches had any organs at all by the time the Civil War broke out (*The Organ* 29, 1928: 88). Hundreds of parish church records, from London and other parts of the country, have been examined, and have yielded very few references to choirs or organs at any time during the reigns of James I or Charles I (Pearce, 1909; Cox: 195–210). We must conclude that these musical aids were exceptional during the period.

Parish clerks, also, had reached a low point in their history. Inflation had devalued their small wages, and few parishes increased them: the wage was often £2 or less in this period (Baigent: 507; Peter & Peter: 318). 'Clerk-ales,' or Sunday fairs designed to raise additional money for the clerk, were frequently put down by puritanical magistrates (Hutton: 108). It is not amazing, in such circumstances, that men of ability and energy rarely chose to become parish clerks.

In most churches the people were left to sing their metrical psalms without help and without encouragement. There was little interference of either a positive or a negative description. Gone was the fervour of early Elizabethan times. George Wither complained in 1619 that the psalms no longer evoked sincere devotion and piety. 'The little reverence that is used amongst us oftentimes in singing the psalms, especially in some private families (I dare not say, in our churches) is much to be blamed in many respects' (Wither: 134). Among the causes of this decline, he said, was the poverty of Sternhold and Hopkins's version, which was so well entrenched that no congregation would allow any other to be substituted (:9); hence the psalms themselves fell into disrepute among cultivated people.

Because the elegancies of these sacred poems have in our language been over-meanly expressed (or rather for that the prayers of God make tedious music in the ears of most men) they have seemed unto many but barren and simple poesy; and the greater number ... sing or read them with the same devotion, wherewith (as the proverb is) dogs go to church. (:68)

Humphrey Sydenham, in a sermon preached at the dedication of the new organ at Bruton in 1637, actually said: 'Singing in private families, or congregations, have a taste, questionless[,] of *Geneva*; but *singing aloud* relishes too much of the *Romish* synagogue' (:15).

In some circles there was already a disdain for metrical psalms because of the humble standing of those who sang them. An unidentified high churchman of the period blamed the Puritans for replacing the ancient hymns of the Church with 'songs of their own altering and composing, to be sung instead of them, by a company of rude people, cobblers and their wives, and their kitchen-maids and all, that have as much skill in singing, as an ass has to handle a harp' (Nicholls: fol. Fffflr).

Left to themselves, the people continued to sing the familiar tunes, and they gradually evolved the slow and strange manner of singing which was described and attacked at the end of the seventeenth century. At no period after the Reformation did parish church music receive less attention, and this fact is reflected in the scarcity of references to it, whether in official documents, in church archives, in printed books, in private letters and diaries, or in literature. Psalmody had entered a long sleep from which it would hardly be aroused by civil war, Commonwealth, or Restoration.

'The whole book of psalms'

The rapid disappearance of parish choirs after the early years of Elizabeth's reign is naturally reflected in the provision of printed music. John Day (Pl. 7), who in 1559 obtained a royal privilege in the printing of music, prepared three books of church music in the first few years of the reign. One was *Psalms of David*, an expanded version of the Geneva metrical psalm book, first printed in 1559 and completed as *The whole booke of psalmes* (PC 9), in 1562, with monophonic tunes provided for the metrical texts. Next was *The whole psalmes in foure partes* (PC 10), a set of four part-books published in 1563, which provided harmonised settings (ex. 12), some for men's voices alone and some for men's and boys' voices, of all the tunes in *The whole booke of psalmes* and some others as well, with the tune generally (not always) in the tenor; a few prose anthems were added. The third was *Certaine notes* (PC 11), also in four part-books; the printing of them was begun in 1560, but they were not issued until 1565. This work contained settings of the sung portions of the liturgy and anthems, including 14 items that had appeared in the Edwardian Wanley partbooks. They are simple in style, and ofter half are for men's voices only (exx. 6a, b).

It is clear that all three books were planned, at least in part, for parish church use, though only the third explicitly mentioned singing in church: 'to be sung at the morning communion, and evening prayer, very necessary for the Church of Christ to be frequented and used' (1560 title), 'to be sung in churches, both for men and children' (1565 title). Evidently there was still some uncertainty about the use of non-liturgical texts in church, though

The whole book of psalms claim to be 'faithfully perused and allowed according to the order appointed in the queen's majesty's injunctions'. The explicit claim, 'set forth and allowed to be sung in all churches, of all the people together, before and after morning and evening prayer, as also before and after sermons', first appears in an edition of 1566 (STC 2437).

The most significant fact about these books is that while the monophonic psalm book was reprinted over and over again, running to nearly 500 editions with music over the next 125 years, the other two books were never reissued at all. Cathedral choirs would rely chiefly on manuscript part-books until well into the nineteenth century – though very few sources of cathedral music in any form survive from the Elizabethan period. It was not worth while to print choral music unless it was to be used in parish churches. After *Certaine notes*, the next printed collection of polyphonic music intended for parish church use would be Henry Playford's *Divine companion* (1701). In the intervening period no parish choir books were printed because there were no parish choirs in any significant numbers. Even collections of harmonised psalm tunes published later in the reigns of Elizabeth I and James I were explicitly designed for domestic use (Temperley, 1972a: 333, n. 12), with some important exceptions to be discussed later.

One manuscript source survives that can be identified with parochial music from early in Elizabeth's reign (MS 26). It is a treble part-book. The first part of it (fol. 1–66v) consists of settings of Sternhold and Hopkins's psalm versions by John Shepherd. The texts follow the wording of the Edwardian editions without Whittingham's revisions, and moreover the selection and order of the psalms is the same as that in the editions of 1549–54. It is unlikely that these earlier editions (other than the suppressed 1559 one) would have been used after 1560, when the first Elizabethan edition appeared. The music of these settings is mildly polyphonic, like those in the Wanley partbooks or Tye's *Acts*. That of Psalm 1 is also found in the Mulliner Book (MS 27). Later in the book are the nine tunes by Tallis that appeared in Parker's *Psalter* (fol. 67v–69v), various prose anthems and hymns, some of which are duplicated in the Wanley books or in *Certaine notes*, and (at fol. 73v–74v) three settings of psalms taken from Elizabethan editions of Sternhold and Hopkins. In each of the last-mentioned cases the treble part in the manuscript fits the tune printed in the psalm book, and one of these tunes (F. 36) was not printed before 1561. We have here, in all probability, a book that was compiled between 1559 and about 1565 for the use of one of the small choirs that still existed in some parish churches.

Only one book had any lasting importance in the parochial music of Elizabeth's reign – and, for that matter, in that of the seventeenth century. This was the completed edition of Sternhold and Hopkins's metrical psalms, printed and published by John Day, and known from the Commonwealth onwards as the 'Old Version' (for fuller details of this work see Frere and Frost: 31–46; Julian: 857–66; Livingstone: 8–50.) With the Geneva books as the starting-point, both textual and musical, it was rapidly expanded early in the reign and earned the title *The whole booke of psalmes* in the edition of 1562, which contained translations of all 150 psalms.

Details of the early Elizabethan editions are as follows:

PC 5 (1559)	[no copy survives]	
PC 6 (1560)*	65 psalms:	7 (?)* hymns:
	62 from PC 701 (1558)	
	1 from 'Wesel'†	6 from 'Wesel'†
	2 by Wisdom	1 new, anon.
PC 7 (1561)*	83 psalms:	17 hymns:
	62 from PC 6	7 from PC 6
	1 from STC 16561a	1 from 'Wesel'†
	3 by Sternhold	1 by Wisdom
	2 by Beacon	1 by Grindal
	15 by Hopkins	3 by Norton
		1 from prayer book
		3 new, anon.
PC 9 (1562)	151 psalms:	21 hymns:
	73 from PC 7	17 from PC 7
	9 from STC 16563	1 by Markant
	(by Kethe)	3 new, anon.
	40 by Hopkins	
	25 by Norton	
	4 by Markant	

Although much of the Geneva books had been retained, there was a clear shift towards the Anglican side by the addition, from 1561 onwards, of non-scriptural texts, including versions of the Te deum, the Veni creator, and the Athanasian creed. The 1561 edition also contained 'A short introduction to the science of music' with woodcuts of the gamut and musical notes. The 1562 edition added a lengthy 'Treatise of Athanasius the Great' on the use of the psalms: an appeal to one of the early fathers of the Church was calculated to persuade religious conservatives of the value of psalm singing.

Seven more alternative versions, omitted in 1562, had been restored by 1565, two of them with tunes. The last textual addition, an alternative version of Psalm 136 by Robert Pont (taken from the Scottish psalm book), did not appear until an edition of 1573. From then on the verbal content remained stable until the eighteenth century:

159 psalms (Of the 9 alternative versions, 6 appeared in numerical sequence in the main body of psalms; one, Psalm 95, was among the canticles as the Venite; and two, Beacon's Psalms 117 and 134, were printed immediately after Psalm 150 as 'exhortations to the praise of God' to be sung before morning and evening prayer respectively).

7 other scriptural texts (2 versions of the ten commandments, 2 of the Lord's prayer, and one each of the Benedictus, Magnificat and Nunc dimittis).

5 liturgical texts from the *Book of common prayer* (Veni creator, Te deum, Benedicite, Apostles' creed, and Athanasian creed).

9 original hymns.

Certain prose items (the treatise of Athanasius, musical introduction, and prayers for domestic use) varied from edition to edition.

* The only surviving copies of PC 6 and 7 are incomplete.
† See bibliography under Sternhold *et al.*

In the permanent contents a nice balance had been struck. Calvinists would find a preponderance of scriptural texts, including every psalm, some in versions directly inspired by the French psalter; there were original hymns for those of Lutheran bent, including some taken from Lutheran sources; while the Anglican party could find in the book a mirror of the *Book of common prayer*, including all the hymns and canticles appointed for use in morning and evening prayer.

Some editions from 1601 onwards (PC 15) were printed with the prose psalms in small print in the margins. These were known in the printing and publishing trades as 'Middleburg psalms' because they were first copied from a pirated edition of the English psalms (PC 702) printed by Richard Schilders at Middleburg in the Netherlands in 1599 (Temperley, 1976). This innovation was distinctly 'Puritan' in character, for it allowed the singer to understand more exactly the original word of God; the prose version was the one from Whittingham's Geneva bible, the most popular translation in England though not the one officially authorised for use in church. Moreover the 'Middleburg psalms' at first omitted all the hymns, alternative versions and prayers. In many later editions these supplementary materials were printed on additional sheets at the end of the book, so that a purchaser could choose whether to buy them or not.

There is no doubt that 'Sternhold and Hopkins' was used universally in public worship throughout the period in question. Holding a well-enforced monopoly in the printing of metrical psalms, Day and his successors had no interest in publishing alternatives; and *The whole book of psalms* was soon firmly entrenched in the public consciousness, as George Wither found out when he tried to dislodge it. The Company of Stationers, which was granted the monopoly by James I in 1603, was even more vigilant in protecting its rights. Though many other poets versified psalms (H. Smith; Campbell: chaps. 4–6; Huttar), they could not compete in the domain of public worship. Day could not well refuse Archbishop Parker, whose version he printed in the 1560s with nine tunes by Thomas Tallis, as *The whole psalter translated into English metre*. But Parker explained in the preface that he intended his psalms for private use only, and had been persuaded by friends to have them printed. The book was never offered for public sale. The next metrical psalm book of importance was that of Henry Ainsworth, the leader of an English Separatist community resident in the Netherlands. It was printed at Amsterdam in 1612. Some copies no doubt found their way (illegally) to England, and were used at secret meetings of Separatists and other dissenting bodies; others, it is said, were taken to America by the Pilgrim Fathers on the *Mayflower* in 1620.

Wither himself published two sets of paraphrases, *The songs of the old testament*, 1621, and *The hymnes and songs of the church*, 1623, with tunes and basses supplied. The second, whose tunes were mostly the work of Orlando Gibbons, found such favour with the king that the author obtained a 51-year royal privilege for its publication. The patent ordered that the book be bound in with every copy of the psalm book. But the Stationers' Company managed to evade this command by argument, delay and sheer inactivity, despite Wither's energetic efforts on his own behalf (Farr). His *Psalmes of David translated as lyrick verse*, 1632, fared no better, though they were 'confined ... to such kinds of verse as I found in the old Psalmbook; fitting them in such manner, that every psalm in this book, may [be] sung to some tune formerly in use'.

The universality of the Sternhold–Hopkins version, with its great preponderance of common-metre verses, 'had an important influence in strengthening the iambic tendency of English verse and in establishing a kind of norm for plain diction in verse' (H. Smith: 271). The metrical psalms, as well known as many folk songs, were one of the 'great commonplaces' of English language and culture. Their literary shortcomings would be deplored and ridiculed by Wither and Dryden, Pope and Addison, Warton and Bridges, yet for a full three hundred years they would remain a treasured possession of the public. As literature they have little to recommend them except accuracy of translation and an absence of flowery conceits. Their place in the hearts of the people must have been due in great measure to the charm of singing them. 'Where one person has been refined and enriched in mind by the poetry of Milton, or Wordsworth, or Tennyson, a thousand have been comforted, inspired, and transformed by Sternhold and Hopkins, Watts, or Wesley' (Lorenz: 55).

The official tunes

The whole book of psalms was equipped with a number of tunes which, from 1562 until 1586 at least, varied little from one edition to another. Not every psalm and hymn was supplied with its own tune (as had been the case in the Geneva edition of 1556); many were referred to the tune of another. Later publications show, however, that the tunes became strongly associated with the psalms with which they had been actually printed, and were referred to in that way, for example 'Magnificat tune', 'Hundredth psalm tune proper' (later 'Old Hundredth'), and so on.

The fortunes of these tunes are dealt with in detail elsewhere (Frost). Those of the 1556 psalm book were considerably changed in subsequent editions:

PC 701/1556	52 tunes:	3 adapted from French
		49 new
PC 701/1558	42 tunes:	25 from PC 701/1556
		7 adapted from French
		10 new
PC 6 (1560)	48 tunes:	41 from PC 701/1558
		3 from German sources
		4 new
PC 7 (1561)	40 tunes:	24 from PC 6
		1 from STC 16561a
		2 from German sources
		1 from STC 2428/16563
		12 new
PC 8 (1562)	64 tunes:	38 from PC 7
		1 from PC 6
		1 from PC 11/1560
		7 from STC 2428/16563
		17 new

Three times, in 1558, 1561 and 1562, almost half the tunes in the preceding edition had been rejected and replaced by new ones. After 1562 the selection settled down, with only minor exceptions, until from 1585 onwards a new type of short tune began to appear: this will be described later. There were 67 tunes in the fullest edition (1570, STC 2441).

It seems more than likely, though there is no proof of it, that John Day himself was mainly responsible for the selection and editing of the tunes. In his pruning of the tunes brought from Geneva he left out most of the unstructured ones and those of the most markedly modal character. The new tunes brought in in 1561 and 1562 were mostly of the same general character, but with more structural features, such as repetition of short phrases at the same or a different pitch, and more in the modes on D and F with one flat, tending towards the modern major and minor. Many of the most superior new tunes were of French or German origin, notably a group of seven imported in 1562, with their texts by William Kethe, from the Anglo-Genevan edition of the previous year (STC 2428/16563). These included the tune which was to become the battle song of the Huguenots (F. 125), taken by the French compilers from the German Reformed psalm book of 1526, and now set to Psalm 113; and the Lutheran 'Vater unser' set to Cox's version of the Lord's Prayer (F. 180). The 'Old Hundredth' itself (F. 114) reached the English psalm book in 1561, was omitted in 1562, and made a permanent return in 1563.

Among the newly printed English tunes, there was a strong group in the D mode with one flat which share a strength and shapeliness found in few of the 1556 tunes:

F. 1   *Veni Creator*
F. 10   *The lamentation of a sinner*
F. 15   Psalm 1 (ex. 9d, replacing ex. 9b)
F. 95   Psalm 78
F. 156 Psalm 136

Possibly they are modelled on the tune for Psalm 119 (F. 132), itself adapted from a German melody (Zahn 7971). Other superior tunes are:

F. 12   *The ten commandments*
F. 150 Psalm 132
F. 163 Psalm 141

Each of these eight has some structural repetition or other memorable characteristic (such as the dotted figure in F. 163) and a strong major or minor 'tonality'; and each was to enjoy a long spell of popularity. So we can see in this group, as early as 1562, a slight tendency to a change in style.

One tune stands out from all the others: the one for Psalm 81 (F. 99, ex. 9e), first printed in 1562. Where the others are stern or dull, this one is gay. It is in a clear triple time, has a clear tonality of F major, and is sequential in its melodic structure. It is the only one of the official tunes that strongly suggests a 'modern' secular folk tune – or an earlier carol or courtly song. And it may have been the most popular of them all. Another version of the tune, not in triple time, was simultaneously printed with Psalm 77 (F. 93), while a third and condensed version (F. 135) appeared with Psalm 120 from 1569 onwards. What is more, the tune was singled out for the special accession hymn in 1578, as recorded above; and it appears to be the ancestor of more than one of the popular short tunes of later date, including 'Winchester', associated in Britain since 1861 with the Christmas hymn 'While shepherds watched their flocks by night' (Temperley, 1972b).

Another purposeful and structured tune used by Day was the one for the hymn called *A lamentation* ('O Lord, in thee is all my trust', F. 186). It had appeared in *Certaine notes* (1560) in a setting by Thomas Tallis, and may well have been composed by him. This, too, was to have a long spell of popularity.

Later editions of the psalm book show which tunes were most widely used. Some began to be dropped, either to save costs or to make way for new short ones. First to go, in the solfa edition of 1569, were those for Psalms 6, 35 and 95 (F. 21, 57 and 113), the last a particularly aimless specimen. Further reductions were made in some editions, of which the prototypes were the following:

STC 2446	1576
STC 2450.5	1578
STC 2468	1584
STC 2511.7	1603

On the other hand, some psalm tunes, together with most of the hymn tunes, survived all revisions and appeared in every musical edition from 1562 until 1687 (the last). These are listed in Table 1. Most of them were slightly revised from time to time. A few notes would be deliberately altered, usually to remove an awkward melodic leap or to modernise a cadence. Such changes are not likely to have been made with a view to 'improving' the versions in use, since the tunes were sung congregationally and learned largely by ear. More probably they were made to bring the printed versions into conformity with practice. If so, they record changes already made in the process of oral transmission, and thus tend to confirm that the tunes were still surviving in use as well as in print.

We have seen that psalm singing, when first introduced in London, quickly caught on, perhaps because some of the tunes were already familiar. But the tunes printed in the book, as I have suggested, were chiefly of foreign or courtly origin, and it is unlikely that many of them were widely known to the common people. Various methods were devised for teaching them to congregations.

One way of doing this was by means of choirs and organs, where such were still available. Within a year after the publication of *The whole book of psalms* in complete form, Day printed his harmonised collection in the form of four part-books (PC 10). Here the same tunes, and some others, were arranged for four-part choir of men and boys, with the tune generally, but not always, in the tenor. Some settings were faburden-like, note for note (ex. 12a), others had a little variety of rhythm in the supporting parts (ex. 12b). One or two were free fantasias on a tune, like Richard Brimley's on Psalm 44 (ex. 12c): the tune wanders from part to part and sometimes disappears altogether. We do not know whether these settings were used by

Table 1. *Tunes found in all musical editions of* The whole book of psalms *(1562–1687)*

Frost no.	Metre	Text (author of version)
1	DCM	Veni creator (Cranmer?)
2	DCM	Te deum (?)
3	DCM	Benedictus (?)
4 (ex. 13)	DCM	Magnificat (?)
37 (ex. 7b)	DCM	Nunc dimittis (?)
6	84X	Benedicite (?)
8	DCM	The humble suit of a sinner (?)
9	DCM	Athanasian creed (Norton)
10	DCM	The lamentation of a sinner (?)
11	TCM	The Lord's prayer (Norton)
12	DCM	The ten commandments (Norton)
15 (ex. 9d)	DCM	Psalm 1 (Sternhold)
17	DCM	Psalm 3 (Sternhold)
36	DCM	Psalm 18 (Sternhold)
63 (ex. 9a)	DCM	Psalm 44 (Sternhold)
69	X^4Y^2	Psalm 50, 1st version (Whittingham)
71	DLM	Psalm 51, 1st version (Whittingham)
86	DCM	Psalm 69 (Hopkins?)
93	DCM	Psalm 77 (Hopkins)
99 (ex. 9e)	DCM	Psalm 81 (Hopkins)
114 (ex. 76)	LM	Psalm 100, 1st version (Kethe?)
117	DCM	Psalm 103 (Sternhold)
125	8^{12}	Psalm 113 (Kethe)
132	DCM	Psalm 119 (Whittingham)
137	$(668)^2$	Psalm 122 (Kethe)
139	X^5	Psalm 124 (Whittingham)
145a	Z^4X^2	Psalm 126 (Kethe)
149a	$(76)^4$	Psalm 130 (Whittingham)
157	DCM	Psalm 137 (Whittingham)
174 (Fig. 2)	6^44^4	Psalm 148 (Pullain)
178	LM	The ten commandments (Whittingham)
180	8^6	The Lord's prayer (Cox)
183	$(87)^4$	Da pacem, domine (Grindal)
184	LM	Preserve us (Wisdom)
185	6^8	The complaint of a sinner (?)
186	DLM	The lamentation

The order of the tunes is that in which they are most commonly found in the psalm books.

Metres are described as follows. Digits refer to the number of syllables in each line of verse: $X = 10$, $Y = 11$, $Z = 12$. Repeated patterns are shown by indices: $X^5 = 5$ lines of 10 syllables, $(76)^4 = 4$ pairs of lines of 7 and 6 syllables each.

Traditional abbreviations are used for some of the commonest metres:

CM (common metre)	8686	SM (short metre)	6686
DCM (double common metre)	$(8686)^2$	DSM (double short metre)	$(6686)^2$
TCM (triple common metre)	$(8686)^3$	LM (long metre)	8^4
		DLM (double long metre)	8^8

cathedral or parish church choirs; the title page contains no reference to their use in church at all, but rather suggests domestic performance – which, of course, was another way of spreading knowledge of the tunes: *The whole psalmes in foure parts, which may be song to al musical instrumentes, set forth for the encrease of vertue: and aboleshyng of other vayne and triflyng ballades.* This type of collection was followed, later in the century, by those of Daman, Cosyn, and Allison, all based on the tunes in Sternhold and Hopkins.

But a more important way of spreading the tunes was by means of the psalm books themselves, which had the official tunes set out without accompaniment. Most parish churches had at least a parish clerk who could read music, and whose duties still included singing; and it was for parish clerks, and any others able to read music, that the book was doubtless primarily intended. Editions from 1561 carried the musical introduction which sought to teach the skill of sight-singing by way of the traditional gamut, at the same time pointing out the value and virtue of psalm singing. In later editions, from 1569, this was often replaced by a much simpler introduction using six solfa letters, and the tunes were printed with one of these letters alongside each musical note (Fig. 2). For the ordinary reader this system was easier to deal with than the standard musical notation that had been explained in the cumbersome introduction of the earlier editions. No doubt the decline in competent parish clerks had led Day to provide some direct assistance to the literate portion of the congregation.

A few records of parish churches buying copies of metrical psalms have been found:*

St Michael, Cornhill	'8 Geneva books' bought, 1560 4 books ruled for music bought, 1562 Copyist paid for 'pricking 27 songs', 1562	A. Smith: 290
St Margaret, Westminster	'4 books of psalms in metre for the choir' bought in 1562	Wallcott: 60
Smarden	'2 singing psalter books in metre' bought in 1564	Haslewood: 234
St Botolph, Aldersgate	'2 books of psalms for the choir' bought in 1570	A. Smith: 293

Since most parish churches had to buy the prayer book and prose psalter as well as the metrical psalms, these were frequently sold in a single volume. The earliest such combined volume surviving in its original binding is in

* The word 'psalter' by itself in church records is more likely to refer to the prose psalter, which was printed separately from the prayer book.

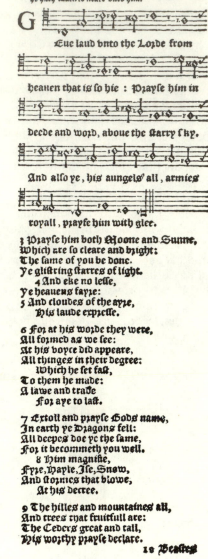

Fig. 2 Psalm 148 with solfa notation *(Whole book of psalms,* STC 2439.5, London, 1569, p. 107)

folio format and dates from 1565 (British Library, C.12.i.1). One unusually specific inventory of 1566 lists a volume of this kind: 'a book containing the ... order of common prayer, and the psalms as they are appointed to be read; with the psalms in metre, appointed to be sung' (A. Smith: 379). A similar early volume combining these three items (the metrical psalms being dated 1567) has an original binding tooled with the name of Sir William

Alyn, lord mayor of London in 1571: perhaps it was used at the Guildhall chapel, or at St Lawrence, Jewry, nearby (see *British Museum general catalogue of printed books: Five-year supplement 1966–1970*: III, 123, and XV, 313).

Another way of familiarising the people with the new tunes was to teach them to the schoolchildren. At many grammar schools the pupils were expected to learn the psalms and then attend the local parish church or cathedral to lead the singing. Provisions of this kind have been found in the statutes of Worcester free school (1561), Sevenoaks grammar school, St Saviour, Southwark, parish school (1562), St Olave, Southwark, parish school (1566), and Kirkby Stephen grammar school (1566) (A. Smith: 379); also at Burford grammar school (1571) (Historical Manuscripts Commission, *Report*: I, 54–5). The statutes at Kirkby Stephen were precise:

Every morning and evening at six of the clock, which are the days for learning of scholars, and keeping of school, the scholars by two and two, and the schoolmaster shall go from the school house into the parish church, and there, devoutly upon their knees before they do enter the choir, say some devout prayer, and after the same they shall repair together unto the chapel or choir ... and there sing together one of these psalms hereafter instituted, such as the schoolmaster shall appoint – so as every one of the said psalms be sung within fifteen days together, viz: [Psalms] 103, 130, 145, 46, 3, 61, 24, 30, 90, 96, 100, 51, 84, 86, 45. (Watson: 42)

This is interesting as being one of the few indications of *specific* metrical psalms sung at any time in Elizabeth's reign. A study of the 13 psalms in the list proves disappointing, however. They seem to be chosen at random: they include psalms long and short, jubilant and penitential, of various metres, some with proper tunes and some without. If anything it suggests that the official printed tunes were not used in this case.

As to the manner in which the tunes were sung, there is unfortunately no description extant, but a few clues can be pieced together. The psalms vary greatly in length, from 8 lines (Psalm 117) to 704 lines (Psalm 119). Selections were made from the longer ones, which were divided for this purpose into 'parts', each of from 32 to 48 lines, or 4 to 6 verses of an 8-line tune. This was probably the typical length of text actually sung (Wither: 136). At first the tempo was lively, judging by the nickname 'Geneva jigs'. The time signature is usually ₵. The tunes are made up chiefly of two note values, the semibreve and the minim, with a long for the final note only. But the semibreves and minims are distributed in such a way that in many cases the tune does not follow any regular beat. In many but not all tunes there is a semibreve or minim rest after every line. Many begin with two or three long notes in a rhythm not repeated later in the tune: perhaps the object of these was to give the congregation time to catch up with the leaders (see ex. 13).

After John Day's death in 1584, a number of editions were carefully revised and brought up to date. Many more changes were made in rhythm than in melody, and most of them tended to standardise the rhythms so that a regular beat could be detected (ex. 13b). From 1621, when Ravenscroft's *Psalms* appeared, further revisions were made under its influence. The time signature was now altered from ₵ to C, and bar-lines were printed at the end of each phrase. Rhythms were further standardised. Most 8-note lines were now printed in the form of six minims and two semibreves: the semibreves were usually the first and last notes, but sometimes there was a syncopated rhythm. Similarly with the 6-note lines. Tunes of irregular metre were revised in much the same way.

These changes are indications of a considerable slowing-down in the tempo of psalm singing – which is exactly what one might expect during a long period of unaccompanied performance and oral transmission. We have already noted that metrical psalms started off as sacred analogues to ballads, both derived from court or theatre songs, and I have suggested that the psalm tunes were originally sung with lute or other instrumental accompaniment. But by the early seventeenth century psalms were no longer being sung at the same tempo as folk ballads. When Ravenscroft printed a number of secular folk tunes in *Pammelia* (1609), *Deuteromelia* (1609), and *Melismata* (1611), he used the crotchet as the normal unit of melody and a time signature of ₵. But for the tunes in his *Psalms* of 1621, he retained the minim as unit and changed the time signature to ₵. The general slowing-down of musical notation, which had been going on for centuries, necessitated the substitution of crotchets for minims as the unit of ordinary melody. But the psalm tunes, unlike other music, had slowed down in actual speed of performance; so the minim, though 'devalued' by comparison with its meaning in 1562, was still the best unit for writing the psalm tunes in 1621. The time signature was altered because a minim now represented two beats instead of one: a 'beat' being the ordinary tactus of somewhat under one second. In Playford's *Introduction* (1658 edition onwards) we find, in the same book, psalm tunes printed in minims and semibreves, and songs and dances printed in crotchets and quavers. There is no doubt that ₵ indicated a slower tempo than ₵ in the seventeenth century. Praetorius said that ₵ denoted 'lento:tarde:langsam' while ₵ denoted 'presto:velociter:geschwindt' (Herrmann-Bengen:44).

Thus in the course of Elizabeth's reign, psalm tunes had gradually become a distinctly slower kind of music than the secular songs to which they had once been closely related. The solemnity associated with church music, and more particularly with congregational psalm (later hymn) singing, can be seen to date from this time: already there was a sharp distinction between the sacred and the secular modes of performance. When comparing a tune of 1562 with a version of the same tune printed fifty years later, we should halve the note-lengths of the earlier version to make the comparison realistic (see ex. 13d).

It is obvious that in the conditions under which the psalm tunes were generally sung in parish churches, rhythms could not have been precise, and this accounts for both the disappearance of old rhythmic distinctions, and the appearance of new ones. As early as 1562, two versions of the same tune were printed in the same book in different rhythms – one (F. 93) in common time, the other (F. 99) in triple time. Some members of a congregation would tend to wait for others to give a lead, and would follow them, perceptibly later, to the next note of the tune. This produced a general tendency to slowness. It had other effects also, which will become evident at a later period.

Another question of performing practice concerns *musica ficta*: specifically, the sharpening of the leading note in the D, G, and A modes. (There were no tunes in the E mode from 1562 onwards.) It is well known, of course, that the leading note in these modes tended to be sharpened in performance, even when no sharp was written; this was especially true in harmonised music, where the sharpening produced a major instead of a minor triad on the dominant. On the other hand many folk songs survived into the twentieth century and were recorded with these notes still unsharpened. The sharpening tendency was one of art music, not folk music. As we might expect, there is little likelihood that it took place in parish churches at this period. In some editions of the psalm book from 1569 onwards, Day, as already mentioned, printed solfa letters (VRMFSL, for ut, re, mi, fa, sol, la) beside the notes as an aid to the untrained reader (Fig. 2). The purpose of solmisation, on which these letters were based, was to distinguish between whole-tone and half-tone steps. The key syllable was *mi* (letter M in Day's system): it told the singer that the next upward step was to be a semitone, and the other letters told him where he was in relation to this semitone step. In all the tunes in the D, G, and A modes, the leading note in these editions is represented by V, F, or S, showing that it is a whole tone below the final or tonic. It seems certain that Day, at least, meant them to be sung in that way. To apply *musica ficta* to the solfa letters themselves would defeat their only purpose. In the few tunes where 'accidentals' are required – the same degree of the scale treated as both natural and flat – a different letter is used to distinguish the two pitches.*

Sharpened leading-notes appear in all harmonised tune books from Day's (1563) onwards, but they are found rarely and sporadically in the common psalm books, until the revisions of 1622 under the influence of Ravenscroft's harmonised tune book. The solfa printings were never revised. They continued to appear in editions or parts of editions until after 1630, but with so many errors that they cannot have been much used after 1600.

The official tunes of Sternhold and Hopkins remained a part of parish church music throughout the seventeenth century, and a hard-core group of them survived well into the eighteenth. They were gradually shorn of archaic features (as were the texts), by *musica ficta*, and by the straightening out of their rhythms into a series of solemn equal notes. But on the whole they remained a conservative bulwark against further inroads of tunes and styles from secular art music.

The 'common' tunes

The evidence presented strongly suggests that the official tunes printed in the psalm books were not well known when they were introduced to the

* The three tunes are those for Psalms 126, 130, and 148 (F. 145a, 149a, 174). Two of them are originally from the French psalter and the third, shown in Fig. 2, from the Anglo-Genevan book of 1558. In each case the letter M appears with a note (B or E) when it is to be sung as a natural; later, the letter F with the same note indicates a flat. This interpretation is confirmed by flat signs before the notes concerned, either in the same source or in another source of the same tune.

public, and that the Puritan leaders sought to promote or impose them by various means. But the early descriptions of congregational singing show that it spread very quickly and was taken up by thousands of people. Such evidence tends the other way: it points to well-known tunes, or at least tunes of a popular kind.

A new, dance-like kind of tune, instrumentally accompanied, strongly measured, often of only four lines, was fast taking over the popular ballad, and at the same time earning the contempt of cultivated people, as may be discovered from George Puttenham's *Arte of English poesie*, published about 1570:

Note also that rhyme ... is not commendably used both in the end and middle of a verse [i.e., of a line of verse, such as a 14-syllable line in common metre], unless it be in toys and trifling poesies, for it sheweth a certain lightness either of the matter or of the maker's head, albeit these common rhymers use it much ... so on the other side doth the over busy and too speedy return of one manner of tune, too much annoy & as it were glut the ear, unless it be in small and popular music sung by these cantabanqui upon benches and barrels' heads where they have none other audience than boys or country fellows that pass by them in the street, or else by blind harpers or such like tavern minstrels that give a fit of mirth for a groat, & their matters being for the most part stories of old time, as the tale of Sir Topas, the reports of Bevis of Southampton, Guy of Warwick, Adam Bell, and Clymme of the Clough & such other old romances or historical rhymes, made purposely for recreation of the common people at Christmas dinners and bridals, and in taverns and alehouses and such other places of base resort, also they be used in carols and rounds and such light or lascivious poems, which are commonly more commodiously uttered by these buffoons or vices in plays than by any other person. (Puttenham:83–4)

With such associations perhaps some Puritans did not want ballads to provide the music of the psalms. And yet the great majority of Sternhold and Hopkins's psalms are in exactly the metre of the ballads which Puttenham scorns, and can easily be fitted, for example, to the tune 'Guy of Warwick' mentioned by him, or to 'Rowland' (ex. 8). It seems reasonable to suppose that tunes like these were used when London congregations began to sing the metrical psalms in 1559.

By the seventeenth century the singing of psalms to actual tunes associated with dancing, sexual love, profanity or the theatre was anathema to church authorities of any shade of opinion. The Puritan George Wither condemned the impiety of using 'those roguish tunes, which have formerly served for profane jigs' for psalms, which he said was as bad as using psalm tunes with profane words (1619: 87). The suppression of Howes's reference to 'galliards and measures' has already been mentioned. In 1630 the court of high commission censured William Slatyer, rector of Otterden (Kent), for attaching to a book of metrical psalms 'a scandalous table to the disgrace of religion, and to the encouragement of the contemnors thereof' (A. Wood: III, 27). The book is entitled *Psalmes, or songs of Sion: turned into the language, and set to the tunes of a strange land ... intended for Christmas carols, and fitted to divers of the most noted and common, but solemne tunes, every where in this land familiarly used and knowne.* The 'scandalous table' at the end gives the tunes of many ballads and other secular tunes, as well as a few tunes from the psalm book.*

In Scotland, Wedderburn's psalm collection, *Ane compendious buik of godly and spirituall sangis* (1567), had set psalms to popular tunes, but no such publication had been sanctioned in England at that time. If the psalms were sung to such tunes, the proceeding was unofficial. On the other hand there was much less reason to object to the use of tunes of similar style and type to the new ballad tunes, provided they did not have 'profane' or 'lascivious' associations.

It is significant that the psalms early acquired the nickname 'Geneva jigs'. It is said to have been used by Queen Elizabeth herself (Davies: I, 387); it was certainly used by John Trevelyan, a Catholic gentleman of Cornwall (J. P. Collier: 116). The term 'jig' itself was comparatively new. The jig was closely related to the ballad: it was, in fact, a kind of ballad in dialogue, presented on the stage with song and dancing (Baskervill: 3–4, 28). It was criticised by Roger Ascham as barbaric and primitive, and was attacked by Puritans (Baskervill: 31). To call psalms 'Geneva jigs' showed not only contempt for their homely, popular character, but a recognition that they had some likeness to the jig proper. It is hard to reconcile the phrase with the official printed tunes such as those in exx. 9 and 12.

The tunes composed by Thomas Tallis for Archbishop Parker's *Psalter* in the 1560s (Frost: 376–93), though very severe, do have the kind of metrical regularity and structure lacking in the official tunes printed by Day. One of them, 'Tallis's Canon', later shortened from eight lines to four, was to become truly 'popular' (Temperley, 1971: 375–6), and it may even have been linked with an early ballad tune. The tune 'Who liveth so merry', printed by Ravenscroft in *Deuteromelia* (1609), is a simple tune very similar to Tallis's, and is also a perfect round; its words are found in broadsides as early as 1557–8 (C. Simpson: 776). The official tune to *A lamentation*, possibly by Tallis, also shows signs of the new style, and so does the official tune to Psalm 81, already mentioned, which tended to generate other tunes, shorter than their ancestor: many of them are four-line tunes in common metre.

The kind of tune that was to prevail in the end was a four-line one, only half the length of the 'official' tunes. It came into print by way of cultivated domestic music-making, where it was, at first, indistinguishable from the strophic secular song tune. *The psalmes of David in English meter, with notes of foure partes set unto them* (1579), compiled by William Daman on commission from John Bull, a London goldsmith, was intended for 'the use of godly Christians for recreating themselves, instead of fond and unseemly ballads'. It contained many of the standard psalm tunes in four-part harmonisations, but also two tunes which, under the names 'Oxford' and 'Cambridge' (F. 121, 42), were to be among the most popular psalm tunes in church use. They were reduced to regular triple time. Two others, 'London' and 'Windsor' (F. 45, 129), appeared in Daman's next collection, dated 1591; this time he claimed it contained 'all the tunes of David's psalms, as they are ordinarily sung in the Church'. The two settings (transcribed by

---

* Chappell (I: 110, 122, 240, 310) knew of this book, but only in the British Library copy which lacks the table: the table is intact in the copy at Cambridge University Library. Le Huray (:383) gives the erroneous impression that the book includes the music of the ballad tunes.

Frost) are mildly polyphonic, with each phrase of the tenor tune introduced by imitative entries in the other parts. An alternative arrangement placed the tune in the treble. Allison's *Psalmes* of 1599 is even more clearly 'domestic', for the tunes are set like airs in the treble voice, with accompaniment for lute or voices or both. It includes many of the newly popular short tunes, with the rhythm of each line strictly organised in measures of common time.

We have Thomas East's word for it that before the end of the sixteenth century (1594) all the psalms were sung to one of four tunes 'in most churches of this realm' (Fig. 3). But, as he pointed out in his 1592 preface, these tunes, 'which are commonly sung nowadays', were 'not printed in our common psalm books with the rest'. All were short, or four-line tunes, one in short and the other three in common metre. Not *all* the psalms could be sung to these four tunes without distortion or adaptation; but a great many could (123 psalms and 13 'hymns' in common metre; 6 psalms in short metre), while the others, in unusual metres, were increasingly neglected

Fig. 3 Table of incipits from East's *Psalms*, 1594 edition (PC 13/2, p. 1)

(Dod: preface). The short tunes had several advantages over the official, long tunes. They were simple and direct; they had a tendency to fall into a periodic rhythm; they had only two cadence points, one generally on the dominant or supertonic, the second on the tonic; they were easy to memorise. In short, they were modern, more like ballad tunes derived from court songs and dances. And they could be sung more often, since they were free of association with any particular psalm: they were 'common' rather than 'proper' tunes. For this reason they could not be referred to by the name of a psalm or hymn, but had to be given names of their own, such as the names of cathedral cities. It is usually said that the custom of naming tunes was the invention of Thomas East, and it is certainly true that East's psalm book of 1592 was the first to print tune names. But the names were current independently of any action by East. For example Dod, in the preface to *Al the psalmes of David* (1620), recommended 'at the least X or XII other usual & good tunes, which were never entered into the said common book (to wit) the Scottish tune, the Cheshire tune, the Bristoll tune, the Banburie tune &c.' Of these names only 'Cheshire' had appeared in East, while only 'Bristol' was to appear in Ravenscroft's *Psalms* published the following year.

Only four of the official tunes had been of the short or four-line variety,* and none of these was in common metre; all were of French or German origin, and two (the 'Old Hundredth' and the 'Ten Commandments' tune) were among the most popular of all the official tunes. To sing the great majority of versions to short tunes, however, common-metre tunes were needed. Four of them made their first appearance in *The whole book of psalms* in an edition of 1588 (STC 2475.2), printed by Henry Denham; in one form or another all four of these had previously appeared in print, two of them in Daman's book. Others were first printed in East's *Psalms* of 1592. Some of them seem to be derived from earlier, longer tunes. One or two are similar to known secular songs of the period: for example 'Windsor' (F. 12a) resembles 'How should I your true love know' (Chappell: 56, 236).

The most interesting, as well as the earliest, of these tunes is the one that Ravenscroft christened 'Oxford' (ex. 14, verse 1). It first appeared in print with a new version of Psalm 108 by John Craig, in the Scottish psalm book of 1564.† But it may very possibly have been current in England before that time. Damon printed it in 1579. It is a distinctive tune, and a very strange one, for it begins on F and ends on G. Thomas Campion in 1618 found it 'quite contrary to nature' and attributed its popularity to the ignorance of parish clerks. He suggested emending it by changing the first note to F sharp and harmonising it on the dominant of G minor: this solution was adopted by Ravenscroft. Even with this change the tune is unusual: how many psalm or hymn tunes begin on the leading note? Its repeated notes and almost exclusively stepwise motion might suggest a Gregorian psalm chant, and it is possible, indeed, that it had its origin in the 6th psalm tone. (It has already been noted that in Edward VI's time metrical psalms were chanted to the psalm tones.) But a more attractive theory (from the point of

* Tunes to Psalm 100 (F. 114), Psalm 134 (F. 153), the ten commandments (F. 178), and 'Preserve us' (F. 184). The Benedicite tune (F. 6) had three lines.
† See bibliography under 'Church of Scotland'.

view adopted here) would derive it from the well-known court song 'Pastime with good company' (ex. 10a), attributed to Henry VIII but also found as a French chanson first printed in 1529 (Ward, 1960: 123). There is also some resemblance to the reconstructed tenor tune of ex. 4, particularly the first line.

If the origin of 'Oxford' is ambiguous, it at least has characteristics similar to those of measured art songs. It is no masterpiece, but it has character and is easy to sing. Like the other three tunes identified by East as the most common, it has a very limited range. At any rate it must have been widely used. Not only was it set by East to no fewer than 33 psalm and hymn texts, but it generated three other psalm tunes which became popular in their turn, as we shall see later.

The 'common' tunes – there were only eight in East's book* – had a corporate character clearly descended from earlier art songs. Their square rhythm, small compass, and regular cadences are strongly reminiscent of some of the songs from Henry VIII's time (see, for instance, ex. 10b, bars 9–17), or the Edwardian choir settings of Sternhold's psalms (ex. 4). They reappeared in dozens of seventeenth-century psalm collections and tune books. This relatively small number of tunes, occasionally varied by one of the old 'official' ones, had already become the core of English congregational singing, and was to remain so for over a century. Ravenscroft's *Psalms* of 1621 attempted to introduce a large number of new short tunes, some of them from the Scottish psalm book, but only a few of these caught the public fancy, notably 'York', 'Martyrs' and 'St David's'. Barton in 1644 claimed to 'have collected the most choice and exquisite tunes that are or have been used in all England', but 'leaving multitudes of tunes (in *Ravenscroft*) as unnecessary and burdensome' (PC 20: preface). Playford in his collections after the Restoration had very few new tunes to add to the common stock, and those he did were probably derived from others already known (Temperley, 1972a: 359, 371). Throughout the seventeenth century only one tune of more than four lines entered the popular domain: the magnificent tune to Psalm 104 first published by Ravenscroft and probably composed by him (F. 119). This, together with a handful of the short tunes he introduced, was inserted into some editions of Sternhold and Hopkins from 1621 onwards.

Another kind of 'popular' tune was one derived from an official tune by evolution in the course of oral transmission. Several short tunes seem to have come from the first half of a long tune printed in the psalm book, or some other collection such as Tye's *Actes of the apostles* (e.g. F. 19, 129). This process is also found in secular folk song. It is due, no doubt, to lapse of memory on the part of a body of singers. The well-known carol tune 'The first nowell' is probably an example of this type of derivation (Routley, 1958: 97). A further possibility is the adaptation of a tune in one metre to a text in another; this, too, generally involves omission of notes, as the tune goes most frequently from the longer to the shorter metre. We know that parish clerks sometimes chose a tune in a metre that did not fit the words (see p. 92): this would inevitably produce a 'new' tune derived from the

---

* F. 19, 42, 45, 103, 109, 121, 129, 172. See Fig. 3.

old. Probable examples are as follows, with dates of first appearances in print of each version:

F. 93/99	DCM	(1562)	became	F. 103	CM	(1592)
			and later	F. 154a	SM	(1671)
F. 10	DCM	(1561)	became	F. 209	CM	(1615)
F. 42b	CM	(1588)	became	F. 45	SM	(1591)
F. 172	CM	(1592)*	became	F. 65	SM	(1579)
F. 93/99	DCM	(1562)	became	F. 135	6^6	(1569)
F. 143a	LM	(1599)	became	F. 143b	CM	(1677)
F. 362a	LM	(1623)	became	F. 362c	CM	(1677)

Harmonised psalm books: East and Ravenscroft

Several books were published in the Elizabethan and Jacobean periods in which the metrical psalms and their tunes were made the basis of simple or elaborate settings in four, five or six parts. Some used the Sternhold and Hopkins versions, others did not (le Huray: 379–82, 386–401, 403–5; Temperley, 1979). They were for domestic use, in most cases explicitly so, and they did not include the full text of the psalms. Those of Day, Daman and Allison have already been described. A very different kind of book, and the first of its kind, was Thomas East's *The whole booke of psalmes: with their wonted tunes, as they are song in churches, composed into foure partes: all of which are so placed that foure may sing ech one a several part* (1592: PC 13). As the title implies, this was a psalm book, containing the entire texts of all the psalms and hymns of the standard version. This alone suggests that it was intended for use in church as well as for the recreation of devout families. There is no explicit indication of this, probably because East wanted his book to be as widely accepted as possible. Even if the queen had overcome her early distaste for metrical psalms, it is certain that many Puritans kept up their opposition to 'curious' or 'exquisite' music, which they associated with 'popery'.

East's settings were largely note-for-note, in four parts with the 'church tune' in the tenor. The parts were set out separately, but were all printed in the same opening of the book; the first verse of each psalm was underlaid, the rest printed below or on subsequent pages. East left the official tunes with their usual psalms, but for most of the psalms not provided with proper tunes in the common psalm book, he ignored the cross-references and provided new four-line tunes, choosing for the great majority of psalms one of the four tunes he designated as most popular.† The settings were 'compiled by sundry authors, who have so laboured herein, that the unskilful with small practice may attain to sing that part, which is fittest for their voice'. Allison, Cavendish, Dowland, and Farmer are among the musicians he called on: le Huray has pointed out that none of these were church musicians (:381).

* The fact that the shorter version was printed before the longer does not, of course, mean that it must have existed first. In general the printing dates support the theory that the shorter versions derived from the longer.

† The 1592 edition had 98 out of 190 psalms and hymns set to the new four-line tunes, 92 of which used one of the four 'popular' tunes. In the 1594 edition the figures were 110 out of 190, with 104 to the 'popular' ones.

The book was popular, running to four editions (the last published in 1611), and a 'pocket version', similar to the 1594 edition, was published by William Barley in about 1599 (Illing, 1968). The four-part settings are very likely to have been sung and played in religious homes, and they may well have been used by cathedral and collegiate choirs. Were they also used in ordinary parish churches? We have seen how very few parish choirs remained by the end of Elizabeth's reign. And yet the book seems well adapted for a choir to sing in harmony, while the congregation sang from the ordinary psalm books. The new short tunes were already known to most churchgoers; the less familiar long tunes were printed in their common psalm books.

In one series of editions, the tunes were altered in conformity with East's selection. These were the octavo 'Middleburg' editions (Temperley, 1976). The prototype was printed by Richard Schilders at Middleburg in 1602 (PC 702/1602). It contained the complete texts of all 150 metrical psalms (but without the 6 alternative versions or the 24 'Divine Hymns'). Ninety-three of them were furnished with tunes, in every case identical with the tunes selected by East for the psalms concerned. In 1605 the Stationers' Company printed a copy of this book (PC 15/1605), with all its tunes, and restoring four old tunes omitted by Schilders. It was reprinted five times. Apart from this edition, however, East's book had little influence on the music of the common psalm books. The 16mo 'Middleburg' edition was only mildly influenced by it; a few other editions incorporated a handful of the short tunes; and that is all.

It may be significant that the octavo 'Middleburg' edition, the only one that could be used precisely in accordance with East's *Psalms*, was a book of strongly Puritanical cast, as we have already seen. It looks as if note-for-note harmonisations such as East provided were particularly favoured in educated Puritan circles.

The next harmonised edition, and the last of its kind, was Ravenscroft's *The whole booke of psalmes: with the hymns evangelicall, and songs spirituall. Composed into 4. parts by sundry authors* (1621: PC 16). It was very similar to East's book in appearance, layout, and intention; some of its music was actually printed from the same typesetting, which has led Robert Illing (1969) to claim that it should be regarded as simply a revised edition of East. Illing has distinguished three issues of this publication, which vary in their title pages and prefatory matter. Some have a preface, 'Of the praise, virtue, and efficacy of the psalms', which forcefully defends the singing of harmonised psalms in church. The tunes, Ravenscroft declared, were 'so composed, for the most part, that the unskilful may with little practice, be enabled to sing them in parts, after a plausible manner'. This preface was missing in the advance or dedication issue, one of the dedicatees being the Archbishop of Canterbury: Illing explains the omission on grounds of haste, but it may have been to avoid offending ecclesiastical prejudice. The title page of this issue contained the words 'That all clerks of churches may know what tune each proper psalm may be sung to', which can only refer to the list of named tunes on page 1, headed 'An index of such names of the tunes of the psalms, usually sung in cathedral churches, collegiates, chapels, &c. As also, the foreign tunes sung in Great Britain'. The names allotted by Ravenscroft include all the cathedrals of England and Wales, and a few other towns or institutions where collegiate choirs existed (Cambridge, Christ's Hospital, Windsor or Eton, Ludlow, Manchester, Southwell, Wolverhampton; see Appendix 1); otherwise they are from the Scottish psalter (Glasgow, Martyrs) or suggest a geographical origin for the tune (Low Dutch). All this suggests an interest in choral rather than congregational harmony. On the title page of the standard issue, the phrase quoted above was altered: 'That all clerks of churches, and the auditory, may know what tune each proper psalm may be sung to'.

As we have seen, Ravenscroft introduced many new tunes in his book, but few of them were generally adopted (Temperley, 1972a: 336). For his settings he reprinted some from East and Barley, and for others went back to Day's book of 1563; from Parker's psalter he took Tallis's Canon, reduced to half its original length; and he used new settings by ten living composers, many of them cathedral musicians (le Huray: 382); the greatest number, however, were by himself.

The book lasted long in the estimation of well-educated musicians, and had much influence. A second edition appeared in 1633. Samuel Pepys, at home on a Sunday evening in 1664, took part in a sing-through of 'Ravenscroft's four-part psalms, most admirable music', with two other men and a boy (Pepys: 27 November 1664). In the 1670s John Playford 'was much importuned by some persons in the West Country to set out a new edition of Mr Ravenscroft's Psalms' (PC 29: preface). Later compilers frequently turned to it for material, and it was republished twice in the eighteenth century and once in the nineteenth.

Nevertheless, there is little to suggest that it was widely used in parish churches during the period following its first publication. As with East, one of the 'Middleburg' editions of the common psalm book (this time the 16mo) was brought into conformity with it (Temperley, 1976). A few of Ravenscroft's tunes and revisions – notably the new tune to Psalm 104 – found their way into some other editions. A wholehearted effort to teach Ravenscroft's tunes to the public was not made until 1688, in the edition by Thomas Mathew (PC 33).

We must conclude that four-part harmony was more than ever a rarity in parish churches, now that organs and choirs had largely disappeared from them. There is certainly no evidence to support one writer's claim that 'by the middle of the seventeenth century four-part singing was, where possible, looked upon as normal... This, of course, did not imply that congregations sang in four parts, but that there was an accompaniment and probably some body of singers more skilled than the rest' (C. Phillips: 130). After Ravenscroft's, no other edition of Sternhold and Hopkins with harmonised tunes was to appear until Playford's of 1677.

Popular harmony: descant

Despite the general absence of choirs, and the failure of East's and Ravenscroft's settings to take root in parish churches, the singing in some churches was not totally without harmony. There was a tradition of improvised descant, perhaps derived from the practice of faburden, in which a second part, generally higher than the tune, was sung with it in note-for-note fashion, moving usually to the nearest available consonance, with an occasional cadence suspension. The evidence for the existence of this tradition is indirect, but it is highly persuasive.

Among the four-line tunes that were popular at the end of the sixteenth century are some that can be sung note-for-note against other tunes, forming good harmony. For example the tune 'Glassenburie' (F. 109) fits almost perfectly as a descant to 'Oxford'. A third tune, 'Kentish' (F. 111), though it will not fit 'Oxford', makes a perfect descant to 'Glassenburie'. In each case the fit is note-against-note, independent of rhythm (ex. 14). All three tunes are found in East, where they are independently harmonised. Each tune was popular in its own right, and they all appear from time to time in later collections, including Playford's of 1677.

It might be argued that these tunes fit together by pure chance. But there is in this case definite evidence that the tunes were related to each other harmonically. Charles Butler stated that the mean and tenor of 'Oxford' had been 'made two several tunes, (under the names of Glassenburie and Kentish Tunes) with other parts set unto them' in East's *Psalms* (:44), though in setting them out in musical notation he confused the names.

Another tune (F. 25), popular at a somewhat later date, is also an exact fit to 'Oxford', and in view of the clear evidence that such things happened, we can hardly doubt that this was its origin. It was variously known as 'London', 'London Old' or 'Litchfield', and was frequently printed between 1650 and 1750 (Temperley, 1971: 488–9). Like its parent 'Oxford' it is curiously ambiguous in tonality, and provoked comment on this account: Thomas Twining, a correspondent of Burney's, wrote the tune down and sent it to him in 1777, with the comment: 'Here is a most curious piece of barbarism for you. This psalm-tune is often sung at Colchester... I never heard anything so horrible and strange; 'tis worse than a Greek fragment' (Twining: 54).

Other cases of 'harmonic derivation' of tunes can be traced. William Barton in his *Psalms* of 1644 prints 'Dutch bass tune, used commonly in Cambridge, and of late in [St Mary] Aldermanbury [London], it agrees in consort with the tune following, so that it is all one whether you take, for they may be sung both together'; the 'tune following' is 'Low Dutch' (F. 19). In this case the match is less perfect, the two tunes occasionally moving in consecutive unisons or fifths. In the case of 'Coleshill' and 'Windsor', whose relationship was noted by Erik Routley (1957: 52), more than half the notes are identical in the two tunes (see ex. 15a).

Apart from Butler the only known publication that actually shows this type of harmonisation in musical notation is a rare collection of Latin metrical psalms published at Oxford in 1681 for use at university and college sermons.* It contains ten tunes, all standard ones used with English metrical psalms; some of them have alternative or 'choosing notes', as they were later known, which amount to partial descants (ex. 15a).

---

* *Psalmi aliquot Davidici in metrum Latini traducti* (1681). See bibliography, p. 409.

The phenomenon of harmonic derivation tells us a good deal, by inference, about the way metrical psalms were sung in the late sixteenth and early seventeenth centuries. It may be noted, first, that the one source describing the process (Butler) and the one source providing examples for simultaneous use (the Oxford Latin psalm book) are 'learned' in their associations. The ability to improvise descants had originally been part of the training of chantry priests and parish clerks; with their disappearance or decline, it would be found only among educated men, who might exercise it in church to bring some variety to a dreary occupation. But we have found, in several cases, the descant detaching itself from the original tune and establishing itself as a tune in its own right. In all known cases the newer tune was the *upper* strand in the two-part harmony. We may easily reconstruct what happened. A well-known tune was set; a few skilful singers improvised a descant above it; this became, in one church, a standard practice every time the original tune was sung; some of the less educated members of the congregation began to think of the upper line as the real tune; they sang it with the descanters, learned it, and began to sing it elsewhere; and so it spread to other churches, where nobody knew its connection with the first tune.* In the case of 'Kentish' this had apparently happened twice in succession by the time East printed the tune in 1592. In the case of 'Oxford' and 'London', John Playford printed them side by side, with mutually incompatible basses, and was apparently unaware of the connection between them. Sometimes, as with F. 25, the new tune was a complete counterpoint to the old. But in many cases the new tune only diverged from the old for parts of its length. Again, this is easily explained if we imagine an unskilled congregation attempting to follow a two-part harmonisation sung by a few skilled members. At times they would follow the original tune, at times the descant. If the new tune has enough in common with the old, it is usually perceived by editors as another 'version' of the 'same' tune. For example, the tune called 'Canterbury' by Playford (F. 19a, 19b) has close similarities to the earlier tune called 'Low Dutch' by Ravenscroft (F. 19). Frost explained this relationship by stating that Playford 'recast this tune twice, giving it the name Canterbury' (Frost: 71). For this and similar changes Playford has been called 'an "improver" who anticipated by two centuries the often nefarious activities of Monk' (Routley, 1957: 45). But Playford explained in his preface his desire to record the tunes as they were actually sung at the time (Temperley, 1972a: 366). Ex. 15b shows how 'Canterbury' could have evolved from 'Low Dutch', sung with a descant (or, as it might have been called, a 'counter') that was sometimes above, sometimes below the tune.

Summary and evaluation

At the beginning of Elizabeth's reign, much survived from older musical practice. But despite her own love of ceremony, and her express injunction

---

* Some corroboration for this theory may be seen in a statement made early in the seventeenth century in a treatise on church music: 'Through ignorance men do often sing children's parts' (MS 36: fol. 9).

to preserve the endowments for choral music, the surviving parish choirs and organs gradually disappeared, leaving congregations to the mercy of the parish clerk, who could no longer, in most cases, be relied on for musical leadership. In parish churches, as opposed to cathedrals, the Puritan ideal for music scored a decisive victory. The resulting clear separation between cathedral and parochial music was not seriously challenged until the eighteenth century.

Unaccompanied congregational psalm singing spread quickly after its introduction in 1559, and was soon a treasured part of popular culture. Only one version of the psalms was used: *The whole book of psalms* of Sternhold, Hopkins and others, put together by John Day from a variety of sources. Although its poetic merit was small, it was a considerable achievement. Its chief virtue was homeliness, which brought religious expression within reach of the common people. For the first time they experienced communal participation in public worship.

The psalms were at first probably sung to well-known popular tunes in which all could join. The Puritan leaders then tried to introduce the tunes that had been used by the exiles on the Continent, and which had originated probably in accompanied songs known only to a small circle. They printed them in the psalm books, but were only partially successful in spreading a knowledge of them over the country. The main reason, no doubt, was that these tunes, deprived of instrumental accompaniment, were not very suitable for popular singing; they lacked features to make them catchy or memorable. There were exceptions, however, and some of the 'official' tunes did become widely known. They were taken over into an oral congregational tradition, and lost what was left of their original rhythms, as can be seen from modifications in the later editions of the psalm book.

But the better-known kind of tune, also originating in court or theatre songs but simpler, more up to date in style, more obviously rhythmical, and shorter by half, overtook most of the official tunes in popularity, and gradually found its way into the psalm books. These new tunes were similarly changed by oral transmission, and also generated other tunes by descant, in which both skilled and popular processes played a part.

The short tunes, which were the real core of parish church music at this time, were excessively restricted, not only in their shape and rhythm but in their melodic resource. Tunes with large range or wide leaps tended to be ironed and flattened by hard use. Within these limits, however, several of the tunes have a classic depth and simplicity that have carried them through all the succeeding changes.

By the early seventeenth century, psalm singing was deeply entrenched, independent of theological theories or of parties in Church and State. It rolled on slowly with irresistible momentum, gathering traditions on its way. There is no evidence that the harmonised psalm books of East and Ravenscroft were widely used in church. Instead, improvised harmonies, seldom in more than two parts, were sometimes added by resourceful amateurs. The tunes had slowed to half their original pace, and were reduced to a small number, mostly of the short variety. Such was the national form of religious and musical expression on which the musicians of later times were obliged to build.

4 Commonwealth and Restoration (1644–1700)

The Puritan ascendancy and the parish church

England was now to undergo another period of turmoil in which religion was a paramount issue. The attempt of Archbishop Laud, with the full backing of the king, to enforce detailed conformity to the ritual prescribed by the prayer book was one of the arbitrary exercises of authority that united and strengthened the opponents of the royal government. When the Long Parliament met in November 1640, it used its unprecedented power to carry out drastic religious reforms. The Scots, whose army was the chief basis of that power, insisted on the establishment of Presbyterianism. In January 1643, therefore, the bill for the abolition of episcopacy passed both houses. In August of the same year, the Solemn League and Covenant expressing the Presbyterian philosophy was approved by the Westminster Assembly of Divines which parliament had set up, passed by both houses, and on 2 February 1644 ordered to be subscribed by all men over the age of eighteen. Naturally, the Covenant did not receive the royal assent. Since it was clearly incompatible with loyalty to Church and king, many parish clergy resigned or were ejected from their livings, probably as many as 2000. The Assembly prepared a *Directory for the publique worship of God*, which was passed by Parliament, to come into force on 3 January 1645: the *Book of common prayer* was abolished, and its use from then onwards made illegal. A later and more effective ordinance (23 October) required the distribution in churches of copies of the directory, penalties for its non-use, and removal of copies of the prayer book (W. Shaw: I, 356). On 19 August 1645 a Presbyterian system of church government based on Calvinistic principles was established by law. It provided that 'all parishes and places whatsoever, except peers' chapels, shall be brought under the government of congregational, classical, provincial, and national assemblies' (Hutton: 156). However, the victory of Cromwell's army over parliament ensured that this system would never be fully enforced. Toleration was extended to Independent sects of all kinds, and even to Jews, who were readmitted to the country in 1655; but it was still denied to Anglicans and Roman Catholics.

It was hardly possible during this period for a conscientious Anglican priest to retain the incumbency of a parish church, though there were a few cases of clandestine services. Evelyn's diary records that he 'heard the common prayer (a rare thing in these days) in St Peter's, at Paul's Wharf, London' on 25 March 1649. In 1655 a still more severe proclamation by Cromwell went into effect, and on 3 August 1656 Evelyn 'went to London, to receive the blessed sacrament, the first time the Church of England was reduced to a chamber and conventicle; so sharp was the persecution. The

77

parish churches were filled with sectaries of all sorts ... Dr Wild preached in a private house in Fleet Street.' On 25 December 1657 Evelyn and others were arrested by soldiers when receiving the sacrament in Exeter Chapel, London: the celebration of Christmas had been specifically forbidden by parliament in 1644.

The deprived Anglican parish priests were replaced by Presbyterian ministers, some of whom later made way in their turn for Independents elected by the congregations. The order of the public services was laid down in the *Directory* (:10–39), and was as follows:

1   Introductory prayer
2   Bible readings
3   Psalm
4   Prayers
5   Sermon
6   Prayers
7   Psalm (optional)
8   Blessing and dismissal

This form will be seen to have much in common with that of the Puritan exiles of the previous century, and it has been the basis of most Presbyterian worship since that time. It gave the sermon pride of place in a nearly symmetrical design; it did away entirely with all set forms, leaving the choice and wording of spoken parts of the service to the discretion of the minister; and, for the first and only time in English history, it gave metrical psalms a full place in legally established worship. In another section, 'Of singing of psalms', it was laid down unequivocally that 'it is the duty of Christians to praise God publicly, by singing of psalms together in the congregation, and also privately in the family' (*Directory*: 83). No psalms were mentioned in the orders of service provided for communion, baptism, marriage, or public fasting. For public thanksgiving, 'because singing of psalms is of all other the most proper ordinance for expressing of joy and of thanksgiving, let some pertinent psalm or psalms be sung for that purpose, before or after the reading of some portion of the Word suitable to the present business' (:81).

Metrical psalms had always been cherished by Puritans as one of the features of their own brand of worship, and were still to some extent a symbol of their ideals. Thus in November 1640, at St Margaret, Westminster, the Commons attended church according to custom; 'and here, while the second [i.e., communion] service was reading at the communion-table, the audience began to sing some of Hopkins's metre, and disturbed the office ... The Commons, it seems, had a mind to acquaint the people with part of their design' (J. Collier: VIII, 194).

But the psalms had long since ceased to be the sole property of the Puritan party, and were a treasured possession of the people at large. They could serve equally as a symbol of the royalist cause. Thomas Mace declared that the best church music he ever heard was at York Minster in 1644, when the city, loyal to the king, was under siege. Before the sermon the whole congregation sang a psalm according to custom, with the choir and 'a most Excellent-large-plump-lusty-full-speaking-Organ' that had cost £1000 (Mace: 19).

The desirability of psalm singing was discussed in a number of lengthy tracts in this period, particularly during the early 1640s. The moderate Puritan view was best summed up by Nathaniel Holmes in *Gospel musick. Or, the singing of Davids psalms, &c. in the publick congregations, or private families asserted, and vindicated* (1644). He gave both scriptural and *a priori* justifications for the 'necessariness of singing with other ordinances': 'Before sermon the churches sing, to quicken their hearts to prayer. After communion they sing, to raise them up in praise... The psalm after a sermon sometimes hath done that which the sermon alone could not do.' He pointed out that singing is the only 'active vocal prophesying' allowed to women in church, and that it may also bring religion home to many who would otherwise be deaf to it: he cited the Indians in New England as an example.

In the customary manner Holmes then proceeded to deal with possible objections to the singing of psalms. One of the most significant was the third: 'From the *form*... that it is liturgical, and cathedral, as in Pauls and Westminster, &c.' He answered in this way:

David's psalms sung in our English metre differ much from cathedral singing, which is so abominable, in which is sung almost everything, unlawful litanies, and creeds, and other prose not framed in metre fit for singing. Besides they do not let all the congregation, neither sing, nor understand what is sung; *battologizing* and quavering over the same words vainly. Yea nor do they all sing together, but first one sings an anthem, then half the choir, then the other, tossing the word of God like a tennis-ball. Then all yelling together with confused noise. This we utterly dislike as most unlawful. (Holmes: 19)

We see from these familiar arguments that as far as church music was concerned, the main animus of puritan hostility was still against the use of nonscriptural texts and against elaborate music in the cathedral style. Indeed cathedral services had been entirely wiped out by about 1647 (le Huray: 53–4). Many cathedrals were used as ammunition warehouses or military staging posts. In parish churches, though the liturgy was entirely abolished, the musical part of the services remained essentially unaltered. It is true that organs were ordered to be dismantled or destroyed by parliamentary ordinance on 9 May 1644, but we know that the great majority of parish churches were not using organs anyway. One or two country churches managed to keep their organs hidden away, to be brought back after the Restoration.

Psalm singing continued to be encouraged by spokesmen for the official Puritan policy. Instrumental accompaniment was approved for home singing; William Barton, in the preface to his psalm book authorised by the House of Lords in 1644, wrote that 'company and custom, the use of an instrument, or observation of a chime, are excellent and speedy means to learn tunes'.* Philip Goodwin in 1655 urged the revival of family psalm singing in the home, which he said would make it more lively in public worship (Goodwin: 306). Psalm settings with instrumental accompani-

* It is possible that chimes were sometimes even used in church to assist the singing. The annual inventory of church goods at Basingstoke from 1645 lists 'a pair of chimes' in place of the former 'pair of organs' (Baigent: 510n.).

ment for domestic use were published during the Commonwealth period, including sets by Henry and William Lawes, William Child, and John Playford.

Psalm tunes were still taught to children at many schools. At Lewisham in 1652 a grammar school was founded by Abraham Colfe (vicar of Lewisham from 1610 to 1657), with places for 31 boys who were to be taught reading, writing, psalm singing, and 'the accidence' (Watson: 215; *DNB*).

The practice of Independents in parish churches during the 1650s is difficult to ascertain, because each congregation was its own master and thus there were no official pronouncements as to their practice. Throughout the seventeenth century there was controversy among Independents, Baptists, and Quakers as to whether the singing of any set form of words could be a true manifestation of the spirit. Thomas Ford, Independent minister at Exeter, followed John Cotton in concluding that only by means of written words could the scriptural injunctions to sing psalms be observed: 'a man cannot conceive and sing a psalm, it being impossible at once to contrive the matter and metre, and be devout too' (T. Ford, cited Curwen, 1880: 42). Psalm singing was allowed by resolutions made at the institution of an Independent Society at Cockermouth church in 1651. At Beccles singing of psalms was begun in 1657, between prayers and sermon on Sunday mornings and afternoons: at communion a psalm was also sung, in the 'New England translation' [i.e. Cotton *et al.*] (Curwen, 1880: 43).

We can see that psalm singing, in itself, was one of the least likely of Puritan institutions to excite opposition, for the simple reason that it had long been a widespread and popular part of worship, the only kind of music ever heard in the ordinary parish church. The Presbyterian authorities, however, also desired to reform or improve psalm singing in certain respects, and here they came up against the conservatism of public taste and feeling.

Efforts to reform the psalms and their performance

The Sternhold and Hopkins version of the psalms had long been under attack, especially in Calvinist circles, for its departures from strictly literal translation of the Hebrew texts. Whittingham had 'conferred with the Hebrew' and emended Sternhold's translations, but once the version had been printed and widely adopted it was difficult to change it further without the authority of the government. Now, with the ascendancy of the Long Parliament, such an opportunity seemed to be at hand; and for encouragement there was the recent example of the 'Bay psalm book', printed at Cambridge, Massachusetts, in 1640 (Cotton *et al.*). William Barton was invited to prepare a revised translation, which he brought out in 1644 (PC 20). In the preface he justified a freely poetic method of translation, for, he said, poetry 'is most necessary for such a work as this, wherein much majesty and gracefulness, together with plainness, sweetness, clearness (suitable to the capacities of vulgar people, and even so many women) is required'. Nevertheless the title claimed that the versions were 'close and proper to the Hebrew'. Thirty-five of the versions, and parts of others, were taken from Sternhold and Hopkins. In a second edition of 1645, the book appeared with an additional thirty of 'the old psalms' incorporated. Among the 'benefits of the following translation' listed in this edition were '1. Nearness to the Hebrew, as far as English and good verse will well allow... 4. The quantity [i.e., metre] of the old psalms retained (though the words (where need is) altered) so that they may be sung, while others (wedded to custom) sing the old.'

However, there was a rival for the privilege of adoption as the official version. Francis Rouse's translation, also 'fitted to such tunes as have been found by experience to be of most general use', was first published privately at Amsterdam, then revised and approved by the Westminster Assembly, and enjoined for use in worship by the Commons on 15 April 1646 (W. Shaw: I, 382). The revised version was officially published by the Stationers' Company later in the same year (MS 73, C: fols. 224v, 234). But the House of Lords never agreed to Rouse's version, because the Independents wanted no specific version enjoined, while others preferred Barton's (W. Shaw: I, 384). The result was that neither Barton's nor Rouse's was legally imposed in England, though in Scotland Rouse's, very much altered, became the basis of the new official version of 1650 (M. Patrick: 90–5).

It is extremely doubtful whether a new version could have been forced on the public even if one had been agreed on by the authorities, but in the absence of a clear directive most congregations simply went on singing Sternhold and Hopkins, which now began to be known as the 'Old Version' (MS 73, D: fol. 5v, 6 August 1655). The most persuasive evidence for this is the evidence of publication. Throughout the period of the Commonwealth, editions of Sternhold and Hopkins continued to appear: not, indeed, in such quantities as in the preceding decades, but still far more frequently than any rival version. What is more many such editions were bound up with bibles just as they had always been, though the *Book of common prayer* was of course lacking. Other versions also appeared in print, including that of Henry King, Bishop of Chichester (PC 22); and other publishers entered the field in rivalry with the Company of Stationers, whose privilege was now more difficult to enforce (Temperley, 1972a: 341, n. 32). As of old, it was clearly in the interests of the Stationers to discourage new translations that might rival the Old Version in popularity. It is noticeable, and perhaps surprising, that the Commonwealth period saw a marked decline in the publication of metrical psalms in general (see Table 6, p. 122).

So the effort to establish a revised version of the psalms failed. But in one other respect parliament did succeed in effecting a reform. The *Directory for publique worship* had this to say 'Of singing of psalms':

In singing of psalms, the voice is to be tunably and gravely ordered; but the chief care must be to sing with understanding, and with grace in the heart, making melody unto the Lord.

That the whole congregation may join herein, every one that can read is to have a psalm book; and all others, not disabled by age or otherwise, are to be exhorted to learn to read. But for the present, where many in the congregation cannot read, it is convenient that the minister, or some other fit person appointed by him and the other ruling officers, do read the psalm, line by line, before the singing thereof. (*Directory*: 83–4)

In this way was introduced the practice of 'lining out', which was to have far-reaching consequences of a kind undreamed of by the assembled divines. It is not very likely that lining out had been practised to any significant extent before it was enjoined by the Assembly, and it may even have been a completely new idea. Bishop Wren, writing some notes in 1660 on the revision of the *Book of common prayer*, proposed the omission of the words 'saying after me' for the general confession, partly on the grounds that 'it gives some countenance to another uncouth and senseless custom, not long since brought in by some factions, one to read a line of a psalm, and then all the rest to sing it' (Jacobson: 55). Playford spoke of 'the late intruding *Scotch* manner of reading every line by the clerk before it is sung' (PC 29: fol. A3r), but although the Scots had certainly taken up the custom, it is improbable that it was of Scottish origin, for the commissioners of the Church of Scotland had opposed the move to allow it when the matter was debated at the Westminster Assembly (W. Shaw: I, 351n.). It quickly became a normal practice. By 1662 it was 'a custom generally used in most if not all parish churches of this kingdom, as well among Presbyterians as others' for 'the psalm that is sung before and after sermon' (Durel: 183). But it was doubtless a Puritan innovation, designed to make sure that the people sang and understood the words of the psalms, as well as the tunes they knew by heart. In addition it facilitated the introduction of a new version of psalms (Rouse: preface; PC 22: preface).

In the matter of tunes the directory had nothing to say, and all the versions printed during the Commonwealth were tailored to fit the tunes associated with the Old Version. Table 2 gives a complete list of the psalm tunes published or recommended during the Commonwealth period (1644–60), other than those in the few musical editions of the Old Version. The only new tunes were published by Barton. Those in his 1644 book are so badly printed that several are unrecognisable (see Frost: 453–6), and at least four of the nine new tunes are descants, basses or combinations of existing tunes. Playford, whose settings of psalm tunes for cithern in 1652 were meant for domestic use, in 1658 began to cater for church use as well. In the edition of his *Introduction to music* printed in that year he inserted a modest collection of standard tunes, each underlaid with the first verse of a Sternhold and Hopkins psalm:

These following tunes of the psalms are of much use, not only for young practitioners in song, but for those parish-clerks which live in country towns and villages, where their skill is as small as their wages: but to them of this city of London, which are most of them skilful and judicious men (in this matter) it will add little to their knowledge; yet I hope and wish it may to some of their congregations, who I am very sensible have great need of instruction herein.
There are many more tunes than I have here set down, but these I chose rather from the rest, as being all of them such as the congregation will join in, and are better acquainted with these than the other tunes. (PC23)

Table 2. *Psalm tunes printed or recommended during the Commonwealth (1644–59)*

Source:	Barton 1644 (PC 20)	Barton 1645 (PC 20)	Roberts 1649	King 1651 (PC 22)	Playford 1652	Barton 1654 (PC 20)	Playford 1658 (PC 23)
Frost no.							
Traditional long tunes (DCM unless otherwise stated)							
2	x						
4	x						
8	x	x					x
15			x				x
71 (DLM)	x	x	x	x		x	x
99		x		x			
125 (8^{12})	x	x	x		x	x	x
132	x	x		x		x	x
174 (6^{4}4^4)		x			x		
180 (8^6)		x					
185 (6^8)	x						
186 (DLM)				x			
Traditional short tunes (CM unless otherwise stated)							
19	x	x			x	x	x
42	x	x	x		x		x
45 (SM)	x	x		x		x	x
65 (SM)	x				x		
103					x		x
111					x		
114 (LM)	x	x	x	x		x	x
121	x	x			x		x
129		x		x	x		x
172		x					
178 (LM)	x	x	x	x			x
205	x	x					x
206		x					x
209	x	x					x
234	x	x					x
New short tunes (CM unless otherwise stated)							
25		x					x
390	x	x					
391	x						
392	x						
393	x						
394 (SM)	x						
a (LM)	x					x	
b		x					
c		x					

Tune *a* is part of F. 125 combined with part of F. 174; tunes *b* and *c* are unidentified. All tunes are in common metre unless another metre is specified.

Barton, 1644 and 1654, and King have tunes unaccompanied; Playford, 1658, has tunes with basses; Playford, 1652, tunes arranged for cithern; Barton, 1645, has tune incipits only; Roberts has tune references, such as 'Sing this as Psalm 51'.

A few editions of Sternhold and Hopkins's *Whole booke of psalms* with tunes were printed during this period; these have not been included. The tunes were the same as in pre-Commonwealth editions.

The Restoration of Church and King

The triumphant return of King Charles II in 1660 brought with it an automatic restoration of the Church of England. The future direction of the Church was for a time uncertain, however. Before his return the king had made a declaration from Breda that he would grant religious freedom to all parties (J. Collier: VIII, 399). To honour it, he summoned the Savoy Conference, at which all parties were represented, to review the liturgy. The Presbyterian divines at the conference recommended drastic reforms (Procter: 172–89), including the revision of the Sternhold–Hopkins psalm versions. (To this the bishops replied: 'Singing of psalms in metre is no part of the liturgy, and by consequence no part of our commission.') None of the proposals were accepted. Parliament and public opinion, as well as the king's private inclination, were anti-Puritan at this point. The revisions made were mostly of a minor character, and, if anything, in the opposite direction to that desired by the Presbyterians.

The revised *Book of common prayer* was annexed to the new Act of Uniformity, which became law on 19 May 1662 and has been in force (though amended) to this day. In this Act the tolerance expressed by the King at Breda had been overcome by the vengeful severity of the strongly royalist, high-church parliament. It bound all ministers to take an oath not only of allegiance to the king, but of assent to everything contained and prescribed in the prayer book. The penalty for refusal was deprivation of living. On St Bartholomew's day, 24 August 1662, the day when the Act was to come into effect, more than two thousand Puritan rectors and vicars gave up their livings rather than subscribe to the new oath. An Act for regulating select vestries (1663) required vestrymen in London and 'all other towns, cities and boroughs where select vestries had been established' to make the same declaration, so that the government of many parishes was placed entirely in Anglican hands (Burch: 42). The Act against Conventicles (1664) made it unlawful for dissenting clergy to conduct religious meetings at all (or for any person to attend or assist such meetings), while the 'Five Mile Act' (1670) banished them from the neighbourhoods in which they had formerly been incumbents. These and other severe measures against dissenters remained in force throughout the reigns of Charles II and James II, though active persecution was greatly reduced after 1672.

The Act of Uniformity thus severed from the Church, at one blow, its most vocal and passionate Calvinist wing – those who were willing to place their convictions above their own worldly comfort and security. Among the majority of the clergy who remained would be found, certainly, some equally passionate Episcopalians; but also some Vicars of Bray who would hold on to their livings at all costs, and some sincere Presbyterians who yet lacked the strength of character to stand up to the force of law backed by public opinion. The last group, of course, leaves no documentary record of its existence. But it was probably numerous, judging by the practice of many clergymen during the latter part of the seventeenth century. Here and there a strong-minded Presbyterian was able to maintain his position openly in the face of the law (Addy: 14).

One more serious attempt was made to embrace the dissenters within the

Church. This was after the revolution of 1688, when William of Orange and his wife Mary ascended the throne on the defeat of James II. Like Charles II, William had issued an advance declaration in which he had promised 'to endeavour a good agreement between the Church of England and protestant dissenters'. A commission prepared an elaborate set of proposals which it was thought would be sufficient to bring the bulk of dissenters back into the church (Procter: 209–21). But, once again, parliament refused to endorse the proposition. It did, however, pass the Toleration Act (1689) which removed the worst disabilities of dissenting ministers, and allowed them to conduct services in licensed places of worship. At this time also a high-church section of opinion was cut off from the Church: the Non-jurors, a group of some four hundred priests (including Archbishop Sancroft and eight bishops) who felt so bound by their allegiance to James II that they could not after his deposition take the oath of allegiance to William and Mary. So the Church was purged of conscientious extremists at either end, and came to a time of broad agreement and toleration in religious matters, which was reflected in the relative stability of worship practice during the eighteenth century.

Interest in the Restoration period among musicians and musicologists has focussed on cathedral music, and especially on what Fellowes called 'the romantic activities of the chapel royal in the limelight of the court of Charles II at Whitehall' (:130). The totally different situation in parish church music has been neglected. Yet this was in truth far more representatively 'English' at the time than the developments at the chapel royal. The king was politically in a very strong position, and he made it clear from the start that he would have whatever he wanted in the services of his chapel, let the Puritans think what they liked. He was prepared to spend money to make those services colourful and artistic. The English liturgy had been kept up in all its ceremony in his chapel abroad during the time of his exile; so that he and his immediate circle, unlike many of his subjects, were familiar with it as a living tradition. In addition he had developed a continental taste in art and music that had not as yet made much headway in England. A brilliant musical tradition quickly developed at the chapel royal (Fellowes; Long). As early as 8 July 1660 Pepys wrote in his diary: 'To Whitehall chapel... Here I heard very good music, the first time that ever I remember to have heard the organs and singing-men in surplices in my life.' (Pepys was born in 1633 and brought up at Brampton, near Huntingdon.)

Private noblemen and cathedral chapters imitated the music of the chapel royal as far as their resources allowed. In most cathedrals organs had to be rebuilt, and there was a difficulty in finding adequate choir boys to perform the choral service. Even the older lay-clerks who were still available must have had difficulty at first in picking up the threads of the old musical tradition. But they were supported on the whole by the desire of the upper clergy to blot out the effect of the Puritan interregnum. And they were not subject to democratic control: funds could be made available from cathedral endowments to set the choirs on their feet.

None of these conditions existed in the parish churches. Some of the people, as well as some of the clergy, were opposed to liturgical worship, but they continued to attend the parish church, since no other place of worship was permitted. Already the words of the prayer book were archaic, and remote from the language of ordinary people; they had hardly been heard for fifteen years; the younger generation had never heard them. Though the liturgy must by law be observed, it struck only a weak chord of response in many worshippers. The people's parts in the services were often 'so little heard, that it seems to one that comes into the church ... as if the minister read a verse, and then stopped a while and read again ... especially if the clerk be absent, as he may have often occasion to be, where prayers are read every day' (Seymour: 20). The responsorial mode of reading the service had long been used in the psalms and canticles (though without rubrical authority) as well as in the versicles and responses, but now it was turning into a duet between the minister and the parish clerk, which was to be the usual thing in the eighteenth century. Often the service was read so quickly that no audible break was made between lessons and psalms, or between psalms and prayers. Bishop Wren suggested that the minister introduce the Te deum thus: 'Let us now give praise to almighty God, and say We praise thee, O God, we &c.'. He explained:

Very requisite it is that some such words of exhortation be appointed wherewith to stir up the people to thanksgiving after every lesson, because very many are not quick enough of themselves to mark how the church passeth from reading to praying. (Jacobson: 47–8)

The mode of reading, at least by some clergy, seems to have been close to intoning. Thomas Seymour, a high churchman anxious to improve the manner of performing the liturgy, wrote:

I wish that people had the art to speak in some kind of concord with the minister, either that their voices might be unisons with his, or a fifth or an eighth from it: for there is a *speaking* as well as *singing* together, that is very harsh, by reason of a discordancy in the voices of those that perform it. (Seymour: 20)

Some clergymen even used a singing tone for preaching. The puritan Cuthbert Sydenham had urged that a careful distinction be made between singing, preaching, prayer and exhortation; 'for no man will say, when a man merely speaks or preaches, he sings, without his tone do make them call him a singing preacher or talker, as too many either out of affection or custom, have given just cause to suspect' (:168).

The interregnum had completed a process of alienation between the liturgy and the people which was probably well advanced even before 1640. Increasingly, they would be mere spectators to a performance by the minister, assisted by the parish clerk; and a service which was originally designed to take full advantage of the possibilities of variety and of congregational participation would become a monotonous and tedious duty, fully open to charges of empty formality, despite occasionally successful efforts of high-church clergymen to revive its full meaning.

Nothing of the kind had taken place with respect to the singing of metrical psalms. They had long been the special province of the people, and had remained so throughout the civil war and Commonwealth; they needed no revival at the Restoration. Most congregations no doubt had a common stock of tunes, even if only half a dozen or so, which they could sing without assistance. The Old Version was still there at the back of the bible or prayer book; the illiterate knew some of the psalms by heart, and could sing the rest with the help of lining out. For those of Puritan leanings there was the additional attraction that metrical psalms, unlike the liturgy, were approved and encouraged by their own party.

Although metrical psalms were sung by moderate Anglicans, their primary association with Puritanism still remained, and with it went a definite identification with the common people. This in turn deprived parish church music of the most powerful resource available: the support of the landed gentry. Gone were the days when every devout father, from country squire to poor labourer, would conduct family prayers and psalm singing (N. Tate: 10, 31). The idea was fast taking root that an English gentleman should have nothing to do with music of any kind, and particularly with a kind that had such an unsavoury odour of democracy. He should rather leave the singing to his inferiors, and maintain for himself an attitude of dignified indifference. Rarely did a nobleman or a wealthy squire or merchant see fit to present his parish church with an organ, or endow a parish clerkship, or even accept the dedication of a collection of psalm tunes.

By the end of the century, class discrimination in church music was known and accepted (N. Tate: 10). Daniel Warner, in a preface to a collection of psalms, recited the usual biblical exhortations to sing, but continued: 'This kind of devotion the common people are most intent upon; to instruct whom, was the main design of this book' (PC 35: preface). Another musician compiled a book 'for the good of the many young persons, in and about these parts of the county of Lancaster, whose purses are not able to purchase the books now extant; that is, not so many books as are necessary, before they can be furnished both with directions how to sing, and tunes proper for the singing of the whole book of psalms: few or none but the poorer sort having yet espoused that heavenly employment' (PC 47: preface).

It was inevitable that the aristocratic indifference to church music would be shared by many of the clergy, who were beginning to aspire to equality of social status with the country gentry (Addison: 72, 96). This was the decisive fact that led to the almost complete separation of psalmody from cultivated influences, including the influence of art music. 'It would be much to the advancement of this divine service of singing psalms,' wrote Playford, 'if the clergy would generally more addict themselves to the study of music, and give themselves some little trouble in assisting their several congregations with their skill. And also if they would make choice of such proper persons for their clerks to have either some skill in song, or at least a tunable voice and good ear to learn' (PC 29: fol. A2v).

There was no law or rubric that required a minister to play any part whatever in the singing of metrical psalms. The only times when they could be legally sung in church were still those listed in the Injunctions of 1559 – before and after service; but by custom they were more often sung before and after the sermon. At these times the minister could absent himself from the body of the church, and frequently did so; or he could stand, or even sit, taking no notice of what was going on. Thus William Beveridge, a high churchman who became Bishop of St Asaph in 1704, was commended for his unusual demeanour as rector of St Peter, Cornhill, London: he 'constantly stood with reverence while he sung the praises of God;... and when he went into the pulpit, he neither altered his posture, nor forbore to join with the congregation till the psalm was finished' (Nelson: 63). The average parson, however, openly dissociated himself with the singing, and the habit persisted into the nineteenth century (E. Miller: 1791, 13–14; Latrobe: 74–5.)

Music played no part in the training of the clergy; indeed in the twentieth century this was still true, and was mentioned as one of the reasons for defects in parish church music ('Church choirs': 111; Stewart: 11). A minister, if he was a Puritan, had been taught that music was inessential and should in any case be congregational; if he was a high churchman, he would give no encouragement to something that was not a part of the liturgy. And if he was that rare species, a clerical musician, he would be more probably found in a cathedral (like Robert Creyghton, precentor of Wells) or at a college (like Henry Aldrich, dean of Christ Church, Oxford) than in a humble parish church.

So it was that the clergy washed their hands of parish church music, and, with honourable exceptions, remained aloof from it until the Evangelical movement roused their consciences from a long slumber. More than ever, the people were left alone with their singing. Organs were still very rare in a parish church: only a few wealthy town parishes could afford the double expense of acquiring an instrument (for hardly any church possessed one at the Restoration) and of paying to have it played, tuned, and kept in repair. The time for using other instruments had not yet come. A church in a fashionable district might boast a few parishioners who could read musical notes, but in any ordinary church there was no-one but the parish clerk who could even pretend to musical expertise.

With the parson declining to lend his authority, the parish clerk came forward as the natural leader of the singing. In times not quite forgotten he had been a trained musician, in times more remote he had been at the head of a substantial choir. Though very few clerks had any kind of professional training in music, their right and duty to take charge of the music in the church was not questioned. The parish clerk was the person entrusted with lining out the psalms; and, increasingly, it was left to him to choose what psalm should be sung, as well as to 'set' the psalm to an appropriate tune. A guide for clerks first published in 1685 gave advice in the important duty of choosing psalms, and even provided an alphabetical index of subjects with psalms suited to each. The index included Angels, Assizes, Atheists, Blazing stars or comets, Conspiracies, Dark cloudy weather, Earthquake, Idolatry and its punishment, Promises made good, Prosperous estate of wicked men, Watchfulness over the tongue, and Whirlwinds (Payne: 21–4, 37). In this way psalms could be related to folklore and superstition, important local events, and everyday human problems. A clerk by his choice could make a psalm an expression of current popular feeling, whereas a parson would have linked it, if he was high church, with the season of the church year, or, if he was low church, with a point of doctrine in the lesson or sermon. In 1724 the Bishop of London, in his charge to the clergy of the diocese, urged them to recover from their parish clerks the responsibility for choosing the psalms, and suggested a course of psalms to cover the church year (Gibson, 1724). He was not entirely successful.

As well as choosing the psalm the clerk was expected to take the lead in singing it. He would begin by announcing the psalm in these words: 'Let us sing to the praise and glory of God the ——th psalm.' The origin of this custom is unknown (Payne: 31). It certainly existed before the interregnum, and the high churchman Heylyn attributed it to Puritan innovation (:ɪ, 271). The custom lasted as long as clerks retained their musical function (Vaux: 244; Macdermott, 1922: 41).

Having named the psalm for the sake of those who could follow it in a book, the clerk then had to line it out for the benefit of those who could not. Although the original purpose of this usage was didactic, and possibly anti-aesthetic (since it tended to destroy the poetic and musical integrity of the singing), it was rapidly taking on the character of a performance, as may be seen from this curious advice in Payne's *Guide*:

Let us . . . so read the psalm, that as much as in us lies we may preserve harmony and decency . . . For which purpose, . . . read it tunably, i.e., in a singing tone, and after the manner of chanting, say,

Psal. 23   The – Lord – is – on ᴖ— ly – my – sup – port,
                and – he that – doth ᴖ— me – feed, &c.

allowing the time of a crotchet or pulse-beating to each syllable in reading, and that the break betwixt the falling from one line to the taking up of the next, may be so quick, as that due harmony may be kept in some measure, notwithstanding the reading . . .

I have put a crotchet-rest after the first four syllables, to denote a little pause; which, if carefully observed in reading, the same will appear musical, much after the manner of the plainsong used in cathedrals, or the chanting of the psalms . . . This way of reading the psalm was constantly practised and commendably performed by the ingenious Mr. John Playford, clerk to the honourable society of the Temple. (Payne: 29–31)

In the Church of England, lining out disappeared in the course of the eighteenth century together with the 'old way of singing' with which it was associated. In Scotland, however, it was allowed to develop freely, leading eventually to an elaborate, integrated, responsorial style such as that recorded at Strathpeffer by Joseph Mainzer in 1844 (Curwen, 1880: 72). It survives to this day in many churches in the United States: William Tallmadge in 1975 found evidence of its use in 255 baptist churches of the Southern states with a combined membership of 15,593 persons (Tallmadge; see also Evans). In these examples the lining out resembles a psalm chant, with ornaments revolving around a single note; it does not anticipate the forthcoming musical phrase.

The clerk, after reading a line or a pair of lines, then led the congregation in the singing of the same words. In the absence of an instrument he had the responsibility of determining the pitch of the tune: advice on this subject was given in contemporary guides and prefaces. Presumably the people took their note from the clerk after he had begun to sing.

It can be seen that the clerk, particularly in smaller churches with no organ and no members skilled in music, bore a heavy responsibility for keeping up the quality and vitality of the singing in his church. Unfortunately he was all too often incapable of discharging it adequately. The days when an educated man might be willing to be a parish clerk were long since gone. The wages for the job were a miserable pittance, so that it was 'unreasonable to expect that those who have already been at the pains and charge of qualifying themselves, will ever take up with so poor a subsistence as is to be had in most parishes of our kingdom' (N. Tate: 33). The duties included menial tasks, and in some churches the clerk and the sexton were the same person. Playford in 1671 bewailed the neglect of many of the best psalm tunes:

nor must we expect it otherwise, when in and about this great city, in above one hundred parishes, there is but a few parish clerks to be found that have either ear or understanding to set one of these tunes musically as it ought to be: it having been a custom during the late [civil] wars, and since, to choose men into such places, more for their poverty than skill and ability. (PC 26: preface)

The motive for choosing poor men was financial. A poor man who could not work by reason of age or unfitness would be a charge on the parish in any case: by appointing him clerk, instead of paying an able-bodied man, the parish could save itself some money (Payne: 3; Seymour: 28). In many parishes the clerk was elected by the vestry, the same body which levied church rates. There was no retiring age, and he could be dismissed only for gross incompetence or neglect of duty.

It is clear that in country churches and many town churches as well, the congregation was virtually left to its own devices in singing the psalms. In some places the singing almost died out, as at Ubley (MS 84, fol. 3r). Elsewhere it remained vigorous, but without artistic guidance. The effect of the clerk's leadership (if any) would not be in the direction of conformity with the current standards of taste in art music. The singing was indeed beneath contempt by these standards. In Shadwell's play *Epsom Wells* (1676) Lucia complains of being in the country, 'never to hear better singing than a company of peasants praising God with doleful untunable hoarse voices, that are only fit to be heard under gallows' (Harley: 96). Thomas Mace found it 'sad to hear what whining, toting, yelling, or screeking there is in many country congregations'. He could 'confidently affirm that 'tis absolutely *impossible* ever to have the *psalms rightly* and well performed according to the common way used throughout the nation'. His remedy was to obtain an organ and teach the clerk to play it; alternatively he suggested that children should learn how to sing from a music teacher, but he admitted that there was little possibility of this in the country (Mace: 5, 11). In many town churches the situation was similar. Even in London 'this part of God's service hath been so ridiculously performed in most places, that it is now brought into scorn and derision by many people' (PC 26: preface). Only a few churches with wealthy congregations began to take measures to 'improve' the singing, and we shall see the results in Chapter 5. But first we will explore the musical consequences of the neglect of psalm singing by the educated classes, including the clergy.

Few descriptions survive of the singing in country parish churches in the later seventeenth century, and they are almost wholly unfavourable, being written from the point of view of a professional musician (such as Mace or Playford) or an educated person familiar with art music (such as Shadwell). An extreme example is the following, which Elias Hall in 1706 attested to have been true 'till of late years in most churches and chapels* around Lancashire':

> Then out the people yawl an hundred parts,
> Some roar, some whine, some creak like wheels of carts:
> Such notes the gamut yet did never know,
> Nor num'rous keys of harps'cals [harpsichords] on a row
> Their heights or depths could ever comprehend.
> Now below double *A re* some descend,
> 'Bove *E la* squealing now ten notes some fly;
> Straight then, as if they knew they were too high,
> With headlong haste downstairs they again tumble;
> Discords and concords, O how thick they jumble,
> Like untamed horses, tearing with their throats
> One wretched stave into a thousand notes.
>
> (PC 56: preface. Punctuation modified.)

Certainly this is an exaggeration; if we believed it literally we would have to credit seventeenth-century congregations with a compass of five octaves! The writer was selling a book of music for parish church use. He had a financial, as others had an aesthetic or religious, interest in denigrating the 'old way of singing', and in promoting the 'new way' of the early eighteenth century, which involved teaching young men to sing from notes.

There is no doubt that the old way was uncouth and discordant. Yet it filled an important role in the worship of the people, and they strongly resisted the efforts of well-meaning reformers to get rid of it. This was appreciated by John Patrick, in one of the rare allusions that show some sympathy for the psalmody of the time (:fol. Alr, Alv).

Before we can understand or evaluate this tradition, we must attempt to gain an unprejudiced idea of its nature. For this purpose, even the most hostile descriptions can serve as sources of factual information. We can turn also to descriptions of the very similar tradition that existed in New England, where at a slightly later date the same kind of reforms would take place; to surviving examples of this type of singing; and to certain kinds of direct musical evidence that have survived from the period in question.

One of the most striking characteristics of the 'old way of singing' was its tempo. We have already noted a tendency for psalm singing to slow down, even before 1600. By this time the process had continued to a point where all sense of rhythm and accent had disappeared. Precise evidence of tempo from the period is very scarce, but the diary of Samuel Pepys gives some assistance. He described the singing at St Olave, Hart Street, London, a church that had no organ:

---

* A 'chapel' at this date was an Anglican, not a nonconformist, place of worship.

6 January 1661: To church again, where, before sermon, a long psalm was set that lasted an hour, while the sexton gathered his year's contribution through the whole church.

5 January 1662: To church, and before sermon there was a long psalm and half another sung out, while the sexton gathered what the church would give him for this last year ... but the jest was, the clerk begins the 25th psalm, which hath a proper tune to it, and then the 116th, which cannot be sung with that tune, which seemed very ridiculous.

The 25th psalm has 22 stanzas short metre and the 116th has 16 stanzas common metre. Assuming then that the sexton took about the same amount of time to collect his dues in 1662 as in 1661, it took an hour to sing about thirty stanzas. This works out at half a minute for each line of six or eight notes, probably including the time taken for the clerk to read out each line before it was sung. Thus the speed of singing would have been two or three seconds to a note.

At first sight it seems unbelievable that psalms could have been sung at a speed of two seconds or more to a note. Yet there is abundant evidence to confirm it, though of rather later date. The prefaces of many eighteenth-century psalmody books define the speed of the 'slowest mood of common time' (signature $\mathbb{C}$) as four beats of a large pendulum clock. In some cases this is stated specifically to mean four seconds, as for example in Davenport's *The psalm singer's pocket companion* (1755). According to a Scottish writer of 1787, 'The semibreve in common time ... is as long as one can conveniently sing without breathing.' (Taas: 35).

The first collection of psalm tunes to incorporate metronome speeds, Benjamin Jacob's *National psalmody* (PC 344a), shows that these extremely slow tempi survived into the nineteenth century. His speed for 'Old Hundredth', which is still printed in minims, is '♩ = 60. Rather slow'. And J. A. Latrobe complained in 1831 of the intolerably slow performance of the old plain tunes, in contrast to the quickness of ornate modern ones. The 100th psalm, he said, is 'generally sung with such deliberation, that the breath is more than expended upon each word, and instead of a mutual connection and dependence, the notes stand apart and disunited' (Latrobe: 222). By comparison, Henry Smart in the later nineteenth century recommended a speed of ♩ = 45 for the 'Old Hundredth' (Curwen, 1880: 170), and Vaughan Williams in 1906 marked it 'Slow and dignified ♩ = 66' (PC 411: 506). Thus in less than a century the tempo regarded as 'slow' had more than doubled. For us today the excessively slow manner of singing hymns is almost unimaginable.

Yet it is not difficult to see how it came about. When singers depend on other singers for the pitch of the note they will sing next, they naturally tend to wait until they hear the note before they venture to sing it. The result is a 'drag'. It is corrected by instrumental accompaniment, or by dancing or even foot-tapping such as often accompanies secular folk song. In church there was nothing to keep the rhythm going, and in addition there was often an echoing building to prolong each sound still more. Over many years the effect was cumulative. Each generation would aim to sing only as fast as it had learned to sing, but would insensibly slow down the 'norm' that it passed on to its successors. A similar process took place in the singing of plainsong over the centuries. By the early nineteenth century, before the reforms of Regensburg and Solesmes, it had become a ponderous recitation in long, slow notes of equal duration, parodied in the 'Dies irae' of Berlioz's *Symphonie fantastique*.

One effect of the slowing down was loss of rhythm. We have seen how the complex rhythms of the psalm tunes tended to be ironed out in later editions of the psalm book. By the time Playford came to print the psalm tunes in his *Introduction to music* (1658) and *Whole book of psalms in three parts* (1677), the rhythm of many tunes had become standardised: each line began and ended with a semibreve, with minims between. Other editors followed popular practice still more closely in their notation. Thomas Smith printed all tunes in minims, with barlines after every second note regardless of stress (PC 42). Thomas Mathew provided an enlightening discussion of the question, in a passage from the preface to his psalm book of 1688, in which all the psalms were fully underlaid with tunes from Ravenscroft. He said that three notes were in use in psalm tunes, the breve, semibreve and minim; he defined their duration as eight, four and two 'pulses at the wrist of a person in good health and temper'.* 'But', he went on, 'the clerks are seldom so exact as to keep these distinct times in the churches: they do generally observe but one time, as indeed is most easy, and therefore most agreeable to the capacities of the greater number in congregations and families, and that is (usually) about a minim and a half, or three pulses, or three quarters of a semibreve' [i.e., perhaps three seconds] (PC 33: preface). Still more extreme distortions of time were suffered in remote places. Thus in Yorkshire in 1718:

The singers in most country churches go quite out of rule, by drawing out the sound of some notes twice or thrice longer than they ought to do, thereby spoiling the music, and this so affectedly too, that they seem to think it makes the very finest harmony: so I have observed them in some places to strain themselves in forcing out some, and especially the last note in a line, that they have hardly had strength to begin again: and whereas they should have sounded the longest of their notes no longer than a *semibreve*, and the rest proportionably; they have made no difference in singing five or seven notes together, but have sounded each of them so long, that I could distinctly count five or six; but whilst they were sounding the last note, I could count nine or ten, which is most irregular, tedious, and intolerable, and takes up as much time in singing what they call two staves, as would serve very well for five or six. (PC 72: x)

It must be remembered that the singing was also interrupted by the lining out between phrases. Any sense of the tune as a whole, and as originally conceived, must have been almost completely lost.

The long duration of time between one note of the tune and the next was not without incident. Additional notes were often inserted, making a kind of ornamentation which is the other main characteristic of the 'old way of singing'. Musicologists have studied this practice chiefly in connection with early American psalm singing (Stevenson: 27; Buechner). During the

* Stainer (:33) misunderstood Mathew's speeds, taking them for twice as fast as they actually were.

controversies between the old and the new ways in New England in the 1720s, it was said of the old or 'common way' that 'they use many quavers and semiquavers, &c.' (Chauncey; cited Chase: 24), and that the tunes 'are now miserably tortured, and twisted, and quavered, in some churches, into an horrid medley of confused and disorderly noises' (Walter; cited Chase: 26). In reconstructing the practice Gilbert Chase realised that it closely paralleled the practice of psalm singing in England and Scotland, and he turned to Mainzer's *Gaelic psalm tunes* of 1844 to discover a record of the style in actual musical notation (Chase: 30). However, there are contemporary English records of the 'old way'. The earliest dates from 1686, and is found in a small anonymous book called *A new and easie method to learn to sing by book* (PC 31). The author first set out the tune 'Southwell' in the ordinary way, then went on to say: 'The notes of the foregoing tune are usually broken or divided, and they are better so sung, as is here pricked [printed].' What follows is clearly an effort to show the 'old way of singing' in musical notation (ex. 16). Other such attempts can be found in later collections. One dates from 1733, when Robert Barber laid out a florid version of the tune 'York', which he headed 'Psalm IV, called the old way of singing' (ex. 17). The different versions of the style are not entirely consistent, but they all have certain things in common. The principal notes of the tune always begin where they are supposed to begin – on the beat; any additional notes occur between beats, and consist largely of stepwise connecting notes. Often they form a simple scale linking one note of the tune to the next; but sometimes they go beyond the next note and return to it. Conspicuously absent are the appoggiatura, turn, shake and other ornaments characteristic of eighteenth-century art music, which begin on the upper note and delay the main note until after the beat.

To hostile critics of the time, this ornamentation of the tunes seemed to be occasioned by the whim or fancy of the singers. Thomas Walter wrote that 'our tunes are . . . left to the mercy of every unskilful throat to chop and alter, twist and change, according to their infinitely diverse and no less odd humours and fancies'; Thomas Symmes explained the development as follows:

The rules of singing not being taught or learnt, every one sang as best pleased himself, and every leading-singer, would take the liberty of raising any note of the tune, or lowering of it, as best pleased his ear; and add such turns and flourishes as were grateful to him; and this was done so gradually, as that but few if any took notice of it. (Chase: 26–8)

From these and similar suggestions has come the prevailing notion that the flourishes of the 'old way' were introduced deliberately, as an artistic embellishment of the tunes, and perhaps as a way of reducing the tedium of the slow progression from one note to the next; one could compare the medieval practice of troping. Such an explanation must assume, however, the presence of individual musical leaders, more skilled than the rest of the congregation, who could impose their musical ideas on the majority. It is certainly true that musical leaders nominally existed; in English churches they were called parish clerks. But I have suggested that it was precisely the lack of effective musical leadership that accounted for the developments that have been described. If there were skilled musicians to lead the singing, why did they not preserve the written forms of the tunes, and enlarge the dwindling stock by reviving old tunes or introducing new ones?

In truth there is no need to assume any arbitrary 'fancies' on the part of the parish clerks or other singers. We can account for the facts without them. The very same circumstance that explains the slowing down of the tunes can also explain their 'ornamentation'. For we know that the tunes were ordinarily transmitted by ear alone. This must mean that in any congregation some singers knew the tunes well, while others younger or less confident had to follow as best they could. At any point in the tune, the next note would be sung first by the experienced singers; the rest would then copy them, but would vary in the amount of time they took to reach the new note. Some of the less musical would raise or lower their voices gradually towards the new note, stopping only when they were aware of being in tune with it; occasionally they might even overshoot it. By the time the laggards had got there, the leaders might already have moved on. Walter observed that 'in many places, one man is upon this note while another is upon the note before him'. In extreme cases total chaos might result, giving the impression of Walter's 'five hundred different tunes roared out at the same time' or of Hall's 'an hundred parts'. As long as reasonable order was preserved, however, the principal effect would be of people sliding gradually, and in their own times, from one note of the tune to the next. This 'pitch-matching' process is strikingly consistent with the quoted description by Hall: 'Straight then, *as if they knew they were too high,*/With headlong haste downstairs they again tumble'.

One can understand that this kind of singing defied exact representation in musical notation. The few surviving musical examples of it can be seen as varying approximations. Our notation is based on discrete pitches, and is specially apt for woodwind, fretted string, or keyboard instruments. But it developed from neumes which represented only the upward or downward motion of the voice. Singers tend to glide from one pitch to the next, and may have sung plainsong in that way before organs accompanied them. Similarly, many ornament signs, such as the appoggiatura or the slide, were probably at first meant to represent a gradual change of pitch that could not adequately be indicated on the stave. When instruments of discrete pitch imitated the voice, they played these ornaments as written. In just the same way compilers of psalmody books strove to indicate the traditional way of singing, with its scoops and glides joining the notes of the tune, by an idealised notation that showed the intervening pitches of the diatonic scale. And as we shall see, organists did the same thing when they came to imitate the 'old way of singing'. But the main notes of the tune remained firmly established, as the points of repose at which all the singers were meant to reassemble before starting out on their various paths to the next note.

Once the meaning of this notation has been recognised, we can see other examples of it where no explicit illustration of the 'old way' was intended. From Playford onwards, we find in psalm tune collections increasingly ornate versions of the traditional tunes. The ornament generally is of the type already described – a filling-in with shorter notes of the intervals between the main notes of the tune. Some tunes move largely by step and allow for very little of this notated ornament; others, such as 'York' (ex. 17), call for a great deal of it. It is quite distinct from the later eighteenth-century type of ornamentation, which reached hymn tunes from art music.

Another element besides the 'pitch-matching' process may have played a part in the old way of singing – a harmonic element, related to the improvised descant discussed in the last chapter. Ex. 18 shows another representation of the style, this time from a book printed in 1718 (PC 71). It is headed 'Those psalms which the clerk gives out line by line, are generally sung in these tunes; which is called the old way of singing.' Two tunes follow, written in $\frac{6}{4}$ time, and supplied with plain basses. The second, set to Psalm 89, is clearly a version of 'Martyrs' (F. 209). The first, however, shown in ex. 18, is of less certain origin. As the example shows, it could be derived equally well from 'Windsor' (of which an imperfect version is F. 129) or from 'Coleshill' (F. 392a), a tune which it has been suggested was derived from 'Windsor' by improvised descant. The ornate version seems in many places to oscillate between one tune and the other: this is particularly striking in the penultimate bar. When we remember that the 'old way' frequently involved different pitches being sung at the same time by various members of the congregation, 'according to their infinitely diverse... fancies', it is easy to imagine that the notation shown in ex. 18 was an attempt to represent in a single melodic line a performance that was partly in two-part harmony. Indeed some of the singers may have actually followed 'Windsor' for a few notes, and then, hearing someone singing 'Coleshill', have transferred to the other tune. In general these early transcriptions of the 'old way of singing' frequently emphasise notes that are a third above or below the main note of the tune, and hence harmonise well with it. There are certainly several notes in ex. 18 which cannot be explained as 'pitch-matching' or filling-in of intervals in the tune.

The 'old way of singing' gradually died out in Anglican churches, but it survived in Presbyterian churches in Scotland and Canada, and in Primitive Baptist churches in the southern United States; in both cases it was generally associated with lining out. In these churches remote rural congregations religiously resisted efforts to reform their singing, which they wished to preserve in its traditional purity (Cooke). One can hear, in recordings made at Sparta, North Carolina, hymns lined out by Elder Walter Evans and sung by the congregation in long, slow notes, 'ornamented' in ways that are much like what has been described (Evans). The tunes are not those of the Old Version, but are in the revivalist tradition, being largely pentatonic and derived from Anglo-Saxon folk melodies; they are sung largely to Methodist hymn texts. Although there is not so great a degree of heterophony as the earlier descriptions suggest, the added notes are very much of the same character, and in some cases seem partially to harmonise the tunes.

Nor is this kind of singing peculiar to Anglo-Saxon culture. A strikingly similar phenomenon has been found among the Old Order Amish, a subdivision of the Mennonites, who were descended from the Anabaptists of southern Germany. Like the Primitive Baptists, and the Free Presbyterians in Scotland, they represent the most conservative group after a number of splits and schisms have taken place, and seek to preserve unsullied the traditions of their forefathers. Each syllable of their hymns is sung to a long melisma, and George Jackson, who studied their singing, believed that the first note of each melisma was the original note of the tune (G. P. Jackson: 285). Nettl suggested that their singing is 'a survival of a style which was common in European hymnody in some locations, and which has been abandoned there' (:327).

It is clear that this type of singing is extremely conservative in nature. Deliberate innovations were no part of the old way of singing, for no self-conscious or creative musicians were involved in it. New tunes were neither wanted nor expected. So Pepys on 9 August 1663 wrote: 'I was amused at the tune set to the psalm by the clerk of the parish, and thought at first he was out, but I find him to be a good songster, and the parish could sing it very well, and was a good tune. But I wonder that there should be a tune in the psalms that I never heard of.' Pepys assumed that the body of tunes 'in the psalms' was fixed. If he did not recognise a tune, it did not occur to him that someone had tried to introduce a new one.

Because the old way of singing was a purely oral tradition, we do not find printed music associated with it, save in the rare cases mentioned above. On the contrary, the tunes printed with the Old Version had ceased to serve any purpose, and were no longer included in ordinary editions. In 1661 Playford revised the large folio black-letter edition printed by the Stationers' Company, bringing the tunes up to date (Temperley, 1972a: 346–53). The book was printed in this form several times more, the last time in 1687; but it was intended for parish clerks (:353, n. 53), and was clearly one of Playford's efforts to reform the current mode of singing the psalms. Fewer than 6000 copies were sold between 1663 and 1696, compared with over 400,000 of the 12mo edition without music (:343). All Playford's psalm tune collections were partly reformative, including his 1677 harmonised psalm book, which will be described later. Other printed collections of psalm tunes from this period were either reformative, like those of Mathew and Smith (PC 33, 42), or were attempts to introduce new translations of the psalms with the old tunes unreformed (this description applies to all the new translations from Barton's to Tate and Brady's). Towards the end of the century books for the use of town churches with organs began to appear. It is in these that the few new tunes of the period are to be found.

In the later seventeenth century the tradition of parish church music began to split into two streams, which I will call 'town psalmody' and 'country psalmody'. For reasons which will emerge, there was a growing wish to modify or eliminate the 'old way of singing'. In the town churches the main instrument of reform was an organ; while in country churches, where for financial or other reasons an organ was not available, voluntary choirs were formed, to be joined later by bands. A century after the Restoration the distinction between the two traditions was clear-cut, and was outlined by John Arnold in *Church music reformed*:

In the churches of *London* and *Westminster*, which abound chiefly with large congregations, it is customary for the people, who chiefly sing by the ear, to follow the organ, in those churches that are furnished with that most excellent instrument;

but, in churches where there is no organ, they generally follow the clerk, who sings the melody of the tune ...

In most country churches the psalms used to be sung formerly much after the same manner as is now used in the churches in *London*, &c.... till about half a century ago, when several books of psalmody were printed and published, containing some very good psalm tunes and anthems in four parts; of which the people in the country soon became particularly fond, so that in a few years almost every country church had one belonging to it; which, in some places had the distinction of the *choir of singers*, in others the *society of singers*; and, in very remote places where they were not quite so polite, they had the appellation of *the singers* only, being, for the most part, placed in a gallery or singing pew, erected for that purpose. (PC 190: iii, v)

Arnold saw the change in country churches as being greater than in the towns, and in one sense it was, because it involved the introduction of completely new kinds of music. In town churches the same old psalm tunes continued to be sung, though the introduction of an organ would obviously have an immediate and drastic impact on the effect of the music, setting a new professional standard.

The eighteenth century is a complex period in the history of parish church music. The two basic types were not absolutely separate, and there were many intermediate possibilities. Nevertheless it is probably best to deal with the two traditions separately, and then to consider their interaction. The simplest way of separating them is the organ. For most country parish churches, an organ was outside the realm of possibility: even if some generous person presented one, it would be difficult to keep it in tune and repair, and to find and pay a qualified organist. Until well into the nineteenth century, therefore, we shall not expect to find organs in country churches. They had their own ways of reforming their music, which will be described in Chapter 6. In many towns, however, it was found possible to acquire an organ and to employ a professional organist. In the course of the eighteenth century more and more town churches aspired to this distinction, with effects on their music which we will investigate in the next chapter.

Summary and evaluation

The second period of upheaval in the national Church had only minor effects on parish church music. The existing usage was firmly established, and in any case conformed quite closely to the views of the Puritans. The only novelty they succeeded in introducing was the practice of lining out. It would have had a destructive effect on any kind of artistic musical performance: but in most churches the mode of singing was already so slow and halting that the interruption of reading the words would have had little effect on the music.

Indeed the singing of metrical psalms had already lost most of the significance which it had had for the early reformers. To them, it had been partly didactic in purpose: the people were to be made familiar with the psalms by singing them to their own ballad tunes, or to other lively tunes.

But the singing had become a ritual, performed without intellectual understanding of the words, and the singers were preoccupied with this ritual in itself, which seemed to express emotions not specifically Christian in character. To correct this, the Puritan leaders had first propagated 'Middleburg' editions with the prose psalms in the margin: but this could have affected only the literate minority. Now, the Westminster Assembly proposed lining out, a more direct means of forcing attention to the meaning of the words sung, and also an aid to the introduction of new and more literal translations. In both objects it failed. The lining out itself became a kind of chant, and was absorbed into the ritual of the 'old way of singing', persisting in the anti-Puritan period of the Restoration.

No period of parish church music is today more remote than this one. Its habits of singing have long since disappeared, at least in the Church of England. It has left no original music for us to study and evaluate. The 'old way of singing', together with the lining out that went with it, was unacceptable or laughable to educated people of the time, as it probably would be to us today. It was the result, indeed, of a long period of neglect of church music by the educated portion of society. But it was genuinely popular in a way that the reformed music of the succeeding period was not. The reformers could get rid of the old way, but could not easily replace it with a musical tradition which the people would feel to be theirs. Not until the Methodists brought a second wave of folk tunes into the churches would genuinely congregational singing be heard again.

5   Urban parish church music (1660–1790)

Motives for reform

The reform of urban church music after the Restoration was dictated by two quite distinct classes of motive. One was religious: sacred music, both in church and out of it, should be an expression of piety, and a weapon in the general raising of standards in religion and morality. The second was aesthetic and materialistic: the old way of singing gave offence, and must give place to something more appropriate for the public celebrations of a prosperous and successful society. These two aspirations sometimes worked towards the same practical goals, sometimes in opposition to each other; they can be distinguished in other periods of our history, such as the nineteenth century. In the eighteenth century the second was predominant.

A leading historian of religion in England has said that the spirit of this age was 'not conducive to worship in general, and was particularly opposed to liturgical forms' (Davies: III, 52). Material prosperity had induced a satisfaction with life in this world, and a proportionate easing of anxiety about life in the world to come. The successes of science and mathematical logic had led to a belief in the power of reason to overcome all difficulties; since man, alone of all creation, possessed this power, there was the less need to invoke the help of supernatural forces. The strongly rational emphasis of the age played down the value of mysticism, of ceremonial, of tradition, and of sentiment. God was acknowledged as the creator of the world, but the natural laws which he had ordained, and which scientists had recently clarified, were not seen as conflicting with the tenets of a rational form of Christianity. Worship should reflect and express this philosophy. 'Men, who are reasonable creatures, praise him in a reasonable manner' (Burnet: 268). Often enough, indeed, worship was seen as a mere introduction to a sermon, in which reason, allied to carefully chosen biblical texts, was used to justify conventional morality, charity and good works, and the existing order of church and state. Little thought was given to the emotional and spiritual needs of the common people.

Davies sums up the ideal of Georgian Anglican worship with the word *decorum*:

Decorum is the enemy of extremes, of enthusiasms, of spontaneity, and often of sincerity. It is seen, symbolically, in the whitewash with which the dark corners of the Gothic churches were covered up, ... [and which], according to Dean Sykes, ... possessed for that age a symbolic value as typifying the dispersal of mysticism and obscurity by the penetration of the pure light of reason. Metaphorical whitewash is a term that may be used to suggest the posturing that often did duty for real religion for many during this century ... The perfunctory tones of the clergyman, who might be wearing his hunting clothes and spurs beneath his cassock and Genevan gown as he raced through the service in his eagerness to get to the social diversions of the day, seemed often to reduce the liturgy to mere play-acting, in which the fashionable members of the auditory acquiesced. (Davies: III, 74–5)

In many cases it must be admitted that the main function of an organ was to provide a kind of musical whitewash, so that decorum could be attained for the ear as well as the eye. So much was stated in explicit terms in a sermon preached by Gabriel Towerson at St Andrew Undershaft, London, on 31 May 1696, the day on which the organ was opened. After recounting the biblical and rational justifications for the use of instruments in church, he went on:

The organ, in particular, both by the *loudness*, and the *harmoniousness* thereof doth, with a kind of grateful violence, carry the voices of men along with it, and not only prevents any such indecent discords as might otherwise arise, but makes their voices indeed and in truth to answer that melody, which is here exhorted to, and is, it may be, the only instrument that can with any certainty procure it. (Towerson: 26)

The same points were made in sermons at organ openings at Bridgwater in 1700, and at Isleworth in 1738 (Shuttleworth; Coleire). Dr Richard Banner, of University College, Oxford, was even blunter in a sermon delivered at a meeting of the Three Choirs Festival at Worcester Cathedral in 1737. After criticising the current versions of the metrical psalms, he continued by advocating the introduction of an organ:

For why should the harsh unpleasing voices, and unskilful singing of the common people, be thought more agreeable to *gospel worship*, than the grave and melodious instrumental music? which tends to regulate the time, and rectify the tune, checks and prevents the over eagerness of some, drowns and mollifies the clamorous harshness and untunableness of others... And would men bestow as much of their time and pains in being instructed in the *more sublime* parts of church music, as they do in this *low branch* of it, they might with the assistance of an *organ*, and those other helps which always attend it, be able to revive the practice of our first reformers, and to make our *parochial* music in some sort resemble that of the *cathedral* or *mother* church. Happy should we be were we in such a case. (Banner: 14–15)

But it was one thing to silence the discordant multitudes, quite another to produce a more decorous kind of singing. The common people could not rise to the standards now required; while the gentry would not so far demean themselves as to sing in church. The answer, clearly, was to dip still further into one's pocket, and with Christian charity to endow a school for poor children who, in return, would be trained to provide a more elegant song of praise. It did not matter that young children could hardly be expected to mean what they sang (John Wesley would later condemn 'the screaming of boys who bawl out what they neither feel nor understand', Telford: III, 226).

The new music would represent, in several ways, the worldly success and status of those who financed it. The richness of the gilded organ case and pipes, like that of the rest of the church, showed not only the generosity of the donors (often commemorated by a plaque) but their wealth; the uniforms of the charity children marked their subservience, which was also hammered home in the specially written hymns and anthems they were asked to sing on the occasion of the annual or twice-yearly charity sermon (described in more detail below, p. 133).* There was something aristocratic in the notion of paying for one's musical entertainment, and the new psalmody approached the music that was heard in the great houses of the nobility – not only in outward conditions but in style as well. For the successive waves of Italian influence had led to a profound change in the musical taste of the aristocracy.

Their music must now be treble-dominated and 'airy'. The admired texture was that of the violin sonata, or the operatic aria or duet: one or two high voices with a light continuo accompaniment. Such a texture could well be achieved by organ and charity children, and the old tradition of keeping the psalm tune in the tenor voice must now be laid aside, so that the music in church could please cultivated persons by its resemblance to fashionable art music.

The Italian manner could reach the parishioners of even such a remote town as Ashbourne, Derbyshire. When the organ built for the church by Henry Valentine was almost complete, in August 1710, the vicar, Nathaniel Boothouse, wrote in the parish records that 'Thomas Cook of Trusley Esq. and his servant and Mr Richard Bassano came in the afternoon' one Sunday, and 'after evening prayers and sermon ended they first played a grave sonata as voluntary, then Mr. Bassano before the church full of people sang the 121 psalm – "I will lift up mine eyes" – as an anthem.' The following month,

the great organ in the church being now completed and put in tune, and the iron standard rods and curtains of the organ loft being set up it was opened and dedicated in the manner following. On Sunday the Vicar preach[ed] from Psalm 92 [verses] 1, 2, 3 ... But in the afternoon Mr. Mathew Haines, one of the singing-men of the choir at Lichfield [cathedral], gave a fine long anthem just after the Italian manner. The anthem has much variety of music in it, and is contrived with intermixture of frequent symphonies or ritornels, which ritornels were touched and played upon two violins by two gentlemen who stood behind the curtain in the organ loft. This performance was very fine as well as grave and solemn. (Cox: 204; Sadler: 45)

Of course, the music was especially elaborate at an organ opening, but it served then to set a new standard to be aimed at. Organ voluntaries were one of the assets that now became available, and here, too, Italian influences prevailed (see pp. 135–9). The taste of the time demanded a bright and easily melodious style, having little to do with the traditional styles of religious music, and an occasional display of brilliant technique.

* At Chelsea a charity school was founded in 1707 by William Petyt, and the school building included a special 'cloister' or covered arcade, three arches in length, facing the street. Here the scholars were to stand after service twice each Sunday 'with their caps off... until the congregation passed by', and were to 'be given to understand who are their benefactors and instructed that as often as they pass by any of them they pull off their caps and make them a bow' (*Survey of London* xxii, 1950: 103).

Those who still took their religion seriously were offended by the frivolity of the new voluntaries.

These worldly and superficial attitudes to church music, and to religious worship in general, were the prevailing ones. They triumphed especially after the accession of George I in 1714, when any religious zeal tended to be associated with Jacobitism, and when bishops were chosen not for their piety and learning but for their supineness and safe Whig political opinions (Allen & McClure: 127–8). Before that time, however, there was a notable high-church movement that strongly opposed the growing rationalist tendencies, and placed great emphasis on the traditional ceremonies of Anglican worship as an expression of religious piety, reinterpreting the Book of common prayer in a Catholic direction (Pl. 5). This movement, not widely known outside the ranks of church historians, reached its culmination in the reign of Queen Anne (1702–14). It was a direct forerunner of Methodism and Evangelicalism, and has even been equated with the latter (Wilson: 42–3). It expressed itself most strongly in the formation of religious societies.

The first of these were founded in London as early as 1678. They were made up of young men of a parish, who met only under the direction of a clergyman, for private devotions (often including the singing of a psalm) and to inculcate goodness and pious living. The societies were exclusively male, and were largely made up of the lower classes. Archbishop Tenison in 1699 praised the 'noble zeal' of the societies, but regretted the refusal of the upper classes to give the movement any support: 'Gain over the persons who have the greatest *esteem* and *authority* in their parishes,' he advised the bishops of his province; 'for if the better sort can be brought up to such a seriousness and sobriety, the rest will more easily follow' (Portus: 63). But there is no sign that this took place. Of the 254 members of the society of St Giles, Cripplegate in 1718, only seven were described as 'gentlemen', and five of these were clerks (:22).

The movement was greatly strengthened in 1698 by the foundation of the Society for Promoting Christian Knowledge, which soon took the local societies under its wing, and actively worked to spread them throughout the country. The S.P.C.K. was also prominent in the founding of charity schools, and in some cases the school was under the control or influence of the religious society in the parish (:81, 135, 201).

In 1697 the Reverend Josiah Woodward, a leading figure in the movement, published *An account of the rise and progress of the religious societies in the City of London, &c.*, in which he praised the work of the societies in improving the spirit and effect of public worship. 'Their zeal hath in many places given new life to the celebration of the *Lord's supper, public prayer, singing of psalms*, and *Christian conference*, duties which were in many places almost disused, or performed in a cool and languishing manner' (Woodward, 1698: 63). The conferences often included psalm singing. Woodward provided 'directions suited to such religious conference' which consisted chiefly of a shortened and modified version of morning prayer, omitting the absolution and other functions exclusive to an ordained priest, so that a lay 'steward' could lead the devotions. This was followed by directions to sing a psalm, then the religious conference, and finally a second psalm (:172, 186). A London society, not identified, published in 1713 *A form of publick devotions* which was closely modelled on Woodward's. (For some further details of the activities of a religious society, see below, p.142.)

In addition to their private meetings these societies of young men took upon themselves the duty of supporting and enhancing the services of their parish church. In 1714, out of 99 London churches at least 27 were dependent on religious societies in the parish for the conduct of some of their services (Paterson; cited Portus: 19). In particular they took the lead in singing the psalms, for which they earned the praise and gratitude of Arthur Bedford (1733: dedication) and George Whitefield (1771–2: v, 167).

If the organ was typically symbolic of the materialistic motive of reform, and the male singing society of the religious motive, then the choir of charity children served both at once. This was a period of great activity in the founding of charity schools. They were founded for reasons that had nothing to do with music. They were meant to inculcate morality, to shore up the Church of England against the inroads of Catholics and dissenters, and to teach the children a trade by which they could earn an honest living. The school at St Margaret, Westminster, founded in 1688 just after the protestant succession had been secured by the defeat of James II, was called 'the first institution of this kind against Popery' (*Gentleman's Magazine*, LV (1), 1785: 390), and it was followed by a large number of similar foundations in the next fifty years, both in London and in provincial towns (Pl. 13). The S.P.C.K. was a leading force, helping to collect funds for the schools, providing them with books, and publicising their efforts and successes. It became common for the school children to be taught to sing. A list of books recommended for charity schools published with the S.P.C.K.'s annual report in 1713 included a 'common prayer book with the singing psalms', 'some book of psalmody', 'Dr. Bray's *Baptismal covenant*' (which had ten psalm tunes in an appendix), and 'Hymns for the charity-schools' (Allen & McClure: 185–6n.). In 1733 it was said that 'the boys and girls in all the charity schools learn the common plain *psalm-tunes*' (Bedford, 1733: 31).

It was natural that the children would also sing in the parish church, which they were required to attend on Sundays and holy days. And it was found that their singing was a powerful attraction, providing, as I have already suggested, exactly the kind of music that many less pious worshippers desired. As the schools depended entirely on voluntary contributions, it became usual for each parish church to have an annual 'charity sermon', at which a prominent clergyman would urge the value of charity and religious education, and the children, in their fine uniforms provided by the charity, would then do their best to melt the hearts of the congregation with their singing. Before long special hymns and anthems were being composed for these occasions, with texts chosen or specially written for the purpose in hand. From 1704 onwards an even more effective fund-raising event was staged: the annual meeting of all the charity children of London in one church. The ceremony took the form of a service with a charity sermon, but the great attraction was the singing of metrical psalm tunes (later, hymns and chanted psalms) by several thousand children. The excitement of the occasion undoubtedly stimulated the children's musical efforts, and raised large sums of money in their support (Pl. 21).

The high-church view of public worship was spelt out in detail by the influential Dr Thomas Bisse, in a series of sermons on 'The beauty of holiness in the common prayer', first published in 1716. He dwelt primarily on the liturgy itself, and described its correct mode of performance in minute detail. Metrical psalms, being outside the liturgy, were less important than the prose psalms, and were best placed after the third collect, where a rubric provided for an anthem 'in quires and places where they sing':

And since the singing psalms are only permitted [i.e., not required] in our Church, this seems the most proper place for singing a psalm, rather than after the second lesson; and thus I have known it practised in some parishes, and it were to be wished, it were done so in all, especially where they so far resemble quires [i.e., cathedrals], as to have organs. 1st. Because parish-churches should as much as possible, conform to the customs of the cathedral churches, which are as the mother-churches to all the parish-churches within the diocese, and should give the rule to them. 2dly. Because after the second lesson there is a proper [prose] hymn or psalm appointed, which is interrupted by a singing psalm coming in between. (Bisse, 1716: 89–90n.)

Bisse's work ran to several editions, and gave rise to a lively controversy in the form of tracts and pamphlets. The idea that parish churches should imitate cathedrals was new, but it was taken up by many musicians in town and country during the next hundred years, and would gather further strength in the early decades of the nineteenth century.

Of the three possible agents of change in the music of the town parish church, organs, charity children, and religious societies, the first two, at least, cost money, and were also open to possible objections on religious grounds. An organ in this period cost several hundred pounds to buy, and an annual sum of £20 or so to pay the organist, with perhaps a further £5 to cover tuning, minor repairs, and the wages of the bellows blower. In all the equivalent of £1000 in capital was about the minimum that would be required. Such a sum was beyond the means of all but the wealthiest parishes, and it was by no means clear that parish funds could legally be used for this purpose. Legal obstacles were available to those who had puritanical prejudices against the use of an organ, or who simply had a conservative attachment to the old way of singing. Once an organ was obtained, there might be disagreement as to what and when it should play, and who should sing. To understand fully these interrelated factors it is necessary to look more closely into the system of parish government that existed in this period, and to see how it operated in determining the musical character of the services.

Parish church government and finance

The conduct of worship, as always, was governed by law, as expressed in acts of parliament, royal injunctions and canons of the Church. In many matters that concerned music, however, the law was imprecise, and the rubrics were silent. The responsibility for decisions concerning music was divided between the incumbent (the rector or vicar of the parish), under the supervision of the ordinary (the bishop of the diocese), and the parish vestry, which theoretically represented the wishes and interests of the parishioners, but was not always democratically elected. In the course of the eighteenth and early nineteenth centuries several court cases defined the boundaries between these two sources of authority.

There was little doubt that the incumbent had complete discretion to decide whether, and at what points in the service, music should be admitted, so long as he made no departures from the prescribed liturgy and rubrics. This right was confirmed by judgments in the ecclesiastical courts. At St Botolph, Aldersgate in 1792, the churchwardens 'prohibited, by their pretended authority, the singing of the Gloria Patri in prose at the conclusion of the psalms of David, and in other parts of the divine service', on the grounds that they paid the organist and managed the children in the choir. The Consistory Court of London ruled in favour of the incumbent: 'The minister has the right of directing the service, e.g., when the organ shall and shall not play, and when children shall and shall not chant' (*Hutchins v. Denziloe & Loveland*; Haggard, 1832a: I, 170–80).

More complex questions arose over the financial provision for music. The maintenance of an organ and the salary of an organist could not be charged to the parish without its consent, and in many parishes the inhabitants were unable or unwilling to tax themselves for this purpose. At Poulton-le-Fylde in 1781 it was agreed that all charges in connection with the organ would be defrayed by voluntary subscriptions only (Fishwick: 92). At Kettering in 1817 the vestry refused to reimburse a churchwarden who had paid for organ repairs (Peyton: 61).

When the incumbent or a group of parishioners wished to install an organ, they had to apply to the bishop for a faculty. The bishop, or his deputy in the diocesan court, invited objections from parishioners, and then decided whether to grant the faculty. When an organ was proposed for the parish church of St Luke, Chelsea, in 1745, a voluntary subscription raised £143 for its purchase. A zealous churchwarden put up the organ although the faculty had been refused (because of objections by some parishioners), and had to take it down again. In 1752 the select vestry again applied for a faculty, and raised a further £20 a year for the organist's salary. This time the faculty was granted over the objections of 64 parishioners, but on appeal the Court of Arches reversed the chancellor's decision (*Randall & Hodson v. Collins & Ludlow*; Phillimore: II, 217–28).

The parish could refuse to pay for an organ, but could not so easily refuse to receive one that was otherwise provided for. In one case, concerning Halifax parish church (Pl. 26), some inhabitants in 1765 had continued to oppose the erection of an organ even when an assurance had been given that the parish would never be charged with any expenses connected with it (*Butterworth & Barker v. Walker & Waterhouse*; Burrow: III, 1689–92). Many faculties included a clause providing against any future expense falling on the parish. But at a later date (1830) it was ruled that no such clause was necessary, since the parish could not, in any case, be bound to maintain an organ even if it had at an earlier time decided to do so (Haggard, 1832b: 4–17). The parish could be *compelled* to pay only essential expenses. 'Most certainly an organ is not necessary in a parish for the decent performance of divine worship; therefore, the parishioners are not bound to provide an organ: but though it is not necessary, it is extremely decent, proper, and even customary in a parish... of extent and opulence.' So said Sir John Nicholl in the Court of Arches in 1830, on an appeal from the commissary court of Surrey by the churchwardens of Clapham (*Pearce & Hughes v. Rector of Clapham*; Haggard, 1832b: 12). If the request for a faculty proposed that the expenses were to be paid out of the parish rates, the court would often deny it, as at St Mary-le-Strand, London, in 1790 (MS 76b: 191). At St Swithin, London, the vestry in 1703 turned down an offer from a wealthy parishioner to give the church an organ, even when he offered to pay for the building of a gallery to hold it (Wren Society XIX, 1942: 54). The church did not acquire an organ for more than a hundred years after this episode.

In practice, the commonest pattern was for an organ to be donated or bequeathed, or paid for by voluntary subscription, while the parish undertook the expense of maintaining the instrument and paying the organist and bellows blower. It was not often that a rich person had sufficient interest in church music to give an organ, so a subscription was a much more common method of raising the money; and this depended on finding enough people of ample means, who resided in the parish and attended the parish church, and who felt enough pride and interest in the services there to contribute to the musical expenses. The existence of these conditions depended, in turn, on the population and make-up of the parish.

The parish system was one of many institutions that had been allowed to survive more or less unaltered from a remote period when conditions had been entirely different. The boundaries between parishes, and the system of parochial government by vestry, involved matters of more vital concern to the ruling classes than church music. They were allowed to survive unreformed until the nineteenth century because private interests and abuses were protected by them (Webb: I). The effect on church music was a chance by-product.

The system worked well in parishes of small or moderate size and with a stable population, where there was a well-understood relationship between the oligarchy of the leading citizens (the squire and principal landowners, the incumbent, the justice of the peace, and so on) and the ordinary parishioners, and where there was a reasonable proportion between the taxable resources of the parish and the expenses to be met. These circumstances remained true of many rural and some urban parishes in the eighteenth century; but in others there was an obvious imbalance, as large movements of population and wealth took place.

In the areas of change, balance could have been maintained by dividing some parishes and amalgamating others. But this could be done only by act of parliament. The Church Building Acts of 1711 and 1818 made general provision for the division of parishes (the first in London only). Apart from this, special acts had to be procured; this was not only a ruinously expensive process, but, in an age of political corruption, it could often be defeated by well-financed vested interests opposed to the change. As a consequence, parish boundaries in large part remained the same as they had been before the Reformation, however inappropriate they might be to the changed conditions.

Provincial town churches

Towns that had been important in the middle ages, especially cathedral cities, suffered now from a superfluity of parishes. For instance:

	Parishes	Population
Norwich	42	36,800
York	28	16,100
Canterbury	14	9,700
Winchester	11	5,800
Hastings	6	3,000
Wallingford	4	1,700

(1801 census)

Before the Reformation towns like these had been points of concentration for the immense wealth of the Church and of the religious orders. There were endowments for music, and often a church could employ several chantry priests and other musicians. The Reformation took away most of the endowments, leaving the ratepayers to bear the full burden of maintaining the services. It is hardly surprising that in parishes of this type very little money was spent on music. Choirs and organs disappeared soon after Elizabeth's accession, not to return for three centuries in many cases.

As an example we may take the venerable city of York, which had been the virtual capital of the north of England, a centre of civil as well as ecclesiastical government, and a crossroads of trade and communications. Only one parish church in the city acquired an organ before 1700: this was the church of St Michael-le-Belfry, next to the cathedral. A guide book of 1831 called it 'the largest and most elegant sacred edifice in York, excepting the cathedral ... The organ, the first which belonged to any parish church in York, came from the Popish chapel in the Manor, and originally from the church of Durham' (*Views*: no. 13). It is not known whether the organ was given to the church or purchased by subscription; the churchwardens' accounts show only a payment of £2 2s for the organ case (1687) and subsequent payments for the organist's salary and occasional repairs. It was more than a century before a second York church had an organ: in 1791 All Saints, Pavement obtained one from Hazelwood Castle, probably· as a gift (see Table 3, p. 112). At Norwich the situation was much the same (MS 80/440). In these and similar cities, all but one or two of the ancient parishes were in circumstances varying from moderate to extreme poverty. They had few wealthy members, and their populations of less than a thousand were in no position to tax themselves to support professional music of any sort.

The opposite problem existed in rapidly growing industrial regions, where the ancient parish church was called upon to serve a population far too big for it. In the north of England, where the old parishes had always been large in area, the problem was especially acute. Until 1699 the entire borough of Liverpool was only a district within the immense parish of Walton: in that year a separate parish of Liverpool was created by act of parliament (Webb: 135). Manchester, already in the early eighteenth century the largest manufacturing centre of the kingdom, was a parish of 54 square miles, containing no less than 30 semi-independent townships, one of which was also called Manchester and contained the ancient town centre (:69–70). By 1801 its population was over 120,000. The parish church was fortunately endowed as a collegiate body (see Appendix I), but the chapels in the outlying districts were dependent for financial support on the parish vestry, an enormous and increasingly turbulent body involved in a succession of political battles. In these large parishes it was sometimes difficult to find a majority in the vestry to support payments for music even in the central parish church, for most of the ratepayers attended their local chapels. When in 1785 the Archbishop of York issued a citation calling on parishioners of Bradford to show cause why a faculty to erect an organ in the parish church should not be granted, the inhabitants of Haworth objected, because they did not want to pay their share of the rates for this purpose. The faculty was granted on condition that the people of Haworth should not be charged, but the matter was a cause of dissension for forty years or more (Cudworth: 113). In some newly populated areas there was no Anglican church or chapel at all, and the inhabitants would attend a dissenting meeting-house or go without worship altogether. It is notorious that until Victorian times the Church of England totally failed to meet the challenge posed by the growing industrial and urban population. The musical problems confronting industrial parishes grew more pressing at the end of the eighteenth century, and will be discussed in a later chapter.

The most fortunately placed churches in this period were those of ports and market towns, without a cathedral but with a single, large parish church. They were now benefiting from the improvements in agriculture and the general growth of commerce, so that a moderate increase in population was accompanied by a considerable increase in wealth. Many such churches were able to acquire a good organ in the late seventeenth or early eighteenth century, to pay a reasonable salary to an organist, and to support a charity school which would provide children to lead the psalm singing. In most cases the bulk of the payments for music were supported by voluntary subscriptions. It often happened that the parish church, in the absence of a cathedral, attracted a good deal of civic pride, and aldermen and leading citizens took pleasure in contributing to the decoration of the building and the adornment of the services. At Hull the organ was purchased in 1711 for £586, and the money was raised by subscription through the efforts of the mayor and the M.P. for the borough. The vestry decided to pay the organist's salary of £20 by doubling pew rents (G. H. Smith: 7). At Bungay, a prominent citizen died in 1728 and left £200 to build an organ in St Mary's church, and a house, the rent from which was to go towards paying an organist (MS 3: 48). In some towns the municipal corporation contributed to the cost of an organ, as at Lancaster (Roper: 617) and at Basingstoke (Parliamentary Papers, 1835: XXIV, 1105), or to the organist's salary, as at Bedford, Doncaster, Scarborough and elsewhere. At Liverpool the corporation went further, building several additional churches and paying for their upkeep and for the salaries of the clergy and other functionaries, to a total of nearly £6000 in the year 1832 (Parl. Papers, 1835: XXVI, 2730–4). At Lostwithiel, on the other hand, the entire expenses of the church, including the organist's salary, were traditionally paid by the Earl of Mount Edgcumbe, patron of the borough (Parl. Papers, 1835: XXIII, 547).

A typical organ of the period was the one erected by John Harris at Doncaster parish church in 1738–40. A copy of the agreement, with details of the specification, survives in the vestry minutes (MS 93: 19/4). The cost of £525 was raised by a subscription, and an organ loft was built at the west end of the church at the expense of the parish, for which a special 3d rate was raised. There were to be two independent manual organs, the Great having 12 stops based on an 8 ft Open Diapason, with 52 keys extending from G below the bass stave to D above the treble stave, and including two Trumpet stops and a Clarion. The second manual controlled the Chair and Echo departments, with the same compass but the Echo stops in the treble range only. There were 4 Chair stops (Stopped Diapason, Flute, Fifteenth and Bassoon), and six Echo stops (Open Diapason, Stopped Diapason, Principal, Cornet (3 ranks), Trumpet and Hautboy). The Echo organ was to 'echo and swell to express passion in degrees of loudness and softness as if inspired by human breath'; in other words it was enclosed with a swell-box, a relatively recent English development. There were 1339 speaking pipes in all. English organs practically never had pedals before the second quarter of the nineteenth century.

At Wigan the records show traces of a long contest between the 'country' and 'town' ideals of psalmody, which was ultimately decided in favour of the latter by the acquisition of an organ. In 1696 the general vestry decided to have an organ, but there was opposition to the plan, and instead a gallery for singers was erected at the west end of the church. In 1707 Edward Finch, fifth son of the Earl of Nottingham, became rector. He was a rare example of a musical clergyman.* Though he had been a prebendary of York since 1704, he chose to reside at least part of the time at Wigan (unlike his predecessor) and took an interest in the music of the church. He was unimpressed by the efforts of the gallery singers, and when in 1707 a parishioner died leaving £200 for the purchase of an organ, Finch offered to pay for its erection out of his own pocket. Backed up by the churchwardens he decided to place it between the nave and the chancel, though this meant turning the mayor and corporation out of their accustomed seats. There was a prolonged legal battle. Finch pointed out that the organ, when built, 'will be able to keep those that sing so much better in tune that it will no longer be needful for them to sit together, and upon this account will be a work of great use and ornament, and add much decency and solemnity in the worship of God'. The faculty was granted, and was sustained by two higher courts. The case was finally decided in 1712. But Finch, perhaps

---

* A Te deum and an anthem by him survive in the Tudway manuscripts (MS 34a), and he also wrote a 'grammar of thorough-bass' (*DNB*).

discouraged by the protracted quarrel, resigned his office shortly afterwards, and it fell to his successor to preside over the opening of the organ, and to appoint the first organist, Edward Betts (later organist of Manchester collegiate church). The mayor and corporation now installed themselves in the west gallery; additional sums were voted for improving the organ and paying the organist. Wigan settled into a typical pattern of 'town' psalmody, and boys of the Bluecoat School were soon brought in to lead the singing (Bridgeman: 591–621).

The parish of Leeds, in the earlier eighteenth century, before it was overwhelmed by rapid increases in population, was governed by a stable, benevolent oligarchy (Webb: 50) that was conducive to the successful development of town psalmody. The parish covered 32 square miles and was coterminous with the municipal borough; it had a population of about 13,000. The authorities built chapels of ease in outlying parts of the parish, and free schools for the education of poor children. The Leeds Charity School was founded in 1705. Its regulations provided for twice-daily prayers and psalm singing on schooldays, and for the children to attend the parish church on Sundays (Sylvester: 187–8). In 1711 the school took 28 boys and 12 girls, and had an income of about £208 per year, including money from collection at communion and donations from 'gentlemen' and 'merchants' (:175). An organ was erected in the parish church in 1713 (Hargrave: 320, 324). The organ was used for playing voluntaries as well as accompanying metrical psalms; the children led, or possibly monopolised, the psalm singing; on special occasions, such as the opening of a new chapel of ease, they were capable of singing an anthem (Thoresby: II, 275, 285, 334, 354). It is clear that financial contributions by a number of leading citizens had led to a transformation in the music of the church.

London churches

London was in a class of its own, and within itself contained extreme contrasts of rich and poor which were reflected in the nature of the parish church music. The area loosely known as 'London' can be defined during this period as the jurisdiction of the Company of Parish Clerks, or the 'Bills of Mortality'. It consisted of the City of London (parishes both inside and outside the ancient city walls), the town of Westminster (not to become a 'city' until 1900), and certain parishes adjoining, including those south of the river in the borough of Southwark. In this area the parish clerks were required to return statistics of death (an activity which kept them particularly busy in 1665, when 70,000 people died of the plague out of a total population of some 500,000). This was why the area was called the 'Bills of Mortality'.

The City of London proper had much in common with other ancient cathedral cities, though on a larger scale; it was at the time of the Restoration a warren of over a hundred small parishes with poor populations, clustered round the great gothic Cathedral of St Paul's. (We have seen how in 1637 a City parish claimed to be too poor to restore its organ.) Though the City was the country's main centre of business, containing great dockyards and markets as well as the budding financial organisations that would soon dominate the commerce of the world, its resident population was already on the decline, and its richer merchants were learning to commute. Outlying suburbs were developing, each with its own character and purpose, in the regions of Covent Garden, Bloomsbury and St James's. The Great Fire of 1666 destroyed most of the City's churches as well as many of its houses and places of business. As is well known, the disaster forced a fresh start which ultimately led to unparalleled prosperity. In the matter of parishes, the opportunity was taken to give London the reorganisation for which other ancient cities had to wait another two hundred years. Parishes were joined together; many old churches were not rebuilt, and one new church was made to serve where two or three old ones had been before.

But even these amalgamated parishes were often small and poor. In 1732 there were sixty-two parishes in the City, but the number of dwelling houses averaged only 183 per parish. By contrast, Westminster had only nine parishes, with an average of 2089 houses per parish – more than ten times as many. The adjoining parishes (those within the Bills of Mortality but not in either the City or Westminster) were intermediate in average size (see Table 3). Westminster, containing the court, parliament and executive departments, had attracted the rich and the powerful. As it enclosed more and more villages and meadows during the rapid expansion of the period, it filled with large prosperous houses parishes which had once been sparsely populated, and hence were large in area. The reorganisation thus took the opposite direction to that in the City of London. Old parishes were carved up, and churches built to provide for the new ones.

Quite apart from their greater size the parishes of Westminster had every

Table 3. *Incidence of organs in parish churches of selected areas in 1801*

Area	Total population	Number of parishes	Average population per parish	Number of parishes with organs	Percentage of parishes with organs	Persons per parish organ
A. London:						
Bills of Mortality	694.8	110	6.3	91	*82.7*	7.6
City of London	63.4	62	1.0	45	*72.6*	1.4
Outparishes and parts adjoining	479.8	39	12.3	37	*94.9*	13.0
Westminster	151.6	9	16.8	9	*100.0*	16.8
B. York (City)	16.1	29	0.6	2	*6.9*	8.1
C. West Riding of Yorkshire	565.3	190	3.0	16	*8.4*	35.3
D. Dorset	115.3	273	0.4	6	*2.2*	19.2

Note: The statistics for organs are not complete for areas C and D. Other parishes in these areas may have had organs of which no record has been found. This is much less probable in areas A and B. The numbers in the first, third and last columns represent thousands.
Source: Temperley, forthcoming.

advantage over those of London proper. Instead of growing up over centuries they were purposely designed (Pl. 11). Most of them were headed by a number of prominent and powerful citizens, who not only had money to spare but also influence to exert on behalf of their parish. The poor (most of whom were servants or caterers to the rich) were better looked after, the streets and squares were spaciously planned, the schools better built and endowed, the churches more richly furnished. Concessions could be obtained from the Crown or the government, including the creation of new parishes by act of parliament. When, after the deposition of James II, the organ at Whitehall chapel (formerly used by a series of Catholic queens consort for their private devotions) was no longer needed, it was presented not to a poor parish in the City but to the new parish of St James, Westminster – possibly the wealthiest in the kingdom. The organ from the Queen Dowager's chapel was given to St Anne, Westminster, in 1700; George I presented an organ to St Martin-in-the-Fields in 1726, at a cost of £1500. If royal bounty was not forthcoming it was no great hardship for the parishioners to provide an organ by subscription. Similarly they maintained large charity schools for poor children, which became a source of choristers. Organists were generously paid, and were often well-trained professionals attached to the chapel royal or the Abbey. Money was available to buy books, or even to have them specially printed. Seats or pews were rented at high rates: Defoe was scandalised at the charges made at St James, Westminster, 'where it costs one almost as dear as to see a play', as he significantly remarked (Chancellor: 76). For all these reasons it is not surprising that the churches of Westminster led the way to an 'improved' kind of town psalmody, which was respectable or even elegant by educated standards and in fairly close touch with the developments of cathedral music and of secular art music.

An important ingredient in the success of these musical changes was the select vestry. Not all parishes had a general vestry in which every male ratepayer had the right to attend and vote. In some, the vestry consisted of from ten to fifty 'principal inhabitants' of the parish, who served for life, any vacancy being filled by co-option. Select vestries had existed in some English parishes by immemorial custom, especially in two areas: the counties of the extreme north-east, and London (Webb: 174). Newly formed parishes in the London area were nearly always given select vestries by the Act of Parliament that established them: this was the case with all 11 formed under the Church Building Act of 1711 (:199). Of 110 parishes in the Bills of Mortality in 1732, at least 42 had select vestries (see Table 4), and this included all the Westminster parishes.

A select vestry naturally tended to be dominated by the rich and the aristocratic. It could exclude undesired elements from any influence in the running of the parish and the church. Select vestries were usually made up entirely of Anglicans: an Act of 1663 excluding all but Church of England supporters from all vestries expired in 1670 (Webb: 242), and in course of time many open vestries would come to be controlled by a majority of dissenters, with damaging effects on the finances of the church, but select vestries could avoid this problem. They tended to adopt paternalistic attitudes to their parish, with sometimes beneficial effects: the vestry of St

Table 4. *Percentage of London parishes having organs and charity schools in 1732, in relation to certain other variables*

	Parishes with							
	General vestry	Select vestry	Charity school	No charity school	1–200 houses	201–1000 houses	1001 or more houses	All parishes
Churches with organs	39.2	67.6	61.1	27.0	26.0	43.3	62.5	47.9
Churches with a charity school	42.8	77.5	100.0	0.0	28.0	80.0	95.8	57.9
1–40 children in charity school	12.5	15.0	22.6	…	16.0	13.3	4.2	13.1
41–70 children in charity school	8.9	17.5	27.5	…	4.0	36.6	12.5	15.9
71–100 children in charity school	17.9	25.0	33.9	…	6.0	23.3	45.8	19.6
101 or more children in charity school	3.5	20.0	16.1	…	2.0	7.7	25.0	9.3

Note: For the purpose of computing each percentage figure in the body of this table, only parishes for which all relevant variable quantities were precisely known are included.
Source: New remarks of London

George, Hanover Square, largely made up of noblemen, was free of the corruption that plagued many London vestries in the eighteenth century (Webb: 240). But they tended to run the church for the benefit of their own class, at the expense of poorer worshippers. As far as church music was concerned, they held a patrician view of its function, paying professionals to provide elegant music for the congregation to listen to, and discouraging the traditional congregational singing.*

The parish of St Martin-in-the-Fields had been in medieval times a large area of countryside adjoining the City of London to the west. In the course of the seventeenth century it rapidly filled up with commercial and residential neighbourhoods. The chapel of ease built in Covent Garden in 1633 was made a new parish of St Paul in 1645. St Anne, Soho, was another new parish carved out of St Martin's; the church was built in 1676–86 out of a donation of £5000 left by a lady to the Bishop of London (Cardwell *et al.*: 2). The most elegant of the new parishes, St James, Westminster (Pl. 11), had a church built as a chapel by Lord St Albans in 1680, and made a parish church in 1685, now known as St James, Piccadilly. The guiding spirit in this development was Thomas Tenison, vicar of St Martin-in-the-Fields from 1680, and then also rector of St James. He refounded free schools in the parishes of St Martin and St James, for boys who were to be taught religion, reading, writing, arithmetic, Latin, Greek, and psalm singing (A. G. Jackson: 10–11). They were supported entirely by funds collected at the offertory, especially at the annual charity sermon. At St James's, a pew in the north gallery was allocated to the use of the schoolboys (*Survey of London*, XXIX, 1960: 54) (see Pl. 12). Further expansion soon followed. A temporary 'tabernacle' was built at King Street in 1688, and was endowed as a chapel of ease in St James's parish in 1700; a new building was erected in 1702. It had its own school for 36 boys, who attended services at the parish church on catechising days and at the chapel on Sundays and festivals; 'so many of them as were capable were taught to sing the common psalm tunes used in the church and chapels of the parish' (A. G. Jackson: 19).

Tenison became Bishop of Lincoln in 1691 and Archbishop of Canterbury in 1694. He did not forget his interest in the parishes of Westminster, but his duty there was more and more often discharged by curates. The typically eighteenth-century custom of performance by deputy even descended to the parish clerks. In 1685 Hugh Ellis was 'appointed clerk of this parish [St James] who is in priest's orders, . . . and to find one under him to set the psalms, to whom he shall allow £10 p[er] ann[um]', a comparatively large sum for the times (MS 76: 7 July 1685). The deputy was known as the 'psalm clerk'. His opposite number at St Martin's was instructed in 1691 'every morning and afternoon on sermon days (fast days excepted) [to] give notice in writing to the organist, before the service begins, of the psalms and number of verses he intends to sing and also what tune' (MS 76a: 3 May 1692). An organ had been put up in St Martin's in 1667; in 1691 St James's acquired the one from Whitehall chapel (Pl. 12).

---

* The conflict over the organ at Chelsea, already related, was an example of a select vestry taking decisions against the wishes of most of the parishioners.

The first organist at St Martin's was the organ builder, 'Father Smith'; later came Robert King, a notable composer and musician of the royal household; he was dismissed in 1714 because of 'several complaints' and later replaced by John Weldon, organist of the Chapel Royal (McMaster: 154–7). The organist of St James was Ralph or Raphael Courteville, also a noted composer and a political satirist.

The vestries of both parishes were select – St Martin's by 'immemorial custom' and St James's by express parliamentary provision (Webb: 198). Both were dominated by the aristocracy. That of St Martin's in 1724 had five noblemen, four baronets or peers' sons, and thirteen esquires, out of a total of forty-eight. They had strong connections with the most powerful figures in church and state: three rectors of St James, including Tenison, became archbishops of Canterbury (Chancellor: 76). St George, Hanover Square, was another offshoot of St Martin-in-the-Fields, formed into a separate parish in 1725, with a select vestry 'composed of the chief nobility in England'. By 1732 it had already four chapels-of-ease, and a parish school for over 80 children; the organist, Thomas Roseingrave, received the large salary of £50 (*New remarks*: 260–2). St John the Evangelist, Smith Square (Pl. 20) was created a parish in 1728.

In 1688 appeared a small booklet called *The psalms and hymns usually sung in the churches and tabernacles of St. Martins in the Fields, and St. James's Westminster*. It consisted of selections from the Old Version, with tunes in three-part harmony. Later editions, from 1697 to about 1750, left out St Martin-in-the-Fields from their title. The selection was possibly made, and undoubtedly approved, by Tenison. It set a new precedent in being designed for use in a particular church. In the next 150 years hundreds of similar collections would be printed for other churches, some with music included, some without. The nature of the music will be considered later. At present the point to be emphasised is that a highly fashionable church was setting the tone for a new kind of church music, one in which the congregation, instead of praising God directly, would pay to have his praise sung by poor school children and played on an organ. It can be said that this was a reversion to the age-old practice of pre-Reformation times, or an imitation of the cathedral practice: in either case it was a defeat for the puritan ideal of congregational song.

Considering the cost of buying an organ and maintaining a free school, and remembering the relative poverty of many parishes in the London area, it is surprising that so many parishes in the Bills of Mortality were able to follow the example of St James, Westminster during the following century (see Table 5). In 1732 a good proportion of the churches had both organs and charity schools (Table 4); as often as not the two went together, while quite a number of churches still had neither. A church with a select vestry was nearly twice as likely as a church with a general vestry to have both. This clearly reflects the aristocratic or upper-middle-class nature of the new 'town psalmody'. Most ordinary parishioners, if they had their way, would just as soon go on singing their own psalms; but in a parish with a select vestry, they would not have their way.

A more sinister factor may also have played a part in the fairly rapid growth in the number of organs. Many vestries in the London area were

Table 5. *Number of London parish churches having organs at the end of each decade (1660–1830) and the same expressed as a percentage of the number of functioning parish churches.*

	City		Out-parishes		Westminster		Total	
	No.	%	No.	%	No.	%	No.	%
1660	0	0.0	0	0.0	0	0.0	0	0.0
1670	1	7.1	1	4.2	1	25.0	3	7.1
1680	3	8.6	7	26.9	2	66.7	12	18.8
1690	9	15.8	9	33.3	3	50.0	21	23.3
1700	12	19.4	12	42.8	5	83.3	29	30.2
1710	15	24.2	15	51.7	5	83.3	35	36.1
1720	20	32.8	16	55.2	5	83.3	41	42.7
1730	23	37.1	17	47.2	7	77.8	47	43.9
1740	26	41.9	22	59.5	7	77.8	55	50.9
1750	30	48.4	23	59.0	8	88.9	61	55.5
1760	31	50.0	24	61.5	8	88.9	63	57.3
1770	34	55.7	27	69.2	8	88.9	69	63.3
1780	39	65.0	31	79.5	8	88.9	78	72.2
1790	44	74.6	33	84.6	9	100.0	86	80.4
1800	44	72.1	37	94.9	9	100.0	90	82.6
1810	48	78.7	37	94.9	9	100.0	94	86.2
1820	52	85.2	37	94.9	9	100.0	98	89.9
1830	55	90.2	36	94.7	9	100.0	100	91.7

Source: Temperley, forthcoming.

specially prone to corruption. 'Parish after parish would, like St. Sepulchre's, or Christ Church, Spitalfields, go in for extravagant building or repairing of churches, often, as the evidence clearly shows, with the express object of securing for individual members of the vestry a series of profitable contracts at the parish expense' (Webb: 235). 'These select vestries', it was said in 1828, 'are a focus of jobbing: the draper supplies the blankets and linen; the carpenter finds the church pews constantly out of repair; the painter's brushes are never dry; the plumber is always busy with his solder; and thus the public money is plundered and consumed' (*Considerations*: 49). It is not unlikely that organ builders profited from the same system, though no case has come to light. One may suspect something of the sort at St Saviour, Southwark, which had a particularly corrupt select vestry in which the vestrymen openly spent large sums of public money on their individual private interests (Webb: 187–8). In 1703–4 the church was 'beautified' at parish expense amounting to £2600; the following year an organ was purchased (MS 48).

One of the first London churches to secure an organ after the Restoration was St John, Hackney, in 1665. Pepys in his diary (4, 21 April 1667) commented on its excellence. At St Dunstan-in-the-West in 1674, the vestry ordered 'that the organ be used on every Sunday both in the forenoon and afternoon, and all other holy days appointed to be kept by the Church of England, and days of Thanksgiving only in the afternoon but both if two sermons' (MS 52: 14 December 1674). Similar terms were frequently inserted in organists' contracts. In the later eighteenth century some vestries agreed to a kind of 'package deal' with an agent, who agreed to provide an organ, keep it in tune and repair, and play it, in exchange for a life annuity. William Warrell or Worrell concluded an agreement of this kind with the parish of St Mary-le-Strand in 1790 (MS 76b: 187, 191, 196) and with St Olave, Old Jewry in 1814 (MS 59: 12, 24 August 1814). Some organists imitated their superiors by having their duties carried out by deputy; in this way they could be organists at several churches. This frequently brought criticism from the vestry. At St John, Hackney in 1753, when six organists competed for the post, Edward Henry Purcell, the winner, undertook to 'attend every other Sunday, and from Michaelmas to Lady Day also in the afternoon of each other Sunday'; at other times he would 'appoint a deputy satisfactory to the vestry' (MS 47: 22 September 1753). In some churches music was not diligently performed every week. In an effort to mend this fault, Simon Mitchell in his will dated 1748 left provision for his organ to remain in the church of St John, Clerkenwell, on condition that 'whensoever the said organ shall not be kept in order and fit for use or not be used as aforesaid by the space of eight Lord's days successively or twelve Lord's days within the compass of any one year, then' the organ would revert to his heirs (MS 46: fol. 65v–67).

Organs were usually placed at the west end of churches, in a gallery which was either specially erected or converted for the purpose. The organ acquired for St James, Clerkenwell in 1734 was placed in 'the old gallery where the charity children sit, enlarged to fix it in... for the more commodious placing of them on each side' (MS 45). More and more frequently the children sang from the organ gallery (Pl. 14), not from their own separate gallery or pew. At St Katherine-by-the-Tower in 1782 the original architect's design had to yield to the necessity of placing children on each side (*Gentleman's Magazine* LIV, 1782: 481n.). The reason, no doubt, was to place them directly under the organist's control.

Organs at London churches in this period varied greatly in size and power. Many City organs had only one manual with half a dozen stops, such as the Renatus Harris instrument at All Hallows, Lombard Street, built in 1695 and unaltered until 1866 (*The Organ* 21, 1926: 10). Two- and three-manual organs were common: by 1800 there were at least 30 London church organs with three manuals, generally controlling independent pipes. The most ambitious parish church organ of the period was that of St Magnus, London Bridge, built by Abraham Jordan in 1712. It had no less than four manuals, 'one of which is adapted to the art of emitting sounds by swelling the notes, which never was in any organ before' (*The Spectator*: 8 February 1712). The swell-box, which was imitated in later English organs, may have been anticipated in Spain and Portugal (Clutton & Niland: 86). British organs of this period differed notably from those of the continent. They were based on a rather sweet, smooth diapason tone; this could be transformed to brilliancy by the addition of powerful mixture stops, which had an 'agreeably silvery quality. They certainly bear no resemblance to the powerful contemporary German mixtures' (:87). There was nothing to compare with the towering mass of the north German organ, nor with the triumphalism of Bach's organ music. English organs had no pedals (the only known exception in a parish church was at St Mary Redcliffe, Bristol, where the organ built in 1726 had 13 pedals). They still used meantone temperament, which restricted the choice of keys and the use of chromatic harmony (Temperley, 1974).

The parish clerk still had an important role to play in the psalm singing, though naturally this tended to diminish when an organ and charity children were present. Parish clerks in London kept up a modicum of prestige and status when their counterparts in the country had become 'mean and inconsiderable' (Brewster: 399). In great measure this was due to the existence of the Company of Parish Clerks of London, the direct descendant of the pre-Reformation Guild of St Nicholas mentioned earlier. The Company's charter had been renewed in 1612, 1635 and 1640, when its geographical orbit was gradually extended to cover Westminster, Southwark and the adjoining parishes (Christie: 122–3). The clerks sang at an annual service in the Guildhall Chapel after the election of the Lord Mayor. Soon after 1660 the Company acquired an organ 'the better to enable them to perform a service incumbent upon them before the Lord Mayor and Aldermen of the City on Michaelmas Day, and also... in performing their duties in the several parishes to which they stand related' (Ditchfield: 121). They met for practice on Tuesday afternoons, and the custom continued at least until 1813; the organ was taken down in 1828 (Christie: 197).

John Playford, who was clerk to the Temple Church (not a parish church) from 1653, was much concerned in the Company's efforts to improve the parish clerks' musical skill. The tunes he printed with basses in his *Introduction to music* from 1658 onwards were intended mainly for country parish clerks, as he said in his preface (already quoted); nevertheless he gave three copies to the Company of Parish Clerks of London, and they later acquired 25 more (Ebblewhite: 76). In 1671 he published his *Psalms & hymns in solemn musick*, with the tunes set for four male voices, partly with the object of teaching the clerks of London to sing in harmony at their weekly practices (Temperley, 1972a: 357). Manuscript part-books, copied from the printed edition presented by Playford, survived in the Company's Library until it was destroyed in the Second World War (Ebblewhite: 76–80). Benjamin Payne in *The parish clerk's guide* said that Playford was 'one to whose memory all parish clerks owe perpetual thanks for their furtherance in the knowledge of psalmody' (Harley: 102).

However much the clerks may have learned about psalmody from these weekly practices, they cannot very well have sung in harmony in their churches, for each church had but one clerk. Their main function continued to be the leadership of monophonic singing: they chose the psalm tunes, set the pitch, lined out the verses, and led the singing. Nahum Tate wrote in 1710, 'Another detriment to psalmody, has been the choice of unskilful parish-clerks: for, as a good clerk, by degrees, removes all obstacles, an insufficient clerk not only puts a full stop to all improvements in psalmody, but occasions a relapse, by making the people forget the good tunes they had learned, for want of practice: for as the clerk sings, so generally sings the parish.' But he acknowledged that few good clerks were to be found, a fact he attributed to the 'poor, small encouragement' they were offered, 'unless it be at London, and some few places more throughout our nation' (N. Tate: 32–3). In London the clerk's salary was often greatly augmented by fees and perquisites.

It was rare for a musically well-qualified parish clerk to be appointed to a London church during the eighteenth century. Almost the only one known to have had any musical skill was Joseph Fox, clerk of St Margaret, Westminster, who in 1752 published a revised edition of Payne's *Guide* under the title *The parish clerk's vade-mecum*, and in 1757 a revised edition of Playford's *Whole book of psalms in three parts*, with many musical innovations including anthems. Vestries generally appointed clerks 'more for their poverty than skill and ability' (Hawkins: IV, 362, quoting PC 26: preface; see also PC 186: 21–2). When the appointment was vested in the incumbent he often treated it as a minor piece of patronage. Some chose their curates, 'who though sometimes are very sufficiently paid by what arises from the parish-clerk's salary, fees and perquisites, are, notwithstanding, displeased with their title... And as the dignity of their order exempts them from officiating as such, they of necessity must have deputies, who are often chosen from the menial servants of the church' (Riley: 20). The rector of St Botolph, Aldersgate, gave the job to his uncle's footman, who was not even resident in the parish (MS 42, facing p. 16). It was not unknown for a woman to be appointed, though she would usually have the work done by a deputy. In general, performance by deputy increased. A writer in 1801, complaining of this, suggested that while in the country the parish schoolmaster was the best person to be clerk, in London the job should be given to the undertaker (*Gentleman's Magazine* LXXI, 1801: 1090).

In a sermon to the Company of Parish Clerks in 1712, Luke Milbourne told them: 'You, my brethren, are masters of our parochial music, especially where an organ is wanting' (Milbourne: 33). But even with an organ and charity children, the clerk continued to play his part. Thomas Busby remarked about 1800 that 'the vocal part of our parochial church service is generally so ill performed, that an organ decently played, and loud enough to drown the voices of the clerk, charity children, and congregation, is a blessing' (D. E. Ford: 91n.). As late as 1877, at St Pancras, Euston Road, William Spark attended a service at which a congregation of over two thousand was led in the responses and hymns by the parish clerk, 'a character that I thought had long ago vanished' (Spark, 1892: 47).

Metrical psalms and hymns

Throughout this period numerous metrical versions of the psalms were published, but none succeeded in dislodging the Old Version from its hold over the affections of ordinary people. In the Church of England there was a well entrenched belief that the Old Version was the only one authorised by law for use in church, though this view was challenged by Richard Goodridge in the preface to his version of 1684 (PC 30). John Patrick's version, completed in 1692, represented a new departure in that it aimed not at literalness but at an evangelical interpretation of the psalms (L. Benson: 52–5). It quickly became popular among dissenters, although Patrick himself was a loyal Anglican, preacher to the Charterhouse and the brother of a bishop. Daniel Warner, the singing teacher, remarked in his *Collection of some verses out of the psalms* (1694) that he 'was advised by some friends to make use of Dr. Patrick's version, who told me, there would be very speedily an Act of parliament for the annexing it to the bibles' (PC 35: preface). But no such act was forthcoming, and in the absence of authority, Patrick's version stood no chance of widespread adoption within the established Church, but it became almost the 'official' psalm book of Independents until displaced by Isaac Watts's version of 1719, frankly entitled *The psalms of David imitated in the language of the New Testament*.

In 1696 appeared *A new version of the psalms of David, fitted to the tunes used in churches*, by Nahum Tate and Nicholas Brady. Tate was a layman, poet laureate and the librettist of Purcell's *Dido and Aeneas*; 'he is said to have been a man of intemperate and improvident life' (Julian: 920). Brady was a prebendary of Cork, a doctor of divinity from Trinity College, Dublin (for 'services to the Protestant cause'), and incumbent of St Katherine Cree, London; he, too, was a writer of plays. The New Version was launched under favourable auspices: dedicated to William III, and on 3 December 1696 'allowed' by the king in council and 'permitted to be used in all churches, &c., as shall think fit to receive them'. Although this order was ultimately found to have no legal effect (J. Gray, 1821), at the time it was a valuable asset in a Church which was intensely loyal to the Crown and tending increasingly to identify itself with the English nation. Its first use in church was apparently at St Martin-in-the-Fields in January 1699 (*The Post-Man*: 8 January 1699).

The New Version was almost immediately endorsed by influential clergymen, such as Thomas Bray, a leading spirit of the religious societies, who printed several selections for use in family prayers in the appendix of *A short discourse upon the doctrine of our baptismal covenant* (1697), with traditional tunes. It was recommended by the Archbishop of Canterbury and the Bishop of London, and seemed to some to represent an official settlement of the longstanding dissatisfaction with the Old Version. But there was also considerable opposition, notably from the high-church Bishop Beveridge, who was perhaps prejudiced by the secular connections of the translators. Sarcastically, he called it 'fine and modish', 'flourished with wit and fancy', 'gay and fashionable': by contrast the Old Version was faithful to the Hebrew and close to common speech. Benjamin Payne, a spokesman for the Company of Parish Clerks of London, also came out in defence of the Old Version, which was unobtrusively revised during the closing years of the seventeenth century to meet some of the criticisms that had been made against it.

Conservatism won the day. Table 6 gives an indication of the popularity of the three leading versions by the number of editions of each held by the

Table 6. *Editions of the complete metrical psalms found in the British Museum Catalogue in 1971, by decade of publication (1541–1900)*

Decade	Sternhold & Hopkins (1562)	Tate & Brady (1696)	Watts (1719)	Other	Total
1541–1550	—	—	—	1	1
1551–1560	—	—	—	0	0
1561–1570	6	—	—	0	6
1571–1580	12	—	—	0	12
1581–1590	14	—	—	0	14
1591–1600	20	—	—	0	20
1601–1610	28	—	—	0	28
1611–1620	30	—	—	1	31
1621–1630	54	—	—	1	55
1631–1640	66	—	—	9	75
1641–1650	40	—	—	8	48
1651–1660	19	—	—	3	22
1661–1670	26	—	—	4	30
1671–1680	25	—	—	4	29
1681–1690	26	—	—	2	28
1691–1700	16	8	—	9	33
1701–1710	26	6	—	7	39
1711–1720	22	3	1	4	30
1721–1730	24	13	2	3	42
1731–1740	21	9	2	1	33
1741–1750	21	13	1	1	36
1751–1760	28	19	5	4	56
1761–1770	30	20	7	6	63
1771–1780	25	30	10	2	67
1781–1790	20	22	12	8	62
1791–1800	13	30	8	7	58
1801–1810	13	37	19	9	78
1811–1820	8	36	22	9	75
1821–1830	4	35	10	20	69
1831–1840	0	24	9	20	53
1841–1850	2	32	4	19	57
1851–1860	1	21	8	18	48
1861–1870	1	1	0	11	13
1871–1880	0	0	0	6	6
1881–1890	0	0	0	4	4
1891–1900	0	0	0	4	4

Harmonised psalm books such as East's and Playford's, and psalm books for use in the Church of Scotland, are excluded.

British Library. It would seem in general that a version reached the peak of its popularity about a century after its first appearance. Certainly the Old Version was in no sense 'replaced' by the New in 1696, as Davies baldly states (:II, 281). At first it was accepted in only a few London churches; at

Brady's own church of St Katherine Cree it was cast out by the vestry (Frere & Frost: 84). The two versions existed side by side, and many books contained selections from both; but as Table 6 shows, the Old Version retained the hegemony for most of the eighteenth century. Edward Miller said that it was 'at present used in more than half the parish churches in the kingdom' (E. Miller, 1791: 27). Naturally, it tended to survive longest in country churches. But a writer to the *Gentleman's Magazine* in 1801 pointed out that it was still in use at the chapel royal, Whitehall, the Temple church, seven specified city parish churches, 'and probably elsewhere' in London (*Gentleman's Magazine* LXXI, 1801: 811). He went on to challenge the view that the Old Version was enjoined by law, in preference to other psalm versions or to hymns. Ralph Guest in 1808 or 1809 wrote that the New Version had 'now become of general use in the Church of England' (PC 335: preface). But as late as 1831, even after the decision in the Cotterill case (see p. 208), many clergymen declined to use any except the Old or New because of the supposed illegality of other versions, and the Old Version was still used in some places (Latrobe: 191–2). The New Version enjoyed several decades of primacy in the early nineteenth century before both were swept aside by the tide of hymns. Still Tate and Brady lingered on in a few places: at All Saints, Knightsbridge until 1870 (Mackeson, 1866–95); until 'well into the seventies' at Fulbourn (Ditchfield: 279); at St Thomas, Southwark until 1879, where the psalms were still sung without choir or organ (Mackeson, 1866–95).

No version other than the two 'authorised' ones had more than a negligible following in the Church until the rise of the Evangelical movement, though isolated psalms, such as Addison's Psalm 23, won some acceptance. Still less was there any wholesale use of hymns. Although a great many hymns had been written at all periods since the Reformation by Anglicans of all shades of churchmanship (Parks, 1972; L. Benson), the vast majority of them were intended for private devotions only. Yet hymns had never been altogether banished from the Church. Neither the doctrines of Calvin nor the Injunctions of 1559 had excluded them, and a certain number were in the Old Version and were regularly used. The New Version was followed in 1700 by a *Supplement* (PC 48) which provided not only some alternative psalm versions and new translations of many of the scriptural and liturgical texts found in the Old Version, but also six new hymns, one for Christmas Day (the familiar 'While shepherds watched their flocks by night'), two for Easter and three for communion. The *Supplement*, like the New Version itself, was 'authorised' by the queen in council (30 July 1703), so it seemed that a limited use of hymns was not disapproved by the authorities. A great many parochial collections in the eighteenth century contain a few hymns, including especially the morning and evening hymns of Bishop Ken (originally written for the scholars of Winchester College). In the late eighteenth century these two hymns were often added to editions of the New and even the Old Version, and the evening hymn, 'Glory to thee, my God, this night', had become a usual introduction to Sunday evening service in many country churches. Both remain favourites today. The tradition of the communion hymn during the people's communion remained alive on 'sacrament Sundays', which usually occurred once a month, or even less frequently by the later eighteenth century. A selection of metrical psalms for the parochial chapel at Gosport, published about 1745, was soon afterwards supplemented by a book of *Hymns for the festivals, and on other solemn occasions*, with tunes in two vocal parts. A table showed the psalms and hymns to be used 'for a course of two months', with the tunes. Two were sung at morning service (Fig. 4), two at evening. The tunes appear to be the determining factor: alternative psalms are suggested for most of them. Where the old 'proper tune' (F. 132, DCM) was used for Psalm 119, the 4-line metrical doxology had to be sung to a different tune, the 4-line 'St. David's'. Two different communion hymns are proposed, one for each month, both sung to the tune 'York'. Evidently the communion hymn replaced the second psalm which would otherwise have followed the sermon.

As to the placing of psalms or hymns in worship, the Injunctions of 1559 remained in force, but were not strictly carried out. The authorised times to sing (before and after service), though they were sometimes observed in country churches, were generally taken up with organ voluntaries in churches that had organs. The most common positions for psalms in town churches were 'between services' in the morning (that is, between the litany that concluded morning prayer and the beginning of the communion service, which was performed, according to rubric, whether the sacrament was celebrated or not) and before or after the sermon itself* (Payne: 46; Nelson: 63; *Spectator*, 8 December 1714; E. Gibson, 1724: 8–12; Johnson: 14; Ditchfield: 6, 9, 279). In some churches the custom grew up of singing a psalm after the second lesson (Reeves: fol. C8v; Bisse, 1716: 89n.) The usual number of psalms was two in the morning and one in the afternoon or evening, with sometimes an additional one on great festivals or at charity sermons (E. Gibson, 1724: 8–12).

The *New Version* itself contained no music, and its verses were explicitly designed to fit the old tunes, most of which were provided in the 1700 *Supplement*. But the sixth edition of the *Supplement* (PC 57), published in 1708, contributed many new tunes, of which the most important were 'Hanover', 'St Anne' (ex. 83) and 'St Matthew', printed anonymously but attributed on reasonably sound evidence to William Croft. They have a majestic dignity that contrasts with the emotional fervour of Jeremiah Clarke's tunes in *The Divine Companion* (see T. Taylor: 20–4). For the first time it is possible to speak of individual character in psalm tunes: they begin to be miniature works of art.

Choir and congregation

The original object of teaching schoolchildren and members of religious societies to sing psalm tunes from the notes, disregarding any inward benefit they might derive from the exercise, was to enable them to lead the

---

* Psalms were sometimes sung during collections of money after the sermon (Pepys: 6 January 1661; Thoresby: II, 28). This was often in effect the end of morning service, since the prayer for the Church Militant, despite the rubric, was generally omitted when there was to be no celebration of the sacrament (Bisse, 1723; C. Benson).

A List of Tunes for a Course of two Months, as Sung at present in Gos.t Chap.l

Morning Service

Sund.	Tunes	Pſ.ms adapted to each Tune
1	St. Ann's Old York	42. Verſes J. 2 { Communion Hymn { All ye &c.
2	Oakingham Proper Tune St. David	33. 66. JJ9. Glo. Patri Comn Meaſure
3	London New Weſtminſter	JJ7. J34. J38. J46. J47.
4	St. James St. Alban's	J5. J. 64.
5	Winſor York	J9 3 laſt Verſes { Communion Hymn { Thou God &c.
6	Falmouth St. Mary	29. 57. 95. 8. 94. JJ5. J2.
7	Meer { Mancheſter { or { French J00 d	34. 92. 27. 7J. 47. 89. J04. J5C
8	Proper York	63 JJ6
9	Bedford { Southwell New { or St. Peter's	37. 50. 25. 3J. 5J. J43 67. J30.

Fig. 4 A course of metrical psalms and hymns for 9 Sunday mornings at Gosport, Hants, *c.* 1745 (PC 128, p. 55)

congregational singing in church. This was a new concept. As far as we know, earlier choirs (before and just after the Reformation) had not pretended to do other than sing alone. In course of time it was found that the new choirs, too, wanted to monopolise singing, and they may well have been encouraged in this attitude by members of the congregation, who

125

desired the 'musical whitewash' of choir and organ. The course of events at Wigan, described earlier, may be seen in this light.

There were certainly some town churches in the early eighteenth century in which a voluntary male choir, associated with a religious society, joined with the charity children to form a full choir. A few collections of the period contain psalm tunes arranged for four voices with the tune in the treble, which was an innovation at this time. One such was attached to the New Version in an edition of 1698 (PC 37). Another was Thomas Wanless's book for the use of St Michael-le-Belfry, York (published 1702), 'taught by Mr. Thomas Chippindell'. There was a society in York (Portus: 132), and there was a charity school in the parish (MS 107). Wanless was also organist of the cathedral, and this perhaps influenced his preference for treble-led settings. It was not until late in the eighteenth century that this arrangement of voices became common, but it is found in a series of collections used in town churches in the Birmingham area (PC 108, 122, 139a, 149, 156, 201, 224). One of these was compiled by John Barker, who had been a chapel royal chorister.

If societies did sometimes combine with charity children to lead the psalms with organ accompaniment, they rarely attempted to sing choral music. One such case was at St Nicholas, Deptford. William Richardson, also a former chorister of the chapel royal and a pupil of John Blow, became organist there in 1697, and in 1729 brought out *The pious recreation ... with six hymns for the use of societies and charity-children, likewise anthems for two and three voices, after the cathedral manner* (PC 97). The hymns and anthems, some of which are on subjects connected with charity, have solos for treble, bass, and 'tenor bass' (baritone), choruses for two trebles and bass, and independent organ accompaniments; there are no alto or tenor chorus parts. Some of the hymns have alternating sections for 'boys' and 'girls'. But the exceptional nature of this collection is revealed in the preface.

The separation of the choir from the congregation began to meet with protests. But the objection was not so much to the occasional hymn or anthem, as to the tendency to deprive the congregation of its right to sing the psalms. Arthur Bedford, who had at first enthusiastically supported the efforts of societies to improve and lead the singing, protested in 1733 against the monopolisation of the singing by the voluntary choir. To correct this abuse he proposed that the singers should disperse themselves around the church, and sing in unison until they had taught the congregation any new plain tunes they wished to introduce. Only then should they gather in one place, give out the first line of the tune in unison, and sing in full harmony while the congregation sang the tune, lined out by the clerk. Bedford thought that 'if the congregation can be prevailed with not to sing too loud ... it will soon be as pleasant as an organ, and much more grave and serious than such, as they are generally managed'. After or before the service, the singers might sing any psalms, hymns or anthems they liked, 'because every one might take his choice either to tarry or withdraw' (1733: 28–30).

In 1736 an anonymous compiler (probably Bedford) began a quarterly periodical called *Divine Recreations* which was clearly designed to cater for the singing of religious societies. Its high-church slant is shown by the other books advertised in its pages, including *The Christian's pattern* by Thomas à Kempis, 'corrected' by John Wesley; *The right use of Lent: The Church of England men's companion in the closet* collected from the writings of Laud, Andrewes, Ken, Hickes and others; and Bedford's *The excellency of divine music*. Several of these books were distributed by the S.P.C.K. The preface to the first number sets out the purpose of the periodical, to provide all 'who have dispositions and capacities for divine harmony (as there are many such in town and country)' with texts and music for the praise of God in psalmody; 'and by this means that heavenly exercise may take place instead of those *wanton* and *profane songs* and ballads with which we are continually disturbed in every corner of our streets'. Each number contains a few psalms set to tunes in four parts, with the melody in the treble, with a few alternative settings in 'four parts close', alto, two tenors and bass, with the melody in the alto: presumably the former are for use in church with the children, the latter for meetings of the societies. There are also hymns (carols in the Christmas number), catches, and canons. Some of the texts are from the sacred poems of George Herbert. Some of the music is of secular or theatrical origin, but with a sacred text substituted, exactly in the manner that would soon be adopted by the Methodists. For example, a dialogue between Cupid and Bacchus by Purcell is taken from *Orpheus Britannicus*, and the words changed as follows:

Come, let us agree,	Come, let us agree,
There are pleasures divine	There are pleasures and charms
In wine and in love,	In anthems and hymns,
In love and in wine.	And also in psalms.

But the religious societies were in a less flourishing state than they had been in Queen Anne's day, partly because of active persecution by the government, which suspected them of Jacobite tendencies. Many continued to meet, but had lost their early fervour. Whitefield in 1737 found that those still in existence were spiritually in a low state, having become little more than social clubs. He succeeded in reviving their enthusiasm, which passed, together with their musical traditions, into the Methodist movement (Portus: 201). By this time the 'choir' of most town churches had been reduced to the charity children alone, with the clerk remaining as nominal director of the congregational singing.

The devout high churchman's ideal of church music remained intact, even though it could not often be realised in practice. An eloquent statement of this goal, and of frustration with the general apathy on the subject, is found in a sermon preached by Luke Milbourne to the Company of Parish Clerks. Milbourne had published his own metrical version of the psalms in 1698, in the preface to which he had called for the establishment of an authorised book of metrical psalms for church use, selected from various versions already in existence, 'now that *singing of psalms by rule* [i.e., by reading musical notation] grows so much in fashion' (PC 39: fol. A9v). In 1704 he became rector of the tiny, organless church of St Ethelburga, Bishopsgate Street, said to be the smallest in the City (it measured 60 ft by 30 ft). In November 1712 he preached at St Alban, Wood

Street to the parish clerks on the subject 'Psalmody recommended'. He repeated his sermon at St Giles-in-the-Fields, replacing the part particularly addressed to clerks with more general remarks about psalmody: the published sermon is a conflation of both versions (Milbourne: iv). He dedicated it 'to the Gentlemen of the Society for the Promotion of Christian Knowledge in and about the City of London'.

Milbourne's message was 'that as psalmody is an important part of *divine public service*, so it may be performed in a pertinent, serious, reverent, and agreeable manner': and he firmly placed the responsibility for seeing that this was so on the shoulders of the parish clergy. Clerks and congregations depended on the priest for example. They should be encouraged to stand during the singing, following the example of Bishop Beveridge at St Peter, Cornhill. The Old Version should be replaced by a better translation (Milbourne made no mention of the New Version of Tate and Brady, published in 1696); lining out should be dropped (:ii–iii, vii–ix, 33–4).

Milbourne pointed out that 'both the *High and Low Dutch*, and French, have taken more care of their *ordinary psalmody* than we have'. He blamed the low state of English psalmody on the leaders of society: 'our *gentlemen and great men* are generally above such *humble dispensations*, and the *music of the theatre* is more grateful to their ears . . . Many are willing to gratify an *eunuch* singing an *opera*, in a much more liberal manner than a *teacher of psalmody*', and tend to laugh at the blunders of the singers instead of encouraging them. He went on to describe the wonderful effect of psalms sung by a large and enthusiastic congregation, and hoped to see a gradual improvement, until 'men of the *highest quality* be ashamed to sit silent, when all the congregation . . . are, with a loud voice and earnest devotion, singing praises to their maker' (:24–8).

This ideal of robust congregational psalm singing led by a skilful clerk was certainly not realised in most eighteenth-century churches, at least until the Evangelical movement gained momentum at the end of the century. Beilby Porteus, bishop of London, told the clergy of his diocese in 1790 that of all the services of the Church, none was 'at so low an ebb' as psalmody (Porteus; cited Kennedy: 25). Occasionally, improvements were successfully introduced, as at St Nicholas, Newcastle upon Tyne, which in the mid-eighteenth century had the unusual advantage of possessing both an enlightened vicar and an able organist. There had been an organ from about 1670. Charles Avison, who was organist from 1736 until his death in 1770, has left in his renowned *Essay on musical expression* a clear statement of his ideas about congregational singing: the secret, in his view, was to restore the proper rhythm and tempo to the tunes, and in support he quoted Isaac Watts. Like Milbourne, he alluded to the superiority of singing in Protestant churches abroad, but he put it down chiefly to 'the exact *measure*, in which those tunes are sung, and not to their *harmony*', the old English psalm tunes and their harmonies being just as good as any others. He confessed to having been 'uncommonly affected' with hearing thousands of voices singing in solemn unison, but he regretted that organists often ruined the effect with 'absurd graces, and tedious, and ill-connected interludes' (:89–92). It was no doubt at Newcastle that Dr John

Brown, vicar there from 1761 until his death in 1766, witnessed or participated in the moving and satisfying psalmody he described in his *Dissertation on . . . poetry and music,* in writing which he had Avison's assistance:

The performance of our parochial psalms, though in the villages it be often as mean and meagre as the words that are sung, yet in great towns, where a good organ is skilfully and devoutly employed, by a sensible organist, the union of this instrument with the voices of a well-instructed congregation, forms one of the grandest scenes of unaffected piety that human nature can afford. (J. Brown: 213; cited Legg, 1914: 187)

Unhappily, such a result was rarely achieved.

Organ and charity children

It is clear that the typical resources for music in a prosperous town church of this period were an organ, played by a professional organist, and a group of charity children who were given some instruction in singing the psalms. The parish clerk was generally unmusical, while the clergyman and an increasing proportion of the congregation were silent. The societies of young men were a factor in some churches between about 1690 and 1740, but they then disappeared from the scene, leaving a choir of trebles only.

The earliest printed organ settings of psalm tunes appeared in the 1660s (PC 24, 25). They provide massive block harmonies with few ornaments, and they probably represent an earlier style of accompaniment, such as that used by Tomkins at Worcester cathedral in the 1630s (ex. 19). Most organists after the Restoration probably improvised their accompaniments, either from the tunes alone (which in any case they knew by heart) or from copies in which the tune and bass alone were printed. They also were required to 'give out' one verse of the tune before the singing. It is not known when this practice began, but it tended to be treated as an opportunity for display; interludes were played between the verses or between lines, perhaps during the clerk's lining out (Moorman: 287), and ornaments added to the notes of the tune. Bedford complained of this in 1711:

When . . . the clerk names the psalm, the organist ought so to play the tune, that it may be plainly understood; and the interludes, that the congregation may know when to begin, and when to leave off. But now the notes are played with such a rattle and hurry instead of method, with such difference in the length of equal notes, to spoil the time, and displease a musician, and so many whimseys instead of graces, to confound the ignorant, that the design is lost, and the congregation takes their tune, not from the organ, since they do not understand it, but from the parish clerk, or from one another; which they could better have done, if there was no organ at all. (Bedford, 1711: 212)

Similar complaints were made elsewhere (*Gentleman's Magazine* I, 1731: 51). Several collections of psalm tunes written out for organ in this way have survived from the early eighteenth century (PC 73, 103, 145). The setting of 'St David's' by Daniel Purcell (1718) is a sample of a number of very similar arrangements, and is the nearest English equivalent to the German organ chorale or chorale prelude (ex. 20). It may be noted, first, that the plain harmonised setting of the tune has no ornaments, and is spaced in a more 'modern' way than ex. 19. The interludes between the lines are mere padding, but are apparently designed to be played in the same tempo as the lines of the tune, which, as we know, were sung extremely slowly. The 'giving out' has a very thin texture, clearly calling for the use of two manuals, with a solo stop (perhaps a Cornet) for the right hand. Close attention should be given to the style of ornamentation. Although there are a few signs indicating shakes or beats, chiefly on the last notes of phrases of the tune, the written-out ornaments are largely a matter of filling in the intervals between successive notes. There is a conspicuous absence of appoggiaturas or other ornaments that delay the principal note. The lack of these fashionable ornaments may have led Bedford to complain of 'so many whimseys instead of graces'; but to us it inevitably recalls the old way of singing, which tended to persist even where efforts were made to reform it. Here we have, surely, nothing other than an attempt to imitate this style of singing on a keyboard instrument.

Later eighteenth-century givings-out tended to preserve the principle of sounding the main note on each beat, for the assistance of the singers, while bringing the style of ornamentation closer to accepted canons of taste. Interludes between the lines disappeared, while those between the verses were frequently extended to a short independent piece (ex. 21). Sometimes there was only one interlude, before the last verse or doxology. Printed collections of preludes and interludes continued to appear until about 1830. A new principle, very obviously originating in art music, is found in Francis Linley's advice of about 1800:

There are three different modes of giving out psalm tunes, viz. on the Stop Diapason and Flute, which is proper for all minor and plaintive airs; on the Cornet, which is more generally used for lively tunes; and on the Cornet and Swell alternately, which I conceive to be the most elegant, as the contrast is admirably calculated to attract the attention of the congregation. I would advise the performer to give them out with as few embellishments as possible; and if he is disposed to show his taste and abilities, he may do it with more propriety on the cadenza note of the last line, than (as is too often the case) by overwhelming it with graces and cantabiles in all parts indiscriminately. (Linley: I, 6)

He gives a number of specimens, one of which is on 'St. David's' (ex. 22).

All these collections provide arrangements of the well-known tunes of the Old Version, with the gradual addition of a few newer tunes as they became widely popular. As long as the singing was largely congregational, new music could not easily be introduced, and no printed voice parts were needed. Charity children, as well as congregations, knew only the common tunes. But adults began to practise, and learn new tunes with the object of improving the singing in church; it became necessary to provide music for them. Until near the end of the seventeenth century, John Playford (Pl. 8) was almost alone in attempting to cater for this need. His *Psalms & hymns in solemn musick* of 1671 was planned chiefly for domestic use, for parish clerks at their weekly practices, and perhaps for his own Temple Church, but he may have hoped it would be used in parish churches as well.

The book was not a success (Temperley, 1972a : 361–3). His next venture (PC 29) was bolder and more innovative, for he provided a complete edition of Sternhold and Hopkins with a tune for every psalm harmonised in *three* parts (Fig. 5). He called the three parts 'cantus, medius and bassus'; the two upper ones were in the modern G clef, and could thus be sung either by women or children at the written pitch, or by men an octave lower, 'it being usual and common for men to sing the songs which are pricked in a treble [clef] an eighth lower, where the parts are so composed, that they do not

Fig. 5 John Playford's setting of 'Manchester' to Psalm 102, Old Version, 1677 (PC 29/3, p. 172)

interfere with [the] bass' (J. Playford, letter dated 26 August 1672, in Locke: 86). He explained in the preface that the tune was in the cantus part, but that 'all three parts may as properly be sung by men as by boys or women'. The bass part appeared separately, but also under the cantus, 'as most proper to join voice and instrument together, according to holy David's prescription *Psalm 144.9*. And since many of our churches are lately furnished with organs, it will also be useful for the organist; likewise to all such students in the universities as shall practice song, to sing to a lute or viol.'

This well thought out volume was flexible enough to cater for a number of possible developments, some of which Playford may have foreseen. Eventually it would prove valuable for both town and country psalmody. At first, however, the response was slight: a thousand copies were printed, but it was not found necessary to bring out a second edition until 1695, several years after Playford's death. Then it caught on fast. Six more editions followed in rapid succession, and at least 15,000 copies were sold in the next seven years. There were twenty editions altogether, the last in 1757 (details in Temperley, 1972a: 374).

This sudden demand for Playford's *Whole book of psalms in three parts* at the turn of the century coincided with a flurry of other publications designed for much the same purpose. Playford's three-part arrangement was adopted in *A new and easie method to learn to sing by book* (PC 31), which explicitly catered for a choir of 'six, eight, or more, sober young men that have good voices'. Daniel Warner, an Oxfordshire singing teacher, brought out a collection in 1694 with the intention of instructing the 'common people' (PC 35). He acknowledged Playford's improvement over Ravenscroft, in the use of only three parts with treble clefs, but explained that he himself had 'pricked only two parts, ... it agreeing with modern practice'. The two-part plan was not original, of course, having appeared in Playford's *Introduction* and before that in Wither's hymn books. It was adopted by several other compilers (see PC 38–65) and had the great merit of being equally suited to childrens' choirs with organ (continuo style), or to two-part men's choirs. Abraham Barber, parish clerk of Wakefield, used this disposition when he revised his 1687 collection for the third edition of 1698; it was also used for the *Supplement to the New Version* of Tate and Brady, from 1708 onwards, and for the later editions of Barton's, Patrick's and Watts's psalms and hymns, used by dissenters.

Playford's three-part arrangement was copied in *The psalms and hymns, usually sung in the churches and tabernacles of St. Martins in the Fields, and St. James's Westminster* in 1688 (PC 34). In the editions of 1697–1704 for St James only, the two-part arrangement was used, the upper voice being definitely designated 'treble'. In 1709 a third part was resumed, and the two upper parts named '1 Treb.' and '2 Treb.'; subsequent editions were much the same. We have in this book the first clear example of psalm tunes arranged for charity children alone, accompanied on the organ. The tunes are printed separately, and there are some 15 of them, largely the familiar short tunes with a few of the old proper tunes still included. The 1697 edition introduced two new tunes in traditional style, one of which, 'St James's' (ex. 23), by the organist of St James's church, Raphael Courteville, soon spread to other publications and entered the permanent repertory. The psalms were selected and arranged to provide for four each Sunday, two at morning prayer and two at evening. The 1688 book covers six Sundays; the 1697 and subsequent cover 13 Sundays, with '55 select portions of psalms, which are sung over in their order with the organ once in every quarter' (PC 36: verso of title page). A few of the metrical hymns and canticles from the Old Version were included in the scheme in 1688, but these were eliminated for Sunday use in 1697 and consigned to an appendix. 'Extraordinary psalms' were appointed for various feast and fast days, and for 'the charity sermons' a psalm and the metrical Benedictus in the morning and two psalms in the afternoon. Revised editions continued to appear until about the middle of the eighteenth century.

Many town psalmody collections were remarkably conservative in their choice of tunes, especially by comparison with the country psalmody books to be described in the next chapter. For example John Church, in his popular collection of 1723 (PC 83), begins with 18 tunes in three parts, and 12 in four parts (the tenor being optional), all taken from Playford's 1677 collection, which itself was largely made up of the Elizabethan tunes of the Old Version and the slightly newer four-line tunes. Church follows with six tunes 'in four parts composed by Mr. Tho: Ravenscroft', the harmonisations being altered so that the tune is in the top part, and three others, also from Ravenscroft or Playford. Not one tune was less than a century old; and Church claimed in his preface that he was 'pretty certain that there is scarce any tune that is usually sung (where there is an organ) that is omitted', clearly acknowledging that the continued use of the old tunes could only be assumed in churches that had organs. The same conservatism is found in most town collections until late in the century.

In such books the tunes were usually printed in their plainest form. One of the reasons for introducing an organ and charity children was to suppress the old way of singing with its slides, trills and 'quaverings'; and although the organist was evidently permitted to 'give out' the tune in ornate style, the accompaniments were in plain block harmony, and the school children were firmly taught to sing the tunes unadorned. The changeover to the plain style is illustrated in the various collections published by Michael Broome at Birmingham. Some were designed for country churches, but in one published about 1735 (PC 108) he was clearly catering for town churches in the Birmingham area. The tunes are the old ones, in four parts with the melody in the treble and a figured bass, but they are set out to represent the old way, with many ornaments of the gap-filling type, made to conform roughly to the rules of harmony and counterpoint. But later collections have the same tunes perfectly plain, shorn of all decoration (PC 122). In a book of 1753 (PC 149) Broome clarified the position in a preface: the first 21 tunes, with treble melody and figured bass, were those 'made use of in all the churches in *London*, and in most of the capital towns of this kingdom, and especially where there is an organ'. But the other seven tunes, 'for the use of societies', are elaborate tunes of the fuging type, with the melody in the tenor. The title page shows that the book was 'for the use of the churches in and near Birmingham', and Broome had to provide both town and country psalmody to attain this object.

But if plain old psalm tunes were the ordinary fare in town churches, the charity children were allowed to aspire to more ambitious music from time to time, especially on the three great festivals of the church year and at the time of the charity sermon. Many collections include a few charity hymns in extended settings, to provide for these occasions: Richardson's *The pious* *recreation* (1729) has already been mentioned. In the Midlands John Barker, organist of Coventry parish church, published about 1756 *A select number of the best psalm tunes, extant, for the treble, counter-tenor, tenor, and bass* (PC 139a). The tunes are in the usual layout. In addition there are six charity hymns. Four are by Dr Croft, who probably composed them for a London parish church.* One of them is shown in ex. 24. In it the children were obliged to sing: 'To psalms and hymns we may aspire, Though anthems are too high.' However, anthems were not always considered 'too high' for charity children. As early as about 1710 Dr John Reading, organist of several London churches, published a book of anthems apparently catering for a choir of children. The music is on two staves, with 'verses' for solo voice of high range in the G clef, 'choruses' also in one part in the G clef, and organ 'ritor[nellos]' (PC 59a). Richardson's *Pious recreation* (1729) includes anthems for two trebles, bass and organ; they retain the 'Restoration' cathedral manner, but appear to be expressly designed for the town parish church (St Nicholas, Deptford) where he was organist from 1697. One of these (ex. 25) begins in solemn fashion, but indulges in tricks of word setting, which become quite playful in the final section with its comical text. John Alcock, soon after becoming organist of St Andrew, Plymouth, in 1737, wrote two anthems 'for the use of the charity-children . . . the solo parts being sung by one of them, and the treble-part of the choruses, by all the rest': when he published them later he added the lower parts (PC 207: preface).

William Gawler, organist of the Asylum for Female Orphans, London, published in 1781 a typical collection of town psalmody called *Harmonia sacra* (PC 248). The list of subscribers includes both archbishops, 15 bishops, and many titled persons, but also five organists of London churches, the rector and organist of Richmond parish church, and the masters of four London 'academies' (charity schools). All the psalm tunes are for one voice line in the treble clef with a figured bass, and each is followed by an organ interlude on two staves (ex. 26). There are hymns that are almost arias, still with only one voice line; and one anthem, 'Call to remembrance', ('sung by the charity children'), for two treble solos, four-part choir, and organ. This anthem is the only music in the book with lower voice parts, so presumably a special effort was made on the occasion of the charity sermon. The anthem is by Henry Heron, organist of St Magnus, London, who in 1790 brought out his own *Parochial music corrected: intended for the use of the charity-schools of London, Westminster, &c.*, dedicated to Richard Till, treasurer of the [Association of] Charity Schools. By this time it is clear that in the more elegant town churches the music provided by the children and organist must conform to the taste of their patrons. The tunes are now quite ornamental again, not in the old way, but in the way of classical music, with appoggiaturas, turns and shakes.

* Barker was a chorister under Croft at the chapel royal, *c.* 1720, and seems to have come into possession of several of his master's compositions, some of which he copied. He was organist of Holy Trinity, Coventry from 1731 to 1752. Croft may have been organist at St Anne, Soho from 1700 to 1711, as Watkins Shaw reaffirmed in *The Musical Times* CXIX, 1978, p. 668. (See also Temperley, forthcoming.)

Solos on the organ occupied a prominent place – in the views of many, too prominent a place – in the town church service of the eighteenth century, and for this reason must be given some attention here. The term 'voluntary' implies an improvised performance, which was indeed the origin of the genre, and which tended to prevent the development of any strict formal structure: throughout its history the voluntary has had no set form. But the voluntary was not merely, as is often thought, an idle filling-in of time before and after the service, though it could have that function. It had also, until comparatively recent times, a place in the liturgy itself, despite the fact that there was no mention of it in the prayer book. Wherever an organ was used, it was customary to play a short voluntary either before or after the first lesson at morning and evening prayer.

This practice was not spelled out specifically until the Restoration, when James Clifford gave 'brief directions for the understanding of that part of the divine service performed with the organ in S. Pauls cathedral on Sundays and holy days'. For morning prayer there was 'after the psalms a *voluntary* upon the organ alone'; similarly for evening prayer (Clifford: 1). But although organists and church authorities may have needed reminding of the custom, it was not an innovation. It had certainly existed in Elizabethan times. Francis Bacon addressed James I, soon after his accession, with 'Certain considerations touching the better pacification and edification of the Church of England'. He pointed out that

after the *reading* of the *word*, it was thought fit there should be some pause for holy meditation, before they proceeded to the rest of the *service*: which pause was thought fit to be filled rather with some *grave sound* than with a *still silence*; which was the reason of the playing upon the organs after the scriptures read. All of which was decent, and tending to edification. But then, the curiosity of division and reports, and other figures of music, have no affinity with the reasonable service of God, but were added in the more pompous times. (Bacon: 245–6, punctuation modernised. See also le Huray: 115)

Bacon's theory of the origin of the custom seems improbably rational. It is more likely to have been a survival from pre-Reformation times, when an organ solo may have replaced the singing of responds after the lessons read at the office. At all events, references to this 'middle voluntary' can be found in many sources until late in the nineteenth century (Bedford, 1711: 212; PC 110 (Tans'ur, 1734): v; E. Miller, 1791: 38; *Gentleman's Magazine* LXXX, 1810: 528, 610; Warner: fol. E2r; Latrobe: 9, 370–2; *What can be done*: 15; Vaux: 341). As late as 1885 it was not unknown, though 'now, happily, almost obsolete' (Bridge: 18). Blunt called it 'customary in many churches' in 1882, and the remark was not altered in a revised edition of 1907 (Blunt: 188n.).

Another frequent place for a voluntary, also mentioned by Clifford, was between morning prayer and communion. Since these two services were generally performed without a break, any music at this point was 'liturgical' at least in its effect. The congregation did not leave the church until the sermon was over.

Before the Commonwealth, voluntaries were chiefly performed at cathedrals, where the largest organs and the most skilful organists were to be found. In this situation it was not worthwhile to publish voluntaries, and each player doubtless improvised his own, though a number composed by cathedral organists survive in manuscript (Routh: 112–26). By the eighteenth century a growing number of town churches had organs, and an organ voluntary was one way in which the subscribers could benefit from their own munificence. Consequently we find an increasing output of published organ voluntaries. Some of the earliest were Italian in origin, such as a collection of *Voluntarys and fugues made on purpose for the organ or harpsichord by Ziani, Pollaroli, Bassani, etc.* published by Walsh in 1710, which was directly lifted from an Amsterdam publication in which the pieces were called 'sonates da organo o cembalo'. Philip Hart's *Fugues for the organ or harpsichord* (1704) were not necessarily for church use, though he himself was organist of several London churches. The first unequivocal set of published English voluntaries seems to have been that of Thomas Roseingrave, *Voluntarys or fugues made on purpose for the organ or harpsichord* (London, [1728]): Roseingrave was organist of St George, Hanover Square from 1725 to 1737. Handel published 'Six fugues or voluntarys' in 1735. The two-movement voluntary was established by John Stanley, the blind organist of St Andrew, Holborn (1726–86) and of the Temple Church (1739–86): his three sets, Op. 5–7, were published between 1748 and 1752. In the second half of the century dozens of sets were published. Though some were the work of cathedral organists, the majority were by the organists of town parish churches. Among the more important were those of Jonathan Battishill, John Bennett, William Boyce, John Keeble, William Russell, John Travers, and John Worgan, all organists of London parish churches. The following organists of provincial town churches published voluntaries in this period:

Dr John Alcock	Tamworth; Sutton Coldfield
John Alcock, jun.	Walsall
Robert Broderip	St Michael, Bristol
Charles Burney	King's Lynn
George Guest	Wisbech
Matthias Hawdon	St Nicholas, Newcastle upon Tyne
Henry Heron	Ewell
Edward Miller	Doncaster

Anthologies of voluntaries by various composers began to appear, and also, increasingly, arrangements of choruses and overtures by Handel and other composers, for use as voluntaries (Routh; Schnapper).

The typical, but not universal, form of these voluntaries was in two movements: a slow, homophonic one generally for diapasons, followed by a quick one, either fugal in character or designed to display a brilliant solo stop, perhaps a Trumpet or Cornet (Routh: 157–8). A strong Italian influence was evident, partly from Italian keyboard pieces (some of which, as already stated, had been published in London as voluntaries), but perhaps more from the fashionable Italian operas and concertos that were rapidly bringing English art music into closer conformity with the continental mainstream. Many of the later eighteenth-century voluntaries were pleasantly tuneful in the galant manner; others maintained the baroque contrapuntal tradition.

Frequent complaints are found in eighteenth-century writings about the frivolity of voluntaries, and especially about the influence of operatic and secular styles. It seems likely that improvised voluntaries were generally much less substantial than published ones, for they would not have to face the scrutiny of professional musicians. The *Spectator* in 1712 said that the religious feelings induced by a good sermon and an appropriate psalm were 'all in a moment dissipated by a merry jig from the organ' (*Spectator*, 28 March 1712). Bedford (1711 : 216–17) wrote of 'the corruption of our music by the organists of our cathedral and parochial churches' through the influence of 'profane' music. These criticisms were echoed by Avison (:88), Riley (:32–3) and many others. The fullest treatment of appropriate style in the playing of voluntaries was offered by William Mason, precentor of York cathedral, in an essay 'On instrumental church music' published in 1795. He suggested that a voluntary should be designed to induce 'tranquillity' in the congregation, especially when 'preparative to devotion'. The older learned style need not be exclusively adopted; a voluntary with some 'air' in it might be played, provided it did not imitate 'common and trivial melodies', or music that is 'too strongly accented' or 'too regularly rhythmical'. But in improvising a prelude to an anthem, or playing at the end of a service, Mason approved more licence in the style of playing. A march might be used, provided it was not too military; or a siciliana, if suitably restrained. 'The organist, who feels what he performs, and recollects the place and occasion of performance, will not fail to throw in those appoggiaturas and delicate notes of passage, which from accentual change it into fluent melody.'

Mason went on to ask whether musicians of the present day could be expected to provide 'this attention to strict propriety', and replied:

Certainly not. Brilliant and rapid executive powers are what they chiefly aim at, and what their audience almost exclusively applaud ... It were to be wished, therefore, that in our established Church extempore playing were as much discountenanced, as extempore praying; and that the organist was as closely obliged, in this solo and separate part of his office, to keep to set forms, as the officiating minister; or as he himself is, when accompanying the choir in an anthem, or a parochial congregation in a psalm.

A good preluder might occasionally 'discant on certain single grave texts, which Tartini, Geminiani, Corelli, or Handel would abundantly furnish, and which may be found at least of equal elegance and propriety in the largo and adagio movements of Haydn or Pleyel'. But he doubted whether congregations would be 'affected so forcibly with ... truly devotional strains, as they formerly were with music of far inferior efficacy' (Mason: 57–70).

Although writers from Bacon onwards repeatedly urged that voluntaries should be suited to their religious context, most organists continued to use the occasion of a voluntary to display their manual and pedal dexterity, the power and variety of the instrument, or at least their skill and learning in the arts of harmony and counterpoint. The development of the organ voluntary in the nineteenth century was to remain largely unaffected by the religious movements of the time. The chief influences were secular, in the growing tendency to imitate orchestral music; and antiquarian, particularly in the revival of the organ works of Bach.

Unreformed church music

There were many churches, of course, both in town and country, where the singing was not reformed, either by means of an organ or by the formation of a choir. Even in London some churches remained without organs into the nineteenth century (see Table 5, p. 117): the last such was probably St Thomas, Southwark, which was still without one when it ceased to be a parish church in 1901. At that church Tate and Brady's psalms remained in use until 1879, as already mentioned, and there was no choir. In other cathedral cities the smaller churches were often without organs or choirs until the mid-nineteenth century, and there were certainly many small country churches in the same situation, especially in parts of England that had no very strong choral tradition (for example, the far north).

The general tendency in such churches was for the congregational singing to decay gradually and eventually die out altogether. The parish clerk was then left to carry on the singing alone. Vincent wrote in 1787: 'In those congregations of the metropolis where there are neither children nor organ, it must be confessed that the cause is almost hopeless. The clerk commences his stave, and goes through it almost wholly unaccompanied, or perhaps joined towards the close, by the feeble efforts of a single voice or two' (:29). At Northleach in 1784 'the clerk sang with a melodious voice, and for some time alone, till joined by a very soft female note. I looked round for the second, and found it to be a rough blacksmith who sang in a feigned voice, that would have graced the Opera House' (Torrington: I, 123). At Flockburgh chapel, Cartmel in the early nineteenth century, 'the psalms were sung... by the clerk *altogether alone*; who, leaving his desk, stood with pitchpipe in hand near to the communion table; when, the congregation all devoutly standing, and *entirely mute*, he deliberately sounded the key note; and then commenced and continued to drawl out, in the most doleful way, the whole of the verses of the psalms of the day.' The word 'drawl' suggests a survival of the old way of singing, and there may have been something of the kind in some churches where the clerk had not followed the congregation into silence. In a small church 'just on the borders of the diocese of Ely' at about the same period,

all the singing was done by the clerk. There was not even a school child to help him. He used to stand up and give out two lines of an hymn and then sing it, after which he read out two lines more, and so on. The good old man was a blacksmith, and used to practise his psalmody whilst blowing the bellows at his forge. Among other embellishments with which he used to adorn his performance, was an extraordinary shake, which he was accustomed to execute at the end, or wherever else it was required to give effect, and which used to astonish and delight the congregation greatly. (*Church Congress*, 1864: 310)

As late as 1870 a similar tradition existed at a small district church in the parish of Wing, where the clerk 'chanted the canticles and hymns most lustily, and was altogether a remarkable singer'. He told the new curate he was 'accustomed to conduct the singing unassisted, and would rather he did not sing' (Shearme: 99).

Although, as one would expect, such survivals lasted longest in the country, there were town churches where the clerk sang alone, for example St Alban, Worcester, in 1848 (*Parish Choir*: II, 100) and also apparently at several churches in York (MS 106). But many parish clerks were incapable of singing, and in such cases the music ceased altogether. Lord Torrington in his tours reported that this had happened at two churches, Bosworth and Sherburn-in-Elmet (:II, 95; III, 34) and Joseph Bennett remembered the same situation at Oldbury-on-Severn, 'although a capacious "singing-pew" at the east end of the south aisle' showed that there had been music at one time (:655). At an East Anglian church in about 1825, while the parson was 'climbing up into the pulpit, the clerk used to give out . . . "let us read to the praise and glory of God, three verses of the first (or some other) psalm"', and then proceeded to do so (*Church Congress*, 1864: 309). No authenticated case of a town church without any music has come to light, but there may well have been some in the later eighteenth century.

Summary and evaluation

The urban church music of this period shows the first wave of cultivated and professional influence upon the popular musical tradition that was a legacy of the Reformation. In some churches the transition to a more acceptable music was effected gradually, where a choir of young men regulated the singing of the congregation. Elsewhere the people found themselves abruptly supplanted by organ and charity children, who 'performed' the metrical psalms and voluntaries in a modish Italianate manner.

With art came artificiality, and the loss of that deep integrity and spirituality that resides in a church full of people singing to God in their own way, however uncouth. (Occasional exceptions are on record, as at Newcastle upon Tyne.) The art music of the period was capable of the highest religious expression, as the works of Lalande, Purcell, Bach, Handel, and Pergolesi undeniably demonstrate. Above all, in the cantatas and Passions of Bach is found a supreme synthesis of learned and popular musical forms. Such a combination was never possible in England, because the educated classes and clergy had long dissociated themselves from the music of the people. Cathedral music had flourished. But in the parish church, without organs, without direction by musicians, and without involvement of cultivated amateurs, popular psalmody had failed to follow the stylistic developments of art music. The two ways had diverged beyond reconciliation. Under the growing pressure for greater decorum in church, a clean break was made, and a new kind of music introduced. The organ was the usual instrument for this operation.

The change was not, at first, in the music itself, but in the manner of its performance. The traditional tunes were still used, but they were now sung 'correctly' as printed, though still very slowly. Instead of undirected and wayward singing by all the people in their own time, there was now punctual, disciplined singing by rehearsed schoolchildren, and an organ to supply harmonies, decorations, interludes, and brilliant voluntaries. The fashionable could listen with pleasure; the humble must listen with respect.

Organists took the opportunity to compose original music for the new circumstances, and the eighteenth century is prolific in psalm tunes, hymns, and even anthems written with treble choir and organ in mind. Quite elaborate music was often provided for the great festivals and for charity sermons. Some accomplished anthems, set pieces, and voluntaries were composed for this purpose. The new tunes are melodious, elegant, balanced, cheerful, sometimes touching. They lack the force and monumentality of the traditional tunes, and they lack also the religious sincerity of the best of the Victorian period.

6 Country psalmody (1685–1830)

Reforming psalmody without an organ

In the country as well as the towns, there were forces tending towards reform of the old way of singing psalms. But they appeared in weakened forms. The desire for greater decorum in worship, born of the social tensions of a growing urban society, was less pressing in the village environment. Older patterns and values were not yet greatly changed, and the country squire and parson, sure of their place in the local order, had little need to impress anyone with the elegance of the parish church and its services. Religious societies spread to the country, even to remote villages, but their impetus died away more quickly than in places where they were constantly stimulated by contact with energetic religious leaders.

However, there was a rural movement for the reform of church music; and because country churches could not normally afford organs, it took quite a different course from the corresponding movement in the towns. Thomas Mace had early recognised the difficulties that stood in the way of reform in country church music. John Playford, though he designed his collections chiefly for London use, hoped that the simplification of tunes and harmonies in his 1677 book would place it within reach of country churches. But no effective reform was possible until some members of the congregation could be brought together to be taught how to read music, and to give a lead to the rest when the psalms were sung in church. The anonymous author of *A new and easie method to learn to sing by book* (1686) had just this object in view, 'whereby one (who hath a good voice and ear) may, without other help, learn to sing true by notes'. Recognising that the old gamut, the traditional tool for teaching musical notes, was no longer useful, he discarded it, substituting his own simplified system, and also showing how notes can be played on a 'bass-viol'. A 'master', he said, would help 'in the more speedy and easy attaining their ends'. He also discarded the C clefs, using only the treble and bass clefs.

In the conclusion, for a *praxis*, I have added several psalm tunes in three parts, with directions how to sing them, to promote that most harmonious and delightful kind of singing. This requires somewhat more skill than the common way, yet is easy enough, at least for a select company of persons, with good voices, to attain to. It would therefore be a commendable thing if six, eight or more sober young men that have good voices, would associate and form themselves into a choir, seriously and concordantly to sing the praises of their Creator; a few such in a congregation (especially if the clerk make one to lead) might in a little time bring into the church better singing than is common, and with more variety of good tunes, as I have known done. (PC 31 : fol. A7v, A8r, punctuation modified)

Although the arrangement for three voices, with two staves in the treble clef and one in the bass, was taken from Playford, this is the first description

141

extant of the actual formation of a voluntary parish choir. The book was licensed for publication on 29 January 1686, and entered at Stationers' Hall on 20 April that year by William Rogers, a London bookseller (*Transcript*: III, 304). Nothing is known of the compiler, nor in what region he may have 'known done' what he described. It will be noticed that he suggested a choir composed of young men, and that the parish clerk was also to take part in the singing.

The following year Abraham Barber, parish clerk of Wakefield, published at York *A book of psalme tunes in four parts* (PC 32). In a preface addressed 'To all the lovers of psalmody, within the town and parish of Almund-bury, in the West Riding of the county of York', he apologised for his audacity in publishing such a work, 'knowing there are so many excellent song-men in your parish and neighbouring parishes about'. The music is in four-part block harmony, with the tunes in the tenor; Barber did not tell his readers that he had taken it almost unaltered from Day's harmonised psalm book of 1563 (PC 10).

The formation of a choir was often associated with a religious society. The vicar of Old Romney described what had happened in his parish in a letter written to Woodward in December 1700:

When I first came to my parish, about 10 years ago, I found, to my great grief, the people very ignorant and irreligious; the place of divine worship indecently kept; the public services neither understood, nor attended; the ministration of the Lord's supper supported only by the piety of three or four communicants, and the divine ordinance of singing psalms almost laid aside. Now, whilst I considered by what means I might redress this general neglect of religion, I was of opinion, that the setting up of such a religious society, as I had known in the city of *London*, would be very proper, but I feared it would be impracticable in the country; so that at first, I began to teach three or four youths the skill of singing psalms orderly, and according to rules, which greatly tended, through the grace of God, to awaken their affections towards religion, and to give 'em a relish of it.

Other young men followed this example, and soon the minister had his religious society, 'by whose means, a general reviving of piety, and a solemn observance of the public ordinances of God, hath been produced among us'. (Woodward, 1701: 41–3)

The minutes of a meeting of the Old Romney Society in 1701 show that the society assisted at divine service in the singing of Psalm 6 (Bristol tune), Psalm 25 (Southwell tune) and Psalm 40 (Westminster tune), and also in the singing of the ten commandments (presumably in metrical form) (MS 41). In 1703 this society published *The Christian's daily manual of prayers and praises*, which included *Select psalms and hymns, with their proper tunes. For the use of the religious society of Romney* (PC 53). Most of the psalms were taken from the New Version of Tate and Brady; 26 hymns followed. The tunes were familiar standard ones, arranged in three parts (two tenors and a bass) with resourceful harmonies. The book was circulated to parish church libraries by the S.P.C.K. (Allen & McClure: 166–8).

Nahum Tate, one of the translators of the New Version, approvingly quoted the letter from the vicar of Romney in his *Essay for promoting of psalmody* (1710), and added a similar narrative from Dr Thomas Bray, the high churchman who had devoted so much energy to the founding of parish church libraries, and also to the welfare of the Church in Maryland. Tate reported another 'reverend divine' as saying that 'since our youth, of late years, in many parts of this kingdom, have learned to sing psalms by *notes*, . . . they have more duly and devoutly attended the house of God, and have taken greater pleasure in the public worship, &c.' (:29).

It will be perceived that the arguments given here in favour of a choir are calculated to appeal to the clergy, many of whom were suspicious of an innovation which they tended to regard as a distraction rather than an aid to worship, or even as a step in the direction of 'popery'. Bedford, himself a minister, quoted the entire passage from Tate's *Essay* in a book about church music, then slyly added a further reason for the encouragement of psalmody, given to him by 'an ingenious and religious clergyman': 'I may add one advantage to my self, *viz.* the cheerful payment of their tithes, upon which I have had no trouble, to the great wonder of my neighbours' (1711: 234).

A religious society and choir existed at Epworth soon after Samuel Wesley, father of John, became rector there in 1697. In this case it appears that the choir existed first, for Wesley, describing his formation of the religious society in a letter to the S.P.C.K. in February 1702, said that he had begun by telling his plan to 'the most sober and sensible man among my singers' (Allen & McClure: 90). Writing to his curate in about 1726, Wesley said 'our people here did once sing well, and it cost a pretty deal to teach them; but are, I think, pretty much fallen off from it'. In early days the village schoolchildren had joined the young men (T. Jackson: II, 509).

The support or at least indulgence of the incumbent was an essential condition for the success of any musical innovations. This is clearly recognised in an interesting manuscript account written by a parish clerk of this period. Edmund Dirrick, clerk of Ubley, Somerset, in 1696 wrote out *A booke of psalme tunes with directions by the rull how to sing them taken out of the works of John Playford*. He may have intended it for publication, as it is marked 'price 2d', but no printed copy is known. It contained simply-worded instructions for learning to read music, and thirty psalm tunes harmonised for counter, tenor and bass. By 'the rull' Dirrick meant, simply, musical notation. In dedicating the book 'to his very good friend and master, Benjamin Jouxson' (who was rector of Ubley from 1692 to 1716), Dirrick wrote:

I thank my God always on your behalf, for the mercy of God, given to me, that I now live under such a master, who is not only the approver of, but also the promoter of good exercises. And amongst many other, that of singing of psalms, an exercise wherein I have taken much delight myself, and made it part of my practice to teach to others, hoping that some may receive comfort by it, and God may have the more glory.

This exercise was formerly well approved of, and promoted by your predecessors, but of late was much decayed, and almost come to nothing. Partly for want of motives and encouragements to that purpose, by them in your place, and partly by reason of discouragements, from them that do disapprove of it. But now by the mercy of God, and your means, [it] is renewed again not only in our church but elsewhere.

Dirrick enlarged on the opposition he had met from those who said 'This is
no good way of singing.' Evidently part of the objection was on Calvinistic
lines:

Again they will say that we do sing by a form, I grant it, we do at the first, and I hold
that best. I hold the same concerning singing, as I do concerning praying. The best
way for a young Christian to learn to pray with the spirit is first by a form . . . The
best way for a young singer to learn to sing with the heart is first by a book.

One argument more they have and that is this. The company, say they, is rude and
profane. I wish with all my heart that it were not true, but I hope that if some are, yet
all are not so, and those that are, may one time or other be convinced. (MS 84: fol.
3r–5r, punctuation modified)

The idea of psalmody as an inducement to greater virtue, or at least as an
alternative to vice, had been spelt out in prefaces and title pages from the
earliest days of the Reformation, and it was still brought forward as
another means of persuading the clergy to tolerate a more artificial kind of
music. So Elias Hall, in the preface in which he gave the rhymed invective
against the old way of singing (quoted above, p. 91), suggested that people
ought to sing music according to rule, as a better way of passing spare time
which 'they often spend in worse employment, in obscene discourse, profane
songs, despising the aged, decrepit and deformed, and the many other
enormities this age abounds with. Now if this duty was performed, how
would the degenerate temper of youth be refined, even to a joyful
admiration!' (PC 56: 3). In this way the classical belief in music's ethical
powers was set up against the old puritanical suspicion of its strength over
the emotions. So long as the new choirs were formed with the clear
objective of helping the people at large to sing heartily and with
understanding, they won widespread toleration and, here and there, active
support from the clergy.

One of the most influential books of country psalmody was compiled by
a man who was himself a clergyman, John Chetham, curate of Skipton. In
the preface to the first edition of his *Book of psalmody*, published in 1718, he
echoed the words of Dr Bisse, already quoted, in defining the aim of his
book: 'to keep up an uniformity in our *parish churches*, and bring them as
much as may be, to imitate their mother churches the *cathedrals*' (PC 71:
preface). These words were copied in many later collections. Chetham's
book was the first to include chants for the prose canticles as well as
anthems, and there is evidence that many parish churches, especially in
north central England, attempted a fully choral service during the next fifty
years. Chetham showed his sensitivity to high-church clerical opinion
when, in his third edition of 1724, he greatly modified the elaboration of
psalm tunes in response to the strictures of Bishop Edmund Gibson (see
below, p. 181).

The practical needs of these choirs involved a modest outlay of money.
They needed a teacher, at least in the early stages; books of instruction, and
collections of tunes; a means of finding and keeping pitch; and a place to
sing in the church. Very few records of payments from church accounts for
the first three objects have been found in this early period:

Hartland	6s. 'spent upon Bideford men for singing', 1696–7	Riley: 575
St Ives (Corn.)	2s. spent on a singing master, 1698	Mathews: 293
Hope	3s. paid for two books and £3 18s. 2d. on a singing master, 1707 12s. spent on meat and drink for singers from Bakewell, Bamford and Castleton, 1713–14	Porter: 80–1
Lymington	£1 1s. for Fordingbridge singers and £1 to the singing master 'for learning poor boys', 1723	Bostock & Hapgood: 61

Several of these recorded payments are for visiting singers. Other examples would emerge from a more exhaustive study of church records, but the majority of choirs evidently existed without financial assistance from parish funds. Probably their expenses were paid by the clergyman in many cases. This would seem to have been the case at Ubley, judging from the wording of Dirrick's dedication quoted above. Elias Hall's collection of 1706 was dedicated to the Reverend Henry Piggot, rector of Brindle and vicar of Rochdale (both in Lancashire); the dedication emphasised Piggot's skill in music and his 'more than common respects to my fellow singers', suggesting that he was one of those clergymen who encouraged psalmody. Tenison, rector of St James, Westminster, was another, and he (as Bishop of Lincoln) was the dedicatee of Daniel Warner's book in 1694 (PC 35); similarly Israel Holdroyd in about 1724 inscribed his book to the Reverend Mr Topham, vicar of Klidwick in Craven, 'because I am conscious it needs the influence of such a *patronage*' (PC 88). Occasionally a benevolent local magnate would help. Sir Benjamin Madox of Little Bookham, who died in 1710, 'left a benefaction to the parish, one moiety of which was to be paid to the rector, and the other to be divided into four parts, ... [of which] one to the parish clerk for the better setting and singing the psalms in church' (Style: xxx; this does not necessarily imply support for a choir, of course). Addison made his fictitious but perhaps not unrepresentative squire, Sir Roger de Coverley, provide assistance:

At his coming to his estate he found the parish very irregular; and ... in order to make them kneel and join in the responses, he gave every one of them a hassock and a common-prayer book; and at the same time employed an itinerant singing-master, who goes about the country for that purpose, to instruct them rightly in the tunes of the psalms; upon which they now very much value themselves, and indeed outdo most of the country churches that I have ever heard. (*Spectator*, 9 July 1711)

The right to use parish funds for church music was debatable, as we saw in the last chapter; and there were many – in some parishes probably a majority of the ratepayers – who were either hostile or indifferent to the reforms proposed, as Dirrick's narrative shows. Choirs often had to find a patron, or, failing that, pay their own expenses, as many certainly did.

The identity of the teachers who initiated these early parish choirs into the mysteries of musical notation is seldom easy to establish. In some cases, such as that of Dr Woodward's correspondent, the clergyman himself taught the singers, though this must have been unusual in view of the general ignorance of music among the clergy and their growing tendency to dissociate themselves from psalm singing altogether. Theoretically, the parish clerk was the obvious person to undertake the task. Edmund Dirrick did so at Ubley; Abraham Barber may have done so at Almondbury, and at Wakefield. Later, William Knapp not only directed the choir at Poole, where he was parish clerk, but probably taught choirs in neighbouring parishes. But these were exceptional. As we know, very few clerks could even sing the tunes properly themselves, let alone teach others; and in fact, few of the eighteenth-century teachers who brought out psalmody collections were in fact parish clerks, though many clerks combined their traditional duty of 'setting the psalms' with membership of the choir (Pl. 16, 17).

The gap was filled by men who simply offered themselves as singing teachers, and found an increasing demand for their services. One of the first of these was Daniel Warner, of Ewelme, whose occupation is otherwise unknown. In 1694 appeared *A collection of some verses out of the psalms of David . . . collected by Daniel Warner for the use of his scholars . . . revised by Mr. Henry Purcell* (PC 35). It was published in London, but was suited for country churches. It contained the ordinary tunes in two parts, largely drawn from Playford's collections. A similar book of 1711 called *The devout singer's guide* (PC 62), compiled by S. Shenton, was 'recommended by Daniel Warner, singing teacher', and a 1719 edition of the same work was 'recommended by P. Joynson, D. Warner and other singing-masters'. These collections included several pages advertising devout Anglican books published or distributed by the S.P.C.K., suggesting a connection with religious societies, either in London or in the country. Thomas Batten is mentioned as a teacher of singing at St Laurence, Reading, in a collection published in 1710 (PC 59), while three Yorkshire teachers (J. Hall, E. Micklethwait and R. Sowerby) appear in another of 1719 (PC 76). Later in the century many itinerant teachers published their own books, which they sold as they journeyed from parish to parish.

Bedford in 1711 referred in unflattering terms to the existence of these teachers:

The good effects of divine music are evident from many places in the country, where the inhabitants learn to sing psalms in consort, though from a mean artist: and if it is thus with psalms, the meanest part of divine music, what might we expect from finer composures, taught by such, who are better skilled in so noble a science?

Common experience tells us, that such a singing of psalms in many country places hath wonderfully increased the congregations. (:229)

Some valuable information is to be found in an unexpected source – the works of Alexander Pope. In 1727 he published 'Memoirs of P. P., Clerk of this Parish', an amusing satire on the gossipy memoirs fashionable at this time. The work is thought to have been written jointly by Pope and John Gay between 1714 and 1718 (Kerley-Miller: 47–8). It contains this passage (the narrator is the supposed editor of the parish clerk's memoirs):

The next chapter contains what he calls a great revolution in the church, part of which I transcribe.

Now was the long expected time arrived, when the psalms of king David should be hymned unto the same tunes to which he played them upon his harp; (so I was informed by my singing-master, a man right cunning in psalmody:) now was our over-abundant quaver and trilling done away, and in lieu thereof was instituted the sol-fa, in such guise as is sung in his majesty's chapel. We had London singing masters sent into every parish, like unto excisemen; and I also was ordained to adjoin myself unto them, though an unworthy disciple, in order to instruct my fellow-parishioners in this new manner of worship. What though they accused me of humming through the nostril, as a sackbut; yet would I not forego that harmony, it having been agreed by the worthy parish-clerks of London still to preserve the same. I tutored the young men and maidens to tune their voice as it were a psaltery; and the church on the Sunday was filled with these new hallelujahs. (Pope: x, 440)

The unctuous tone and biblical language of the clerk are satirised, and also his gullibility in taking at face value the boasts of the singing teacher, who claims that his music has scriptural authority and is as good as that of the chapel royal. It is also clear that the new psalmody is a reforming influence (a 'great revolution in the church'), replacing the old way of singing ('quaver and trilling'). The singing masters, it seems, came from London, and passed on their knowledge to the local parish clerks, who then taught the younger members of the congregation. (There is also an allusion to the weekly psalm-singing practice maintained by the Company of Parish Clerks of London.)

It may be noted that 'maidens' were in the choir as well as 'young men', and this was a possibility also recognised by the compilers of psalmody books. Children might also join the choir in some parishes. Playford in his 1677 collection had suggested that any of his three parts (TTB) could be sung an octave higher by 'boys or women'. The three-part arrangement was followed by some compilers. A collection published in 1700 for 'young persons in and about the county of Lancaster' gave instructions for singing by men, women and children (PC 49). But men's voices took the lead.

An immediate difficulty confronting psalm singers in the absence of an organ was that of finding and maintaining the right pitch. Indeed this problem existed before choirs were formed. John Playford, in the 1660 edition of his *Introduction to music*, gave instructions for parish clerks on choosing the proper pitch for each tune, 'that thereby you may give the *tune* of your first *note* so as the rest may be sung in the compass of the voice, without *squeaking* above, or *grumbling* below' (PC 23/1660: 55). These instructions were copied in countless later collections, both English and American, often with the same colourful phrase about squeaking and grumbling. Harmonised collections sometimes had instructions for giving the pitch to each voice in the harmony. There is no mention of pitchpipes until after the middle of the eighteenth century, when they began to be a common acquisition, usually kept on or under the clerk's desk (PC 186: 12–14). An illustration of the 1770s (Pl. 16) shows a choir of young men, all singing from the same book, while the parish clerk gives them their note on a pitchpipe. The artist has distorted the singers' mouths so as to suggest uncouth and insensitive singing.

Even if the singers started at the correct pitch, it must have been difficult for them to maintain it. From very early in the history of parish choirs, we find suggestions for instrumental support. Benjamin Hely's *Compleat violist or an introduction to ye art of playing on ye bass viol* (1699) includes 'a collection of the psalm tunes set to the viol, as they are now in use in the churches where there are organs'; but it is not certain that Hely meant the viol to be played in church. The tunes are written in the treble clef, with numerous ornament signs. On 27 June 1699 Henry Playford advertised a new instrument called The Psalmody, 'invented by Mr. John Playford, deceased, ... fitted by letters for the meanest capacities', together with a small book of directions (Tilmouth: 29). If indeed this instrument was invented by John Playford, it existed before 1687, and may perhaps have been tried out by him at the Temple Church, London, which had no organ before 1684. No example of the instrument has survived, nor has any copy of the instructions published with it. Philip Hart, a London organist, in 1716 published a collection of psalm tunes for organ, with more ornate versions arranged for the 'flute' (i.e. the recorder) (PC 69). In 1725 appeared *An help to the singing [of] p[s]alm-tunes by the book ... with directions for making an instrument of one string* (PC 91). The compiler, 'W. S.' (his last name is thought to have been Sherwin), acknowledged the help of the Reverend John Rastrick, 'minister of the gospel' at King's Lynn (perhaps a dissenter), who 'about thirty years ago' had made and sent him an instrument of this kind with a book of instructions: quite possibly these were Playford's. A variant was James Leman's *A new method of learning psalm-tunes, with an instrument of musick call'd the psalterer*, 1729 (PC 96). Whereas the 'psalmody' had one string, probably fretted and with the frets labelled by letter, the 'psalterer' had two, tuned an octave apart, also with lettered frets. It was held as a 'bass viol', between the knees, and bowed. Leman provided a simple tablature notation for the tunes and their basses, but these could not be played simultaneously on one instrument. The tune of 'Martyrs' (F. 209) looked like this:

```
A   D   A   H   D   C   A   H
H   L   H   K   N   H
H   L   F   H   D   C   A   H
L   K   F   K   H   A
```

'A' stood for the open string (which could be tuned to any convenient pitch), and the other letters for the frets which were evidently tuned chromatically in semitones, as on a lute or guitar. Later in the book a more complex notation was explained, including signs to indicate rhythm. Leman offered his instrument to 'church-clerks' and others who knew few tunes, or had a poor ear.

No direct evidence exists to show that any of these special instruments was ever used in a church. In fact there is nothing to show that any parish choirs were supported by instruments before the 1740s (see Tables 7 and 8), though the impression is sometimes falsely given that bands were common throughout the century (Pearce, 1921–2; Langwill: 11; Macdermott, 1948). Charles Cox, who studied hundreds of early church accounts, quotes no reference to instruments before 1742. The first known reference to a bassoon dates from 1748. Of course, instruments may have been in use before these dates at the expense of their owners, or instruments originally

Table 7. *Evidence of instruments in church from parish church records up to 1785.*

Date	Parish	Details	Source	Bass	Treb.
1742	Youlgrave (Derbys.)	'For hairing the bow of the viole, 8d'	Cox: 205	x	
1748	Rodborough (Glos.)	A bassoon was the only instrument allowed in the gallery	*Choir and Musical Journal* XVIII (1927): 67–9	x	
1751	Youlgrave (Derbys.)	Reeds for bassoon, 3s 0d	Cox: 205	x	
1759	Hope (Derbys.)	Vestry agreed to pay 16s 6d towards bassoon and oboe which would remain the property of the parish	Porter: 91	x	x
1762*	Bunbury (Ches.)	Bassoon purchased, £5 5s 0d	R. Richards: 81	x	
1763	Stapleford (Notts.)	Bassoon dated 1763 is preserved in the church	Macdermott, 1948: 26	x	
1765	Poulton-le-Fylde (Lancs.)	'Spend receiving bassoon 1s 6d'	Fishwick: 91	x	
c.1765	East Stoke (Dorset)	Subscription list for 'bass viol'	MS 13	x	
1767	Beaminster (Dorset)	Bass viol mentioned	Hine: 34–5	x	
1769	Hope (Derbys.)	'Paid for a bass viol £1 10s'	Porter: 94	x	
1769	Brailes (Warks.)	Bassoon labelled 'Cahusac, London, 1769' preserved in the church	Macdermott, 1948: 26	x	
1771	Dorchester (Dorset): St Peter	£1 1s 0d paid towards cost of 'bass viol'	MS 12	x	
1771	Ticehurst (Sussex)	'For mending the bassoon and reed 11s 3d'	Hodson: 180n.	x	
1772	Charmouth (Dorset)	'For a set of strings for the bass viol as usual'	MS 16a	x	
1772	Hayfield (Derbys.)	Bassoon 'came'	Cox: 206	x	
1772	Over Peover (Ches.)	Bassoon first mentioned	R. Richards: 272	x	
1773	Ribchester (Lancs.)	'To two Hautboys £1 1s 0d; to mending, and new Bazoon £2 17s 0d'	Smith & Shortt: 100	x	xx
1774	Eastham (Ches.)	Bassoon purchased; played in church with 'bass-viol' and clarinet	R. Richards: 152	xx	x
1775	Over Peover (Ches.)	Oboe first mentioned	R. Richards: 272		x
1775	Tendring (Essex)	Bass viol purchased	Boston & Langwill: 112	x	
1776	Milford (Hants.)	Bassoon purchased for £4 8s 7d	Boston & Langwill: 112	x	
1777	Over Peover (Ches.)	'Bass viol' first mentioned	R. Richards: 272	x	
1780	Macclesfield (Ches.): St Michael	'Bass vial', £1 1s 0d; oboe 10s 6d	R. Richards: 396	x	x
c.1780	Boldre (Hants.)	Bassoon made by G. Astor about 1780 preserved in the church	Macdermott, 1948: 26	x	
1781	Tadmarton (Oxon.)	Bassoon reeds purchased	Byrne: 90	x	
1782	Lymington (Hants.)	'To a bassoon for the singers, £1 11s 6d'	Bostock & Hapgood: 24	x	
1783	Swalcliffe (Oxon.)	Oboe (10s 6d), vox humana (18s) and bassoon (£5 5s 0d) purchased	Byrne: 90	x	xx
1785	Farndon (Ches.)	Bassoon purchased 1785, made by 'Millhouse, London'	R. Richards: 155	x	
1785	Swalcliffe (Oxon.)	'Bass viol' purchased by subscription	Byrne: 89	x	

* The date of this entry is wrongly given as 1712 by Langwill (:11), who is followed in this by Macdermott (1948: 26) and Boston & Langwill (:111).

Little significance can be attached to the geographical distribution of the entries in this table. All examples known to the writer are included, but some areas have been more exhaustively searched than others.

The x's in the last two columns indicate the number of distinct instruments referred to.

intended for other village activities may have been borrowed for use in church. At Youlgrave, for instance, although the parish paid for rehairing the bow, it did not acquire a 'bass viol' of its own until 1785, when it was decided at a vestry meeting that the instrument should be used only in church, 'and not be handled about to wakes or any other places of profaneness and diversion', except the club feasts of Youlgrave and neighbouring parishes (Cox: 205). Nevertheless, it is unlikely that many choirs used instruments before about 1740. If they had, some evidence of

Table 8. *Evidence of instruments played in church from printed collections of parish church music up to 1800*

Date	PC	Compiler	Details	Bass	Treb.
c. 1748	134	W. East	Introduction has scales for bassoon and oboe (? for church)	x?	x?
1750	138	Moore	Introduction says parts have been printed in G clef partly because 'more commodious for persons who play on the violin flute, hautboy, and many other instruments' (? in church) and mentions 'those companies where they have no organ or other instrument to regulate and fix the pitch'.	x?	x?
c. 1755	158	Pratt	Preface says instrumental bass parts are for bassoon or cello; one anthem has parts for two bassoons	xx	
1761	117/5	J. Arnold	Preface: 'The bassoon being now in great request in many country churches' (no other instrument mentioned here)	x	
1770	200	Harrott	Preface mentions oboe and bassoon	x	x
1770	202	A. Williams	Part for bassoon or cello	x	
1771	208	Wise	Part for bassoon	x	
1774	214	Langdon	Preface says 'auxiliary bass' part is for cello or bassoon, 'which, though not essential, may be used in those churches where there is no organ'.	x	
1775	219	Newton	Introduction condemns use of 'German flute' for psalmody		x
c. 1775	227	Stephenson	Part for bassoon	x	
1776	229	Key	Parts for violin, oboe, trumpet, 'basso'	x	xxx
1777	232	Alcock jun.	Parts for 2 bassoons in one piece, 2 treble instruments and bass in another	xx	xx
1777	233	J. Arnold	Preface refers to use of 'violins, oboes, clarinets, vauxhumanes &c.' to accompany voices in country churches		x
c. 1777	234	Alcock jun.	Parts for oboes and bassoons	x	x
1784	251	Billington	Preface: 'A bassoon or violoncello will be the properest accompaniment'	x	
c. 1790	275	W. Dixon	Parts for flute, oboe		xx
c. 1790	276	W. Dixon	Parts for flute, 2 oboes (3 in one piece), bassoon	x	xxx
c. 1790	279	Key	Parts for 2 oboes, bassoon	x	xx
[1794]	295a	Alcock jun.	Parts for 2 oboes, bassoon	x	xx
–1797	307	Gresham	Preface: alto part is often doubled by 'a clarinet or two, and in the treble octave'		x
1799	314	Willoughby	Preface gives detailed rules for instruments to play the organ and voice parts: mentions first and second violins, viola, hautboy, flutes, bassoon, cello	x	xxx
c. 1800	323	Key	2 treble instrumental parts (unspecified), one bass	x	xx

The x's in the last two columns indicate the number of distinct instrumental parts printed or referred to.

their use would surely have appeared. Many people wrote about psalmody, and many others printed collections of music, but nobody mentioned instruments in actual use in church. Pitching instructions, a sure sign of unaccompanied singing, are found in the introductions to many psalmody books. In some the pitch recommended for each piece is different from the written pitch, so as to avoid difficult key signatures; for instance every piece in Davenport's *The psalm-singer's pocket companion*, in all editions (the last dated 1785), is written in G major, A minor or E minor, and the introduction gives directions for setting the pitch. In Caleb Ashworth's *A collection of tunes* [*c*. 1760] the interval of transposition is even changed in the middle of one anthem ('I will cry unto God'). The first part is printed in E minor, with the direction 'pitch C♯'; the second is printed in C major, with this note: 'N.B. Let the contra and bass begin this part exactly on the height at which each ended the last, only observing that the key changes from flat to sharp.' Thus while the written key changes from E minor to C major, the sounding key changes from C sharp minor to C sharp major.

Some choirs continued to sing unaccompanied throughout the period of church bands and barrel organs, until they were wholly superseded in early Victorian times (Pl. 18). The pitchpipe at Cartmel Fell was still in use in 1867, when a harmonium was given to the church, while the one at Hook was used until 1856 (Macdermott, 1922: 43). So the church band, though a colourful addition to the country choir and a help in maintaining pitch and rhythm, was never essential. The fundamental medium of country psalmody was the unaccompanied choir, dominated by the tenor voice.

Nevertheless, in many churches between about 1740 and 1770, a bassoon or cello was introduced. Its function was generally to double the bass voice part. John Arnold, in a detailed account of church music written in 1761, said that the bassoon was 'now in great request in many country churches . . . It makes an exceeding good addition to the harmony of a choir of singers, where there is no organ, as most of the bass notes may be played on it, in the octave below the bass voices: The bassoon requires a pretty strong breath to blow it, but is not at all difficult to learn to play upon, all the instructions, belonging to it, being only a scale of its notes' (PC 117/5: iv). Although Arnold mentioned flutes,* violins etc. in the same paragraph, he said nothing about their use in church. He mentioned also organs 'in many of our market-towns' and even suggested barrel organs for 'churches in remote country places'. The figured basses found in some country psalmody books may have been provided for the rare country church that had an organ, but a more practical purpose was for practising the psalmody at home or in a singing society with a harpsichord accompaniment. For some time the bass instrument was generally the only one in use. Higher instruments have not been found in church records before 1759, and they are not common before 1770. The parish church 'band' did not really exist before the last thirty years of the eighteenth century, and I will defer its discussion until later in this chapter.

Separation of the choir: the singing gallery

From the very beginnings of the parish choir we can find the seeds of disagreement as to its function. The religious societies, and those clergy who supported or tolerated the choirs, wished primarily to stimulate and improve congregational singing. If an organ was too expensive, they hoped

---

* By this time the transverse flute, not the recorder, was probably meant.

to procure a similar effect by instructing some members of the congregation in 'correct' singing, and thus spreading the new music throughout the church. Advice from the S.P.C.K. in London suggested that this could be done.

But for musicians such as Playford, the ideal was that of 'psalms and hymns in solemn music' – choral harmony, in which the congregation would play no part. And the choirs, once formed, were encouraged by singing teachers (who had their own motives) to strive for this ideal, and even to imitate cathedral choirs. They wanted to sing anthems after the service, then to sing the liturgy; ultimately, to choose elaborate psalm tunes in which the congregation could not join.

When this was seen to happen, the clergy began to obstruct the activities of the choirs. Edmund Gibson, bishop of London, included the following passage in his charge to the clergy of his diocese in 1724:

But when I recommend the bringing your people, whether old or young, to a decent and orderly way of singing, I do by no means recommend to you or them the inviting or encouraging those idle instructors, who of late years have gone about the several counties to teach tunes uncommon and out of the way (which very often are as ridiculous as they are new; and the consequence of which is, that the greatest part of the congregation being unaccustomed to them, are silenced, and do not join in this exercise at all), but my meaning is that you should endeavour to bring your whole congregation, men and women, old and young, or at least as many as you can, to sing five or six of the best known tunes in a decent, regular, and uniform manner, so as to be able to bear their part in them in the public service of the church. (E. Gibson, 1724; cited PC 134: preface)

These remarks were very influential, and were frequently quoted or imitated. But it is doubtful if they had much effect in the long run. Country psalmody had quickly gathered a strong momentum of its own, and could not easily be restrained.

One of the main issues in the growing controversy about the new psalmody concerned the physical separation of the choir from the congregation. Some of the clergy felt that such separation would encourage the tendency of the choir to give a 'performance', as indeed it did; they saw that by obstructing the physical arrangements for such a separation they could maintain greater control over the activities of the choir. So we find them resisting the pressure to build special galleries or pews for the choirs.

In fact, however, this attitude showed their lack of understanding of practical musical necessities. The singers needed to be separated from the congregation even if their sole function was to lead the congregational singing. For this purpose alone, some remodelling of the interior furnishings of the church was generally necessary.

A group of parishioners would meet together, perhaps in the vestry or outside the church altogether, to learn the principles of music notation from a travelling teacher or from the parish clerk, and to rehearse psalm tunes in harmony. Whether this was treated as a religious exercise (as it would be if organised by a religious society) or merely as a musical one, the singers, when they felt ready to sing at the church services, would naturally need to be together in the church, so that they could give each other confidence and reproduce as nearly as possible the conditions under which they had learned to sing. An individual singer, recently taught the rudiments of music, could not be expected to maintain the new or 'correct' style when surrounded by uninstructed people singing in the old way. The choir could only regulate the rest if it sang as a body.

But the traditional seating of parish churches made no allowance for any such arrangement. The vast majority of parish churches outside London were survivals from before the Reformation, and therefore contained a chancel, which in medieval times had been used by the clergy and by such semi-clerical officials as parish clerks and chantry priests. There the liturgy had been sung, while the people listened from the nave. With the change in emphasis at the Reformation, however, chancels soon fell into virtual disuse outside cathedrals and collegiate churches. Instead of an altar, a communion table was set up in the nave (Pl. 4), and the priest read the services from his desk near the east end of the nave, where all the people could hear and understand him. If the church became overcrowded, the chancel was used for additional seating, and people sat in it facing the priest, with their backs to the altar. At St Martin-in-the-Fields, London, parishioners put their hats on the old altar and even sat on it (Davies: III, 39). When during the ascendancy of Archbishop Laud the altar was restored at the east end of the chancel, and often raised on several steps to emphasise its function as the chief focus of divine worship, chancels once again came into their own, but were only in actual use during the communion service. The medieval plan was now adapted to form a two-chamber church, 'taking the communicants into the chancel for the Eucharist, so that they can be within sight and hearing of the priest at the altar; and . . . bringing down the priest from the chancel to the nave so that he could be amongst his people for morning and evening prayer' (Addleshaw & Etchells: 45). This quintessentially Anglican principle was partially reinstated after the Restoration (Pl. 5, 6). In many of the new classical churches, above all those built by Wren in London after the fire, the chancel was minimised, or altogether done away with; great prominence was given to the pulpit, and Wren took special care that all the congregation could easily see and hear the minister (Davies: III, 40–1). In old churches the chancel was again used for communion, but as both the frequency of communion services and the attendance at them declined steadily during the eighteenth century, many chancels fell into disuse once more, or were diverted to other purposes such as schoolrooms or storage areas.

A characteristic piece of church furniture in the Georgian period was the three-decker pulpit (see Pl. 14, 17). The clerk sat at his desk at the lowest level, with the parson's reading desk above him, and there the two men would read the services in the customary duet. For the sermon the parson would retire to the vestry, exchange his surplice for a black 'Geneva gown' while the psalm was singing, and return to mount the steps to the pulpit itself, on the highest level. (Ante-communion as well as morning and evening prayer were read from the desk.) Only on the infrequent 'sacrament Sundays' (once a quarter in many country churches) would he approach the altar.

Before the advent of parish choirs, the singing naturally took place in the nave, with the clerk announcing the psalm, setting the tune, and lining out from his desk, facing the congregation. When voluntary choirs began to appear, there was no reason to place them in the chancel, even if by chance the medieval choir stalls had escaped destruction. As far as most of the clergy were concerned, choirs were admissible, if at all, only on the basis of leading the singing of the congregation. To fulfil this purpose, they must be placed among the people. But they had to be close together to be effective. In the case of a mixed choir this presented a special problem, for in many churches the sexes were traditionally seated separately (Vaux: 31–6).

An illustration of 1700 (Pl. 15), forming the frontispiece to a collection of psalm tunes originating in Lancashire (PC 47), shows an interesting early solution. The church is a classical one. The railed chancel, though minimal, establishes that this is an Anglican building. The congregation sit facing the centre of the nave, in the manner of a college chapel (perhaps this is merely an artist's licence to allow their faces to be shown). The sexes are separated, the women sitting in pews or low galleries along the north and south walls, the men on seats in front of them, and children on low benches along the aisle. The singers stand in a group in the centre of the aisle, facing east. They seem to consist of two women and eight or more men. The pulpit is conspicuous, but there is no sign of parson or clerk. Perhaps the parson has retired to change his vestments, while the clerk is leading the singers. The singers are further west than any of the congregation, and the heads of the listeners are therefore turned towards them and away from the altar. All the congregation have open books in front of them, but they do not appear to be using them. As far as one can tell, their mouths are shut. Presumably the singers returned to their places when the music was over.

It is not surprising that singers were not long content with such an arrangement. Each singer needed to see two books – the words of the metrical psalms (whether Old Version of New) and the book of music, printed or manuscript; later on, some of them would have instruments. In any case sitting was the usual posture for psalm singing (Abbey & Overton: 472). In many churches it became necessary to provide the choir with a gallery or pew, with seats and reading desks.

Galleries had long since been added to Gothic churches, for the purpose of accommodating more people: the earliest is believed to date from 1550 (Cobbe:.235, n. 3). They were a feature of most new churches, as they had the great advantage of bringing more people within auditory range of the minister. Organs, where they existed, were accommodated in galleries, most usually at the west end of the church, and these often contained seats for the charity children (Pl. 12, 14). It was natural therefore to consider a gallery as a possible place for a voluntary parish choir. Sometimes a gallery originally built to house an organ was left unoccupied when the organ was removed or destroyed, and was now available for the singers. This was the case, for example, at Prestbury (R. Richards: 282). Many churches, even small ones, had singing galleries by the early nineteenth century (see Pl. 16–20, 22, 24). Some still survive. The one at Lamberhurst has two upright grooved holders for the desk of the conductor, who stood facing the congregation as in Plate 12 (Macdermott, 1948: 13). At Puddletown (Pl. 19) is a gallery which was built in 1635 for additional seating, but was later used to hold the singers, who were joined in the late eighteenth century by as many as eight instrumentalists, among them Thomas Hardy, whose grandson, Hardy the novelist, called Puddletown 'Weatherbury' in his Wessex romances. The band was replaced by a barrel organ in 1845, and later by a pipe organ which still stands in it today (Helps: 12–13). At Birtles a singing gallery was made as late as 1840, when the church was built as a private chapel for the Birtles Hall tenants. It became a parish church in 1890, and the choir were still using the gallery in 1947 (R. Richards: 61). In other churches the singers were accommodated in a 'singing pew', such as the one at Selsey, which was the front pew and had a special high desk in front of it to hold the music (Macdermott, 1948: 14).

To provide a special pew or gallery for the singers cost money. If a new accommodation was built, it must be paid for; if existing places were taken over for singers, there would be a loss of 'pew rents' which were normally charged for seating in church. At Lancaster in 1724 it was resolved that an additional gallery be built at the west end 'and that a convenient number of the seats be appropriated to the use of the singers and the rest be disposed of to defray the charges of erecting the said gallery'. But a few years later an organ was put up, and charity children soon replaced the 'singers' (Roper: 616–42).

The possible conflict between the needs of the singers and the rights of those who had contributed to the cost of the gallery were explored and resolved in detail at Cuckfield, in the form of 'Rules agreed on by the vicar and divers of the chief of the parishioners and other persons that contributed to the building of the new gallery for singing psalms for the better order of those that sit and sing in it', dated 16 February 1700. The rules included the following:

This gallery being built only for the singing of psalms by those that have learnt, and for their singing them together, therefore 'tis agreed that it be used ... by such only ... and by no other, though proprietor, till approved singers.

[Rules 2 to 8 give detailed arrangements for seating, according to their singing voice (only tenors and basses are mentioned) and their rank.]

9. Since the singers are a running body and sometimes a family of the proprietors may have more or less, or none that can sing well, and since if they all had a competent number of singers there would not be enough places for them ... they must take their lot without murmuring. ...

15. That as the bishop enjoins in his faculty divers of the singers ... disperse themselves in the congregation ... to assist others to sing. (Macdermott, 1922: 17)

This is the earliest known example of a condition that the authorities sometimes inserted in the faculty to build a gallery, and it shows that already there was some concern lest the singers should be tempted to give a mere 'performance' instead of leading the singing of the congregation. Similarly at Mayfield in 1731 the archbishop's faculty ordered 'that some of the singers of the said parish who may have a right to sit or be placed in the said gallery do sometimes disperse themselves into the body of the said church for the direction and assistance of such persons as shall have a pious intention of learning to sing' (Bell-Irving: 106).

At Wigan, as we saw in the last chapter, one of the advantages the rector saw in the acquisition of an organ was that 'it will no longer be needful for [the singers] to sit together'. It was the provision of a special singing gallery, more than anything else, that decisively turned the 'singers' into a choir rather than a leading portion of the congregation. But to the singers themselves a gallery was highly desirable, adding to the greatly increased prestige which they had begun to enjoy. They had acquired enviable skills denied to the rest of the community; they had a captive audience to display them to; a gallery was the crowning reward, giving them a commanding and privileged physical position in the church itself. Such sentiments, though very far from those that the clergy had had in mind when they first encouraged the formation of singing societies, were very natural in people whose lives otherwise offered little in the way of challenge, excitement, or exaltation of status. So we soon begin to hear of the conceit of singers: 'they very much value themselves,' as Addison put it (*Spectator*: 9 July 1711); 'they think more highly of themselves than they ought to think', it was said to Whitefield in 1737 (Whitefield: v, 167) (see also Pl. 16). Their manner of singing became increasingly ostentatious and affected; they began to demand the right to choose the tunes or even the words of the psalm; and they became ambitious to perform elaborate music on their own. We have already seen that Bedford objected to their tendency to shut out the congregation from the singing. Some choirs went even further in aggrandising their importance. A crisis was reached at Hayes in 1749, when 'the company of singers, by consent of the Ordinary [the bishop], were forbidden to sing any more by the minister, upon account of their frequent ill-behaviour in the chancel and their ordering the carpenter to pull down part of the belfry without leave from the minister and churchwardens'. No doubt they wished to extend the space allotted to them in the west gallery. A few weeks later at a Sunday service 'the clerk gave out the 100th psalm, and the singers immediately opposed him and sung the 15th, and bred a disturbance. The clerk then ceased' (Thomas). At Castle Cary in 1769, the curate, James Woodforde, wrote in his diary:

I was disturbed this morning at Cary church by the singers. I sent my clerk some time back ... to desire that they would not sing the responses in the communion service, which they complied with for several Sundays, but this morning after the first commandment they had the impudence to sing the response, and therefore I spoke to them out of my desk, to say and not sing the responses which they did after, and at other places they sang as usual. [Two Sundays later:] No singing this morning, the singers not being at church, they being highly affronted with me at what I lately had done. (Woodforde: I, 92–3)

At Camerton, near Bath, in 1822, the rector, John Skinner, who was constantly at war with the Methodists in his parish, recorded the following incident:

During the evening service [on Sunday 14 July] the church was crowded; and the singers, who have been in a state of constant intoxication since yesterday, being offended because I would not suffer them to chant the service after the first lesson, put on their hats and left the church. This is the most open breach of religious decorum I have ever witnessed ... There could not have been less than twelve or fourteen who quitted the church at the same instant, thinking I should miss their aid when the psalm was to be sung before the sermon. But I was fully prepared to go through the whole service, even without the assistance of the girls, whom I ordered to sing the hundredth psalm. The sermon followed.

The schoolgirls, who did not sit in the singing gallery, had not joined the rebels. Next day the rector learned, in the course of visiting in the village, that the singers 'had gone from the church immediately to the Red Post public house, and had determined to sing in future at the [Methodist] meeting house, where the gallery was to be enlarged for their accom-modation'. Next Sunday

the girls sang both morning and evening, and much more to my satisfaction than the great Bulls of Bashan in the gallery used to do, who, though never in tune or time, were so highly conceited of their own abilities they thought of nothing else the whole time of the service. If they choose to withdraw themselves, we shall do better without them.

The following Sunday, however, 'before church two of the singers, White and Harper, both under-bailiffs of the coal works, called to say they were very sorry for their behaviour', and asked to be allowed to sing again. The rector let them 'after due admonition'. A few years later the singers were joined by a band, which attracted a large congregation. Skinner confessed to his diary: 'I do not like their mode of performing this part of the service near so well as that of the schoolgirls; but if it induces the people to come to church, I will bear with them patiently' (Skinner: 8–22, 235).

On occasion the singers stepped altogether outside their legitimate concerns. At Aldingbourne, some time in the early nineteenth century, a newly appointed vicar decided to introduce a sermon at matins, but was defeated in his intention by the choir.

Knowing that there was never much time to spare for the parson to have his lunch and make the journey to Oving [where he was also incumbent] between the two services, on the first Sunday that he went into the pulpit to preach they started singing the 119th psalm, and refused to stop when the would-be preacher wished. In vain the vicar looked up at the gallery and held up his written discourse, in vain he coughed and hum'd and ha'd; the singers would look at nothing but their 'Old Version'. Verse after verse they bawled out, lustily and slowly, till at last the vicar's patience and time were completely exhausted, and he had to climb down, literally and metaphorically, and leave the church without delivering a discourse at all. (Macdermott, 1922: 8)

These clergymen had to deal, with greater or less success, with an established institution, which for good or ill had become generally accepted in country churches by the middle of the eighteenth century. Probably the attitude of resignation eventually reached by Skinner was their most usual response. Especially after the rise of Methodism, whose music had certainly beguiled large numbers from the established Church, few incumbents could afford to abolish a feature which (we may note from Skinner's narrative) was popular among the listeners as well as the performers.

The church choir had indeed become one of the main attractions of village life. It did not include the gentry, but it might well include smaller landowners, shopkeepers, and domestic servants, many of them leading figures in the village. Woodforde listed the singers of Castle Cary who had walked out on him that Sunday in 1769: 'John Coleman, the baker, Jonathan Croker, Willm Pew Junr., Thos Penny, Willm Ashford, Hooper the singing master, James Lucas, Peter, Mr. Francis's man, Mr. Melliar's man James, Farmer Hix's son, Robert Sweet and the two young Durnfords' (Woodforde: I, 69). At Welford in 1770, the choir was led by 'Mr. Archer's steward, honest John Heath', while the gamekeeper played the hautboy and the gardener the bassoon, with eight or ten voices (Houblon: II, 147). For most people of this sort the singing or playing in church was the highest accomplishment of their everyday lives. Small wonder that any attempt to interfere with it met with the strongest resentment and resistance.

The 'musickers' were often ignorant, sometimes without musical talent, frequently poor executants and generally somewhat irreverent; but they were always burning, and well-nigh bursting, with zeal in matters musical. They practised singing several nights a week at home or in church; or they learned their instruments slowly and laboriously ... devoting most of their time to this one and only hobby; or they spent hours of painstaking labour in the writing of volumes of manuscript music. And their enthusiasm for their tasks equalled their industry ... Their daily toil was but a graceless necessity of existence; their true mission in life was to excel in the minstrels' gallery in the parish church of their native village. (Macdermott, 1922: 8–9)

In some parishes in the later eighteenth century, the existence of the singers was formally recognised and articles of association drawn up: documents of this kind have survived from several parishes (W. E. Tate: 168). From this time, too, we begin to find more frequent references to payments from parish accounts for the singers' expenses, though they seem to have expected no direct reward except an annual feast (:168), which survives to this day in some villages, or a tip from the parson at Christmas (Woodforde: IV, 22). Often the church choir was essentially the same body of singers as the village waits, who visited houses at Christmastide and expected to be rewarded with food, drink and money (Macdermott, 1922: 10–11; Hardy).

Choirs frequently visited neighbouring churches to sing, and we have already noted payments for the refreshment of visiting choirs quite early in the period. In the early nineteenth century itinerant choirs would sometimes be formed of the best singers from several parishes in a neighbourhood (Ditchfield: 216).

Country choirs did not develop equally in all parts of England. A very strong region throughout the period, but particularly in the earlier decades, was the southern and industrial part of the West Riding of Yorkshire, with the adjoining areas of south Lancashire and the north Midlands. A substantial proportion of the earlier printed collections of country psalmody come from that region (see PC 32–88). At a slightly later date (from the 1730s) East Anglia developed a strong psalmody tradition, as did the southwestern counties of Somerset, Dorset, Devon, and Cornwall; it was in the latter region that the last country choirs and bands remained at the end of the nineteenth century. Thomas Billington singled out the country singing in Devon, Derbyshire and Lancashire for special mention in 1784 (PC 251: 3). Lincolnshire and Leicestershire formed another important region.

William Knapp, Dorset parish clerk and compiler of psalmody books, wrote an introductory letter of commendation for his colleague Joseph Stephenson's psalmody collection in 1760:

> Had this excellent performance made its appearance in the world some years ago, I am very sensible it would not have met with that kind reception, nor the approbation it deserves; church music not being so much in vogue nor understood (especially in parish churches) as at present.
>
> But now it is arrived to that perfection, that there are but few congregations where there is not a choir warbling forth praises to the Almighty Being, in psalms, hymns, spiritual songs, and melodious anthems; with all which this book will abundantly supply them. (PC 171: preface)

Making due allowance for hyperbole, a fault to which psalmody compilers seem to have been especially prone, we can agree that choirs were found in most country churches by the later eighteenth century. The one region where there is little evidence of them is the extreme north of England. Doubtless there were also many small churches where not enough singers could be found to form a choir, and the singing continued to depend on the clerk alone. Occasionally a parish clerk was so skilled at singing that no choir was needed. John Kent (died 1798) was for 52 years clerk of the parish church and abbey of St Albans (now the cathedral), and apparently had few of the usual faults of his calling:

> His knowledge of psalmody was unsurpassed, his voice was strong and melodious, and he was a complete master of church music. Unlike many of his confreres, he liked to hear the congregation sing; but when country choirs came from neighbouring churches to perform in the abbey with instruments, contemptuously described by him as 'a box of whistles', the congregation being unable to join in the melodies, he used to give out the anthem thus: 'Sing *ye* to the praise and glory of God...' (Ditchfield: 88–9)

There was no organ in the church until 1820 (MS 80/449: 14–20).

Another outstanding singer was Samuel Roe, clerk of Bakewell from 1747 to 1792. His epitaph states that 'his natural powers of voice, in clearness, strength, and sweetness were altogether unequalled'. He was succeeded by his son, who held the office from 1815, and who was commemorated with these touching verses:

> The vocal powers here let us mark
> Of Philip our late parish clerk,
> In church none ever heard a layman
> With a clearer voice say 'Amen'!
> Who now with hallelujah's sound
> Like him can make the roof rebound?
> The choir lament his choral tones,
> The town – so soon lie here his bones.
> Sleep undisturbed within thy peaceful shrine
> Till angels wake thee with such notes as thine.

(Ditchfield: 94–5)

159

Evidently this clerk had played a leading part in the choir. It was not uncommon for the clerk to announce the psalm from his desk below the parson's, then march down the nave and up to the gallery to assist or lead the singers (Ditchfield: 214; Macdermott, 1922: 16; Eliot, 1859: 199).

What was the singing of country choirs like? Canon Macdermott spent many years learning about the old church choirs and bands, much of his information coming from former singers and players who were still living early in the twentieth century. He points out that descriptions and opinions have diverged widely. 'No praise was too high on one hand, no contempt too great on the other. The eulogies were generally bestowed on each other by the singers themselves ... while the scorn was heaped upon the vocalists, by the compilers of tune-books or by non-vocal members of the congregation.' He gives examples of each extreme (1922: 20–8). More disinterested praise can be found here and there, however. The Reverend Stotherd Abdy, when he took temporary duty at Welford in 1770, found 'their manner of singing psalms ... particularly pleasing. The tunes are solemn but exceedingly melodious' (Houblon: II, 147). Woodforde occasionally approved the performance in his own church at Weston in the 1790s (Woodforde: III, 386–400; IV, 81–97). More significant than these clergymen's opinions, however, is that of professional musicians. John Alcock, a doctor of music and organist of Lichfield cathedral, in 1756 published a collection for the use of country churches. He had this to say in his preface, addressed to 'all lovers of psalmody':

I hope I shall not be suspected of flattery (a crime which I fancy even my most inveterate enemies will scarcely accuse me of,) if I assure you that I have frequently had the pleasure of hearing several *psalm-tunes, hymns, anthems*, &c. sung by companies of singers in the most exact manner possible, particularly at *Stockport* in *Cheshire*, (at the opening of the organ) where I heard Mr. *Purcell's Te deum* and *Jubilate*, and two *grand anthems*, with all the *instrumental parts*, performed by tradesmen (most of them from *Manchester*,) amongst which were only two professors of *music* [i.e., professional musicians]: And at *Dudley* in *Worcestershire*, when that *organ* was opened, the same *Te deum, Jubilate*, and a *grand anthem*, were performed when not more than two or three masters assisted. (PC 161: ii)

Of course these were not ordinary occasions when a country choir sang without assistance. But Thomas Billington, an experienced performer and composer with an established London reputation, wrote a discriminating preface to his Service in D for men's voices (PC 251), a work which he said was 'composed at the request of a number of friends in the country'. His instructions are worth quoting in some detail since they give a good picture of the standard and character of performance in ordinary country churches at the time (1784).

He begins by stipulating that the work is 'only meant for those who have other requisite for singing but *a good manner*'. Then he explains how this is to be acquired. He condemns the addition of ornaments and graces to music in more than two parts, and the use of excessive vibrato, trills and beats.

I must here observe, one other bad habit that I think is rather peculiar to bass singers, that of taking a fourth below the *note* that ought *only* to be sung; and so they have slid up to it; which has always reminded me of the yell of the Ghost in King Richard the Third ... Bass singers generally appear to be in a passion also, as if a gruffness of manner was necessary, or added more weight and dignity to the performance.... Contra-tenor and tenor singers have equally as bad a habit, which is that of falling a fourth preceding a rest ... I have just touched upon solo singing; as it often happens, that in anthems in three and four parts, there are solos introduced ...

As I imagine it will be performed in churches by more than three voices, I must observe that the parts should be equally distributed, or if any thing, to support the two extreme ones. For I know that the tenor is apt to be the most supported which stands the least in need of it.... I suppose that upon an average there are four tenor singers to one contra-tenor. Neither are basses so numerous as tenors, it being the natural voice of men in general. If there should happen to be a female singer who has a low compass of voice, she can join the contra-tenors in their part. A bassoon or violoncello will be the properest accompaniment.

Such patient and detailed criticisms are less often found than sweeping condemnation, particularly, as Macdermott said, from compilers of collections of church music, who were keen to point out the need for improvement which they themselves could supply. Attention was usually focussed on the performance of psalm tunes rather than anthems.

In country parishes, the psalms are chosen, that consist of four parts, and it is thought by the people who form themselves into a choir, that their performance will be very defective, if they do not contrive to fill them all. There are men who travel, and style themselves professors of, and instructors in psalmody; they are furnished with books of their own selection which are seldom correct, and these are disposed of in every place where they go. While such measures are countenanced, it is impossible to expect, that their disciples, should ever arrive at any degree of perfection. (PC 251: preface)

John Brown, vicar of Newcastle, wrote that 'in country churches, wherever a more artificial kind [of music] hath been imprudently attempted, confusion and dissonance are the general consequence' (:213); and a later writer, enlarging on Brown's views, was even more outspoken. He said that the 'select band', or choir, must be induced

to discard every kind of anthems, singing in parts, new and varied compositions; and if this were once effected, the bad habits of delivering the voice through the nose instead of the mouth, the unnatural shrillness of the upper voices, and the tone of provincial utterance (which are the evils chiefly complained of) would be readily corrected by instruction and practice. One cannot readily account for the introduction of anthems, and varied compositions into the parochial service; it has certainly done no good, and as it throws the rest of the congregation out of all possibility of partaking, it evidently does harm. (Vincent: 21)

A number of writers followed Brown and Vincent in criticising parish church music, and the demand for reform became more and more urgent (Wharton; Cole; Kennedy; D. E. Ford). When reform was under way, critics of the old ways grew more zealous than ever in rounding up the laggards, and the harshest, most censorious attacks are found in the 1830s and 1840s, in some of the many articles, tracts and books about church practice that flooded the presses in those times (e.g., Latrobe; T. Williams;

161

Druitt; Plumstead). Then a more lenient attitude set in, and even, as in Vaux and Macdermott, a sentimental regret at the passing away of old traditions.

There is no question that much of the opposition to country choirs had nothing to do with the music they sang, but was due to the irreverent behaviour of the singers and the clergy's inability to control them. A good account of this problem is given in a popular tract called *The singing gallery*, by Lucy Cameron, published anonymously in 1823 (see Pl. 18). Its message is in the form of a short story, in which the pious Mrs Read is asked by the vicar to undertake the reform of the singers in the parish church. Mrs Read attends in the gallery at a morning service (she is seen at front left in the illustration), and notes the behaviour of the choir. The Sunday school children behave well, but the young men and women show disrespect towards the clergyman, argue about what tune is to be sung during the lessons and prayers, and indulge in flirtatious horseplay during the sermon. 'Mrs. Read felt so much grieved, that she could frequently have shed tears; to see the sanctuary of God so profaned' (Cameron: 6). She says nothing at the time, but invites the older girls, who are 'all poor girls' (:8), to tea at her house, where she shows them the evil of their ways, while the vicar tackles the young men. A great improvement is effected, though 'one or two young people, ... who had come merely for their amusement, soon afterwards quite forsook the church' (:14). The improvement, it is clear, is not in the singing, but in the subordination of the singing to worship, and the consequent improvement in the attitudes and characters of the singers: they sang now 'not only with their lips, but in their hearts' (:15). Mrs Cameron's story may well have been rooted in her own experiences as the wife of the curate in charge of a parochial chapel in a Shropshire colliery town (*DNB*: IV, 753).

On the whole it seems probable that the performance of the Georgian country choir was rarely such as would satisfy an educated musician. Some of the music they were asked to perform, as we shall see, makes little sense by the standards of the elite music of the time. But it is possible nowadays to regard it from a different standpoint – to think of it as a form of folk music, as it would surely have been considered had it survived in use until the present time. Although we can never experience it as a living tradition or hear an authentic performance, we can at least study the music in the written and printed forms that have survived.

Anthems for country choirs

A large body of music survives in print, from the eighteenth century and the first few decades of the nineteenth, that was designed to cater for country choirs of the kind we have been considering. Well over three hundred such collections are available, and yet one would hardly suspect their very existence, let alone learn anything about their contents, from reading any recent history of music in England.

The earliest of these books were compiled by London music publishers and professional musicians; soon the trade was carried on by local amateur musicians and singing teachers, who would travel round the villages of an area teaching the local choirs to sing, and selling their books. In both cases the books were a strictly commercial venture, made possible by the growing demand for this kind of music. Although individual clergymen, as we have seen, occasionally lent their support, the Church played no official part in the development and was, on the whole, somewhat hostile to it.

Towards the end of the seventeenth century some collections of psalm tunes were provided, taking John Playford's *Whole book of psalms* as a model, with country choirs specifically in view; some of them (PC 32, 43, 47) were associated with a particular region. But the distinctive development of country psalmody began when elaborate music such as anthems was included. It was characteristic of country choirs that after learning the common psalm tunes they soon wanted to progress to something more difficult. The first step might be to try out simple anthems or polyphonic psalm or hymn settings at their practices: then they would sing them before or after service. Since this would interfere with neither the liturgy nor congregational psalm singing, there was no compelling reason for objection on the part of the clergy. So anthems were introduced in country churches some time before elaborate psalm tunes or liturgical music.

The first book to provide anthems for country choirs was Henry Playford's *The divine companion: being a collection of new and easie hymns and anthems, ... fitted and for the use of those who already understand Mr. John Playford's Psalms in three parts. To be used in churches or private families, for their greater advancement in divine musick* (PC 51). It was published in 1701, and dedicated to the Archbishop of York, in whose province the greatest advances in country church music were taking place. Playford claimed to be following in the footsteps of his father. The music was entirely new, and it catered intelligently to the needs of the new choirs, providing hymns and canons (probably for use at meetings out of church), psalm tunes (six of them by John Blow), and nineteen anthems. As the preface promised, the anthems were specially designed for their purpose, and were not merely simplified cathedral music. A new class of church music came into existence at this moment: the parochial anthem. Playford's models were short, simple, and largely homophonic; six were in two parts only ('cantus', in the G clef, and 'bassus'), the rest had an optional third part, also in the G clef, printed separately from the main two-part score. Of the eight professional composers whom Playford commissioned to write this music, five were organists or singers in the chapel royal – John Church, Jeremiah Clarke, William Croft, William Turner and John Weldon. As one would expect, the anthems are smoothly correct in their harmony and part writing, and well designed for their purpose (ex. 27).

The book was a success. A second and augmented edition appeared in 1707, with additional hymns, canons and sacred songs, and two new anthems, one by Blow and the other by Michael Wise. Three more editions appeared with little change of contents. William Pearson, Playford's successor, brought out a sequel in about 1731 (PC 104). A church musician, John Bishop, compiled *A sett of new psalm tunes* (1710), which had four anthems and a number of psalm tunes, some rather ornate. It was issued in the form of four part-books (soprano, alto, tenor, bass), but this format had only one imitator; Playford's became the norm.

Taking their cue from these publications, country musicians brought out their own collections, containing anthems as well as psalm tunes. Elias Hall (1706) included six anthems, all taken from Playford's *Divine companion*; Abraham Barber began to include a few anthems, from the same source, from 1711; John and James Green and John Chetham took them from both Playford and Bishop. All these collections came from the north of England. Chetham's *A book of psalmody* (1718) was the most enduring of all; it ran to eleven editions in the eighteenth century and 21 more in the nineteenth, and was probably in use at Halifax parish church for more than 150 years. Through these and later books, some of the anthems in Playford and Bishop were widely disseminated, even reaching American collections in the later eighteenth century.*

But the music did not remain in its original form in the course of its journey from book to book, and from parish to parish. Some anthems were transformed almost beyond recognition, and the later versions would actually be unrecognisable if intermediate stages were not available for comparison. Very often the first stage was to leave out one or more voice parts. Thus the anthems taken by Green from Playford in 1713 were reduced to tenor and bass.† At a later stage one or two upper parts might be added, but these would be entirely different from the original ones. At the same time the bass might be altered, the tenor ornamented; the rhythm seems to have been especially vulnerable, and was so distorted in later versions as to suggest oral transmission rather than copying from printed music. Repetitions and cuts are also found. The only elements that seem to have been relatively stable were the text and the associated succession of pitches in the tenor part. These points are illustrated in exx. 28 and 29, which show transformations of Jeremiah Clarke's anthem 'Praise the Lord, O my soul', given in its original form in ex. 27.

Compilers of country collections soon added local products to the material provided by professional musicians. The first anthem of 'country' provenance is 'Hear my prayer, O Lord', in *A book of psalm-tunes* by John and James Green (ex. 30)‡. It occurs in the second edition of 1713; the first edition has not survived. Although in externals it is modelled on the examples in Playford's book, being in two-part homophony, there is a startling difference in style. The music does not satisfy the expectations of a cultivated listener of the time; it has long static sections followed by bursts of activity, stark and unexplained dissonances (the E flat producing a tritone in bar 9 is explicitly indicated in the source), and suggestions of archaic modality. Yet it has a directness and sincerity lacking in the

* For example, Samuel Akeroyde's 'They that put their trust in the Lord', from *The divine companion* (1701), reached Abraham Adam's *The psalmist's new companion* (London, *c.* 1760), from which it was taken into John Stickney's *The gentleman and lady's musical companion* (Newburyport, 1774), where it was attributed to Adams (R. T. Daniel: 81, 168).

† In an extreme case, a four-part anthem by Aldrich (arranged from a Palestrina motet) was reduced to the tenor part *alone*, including rests of several bars' length (PC 84: 90).

‡ A borderline case is 'O God be merciful unto us' in PC 61 (1711). It is not one of the five anthems mentioned on the title page and it is musically similar to the elaborate psalm tunes in the same book, but it has a prose text.

polished specimens of Clarke, Croft and Bishop. The two-part harmony does not seem incomplete, like the two lower parts of ex. 27, but movingly intense.

This anthem recurred, in slightly revised form, in later editions of Green's book, and also in Chetham's *Book of psalmody* (1718), which had three anthems from Playford (via Green), two from Bishop, two from Green, and eight new. As, in many country collections, the new anthems were not ascribed to any composer, later editions tended to attribute them to the compiler of the book from which they had taken them. Three of the new anthems in Chetham, 'O give thanks' (from Psalm 105), 'I heard a voice from heaven' and 'Sing we merrily', were extremely popular, and reappeared, in variously modified forms, in dozens of later collections, often with wrong attributions. The second and third found their way into early American psalmody books, where they were usually attributed to 'Williams' and 'Tans'ur' respectively (R. T. Daniel: 54, 63). Table 9 lists the most popular parochial anthems of the eighteenth century.

Country singing teachers gradually became more ambitious for their choirs. Cathedral anthems were occasionally mixed in with the rest, beginning with 'Lord, for thy tender mercy's sake', now generally ascribed to Richard Farrant, in Green (1713); Pearson brought in anthems by Byrd and Tallis, which were copied in later collections. Newly composed anthems became more elaborate, and took on some of the mannerisms of Restoration cathedral music: verse sections, solo or duet; alleluias for full choir; triple-time passages with dotted rhythms. They became steadily longer, and were frequently divided into several sections in different tempos, marked with repeat signs. More and more singing teachers included anthems in their books, and we must assume that they were sung in more and more country churches. They went further, introducing chanted canticles and service music; but here, as we have seen, they often had to contend with the opposition of the clergy.

Anthems in country churches were not, as is sometimes assumed (Wienandt & Young: 128), generally sung in the place prescribed in the prayer book, after the third collect. Instead they were sung after service, or between morning prayer and communion (Poole, 1842: 11–12; *The Parish Choir*: I, 9), so that (as Bedford had pointed out) nobody was compelled to listen. Sometimes an anthem was sung during the celebration of communion, and a few books have anthems designated 'for the holy sacrament'. Much more common, however, is an anthem for a special occasion. A great many are for Christmas, Easter, Ascension, and Whitsun; others are for national days such as King Charles's martyrdom, the anniversary of the Restoration, and Guy Fawkes' day (each of which had a special service ordained until 1859), the accession and coronation days of the current sovereign, and special celebrations of victories. Knapp's *A sett of new psalm-tunes and anthems* has an anthem to be sung at Blandford on 4 June, to commemorate a terrible fire that afflicted the town on that date in the year 1731. Funeral anthems were also provided, including settings of 'Man that is born of woman' from the burial service. A good many 'anthems' were through-composed settings of metrical texts, either paraphrases of psalms or other scriptures, or original hymns. Strictly

Table 9. *The most popular anthems in parish church collections of the eighteenth century*

Anthem (Forces, key and incipit in earliest source)	Composer	Earliest source		No. of known sources up to 1800				
		PC no.	Date	Distinct collns	Distinct edns	Manuscript sources	American edns	Total sources
Sing we merrily unto God SATB a 3/4 s Amc|G#c.AqBc|Cq.	Henry Purcell?	71	1718	23	53	2	8	63
Behold, the Lord is my salvation SATB G ¢ᵀGm|BmAm|GmAcBc|	John or James Green?	67	1715	30	51	2	–	53
Blessed are all they SATB d ¢ˢAmcGc|Fs|Em＿|Cm	John Bishop?	59	1710	24	51	1	–	52
Great is the Lord (ex. 32, 33) SATB C 3/4 sEccDc|Cm.|Ec. FqDc|	Thomas Everitt	102	–1731	21	35	3	2	40
They that put their trust in the Lord SATB F 3/4 sAc.qqq|cGcAqBbq|Cm.	John Chetham?*	71	1718	15	39	0	1	40
O give thanks unto the Lord, and call SATB C 3/4 ᵀGmEc|Aq.BsqCcDc|Eq.	John Chetham?	71	1718	16	36	1	–	37
Praise the Lord, O my soul (ex. 27–9) SAB g ¢ˢGs|.Am|Bb s|AmGm|F#s|	Jeremiah Clarke	51	1701	12	33	0	–	33
Thou, O God, art praised in Sion SATB G 3/4 BF#mGc|Ac.GqAc|BcGm|	Israel Holdroyd?	80?	[c.1720]	18	29	3	–	32
I heard a voice from heaven SATB Bb ¢ˢBbs|m.Cc|DmCm|Bbs|	John Chetham?	71	1718	13	24	0	7	31
Sing unto the Lord and praise his name SATB a ¢ˢAs|Ccccc|Bs|Cs|Ecc	Vaughan Richardson	90	1725	15	21	0	6	27

* This anthem is modelled on Samuel Akeroyde's (in PC 51), but is nevertheless a distinct composition.

speaking such pieces were not anthems, and they were generally called 'hymns' in eighteenth-century word books used in cathedrals.* To distinguish them from strophic hymns I will call them 'set pieces', a name by which they were quite often known in the eighteenth and early nineteenth centuries.

A continuous flow of parochial anthems appeared in country psalmody collections throughout the eighteenth century and into the first decades of the nineteenth. At the same time, some of those published in the earliest period remained the most popular, and were reprinted over and over again (Table 9). In construction they were clearly based on the cathedral model; but the composers, lacking the skill of trained organists (and lacking also the vocal and instrumental resources of a cathedral choir), developed a simpler, more straightforward manner, and one in which characteristic archaisms and imperfections of technique became part of an established style. The smooth overlapping of sections attained by means of imitative counterpoint in the cathedral full anthem was generally lacking, and the country anthems are frankly broken up into separate sections, often with a stark contrast of texture, tempo, metre, and mood. But although the original model was the cathedral anthem, the country anthem developed independently, retaining its own character. An anthem of 1799 (ex. 35) preserves much the same distance from the cathedral style as one of 1723 (ex. 34). The country psalmody style can be found in some anthems up to the beginning of the Victorian period: some of the last 'country' anthems are to be found in a collection by Shadrach Chapman, of Draycott, 1838 (PC 363), with independent parts for oboe, bassoon, violin and trumpet.

But from about 1800 onwards the set piece tended to occupy as much space as the true anthem in many psalmody books. This was a development connected with the Methodist and Evangelical movements, which will be considered in the next chapter. A writer in 1822 said that 'with a few solitary exceptions on very extraordinary occasions, an anthem in a parochial church is perfectly obsolete' (*Quarterly* IV, 1822: 179–80), though he might not have made such a remark if he had visited some remote country churches. An interesting word book of *Anthems and hymns used in Gateshead church*, dating from about 1815, contains a mixture of cathedral anthems by Samuel Arnold, Ebdon, Kent, and Mason, and parochial anthems by Crompton, Dixon, Holdroyd, and Knapp, with several 'odes' (set pieces) by Madan and others.

Chants and service music

Dr Bisse's invitation to parish churches to 'conform to the customs of cathedral churches' was taken seriously in many quarters. The same book that first took up the challenge, Chetham's *Book of psalmody*, was also the first to include chants, for the Te deum, Benedicite, and Nunc dimittis (1718); in the third edition (1724) was added a single chant for the Venite,

---

* Similarly, a country psalmodist, John Crompton, defined 'anthem' as 'a divine song in prose' (PC 235: cxx).

with the comment 'This, or any other tune of this kind, may suit *the whole book of psalms,* commonly called the *reading psalms.*' Clearly this was an invitation to parish choirs to get into the business of chanting. Nor was it in vain. Already in 1724 Chetham could report that in 'several churches they now' chant the canticles. Dozens of later collections, especially from north and central England, reprinted these chants and added others of their own, and there is no doubt at all that chanting was commonly heard in parish churches in the eighteenth century, a fact which seems to have escaped the notice of church and music historians alike.

Chetham's chant for the Te deum appears to be taken from the third of six four-part chants printed by John Playford, 'composed by Mr. John Blow and Mr. William Turner' and sung at the chapel royal (ex. 31a). But it was evidently not copied from the printed version, but transcribed by someone who had heard it sung: the tune, somewhat altered, is placed in the tenor, in a two-part setting for tenor and bass.* Variations are suggested for some verses, and the single chant is converted into a double chant by having alternate verses transposed from G major into D major and sung by alto and bass. A four-part setting is provided for the last verse. Barber (1723) printed this with the words *in extenso,* and introduced further variety of harmony and much ornamentation in all parts (ex. 31b). When there are many syllables to be recited, they are not, as in modern chanting, sung in natural rhythm to a note of indefinite length; they are provided with shorter notes, so that the total time taken up is the same in each verse – precisely seven bars. As we shall see, there is a good deal of evidence that this was the way chanting was done, not only in parish churches but in cathedrals, in the eighteenth century. The rhythmic vitality and bounce is utterly different from the studied fluidity of present-day Anglican chanting. This Te deum chant was reprinted in a great many psalmody books, and was very popular, as were a handful of similar chants that went with the other canticles. It was even transformed into a hymn tune named 'Sterling', in collections for dissenters, whence it reached Oliver Shaw's *Providence selection* (1815) and other American collections, its source sometimes given as 'an old chant'. From there it crossed the Atlantic again to appear in Mercer's *Church psalter and hymn book* (1864) as a hymn tune revised by John Goss: the index listed its source as 'American' (PC 389/1864: 215, 278).

Robert and John Barber's *Book of psalmody* (1723), from which this setting is taken, continued the process of imitating the cathedrals by providing polyphonic settings of the canticles, a feature that was also copied many times over. The Jubilate, for example, appears in 33 different settings in country collections before 1800, and is commoner than any single anthem text.

The final step was taken in the second edition of the same work (1733), when Robert Barber provided complete instructions for chanting the whole service, including the litany and ante-communion, after the cathedral manner, although mostly in three-part harmony only (see ex. 65a). This

---

* It also bears a strong resemblance to the Sarum chant for verses 1–13 of the *Te deum* (see Harrison: 66). Perhaps it had survived, against all the odds, by oral transmission.

1 Fifteenth-century rood-loft at South Warnborough (Hants)

2 Fifteenth-century chancel stalls at Fressingfield (Suffolk)

Four representations of the sacraments

3 Carmelite friars at mass in about 1395

5 A high-church ideal of communion in Queen Anne's time

4 The Puritan concept of baptism and communion, 1578

6 Communion at an Oxford church in late Georgian times

7   John Day (1522–84), aged 39–40

9   William Tans'ur (*c.* 1700–83), aged 72

8   John Playford (1623–86/7), aged 40

10   Dr Edward Miller (1735–1807), aged about 59

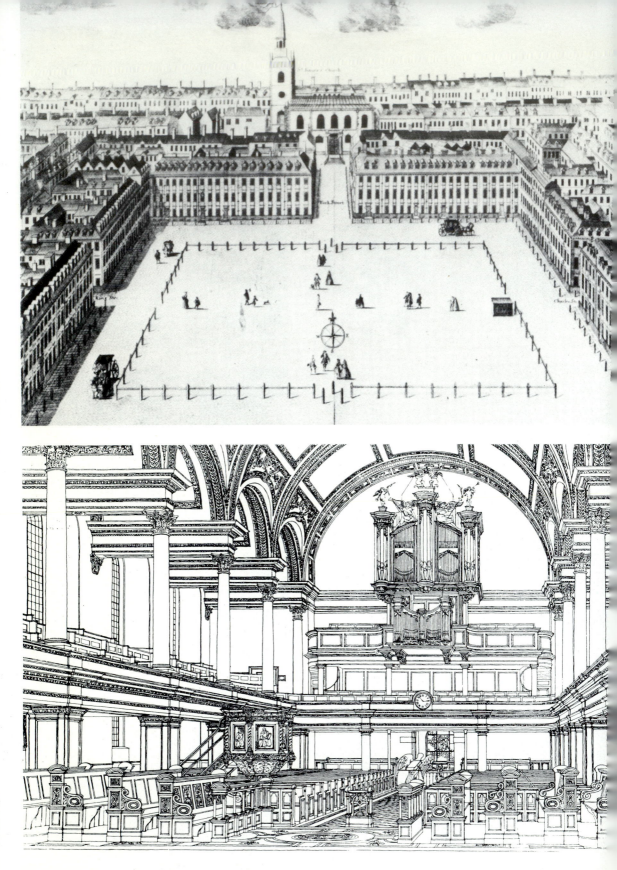

11 St James's square and church, Westminster, about 1720

12 St James's church, Westminster, looking west

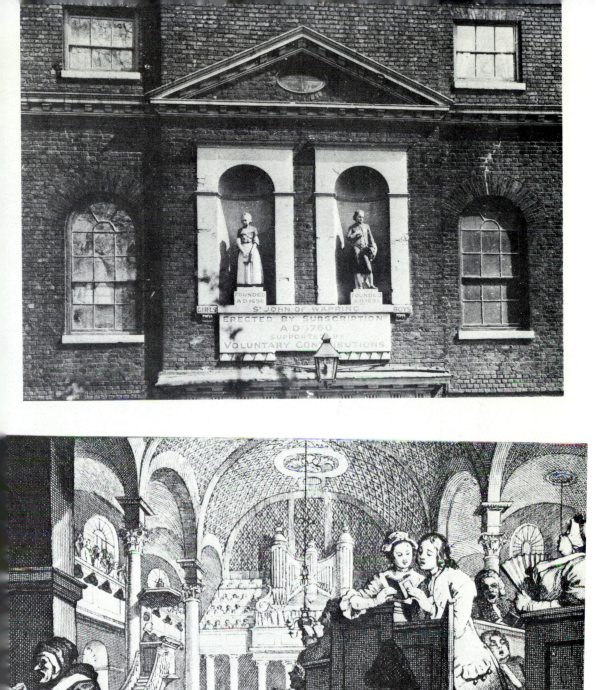

13 The charity school of St John, Wapping

14 A service at St Martin-in-the-Fields in 1747

15 A northern parish choir in 1700

17   Sunday matins in a village church in 1790

18   A country choir in 1823

19   The church at Puddletown (Dorset), looking
      down from the west gallery

20 Morning service at St John the Evangelist, Westminster, about 1830

21 Charity children going to St Paul's cathedral, about 1840

22 The choir at Bow Brickhill (Bucks), about 1840

23 A village choir rehearsal in 1863

24 Singing galleries and barrel organ at Wissington (Suffolk)

25 Barrel organ at Shelland (Suffolk)

26 Halifax parish church looking west, 1840

27   A choral procession in a London suburban church, 1865

28   Opposition to Tractarian innovations, 1866

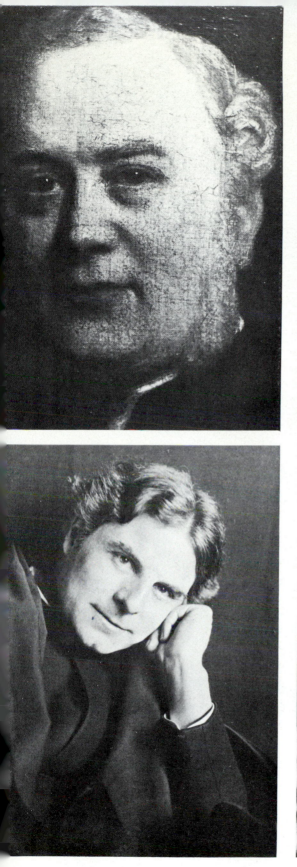

29 The Reverend Thomas Helmore (1811–70)

31 The Reverend Percy Dearmer (1867–1936)

30 The Reverend Dr John Bacchus Dykes (1823–76)

32 Sir Sydney H. Nicholson (1875–1947)

33   The church of St Mary Summerstown, Wandsworth, in about 1910

34   The church of St Mary-the-Virgin, Primrose Hill, Hampstead, in 1937

35 Chalfont St Giles and District Choirs Festival meeting at Amersham (Bucks), 1934

36 The choir of Badwell Ash (Suffolk) in 1972

37   A service at St Luke, Brighton, in 1978

38   The church of Holy Trinity, Twydall (Kent)

feature was copied by only one other compiler, John Arnold of Great Warley, in editions from 1741 to 1779. (Arnold gave the responses in unison only.) The source of Barber's settings is unknown: he, or another country musician, may have tried to write them down after hearing them in a cathedral. Arnold took his from Playford (1674).

A fully choral service was not unknown in northern parish churches at this date. From Selby in 1751, Bishop Richard Pococke reported:

This town is no corporation, and has neither clergyman nor justice of the peace. They chant all their service, except the litany; and the clerk goes up to the communion table and stands on the epistle side to make the responses, and they sing well not only the psalms but anthems. (Pococke: I, 173)

Selby Abbey, whatever its former splendour, was in the eighteenth century an unendowed parish church, and until the first organ was installed in 1825 there was only a voluntary choir supported by instruments (MS 92). The chanting and singing described by Pococke was accomplished by uneducated parish singers, and in 1751 it is likely that they were accompanied only by a bassoon or cello, or not at all. A serpent, preserved in the abbey, dates from a slightly later period.

At Shaw chapel in the parish of Oldham, a society of singers was formed in 1741 by about forty parishioners in association with the minister. They drew up and signed a document entitled 'articles, proposals, and agreements for the better encouragement and propagation of singing chants, hymns, and anthems, and other divine music, in Shaw chapel' (Hudson: 539).

Settings of the responses to the commandments in the communion service are found in several collections, including Tans'ur's *Royal melody compleat* (1754–5), and these were heard in a good many churches (Woodforde: I, 92). There are also settings of the Sanctus, beginning with the introductory phrase 'Therefore with angels and archangels', as for instance in John Everet's *The divine concert* (1757), a Lincolnshire collection, and the short traditional response 'Glory be to thee, O God', used after the naming of the gospel in the communion service, is also found.

Another feature of many psalmody books is the canon. While canons may have been originally intended entirely for the recreation of singing societies, there is some reason to think that they sometimes found their way into services. The best known of all the canons was *Non nobis, Domine*, traditionally attributed to William Byrd. It was printed in many psalmody books. And William Tattersall, in 1791, printed it in conjunction with 'Glory be to thee, O God,' with the remark: 'This and the following tune [*Non nobis, Domine*] have always been sung in the communion office, previous to the reading of the gospel.... They are excellent compositions, very easily learned, and, when parts are filled, have a fine effect' (PC 292).

In several instances, choirs were prevented from singing or chanting the liturgy by the intervention of the clergy. But the practice was not so easy to stamp out. Chanting does appear to have waned: in the later eighteenth and early nineteenth century, fewer country psalmody books contain chants than in the earlier period. Chanting in parish churches was to be revived, in very different conditions, under the influence of the Evangelical movement.

But the singing of canticle settings remained a feature of country services in the north and west of England, especially on Sunday evenings. As late as 1851 William Spark complained of the many bad evening services in use: 'In the west of England I know there is scarcely a village boasting a choir, where they do not perform some favourite service by a local composer, consisting of solos, duets, trios, &c., with noisy accompaniments for clarionets, bassoons, bugles, basses, &c.' (Spark, 1851: 22–3).

Psalm tunes

Anthems, set pieces, hymns, chants, and canticle settings were all subordinate to the principal form of psalmody, the metrical psalms. Here the situation was different, for the country choir had a rival for the honour of providing the music. Congregations had been accustomed, from time immemorial, to sing the psalms at certain conventional points in the service, and it was a privilege that many were loth to surrender. It was one thing for choirs to learn the common psalm tunes 'correctly' and in harmony, so that the congregation could be brought to sing them more tunefully, and to introduce a few new tunes of the same simple type. But elaborate tunes, which the ordinary untutored person could not sing, were likely to meet with resistance, both from the congregation and from the clergy. We have already seen examples of such resistance. They explain why the elaborate psalm tune was slower to develop than the parochial anthem, which established itself almost as soon as country choirs became common.

Indeed some country psalm tunes in the early eighteenth century seem quite deliberately designed to exclude the congregation from taking part in their performance. In the accustomed way of singing, the principal notes of the tune were conceived as equal in time value (whatever their 'correct' value might be). The new type of tune moved in sprightly rhythm, often in triple time, and with a sharp distinction between longer and shorter notes which would tend to bewilder anyone who had not rehearsed the music. At a later stage one syllable might be drawn out in a long melisma, the next quickly passed over (ex. 39).

A still more disconcerting feature was the fact that the tenor could no longer be relied upon to carry the melody throughout a tune, as had always been the case in traditional settings, no matter whether in one, two, three, or four parts. In some of the new tunes, one or more parts (including the tenor) might be silent for some phrases, to allow for solos, duets, and other contrasts of texture. An early tune of this kind, dating from about 1722, occurs in the second edition of John Bishop's *A sett of new psalm tunes* (PC 59). The tune (ex. 36) begins with a line for tenor alone, followed in turn by lines for bass, soprano and alto: this completes the four-line verse. The last two lines of both verse and music are then repeated in a fully harmonised setting in four parts. Bishop was a professional musician, and this particular tune is more or less conventionally correct in its harmony and word setting, bar a pair of consecutive fifths.

This pattern was taken up by the more adventurous country composers. The pattern of solos followed by full chorus was sometimes converted into an alternation of duets and chorus, as in a tune printed by Israel Holdroyd dating from about 1723 (ex. 37). The harmony, as with much country music, is made up of root-position chords, but is 'correct' apart from the startling pair of chords at the end of the second phrase – a survival of earlier practices that was by no means unique, as we have seen. The word setting at first appears distorted, until one realises that the trouble is in the barline notation. If every barline is shifted by one crotchet, the real musical rhythm emerges, and does no violence to the words.

Other tunes (ex. 38) are in full chorus throughout, but the tenor is so full of elaborate melismas that it could not be exactly followed by a large body of singers. A tune like this can, however, be regarded as an attempt to regularise and harmonise the old way of singing, as in ex. 17. But the harmony obviously could not be successfully applied if the congregation was free to sing the tune in the old way, for there would then be no predictable time values.

In one way or another, these new tunes were beyond the reach of an ordinary congregation; only those who had learned the music, or had it in front of them, could know what was going to happen next. Deprived of the opportunity to sing what they had always sung, in a way that required no conscious thought or special skill, people were now compelled to choose: they could join the choir and learn to sing from notes, or they could listen in silence. The response obviously varied from place to place. It is clear that in some parishes, at least, the new style of psalmody was popular. Enough people joined to form a sizable choir, and enough of the rest enjoyed listening to the more pretentious music that was now offered them, or at least were prepared to tolerate it. But several compilers record the hostility that sometimes met their efforts. Chetham (1718) wrote of the difficulty of getting country congregations to forsake what they had been accustomed to: 'What terrible outcries do they make . . . against any alterations; and if their understanding does not help 'em to any arguments against the thing itself, they immediately cry out Popery!' (PC 71: preface). One old woman 'called the singers very opprobrious names, saying they had put her out of her tune that she had sung forty years' (PC 138: iv). Crompton (1778) felt that singers should let congregations have their way

in the choice of the tunes to be generally sung, and consequently prevent such feuds and animosities as have arose . . . amongst many congregations . . . There are always opportunities enough for companies of singers to amuse themselves with light and airy tunes when a congregation doth not want to join them; and yet probably would not think half an hour ill spent (when . . . worship may be over . . .) to hear them exercised in some of their most airy tunes, or fuging pieces. (PC 235: ix–x)

The elaborate psalm tune developed very rapidly when once the first models had spread. It was not long before tunes were appearing that were almost miniature anthems or cantatas. But if they were to be actual 'tunes', rather than 'set pieces', they must be capable of strophic repetition, and it was this that formed the only check on the proliferation of elaborate psalmody. If techniques of word setting were to be borrowed from art music, where verbal repetitions, echo effects, melodic leaps, long melismas and wide variations in syllable duration were used to enhance particular texts, it was almost impossible to write music that was equally suited to each of a number of verses.

One way round this problem was to use a text that had some kind of refrain, and to reserve the most elaborate part of the music for that refrain. Unfortunately, very few psalms offered this possibility. Psalm 136 is the only one that has a regularly repeated refrain (and it is no coincidence that this psalm was used in some of the earliest fuging tunes). The Benedicite has a refrain; a hymn may have one. But the Benedicite had to be sung complete or not at all, and its great length ruled it out for ordinary use; and hymns were still frowned on for regular use in the Church of England. A word like 'alleluia' could be harmlessly added to each verse of a psalm of praise, and this was sometimes done, though some might call it popery. An early example of the new type of tune came from an interesting collection called *Lyra davidica* (1708), whose compiler is unknown but was certainly a competent musician. This was the Easter hymn, 'Jesus Christ is risen to-day', which is still commonly sung to a version of its original tune (for which see Frere & Frost: 214). Each line is followed by an alleluia, which is set to an ornate melismatic phrase, while the rest of the text has mostly syllabic and equal notes. To sing the alleluias one had to perform accurate vocal leaps and distinguish carefully between different note and syllable lengths. It was a tune for choirs, and it did find its way into many country psalmody collections.

A still more elaborate tune of the 'miniature cantata' type is first found in the second edition of Chetham's *Book of psalmody* (1722). Again it is pretty clearly the work of a professional (ex. 39). It has a variety of rhythmic patterns and syllable lengths, melismas, dotted notes, and word repetitions. It is clearly in three sections: a duet for tenor and bass, in the tonic key; a duet for soprano and alto, answered by tenor and bass, that modulates to the dominant key; and a section in the tonic for full chorus. No part carries the 'tune' or even sings throughout, so there is no opportuntiy for the congregation to join in. There is a change of time signature between the first and second sections. There is even a touch of text overlap in the first section, at the words 'the king', though in the absence of rests this is not a true point of imitation. Yet all this complexity is found in a strophically repeated tune.

The trick has been performed by the choice of a very special psalm text, Psalm 24, verses 7–10. It so happens that the two stanzas in the Old Version are identical except for their last three lines. So the word repetition and imitation in the first section are repeated to identical words, while the effective 'question and answer' of the second section also repeats to very similar words. The last section, which is largely homophonic, readily adapts to words of similar rhythm and sentiment. Hence the 'tune' could be called a set piece sung twice with slight variation in the words.

This 'tune' was itself copied (and frequently modified) in many later books, but it had no direct imitators, simply because it was a special *tour de force* that could not be repeated: few, if any, other passages in the psalms lend themselves to such treatment. The touch of counterpoint in the tenor-and-bass section set a precedent that nobody would follow for a quarter of a century afterwards. It produced an overlap of text, never found before in a psalm-tune setting designed for church use. Though barely noticeable in this case, it was open to the objection of obscuring the text. This, even more than 'vain repetition', had been one of the chief objections of the Puritans to choral church music, and it was by no means forgotten now.

The final stage in the elaboration of psalm tunes happened when the 'fuging tune' appeared. Because several collections containing fuging tunes cannot be precisely dated, the priority is difficult to establish. But it is certain that a little before 1750 fuging tunes appeared in several printed books. Probably they had been tried out from manuscript copies some time before, but there is no way of knowing in what part of the country they arose, since the early books containing them come from several regions.

A fuging tune, properly so called, contains passages in which voices enter successively in such a way that more than one part of the text is being sung at one time. Generally, though not necessarily, the entries are imitative: two or more voices enter successively with the same phrase of text and a similar musical phrase. Thus the text would be obscure to some extent, and might be difficult to hear, and moreover the passage might not fit well when the tune was used for other verses of the psalm. Some compilers mitigated these effects in one way or another. The words in the fuging section were often repeated in plain homophony, so that if they were missed once, they would be heard the second time. William Tans'ur, whose first fuging tunes are in his *Royal melody compleat* (1754–5), was even more cautious. In five of the six tunes, the fuging part is a 'chorus' at the end, which repeats two lines of text already sung in block harmony (ex. 41); in the sixth the fuging section is a setting of a refrain, based on additional words not in the psalm. In all cases the tune could be sung with the fuging section omitted, and would end on a full close in the tonic. Tans'ur pointed out in his preface to the third edition (1764–6) that the 'fuging chorus's' may be omitted. He thus anticipated objections, and provided for the possibility that choirs would sing the plain versions in church, but would add the fuging sections for their own diversion when singing the tunes in rehearsal.

So there were technical as well as religious factors to inhibit the growth of the fuging tune 'industry', but once these had been overcome there was a flood of them. The Chetham tune was copied in many collections between 1722 and 1750: sometimes without change, sometimes with a new text or in a different vocal arrangement, sometimes with a reduction of elaboration, sometimes with an increase of the 'fuging' element. It did not become a truly fuging tune until Green, in 1744, rewrote it with three genuine imitative entries, complete with rests and text overlap (Fig. 6; ex. 40). A much greater degree of imitation is found in a Broderip tune of 1745. But the fuging tune did not really arrive until 1749, when John Watts, of Fennycompton, published a collection containing no less than ten examples, all new. The following year William East of Waltham added a second part to his *Voice of melody* of two years earlier, and included 23 fuging tunes. In 1754 he produced the first collection in which all the tunes are fuging. He called it *The sacred melody. Being the newest ... collection of church-musick now extant. Containing a curious and select number of psalm-tunes, in the fugeing, syncopating and binding taste ... as also, services and anthems.* About half the tunes in this book are attributed to John Everet, of Lincolnshire, who later (1757) brought out his own collection.

PSALM XXIV. Verſe 7, 8, 9, 10. Or Pſalm 24, *New Verſion.*

Ye prin-ces o——pe your gates, ſtand o——pe the e-ver-

Ye prin-ces o——pe your gates, ſtand

—laſt——ing, e—-verlaſt--ing gate, for there ſhall en—ter

o——pe the e-ver--laſt--ing gate,

in there—by the kin——

the

Who is the king, is the king, the

Who is the king, the

——————g of glorious ſtate?

k—-——g of glorious ſtate?

174

Continued.

Treble 10th, Contra 8th, from Bass.

(Repieno.)

king of glo——rious ſtate?   The mighty

The ſtrong and migh——ty Lord, the mighty

Lord, in bat——tle ſtout, and tri——al of the ſword.

Lord, in bat———tle ſtout, and tri—al of the ſword.

9 Ye princes, ope your gates, ſtand ope ye everlaſting gate ;
    For there ſhall enter in thereby, the king of glorious ſtate.
10 Who is the king of glorious ſtate ? the Lord of hoſts he is ;
    The kingdom and the royalty of glorious ſtate is his.

Q 2   PSALM XXX.

Fig. 6 Modified version of the Chetham tune for Psalm 24, verses 7–10, Old
Version (see ex. 39) in James Green's *Book of psalmody*, 1744, with manuscript
additions in an unknown hand (PC 123, University of Illinois copy, pp. 114–15)

Meanwhile other compilers including Moore, Milner, Knapp, Davenport, Tans'ur and probably Adams had begun to follow suit.

So the three pioneers of the fuging tune, Watts, East and Everet, were all local singing masters in the depths of the country. They were by no means equals in skill: East's stand out as the most adroit at dealing with the problems involved. By making his points of imitation follow the metrical accents fairly closely, he ensures that the subsequent verses will fit reasonably well (ex. 42). Some composers show a reckless disregard for the fit of the text, even when the additional verses are set out under the tune.

The rage for fuging tunes continued into the 1760s and 1770s, when it spread to the American colonies and was enthusiastically taken up by the New England composers. Fuging tunes met with considerable opposition, among others from John Wesley, who thought them an insult to common sense and a mockery of God's word. By the end of the eighteenth century, though found in many collections, they were clearly on the decline. Their place was gradually taken by a more 'correct' kind of fugal tune, modelled on the glee, which we will meet in the next chapter. In Chetham's *Book of psalmody* the original 1722 tunes survived until 1811; the next revision, 1832, included three fugal tunes of the new type, one of which, 'Comfort' (later attributed to Handel), is well known in the United States to-day as a Christmas carol, 'Joy to the world'.

Not all country psalm tunes were fuging, of course: in fact, the great majority were homophonic, though with a tendency to elaboration. While the fuging tunes all dropped out of use when their style became unacceptable in the nineteenth century, quite a number of their simpler contemporaries have survived. *Hymns ancient and modern revised* (1950) retains about a dozen tunes that first appeared in country collections of the eighteenth century (Frere & Frost: 705). Some of these have remained favourites, and show the country psalmodist's grasp of simple melody:

'Burford'	Chetham, PC 71	1718
'Bedford'	Timbrell, PC 80	*c*. 1725
'Wareham' (ex. 44)	Knapp, PC 115	1738
'St Thomas'	Williams, PC 189	1763
'Rockingham'	Williams, PC 236	1778
'Abridge'	I. Smith, PC 246	*c*. 1780
'Warrington'	Harrison, PC 258	1786

Compilers and composers

The task of identifying the composers of much of the country psalmody of the eighteenth century is not an easy one. The idea of individual authorship of a work of art was little more developed among country musicians, at least in the early eighteenth century, than it was among church musicians of the middle ages. They took whatever was available and remodelled it to suit their purposes. No clear dividing line existed between arrangement and composition. It was not that compilers claimed as their own work music that had actually been composed by someone else: cases of this are extremely rare. It was rather that they made no claim or statement whatever about the origin of most of their music, unless it was believed to be the work of a famous composer such as Purcell or Handel. A name at the head of a piece, which we might take for an attribution to a composer, was much more likely to be an acknowledgment of the immediate source from which the compiler had taken it. To find the composer, we trace the piece back, sometimes through several collections; but when at last we reach the earliest source, there is often nothing in it to indicate the composer's name.

The music of professional composers (who include, of course, many organists of provincial parish churches) is intermixed with that of country amateurs in many country psalmody collections. To start with, there was the music specially commissioned for the purpose by Playford, Bishop, Church and Pearson, some of which was used by compilers of country collections. But in addition many compilers sought out cathedral music from both printed and manuscript sources. The printing of the sung liturgy by Robert Barber and John Arnold has already been mentioned; the chants in psalmody books were probably derived largely from manuscript sources, or by oral transmission. A few services and a larger number of anthems by cathedral composers were also printed in these books, often for the first time. Most of the main cathedral composers from Byrd and Farrant to Greene and Handel are represented by at least one anthem, and we also find adaptations of Latin motets by Palestrina, Tallis and Carissimi, some of them originally made by Henry Aldrich for Christ Church Cathedral, Oxford. In some cases the transcription is remarkably faithful to the original; in others, there are errors, misunderstandings, or deliberate alterations and cuts, even the entire omission of one or more voice parts. At a later date Boyce's and Arnold's published collections of cathedral music were frequently drawn on.

This eclecticism is especially noticeable in the earlier part of the eighteenth century. A singing teacher could virtually corner the market for church music in the region he worked in. When he visited one of his choirs, he offered them copies of the local book, his own or that of a neighbouring teacher. It was unlikely that they would have other sources of music to draw on, unless a rival psalmodist had been travelling the same beat. Hence he could choose materials from the whole range of available music: utility was the only criterion. There was little point in being particular about the origins of the music he used, or in being faithful to the original form of the music if another suited his purpose better. Many compilers even renamed old tunes after local towns and villages. But there was apparently a code of honour among the psalmodists themselves, which frequently constrained them to acknowledge borrowings from other collections. In some cases a compiler offers a fulsome testimonial to one or more of his predecessors in the preface, or prints a verse tribute to himself by one of his colleagues. William East proudly offered readers of his *Collection of church musick* the following eulogy, probably the work of a fellow psalmodist:

> *To the author of the Divine Melody.*
> Accept, my friend, what justice makes me do,
> And your harmonic notes compels me to.
> Great Playford's works immortalized his name,
> And Tans'ur's stretched the blowing cheeks of fame;

Green, Barber, Chetham, Smith, &c. in thought was best,
Yet all these worthies are revived in East.
Great thanks, my friend, we to thy labours owe,
Which makes the paths of music smooth to go.
How many psalmists (who pretend to be)
Instils vile stuff, instead of psalmody?
But here's a well dressed piece, in proper light,
Composed just, collected full as right.

* * *

Go on, great artist, with this earthly choir,
Till body's flat, and soul is raised higher:
Then mayst thou sing with choristers of fame
Celestial hymns to celebrate the same.
 I am, S^r, your humble servant,

John Stanley. (PC 157; punctuation modified)

Thomas Moore in a collection of 1750 mentions a number of other 'books of the like kind', providing an interesting survey of the history of country psalmody up to his time. Occasionally a compiler would include a piece by another country musician in his circle, and name the composer. East's use of fuging tunes by Everet is an example. John Arnold of Great Warley, in his *Compleat psalmodist* (1740), acknowledged taking some tunes by 'James Green, John Chetham, Israel Holdroyd, William Tans'ur, and several others, now deceased' (apart from Tans'ur these compilers had not composed the tunes Arnold took from them). But four other tunes were by 'Mr. Philemon Chalk, one of the [singing] society of Great-Warley'; one by 'Samuel Laisel, of Great Warley'; one by 'John Harwood, leader of the tenor, of Great-Warley'; and forty-two 'are of my own composing'.

A few compilers claimed authorship of all or most of the material in their books: among the first to do so were Josiah Street, William Tans'ur and Uriah Davenport. It is only in such cases that one can easily study the style of an individual country composer. In the later eighteenth and early nineteenth centuries, more composers were inclined to follow this example. A likely reason for the trend was the rapid opening up of country districts to easier communication with the centres of population and commerce. Regions were no longer insulated, and choirs might have access to many sources of musical materials, including some produced and distributed by London publishers. In these conditions it was more important for a composer to claim his work as his own, and for a compiler to emphasise the unique advantages of the particular collection he was offering for sale. We find a growing sense of rivalry among the country compilers of the later eighteenth century. Instead of paying each other compliments they began to attack each other in their prefaces, and to dwell on their own learning and experience and the specially valuable nature of their selection of music. So Tans'ur in his *Royal melody compleat*:

There are many, in this age, that assume the shape of a master, or tutor, who are so very ignorant, as not to say their gamut; and much less to understand it . . . Many of these will also set up for composers, which neither know tune, time, nor concord: and, for all they cut so ridiculous a figure in the eyes of the learned, yet they gain proselytes luckily among the ignorant; which makes good the old saying, 'that they are clever fellows, amongst folks that know nothing'. (PC 155: preface)

Unfortunately, this comes close to being an accurate description of Tans'ur himself.

The great majority of country psalmodists were probably, indeed, men of little education, either musical or general. In some cases nothing whatever is known about a compiler except his name, or his name and location. Many were also printers, publishers and booksellers, at least insofar as they printed and distributed their own books. Most were singing teachers. Indeed most of the books begin with an introduction containing the rudiments of music, based on the increasingly irrelevant gamut. Probably their practical teaching methods had little to do with the lofty theoretical treatment provided, which was generally taken straight out of an earlier publication. The old-fashioned scriptural justifications for psalmody were often included. Some introductions, however, contained lively practical comments which often reveal much about the musical conditions. There are suggestions about the physical placing of the singers, about pitching the music, about striving for 'polite' pronunciation instead of a regional brogue, about matters of performing practice – tempo, dynamics, ornaments, instruments. Many refer to the perennial clef problem, which will be separately treated.

Thomas Moore, issuing a psalmody book from Manchester in 1750, advertised as follows:

As the author intends to make the improvement of psalmody his study and practice, he will be ready to teach that art in any place where he may have proper encouragement, after a new and expeditious method, by which the learner may in a short time be able to sing true at sight, without the assistance of a master. (PC 138)

John Bellamy's book was 'sold by him, at his school in West-Redford, Notts.'; Francis Timbrell's was 'for the use of his scholars'; William East's 'for the use of his schools'. There was nothing of the permanent institution about these singing 'schools', and indeed the essence of the psalmodists' method was that they claimed, like Moore, to be able to teach people how to sing from notes in a short time. In this way they could travel from place to place, 'like unto excisemen' as Pope put it, teaching choir after choir and selling their books as they went. Their journeying was an economic necessity. Only by covering many parishes could they hope to make a living out of the pockets of the poor.

Some began operations in one region, but eventually settled in another. Michael Broome seems to have started in the Chilterns area. His first collection (PC 89), dating from about 1725, has a second title page which is almost identical in its wording to that of Francis Timbrell's book of similar date (PC 80). Several of the tunes in it are named after places in Buckinghamshire and Oxfordshire, including one by Broome himself called 'Wendover'. A copy belonged to 'Richard Minchin at Watlington in Oxfordshire'. The book was compiled jointly by Michael and John Broome, but we hear no more of John. Michael's next book (PC 102) called him 'singing master at Isleworth, Middlesex'. It contains several anthems, not found earlier, by George Gibbs, who later (in 1734) became organist at Bungay (MS 80/444: 125–30). Broome must have been building a connection in East Anglia, too, at this period. A copy of this second book is inscribed 'William Bidwell/Thetford/Anno Domini/1731'. John Buckenham in 1741 acknowledged that 'a considerable part' of the psalmody then known in Norfolk and Suffolk 'was introduced by Mr. Joseph Needham, and Mr. Michael Broom, ingenious teachers of the same' (PC 120: preface). Needham's collection (PC 119) has not survived. Buckenham took a number of pieces from Broome's third book (PC 108). Meanwhile, Broome moved to Birmingham, where he soon became a leading musical personality, and settled down as a bookseller and parish clerk of St Philip's church. Later he founded the Birmingham choral society and musical festival (Sutcliffe Smith: 11, 88–9).

John Hill's first book (PC 166) was published at Lydd in the 1750s, but the list of subscribers in it shows almost as many names from Northamptonshire as from Kent and Sussex. He was evidently building a practice in the Midlands. Later he settled at Rugby, where he brought out *Hill's church music* in 1788–91 (Schnapper mistakenly ascribes it to a different John Hill). This time the subscribers ranged over the Midland counties, and included 23 singing societies (i.e., choirs), thirteen clergymen (four of them incumbents of local parishes), three schoolmasters, one parish clerk, three organists, a music seller, a 'musician', an attorney, three excisemen, an ensign, an auctioneer, a land surveyor, a cordwainer, a maltster, and a Fellow of Magdalen College, Oxford.

Another peripatetic psalmodist was the eccentric William Tans'ur (Pl. 9). Born at Dunchurch about 1700, he issued his books successively from Ewell, 1734–5; Barnes, 1736; Cambridge, 1754, 1776; Stamford, 1756–9; Boston, 1761. He has also been traced at Leicester, Market Harborough and Witham. He dated some of his prefaces from 'the university of Cambridge', but his only claim to a connection with the university was the fact that his son was a chorister at St John's College. Others were dated from 'the ancient university of Stamford', an institution not otherwise on record. The last forty years of his life (1743–83) were 'spent chiefly at St. Neots, where he was a stationer, bookseller, and teacher of music' (*DNB*); he seems to have played no part in the music of the parish church there.

It was comparatively rare for a compiler to have any permanent office connected with a parish church, probably because this would have taken away the mobility that was necessary for his trade. In early days Abraham Barber, parish clerk at Wakefield, taught a choir some 14 miles distant. Broome, clerk at St Philip, Birmingham, distributed his books through 'the men who carry out the Northampton, Stamford, Coventry, and Birmingham papers' (PC 122: title page). He may have had some assistants who actually taught the country choirs in his neighbourhood. William Knapp, in addition to being a glover (H. P. Smith), was parish clerk at Poole. The first edition of his *A sett of new psalm-tunes and anthems* (1736) carried a list of 166 subscribers, who included nine local singing masters; it was dedicated to John Saintloe Esq., of Little Fontmill, Dorset. Editions of the book were published and distributed as follows, according to their title pages:

1st edn (1736) pub. Poole	sold at Wimborne, Sherborne, Dorchester, Blandford and Taunton
2nd edn (1741) pub. Poole	sold at Sherborne, Taunton, Salisbury, Exeter, Reading, and London
3rd edn (1747) pub. London	sold by 'all country booksellers'

We see rather clearly how Knapp's market expanded outside the possible range of his personal control. He was thus able to profit from many editions while retaining his position as parish clerk.

An established local position was held by the compiler of the most important country collection of all, John Chetham of Skipton. He was master of the Clerk's School there from 1723, and curate from 1741 at a salary of £30 a year; he died in 1746 (Frere & Frost: 667). The first edition of his *Book of psalmody* was printed by Pearson in London, but published at Sheffield, by Joseph Turner, in 1718. Although several other psalmodies were available in the West Riding, Chetham's was evidently the most acceptable, its nearest rival being James Green's. The fourth edition (1731) was published at Wakefield and sold at Barnsley, Leeds, Skipton, and Halifax (all West Riding), Chesterfield, and London. York, Bradford, Manchester and Newcastle [under Lyme] were later added to the list.

The wording of the original title page said the music was 'all set in four parts, within such a compass as will most naturally suit the voices in country churches'. Imitation of cathedral music was urged in the preface, and chants and anthems provided in the book, as well as some plain and a few ornate psalm tunes. Perhaps to help smooth the transition to elaborate choir music, Chetham provided also two examples of 'those psalms which the clerk gives out line by line ... which is called the old way of singing' (ex. 18). These disappeared from the second edition (1722), being replaced by the half-fuging-tune, half-set-piece already described. (See Table 10.)

The third edition (1724) saw some surprising changes. References to country churches were removed from title page and preface, and there was nothing about imitating cathedrals. A new, severe tone was adopted, echoing Bishop Gibson's charge of the same year:

The indifference, and even contempt that *psalmody* too often meets with, and that from persons of the best taste, generally arises from the meanness of the performance of it; not only in those places where the *old way* (as they usually term the ancient *psalm-tunes*) is still continued, but more especially amongst those that have been so far imposed upon, by the pretence of a *new method*, as to introduce such a wretched mixture of noise and confusion, as ought never to be heard in a Christian congregation.

Chetham firmly dissociated himself from this 'new method', and continued:

It is evident from experience, that singing in our parish churches and chapels may be improved to a great degree, and that where there is a competent number to learn, and due encouragement given, they may in a short time become masters of the greatest part of this book, and perform the Te deum, Jubilate &c. as in several churches they now do ... and therefore, it is much to be wished, that societies were formed in every parish, to promote this religious exercise that the better sort would not only contenance, but be themselves the first to come into them ...

> In this edition the number of psalm tunes are reduced to twenty, so many as are sufficient for the best part of the psalms in metre, and so few that they may soon be learned, and by being often repeated, the whole congregation become acquainted with them. (PC 86: preface)

The change of emphasis is reflected in the psalm tunes, which are, as the preface suggests, fewer and simpler than in the first two editions. The 'fuging' Psalm 24 has disappeared; many remaining tunes are shorn of decorations.

The severity of the third edition may have been unpopular with Chetham's public. At all events, in the fourth edition (1731) the old preface was restored, and all the fripperies of the new, ornate tunes were brought back. In due course fully fuging tunes were added to the selection, though it retained a core of ancient tunes.

Chetham's *Psalmody* was widely used in the West Riding and beyond. It became firmly entrenched at Halifax parish church (Pl. 26), so much so that when an organ was introduced there in 1766 it did not result, as one might have expected, in the replacement of Chetham by a book designed for town churches. (Chetham furnished his book with figured basses from 1736 onwards.) The first organist, William Herschel, held office for only three months, before leaving to begin his career in astronomy. His successor, Thomas Stopford, served for fifty-three years (1766–1819). During that time three more editions of Chetham were brought out, published at Leeds, the last in 1787. Then, in 1811, Stopford himself revised and added to the book, in an edition published at Halifax. His successor, John Houldsworth, again revised and augmented it in an edition of 1832, which was known as 'Houldsworth's Cheetham's Psalmody' and which, in turn, went into twenty editions, the last appearing in 1868. They were dedicated to the vicar and clergy of the parish of Halifax. Still later organists added supplements, and there is no doubt that in the nineteenth century, at least, Halifax had taken control of a book which was still widely used around the West Riding. Some of the tunes were retained throughout all 32 editions, and it was on the material in this book that Halifax parish church built its exceptionally high reputation for psalmody (Houseman).

Choirs rarely purchased enough copies of a book for each member to use one. The largest number of which a record has been found is 12, which was the number of copies of John Buckenham's *The psalm singer's devout exercise* (1741) 'subscribed for by the gentlemen and other inhabitants' of Sibton and Peasenhall 'to the use of the company of singers', apparently a joint choir for the two villages (PC 120: list of subscribers). More typically a choir would buy one, two or three copies. In Plate 16 a single copy is made to suffice. But then they would often set to work copying the music, either in the form of scores or of partbooks: examples of both survive. Dorset county museum, for example, has five related partbooks dating from about 1765 to 1830, probably used in a Dorset church; they include some psalm tunes and anthems in score (MS 6. See also Millington: 9; Galpin, 1906: 103–4). The music in these books seems almost always to come from a printed collection (often with explicit acknowledgment of the source) so that they could be used by singers or players while the choir leader, parish clerk or organist used the printed book. In Plate 22 (*c.* 1840), books of

Table 10. *Contents of successive editions of Chetham's* Psalmody *and supplements (1718–1885)*

Compiler	Chetham							Stopford	Houldsworth		Frobisher	Gauntlett	Roberts
Edition no.	1	2	3	4–6	7	8	9–11		1	4–20			
Date	1718	1722	1724	1731–41	1745	1752	1767–87	1811	1832	1838–68	1855	1878	1885?
PC	71	71/2	86	86, 111a	111a	111a	111a	338	359	359	389a	406	404
Tunes, etc.													
'Old way of singing'	2	—	—	—	—	—	—	—	—	—	—	—	—
Pre-1690 tunes	20	20	4	21	21	21	21	21	7	7	6	4	3
Post-1690: plain	12	12	7	12	12	15	12	23	20	21	32	104	25
ornate	8	8	5	8	8	9	8	32	57	56	69	3	—
solo/duet	—	1	1	1	1	2	1	12	51	51	11	3	1
fuging	—	—	—	—	—	1	1	5	9	9	4	—	—
Set pieces	1	1	1	1	1	1	1	3	—	—	1	—	—
Metrical chant	—	—	—	—	—	—	—	—	—	—	—	1	—
Anthems, etc.													
Anthems	15	15	11	14	15	15	15	8	1	1	3	5	—
Canticle settings	—	—	2	2	2	2	2	1	—	—	—	6	—
Liturgical music													
Chants	3	4	5	5	5	5	5	9	96	96	90	21	132
Responses	—	—	—	—	—	—	—	1	16	16	13	6	9
Doxologies	—	—	1	—	—	—	—	—	10	10	6	—	—
Sanctus	—	—	—	—	—	—	—	—	—	—	1	—	—
Creed	—	—	—	—	—	—	—	—	—	—	—	1	1
Beatitudes (chant)	—	—	—	—	—	—	—	—	—	—	—	1	—

'*Tunes, etc.*' are settings of metrical texts. 'Plain' tunes are tunes with not more than four melismas, 'ornate' tunes have five or more melismas, solo/duet tunes have variations in texture (one or more parts silent some of the time) but no text overlap, fuging tunes have contrapuntal entries with text overlap. Set pieces have continuous music instead of repeating the same music for each verse. '*Anthems, etc.*' are polyphonic settings of prose texts. 'Responses' means settings of the responses to the commandments in the communion service.

different sizes are being used simultaneously. It may well be that the conductor and the clarinet player are using printed scores, the cellist and the adults in the right background are reading from partbooks, and the children in the front row, singing the tune, have only word books: the children's are open at a page near the end, and the Old or New Version was often bound at the end of the prayer book.

Some printed collections are obviously laid out primarily to provide material for hand-copied part-books, for the scores are printed in such a way that the parts are not in vertical alignment. A greater oddity is a book printed in score with blank staves throughout, with words of psalms *and anthems* carefully underlaid, leaving the purchaser to fill in the clefs and notes by hand. Two books of this sort are extant:*

A choice collection of psalms and hymns, with Timbrel's anthems ... Printed with lines ruled for two and three voices, but without notes, so that any person may adapt what tune they please to the words. Northampton: W. Dicey [*c.* 1740?]. (Copy: Library of Congress, Washington.)

Widdowes, D. (of Calne, singing-master). *The young psalm-singers guide, containing a curious collection of psalms, hymns and anthems. The whole so contriv'd, that all masters and admirers of the heavenly art of musick and divine psalmody, may put what tunes they please to each psalm, hymn, or anthem, in a few minutes. The third edition, with several additions.* Gloucester: printed by R. Raikes [*c.* 1760?]. (Copy: Dorset County Museum, Dorchester.)

Performing practice: the clef problem

Throughout the history of country psalmody, progress was hindered by an ambiguity in the use of clefs, which was the outward sign of a long struggle for predominance between the tenor and treble voices.

From the beginnings of polyphony in the early middle ages, the *cantus firmus* or leading melody had been sung by the tenor voice, and any other vocal or instrumental parts were constructed around it. This naturally reflected the fact that men had done most of the singing before the polyphonic era, so that the traditional chant melodies were sung in the range that suited the average male voice. When polyphony was gradually emancipated from the chant, it became possible to give equal weight to all the voices, with women or trained choirboys in the treble line. But in this situation the ear tends to give its chief attention to the topmost voice. With the growing importance of the audience in the baroque period, therefore, there was a tendency to treat the treble or soprano voice as the leading one, and the lower voices as mere accompaniments.

But in country churches the dominance of the tenor voice continued long after it had declined in art music. There was still a reluctance to let women play a prominent role in singing in church, and children could not be entrusted with the leading part unless they were soundly taught. In town

---

* They are not listed in the bibliography under 'printed collections of music', for they contain no music.

churches after the Restoration, as we know, this object was achieved by the foundation of charity schools, and the result was a new treble-based form of psalmody, often in practice for trebles and organ only. But in country churches this was hardly possible; nor was there ever likely to be a sufficient level of choral skill to allow four-part polyphony to be sung correctly and with a proper balance among the parts. The tenor voice, carrying the tune, was sung loudest, and continued to be the mainstay of the whole performance. The social dominance of men was clearly reflected in this musical imbalance – indeed it was dramatised in the word setting of such a tune as ex. 39. Difficulties arose whenever the country psalmody tradition came into contact with the treble-based style of art music.

The Old Version psalm books had given the tunes in the C clef (variously placed on the stave), and, of course, East and Ravenscroft placed the tune in the tenor voice for all their four-part harmonisations, as did Playford in 1671. But in his 1677 book Playford had begun the new era by setting the tunes on two staves, the upper carrying the tune in the G clef, the lower the bass in the F clef. The medius part (also in the G clef) was printed separately. The two-stave score was beautifully adaptable. It could be played on a keyboard instrument, or sung by voices in either octave, as Playford pointed out in the preface, doubled if necessary by melody instruments. And in fact his book was the ancestor of both town and country psalmody books of the eighteenth century.

For two-part settings, which predominated in the early days of country choirs, this format presented no problem. When choirs aspired to three- or four-part music, they could use scores of the traditional kind, but this would mean that the tenors would have to sing from the now unfamiliar C clef. So there was a tendency to print the tenor part in the G clef. The four-part score either had three G clefs and an F, the alto and tenor both transposing down an octave (this was first tried by Elias Hall in 1706 (PC 56)); or it had G clefs for the treble and tenor, an alto C clef for the alto, and an F clef for the bass (this seems to have been invented by William Tans'ur in 1734 (PC 110)).

But there were several factors encouraging the doubling of the tenor part an octave higher. If the music was a well-known psalm tune, the women and children in the congregation would sing the tune. If the music was new, and had to be learned by the choir, it might well be tried out with the accompaniment of a keyboard instrument, and the player would use the two lower staves as his score, playing the tenor part with the right hand at written pitch. Lacking a keyboard instrument, a melody instrument might be used, and it too would play the tune at treble pitch, as did Hely's viol and Hart's flute (PC 44, 69). If women or children were admitted to the choir, they would find it easiest to sing the tenor part, which was either a well-known traditional tune or at least the most prominent part of the music.

In many performances of such music, therefore, the soprano and alto parts as written would have been overshadowed by the doubling of the tenor part an octave higher. This was actually directed, for instance, in the preface to *The psalm-singer's necessary companion* (1700). The soprano and alto parts, in fact, were often dispensable. Chetham's music was 'all set in four parts . . . but may be sung in three or two, without any disallowances'.

Arnold (1741) in his advice to composers, showed his awareness of the problems of writing music for varying choral forces. He advised composing the tenor first – an interesting archaism. For three parts

you must make a cantus, or a treble, to be sung in the eighth below... keep your cantus rather below the tenor than above... Tunes of four parts may be sung in three, by omitting the contra, and singing the treble an eighth below... Observe, that two [parallel] fifths, or two eighths, may be taken in four parts, rather than spoil the air of the tune, but let it be between one of the upper parts [and] the bass; for if they are between the tenor and bass, it is not so well; for where there are not voices for the two upper parts, there will be a sad disallowance. (PC 117: I, 20–3)

Tans'ur explicitly permitted the omission of either or both the upper voices in his own psalm tunes (PC 110: II, preface). In more than one case, manuscript additions have been found in the tenor part of an anthem or fuging tune, replacing rests, clearly with the object of keeping the music going when the upper voices are lacking: Fig. 6 provides an example. John Crompton in 1778 warned that 'where a congregation chooses to join in general, the engaging in two parts only, viz. the tenor and bass, is most likely to be attended with... agreeable harmony' (PC 235: xxxv).

As time went on the practice of singing the tune in the tenor came more and more to seem primitive or provincial, being out of step with the practice of art music. Some compilers, especially if they wanted to make their music useful for town as well as country churches, firmly placed the tunes in the upper voice, and drew attention to their action: so Michael Broome, John Alcock the younger, James Kempson, and John Barker, all active in the Birmingham region. John Hill, who used the G clef for the treble and tenor parts, added a footnote:

Please to observe that the upper part is the principal throughout the whole book, and where there is no treble voices to sing it, the tenor must, for it must by no means be left out. If any part is omitted, it must be that next the bass. (PC 264: 2)

But the practice of treating the part 'next the bass' as the melody, singable equally by tenors or trebles, was well established in many places, until at last it actually became the treble. Its status is ambiguous in Aaron Williams's *New universal psalmodist* of 1770. He defended his use of the G clef for all three upper parts and 'placing the air next above the bass':

According to the rules of composition, the treble does or ought always to contain the principal air of the piece; but custom has rendered it otherwise, especially in psalm tunes, the air or church part being generally found in the tenor, though it must be allowed that they were originally in the trebles... One thing may be further said of it, that those who play on the harpsichord, &c. will, doubtless, like to have the two principal parts so near together. (PC 202: preface)

Williams's reading of history was doubtful, but his perception of present customs was clear. A certain indication of the transformation that was gradually taking place is seen in successive editions of Chetham's *Psalmody*, as used at Halifax parish church. Though an organ had been acquired in 1766, Chetham's book continued in use, and until the eleventh edition (1787) the music was still printed with C clefs and the 'leading part' in the tenor. Nevertheless, it was evidently sung by trebles as well as tenors.

In Stopford's revised edition of 1811, he added a footnote to Chetham's introduction:

Note. The tenor or leading part and principal air in the old editions, properly belongs to the treble, and is so arranged in this book, and that which was before treble is now tenor; perhaps the treble part being given to the tenor, was to suit congregations, which principally consisted of tenor voices; notwithstanding which the treble part in this edition may still be sung by tenor voices.

He inserted a further note at the end of the introduction:

N.B. In all former editions of Cheetham's Psalmody, the principal air or melody of each tune is in the tenor clef, but in this edition the treble is substituted, with the bass properly figured underneath, which is a great accommodation to performers on the organ, piano-forte, violin, or flute, as likewise to private families and learners, besides facilitating congregational singing. The counter and tenor parts are also in the G or treble clef. (PC 338)

Fig. 7 shows what Stopford actually did to the music. In the anthems the treble and tenor parts changed places on the page, the music remaining unchanged. In the psalm tunes, where there was a distinct 'tune', the treble and tenor parts had actually changed places. The trebles now sang the tune an octave higher, and the tenors sang the old treble part an octave lower. The same thing was done in many psalmody books, and a common format in the early nineteenth century had the voices arranged as in Fig. 7b.

The older method of keeping the tune in the tenor did not persist far into the nineteenth century. In 1797 it was already a curiosity:

The usual method of executing the four parts in country churches is very singular; for the air, or principal part, is uniformly sung by tenor voices, and the other two parts, which should be accompaniments to the air and bass, are sung by treble and counter-tenor voices. (PC 307: preface; quoted Macdermott, 1922: 84)

So he concludes that women and children should sing the tune an octave above the men. By 1827 a writer said that only one work of 'modern date' still placed the tune in the tenor, and insisted that 'the first treble should always be sung by women and children *alone*; or if they cannot be prevailed upon to sing with sufficient confidence by themselves, one soft tenor might be allowed to lead them' (D. E. Ford: 60–1). The change placed the men in difficulty, for they now had to learn to sing subordinate parts. But this is a problem that we must postpone for a later chapter.

There is evidence that in many anthems, as well as psalm tunes, the treble and tenor parts were exchanged in actual performance. Some anthems have survived in two forms, with the treble and tenor parts interchanged. Examples are 'Christ being raised from the dead' (one version in PC 62, 101, the other in some copies of PC 80); 'How long wilt thou forget me' (both versions appearing in the same year, in PC 71, 72). They show clearly that parochial anthems were not, in practice, truly polyphonic compositions in which all voices had equal weight. In them, as well as in psalm tunes (and, for that matter, chants, hymns and set pieces), the tenor had been the leading voice, the upper parts subordinate or even dispensable. When in the later eighteenth century it became more common for women or children to join men in the parish choir, they would often sing the tenor part in

Fig. 7 Comparison between the 1752 and 1811 editions of Chetham's *Book of psalmody*

- (a) psalm tune, 1752 (PC 111a/8, p. 1)
- (b) psalm tune, 1811 (PC 338, p. 1)
- (c) anthem, 1752 (PC 111a/8, p. 167)
- (d) anthem, 1811 (PC 338, p. 215)

anthems, either in two-part harmony, or, if the men had sufficient skill, with the subordinate 'treble' part now sung by tenors.

It is true that, although the tenor part was dominant in anthems as well as psalm tunes, there were occasions when it was silent, as when there was a soprano solo in an anthem, or a line in an elaborate psalm tune for trebles and altos only. How was this performed when there were only two parts in the choir? The answer is provided by Arnold: 'Note, that in some of the anthems in this book the treble sings alone, and where there are not voices to reach that part, the tenor may sing it in an eighth below'.

In all this the bass part was more or less unaffected, but the alto or 'counter' part was also undergoing change. In early times it was intended for male counter-tenors, and was from Playford onwards often printed separately as an optional third part above the basic two-part arrangement of tenor and bass. In some editions, the part remained in the C clef even when the tenor part had been transposed to the G clef, but from 1706 onwards many books had the alto part in the G clef also, but printed (like the tenor) an octave above the sounding pitch, not as in modern use. The confusion that sometimes resulted is exactly described by Thomas Billington (1784):

I also recollect to have heard a very great absurdity in four-part singing, which is, that the composer having thrown the contra-tenor part into the treble clef, merely to accommodate those who should happen not to be acquainted with the contra-tenor [clef], a great error has been committed: For the trebles have naturally caught at what has appeared to be the highest part, and of course have taken the contra-tenor instead of their own... Hence the melody [treble] has been consigned to the tenor, the tenor to the contra-tenor, and the contra-tenor to the treble, which, I need not add, has produced the most horrid effect that can be conceived; and what before were fourths, and of course agreeable to the ear, have become fifths. So that instead of a bar of succeeding sixths [first-inversion triads], I have heard eight succeeding perfect fifths [root-position triads], which is always avoided in composition, and is more grating to the ear than the most complicated discord whatever. (PC 251: 3–4)

Exactly this process took place in one of the best known parochial anthems, 'Great is the Lord', though it may not have been due in this case to confusion about the meaning of the G clef. Two versions were in use over a period of half a century or more, and the chief difference between them was the reordering of the three upper parts. It is likely, though not certain, that the original version was that shown in ex. 32, which is taken from an early collection of Michael Broome's. Later Broome ascribed the anthem to Thomas Everitt, of whom nothing is known, but the five-part Alleluia was based on a passage in Purcell's Te deum in D.

Later (and perhaps earlier too) Broome published the anthem with Everitt's own four-part Alleluia instead (ex. 33). In a version printed by Francis Timbrell, however, the original tenor part was put on the upper stave in the G clef and clearly marked '1 Treable'; the original soprano part followed as '2 Treable'; the original alto, in the alto C clef as before, as 'Tenor'; and the bass remained unchanged. All three versions were copied in later collections, and their vicissitudes can be followed in detail in Table 11. There may have been a geographical boundary separating the use of the three versions (and their later derivatives), but if so it does not emerge clearly from the information in the table.

The addition of instruments doubling the upper parts was one good reason for using G clefs, as Arnold pointed out in 1779 (PC 117/1779: iv). But it could add to the confusion: William Dixon reminded country musicians that '*alto* and *tenor*, but *alto* more particularly, when written in the G clef, if an instrument is made use of, should be played in the octave below; otherwise it will cause an inversion of the harmony throughout, which is generally productive of bad effect' (PC 275: preface). William

Table 11. *Versions of the anthem 'Great is the Lord' (exx. 32, 33)*

Source	Date	Region	Voices	Parts	Alleluia	Attribution	Notes
PC 102 Broome	−1731	Chilterns?	SATB	1234	(1)		ex. 32
PC 107 Broome	*c.* 1733	E. Anglia?	SATB	1234	(2)	Everitt	ex. 33
PC 80/1735 Timbrell	*c.* 1735	Northants.	SSTB	3124	(2)		
PC 118 Sreeve	1740	S. England	SSTB	3124	(2)		
PC 120 Buckenham	1741	Suffolk	SATB	1234	(2)	from Broome	
PC 122 Broome	−1744	Birmingham	SATB	1234	(1)	Everitt and Purcell	
PC 130 Evison	1747	Sussex	ATB	234	(2)		revised
PC 134 East	*c.* 1748	Leics.	SATB	1234	(1)	Everitt'	(a)
PC 117/2 Arnold	1750	Essex	SATB	1234	(2)	Michael Wise*	
PC 138 Moore	1750	Manchester	SATB	1234	(2)		
PC 144 Milner	1751	S.E. England	SATB	1234	(2)		
PC 88/5 Holdroyd	1753	W. Yorks.	SATB	3124	(2)		
PC 155 Tans'ur	1754–5	Cambridge	SATB	1234	(2)		
PC 182a Wilkins	*c.* 1760	Oxon.	SATB	1234	(2)		
PC 174 Adams	*c.* 1760	S.E. England	ATB	234	(2)		(b)
PC 175/2 Ashworth	1765	Midlands?	SATB	1234	(2)		
Bayley, *New Universal Harmony*	1773	New England	SATB	1234	(2)	from Arnold	
PC 239 Addington	1780	Leics.	ATB	234	(2)		(b)
Jocelyn, *The Chorister's Companion* III	1783	New England	SATB	1234	(2)		

'Parts' 1, 2, 3, 4: the four lines of music in the earliest version.

Alleluia (1): in five parts (SSATB), adapted from Purcell's Te deum in D, where it is a setting of the words 'Day by day we magnify thee'. It later appeared separately as 'A chorus for 5 voices' in Josiah Flagg's *A collection of the best psalm-tunes* (Boston, Massachusetts, 1764) and other American collections (repr. Marrocco & Gleason: 59–60).

Alleluia (2): in four parts (SATB), attributed to Thomas Everitt in PC 107

(a) with an added alto part in the 3-part section

(b) transposed to A major.

* Attribution in the 7th edition (1779) only.

Gresham reported that 'for want of sufficient voices, the treble is often omitted, and the counter made completely to overpower the air, by being played on a clarinet or two, and in the treble octave' (PC 307: preface; quoted Macdermott, 1922: 84). The same effect was observed by Canon Galpin when he heard one of the last of the church bands over a century later. The tune, now in the soprano part, was sung by the congregation, but the alto and tenor parts were played an octave above their proper pitch by the clarinet and flute respectively (Galpin, 1893: 32; Galpin, 1906: 102).

The style of country psalmody

Psalmody for country choirs in the eighteenth and early nineteenth century amounts to a very considerable body of music. In printed sources alone we can find over a thousand psalm and hymn tunes, several hundred services, anthems and set pieces, and various chants, canons and miscellaneous pieces. No other class of music exists in greater quantity in English printed sources of the eighteenth century, except the song with keyboard accompaniment (Schnapper: count of items). Yet until recently this music had never been even briefly described by any historian. The detailed studies that do exist (Barbour; R. T. Daniel; Britton; Wienandt & Young) are perceptive and valuable, but they consider the music only as a precursor of early American psalmody, which, of course, it is. These writers acknowledge that the music of the New England psalmodists, once thought to be a purely indigenous American phenomenon (Macdougall: 50), was in fact so closely related to English parochial psalmody that it can be regarded as part of the same musical culture. (This was first conclusively demonstrated by Irving Lowens (:237–48).) But they acclaim William Billings as the one composer, either English or American, who transcended the limitations of this style, and succeeded in creating original works of art by resourceful extension of its possibilities.

Very little English music of the country psalmody period is readily available for study. A considerable number of hymn tunes in modern use have their origins in country psalmody books, as already pointed out, but almost always in greatly modified forms. Ralph Daniel has transcribed five anthems (using American sources):

William Tans'ur	'O clap your hands together'	from PC 110 (1734)
William Knapp	'The beauty of Israel is slain'	from PC 115 (1738)
Joseph Stephenson	'Behold I bring you glad tidings'	from PC 171 (1760)
Benjamin West	'O Lord our governor'	from PC 173 (1760)
Aaron Williams	'I was glad when they said unto me'	from PC 189 (1763)

Otherwise only brief excerpts are available (Barbour: Macdermott, 1948; Wienandt & Young).

A detailed analysis of the style of country psalmody cannot be accommodated in a general history of parish church music. But a few points about it can and should be made. The music under discussion was created by unschooled composers. Their models were provided by professionals, who distilled and simplified the style of art music of the day. Beyond these they could only build on the established popular traditions of psalm singing and folk music, which preserved within them some features of the art music of much earlier times.

It is not surprising that harmony was the side of music that gave country singing teachers the most trouble. However industrious they might be in trying to inform themselves on this subject, they could never acquire such a mastery of harmony as came easily to a cathedral organist. The accepted rules of harmony found in standard treatises, which were often copied by the psalmodists in their introductions, were in themselves quite inadequate as a basis for learning to compose. We find pieces that literally obey most of these rules, and yet lack any feeling for the harmonic style that underlies them. Some of the rules proved too stringent; we find Arnold (already quoted), Tans'ur and others modifying the rule against consecutive fifths in a way that was universally condemned in art music until more than a century later. Other rules actually stated in the introductions were broken in the music, whether deliberately or not.

Yet we certainly cannot accept the judgment of contemporary

professionals that country psalmody was 'incorrect', a judgment implying absolute standards which today are untenable. Obviously, eighteenth-century psalmodists had as much right to change the conventions of musical style as twentieth-century dodecaphonists. Even if some features were originally due to inadvertent errors, they were found acceptable in performance, and were often copied unaltered from edition to edition, and from collection to collection. We must assume that they represent the considered preference of the musicians concerned.

At the same time, much that seems strange or even unintelligible in the harmony of country psalmody is easier to understand if we recollect that it is basically two-part harmony – a fact which was demonstrated in the last section. Some of the music (exx. 30, 31) was actually limited to two parts. In most of the rest of it, the tenor and bass mattered much more than the other parts. Most of the composers probably found it difficult to hear mentally the sound of music in four parts, and many of them were unable to try it out on a keyboard instrument. They began by composing the tenor and the bass (as Arnold recommended). For the sake of variety in anthems or fuging tunes, they might insert a few passages for upper voices only. But in the full four-part sections the upper voices were added to music that was already complete in the composer's mind. They would be constrained to obey the rules as far as possible, but in fact many unexplained dissonances would often appear. (This is obviously the case in ex. 32, especially bars 4–12: the tenor and bass make good sense by themselves, but the whole is unintelligible.) It did not matter very much. Often the music would be sung without the upper voices; if it was sung in four parts, the upper voices would be less prominent than the tenor and bass; performances in which all four parts were sung correctly as written were probably rare. On the other hand after the rise of church bands the full harmony would be more clearly heard, yet there is little sign of any change in harmonic style following this development. Country congregations had heard little art music, and probably treated singers' efforts with unquestioning respect. So the harmonic style became acceptable in a way that is now difficult to imagine (Eden: 17).

The most immediately striking fact about this style is the predominance of consonances, especially at cadences, where open fifths and plain octaves seem to be used just as commonly as full triads. This might come naturally from thinking primarily in two parts, but it can also be interpreted as a survival from an earlier period. Closer analysis reveals that fourths and fifths, in this music, were treated as more or less equivalent to thirds and sixths. So we find a bare fourth treated as a full consonance (ex. 30, bars 21, 27, 35), though in the same work it serves as an expressive dissonance (bar 5). We find also a notable tolerance for consecutive fifths and octaves. In extreme instances one is even reminded of the earliest form of polyphony, parallel organum: there is a passage in 'O God, my heart is ready' (PC 68) where the tenor is accompanied in *parallel* fifths and octaves alone for six notes, and a similar one in 'Christ being raised from the dead' (PC 62, 80, 101).

The root-position triad (or its cousin the open fifth) is by far the most common chord. As R. T. Daniel pointed out, 'it is with Tans'ur almost his only harmonic resource. For example there are only nine inversions in "O clap your hands"' (:56). The same is true of a great deal of this music (exx. 31, 34, 43). Sometimes the only departure is a tonic six-four as the antepenultimate chord at a cadence, or (much more rarely) a 5–4 suspension (ex. 32, bar 27; ex. 35, bar 71). The characteristic phrase ending is a plain, unadorned perfect cadence, often marked to be sung slow (ex. 44). However varied the texture of the music, it is always punctuated by these cadences, the great majority of which are generally in the tonic key.

Some of the country composers were discreet enough to stay within the harmonic domain that they could fully control, and confined themselves either to two parts (ex. 30) or to simple progressions of consonances with only passing notes between (ex. 42). Sometimes the result was a beautiful and moving simplicity, as in the chords of the opening and closing sections of Robert Barber's 'By the rivers of Babylon' (ex. 34). Other composers were more aggressive, and aspired to write full polyphony in four or even more parts. Some sharp and surprising dissonances often resulted. Suspension and resolution were not much used: the dissonances arose through the clashing of melodic lines, with little regard to harmonic effect. Such treatment resembles that of medieval or modern rather than classical music. It is not surprising to find the most extreme examples in passages of imitative counterpoint, whether in anthems or fuging tunes. Lacking the skill to control the harmony and the part-writing simultaneously, they maintained the contrapuntal imitation regardless of the resulting harmony. After a wild passage of this kind the parts always come together again for a strong, straight perfect cadence (ex. 33, bars 7–10; ex. 35, bars 62–72). One might put it that the composer licensed each voice to take off on its own for a space, provided that all was made good in a deliberate show of consonance at the end.

A few of the composers were totally incompetent to deal with the musical problems that confronted them. Benjamin West's tune 'Watford', for example (ex. 43), is comprehensible as a duet for tenor and bass, indeed quite expressive, but the four-part harmony is largely meaningless and must have been almost unperformable in places, though the sounds may prove intriguing to a modern chorus. In the tenor voice in bar 9 the note C flat alternates with B sharp, which makes little sense even when the sharp is taken to mean 'natural'. The use of the key of E flat minor is an example of pretentiousness, also found in meaningless directions which West strews about his scores (such as 'Alemand', 'Concerto grosso', 'Euphony'). Another. extreme example of musical illiteracy is a tune called 'Buckingham' printed in PC 120. The compiler, John Buckenham, says the tune is 'by Israel Holdroyd', and it is indeed taken from a book by Holdroyd (PC 88/3: p. 21). But where Holdroyd clearly intended the first two staves to be sung first, and then the third and fourth, Buckenham puts them together in one score to be sung simultaneously, with excruciating results.

On the other hand, a certain degree of unexplained dissonance was not only tolerated, but apparently prized, for it is found in some of the most popular music of the whole period. An example is the anthem 'Great is the Lord' (exx. 32, 33). Daniel rightly points to 'the primitive character of the whole harmonic scheme' in this anthem, and says 'there are quite a few dissonant combinations which cannot be explained in terms of the usual non-harmonic tones, and many violations of the "rules", such as parallel fifths and octaves'. We have already seen how this anthem was printed and reprinted over a period of fifty years, even reaching American collections. Although it was several times revised in one way or another (see Table 11), the basic harmonies were left untouched, and presumably found acceptable.

Daniel also points out the rare use of an augmented sixth chord at bar 35 of this anthem. Other deliberate chromatic chords are found occasionally, such as the bare diminished fifth (ex. 30, bar 9) or the augmented triad (ex. 34, bar 30), but these are not really typical of the style.

In the interrelated matters of melody, rhythm, and text setting, the country psalmodists also had a style of their own, bearing little resemblance to that of their professional contemporaries. Some of the composers had considerable lyrical power, which is shown at its best in passages that are unfettered by elaborate harmony and counterpoint (ex. 44; ex. 35, bars 44–56). The melody tends to be highly ornate, sometimes incorporating long melismas that may add extra bars to the normal phrase lengths in the case of a metrical setting. Some compilers encouraged further ornamentation of the melodies by including a section on ornaments in their introductions, and others decorated melodic lines of tunes and anthems taken from older collections.

An interesting archaism is the apparent survival of melodic rules of *musica ficta*. For example, in Knapp's original harmonisation of his tune 'Wareham' (ex. 44), the alto part shows a persistent tendency to sharpen the note F when it is rising to G, regardless of harmony. One is tempted to add an editorial sharp in analogous cases, such as bar 6.

Verbal accentuation was a weak point of many country composers, and it has been said that composers such as Tans'ur had 'apparent difficulty in reconciling the chosen metre to the textual, musical, and harmonic rhythms, with a resultant awkwardness in all'. Barbour points out, though, that many apparent anomalies of rhythm are really due to a misunderstanding of rhythmic notation. If one disregards the placing of the barlines, and sometimes the time signature as well, it often turns out that the composer has not produced a false rhythm at all, but has merely notated it wrongly (Barbour: 14–42). The last section of ex. 41, also quoted by Barbour in this connection, is a good case in point. Although Tans'ur has chosen to write this passage in $\frac{3}{4}$, the contrapuntal entries occur at regular intervals of four crotchet beats, and only the last four bars have any real feeling of triple time.

But there are other cases where a change of notation is not enough to show the rhythmic conception. In a fuging tune by East (ex. 42), the voices enter with a similar phrase at three-beat intervals and in triple time; yet the phrase itself is really in common time, judging by the accents of the words and of the poetic metre. We have thus an independent metrical scheme for each voice, and they cannot be combined into a single meaningful barring scheme. Examples of this phenomenon, called 'free rhythm' by Barbour, are common in this music, and they show in another way how the country psalmodists, freed from the strict conventions of art music, could allow the individual voices to take off on their own from time to time.

It was in the matter of texture and form that they showed the greatest boldness and ingenuity. The cathedral anthem provided a model for sectional construction which was followed in the more ambitious parochial anthems: changes of time signature, tempo, and vocal texture were common with each new phrase of text. The practice was extended to elaborate psalm tunes: the model for the fuging tune (ex. 39) already showed how this might be done. But in the anthem there were many opportunities for affective contrasts and musical imagery to illustrate the successive ideas in the text, and the parochial composers were far more direct and uninhibited in taking hold of these opportunities than cathedral composers of the same period. They showed a particular liking for such colourful texts as 'By the rivers of Babylon we sat down and wept' (ex. 34), 'Lift up your heads, O ye gates' (the prose form of ex. 39), or 'O clap your hands together, all ye people'. In their innocence they were not overawed by texts dealing with such sublime subjects as the Resurrection. George FFitch,* in 'Hallelujah, now is Christ risen' (ex. 35), used every device that occurred to him for dramatising the text. At three points (bars 11–26, 27–40, 127–146) the well-worn minor–major contrast illustrates the transition from death to immortality, but it sounds fresh in this context. FFitch also used bouncy dotted rhythms (33–42, 73–85, 160–3) that would have shocked a cathedral chapter, even one accustomed to Restoration anthems, and he repeated phrases of text beyond what was normally acceptable.

The most remarkable passages in this anthem use the chorus in an inventive, surprisingly 'modern' way, concentrating on sheer sound effects often at the expense of melody, harmony, and text intelligibility. At the words 'But we shall [all] be changed, In a moment, in the twinkling of an eye, at the last trump' (1 Corinthians 15:51–2), FFitch changes tempo to 'Allegro ma non presto', and in bars 62–70 provides an astonishing passage in which the counterpoint is largely textual, relying for its effect on the rapid articulation of syllables. At most points in this passage the harmony is quite bare and non-functional. The phrase 'at the last trump' is introduced in the middle, not so much to project the additional words as to make a slight variation in the sound effect. In another rapid passage (147–59), during multiple repetitions of the text 'But thanks be to God', different voices are singled out to sustain the word 'thanks' with its open vowel, another 'modern' effect. By contrast, many passages are in plain chordal homophony, often in a simple yet not quite predictable harmonic progression which greatly enhances the text (e.g., bars 119–34).

This inventiveness and originality in text setting is characteristic of many country psalmody composers, and in itself makes their music worthy of greater attention. However uneducated and even unmusical many of them may have been, they were well versed in the Bible and metrical psalms, and were familiar with many musical settings of them, as were those who sang

---

* The two capital F's were an integral part of this composer's surname, as is made clear in the list of subscribers, which includes several of his relatives. They are equipped with two F's, while other subscribers whose names begin with F get only one.

or heard the music. In spite of this, some, notably Tans'ur, felt free to alter the texts at will (R. T. Daniel: 54–5), an example that was followed by William Billings and other American composers. We may be sure that their audience noticed and appreciated both textual and musical departures from tradition, even if they did not approve of them. In this side of their work, more than in harmony and counterpoint, the psalmodists knew exactly what they were doing.

The church bands

As can be seen from Tables 7 and 8 (pp. 149–50), church bands, including treble as well as bass instruments, were uncommon before 1770, but became rather widely popular after that date (Pl. 17), and were taken into account by some compilers of psalmody books. The most detailed account of the church bands has been given by Canon K. H. Macdermott, whose sympathetic picture of the 'old church gallery minstrels', as he called them, was based on a lifetime of indefatigable investigation. Macdermott studied church records, first in his own county of Sussex and then in other parts of the country; examined old instruments and psalmody books that he found in the churches; questioned dozens of people who had taken part in the singing and playing or who remembered it; and maintained a large correspondence with enthusiasts throughout the country. He published his findings in two books (1922, 1948), and left quantities of papers giving further evidence (MS 23; MS 30).

Unfortunately Macdermott was not methodical enough to provide a really reliable and complete account of the bands. He rarely gave a source or even an approximate date for the many anecdotes he told. His 'table of musical instruments used in Sussex churches in the past' (1922: 91–2) is in itself most interesting, covering 106 churches and parochial chapels and listing well over 200 instruments said to have been played in them. But again no sources or dates are given, and one cannot know which instruments were played together at one time. Another table (1948: 67–70) lists 258 places in 33 English counties that had bands; 91 of them are in Sussex, but Macdermott points out that this is merely because he had made a special study of Sussex churches, and adds that 'probably Yorkshire, Lincolnshire and Norfolk had more than Sussex'. His interest in the quaint and the bizarre leads him to dwell on extraordinary bands, or ones that included unusual instruments, and these are the ones whose composition he gives in full detail in the text.

To gain a balanced impression of the church bands one must turn to other sources. Table 12 provides a sample. It seems that bands usually varied from two to five or six instruments, with occasionally a larger number, perhaps on a special occasion when neighbouring bands united. Whereas some of the earliest bands were formed in the north of England (as Table 7, p. 149 suggests), their last home was the south-west. The band at Winterbourne Abbas, observed by Galpin in 1893, is usually said to have been the last (Trask); but in a survey of church music in the diocese of Truro (i.e., the county of Cornwall) carried out in 1895, 18 out of 219

Table 12. *Make-up of sample parish church bands*

Plate	Dates	Violin	Viola	Cello	Flute	Oboe	Vox humana	Clarinet	Bassoon	Total	Voices	Source
Westbourne (Sussex)	1780–1819	–	–	2	–	–	–	1	–	3		Mee: 190
Swalcliffe (Oxon.)	1785–1815	–	–	1	–	2	1	–	1	5		Byrne
Clawton (Devon)	1780–1830	1	–	1	1	1	–	1	1	5		Macdermott, 1948: 24
Botesford (Leics.)	1789	–	–	–	1	–	–	1	2	4		Torrington: IV, 139
Eaton Socon (Beds.)	1791	–	–	–	1	1	–	–	–	2		Torrington: II, 175
Middleham (Yorks.)	1792	–	–	–	–	–	–	–	2	2	c. 12	Torrington: III, 58
Eccles (Lancs.)	c. 1792–1813	1	1	1	1	–	–	–	2	6	9	Millington: 11
Ellenbrook (Lancs.)*	c. 1800–20	1	4	1	1	1	–	–	1	9	13	Millington: 23
Swinton (Lancs.)*	c. 1805–20	1	–	1	–	2	–	1	1	6	7	Millington: 15
West Kirby (Ches.)	–1807	1	–	1	1	1	–	–	1	5		R. Richards: 350
Cockshutt (Salop)	1818–46	–	–	1	–	1	–	1	1	4		Boston & Langwill: 114–15
Winterbourne St Martin (Dorset)	1820	–	–	1	–	1	–	4	–	6	c. 20	Galpin, 1893: 31
Bere Regis (Dorset)	1830–45	–	–	1	–	1	1	–	1	4		MS 7
Beaminster (Dorset)	–1836	2	–	1	1	2	–	–	–	6		Hine: 34–5
Chedworth (Glos.)	1838	wind and strings								12		Curwen, 1897: 138
Puddletown (Dorset)	c. 1840	–	–	2	1	–	–	2	1	6		Galpin, 1906: 102
Winterbourne St Martin (Dorset)	c. 1840–65	–	–	1	2	–	–	1	–	4		Galpin, 1906: 102
Preston (Rutland)	–1846	–	–	1	1	–	–	2	1	5		Boston & Langwill: 114
Easton-in-Gordano (Somerset)	c. 1847	–	–	–	–	–	–	–	1	1	4	*The churgh-goer: rural rides*: I, 156
Winterbourne Steepleton (Dorset)	–1850	1	–	1	1	–	–	2	–	5		Galpin, 1893: 32
Publow (Somerset)	c. 1850	–	–	1	2	–	–	1	–	4	8	*The church-goer: rural rides*: II, 135–8
Souldrop (Beds.)	–1856	–	–	1	–	–	–	–	–	1		Newbolt: 206
Blaxhall (Suffolk)	–1863	1	–	1	1	–	–	–	–	3		Boston & Langwill: 115
Winterbourne Abbas (Dorset)	c. 1840–98	–	–	1	1	–	–	1	–	3		Galpin, 1893: 32; Curwen, 1897: 137; Trask

* Chapels of ease in the parish of Eccles.

parishes reported 'using orchestral instruments, varying from a fairly complete band down to a single cornet' (Donaldson: 406).

The period when bands were commonest was roughly 1780 to 1830. The most essential instrument was a bass of some kind, generally a bassoon or cello. (The only one of the bands listed in Table 12 for which no bass instrument is recorded is that at Eaton Socon, and in this case it is quite possible that a bassoon or cello was present: the observer, Lord Torrington, said: 'The psalm singing, in a singing gallery, was tolerable, accompanied by a flute and a hautboy.') Some bands had two or more bass instruments (Pl. 22, 23). The other instruments were generally of treble compass. A few bands had one of middle compass, such as viola or vox humana, but it is clear that this was neither common nor essential (Galpin, 1906: 103). Very likely the polarisation of church bands into treble and bass is closely related to the tendency, already discussed, for the tenor and alto voice parts to be sung an octave higher. The tenor voice was doubled by an instrument playing at the written pitch, so that there would be no need for an instrument of tenor compass. Even Macdermott found not a single viola in a Sussex church, though he said they had been found in Dorset (Macdermott, 1922: 44). On the whole it seems that woodwind instruments were somewhat more common than strings, but mixed bands were frequent.

Maurice Byrne has given a detailed account, based on documentary evidence, of the formation of the band at Swalcliffe in the 1780s. Money was collected in four villages within the parish for the purchase of the instruments: there were 66 subscribers, including 14 singers. They sent to London for an oboe, vox humana and bassoon in 1783, and two years later a 'bass viol' or cello and a second oboe were added. The four wind players were a weaver; his younger brother, a woolcomber; and two labourers. Byrne comments that in neighbouring villages the instruments appear to have been made locally.

In addition to the instruments listed in Table 12, others have been found in bands. Among bass instruments Macdermott found in Sussex churches, there were 8 trombones, 4 serpents, 4 double basses, and 1 bass horn (compared with 57 cellos and 28 bassoons). The serpent was recommended for churches without organs in 1822 (Eden: 21). Macdermott also found isolated references to the following: fife, flageolet, tin whistle, cornet, cornopean, French horn, key bugle, tenor saxhorn, baritone saxhorn, euphonium, ophicleide (a keyed substitute for the serpent), bombardon (contrabass tuba), banjo, kettledrum, triangle, flutina (a type of concertina), accordion (1948: 18–36, 42). He does not mention trumpets, but trumpet parts are found in several psalmody books. The most extraordinary instrument, and the one most thoroughly described by Macdermott, was the vamphorn. It was in the form of a plain horn or megaphone, lacking any holes, keys, or effective mouthpiece, varying in length from three to eight feet, and with a bell of diameter from seven to twenty-four inches. Seven specimens were still extant in 1948 (Macdermott, 1948: 33). It would have been impossible to 'play' such an instrument in any way that would have been useful for church music, and it seems that they were actually used to magnify the singing voice. An inscription on a plaque under the vamphorn hanging in the vestry of the church at East Leake read as follows:

This trumpet was formerly used in the gallery of this church for one of the singers to sing the bass through. Having become much decayed, it was saved from destruction and repaired by Ch: Augrave, Esq., of Berwick, Sussex, late of this parish, by whom it was sent to the 'Inventions Exhibition', London, 1885, and replaced in this church 1888.

This method of singing, called 'vamping' in Lincolnshire and elsewhere, was obviously more suited to leading the congregation than to participating in a piece of choir music, and this, no doubt, was what it was for. Vamphorns were used for sundry other purposes, such as calling people or cattle from the fields, giving out the psalms and hymns in church, and summoning assistance in time of danger. (Macdermott gained most of his information from Barr-Brown and Gill.)

The chief function of instruments in church was to double the voice parts, either at pitch or in another octave, to help the singers keep time and tune. The bass line was naturally taken by the bassoon, cello, or serpent, often an octave below the singers. The other parts were divided among the melody instruments, all played at the written pitch, which meant that they played an octave higher than the singers in the case of the tenor and alto parts. There was probably no uniformity about which instrument took which part, but a common arrangement seems to have been for the oboe or violin to take the 'tune', the clarinet the alto part, and perhaps a flute or second oboe the treble or tenor (other than the 'tune').

As time went on more collections began to include separate parts for the band instruments (see Table 8, p. 150), usually in the form of short 'symphonies' or interludes between the vocal sections; occasionally, obligato accompaniments were provided. Symphonies were written either on two staves (treble and bass) or on three (two trebles and bass). Thus, whether or not specific instruments were mentioned, they could easily be played by most bands. No parts for transposing instruments are found; both clarinets and trumpets played in C. In some collections the accompaniment was designed to be played by either organ or band: for example, William Jackson of Masham (1815–66) appended this note to one of his anthems as late as 1848: 'In choirs where there is not an organ, the upper notes of the organ part, may be taken by a violin or clarionet, the notes below forming a second. The bass may be taken on the violoncello or bassoon.' Still later, East Westrop, in the preface to *The universal psalmodist* (1856), warned 'choirs, where instruments are used' that the tenor must be played an octave lower than written, and suggested that the bassoon should play the upper notes in the bass stave of the (two-stave) organ part, the cello the lower notes. It should be emphasised that the proportion of country psalmody books with *independent* instrumental parts probably did not, at any time, exceed ten per cent of those published. They were probably commonest in the first decade of the nineteenth century, the heyday of the church bands. But even in that period the most usual instrumental accompaniment in printed collections was an organ part on two staves.

Valuable information about the part played by church choirs and bands in the growing choral festival movement is to be found in *Sketches of local musicians and musical societies* (1884), by William Millington, himself a bassoonist and cellist of many years' standing. He relates how the four church choirs of the parish of Eccles, not far from Manchester, in about 1792 formed a club which held quarterly meetings at which they performed 'vocal and instrumental music, principally oratorios of Handel, Haydn, and other eminent composers'. In each of the four villages a monthly rehearsal was held. But 'the introduction of organs into the churches and chapels in this district broke up the small bands at each place of worship', and as a result the quarterly meetings ceased about 1820, and the copies of music were divided up amongst the members. One of the clubs, however, the Ellenbrook Monthly Meeting as it was called, was revived in about 1835, reassembled the music, and formed a choir of some 15 men with an orchestra of 7 strings and 3 wind.

Many of its members were handloom weavers, who made music a special study. Many of them were very good copyists and by this means, and constant practice, became good performers, and had a large experience and knowledge of Handel's music, Dr. Croft's, Dr. Greene's, Dr. Boyce's, Dr. Nares', Kent's, Webbe's, and other anthems. At the quarterly meetings the proceeds were divided between the four choirs, with which they generally bought a score copy of some oratorio, or anthem, and from this copy the instrumental parts were copied, and in process of time they got a good library that is in use even at the present day. (Millington: 11, 35, 40–1).

Occasionally several such local choirs, often including nonconformists as well as Anglicans, would join together to give large-scale festivals, with the solo parts being taken by professionals from London; in such a way were the musical festivals of the nineteenth century built. In the north of England particularly, the humble church choirs and bands often reached standards of excellence that brought them into contact with the world of professional music. Millington himself was frequently principal bassoonist at concerts in Manchester, Liverpool and other Lancashire towns, sometimes playing under Hallé; yet he never became a professional musician (Millington: 6). He provides biographical sketches of hundreds of such local players and singers.

Not far from Eccles, at Shaw chapel in the parish of Oldham, similar activities had taken place at an even earlier date. The society of singers was formed in 1741, and it at once purchased a copy of William Croft's anthems (*Musica sacra*, 1724) for use in 'divine service'. The choir of some 40 people evidently felt ready to launch immediately into full-scale cathedral anthems. Later Greene's anthems were added to the library, and a large number of Handel's oratorios, all in full score. The parts for these were copied by a member of the society, Edmund Cheetham, between 1778 and 1788 or thereabouts, and were used at concerts given by the society at the Blue Bell Inn, Shaw Lane. Surviving manuscript parts show that the accompaniments were played by two violins and a bassoon, sometimes assisted by an oboe, with an organ or harpsichord probably filling out the rest of the score. Members of the society, chiefly singers, were frequently engaged to sing at the Ancient Concerts and at provincial festivals; one, Deborah Travis, became a famous singer, and married William Knyvett, a prominent London singer and composer. Another member of the Shaw society, Jonathan Nield, became a gentleman of the chapel royal (Hudson).

William Mason, precentor of York cathedral, in 1795 deplored the overweening ambition of 'our village practitioners... For these, since the rage of oratorios has spread from the capital to every market town in the kingdom, can by no means be satisfied unless they introduce chants, services, and anthems, into their parish churches, and accompany them with, what an old author calls, *scolding fiddles*, squalling hautboys, false-stopped violoncellos, buzzing bassoons, . . . in place of an organ' (Mason: III, 218–19).

Such links with the greater musical world were perhaps largely confined to Lancashire, the West Riding, and the north Midlands, the area which had been the cradle of parochial choirs, as also of nonconformist choral music. In all parts of the country, however, the church musicians, particularly the instrumentalists, were figures of considerable standing in village life. 'One must not imagine that these musicians played only in the church. They were concerned with the whole social and festive life of their village, and took their part in the dance, the harvest home, the Christmas carol, the flower show, the club feast' (Curwen, 1897: 138). This indeed was one of the reasons that prompted the desire to reform the church band out of existence, particularly among the clergy. It came to be felt that the music of worship must be distinct in all respects, including even the identity of the performers, from the song and dance of secular life; and that those who provided it must have God, not music, uppermost in their minds.

Sympathetic accounts of the old church musicians have been written by Thomas Hardy, whose father and grandfather had played in Dorset churches. The best is in *Under the greenwood tree*. Washington Irving also described the bands, in 1820 (:88, 93–4). George Eliot's *Adam Bede* (1859) contains a vivid picture of a service at Hayslope church on a Sunday afternoon in 1799 (:197–206). While the women went into church the men lingered outside in the churchyard, 'and hardly any of them except the singers, who had a humming and fragmentary rehearsal to go through, entered the church until Mr. Irwine [the rector] was in the desk'. As they lingered,

the sound of the bassoon and the key-bugles burst forth; the evening hymn, which always opened the service, had begun, and everyone must now enter and take his place . . . The choir had two narrow pews to themselves in the middle of the right-hand row, so that it was a short process for Joshua Rann [the parish clerk] to take his place among them as principal bass, and return to his desk after the singing was over . . . And now all faces were visible, for all were standing up . . . while good Bishop Ken's evening hymn was being sung to one of those lively psalm-tunes* which died out with the last generation of rectors and choral parish-clerks.

The clerk was better at reading than most of his kind, but 'Joshua himself was less proud of his reading than of his singing, and it was always with a sense of heightened importance that he passed from his desk to the choir.' As a burial had just taken place, the 'funeral psalm' was sung: 'It was in a solemn minor strain they sang . . . "Thou sweep'st us off as with a flood; We vanish hence like dreams"' [Psalm 90, New Version]. The sermon followed. 'Then came the moment of the final blessing, when the forever sublime words, "The peace of God, which passeth all understanding" seemed to blend with the calm afternoon sunshine that fell on the bowed heads of the congregation.'

---

* The tune probably sung in this case was ex. 56 (Temperley, 1971).

Country psalmody (1685–1830)

Summary and evaluation

The congregational singing of metrical psalms had, by the end of the seventeenth century, evolved into something quite other than the reformers had intended. It no longer satisfied Puritan ideals, and it was also contemptible in the eyes of educated people. But to reform it was difficult in small parishes with limited financial resources. The method generally adopted was to form a voluntary choir, wholly or chiefly of young men, who would learn to sing the common psalm tunes correctly from printed music, and would then regulate the singing of the congregation. The innovation was superintended by the S.P.C.K. and at first supported by many of the clergy, but it soon got out of hand. Like its predecessor, it grew into an entirely different creature from the one its inventors had in mind.

When once the choirs were established, they wanted to sing more ambitious music than old psalm tunes and in this they were encouraged by some disinterested musicians and a few clergymen, and exploited by enterprising music publishers and singing teachers. In a short time there came into existence a large repertory of parochial anthems, services, and elaborate psalm tunes of a kind the congregation could not join; and, in the north especially, choirs even began to chant the psalms and liturgy. The ultimate products of this development were the set piece and fuging tune. To help village choirs sing this difficult music at the correct pitch, pitchpipes, bassoons, cellos, and specially designed string instruments were used. Towards the end of the century it became common for choirs to be supported by a small band of two to six wind and string instruments. The congregation listened, often turning round to 'face the music' proceeding from the west gallery.

The music of country choirs was condemned by most professional musicians of the time, and was largely ignored or mocked by the upper classes. Some of the clergy were wise enough to recognise its pastoral value, and its positive influence in the lives of the musicians and even of the listeners. The time is now ripe to re-evaluate it as religious music. Apart from a handful of altered psalm tunes, it is practically unknown today. It is not to be compared with the art music of the eighteenth century, or of any period, nor is it to be faulted for breaking theoretical rules developed by trained musicians. The country composers' imperfect command of musical resources often led them to make imaginative experiments. Some of these were failures, but others produced music of a wonderful freshness and a delightful freedom from cliché. The preponderance of common chords and bare fifths and fourths, with occasional suggestions of much earlier music, imparts a clear, bright quality, especially at cadences. Uninhibited word painting is another strong characteristic.

The rediscovery of eighteenth-century country psalmody has already begun in the United States, where a natural interest in the music of their early forbears has led American scholars to explore colonial church music, and in recent years to revive some of it in performance. The result has been widespread acclamation. William Billings, long acknowledged as an individual composer of genius, is now seen to have been only one (admittedly an outstanding one) of a large school of self-taught composers.

American scholars have acknowledged that this school was directly descended from the English country psalmodists. It may well have reached its highest point in American soil, more remote from European art music and from ambitious reformers; and in Congregational churches, free of episcopal control. But this is a question that remains entirely open. Judgment must be reserved until the music of English country parish churches has been equally thoroughly explored and revived.

7 Reform movements (1760–1830)

The Evangelical movement

In the period that led up to the Victorian age, immense changes were taking place in English society, at an unprecedented pace: changes which led to the modern way of life as it is experienced in advanced countries. At the same time, within the Church of England, two religious movements grew up, which were later regarded as being opposed to each other, but had much in common, and taken together added up to an Anglican revival.

Historians of religion are sometimes tempted to account for the changes that took place in the Church solely in terms of internal religious movements. The Church is theoretically a haven from the forces of the material world. Yet its members live their days in that world, and are moulded by it. The Church of England embodied a tradition of toleration, and of non-interference in the daily life of the laity; it was closely associated with the fortunes of the nation. For most people its services were dignified interludes in a life governed by material considerations, and could appropriately reflect the material progress that was the dominating fact of the age. We have already seen such attitudes in an earlier period, expressed even through the mouths of the clergy. The religious revival which now took place was certainly, in part, a reaction against the growing strength of materialism and the governing rationalist philosophy. It was a reassertion of revealed truth, of traditional modes of worship, and of personal dedication to Christ. It won many adherents, yet in the end was overcome by the secular forces of materialism, allied to discoveries of science which made some of the teachings of Christianity more and more difficult to defend. As far as parish church music was concerned, the idealism of Evangelicals and Tractarians alike was ultimately subordinated to more worldly considerations: their effort to restore a congregational song of praise was frustrated by the growing professionalism of choirs.

The Evangelical movement grew directly out of the high-church religious societies of Queen Anne's time (Wilson: 42–3; Every: 174). It was at first identical to Methodism, which began strictly within the Church of England. John Wesley, whose father had been closely involved in the religious societies, began his work with such a society of young men at Oxford, the 'Holy Club'. In the 1730s he read the works of the early Church fathers, quite along the lines of the Oxford movement of a century later, and believed in strict observance of every detail of the liturgy (Balleine: 7). The chief opposition to his movement came at first from low churchmen or Latitudinarians, who were predominantly Whig, rationalist, permissive, and opposed to intensity or 'enthusiasm' in religion (Balleine: 165). When Wesley and his followers were seen to attract large numbers away from the Church, there was more widespread opposition, particularly from conservative high churchmen. Wesley remained in the Church of England, of which he was an ordained priest, even when he was rejected and forbidden to preach in most dioceses. He timed his open-air or meeting-house services so as as not to conflict with those in the parish churches, which he exhorted his followers to attend; for if they should leave the Church, he told them, Christ would leave them. Near the end of his life in 1788 he made a new avowal: 'I declare once more that I live and die a member of the Church of England; and that none who regard my judgment will ever separate from it' (Telford: XIII, 273; cited Davies: III, 188).

Nevertheless, the Methodist movement gradually drifted away from the Church in Wesley's own time. The outdoor preaching and class meetings took their forms from the dissenting tradition, while the love-feasts and watch-nights were Moravian in origin; and many of those who attended them had no ties with the Church of England, and could not regard it as their spiritual mother (Davies: III, 189–92). In the end Wesley himself was compelled to make a decisive breach with the Church when he ordained ministers to carry on his work in America; only a bishop could perform a valid ordination, according to the Church's law, and only a priest so ordained could administer communion or solemnise a legal marriage. In 1795, four years after the death of their founder, the Wesleyan Methodists became openly Nonconformist. Within a few years they had splintered into a number of rival sects (Davies: III, 212).

Thus it can be seen that in some ways the true heirs of Wesley were the Anglican Evangelicals. They shared his ideal of the revitalising of religion through the fervour of preaching and prayer, and his conviction of the need for personal conversion and submission to Christ; and they also, like him, remained loyal to the Church, its rule and its liturgy. An additional issue which divided both churchmen and dissenters was a theological question, having only an indirect bearing on our story. Wesley was an Arminian, believing that God's grace was universal, and would save any sinner who was reborn in Christ by personal conversion. This belief had been strongly held by some in the Church from the time of Andrewes and Laud: it was on the whole a badge of high churchmanship. But it was in apparent conflict with the original Calvinism of the Church, enshrined in the Thirty-nine Articles to which every Anglican minister had to swear his agreement. This taught that man was helpless to procure salvation, which awaited only those whom God had pre-elected to it. George Whitefield, who began his ministry as a member of Wesley's Holy Club, later founded his own sect of Calvinistic Methodists; they, too, reaffirmed their allegiance to the Church. When their chief protector and benefactress, Selina, Countess of Huntingdon, left the Church of England in 1782, most of her chaplains declined to follow her into exile, and she had to continue her work with unordained ministers (Davies: III, 212–13). Among those who left her was William Romaine, a leading Evangelical; Whitefield had died before the breach was made. The majority of Anglican Evangelicals were Calvinists, and were as strict in their support of the Thirty-nine Articles as in their conduct of every detail of the Common Prayer. But there was a significant minority of Arminians, among whose numbers were several who played a leading part in the revival of congregational singing.

Until the end of the eighteenth century it is impossible to draw a clear line between Methodists and Anglican Evangelicals. The ultimate breach was on the issue of loyalty to a Church that was unresponsive and, for the most part, hostile to their efforts. Before the schism came, it was not necessary for the leaders of the movement to declare their primary loyalty, and few did so. Some, however, were outside the Church from the start. They bluntly condemned the coldness and formality of Anglican worship, and fearlessly criticised the laxity and worldliness of its ministers. They journeyed all over the country, intruding into quiet parishes to conduct disturbing and exciting religious meetings that, whatever Wesley might say, were a threat to the parish church and a rival to the parson for the allegiance of his flock. It is not surprising that the Church authorities did everything in their power to hinder these activities. Licences to preach were refused; bishops declined to ordain followers of Wesley and Whitefield; those who were ordained found it difficult to secure the incumbency of a parish church.

With a few exceptions, therefore, Evangelicals were for long compelled to conduct their ministry from the fringes of the established Church, or even outside it. Some held privately endowed 'lectureships' at parish churches, which allowed them to preach in the church at times other than those of the regular service conducted by the incumbent. The situation often generated hostility. Romaine, the leading Evangelical in the London area, was lecturer at St Dunstan-in-the-West from 1749 until his death in 1795, but after 1758 he was opposed by the new vicar and the churchwardens, who would not provide candles for his evening lecture, until the bishop compelled them to make proper arrangements. In 1764 he became also rector of St Andrew-by-the-Wardrobe, the living of which was in the gift of the parish, so that he could be elected by the parishioners. Evangelical preachers were nearly always popular with the common people, to whom they spoke in simple, direct and often inspiring terms. But most benefices were controlled by local magnates, bishops, cathedral or collegiate bodies, or the Crown. Only one other London church north of the Thames was held by an Evangelical before 1800: St Mary Woolnoth, whose vicar was John Newton from 1779 onwards. The first Evangelical bishop was not appointed until 1815. Many flocked 'to see this great curiosity, a religious bishop'. (Balleine: 41–3, 48, 152)

Another home for Evangelicals was the proprietary chapel, often erected in the eighteenth century in London and other large towns, either to spread a particular religious point of view or even as a commercial speculation. These chapels were not consecrated, but were licensed for Anglican worship by the bishop of the diocese; they were free from direct ecclesiastical control (see *Gentleman's Magazine* LXXXVI, 1816: 232, 582). Examples in London were St John's chapel, Bedford Row; Portman chapel, Baker Street; Bentinck chapel, off Edgware Road; Broadway chapel (now Christ Church), Westminster; Bedford chapel, Bloomsbury; Surrey chapel, Blackfriars Road. The Countess of Huntingdon's chapels at Bath and Brighton were of this character until her break with the Church in 1782. Some of these, towards the end of the eighteenth century, printed their own collections of psalms and hymns (PC 601–661).

A similar status belonged to many hospitals and charities founded by pious benefactors for the good of unfortunate sections of the community. Such were the Foundling Hospital (in full, the Hospital for the Maintenance and Education of Exposed and Deserted Young Children), founded by Thomas Coram and opened in 1741 (its chapel was built in 1747); the Lock Hospital, for venereal patients, founded in 1746 (its chapel was opened in 1762); the Magdalen Hospital, for penitent prostitutes, opened in 1758; and the Asylum for Female Orphans, also founded in 1758 (Rodgers: 26–54). All these charities, like the proprietary chapels, were relatively independent in the conduct of worship, and they nearly always chose an Evangelical chaplain. Some played an important part in the development of parish church music, and must therefore be considered here, although they were not, of course, parish churches (see PC 501–550).

In the nineteenth century the Evangelicals gained influence steadily, but slowly. Laymen played an important part, particularly in the formation of the 'Clapham Sect', which revolved around William Wilberforce. They addressed themselves to important social issues of the day, such as the abolition of slavery, the improvement of education, and the temperance movement. Sunday schools were eagerly adopted by the Evangelical clergy after the first one had been founded at Gloucester in 1780. Their purpose was manifold: to preserve the sabbath from desecration; to teach literacy to children who had to work for money on weekdays; to inculcate Anglican religion and morality; to prevent the growth of a criminal class. Early Sunday school regulations generally included attending the parish church, and in many cases the children could provide a treble choir in churches which had not had one before (Sylvester: 254–64).

Charles Simeon, and after his death his trustees, steadily acquired the advowsons of parish churches and used them to appoint members of their party to the livings. John Crosse in 1784 received the vicarage of Bradford from his father, who had purchased the next presentation for this purpose (J. James: 212). Crosse himself later purchased the perpetual advowson and sold it to Henry Thornton, a prominent member of the Clapham sect, 'in confidence that he will take care to provide after my decease a vicar who will take the oversight of the flock not for filthy lucre's sake, but with a sincere desire to win souls for Christ' (MS 2).

The views of the Evangelical party were aired in *The Christian Observer*, founded in 1802 by the Clapham sect. A second journal, *The Record*, was founded in 1828, but it took up a violent tone which eventually harmed the cause, and paved the way for the rancorous infighting between parties in the Church that was the bane of the Victorian period. The Evangelical party was never more than a minority in the Church. Its one period of power was the decade from 1855 to 1865, when Lord Palmerston as prime minister took the advice of Lord Shaftesbury, a leading Evangelical, in all Church affairs, including the appointment of bishops.

Evangelical aims for parish church music

The Evangelicals combined two apparently opposing objectives for worship: to preserve every detail of the liturgy; and to restore emotion and spontaneity. Where conditions were right, they achieved both. On the one hand, they placed great emphasis on those parts of worship in which the liturgy laid down no form of words: on preaching, whether in the place prescribed in the ante-communion service or in special sermons or 'lectures' not forming part of a prayer-book service; on family prayers, which they succeeded in reviving as a daily practice in devout homes; and on the singing of metrical psalms, hymns, and anthems. In all these they explored to the full the opportunities to revive the spirit of Anglican religion, and we shall, of course, be specially concerned with their influence on singing.

On the other hand, they also strove to make the liturgy itself a living word instead of an empty form, and wherever possible to involve the voices and hearts of the congregation in its performance. 'Pray the prayers, don't read them only', Simeon said to his followers. 'The finest sight short of heaven would be a whole congregation using the prayers of the liturgy in the true spirit of them' (Davies: III, 217–18). They would even begin to induce congregations to sing the prose canticles, psalms, and other parts of the liturgy.

Charles Wesley, with Isaac Watts the greatest English hymn writer of the eighteenth century, must be regarded as an Evangelical quite as much as a Methodist: he was to the end of his life a strict high churchman, disapproving of even the slight departures from church order that his brother permitted himself. In his hymns, it is not too much to say, Christianity was first brought home to the minds and hearts of millions of uneducated people, who had previously known it only as a mysterious rite to which they were expected to conform. Many hymns of lasting value were contributed by other Evangelicals, especially John Newton, William Cowper, and Augustus Toplady. They were first made popular at the informal religious meetings of the Methodists, many of them out of doors; by degrees they were introduced in charities and proprietary chapels, and eventually in parish churches and even cathedrals. Yet among Evangelicals themselves were some who disapproved of hymns in church, taking the old Calvinist view that only directly inspired words should be sung there. Romaine, one of the most conservative, took this position in *An essay on psalmody* (1775; cited Curwen, 1880: 9). He was probably influenced by the old belief that only the Old and New Versions were legally authorised for use in church, which was publicly claimed as late as 1814 (*Gentleman's Magazine* LXXXIV, 1814: 532). This tradition was first cautiously, then blatantly ignored by many Evangelical clergy, until eventually it was challenged in court. Thomas Cotterill in 1819 compiled an eighth and enlarged edition of his *Selection of psalms and hymns*, advanced but not untypical of its date, for the use of his church, St Paul, Sheffield. A group of parishioners brought an action against him (*Holy & Ward v. Cotterill*) in the Consistory Court of the diocese of York, and a thorough investigation of the legal position was undertaken by the chancellor, G. V. Vernon. He concluded on 6 July 1820 that the status of hymns was exactly like that of metrical psalms: neither were part of the liturgy, but both were authorised for use before and after services. This important decision opened the way for the flood of nineteenth-century hymn books. (J. Gray, 1821: 46–53.)

Meanwhile Edward Vernon, Archbishop of York, agreed to prepare a revised selection for use in Cotterill's church, *A selection of psalms and hymns for public worship* (London, 1820), which was distributed in the church, each copy inscribed: 'The gift of his Grace the Lord Archbishop of York'. The unofficial but influential approval thus given to hymn singing, and the practical failure of the action against Cotterill, greatly encouraged the further introduction of hymns into Anglican worship. The 'Archbishop's selection' appeared in many northern parish churches, and went into at least 29 editions (L. Benson: 355, n. 77). A companion volume of music, compiled by Samuel Mather, organist of St Paul's church, appeared under the title *Christian psalmody* (PC 358): Matthew Camidge of York published a tune supplement explicitly to cater for the new metres in the archbishop's selection (PC 351a).

Evangelical hymns were 'songs of individual experience, marking the successive stages of penitence, conversion, justification, pardon, and sanctification in the life of the Christian pilgrim through this vale of sorrow to eternity' (Davies: III, 234–5). Like the Pietist hymns of Germany, they used language that was personal, emotional, immediate in its imagery (ex. 45), and had a vastly greater appeal than that of the old metrical psalms. The most important collection of hymns by Evangelical Anglicans, excluding the Wesleys, was certainly *Olney hymns* (1779) by Newton and Cowper (L. Benson: 336–40), several of which have become permanent favourites. One of the most extreme Evangelical hymns was Toplady's 'Rock of ages, cleft for me' (1776), with its explicitly Calvinist theology, helpless dependence on God's grace, morbid sense of guilt, and disturbing images of the human body which suggest Freudian meanings to the twentieth-century observer. These elements explain both the wide appeal of Methodist and Evangelical hymns, especially among the uneducated, and also the distaste for them felt by many sincere Christians of a more conservative mind and fastidious taste.

The cardinal point about singing for Methodists and Evangelicals was that it should be a heartfelt and spontaneous act of worship by the people. They revived with new intensity all the old objections to the monopolisation of the singing by choirs, and to the tunes that were too difficult for the common people to sing. They insisted that all who could sing should do so, men, women and children; and, following Isaac Watts, the Congregationalist, as well as the high-church Bishop Beveridge, they demanded that everyone should sing standing up. Instead of fuging and elaborate tunes, they introduced simple, attractive tunes that everybody could sing, and enjoy singing. John Wesley himself had very decided views on these matters, summarised in his preface to *Select hymns with tunes annext* (1761) (Lightwood: 26). At the Methodist Conference at Bristol in 1768 he attacked 'complex tunes which it is impossible to sing with devotion' and long hallelujahs, and maintained that 'the repeating the same word so often (but especially while another repeats different words – the horrid abuse which runs through the modern church-music) as it shocks common sense, so it necessarily brings in dead formality and has no more of religion in it than a Lancashire hornpipe' (Lightwood: 35–6). In all his hymn books from the *Foundery tune book* (1742) onwards, he incorporated tunes adapted from secular sources, even from operas: one of the 1742 tunes, for instance, is based on a march in Handel's *Riccardo primo*. Many Wesleyan hymn texts were written to go with well-known secular tunes. Thus Charles Wesley's famous hymn 'Love divine, all loves excelling' is a parody of Dryden's 'Fairest isle, all isles excelling', and was first sung to Purcell's tune from *King Arthur*. Another of Charles Wesley's hymns explicitly defends this policy:

> Who on the part of God will rise,
>   Innocent sound recover,
> Fly on the prey, and take the prize,
>   Plunder the carnal lover:
> Strip him of every moving strain,
>   Every melting measure,
> Music in virtue's cause retain,
>   Rescue the holy pleasure? (PC 186: 4)

The principle of taking popular songs and converting them to religious use was older than the Reformation, as we now know, but in its new form it excited a great deal of opposition from high-church clergymen. In a sermon at a meeting of the Three Choirs Festival in 1753, William Parker, rector of Little Ilford, suggested that the sacred musician should avoid 'levity of notes':

Let him carefully decline the introduction of all such addresses to the passions in his notes, all such complications of sounds, as, having once been connected with words of levity, may naturally recall into light minds the remembrance of those words or their ideas again.

At all events, the singer or listener should endeavour to avoid such associations: 'let him rather study to adapt good ideas to the sound, and thereby correct the judgment of the musician' (Parker: 24–5). William Riley printed a reasoned attack on 'the singing of ballad-tunes in public worship' in 1762 (PC 186: 3–10). A writer in 1819 attributed the origin of this type of adaptation to Whitefield, and there are certainly several examples in *The divine musical miscellany* (1754) which was designed for use at Whitefield's Tabernacle. Wesley approved the setting of 'Christ the Lord is risen today' to Handel's 'See, the conquering hero comes'. One popular hymn tune was based on 'an old public house catch ("How great is the pleasure")', another on 'Drink to me only with thine eyes' (Cole: 90–1). Hymn tunes taken from secular melodies were gradually, after 1800, introduced into Anglican hymn books, despite opposition.

Apart from these borrowed tunes, however, the Methodists quickly established a new *type* of tune, which was popular and strongly secular in style. The first set of original tunes written for Methodists was by the German musician Johann Friedrich Lampe (1746), but they were too florid to gain complete approval from Wesley. His collection of 1761, whose 92 tunes were also published separately as *Sacred melody*, is representative. Collections of hymns and psalms for the charities also began to appear: Thomas Call's for the Magdalen chapel in 1762 (PC 542), which was superseded by an anonymous pirated version (PC 541), to become very popular as the 'Magdalen Collection'; Martin Madan's for the Lock Hospital (PC 531); William Riley's for the Asylum for Female Orphans (PC 501); and the 'Foundling Collection' in 1774 (PC 522). Madan was the most important of the compilers. A member of the Wesley circle, he was both a clergyman and a musician; as chaplain of the Lock Hospital he made the selection of psalms and hymns to be used there, and as musical director he prepared and arranged the tunes, composing some of them himself. His exposure to the horrors of venereal disease induced him to believe in polygamy as a remedy for the social evil of prostitution, and he advocated it in a remarkable book called *Thelyphthora* (1780); as a consequence he was obliged to resign his post.

The first chaplain of the Magdalen Hospital was William Dodd, a colourful Evangelical preacher. 'Imaginative pictures of the scarlet past of the fallen women, the blandishments of their seducers, the anguish of their parents, and their touching repentance, were cleverly drawn in the sermons that were preached each Sunday in the chapel. These Sunday services, to which the public was admitted, soon became famous' (Rodgers: 52). In 1782 there were three services every Sunday, with collections for the charity:

The Magdalens are heard to join the responses, &c. and they also sing psalms and hymns, in which they have been previously instructed, being accompanied by a good organ. There are two galleries for the accommodation of these women, who are, however, concealed from the rest of the congregation by pieces of green canvas, stretched upon frames, and placed at the front of each gallery. (*The London Guide*: 149)

There was an obvious similarity here (apart from the green canvas) to the singing by charity children in town parish churches, and many of the hymns written for the hospital chapels were equally suited to that purpose, including some with special texts connected with charity. Since most of the inmates of hospitals were either women or children, the tunes provided for them were treble-dominated, generally for one or two treble parts with figured bass accompaniment: each hospital chapel had an organ. It was through the hospital collections that the new type of tune, which we may call the 'Methodist' type, began to find its way into the parish churches, together with some of the hymn texts that went with it. Frere, Frost, and other writers have obscured this issue by implying that the Methodist tunes were fuging tunes. They quote a passage from William Riley saying that 'their tunes mostly consist of what they call fuges, or (more properly) imitations, and are indeed fit to be sung only by those who made them' (Frere & Frost: 101), as if Riley were speaking of the Methodists, whereas actually this passage clearly refers to country psalmody teachers in parish churches (PC 186: 1). Riley's condemnation of Methodist tunes is on quite different grounds, namely their secularity and 'profane manner', which he tried to avoid in his own tunes for the Asylum for Female Orphans. We have seen that Wesley himself forbade fuging tunes among his followers; and we find in the hospital collections that the tunes are often florid, theatrical, or sentimental, but never fugal. The text is always quite clear; when more than one voice is singing, they sing the same words, though a line of text is often repeated. The fuging tune, it must be emphasised, was an exclusively Anglican development; whether it is praised or condemned, the Methodists are free of all responsibility. Wesley actually stopped the performance of a fuging tune at Warrington in 1781 (J. Wesley, 1909–16: VI, 312).

The 'Methodist' tune did have some strongly marked features, which were directly derived from the secular music of the time. Typical tunes are 'Hotham', written for Charles Wesley's 'Jesu, lover of my soul' and still often sung to it (ex. 45), and 'Helmsley', designed for another Wesley hymn, 'Lo, he comes with clouds descending' (ex. 46). Both are in the new trochaic metres (7^8 and 878747 respectively) which were the Wesleys' chief contribution to English sacred prosody. The characteristic seven-syllable trochaic line fit squarely into two bars of common time, and gave rise to a standard cadence that was typical of these tunes: three well-defined, obvious chords (tonic 6–4, dominant, tonic), with the melody in plain notes, generally in contrast to earlier passages where the syllables were subdivided into shorter notes. The eight-syllable trochaic line often produced a 'feminine ending'. The ornamentation of the melody included appoggiaturas and trills delaying the main note (ex. 45, bars 13, 14; ex. 46, bars 1, 4); there were also some ordinary passing notes, just as in older psalm tunes. A characteristic type of ornament was one that passed from one chord note to another on the same beat (ex. 45, bars 9–10; ex. 46, bar 1, 2nd beat, bar 4, 1st beat). Such an ornament lacked the functional character of a passing note (which can be explained as deriving from the 'pitch-matching' process in the old way of singing), or the emotional, sentimental effect of an appoggiatura. It was merely pretty or elegant, and it was this that so strongly suggested its origin in secular music, and the 'light' or 'trivial' quality that some found objectionable. One writer in 1819 complained bitterly of the use of 'theatrical embellishments . . . the very refuse of the theatres', and gave as an example the old 'galant cadence', long since obsolete in the theatre, but still common in psalm tunes: worse still, it was found with its second note omitted (as in the last two bars of 'God save the king', which, however, the writer did not mention (Cole: 103–4).)

Another feature of 'Helmsley' and 'Hotham' which was to be associated with the Methodist tune was the repetition of a line or part of a line of text, sometimes twice or three times, allowing the composer a possibility of musical repetition or sequence, which again suggested secular music. These 'repeating tunes' sometimes attracted ridicule, for if they were not applied with care they might repeat a meaningless or ambiguous collection of syllables (Macdermott, 1922: 82–8; and see ex. 45, verses 2–4). The Methodists often had one or more lines sung by women alone, and this tradition survives in one of the few repeating tunes still in general use, 'Adeste fideles' (though it is of Catholic, not Methodist, origin). The contrast between loud and soft was also used between adjacent lines of text (ex. 46), and it is probable that the lines marked 'soft' were sung by women alone. Whitefield's *Selection for the Tabernacle* (1753) included antiphonal hymns, the men on one side of the building being answered by the women on the other. Stephen Addington's *Collection of psalm tunes* (1780), primarily for Congregationalists, laid down that 'where Pia. is over a line it is to be sung soft, or only in women's voices'. Wesley, though anxious for all the congregation to sing, wanted the women to sing the tune in the treble part alone: 'let no man sing with them, unless he understands the notes and sings the bass'. He rather disapproved of repeating tunes, but not so much as he did fuging tunes.

'In 1757 Wesley was able to boast of the superiority of Methodist singing over that of the established Church' (Telford: III, 226–8). The excellence of the Methodists' singing was one of the most powerful attractions of their movement. Just as at the time of the Reformation, ordinary people loved to take part themselves in hearty singing, instead of listening to the strange complexities of a parish choir. William Vincent considered that 'for one who has been drawn from the Established Church by preaching, ten have been induced by music' (Vincent: 15). The message was not lost on the church authorities; Dodd recommended imitating Methodist singing in the Church of England (Curwen, 1888: 21). Beilby Porteus, bishop of London, devoted a part of his charge to the clergy of his diocese in 1790 to an urgent plea for the improvement of psalmody. After condemning both country and town psalmody of the conventional kinds, the bishop suggested that the remedy lay in teaching the common psalm tunes to the Sunday school children, of whom he estimated there were now 300,000 (Porteus: VI, 243; Box: 78–9; Frere & Frost: 108). Thus many clergymen, even though not themselves Evangelicals, were persuaded to adopt some of the methods of Evangelicalism with respect to psalmody, not so much for Evangelical ends but as a defensive measure against the inroads of Methodism and other dissenting bodies.

On the whole Evangelicals discouraged more elaborate forms of music, such as anthems, if they formed part of public worship, but encouraged oratorios or concerts of sacred music, even in consecrated buildings. Wesley himself was ambivalent about anthems. He freely admitted that anthems at St Paul's cathedral had played a vital part in the greatest religious crisis of his life, his 'conversion' in May 1738 (J. Wesley, 1909–16: I, 472, 478–9). His attitudes to anthems later in life varied according to whether he felt the text was heard and understood by the listeners (J. Wesley, 1909–16: v, 283, 512; VI, 182, 337n., 365; Lightwood: 54–6). In *Sacred harmony*, a collection he supervised and had published in 1780, two 'anthems' in three parts were included: 'The voice of my beloved sounds', adapted from a popular song, and Madan's 'Before Jehovah's awful throne' (Dr Watts's Psalm 100), from the Lock Collection. Two more appeared in the second edition of 1787. Nevertheless, anthems were banned at the Methodist Conference at Manchester in 1787. Wesley does not mention this action in his journal, though it could hardly have been taken without his approval (J. Wesley, 1909–16: VII, 307n.). Again the decisive factor was probably intelligibility of text. The 'anthems' in *Sacred harmony* all had metrical texts – in fact they are more strictly to be called 'set pieces'; they have little text repetition and no contrapuntal overlapping of words.

'Vital spark of heavenly flame' (ex. 47) appeared first in Harwood's *A set of hymns and psalm tunes*, published at Chester about 1770 (PC 205): the purpose of this collection is not precisely known, but the emphasis on hymns makes it unlikely to have been for regular Anglican use, while the presence of a figured bass rules it out for dissenting worship at that date. The text, by Alexander Pope, is more sentimental than Christian in its message about immortality, despite its last two lines, and it is surprising that it commended itself to Wesley.* Harwood's piece was enormously popular in Anglican, Methodist and dissenting circles in the first half of the nineteenth century; it was frequently arranged for four voices, and was even adopted by the old-fashioned country choirs and bands: in 1846 a writer complained of places 'where a rustic choir, accompanied with flute, clarionet, bassoon and every other instrument that can be mustered, sing "Vital spark", with other hymns and anthems of a similar stamp, in a gallery' (*What can be done?*: 17). It was even reprinted in an early issue of *The Musical Times*. It is a good example of how far Methodists and Evangelicals were prepared to go in the direction of secularity; for its style, form, text, and flavour are entirely those of the glee or part-song, not at all that of the psalm tune, anthem, or even oratorio movement. It is equipped with a galant cadence (bars 11–12), sentimental appoggiaturas (35–42), passages of coloratura (67, 75), and pauses for cadenzas (44, 73). The changes of mode, tempo, and time signature are just those that one would expect to find in a cantata with an amorous text. This text was, in fact, set to music at least fifteen times, in both Britain and America (Carr), and evidently embodied feelings that were prevalent at the time. Despite the fact that it commended itself to Wesley and other religious leaders, it surely partakes a good deal of the secular materialism that the Evangelicals opposed.

A similar attitude to text setting was held by Richard Cecil, minister of St John's chapel, Bedford Row, London, a leading Evangelical who remained loyal to the Church. 'Anthems, or any pieces wherein the words were reiterated, he disliked, for public worship especially, as they sacrificed the real spirit of devotion too much to the music.' He composed an anthem, 'I will arise', which was to be one of the most popular in both Anglican and dissenting use in the nineteenth century. Its text expressed the repentance that was central to Evangelicalism. It is extremely simple, entirely homophonic, and uses verbal repetitions only for affective emphasis (ex. 48). The style is conventionally correct, and is, of course, far removed from that of country parish psalmody. In feeling as well as text it is typically Evangelical. In many churches and chapels it was probably sung by the whole congregation.

Organ voluntaries were abhorred by Wesley, though even he had to admit being occasionally moved by them (J. Wesley, 1909–16: III, 520; VI, 346). Organs were little used in Methodist meeting houses, though at least three were erected during Wesley's lifetime (Lightwood: 40). He approved one at Macclesfield in 1786. But at Louth in 1790, when Wesley (aged 87) preached at the parish church to large crowds, 'the organ annoyed him. After the first verse [of the hymn] he said, "Let that organ stop, and let the women take their parts." "They cannot sing without it, sir," replied Mr. Robinson, one of the stewards for the Lincolnshire circuit. "Then" he

---

* It was included in the second edition of Wesley's *Sacred harmony*.

retorted, "how did they do before they got one?"' (J. Wesley, 1909–16: VII, 411n.). Among Evangelicals within the Church, however, an organ was often seen as an essential agent in the reform of singing. Crosse at Bradford, Richardson at York, Sutton at Sheffield, Romaine at St Andrew-by-the-Wardrobe, London, all took the initiative in purchasing or restoring an organ soon after they were appointed incumbents. But they wanted it used strictly for the accompaniment of congregational singing. A letter to *The Christian Observer* in 1805 (IV, 212–14) complained about the abuse of organs in parochial services by a frivolous style of playing with too many 'graces', but at the same time noted with approval that some dissenting churches had begun to introduce organs. In 1822 it was noted that those who objected to the voluntary before the first lesson were 'generally, if not universally, found to be of the class usually called Evangelical' (*Quarterly*: IV, 39). It was an offence against liturgical propriety as well as a bar to congregational participation.

By 1800 the Evangelicals were stronger in Yorkshire than in any other part of the country (Balleine: 64; Popham: 65–8). Several important parish churches had come into the hands of Evangelical clergymen, and many took advantage of the strong tradition of singing in that part of the country to reform psalmody in the directions already followed by the Methodists, and by the London hospitals. Henry Venn, vicar of Huddersfield from 1759 to 1771, 'read the service with peculiar solemnity and effect. The Te deum especially was recited with a triumphant air and tone, which often produced a perceptible sensation throughout the whole congregation. He succeeded in inducing the people to join in the responses and singing' (Ahier: 59). An organ was not acquired at Huddersfield until 1812, however.

Doncaster already had an organ (since 1740), an excellent organist (Dr Edward Miller, Pl. 10), and a flourishing tradition of psalmody, when in 1785 it acquired an Evangelical vicar, George Hay Drummond. The psalmody had been until then controlled by a parish clerk, whose 'custom was to send the organist not the *words*, but only the *name* of the tune, and how often it was to be repeated. Strange absurdity! How could the organist, placed in this degrading situation, properly perform his part of the church service? Not knowing the words, it was impossible for him to accommodate his music to the various sentiments contained in different stanzas' (E. Miller, 1804: 88). Drummond soon altered all this, by 'selecting the best stanzas in each psalm, from the version of Tate and Brady,' and arranging them 'for every Sunday and festival throughout the year', with music provided by Miller, chiefly based on 'the most popular of our old and venerable melodies long used in the established church'. The result was Drummond and Miller's *Psalms of David* (1790), a landmark in the reform of town psalmody. The preface condemned various abuses: 'drawling out ... each syllable to an improper and unlimited length'; leaving the choice of words and tune to the clerk; indulging in 'extraneous flourishes, or in running up and down the keys at the end of every line'. Miller recommended that the parish organist 'attend once a week, for a few months, to instruct the *charity*, or Sunday school children. Let him invite such part of the parishioners to meet him, as may wish to learn. But above all, let him persist in playing the old *common* time tunes in quicker measure than at present, according to their original intention, and as they are now sung in the Lutheran churches in *Germany*', by contrast with the churches of England and Holland. The heads of grammar schools and girls' boarding schools should insist on their charges attending these rehearsals; there was no reason why young ladies should not sing in church, since they often sang in company. Psalms ought to be performed standing. 'Many there are, and particularly those of rank and eminence, who do not join at all in this high act of devotion, or do it with utmost indifference.'

The book contains only thirty tunes, repeated often enough to provide for three psalms for each Sunday in the year (two morning, one evening) and a few extra ones for festivals. They are set out on two staves, in a novel manner (elsewhere credited to Domenico Corri (PC 306: preface)) in which the realisation of the figured bass is suggested in small notes (Fig. 8). A few of the traditional old tunes are there, in a livelier rhythm than had been customary, but there are also a number of much more modern tunes. One, 'Messiah', is based on Handel's 'I know that my redeemer liveth'; another, 'Brunswick', on an aria from Handel's *Saul*; a third, attributed to 'Dr. Arne', is undoubtedly taken from a secular work. There are tunes by Dr Burney (Miller's teacher) and C. P. E. Bach. The whole design of the undertaking is clearly to make psalm singing more lively, and to restore choir and organ to their proper function of leading the congregation. Although Miller had been organist of Doncaster since 1756, his efforts concerning psalmody date only from 1790, when Drummond became vicar.

But the importance of Miller's work went far beyond Doncaster itself. *The psalms of David* was, as he claimed, 'the *first* publication of congregational psalmody that has appeared since the Reformation, with a regular arrangement of *words* and *music*, adapted for every Sunday throughout the year' (PC 271: ix), though a course of psalms for three or six months had appeared before (PC 36, 109). Its dissemination was enormous, as can be shown by its extraordinary list of subscribers, which included the king and queen, both archbishops, and a dazzling array of bishops and lords, as well as a large number of organists and parish churches. But these were largely in northern England, or in Miller's native East Anglia; none was in London. Miller's plan was copied in several other influential collections. He also adapted his own collection in two later books, one (*David's harp*, c. 1803) for Methodists, the other (*Sacred music*, c. 1800) for the older dissenting bodies.

At Bradford, John Crosse, as already mentioned, became vicar in 1784. He had been a minister at the Lock Chapel in the early 1760s, where he had come under the influence of Dodd and Madan. At Bradford he soon attracted congregations of immense size, with the result that three new galleries had to be built in the church during the next thirteen years (Fawcett: 14), but even these were not enough to accommodate the thousands who wanted to hear him (Outhwaite: 4). He was much attached to the Methodists and almost became one (W. Morgan: 13). He was an Arminian (W. Morgan: 50; J. James: 213). He delighted in sacred music, especially the old psalm tunes; on Sundays he would allow only the Old

FOURTH SUNDAY after TRINITY
Firſt Morning

Pſalm 18 —Verſes 1. 2. 3. 18.

Old 100 Melody **L.M.** Compoſed by Martin Luther from the authority of Tallis. Blow. Handel and St. John Hawkins.

A Tempo Giuſto

No change of times ſhall ever ſhock My firm affection, Lord to thee;

No change &c.

For thou haſt al—ways been a rock, A fortreſs and de-fence to me.

2
Thou my deliverer art, my God:
My truſt is in thy mighty pow'r:
Thou art my ſhield from foes abroad,
At home my ſafe guard and my tow'r. **18**

3
To thee I'll ſtill addreſs my pray'r
(To whom all praiſe we juſtly owe;)
So ſhall I by thy watchful care,
Be guarded from my treach'rous foe.
Their ſubtle rage had near prevail'd
When I diſtreſt and friendleſs lay;
But ſtill when other ſuccours fail'd,
God was my firm ſupport and ſtay.

Fig. 8 Edward Miller's arrangement of the tune 'Old Hundredth' to selected verses of Psalm 18, New Version, 1791 (PC 271, p. 58)

Version of psalms to be sung, and he agreed with Romaine's views about psalmody (W. Morgan: 155). Crosse himself took the initiative in the purchase of an organ; the faculty was granted in 1785, on condition that the inhabitants of Haworth would not be charged with expenses connected with it; he began a subscription fund, which had raised £1231 by March 1788, including £742 from the sale of seats in the galleries. The organ had three manuals with 22 stops. It was opened in May 1786 with a '"grand oratorio", the circumstances attending which formed the subject of much bitterness at the time' (MS 2; Cudworth: 112–16). Edward Miller wrote in 1791:

A few years since, an *organ* was erected in the parish church of *Bradford*, ... and by the attention of the present vicar to the improvement of *psalmody*, the

217

congregations of the numerous dissenters in that town, and neighbourhood, are lessened; while [those] of the established church are increased in proportion. This information I had from a clergyman born in the town. (E. Miller, 1791: 12n.)

But the most interesting developments took place in York itself, still an important focus of events in the north of England, especially in church matters. William Richardson, an Evangelical minister who took the Arminian theological position, was appointed a vicar-choral of York Minster in 1771, and was given the perpetual curacy of the neighbouring church of St Michael-le-Belfry. He acquired these offices through the agency of William Mason, precentor of York, who, though not explicitly an Evangelical, had similar views on church music (Draper; Mason: 1795). During the next fifty years Richardson made St Michael's a notable centre of Evangelical religion in York. A second centre was established at St Saviour, where John Graham, a close friend and colleague of Richardson's, became vicar in 1796.

St Michael-le-Belfry had possessed an organ since the seventeenth century, but it had not been kept in repair. The organist was John Camidge, who doubtless devoted most of his time to his more important duties at the Minster; the children of the local Bluecoat School sang the metrical psalms. After a barrel organ had been tried out (at Mason's suggestion) in 1782, Richardson determined to install a new organ, which he did by raising a subscription in 1786. Camidge's salary was doubled to £10, and a new pulpit and reading-desk were erected in the middle aisle (MS 107).

In 1788 Richardson published *A collection of psalms* (words only), in which he made a careful selection of verses from the psalms, supplementing the Old and New Versions with those of Isaac Watts and James Merrick. In his preface, after briefly justifying psalm singing as ordained of God, he pointed out that it was in great need of improvement. To emphasise the importance of the way psalms are sung, he laid down these simple rules, which show his concern for effect as well as intention:

Those who possess a musical voice and ear, should learn the tunes perfectly, ... and sing loud ...
Those who have a harsh voice, or an imperfect ear, should sing low ...
Those who are totally without a voice or ear for music, should not attempt to sing, but be content to join in heart and affection.
Lastly: the whole congregation ought to stand up during the singing, as they do in reading the psalms. (W. Richardson: preface)

(The last observation shows that chanting of the psalms was not as yet practised.) Richardson also turned his attention to tunes, recommending one by name for each psalm selection. The 24 tunes he listed included a number of plain old tunes, and some excellent new ones such as 'Darwall's 148th', but avoided fuging and repeating tunes and those adapted from theatre or concert music. Matthew Camidge, who had probably taken his father's place at the organ for many years before he formally succeeded him in 1801, published a *Musical companion* to the collection about 1800 (PC 317), which gave organ settings of these and six other tunes. They were set on two staves, for right-hand chords and bass. By 1817 Richardson's collection was in use in 'at least thirty churches, in and near York', and it had had the effect its author desired (J. Gray, 1817: preface).

Richardson included no hymns, other than the Veni creator (authorised by its inclusion in the prayer book ordination service) and a communion hymn from the *Supplement to the New Version* (authorised by Queen Anne in 1703). As more and more hymns came into use in Anglican churches, he modified this conservative stance, and by 1817 he was willing to sanction a supplement of hymns (J. Gray, 1817). *A collection of tunes* (PC 342) for the hymns was prepared by Philip Knapton, organist of St Saviour. Together the two portions were published as *The York psalm and hymn book*, which went into many editions up to about 1850, the last of which were published in London.

This hymn selection, though published anonymously, was the work of Jonathan Gray, an important figure in our story, though now largely unknown. He was a lawyer by profession; an active supporter of Pitt and Wilberforce; a leader in national issues including slavery, foreign missions, and the treatment of the insane; and a local figure of importance, as alderman, magistrate, and a governor of several institutions. When he died in 1837 he was probably the most widely esteemed man in York (*York Chronicle*, 20 December 1837; A. Gray; Graham). He was also an accomplished amateur organist and composer. When Graham introduced Sunday evening lectures at St Saviour, Gray played the organ, because Knapton's duties covered only the morning service.

Oh, it was a sacred pleasure, to join in the song of praise sung with the understanding by a thousand voices, and attuned to the organ's pealing notes, produced by the hand of one, in whose heart the genial current of holy feeling ran, but stopped alas! too soon for us. (Burgess: 14–15)

Gray added church music to the many causes he supported, and persistently advocated all the improvements desired by Evangelicals. He began to develop his case in *The Christian Observer*, arguing over the signature 'H. G.' that the Old and New Versions had no special authority, and urging a good new selection of metrical psalm translations (such as Richardson's) and the introduction of hymns (XVII (1818), 152–9; XXII (1822), 421). He adapted this article for the preface to his selection, already mentioned, of hymns for use with Richardson's *Collection of psalms*, and it was further expanded in an important and influential pamphlet published in 1821. Here he brought his professional skill to bear in decisively showing that hymns were authorised for use in church, citing the recent case of *Holy & Ward v. Cotterill* to strengthen the case. This pamphlet was quoted as an authority by Latrobe and by later Tractarian apologists, and can be said to have laid the foundation for the Victorian development of Anglican hymnody.

In the same series of articles, Gray developed arguments for another kind of reform: the introduction of congregational chanting. In 1821 he wrote:

There is...little hope of the general restoration of [liturgical] church music in our parochial service. Yet in the parish churches of many of our principal towns, the practice of that music, has, within the last thirty years, been revived; and the congregations join in chanting the Venite exultemus, the Te deum, and Jubilate, the Magnificat (or the Cantate domino), and the Nunc dimittis (or the Deus misereatur), with a happy and devotional effect. In proportion as the usage of primitive ages is copied; in proportion likewise as the rites of the Church are respected, the structure of the poetry attended to, and her music duly appreciated, this mode of singing will be preferred above metrical psalmody. (J. Gray, 1821: 9)

The ideals expressed here for parish church music seem almost Tractarian in spirit, and most people would have difficulty in believing that they were the words of an accredited Evangelical. It has often been stated that the introduction of chanting in parish churches was an achievement of the Oxford movement. A standard history of the English Church in the eighteenth century says that 'through a great part of the eighteenth century chanting was almost unknown in parish churches, and was regarded as distinctively belonging to "cathedral worship"' (Abbey & Overton: 485). Percy Scholes wrote that 'up to the Oxford Movement of the 19th century the Anglican chant was in very little use except in cathedrals and other collegiate churches' (Scholes, 1955: 34), while Bernarr Rainbow defines the original aim of the Oxford 'choral revival' as 'to stimulate congregational chanting of the psalms and responses – sections of the service which had hitherto been read', and credits Frederick Oakeley with its first introduction at a parochial service in 1839 (Rainbow: 14). Scholes and Rainbow both credit Robert Janes, organist of Ely Cathedral, with the first pointed psalter, that of 1837 (Scholes, 1947: 551; Rainbow: 83).

In fact, the introduction of congregational chanting can be wholly attributed to the efforts of the Evangelical party, particularly at York. With their faithfulness to the liturgy and their desire for livelier worship, it is not surprising that they called in the aid of music. They accepted that in cathedrals the service was performed by the choir, but in the parish church they wanted all the singing to be congregational. Hence they conceived the revolutionary notion of congregational chanting. We have seen how, from 1718 onwards, psalmody books often contained chants for canticles and psalms, and sometimes even for the whole service. But these were emphatically intended for the use of the voluntary choirs, in imitation of cathedrals. Congregational chanting was quite another matter. The earliest distinct reference to it dates from 1790. William Vincent describes the psalm chanting by choirs recently introduced in certain churches and chapels in London, but points out that these choirs, instead of singing alone, should be leading the congregation.

A common chant is easily attainable by the ear; and if the same was always used, would soon become familiar to the audience, and all be insensibly led to join in it ... For this purpose, no chant is better calculated than that which the charity children sing at the conclusion of each psalm, at [their massed performance at] St. Paul's [cathedral]. – It is composed by Mr. Jones,* and has been adopted in one congregation with success. (Vincent: 10)

But the great difficulty was that congregations, unlike choirs, could not be expected to learn and rehearse the psalms of the day; nor could they chant

* In all probability this was the chant given in ex. 49.

them directly from the prayer book, since the pointing was inadequate, consisting only of a colon dividing each verse in half.

It was for this reason that congregational chanting was limited at first to the doxology ('at the conclusion of each psalm' in the above quotation) and then to the canticles, which were repeated often enough for regular churchgoers to learn how to chant them with reasonable uniformity. Meanwhile some reformers began to devise methods of pointing that could be used for chanting the psalms, even by an unrehearsed congregation. The first steps were taken in cathedral choirs. John Marsh, an amateur musician of Chichester, proposed in the preface to his *Cathedral chant book* (1804) that the organist and choir of a cathedral should agree on the pointing of all the psalms and underline the last syllable to be sung to the reciting note in each verse. John Christmas Beckwith, organist of Norwich cathedral, in 1808 published *The first verse of every psalm of David, with an ancient or modern chant in score*, but offered no guidance for subsequent verses. Benjamin Jacob, in *National psalmody* ([1817]), laid out the canticles complete under chants, with suggestions for organ registration; they were designed for congregational chanting. Gray, in an appendix to his 1821 pamphlet, printed the Te deum 'pointed to be conveniently chanted in churches', which he had arranged, with the help of Dr Camidge, 'for the church of St. Helen, Stonegate, in York'.

To gain an idea of the manner of this chanting, we may turn to Jacob's version of the Jubilate (ex. 49). He set it to the popular chant by Jones, which has a surprisingly large range for congregational singing, but is harmonised in unisons for the first half of each verse. He explained two points in the preface:

The pause over certain words in the recitative or speaking parts of the chants, is intended to show the emphatic word which gives sense to the whole, and which should be forced and dwelt upon a little; it is also recommended, that this recitative be not hurried, but every word pronounced distinctly. The metronomic figures do not apply to the recitation, which is unmeasured, but to the succeeding bars.

These cautions were evidently necessary, when we recall that the country collections of the eighteenth century had treated each reciting note as a semibreve in strict time, and had divided it up into notes of whatever length was necessary to accommodate all the words. Such a mode of chanting was probably used in many cathedrals in Georgian times. David Weyman, a lay-clerk in both Dublin cathedrals, published a version of the canticles in 1825, set out in much the same way as Jacob's, but with the semibreves divided into shorter notes and fitted to the syllables of each verse. He added a note: 'Several ladies and gentlemen being anxious to join in the chanting during divine service, but finding it difficult to apply the words, particularly of long verses, to the music (as printed in the usual way), the following arrangement ... is ... published agreeably to their wishes' (PC 713: 8). Further evidence that this 'strict tempo' method of chanting was widely used comes from barrel organs, which will be discussed later in this chapter.

It is clear that cathedrals did not need a printed pointed psalter: they had got along without one for nearly three hundred years, and, if they wished to improve the uniformity of their chanting, could do so by rehearsal or by manuscript additions to the prayer book psalter. The need for printed psalters with pointing arose only when congregational chanting became widespread.

There is reason to believe that the congregations of several churches in York chanted the canticles, and in some cases the psalms, during the first thirty years of the nineteenth century, largely because of the efforts of Gray and his friends (Temperley, 1977). Well might Matthew Camidge say on the title page of a collection of church music published in 1823: 'As chanting is becoming general in parish churches the author has subjoined twenty four of his own double chants' (PC 351a). But if York was perhaps in the lead in this practice, there is plenty of evidence that it existed also in other parts of the country. Many parochial collections of the 1820s contain chants, and Edward Hodges, writing in the *Bristol Mirror* in 1822, said that the practice was 'reviving. In many parochial churches the hymns [i.e., prose canticles] following the lessons are regularly chanted, and the congregations begin to take a part in the performance' (*Quarterly* IV, 1822: 175). In 1831 J. A. Latrobe, in a general survey of the practice of church music, said that chanting by choir and congregation had been adopted in 'many parochial churches', especially for the canticles (:265–76). In the same year came the first* fully pointed psalter, J. E. Dibb's *Key to chanting*.

Dibb was an obscure figure: deputy registrar for the West Riding, and apparently centred at Wakefield; his only other known publication is *The sub-diaconate*, a paper read to a meeting of the Church of England Clerical and Lay Association for the Maintenance of Evangelical Principles at Derby in 1866. His *Key to chanting* (1831) is now very scarce. In the prefatory Address to the Reader Dibb wrote:

> The fact is notorious, that very few, except choristers [i.e., choir members], are able to join in this part of the public worship of Almighty God ... Inability, on the part of the congregation to join in this service, chiefly proceeds from their not knowing how much of each verse is to be sung to the first, and how much to be left for the remaining notes of the chant, which latter are to be sung in exact time ... [The Reformers] placed a colon in the middle of each verse, to suit the ancient ecclesiastical mode of chanting; some further arrangement, however, is still required to render the practice easy and pleasant to each member of the congregation. To remedy this defect is the design of the present volume. (Dibb, 1831: iii)

His method simply consisted of separating and italicising the final syllables of each half-verse, thus:

> O come, let us sing un – *to the Lord*: let us heartily
> rejoice in the *strength of our salvation*.

Dibb used a slightly modified form of the crude 'rule of 3 and 5', which simply severed the last three syllables of the first half-verse and the last five of the second, regardless of verbal stress. He allowed two syllables to the last note of each half-verse, where the last syllable was unstressed. He directed that each word should be given 'the same due proportion of

---

* J. Dixon's *Canto recitativo* (PC 341, 1816) set out all the psalms fully pointed, but according to a reformed type of chant of his own devising; they could not be sung to Anglican chants.

emphasis, as if the passage were read', so that his system was actually a radical one, in which the musical accents would be largely subordinated to the verbal (:iii–iv).

This publication prompted criticism in *The Harmonicon*, and in the subsequent correspondence Gray was given the credit for developing Dibb's method of pointing (x, 1832: 27–9, 55). Gray himself shortly afterwards produced another work on the subject: *Twenty-four chants: to which are prefixed, remarks on chanting* (PC 360). He repeated again the arguments in favour of congregational chanting, and described, with examples, four modes of pointing that he had observed at the cathedrals of Lincoln, York, Canterbury and Bangor; it was the second mode that had been so severely criticised in *The Harmonicon*, but, Gray pointed out, Dibb was 'no further accountable than for having exhibited the ancient York method of chanting'. He admitted that 'in those parts of the kingdom which are remote from cathedral churches, ... chanting has not yet been introduced into the parochial service'. During the next fifteen years, dozens of pointed psalters appeared, and congregational chanting of the psalms in parish churches quickly became widespread. In this process the leaders of the Oxford movement played an important part, and added their own emphases and preferences which will be described in due course. But it should not be forgotten that the first initiative came from the Evangelical party, and the first pointed psalter from an Evangelical of Yorkshire. Dibb's psalter was still in use in 1850, despite the existence of so many rivals (*Parish Choir* III, 1850: 148).

It has sometimes been suggested that the Evangelicals were aesthetically impoverished, and failed to understand the religious value of art and music (Elliott-Binns: 436; Davies: III, 326–7). As far as music is concerned there are many counter-examples: the Wesley family; Thomas Haweis, Henry Venn, John Crosse, and William Richardson, who vigorously encouraged music in their churches; Martin Madan and Richard Cecil, who successfully contributed their own compositions to the store of church music; John Darwall, vicar of Walsall, who improved the singing in his church (Whitley: 149) and composed new tunes to all the metrical psalms of the New Version, one of which ('Darwall's 148th'), with its typical 'Methodist cadence', has joined the immortals; Jonathan Gray, though a layman, an indomitable fighter for the best in church music. As a group the Evangelicals opposed the vicarious types of psalmody that had developed both in town and country during the eighteenth century, and restored to the people their right to take part in the singing of praise. It was through them that both the hymn and the chanted psalm became accepted parts of congregational worship in the Church of England.

Traditional high churchmanship

Although Evangelicalism grew out of a high-church movement, it did not carry all the high-church clergy with it. A more conservative, austere party in the Church recoiled from the emotionalism of Evangelical preaching and hymn singing, and fell back on the traditional dignity of Anglican worship

(Pl. 6). The estrangement was complete when the various branches of Methodism separated from the Church, and the Evangelicals became associated with dissent. For the conservative high churchman, loyalty to the Church of England was almost the cardinal point in his religious creed. He despised Roman Catholics and dissenters with equal vigour. For him, the liturgy of the prayer book was the ultimate in religious excellence, and was to be carried out in every detail, adorned with the most beautiful music that could be devised. Dr Bisse's ideal of imitating cathedral music remained the supreme goal, however difficult of attainment.

William Hanbury, regarded as a 'high church Jacobite', used his personal fortune in an effort to maintain this ideal at Church Langton, where he was rector from 1749 to 1778. He founded a trust to assist the precise performance of the liturgy according to rubric, and to provide for its musical adornment; he also presented an organ, built in 1759. However, his funds were diverted to other uses, and were not spent on music until 1864 (*Victoria History of the County of Leicester*: v, 200).

William Jones of Nayland was a late eighteenth-century representative of the 'high and dry' section of the clergy; he happened to be a talented musician, and hence took more interest than many of his colleagues in the music of worship. He held several livings, but resided at Nayland where he was perpetual curate. He led a subscription to place an organ in the church, persuading many of the local gentry to contribute; he formed a choir of the local Sunday school children, and taught them to sing psalm tunes in harmony. But in a sermon on music in 1787 he insisted that their role was merely to lead the congregation, and he favoured the traditional psalm tunes, not modern ones of the Evangelical type. The organist should accompany in plain harmony, and in playing alone must 'take care not to mislead the ignorant into vain fancies, nor to offend the judicious with unseasonable levity. . . . If any anthems are admitted during the time of divine service, country choristers should confine themselves to choral harmony, in which they may do very well; and our church abounds with full anthems by the best masters.' Solos were discouraged. Boyce's *Cathedral music* was recommended as a source for simple anthems (Jones, 1810: iv, 86–7). Two years later Jones was able to boast that with the help of the organ, 'some of the best of our cathedral services and anthems are occasionally heard; and our psalmody, so assisted, is to my ear more affecting than any I ever met with of the kind, from such a number of tuneful children singing the old plain psalms in *different* parts' (PC 268: dedication).

An anonymous writer, calling himself 'A friend to Decency in religious Worship', in 1797 gave an approving description of a country service that was full of the beauty of holiness, at Whilton. The church was 'of modern date', and the present rector (William Holden)

with a large fortune possesses a singular turn of mind – that of beautifying the temple of God; and retains an old-fashioned notion, that the splendour of outward services and ceremonies conspires to raise devotion. He has laid out above £300 in making this church elegantly neat . . . The furniture of the desk and pulpit is rich and becoming; that of the altar splendid, but without any ostentatious finery. A beautiful organ has been lately erected, of sweet tone and full power, which leads a well-instructed choir, consisting of young women in the organ-gallery, and of men in an opposite one; so that there is frequently an alternate chorus, like that of the *decanus* and cantor in cathedrals. (*Gentleman's Magazine* LXVII, 1797: 931–2; see also Baker: I, 235)

At more and more churches in the early decades of the nineteenth century, choirs were asked not only to sing metrical psalms, hymns and anthems, but to chant the canticles, portions of the liturgy, and even the prose psalms. The goal was of course quite distinct from the Evangelical one of congregational singing and chanting. Chanting by parish choirs was challenged in court in more than one case (as described above, p. 106), and was sometimes stopped by the parson, as at Camerton in 1822 (Skinner: 8) or at Sherborne in 1823 (Mayo). But, especially in large town parish churches, chanting was introduced, and the greater efforts demanded of the choirs were rewarded by increasing payments by the parishioners, or in some cases by the municipal corporation. At Doncaster in 1817 (ten years after Miller's death), the schoolchildren were for the first time paid a salary of one guinea each, and three male singers were engaged to assist them, one of whom, a Mr Wragg, was 'to teach the singers and to attend the singing himself at an annual salary of twenty guineas ... Mr. Wragg to attend three times a week' (MS 93/38: 385). The choir was thus equipped, though only just, to chant in four parts in cathedral manner. The annual payments were gradually increased, and the choir by 1832 contained five men and twelve children (:501). In the decade 1822–32 the singers were getting an average total of over £45 per year. In 1833 the payments were severely cut back as a measure of economy, and in anticipation of the approaching enquiry by the parliamentary commissioners (*Doncaster Report*).

In a rural area far from industrialised Yorkshire, at Bridport, an organ was installed in 1815; it was the only one for miles around, and 'it was no unusual thing, for many country people to come to Bridport, on Sundays, purposely to hear the much talked-of organ' (Collins). The choir, rising to the challenge, embarked on an ambitious programme of music on cathedral lines. Three manuscript part-books have survived (one labelled 'No. 22'), dated 1823. Besides metrical psalms, hymns and cathedral anthems, they contain a large number of psalm chants, and 'the service as chanted at Lichfield cathedral' (see ex. 65b). At Falmouth, in the far south-west, four volumes of anthems were purchased in 1808, and were sung by a choir of men and women: in 1826 the organist was instructed 'to obey the orders of the minister for the time being as to all singing, chanting and playing in the church' (Kempthorne: 49–50).

At Leeds, the difficulties of the parish church included a rapidly increasing population, and an open vestry in which a large proportion of the voters (ratepayers) were dissenters, who were not disposed to vote money in support of elaborate church music. Nevertheless, in 1815, when Richard Fawcett became vicar, a professional body of singers was formed to sing the services, and in 1818 a *surpliced* choir of men and boys was installed, i.e., more than twenty years before the date usually given (Rainbow: 27, and n.). They were paid nearly £100 a year, and in 1826, when these payments were called into question at a vestry meeting, the vestry regularised them by a small majority, despite opposition from dissenters, who called the choir a 'relic of popery' (Rainbow: 307–9). It is most probable that this choir's duties included chanting, for John Greenwood, who was organist from 1821 to 1828, published about 1825 (at Leeds) *A selection of ancient and modern psalm tunes, chants, and responses*, containing several chants (PC 354).

The payments for the music were withdrawn by the vestry in 1833, and thenceforward had to be raised by voluntary subscription; the standard quickly declined. But a few years later it was raised to still greater heights, when Walter Hook, the high-church vicar of Leeds, introduced daily choral services along cathedral lines, in a new building in the gothic style, with choir stalls in the chancel. In doing so he relied heavily on the advice of John Jebb, a prebendary of Limerick cathedral, who was strongly opposed to any congregational participation in the singing of the liturgy. In chanting, Jebb felt, 'the roar of the congregation' was entirely out of place, and 'the nicest discrimination' was necessary, 'to be attained only by constant daily practice' (Jebb: 298–9; cited Curwen, 1880: 22–3). The choral service cost six or seven hundred pounds a year, a sum which Hook assumed personal responsibility for raising (W. Stephens: II, 124). In 1842 he crowned the whole effort by appointing as organist Samuel Sebastian Wesley, the most prominent cathedral organist of his generation, at the unheard-of salary of £200 a year. Naturally the 'cathedral' quality of the service became even more pronounced under Wesley's direction. He produced a pointed psalter and an elaborate Service in E major for the Leeds choir, which indeed became one of the most efficient in the country. In 1850 it consisted of 16 boys and 12–14 men on Sundays, a larger number than almost any cathedral could boast at that time; on weekdays there were 12 boys and 8 men (*Parish Choir* III, 1850: 148). The Leeds model of fully choral services was imitated, first at a few churches in London and other large towns, and before long in many small-town and even village churches.

This change, in which the Leeds achievement was the first landmark, took place at the same time as the Oxford movement, and has often been associated with it (Beresford-Hope: 12; Scholes, 1947: 537). Yet the introduction of choral services on cathedral lines, to the exclusion of the congregation, was hardly in accord with the ideals of the movement, as we shall see, and as Bernarr Rainbow has pointed out (:26–42). Hook himself was not a Tractarian (W. Stephens). He was a high churchman of the older school, whose ideal was the 'beauty of holiness' for which the cathedral service seemed to provide the best model. Both he and Jebb entertained the highest religious ideals in choosing this model. But the widespread support that it won, first at Leeds and soon afterwards in London and throughout the country, was probably based on a mixture of motives, in which religious idealism played a relatively small part. It certainly came to be accepted by vast numbers of people who were indifferent or hostile to the Oxford movement (Rainbow: 263–80).

The conservative high churchman based his view of worship and church music entirely on his overriding veneration for the liturgy and traditions of the Church. He did not, like the Evangelical, temper this formality with the charisma of the living word: even his family prayers tended to be liturgical (Davies: III, 220). He saw no reason to depart from the mode of worship that was then traditional in the Church (and this was before scholarly enquiry had led to the revival of still older traditions). Corporate splendour and dignity mattered more than the individual worshipper's state of mind. It was a view that tended to lead to the imitation of cathedral worship advocated by Bisse, and eventually achieved by Hook. But it must still be distinguished from the low-church or materialistic approach, which could also tend in that direction, and which is now to be considered. While the high churchman strove for the greater glory of God, there were many in that age who saw church music as an extension of themselves, and who wanted it to reflect their own progress through the ranks of society.

'Improved psalmody'

A development distinct from either of those so far considered was the 'improved' psalmody of the genteel. They, like the Evangelicals, wanted to curb the excesses of the country choirs, but not with the object of letting the whole congregation sing. On the contrary, they wished to silence the congregation completely, and listen instead to a well-ordered, paid choir, trained and accompanied by a professional organist. Some traditional high churchmen, such as Jones of Nayland, joined the Evangelicals in wanting the people to join the singing of the choir, at least in the metrical psalms, but most members of the wealthier classes were no more willing than they had ever been to join in the homely singing of their inferiors. A correspondent of the *Gentleman's Magazine* in 1781, signing himself 'No Psalm Singer', summarising Thomas Warton's account of Sternhold and Hopkins's version (Warton: III, 176–7), associated it with a dissenting congregation of 'manufacturers and mechanics':

It is certainly better calculated for the spiritual consolation of tallow-chandlers and tailors, than for the pious uses of the liberal and intelligent. Psalm-singing and Republicanism naturally go together. They seem both founded on the same levelling principle. The Republican Calvin appears to have been of opinion, that all people should *sing* in the church, as well as *act* in the state, without distinction or inequality. Hence his necessity of a *vulgar* and *popular* psalmody. There is much philosophical truth in a ludicrous saying of King Charles the Second, that *the Presbyterian worship was not fit for a gentleman.* (*Gentleman's Magazine* LI, 1781: 369)

Isaac D'Israeli (father of Benjamin) claimed that psalm singing 'frequently served as the trumpet of rebellion' (D'Israeli). Such reactions are perhaps only a sign of the panic induced in the landed classes by the American and French Revolutions. But a more formidable opponent of congregational singing was none other than Charles Burney, himself a former parish church organist. In his treatment of protestant church music in the third volume of his *General history of music*, published in 1789, he expressed the view that 'the greatest blessing to lovers of music in a parish-church, is to have an organ in it sufficiently powerful to render the voices of the clerk and of those who join in his *out-cry*, inaudible'. He asked, 'why is the *whole* congregation to *sing* any more than preach, or read prayers?... *Every* member of a conventicle, however it may abound with cordwainers and tailors, would not pretend to make a shoe or a suit of clothes; and yet in our churches *all* are to sing' (:III, 60, 64). His argument was answered with some spirit by Mason two years later (Mason: 197–205). Nevertheless, it gave countenance and respectability to a point of view that was probably held by many, though seldom boldly stated. The facetious snobbery of Burney's account would have appealed to the elegant and fashionable class to which he himself aspired to belong. He described the singing as 'indecorous', recalling the early Georgian period, when, in the name of decorum, the wealthy had paid for organs and charity children to provide their church music. By now the organs were often out of repair, the charity children ill-trained and screechy. It was time to take measures to restore a proper standard of decorum in the singing, and to bring the music up to date. The basis for this kind of improved psalmody remained the choir of charity children in the organ gallery, supplemented, if possible, by adult voices. But there was no desire to have them chant the liturgy, or otherwise imitate cathedral choirs. That is the main point of difference with the traditional high-church party.

A representative figure in this low-church view of psalmody was the Reverend William Tattersall, a pluralist clergyman who was incumbent of both Wootton-under-Edge, where he normally resided, and Westbourne. In a collection of psalm tunes (1791, PC 292) he deplored the contempt into which psalmody had fallen, which he put down to want of encouragement by the clergy and the gentry. As a remedy he proposed the formation of a choir, to be supervised by the clergyman (a significant departure from normal country practice), and to be subsidised by a small fund 'for the instruction and occasional encouragement of the poorer members', partly from parish funds or voluntary contributions and partly from fines for non-attendance at rehearsals. 'In my own parish I have found a plan of this kind attended with the fullest success.' Further, Tattersall proposed reform of both the texts and the music to be sung. Rejecting the homely and commonplace verses of Sternhold and Hopkins, and of Tate and Brady, he provided selections from the 'elegant version' of James Merrick (who, however, in the preface to his version (published in 1765) had said that it was not 'calculated for the uses of public worship'). For tunes, Tattersall advocated simplicity and cheerfulness: 'The serious glees which consist only of three parts, seem to present a perfect model for this species of divine harmony', and he advised those who set Merrick's version 'to confine themselves to this style'. Tattersall acknowledged the help of two professional musicians of distinction, William Parsons and Benjamin Cooke. His collection was later greatly expanded in a work entitled *Improved psalmody* (PC 297), which gives this section its name. It came out in numbers in 1794 and 1795, and its list of subscribers equalled that of Miller's *Psalms of David* in social prestige (not in size), but was weighted to the south of England rather than the north. Instead of Miller's emphasis on sturdy, simple tunes in which the congregation, led by an organ, could effectively take part, Tattersall provided a large number of new tunes of ornate elegance. He obtained them by commissioning the leading musicians of the day,* including Shield, Callcott, Webbe, Parsons, Arnold, Cooke, and even Haydn, who contributed six tunes (ex. 50). Although the congregation was invited to join in the 'upper part' of the two- or three-part harmonisations, these were clearly designed for a choir of trebles, supported by a vocal or instrumental bass (ex. 51). Some of the settings were through-composed set pieces. All were in the glee style that Tattersall advocated, sometimes with contrapuntal imitation of a mild sort, for, as he pointed out, 'many congregations are delighted with tunes where the parts lead off separately'. The music was impeccably correct and professional. Only two old tunes were used, though in an appendix many traditional tunes were provided, together with words from the Old Version, to cater for those who did not want their psalmody improved.†

Tattersall's book was widely adopted, especially in town churches where the resources to pay for an organ, organist and choir were available. At Wakefield, a new chapel of ease, St John's, was opened in 1795, and the minister, Richard Munkhouse, made it a progressive centre for church music, with a large and efficient choir. On 8 May 1796 he preached a sermon 'previous to the introduction of the Rev. James Merrick's version of the psalms, with music provided by the Rev. W. D. Tattersall' (Munkhouse: I, 251). Because the charity children were engaged in the parish church, Munkhouse found children from the Sunday schools and private schools for his choir, following Bishop Porteus's suggestion. Men were also recruited. The choir originally numbered 120; 60 remained in 1797 (Munkhouse: II, 102). All the expenses of the choir were paid by a local landowner and builder, John Lee. In 1799 the chapel organist, Richard Sampson, published a complementary selection of psalms in the Old and New Versions (PC 315) set to traditional tunes, but these were also arranged for two trebles and bass in glee-like fashion and with the addition of ornaments (ex. 52). The selection of texts was made by Munkhouse (:II, 93n.). The choir was at first taught for three months by 'a country singing-master' who used 'Mr. Chetham's method'; but when this was found slow and ineffectual, a simpler and more practical method was devised, and is described in Sampson's preface. The choir rehearsed for four months, several hours a week, before venturing to sing in the church. At a later date they began also to chant the canticles and possibly the psalms. In 1823 a small notebook was begun, to record 'Subscriptions to be distributed to the Boys & Girls who chant and sing at St. John's church intended to encourage them to improve themselves in that department and to reward them for so doing' (MS 98).

Halifax was in this period at the very centre of that remarkable development of choral music in Yorkshire, Lancashire and Derbyshire that has already been mentioned. From 1731 to 1775 it had a low-church vicar, George Legh, 'popular among the dissenters, a disciple of Bishop Hoadley and his coadjutor, in what was called the Bangorian Controversy'

---

* Arnold and Callcott had published their own collection, on similar lines, in 1791, with many 'polite' fuging tunes (PC 291).

† Another quite distinct work, also called *Improved psalmody*, 'sanctioned by the king at Weymouth', was produced by Tattersall in 1802. Here Merrick's versions had been set to adapted selections from the works of Handel, apparently to indulge the tastes of George III.

(Crabtree: 130). He was followed by two moderate Evangelicals as vicars, Henry Coulthurst (1790–1817) and Samuel Knight (1817–27) (Crabtree: 131, 273), and another low churchman, Charles Musgrave (1827–75). The church (Pl. 26) was famous for music, and we can fortunately gain an accurate idea of the music performed there at different times by studying successive revisions and supplements to Chetham's *Psalmody* (see Table 10, p. 183). The edition of 1811, revised by Thomas Stopford (who had been organist for 45 years), was on the whole conservative, retaining a surprisingly large number of the old psalm tunes. It maintained the tradition of chanted canticles and anthems, though there were fewer anthems than in eighteenth-century editions of the book. A new Evangelical influence can be detected in some of the hymns now provided, and many of the new tunes are of the repeating type or otherwise have a distinctly Methodist flavour.

This trend was continued in the next revision, compiled by John Houldsworth (organist 1819–36), and published in 1832. It ran to twenty editions with little modification. The proportion of hymns to psalms was now much increased; many of the older tunes were dropped, and many new ones of an ornate and secular type added, including some actually adapted from popular songs, such as 'Cranbrook' from 'On Ilkley moor baht 'at'. The tunes were given 'in keys best adapted to congregational singing' (PC 359: preface).

On the other hand the book also indicated a marked shift towards choral and away from congregational singing. The number of chants was increased from 9 to 96, and words were set under the chants 'to promote uniformity and to assist choirs, who may wish to introduce chanting into the service'. Directions for chanting were provided for the 'performers'. Houldsworth also provided settings of the responses to the commandments in the communion service, which he said were 'generally left to the choir', and of the doxology in the responses at morning and evening prayer, which 'must be sung in full chorus'. It is true that there were now almost no anthems or service settings in the book. But other evidence reveals that this was caused by an increase, not a decrease, in the amount of elaborate choral music sung at Halifax. For the parish church library contains a large amount of cathedral music, much of it in editions published at the time that 'Houldsworth's Cheetham's Psalmody' was also in use. A pattern of hymn singing by choir and congregation, and psalm chanting and singing of services and anthems by choir alone, was apparently retained until late in the nineteenth century; successive organists prepared appendices and supplements to Houldsworth's book on similar lines, and the church library continued to augment its supply of cathedral music, with an emphasis on recent and contemporary works (MS 20). Not until the 1880s was the local psalmody collection superseded by *Hymns ancient and modern* and *The cathedral psalter*. The organ and choir remained in the west gallery until 1878, when, on the recommendation of Varley Roberts (organist 1868–82), it was moved to its Victorian position in the chancel.

It is clear that at Halifax parish church a continuous tradition of choral singing, including anthems, service settings and chanting, was maintained from early in the eighteenth century until the present day. But the emphasis was on elaborate psalm and hymn tunes, suited to predominantly choral singing with organ accompaniment. The joy of listening to a powerful and efficient choir prevailed over the desire for greater congregational participation, which may have been strong under Evangelical influence in the early nineteenth century. Perhaps because no Tractarian was ever appointed vicar, the Oxford movement had little direct effect on the musical tradition. The church was a leading centre and model for music in its area, as is indicated by the meetings of the Halifax Choral Society from about 1820 onwards (*Harmonicon*, 1833: 33, 109), the ambitious choral festivals held in the church in 1830 and later years (Houseman: 90–5), and the deanery choral festivals held there from about 1880 (festival programmes in the church library). In many choral enterprises the choir of the parish church combined with singers from Nonconformist churches in the area. George Hogarth observed the unbounded enthusiasm for choral music, and the surprisingly high standard of performance attained at these festivals (Houseman: 95–7; *Musical Herald* I, 1846: 34).

An entirely different solution to the low-church ideal of 'improved psalmody' was the choir or quartet of paid concert or opera singers. It is difficult to say whether this was originally in imitation of the Roman Catholic Embassy chapels (the Portuguese chapel, in particular, was famous for its professional choir in about 1800). If so, it is surprising that it seems to have been introduced chiefly in Anglican churches of low-church associations. A more likely model was the Foundling Hospital and 'some fashionable proprietary chapels', where 'there are half a dozen female concert singers, and as many men perched up in a gallery behind a red curtain' (*What can be done?*: 16). At the date of this passage (1846) it was not suggested that any parish churches had followed suit, but a decade later Dickson wrote that 'in very many town churches...a hired "choir" occupies the organ-loft... [consisting of] ladies and gentlemen from the concert-room. It is most painful to me, I own, to witness the display which takes place in such churches, when (the curtains of the organ-loft being noisily drawn aside) a lady, fashionably dressed, proceeds to sing a solo from an oratorio by way of an anthem' (Dickson, 1857: 8). A certain number of London churches maintained such an arrangement until near the end of the century (Mackeson, 1866–95).

Low-church psalmody made no attempt to develop a distinctively 'religious' kind of music. On the contrary, it took over all that was appealing, cheerful, and fashionable in secular music, so that going to church would include a suitable amount of pleasant and rational entertainment. Evangelicals, with somewhat different motives, also adapted the current modes of secular music. William Gardiner, the Leicester stocking manufacturer and able amateur musician, brought this trend to a logical conclusion by publishing a six-volume collection of *Sacred melodies, from Haydn, Mozart and Beethoven* (1812–15: PC 339), in which metrical psalms and hymns were adapted to choice passages from the works of the Viennese masters (ex. 53). Gardiner justified his exploit in the preface, and again in *The music of nature* (:277–84). The Nonconformists, he said, have adapted trivial and unworthy tunes, such as 'The Tyrolese

231

Waltz', to sacred texts. In reaction, 'some musical professors have loudly condemned the introduction of modern music into our churches, and would confine us to the dull and dismal tunes of the last century'. (The chief target for this remark was Dr Crotch, whose opposite views will be considered later.) But beautiful melody, in Gardiner's view, is flowing, and 'the voice, in passing from one interval to another, feels for those stepping stones ... by which it not only moves with greater ease, but with greater certainty. It is only in the works of the moderns that we find these melodies'. Accordingly he adapted a large number of tunes by Haydn, Mozart and Beethoven (ex. 53). Many other adaptations besides Gardiner's found their way into Anglican hymn books. One of the most popular was the tune 'Creation', from a chorus in Haydn's oratorio, which was happily adapted to Addison's metrical version of Psalm 18, 'The spacious firmament on high', by Bishop Simms, organist of St Philip, Birmingham, separately published in about 1810, and reprinted in many collections, including Houldsworth's edition of Chetham's *Psalmody* (ex. 54; see also ex. 50).

Several comprehensive collections of psalmody for low-church use were produced by professional musicians who were thoroughly at home in the secular music of the day. Thomas Greatorex, organist of Westminster Abbey, compiled *Parochial psalmody* (PC 349), which was designed to provide music for Rann Kennedy's *Church of England psalm book* 'selected from the authorised versions' (no hymns were admitted). Greatorex published his book in 1820 and dedicated it to George IV. He commented in the preface:

As most churches are now supplied with a choir of singers, their assistance will be highly useful in giving the proper effect to these psalms, which need not, like the anthems, exclude the congregation from joining in them. Even to the tunes I call congregational (while the melody may be sung by the congregation generally), I have added other parts to be supported by the alto, tenor, and bass voices of practiced singers.

His selection of tunes was conservative, including many of the traditional ones, but they were harmonised in a mellifluous fashion that rather suggested the glee (ex. 55), despite the compiler's view about the 'sublimity' of these ancient tunes, to which we will return in another chapter. Later collections on similar lines were Charles Hackett's *The national psalmist* (PC 365: 1839), dedicated to the Bishop of Ripon and particularly popular in the northern counties; and *Harmonia sacra* (PC 367: 1840), the joint production of the lecturer (John Baxter) and organist (Charles Baldwyn) of St George, Kidderminster, which was widely used in the south and west. Both included some hymns. All three collections included chants, responses to the commandments, set pieces and anthems to supplement the core repertory of psalm tunes.

The attractions of a musical performance by a skilled choir and organist led many low churchmen to accept more and more singing of liturgical music, when they had got over their initial prejudices. (In an imaginary dialogue in *The Parish Choir*, 'Mr. Bray' comments: 'The very word *chant* is connected with some most indefinable objections in my mind. I do not like it, and yet can hardly say why; but I have some notion that there is

Popery lurking at the bottom of it' (:ɪ, 1845: 33).) Hence the gradual move towards choral singing of the liturgy in parish churches, initiated by traditional high churchmen, eventually won the support of low churchmen, who came to see it as the ultimate 'improvement' of psalmody. So it became, in Victorian times, acceptable to the broad majority of Anglicans. Only extremists of one kind or another succeeded in opposing it.

Churches, organs, and barrel organs

The early nineteenth century saw a phenomenal increase in Anglican church building. Partly, no doubt, this was linked to the religious revival, first Evangelical and then Tractarian; there was also a political motive, raised by the cry 'The Church in danger' (Yates; *Gentlemen's Magazine* LXXXV(2), 1815: 45). The French Revolution and the war with Napoleon had led to a desire to shore up national institutions, and to treasure what was traditional in English life. Defections to nonconformity, particularly Methodism, had been large, and it was no longer possible to ignore the religious needs of the new industrial districts. So it was that a reactionary Tory government in 1818 passed the Church Building Act, which not only provided a million pounds in public money to finance the building of new churches, but removed the legal obstacles to the dividing of parishes. The Commissioners appointed to administer the act built altogether 214 churches, of which 174 were in the gothic revival style: their earliest churches, such as that of St Pancras, built 1819–22, were in Greek revival style. The gothic churches built between 1818 and 1833 were mainly sponsored by Evangelicals, and did not show the scholarly and antiquarian attention to detail of the later Tractarian churches (Davies: ɪv, 43–4). They were gothic only in appearance: their chief function, like that of the Georgian classical church, was still that of an auditorium.

The investment of the Commissioners was soon overtaken by the generosity of private subscriptions and endowments. Of 12,000 churches existing in 1851, it was estimated that

8,000 were built before the Reformation
1,500   between 1550 and 1801 (average 6 per year)
  500   between 1801 and 1831 (average 16 per year)
2,029   between 1831 and 1851 (average 100 per year)

The cost since 1801 was estimated as follows:

1801–31: £1.2 million public money, £1.8 million private funds
1831–51: £0.5 million public money, £5.6 million private funds
                                  (*Census of Great Britain* (1851): xxxii–xliii)

Because many of the new churches were in newly created parishes, the incumbent was free both of supervision by another clergyman and of the restraints imposed by long-established local traditions. Thus both Evangelicals and Tractarians frequently found they could make innovations more easily in new churches (*Parish Choir* ɪ, 1847: 166–7). Many of the Victorian experiments in 'advanced ritualism' were carried out in newly built churches, as was the introduction of fully choral services at

Leeds. And in earlier times, as at St John, Wakefield, in the 1790s, a clergyman was sometimes able to plan and execute an integrated scheme of architecture, furnishing, liturgy and music, as a new district and a new church were simultaneously brought into existence (Munkhouse).

There was also in this period a great rush to provide organs in churches. It was now taken almost for granted that any new church would have an organ in it, and by 1820 the great majority of churches in London had organs as did those in town parishes of any size: the small parishes in ancient cathedral cities lagged behind (Table 3, p. 112). But country churches still could not usually afford an organ (Cole: 6); and it could still be said, in 1821, that 'in the majority of churches there are no organs, as they are seldom to be met with except in towns' (Kennedy: 26). In the second quarter of the century the English organ was in transition from the older style of instrument without pedals, and with an F or G compass tuned in meantone temperament, to the 'German' type of organ with pedals, C compass and equal temperament. One of the first of the new type in a parish church was installed at St James, Bristol in 1824 (Galpin, 1965: 172).

For country churches, the problem was not so much to pay for an organ as to find and pay a qualified organist who was willing to attend services regularly. Sometimes the vicar's wife or daughter could oblige, but a professional player was unlikely to reside within easy distance of the church. At Beckenham, as late as 1859, there was a good organ, but the organist walked down from London every Sunday to play at morning prayer, and walked back immediately afterwards, probably to play at another church. At evensong, therefore, the singing was still unaccompanied, led by the parish clerk (MS 97: 45).

The solution, advocated by many and in the end widely adopted, was a barrel organ, which had the pipes and stops of an ordinary organ but was played by a pin-barrel. Alternatively, a mechanism called a 'dumb organist' could be attached to the keyboard of an ordinary organ (Sharp). In either case the operator had only to turn a handle, which on most instruments worked the bellows and the barrel simultaneously (Pl. 25).

Mechanical organs were invented in the middle ages, but their period of popularity began towards the end of the eighteenth century, when they were specially in demand as chamber organs, playing popular tunes for singing and dancing. Boston & Langwill, who carried out exhaustive research on English barrel organs, list very few church barrel organs before 1790, and these few are not well authenticated. Barrel organs were recommended by John Arnold as early as 1761, who pointed out that they could play 'a set of voluntaries, also most of our ancient psalm-tunes, with their givings-out and interludes, &c. which are very commodious for churches in remote country places, where an organist is not easily to be had or maintained' (PC 117/5: preface).

But no barrel organ capable of playing anything so elaborate appears to have survived. William Mason, as already stated, tried one out at St Michael-le-Belfry, York, in 1782 and then installed it in his own parish church at Aston; in his view the great advantage of a barrel-organ was that it played in strict time (Mason: III, 226). Robert Wharton in 1791 advocated a barrel organ where 'the opulence of the parish' could not afford an organ. In his own parish church (Sigglesthorne) a great improvement had resulted from an instrument of 21 notes, capable of playing in the keys of C, G, F, and G minor, with two barrels of ten tunes each: it had cost £21 (Wharton: 10–12, 25–6). From the 1790s until the 1860s, many barrel organs were manufactured and used in parish churches. The geographical distribution (Boston & Langwill: 73–99) shows that they were in use in all parts of England; the apparent bias in favour of Sussex and East Anglia is caused, no doubt, by the special studies of those regions made by Canon Macdermott and Canon Boston respectively.

The barrel organ would generally replace the church band in a country church, and to some extent would also replace the choir (Pl. 24, 25). This, indeed, was what commended it to many clergymen. Bryceson's advertisement of about 1840 clearly set out its advantages:

To those wishful to promote decent psalmody in their congregations, they are a certain guide; the tunes are so correctly set, as to be equal in performance to a finger organ, and will entirely supersede the use of other instruments. In consequence of the great expense of a finger organ, and the salary of an organist, many serious people are deprived of the means of joining in that pleasing part of divine worship, while it is not generally known that an able substitute may be had in one of his barrel organs, and at an expense which almost any congregation can afford – the prices are from 40 guineas to 100 upwards. (Boston & Langwill: 3)

Of course, the singers and instrumentalists were not happy to find themselves abruptly made redundant. Mr Mail in Hardy's *Under the greenwood tree* expressed the wounded feelings of many: 'Times have changed from the times they used to be ... People don't care much about us now! I've been thinking, we must be almost the last left in the county of the old string players. Barrel-organs, and they next door to 'em that you blow wi' your foot, have come in terribly of late years.' Some clergymen objected to barrel organs on the grounds that they were too mechanical and failed to follow the singers, and were associated with trivial uses: they were frequently carried out to the public houses to accompany dances, and there are even anecdotes about the parish clerk playing the 'secular' barrel in church by mistake (Latrobe: 354–7; Macdermott, 1922: 52). F. A. Head, vicar of Awlescombe, in 1840 deplored 'the hopeless endeavour to imitate the perplexed sounds of the damaged barrel-organs', explaining that 'these intruments, when once unhappily introduced into our village churches, are very rarely afterwards either repaired or tuned' (PC 368: 7–8). Certainly many surviving organs, left presumably in the state they were in when last used, produce very defective music, even when put in tune, because of damage to the pin barrels.

Surviving tune lists show that an organ would be equipped with from one to three barrels, each carrying ten to fifteen tunes (Boston & Langwill: 117–20). Any tune on a barrel could be selected, and then played through as many times as needed. For this reason, each tune had to take up one complete revolution of the barrel, apart from the short gap between the end and the beginning. Thus every tune on the barrel would occupy about the same time, unless it was possible to fit in a tune twice through on one revolution. Tunes of standard length were easiest to manage: anthems, set pieces, and long fuging or repeating tunes of the eighteenth-century type could not be accommodated, except on a very large and slow-moving barrel. A tune somewhat longer than average could be managed, but if it was to be played at the same tempo as a tune of ordinary length, the handle would have to be turned slower than usual.

Table 13 gives statistics of the tunes most frequently found on surviving barrel organs. While it does indicate which tunes were most often used in churches with barrel organs, it has only limited value as evidence of the

Table 13. *Tunes most frequently found on church barrel organs (c. 1790–1860)*

Name of tune (alternative names)	Origin	Modern source	Metre	No. of barrels containing tune
Old Hundredth (Savoy)	PC 701/1561; from French Psalter (1551)	AMR 166; F. 114	LM	66
Hanover (Airlie Street)	PC 57 (1708); attributed to William Croft	AMR 167b	XXYY	45
Evening Hymn (Suffolk, Berwick, Magdalen, Tallis)	Altered version of Tallis's Canon, in Parker's *Psalter* (*c.* 1565). See p. 238.	ex. 57	LM	43
Portuguese Hymn (Portugal New, Adeste fideles, Christmas Hymn)	Webbe (1782): by J. F. Wade, *c.* 1740	AMR 593	Irregular	37
Easter Hymn	*Lyra davidica* (London, 1708): altered	AMR 134	$(7474)^2$	35
Bedford	PC 80 (*c.* 1720); attributed to W. Wheal	AMR 320	CM	33
Sicilian Mariners (Mariners, Sicily)	PC 297 (1794)	AMR 410	557557	32
Mount Ephraim (St Helena, Conway)	PC 621 (1768): by Benjamin Milgrove	AMR 531	SM	30
Abridge	PC 246 (*c.* 1780); by Isaac Smith	AMR 300	CM	25
Morning Hymn	PC 501/1785; attributed to F. W. Barthélémon	AMR 3	LM	25
Shirland	By S. Stanley (1767–1822)	...	SM	25
Helmsley (Advent Hymn)	J. Wesley (1765)	AMR 51; ex. 46	87874447	23
St Stephens (Nayland)	PC 268 (1789); by William Jones	AMR 52	CM	23
Irish (Dublin)	PC 175 (*c.* 1760), from S. Powell, *A collection of hymns* (Dublin, 1749), according to Frere & Frost (:287)	AMR 263	CM	22
Wareham	PC 115 (1738); by William Knapp	AMR 245	LM	22
Devizes	By Isaac Tucker (1761–1825)	...	86866	21
London New (New Toun, Magdalen, Exeter)	PC 26 (1671), altered from the Scottish psalter of 1635	AMR 181; F. 222	CM	20

Source: Boston & Langwill: 21–38. (Boston & Langwill's own list of tunes in order of frequency, on p. 19, does not agree with their detailed lists on pp. 21–38.)

AMR: *Hymns Ancient and Modern Revised* (PC 417). See also Frere & Frost.

For a note on metres, see Table 1, p. 60.

general popularity of tunes. This is because the mechanical limitations of the instrument just described amount to a bias in favour of short tunes.

Unfortunately, there was little room for variation of tempo on many barrel organs. This was so on the one from Attleborough, which I was able to play and record. I was forced to turn the handle almost as fast as I could, for if I allowed the speed to slacken, the wind supply began to fail. Table 14 shows the tunes on this organ, and the tempo range possible for each. A few larger instruments had independent mechanisms for the barrel and the bellows, allowing the player to slow the tempo while maintaining the wind supply (Boston & Langwill: 19).

Table 14. *Possible tempo variations of tunes on Attleborough barrel organ*

| Tune | Metre | Time | Crotchet beats | | | Tempo ($\downarrow$/min.) | | | |
			(a)	(b)	(c)	Slow	Mean	Fast	Jacob
1. Morning Hymn	LM	4/4	32	+1	33	42	50	55	72
2. Evening Hymn (ex. 57)	LM	4/4	32	+2	34	43	51	57	72
3. Old Hundredth	LM	4/4	32	+1	33	42	50	55	60
4. Hanover	XXYY	3/4	48		48	61	72	80	88
5. Devizes	86866	4/4	54		54	69	81	90	72
6. Shirland	SM	4/4	28	−1	27	34	40	45	—
7. Portuguese Hymn	Irreg.	4/4	80		80	102	120	133	—
8. Bedford	CM	3/4	42	+2	44	56	66	73	80
9. Mornington Chant (ex. 56) (twice through)		4/4	56		56	72	84	94	[120]*
10. Sicilian Mariners	557557	4/4	64	−2	62	80	93	104	—

The barrel organ, which was used in Attleborough parish church about 1840, is now in the collection of the Reverend Jonathan Boston at Horsford, who kindly allowed me to play and record the instrument. It has one barrel with the ten tunes listed above, all of which (except the chant, No. 9) can be found also in Table 13. It was found that a complete tune (one revolution of the barrel, excluding the short silence at the end of the tune) could be most comfortably played in 40 seconds, could be played in 36 seconds by turning as fast as possible, and could not be played in more than 47 seconds without a loss of wind resulting in wavering pitch.

All tunes have been reduced to crotchets ($\frac{4}{4}$ or $\frac{3}{4}$). The number of crotchet beats in the tune as written is given in column (a); column (b) shows the variation in this number when the tune was played, through shortening of long notes or addition of rests; column (c) shows the resulting number of beats as played. The first three tempos represent the slowest, comfortable, and quickest possible performance as explained above. The last is the metronomic tempo given for the same tune in Benjamin Jacob's *National psalmody* (London, [1817]).

In general the barrel is slower than Jacob's tempos. The exception is 'Devizes', where an extra line has to be accommodated in one revolution.

* Jacob does not include Mornington's chant, but gives this tempo for all chants included.

The tempo problem became acute when barrel organs were used to accompany chanted psalms or canticles. Boston reported successfully accompanying a psalm on one of the two-handled instruments:

the wind was maintained in the organ by the blowing handle or pedal and a note could be held by the turning handle for any length of time during the 'reciting note'; then when the chanting notes came the little handle would have to be simply whirled

237

round. It can be done, for I have done it, and, most certainly, it was done. This is evidenced by the more than seventeen barrel organs which include chants on their barrels. (Boston & Langwill: 19–20)

The most popular chant was one of Lord Mornington's, found on eight organs (see ex. 56). One organ had a barrel of chants alone (:20). But many of the barrels containing chants were made for organs with only one handle, including the Attleborough organ. I found in playing the chant on this organ one could not lengthen the reciting note to any appreciable extent; it would last precisely one semibreve for each verse, as if the chant was being played through before the psalm began. Evidently the choir or congregation would have had great difficulty fitting in the notes of one of the longer verses. For instance, when the Te deum was chanted at Manthorpe, 'the performer had been taught that the great point in playing a barrel organ was to maintain perfectly a uniform pace so that he applied this principle to the Te deum without any regard to the length of the different verses, the singers getting in the words as best they could' (*Notes and Queries*, series 12, 1922: 353; cited Boston & Langwill: 20). It may seem incredible that chanting could have been done in this way at all. But we have already found evidence that it was. Again, Joshua Done, a London organist, found it necessary to explain in a note prefacing a chant for the Jubilate: 'When the verse, or sentence, is of extraordinary length, the time of the accompaniment must be prolonged, in order that each syllable may be distinctly sounded' (PC 357a: 95). In a Worcester church in 1848, an organist was heard to play the reciting note in strict time when accompanying the psalm (*Parish Choir* II, 1848: 99). (See also Hullah, 1865: 296.)

Some barrels also carried music for the responses in the ante-communion service. Others had short anthems and voluntaries (*Parish Choir* II, 1848: 31). A few church barrels contained one or two marches as well as the tunes, which may have been intended for use as voluntaries. The amount of ornamentation added to tunes varied greatly; example 57, from the Attleborough organ, is a precise transcription of the now obsolete tune 'Evening Hymn', a remote descendant of Tallis's Canon. It has a moderate amount of ornament. It also provides information about the style of playing the organ at that time, which allowed very little articulation or phrasing; repeated notes were often tied over with no break at all.

Writing in 1880, J. S. Curwen said that he knew of only one barrel organ still in use, although thirty years before 'there would have been found in the Church of England, all the country over, a considerable majority of barrel-organs over those played by the hands and feet'. He put down the rapid decline to 'the multiplication of piano players', which made it likely that even the smallest village would boast at least one competent keyboard player. Curwen described the one survivor, which had been built for St John, Stratford in about 1837, and soon moved to East Ham, where it had been played for forty years. The old man who played it throughout that time explained to Curwen that 'it was no use ... for any one to play that organ who had no ear for music'. At the reciting notes of the chants he had to pause in his turning; at the end of a hymn he made a *rallentando*; and in the successive lines of a repeating tune he piled on the stops. It was a large instrument, standing 14 feet high, with six stops and four barrels, and it had independent control of the bellows by pedals. The 44 'tunes' included 4 chants, a 'Gloria tibi', and 'I will arise', presumably the anthem by Richard Cecil (ex. 48) (Curwen, 1880: 92–3).

The last surviving barrel organ in regular use appears to have been that at Shelland. The organ dates from before 1823; from 1885 to 1935 it was played by the parish clerk, Robert Armstrong (Pl. 25), and thereafter by his son, who played it for a BBC broadcast on 28 December 1957 (Boston & Langwill: 36). Its unique survival, so long after the general disappearance of church barrel organs, was a curiosity more than anything else. With the encouragement of enthusiasts like Canon Boston, some barrel organs have been restored and brought into use again (Boston & Langwill: 98).

From about 1850, a new type of instrument, the seraphine or harmonium, began to rival the barrel organ as a cheap alternative to the pipe organ for parish church use. As this instrument belongs most characteristically to the Victorian era, it will be discussed in Chapter 9.

The survival of country psalmody

In many country churches, the old country psalmody was allowed to continue with little change; some bands and choirs were still playing and singing in west country churches at the end of the nineteenth century. For the first thirty years of the century, at least, this was still the normal state of affairs in village churches. Latrobe in 1831 said that although there had been some 'improvement' in church music in the towns, there had been none in the country: 'the modern spirit of innovation has not touched it' (:1). In 1857 a description of a typical service in a 'retired village' went as follows:

The tinkling of the bell ceases, and the clergyman commences the morning prayer... The canticles and psalms awaken no note of music; but when a psalm from the metrical version is given out, and a 'choir' in the gallery proceed to sing it to the accompaniment of a flute, a clarionet, and a violoncello, it is difficult to repress a smile. The tune is supposed to be in parts; nay, it is of the nature of a fugue, florid and difficult. We are in doubt whether we hear the tune at all, or only the tenor part of it, sung by a man's voice with an uncomfortable effect of straining and exertion.

Sometimes even services and anthems are attempted, 'with a result which by some minds will be felt as ludicrous, by others as melancholy' (Dickson, 1857: 10).

Nevertheless, changes were taking place in country psalmody. Quite a number of small churches acquired barrel organs, though it is difficult to estimate the proportion that did so. If they did, there was of course an immediate change, not only in the mode of performing the music, but in the nature and style of the music performed. The tunes on the organ barrels were mostly either traditional, or of the kind sung in town churches or dissenting chapels (see Table 13, p. 236). Very few of the eighteenth-century 'country' type of tune are to be found, and these few were generally rewritten and harmonised in a more conventionally correct fashion. After all, the barrel organ was intended as a cheap substitute for a finger organ and organist, and the style of organ music was alien to the style of country psalmody.

Even in churches that retained the old choirs and bands, the musical repertory changed much more than one might imagine from the quoted description of Dickson's. An examination of the books, both printed and manuscript, used in rural parishes in Dorset during this period (for instance PC 343, 348, MS 6, 8) shows that the older type of fuging tune and anthem had largely given way to a newer type of music that was much closer to the art music of the day, or of a somewhat earlier period. Music from town collections such as Miller's *Psalms of David* and Tattersall's *Improved psalmody* found its way into many country churches. A collection for country use printed in 1803 (PC 329) contained tunes selected from 'Playford, Smith & Prelluer, Riley, John Friend, and Dr. Miller' (i.e., probably from PC 28, 105, 186, 302, and 271 respectively). All these sources had organ parts, but the 1803 collection had none, and was entitled *A collection of the psalm-tunes most commonly used in parish-churches*.

A still more popular source for country church music in this period was the Methodist and Evangelical psalmody, and even that of the older dissenting bodies. Tunes and even hymn texts from Wesley's and Whitefield's books, from the Magdalen, Foundling and Lock Hospital collections, and from Stephen Addington and John Rippon's collections used by Congregationalists and Baptists, are more and more often found. Instead of anthems, set pieces were often sung, such as Harwood's 'Vital spark' and Madan's 'Before Jehovah's awful throne'. The fuging tunes which Dickson heard in 1857 may very well have been of the newer and more 'respectable' kind, modelled on the glee, found in Tattersall and other low-church books, and in Methodist collections; there are some examples in Houldsworth's 1832 revision of Chetham's *Book of psalmody*.

The reason for this new influence must be sought in the fact that many country choirs and bands now served both the parish church and one or more dissenting chapels in the same neighbourhood. We have seen an example of 'singers' leaving the parish church in a body and offering to sing at the Methodist chapel, to punish the vicar for his restrictions on their musical activities, at Camerton in 1822 (Skinner: 11). This was far from being a unique situation. Itinerant choirs were common in the early nineteenth century, 'and used to migrate from church to church, and sometimes to chapel, in the district where the members lived' (Ditchfield: 216). At Fulbourn, as late as the 1870s, the band played for the parish church in the morning and the dissenting chapel in the afternoon (:279–80). From about 1760 onwards many collections were at first implicitly, later explicitly intended for both parochial and dissenting use (see PC 182–259). Joseph Major's *Collection of sacred music for churches and chapels* (c. 1825: PC 356) had a list of subscribers that included Nonconformist choirs as well as incumbents of parish churches. Its tunes included many elaborate ones of the Methodist type, but none fuging, and no anthems. Thomas Shoel, of Montacute, was a poor weaver who taught singing to parish choirs in

Somerset (Bowles: 221n.). He published a series of psalmody books soon after 1800 (PC 326–7) clearly intended for country use, but not specifically for church or chapel. The tunes were adapted to the Old or New versions as well as hymns and psalms by Watts, Wesley and Doddridge; there were anthems as well as odes and set pieces, including Shoel's own setting of 'Vital spark'. Many collections aimed at the widest possible market by confining their selection to music that would be acceptable in either Anglican or dissenting worship, and avoiding any specific statement of intended use. Thus commercial interests tended to bring the two traditions together. Because in dissenting churches choirs had not usually been permitted to sing music that the congregation could not join, the trend in country churches was now also towards music of a simpler, more melodious character. Thus when a barrel organ or harmonium took over from the band, the change was not always a drastic one.

Not all country clergy wanted to reform the old choirs and bands out of existence; some, indeed, actively supported them (Pl. 23). In notes added to a sermon preached at the opening of an organ in 1822, John Eden perceptively pointed out that 'the majority of a country congregation is composed of persons, whose taste and intellect are upon a level with those of the singers', and that for the singers themselves psalmody was an innocent recreation and solace, tending to keep them from more harmful diversions. Where the singers had been disbanded they had often abandoned public worship altogether, 'or gone over to some neighbouring conventicle, and carried with them a part of the congregation, which had derived pleasure from their musical performances'. Reform, he concluded, was better than abolition (Eden: 17).

Some clergymen did try to improve the singing of their choirs, and to draw the congregation back into the singing again, perhaps stimulated by Bishop Porteus's charge of 1790. Some suggested reducing the number of choral parts to two, so that all would clearly hear the melody and could easily join in (PC 242: 17–18). Tattersall, on the same principle, reduced the harmony to three parts, and made other suggestions for reform (PC 292: iii–vi), which he said he had successfully put into practice in his own parish. Charles Dunster, rector of Petworth from 1789 to 1816, provided rules for the performance of psalmody in the preface to the selection of psalms and hymns he prepared for his church, rules which sought to regulate the relationship between choir, clerk, band and congregation (Dunster: lxx–lxxi; revised version transcribed Macdermott, 1922: 71).

A similar effort was successfully made by F. A. Head, vicar of Awlescombe (Devon), who in 1840 published *Choral psalmody, a collection of tunes to be sung in three parts, without instruments, by all village choirs* (PC 368). He dispensed with the band, but instead of introducing an organ he trained the choir of six men, six women and twelve children to sing *a cappella*, which they did 'with an ease, precision, and effect, which would not easily be credited'. He set some old, and more new, tunes in three (sometimes four) parts, with the tune clearly in the treble. He suggested, under the influence of 'the gentry or the middle class', daily instruction in musical rudiments 'in the parish school of every village', first with a piano, then with a pitchpipe, until the choir was efficient. 'The result would be the rescue, for ever, of the musical division of our beautiful church service from the degradation into which it has so long and apparently so hopelessly, been sunk in the villages of England' (:1–2). There was no reason why the congregation should not learn to join in such singing, even in parts (:7–9). It is clear, however, that for Head congregational singing was a secondary object.

Similarly William Cecil, rector of Longstanton St Michael, prepared a book of music for his village church or others like it, and published it in 1845 (PC 372a). He said that while such music had been printed for town churches with organs, 'almost nothing, or worse than nothing, has, until very lately, been done' for villages. He complained of monopolisation by the gallery singers: and, he said, 'almost every alternate Sunday, throughout the summer, the chief singers absent themselves from the church, in order to meet their fellow musicians at some feast or wake in the neighbouring parishes'. But he was far from wanting to abolish the choir and band. 'They often perform their parts with a zeal, adroitness, precision, and effect, superior to what is generally found in congregations led by an organ' (:3–5, 16). His collection appeared in four books: a score 'for the organ-player or leader of the band', a tune book 'for the clerk, the school-children, and other treble-singers', and 'second' and 'bass' books 'for any persons in the congregation who can sing or play those parts'.

All but the most remote churches would experience rapid changes in the Victorian period, and the reforms would be linked with matters of churchmanship as well as the inexorable advance of education, communication, and technology. But the old country psalmody, like its predecessor the old way of singing, did not give in without a long struggle.

Summary and evaluation

The era discussed in this chapter was one in which more active efforts to control and reform parish church music were made by clergymen, professional musicians, and others, after a long period in which it had been generally allowed to go its own way. The direction and emphasis of the reforms varied with the different parties in the Church, but their ultimate effect was to prepare the way for the new pattern of worship that would be established in the Victorian period.

The Evangelicals were responsible for reviving the people's role in the music of the service, not only in metrical psalms and hymns, but in the prose canticles and psalms as well. The innovation of congregational chanting was nothing less than revolutionary, for there was no precedent for it either before or after the Reformation. Despite considerable variation, it would persist until quite recent times, and even at this day is probably most people's norm for traditional Anglican worship. In hymn singing, Evangelicals, together with low churchmen, allowed secular influences, and encouraged a more emotional, more spirited type of tune. Unlike low churchmen, however, they insisted that hymns should be sung by the whole congregation with earnest devotion, and for this purpose they urged the introduction of organs.

For all reformers except the Evangelicals (and, later, the Tractarians), the main goal was not to increase the congregation's share in the singing, but to make the music more beautiful. High churchmen set up the cathedral ideal for the parish church, and eventually, at Leeds, achieved a physical arrangement of the choir that imitated the cathedral. Though the surpliced choir in the chancel would be accepted by the Tractarians, it suited their desire for congregational participation less than it suited the low-church liking for paid professional singers. The low-church model for parish psalmody was the glee. Every church now aspired to have an organ, but the smaller country churches more often had to be content with a barrel organ.

The two ideals of congregational participation and musical perfection were not easy to reconcile, but a successful synthesis would be attained in the Victorian service of central churchmanship. But first a more profound, more disturbing movement would take place, one that rediscovered and re-evaluated lost traditions from earlier periods in the life of the Church. The Oxford movement would put forward a new ideal of the nature of the Church itself, from which followed unfamiliar styles of worship and music. Although these never secured acceptance in their entirety, they also had their influence on the formation of the Victorian model of parish church music, and must be separately discussed before we consider the trends of the second half of the century.

8   The rediscovery of tradition (1800–50)

The Romantic movement

The many-sided aesthetic movement called Romanticism is too complex to be fully discussed here, except insofar as it affects our story. In its exaltation of feeling over reason, it was clearly sympathetic to Evangelicalism; while its regard for tradition and antiquity makes it a primary factor in the Oxford movement. Further, all three movements can be seen as facets of the reaction against the advance of secular, rational, urban materialism, whose manifestations in church music were discussed in earlier chapters.

The Romantics, in one phase of their activity, sought out those monumental works of nature, or of earlier ages of civilisation, which seemed to symbolise a more natural human existence. In architecture the Greek Revival, stimulated by Goethe's descriptions of the ruins of antiquity, was followed by the Gothic Revival, more directly patterned on the medieval buildings still abundantly surviving in Western Europe. In aesthetic theory such ideas were summarised in the concept of 'the sublime'. William Crotch, professor of music at Oxford and a leading composer of the time, adapted Sir Joshua Reynolds's theory of painting by dividing all 'scientific music' (art music) into three styles: the sublime, the beautiful, and the ornamental, the last corresponding to Reynolds's 'picturesque' (Crotch: 29–35; Rennert: 43–7). The sublime reached its greatest perfection, in Crotch's opinion, in the music of the sixteenth and early seventeenth centuries, when the 'style peculiarly suited to church music' was developed; it had been on the decline ever since. Rainbow (:62) has emphasised the influence of these ideas on the musical leaders of the Oxford movement.

Crotch was at pains to denounce the assumption underlying the idea of 'improved psalmody' – that the music of the present age was better than anything that had preceded it.

I should tremble for the fate of the sacred style, if modern music in general, or much of that now composed for the church, were to be adopted a hundred years hence. Few productions of the present day will ever become fit for divine service at all. The rust of antiquity will never constitute sublimity ... Let not the musical student, with some writers, ... imagine that music is continually improving; that every age is superior to the preceding; and that every new composer is greater than his predecessor; [a view that] is displayed in the daily practice of your young females who, on entering a music shop, simply enquire if anything new is published. (Crotch: 71, 72n.)

On the contrary, the only hope for a recovery was to revive and imitate the old music. 'The harmonies which Tallis, in the sixteenth century, put to the litany, may have been his own, but the chants themselves are older, and are still used for chanting the prayers in most cathedrals ... They constitute a perfect specimen of true sublimity, totally unlike the music of the present day ... They are, indeed, what the poet calls "the voices of the dead, and songs of other years".'* For hymns and metrical psalms, only the old tunes should be used; 'while all the Magdalen and Foundling hymns, with psalms made out of songs, glees, and quartetts ... in drawling, whining, minuet-like strains, with two or three notes to each syllable, full of modern and chromatic discords, with interludes, symphonies, introductions, shakes, flourishes, cadences, appogiaturas, and other unseemly displays of the organist's finger or fancy, should be denounced and utterly abolished' (:81). Crotch followed these principles in his selection of *Psalm tunes selected for the use of cathedrals and parish churches* (1836: PC 361).

We begin to find, towards the end of the eighteenth century, an entirely new kind of appreciation of traditional psalm or hymn tunes among cultivated persons. Instead of dismissing them as the humble music of 'labourers and mechanics', some began to exalt them as pure specimens of primitive art. The new fashion may have been started by Karl Friedrich Baumgarten, who was organist at the Lutheran chapel in the Savoy from about 1760. At the Covent Garden oratorio concert on 18 March 1801 was introduced 'a hymn, composed by the celebrated Martin Luther, as performed at the Savoy Chapel, with accompaniments by Mr. Baumgarten'. The hymn, entitled 'Great God, what do I see and hear?', was received with 'such unbounded applause' that it was repeated twice in the same season, and many times in later seasons (*The Times*: 18, 25 March 1801).

Thomas Greatorex, who was conductor of the Concerts of Ancient Music from 1793, also played a part in this development. At the concerts in 1797 he introduced *Adeste fideles*, known as the 'Portuguese hymn' from its association with the Portuguese Embassy chapel but actually composed by an English Roman Catholic, J. F. Wade (Routley, 1958: 147–8). This, too, was sung by soloists and chorus with orchestral accompaniment, and was many times repeated. English metrical psalms treated in the same way were Psalm 18, with the tune 'St Matthew' by Croft, sung at the Ancient Concert on 5 February 1806; Psalm 104, probably also with a tune by Croft ('Hanover'), on 19 April 1809; and Psalm 100, with tune 'Old Hundredth', on 28 March 1810. All were in the Old Version, and all were repeated many times in subsequent years.

At the York Festival of 1823 (also conducted by Greatorex), three hymns or psalms were sung by the entire casts of soloists (led by Angelica Catalani), chorus and orchestra: Psalm 18, 'as arranged by Mr. Greatorex for the Ancient Concert'; *Adeste fideles*; and Luther's hymn, no doubt in Baumgarten's arrangement, with a trumpet solo played by Thomas Harper. A commentator said that this hymn

produced the greatest impression during the whole of this extended festival ... The sound of the trumpet, proceeding from nearly the top of the orchestra, appeared as

---

* This quotation is from Reginald Heber's poem *Palestine*, which was set to music by Crotch as an oratorio, published in 1812. He set these words with strikingly modal harmonies.

if it descended from the open space of the tower above; and the thrill of awe, not unmingled even with terror, ... was such as we shall not attempt to describe ... It is in vain to deny the sublime effect of its performance at this time, by which all previously conceived opinions and rules of criticism were wholly overpowered and swept away. (Crosse: 339–40)

Baumgarten's arrangement, which other critics dismissed as 'ridiculous or disgusting', was published in 1805 and several times reprinted: it is reproduced in ex. 58. Whatever one may think of it, it was a new form of romanticism in music, both catering to the mass audience and providing it with an escape from mundane reality. The four-part harmonisation of the tune, no doubt designed for string and wind instruments as well as voices, gives the melody to the trebles and altos in octaves, while the basses are partly independent of the main instrumental bass.

This version of Luther's hymn appeared in many parochial collections with the trumpet part in small notes, and it was undoubtedly performed in many churches with the Trumpet stop of the organ. Charles Thorp, archdeacon of Durham, referred to the York performance in a sermon given at the opening of an organ in the parish church of Gateshead (Durham). He said it showed that 'music communicates sentiment and feeling more strongly than eloquence'. The idea of the text, concerning the day of judgment, was brought home by the music 'in a new and formidable shape, to minds unaccustomed to serious reflection'. Thorp went on to commend some of the older psalm tunes usually sung with the Old and New Versions, and to regret their decline. 'It is observable that the distaste for the ordinary versions and music of the psalms, and the fondness for lighter airs and poetry, began with the decay of true religion; – may it cease with the revival' (Thorp: 18, 23). There was an opportunity here to harness Romanticism, with its appeal to feeling, in the interests of religion.

The traditional tunes had, indeed, rapidly fallen out of use, even in town churches, where they had long been the mainstay of psalmody. A few high churchmen such as Jones of Nayland preferred them. But Miller's *Psalms of David* contained only five tunes composed in England before 1690, with two more in an appendix; Tattersall's *Improved psalmody* had two, with five in an appendix. Their conscious revival (as distinct from mere survival in conservative collections) was begun, appropriately enough, by William Crotch, who published in 1803 *Tallis's Litany* ... [*with*] *a collection of old psalm tunes adapted to the Old and New Version for the use of the University Church, Oxford, and Tallis's 'Come, Holy Ghost'* (PC 330). The book was used in several Oxford college chapels, as well as the university (and parish) church of St Mary the Virgin and other Oxford churches. Crotch's successor as organist of St Mary, William Cross, followed in 1818 with *A collection of psalm tunes* (PC 345), dedicated to the Bishop of Oxford,* 'an encourager of the primitive style of congregational psalmody'. Cross pointed out the unsuitability of modern psalm tunes: 'they carry with them the rhythm and levity of a ballad air, and differ from one in nothing but their time' (:ii). He claimed to have reproduced the old tunes 'as

---

* Curiously, the dedication is to 'Edward, Lord Bishop of Oxford', although the bishop from 1816 to 1827 was Henry Legge.

harmonized by Ravenscroft, etc.', but actually Ravenscroft's harmonies were altered, both by inverting the tenor and treble parts and by actual changes of chord. Greatorex himself, in his *Parochial psalmody* of 1820, favoured the old tunes, which, he said, 'are exceedingly beautiful in themselves, and, when harmonized and well sung, capable of producing the most sublime effect: this has been fully proved at the King's Concert of Antient Music, where several of these tunes are annually performed' (PC 349: iii). John Goss's *Parochial psalmody* (PC 357) for St Luke, Chelsea (1827) used largely old tunes, as did Crotch's *Psalm tunes* in 1836. William Havergal published a complete reprint of Ravenscroft's *Psalms* in 1847, and a more general collection of old psalm tunes in 1849 (PC 378a). Edward Rimbault produced several antiquarian collections, including an inaccurate reprint of East's *Psalms*, during the 1840s. James Burns published four-part psalm tunes by Tallis, Tye, Gibbons, and Ravenscroft in 1842. Most of the early English tunes were thus available by 1850.

The Anglican chant was also a candidate for sublimity, although in its current form it was a much younger phenomenon than most people realised. Jonathan Gray had approved chanting as 'the usage of primitive ages'. Chants may have been sung at London concerts in the later eighteenth century, for instance at the Covent Garden Oratorio on 7 March 1792, when the programme included 'Grant Chorus, Gloria Patri' (*The Times*, 7 March 1792). It was the performance of Jones's chant (ex. 49) by four thousand charity children that had overwhelmed Haydn in 1791, and at the York Festival of 1825 two psalms were sung to the two-note 'grand chant' attributed to Pelham Humfrey. Chants were of course sung daily in cathedrals, but the great attraction of the York performances, as of those of the assembled charity children in London, was that the chants were sung by a large number of voices in unison, producing an impersonal and awe-inspiring effect that suggested the sublime.

As knowledge of early music increased, however, it was realised that Anglican chants were not true examples of ancient chanting, and there began to arise an interest in rediscovering the chant of pre-Reformation times. Hodges in 1822 referred vaguely to

the old Ecclesiastical Chant, which consisted of but a few notes, and was sung of the whole congregation in unisons. This is music of the simplest description, but such as is capable of association with the true sublime. What is much to be regretted, it is rarely now heard, excepting in some parts of the cathedral service, and there but very sparingly; the reason of which may be, that to give it its best effect, it is requisite that it be performed by a vast number of voices. (*Quarterly* IV, 1822: 173)

Even in Catholic chapels, the use of Gregorian chant had almost ceased, though efforts to revive it were being made by Samuel Wesley and Vincent Novello (*Quarterly* V, 1823: 198–206). Crotch had shown, however, that the chanted responses of cathedral service, as distinct from the chanted psalms, were of ancient origin. A complete musical *Order of daily service* with traditional music was published in 1843 by the painter and musical amateur William Dyce (PC 371), partly based on Marbeck's *Booke of common praier noted* (Rainbow: 79–83). Within a very short time these specimens of the sublime were being sung, often congregationally, in many parish churches. Finally, efforts were made to revive the Gregorian psalm tones, and to adapt them to the English prose psalms. As this development was more closely associated with the Oxford movement, however, it will be considered later.

As for the revival of early English anthems and services, there was little sign of it before about 1840. In cathedrals a substantial amount of music by Elizabethan and Jacobean composers was already in use (*Quarterly* VI, 1824: 26–7, 310–17), while the printed collections of Boyce, Arnold, and Page also contained a fair sample.* But it is not very likely that many parish churches availed themselves of these. Anthems were not often performed, services still more rarely; and when they were, more recent compositions were selected. The high-church *Christian Remembrancer* noted with approval in 1841 that 'within the last year or two several societies have been formed for the cultivation of ancient choral music, sacred and secular', such as that of Tallis, Shepherd, Byrd and Gibbons. 'We trust ... that, in this new disposition, there is the best groundwork for a reformation of the music of the Church' (I n.s., 1841: 112). One of these bodies was the Motett Society, formed in 1841 with the object of publishing and performing 'ancient church music' under the leadership of Dyce and Rimbault. Three volumes were produced, two of anthems and one of services; although they included a few examples of early English works, the bulk of the music was by Palestrina, Victoria and other continental composers, adapted to English words. Thomas Helmore tried out several of these works at St Mark's College, Chelsea, in 1843 (Rainbow: 65–7; Grove, 1879–89: II, 376).

The Tractarian *Parish Choir* between 1846 and 1850 provided for its readers three supplements of music for use in a parish church. Each consisted of the complete choral service, with a simple chant-like setting of the Te deum and Anglican chants to all the other canticles and the Athanasian creed; Marbeck's communion service, harmonised; metrical psalms, all of the older type; the Gregorian psalm tones harmonised; chant settings of the marriage and burial services; and about 40 full anthems by English composers from the mid-sixteenth to the mid-eighteenth century, all of a simple description and mostly in four parts, with organ accompaniment, largely doubling the voices, for rehearsal purposes. All this music was ideally to be sung unaccompanied. The only modern compositions were three 'offertories' (short anthems) by W. H. Monk, all in a style superficially imitative of the early English full anthem, complete with flattened sevenths, and cadences with 4–3 suspensions instead of dominant-seventh chords. These harmonies were by now regarded as specially 'ecclesiastical'. A correspondent in 1850 wrote of 'the perversion of ecclesiastical harmony' by organists who wrongly introduced dominant sevenths and chromaticisms (*Parish Choir* III, 1850: 119–20). Henry Gauntlett wrote in 1846:

There are a certain catalogue of harmonies peculiarly proper for Divine Service, and cannot be heard out of the Church: are these to be given up ... because some

---

* The contents of all three collections are listed in Grove, 1879–89, under the compilers' names.

fifty out of five hundred worshippers desire to sing an extempore harmony, to which they have paid no previous attention or study? (PC 373: xxiii)

The notion of a special style of music for the Church, deliberately distinguished from secular music, was precisely opposite to the Evangelical plans to 'plunder the carnal lover', and also to the low-church cultivation of the fashionable styles of art music. It was, on the other hand, entirely in conformity with the Tractarians' concept of the Church as a body apart, owing allegiance to no secular authority. Indeed, by the middle of the century the revival of early church music, and more especially the Gregorian psalm tones, was strongly associated with the Oxford movement, which was already becoming synonymous with the high-church party. But the original impetus had had little to do with any specific theology or party, despite its link with Oxford. It was due to the Romantic interest in 'the sublime', which was felt to be particularly suited to the music of the Church. It was almost a physical response, as illustrated by a letter which Crotch wrote to his grandson in 1835, describing his feelings when asked to write in a lady's autograph book:

I determined to write something which would show what *I* was fond of & I gave a few first bars of Allegri's Mass performed by *voices alone* at the Pope's Chapel on Good Friday while all the lights are extinguished excepting one. These are as follow [a few modal chords and a cadence with 4–3 suspension]. Play them very slow & soft & tell me how you like them William? They make my blood run cold. (MS 82: III, no. 2)

But this was a highly sophisticated taste, a reaction against the conventional musical fashion of the day. It could not be felt by those who were not exposed to that fashion, and would not appeal to those who were trying to acquire that fashion. Hence it made slow headway in parish churches, and even the most convinced and determined Tractarians would find it hard to arouse much enthusiasm for the austerities of Gregorian chant.

The Oxford movement

Enough has been said to show that the Oxford movement was not the sole influence in the transformation of parish church music that took place in the early Victorian period. Many of the innovations often carelessly credited to the Tractarians* – the chanting of psalms, the singing of the liturgy, the interest in ancient music, the surpliced choir of men and boys – were in fact already in existence before John Keble preached his sermon on 'National apostasy' at the university church, Oxford, on 14 July 1833, an event which Newman always regarded as the beginning of the movement.

Nevertheless, the Oxford movement was the most important development in the Church of England during the nineteenth century, and had the greatest ultimate effect on the character of parish church worship, even if its

---

* For the purposes of this study 'Tractarianism' and 'the Oxford movement' are treated as synonymous.

principles were never widely adopted in their original purity. As Owen Chadwick has put it,

> no one doubted in 1860, and few will doubt now, that the clergy of 1860 were more zealous than the clergy of 1830, conducted worship more reverently, knew their people better, understood a little more theology, celebrated sacraments more frequently, studied more bible, preached shorter sermons and worse. (:127)

These changes were in large part due to the vigorous and uncompromising efforts of the Tractarians. In particular, they had enhanced enormously the beauty and impressiveness of worship, so that even their most inveterate enemies were ultimately shamed into putting some of their ideas into practice.

Because of the later enmity between 'high church' and 'low church' parties, in which churchmen of differing views felt obliged to coalesce in one party or the other, it has been assumed by many that the Oxford movement was the antithesis of Evangelicalism. But in fact there were many links between the two (Brilioth; Davies: III, 247–52; Balleine: 170–2). Both were intensely loyal to the Church of England and its liturgy; both, whatever their differences of emphasis, were concerned with the 'undeviating pursuit of holiness, sanctity, salvation' (Davies: III, 248), and were enemies of low churchmen who made mere decorum the highest object in worship, or, worse, treated the clerical calling as a mere profession and source of income. Both were minorities bent on making a greater reality out of the Church. We have already seen that Evangelicals, as well as Tractarians, were concerned to enhance the conduct of the liturgy. Equally Tractarians, as well as Evangelicals, recognised the importance of preaching and of hymn singing. Finally, there were many personal links: most of the leading Tractarians, including Newman himself, had been raised in a strongly Evangelical atmosphere; the Wilberforce brothers, leaders in the Oxford party, were sons of the most famous Evangelical layman of his day; Pusey, who gave the Tractarians one of their pejorative nicknames, himself recognised the debt to Evangelicalism (Davies: III, 249), as did Frederick Oakeley, who was closely concerned in the first Tractarian innovations in worship (Oakeley), and John Bacchus Dykes, the most important Tractarian composer of hymn tunes. Dykes's brother persuaded their Evangelical father that 'the dreaded Puseyites were only enlightened Evangelicals' (J. Fowler: 15).

The Oxford movement was primarily concerned with theology, and its theological ideas were expounded in the series of *Tracts for the times* which emanated from Oxford in the 1830s (Newman *et al.*). The first generation of Tractarians, including Keble, Newman and Pusey, had little interest in the ceremonialism which preoccupied some of their followers. But their overriding concern with Church tradition, the apostolic succession, and the corporate entity of the Church (as contrasted with the Evangelical emphasis on individual salvation and personal religious experience) were bound to have a profound effect on the character of worship. In their rejection of the prevailing liberalism and toleration, the Tractarians sought to recover traditions from an age when the Church's authority was accepted as a matter of faith, and to reimpose these traditions by an exercise of the restored authority of that Church. Ideally they accepted no secular control, and we can discover in the practice of the revived Anglican communities of monks and nuns how Tractarian worship developed when it was free from external constraints (Davies: IV, 131–8). Some Tractarians also rejected the authority of the State in the conduct of public worship, and either seceded to Rome or flouted the law at considerable risk to their personal security. The majority recognised that secular control was a fact of the Established Church that must be lived with, and worked to accommodate the law as much as possible to the innovations they desired.

The details of Tractarian worship were worked out primarily by the Cambridge Camden Society (later renamed the Ecclesiological Society), founded in 1839 by John Mason Neale, then an undergraduate at Trinity College. The society embarked enthusiastically on scholarly research into the traditions of Christian worship. They began to publish their findings and recommendations in *The Ecclesiologist*, a new periodical founded by them in 1841 and entirely devoted to the study of worship and ecclesiastical architecture. It was through this society, above all, that Gothic churches came to be built with a full understanding of the significance, both practical and symbolic, of their various parts. Their influence on Victorian church building and restoration was immense. 'It is doubtful if there is a Gothic church in the country, new or old, which does not show their influence' (Clark: 238). Beyond this, they were concerned to restore every detail of traditional ceremonial that was permitted by law, and expended much energy in minute examination and reinterpretation of acts of parliament, royal injunctions, rubrics, and other historical documents bearing on the case:

Let us endeavour to restore everywhere amongst us the daily prayers, and (at the least) weekly communion; the proper eucharistick vestments, lighted and vested altars, the ancient tones of prayer and praise, frequent offertories, the meet celebration of fasts and festivals (all of which and much more of a kindred nature is required by the ecclesiastical statutes). (William & Harris: 427, cited Davies: III, 272)

The aesthetic of the Tractarians was not closely tied to their theology. They were eclectic in their choice of past traditions for revival. Whereas their theology was primarily based on the early fathers of the Church in the first five centuries of the Christian era, as reinterpreted by the English divines of the seventeenth century, their architectural ideal was the Decorated Gothic (or 'Middle Pointed') of the fourteenth century. Their liturgy was, perforce, of the sixteenth century. Their musical models were the Gregorian chant, believed to date from early Christian times, and the harmonic and contrapuntal style of the Renaissance. Many of their vestments and ceremonial customs dated from the later middle ages. With the help of creative imagination and passionate advocacy, this conglomeration soon assumed a strong integrity, recognised by friends and foes as the outward form of the Oxford movement.

The ceremonial revival was begun at Littlemore, near Oxford. Newman was incumbent there, but the active spirit was his curate, John Bloxam, who began his innovations in 1837. He installed a stone cross behind the altar, and on the altar placed four candlesticks, a bible, and a wooden alms dish. Such an arrangement would not attract attention to-day, but it startled many observers at the time. Peter Maurice, chaplain of All Souls' and New Colleges, Oxford, described his first visit there in a book entitled *The popery of Oxford confronted, disavowed, and repudiated* (1837):

I felt an indescribable horror stealing over me, as I carried my eye towards the eastern wall of the building, and beheld a plain naked cross, either of stone or a good imitation of it, rising up and projecting out of the wall, from the centre of the table of communion. (:53n.)

Bloxam also wore a wide stole of black silk over his surplice. Such innovations were soon copied elsewhere, and others introduced, so that in a surprisingly short time Tractarian worship was entirely different in character from the conventional worship of the Church of England. By the 1850s some Tractarians were using incense, the eastward posture at communion, liturgical colours, eucharistic vestments such as the cope and chasuble, an altar cross and altar lights, and even a processional cross (Davies: IV, 274).

The aim of the Tractarian changes was to involve 'the whole of the nature of man, his body, mind and spirit' in worship, to restore through symbolism a sense of the wonder and majesty of God's presence, and to correct the Evangelical emphasis on individual religious feeling, which had tended to lapse into sentimentality, by restoring forms of expression that had been purified by the attrition of the ages. In dramatising the altar, restoring the chancel, and enriching the vestments of the priest, they desired to turn the thoughts of the worshippers away from themselves and towards the Almighty. In their enthusiasm many moved too fast and too far for the good of their cause, not heeding the cautious advice of their leaders. The conservatism of the average churchman, and the deep-seated hatred of Rome which still burned in English breasts, generated an immediate and predominantly irrational hostility to the new forms of worship. Unfortunately the fears of the majority seemed to be confirmed by two events: the defection to the Roman Church of Newman and many of his followers in 1845, for reasons which had little directly to do with forms of worship; and the re-establishment of the Roman Catholic hierarchy in England by papal edict in 1850. Through fear of a general move towards Rome, Evangelicals were propelled into an alliance with latitudinarians, to form a new 'low-church' party. They found a political spokesman in Lord John Russell, the prime minister, who in an open letter to the bishop of Durham voiced his fear of a plot by Rome to re-establish supremacy over the people of England (*The Roman Catholic Question*, 2nd series: 13; cited Rainbow: 146). Nearly three centuries after the defeat of the Spanish Armada, and at a time when British military and political power were at an unprecedented height, it was still all too easy to revive ancient fears of Roman conquest, and of spies working within the Church. Rallying to the old cry of 'popery', rioting bands invaded the services of Tractarian churches. The long and disastrous ritualistic controversy had begun. Like the vestiarian controversy of the 1560s, it was concerned with superficial differences of practice in worship, which could be precisely observed and defined and were therefore susceptible to legislation and to litigation. In both cases, passions were aroused because these habits of worship were symbols, not only of conflicting theological views, but, perhaps more importantly, of differing sources of loyalty and self-identification.

Tractarian aims for parish church music

The Cambridge ecclesiologists believed that in the Age of Faith congregations had spontaneously sung the people's part of the liturgy to the Gregorian chant, led by robed choirs of men and boys. A number of formidable difficulties stood in the way of restoring (or rather creating) this situation in their own time. The ancient chants were almost dead, surviving only in written or printed documents. No one knew how they were supposed to be sung. They had been sung to Latin words, but if they were to be used in public worship they must be fitted to English. The Tractarians rejoiced in their discovery that many parts of the English liturgy were direct translations of the pre-Reformation Sarum use, but that did not make them easier to fit to the plainsong. They found Marbeck's adaptations, which they eagerly revived, and they made new adaptations of their own. But modern congregations were accustomed to harmony, strong regular rhythms, and organ accompaniment. If these were retained, they would pervert the nature of the chant, and vitiate the purpose of reviving it. If they were removed, the people would be deprived of their accustomed support, and would be hindered in learning to sing the strange melodies. Another problem concerned choirs. There was always a danger that they would forget their function of leading the congregation, and would sing on their own.

In the publications of the early years of the movement, we can see these problems being hotly debated. The Cambridge Camden Society were much troubled to find the right policy concerning organs. They doubted that organs were really necessary, and looked forward to a time when they could be dispensed with. Meanwhile, if there had to be an organ, what should be done with it? In the first edition of *A few words to church builders* (1841), they suggested 'a shallow stone projection at the west end' (:23); in the second edition (1842) they decided that 'there is no occasion for a gallery, for it will sound equally well anywhere else, even on the floor. But if there must be a gallery, it should be a shallow stone projection from the north or south of the nave, or somewhere where no window will be blocked' (:25). The following year they declared that 'few things give more trouble to church-arrangers or church-builders than the position of the organ', and raised objections to every position that had been suggested. An organ was not really necessary, as had been shown by the success of the Reverend E. Shuttleworth at St Mary, Penzance, 'where we have the whole service intoned admirably without instrumental accompaniment'. An organ was the destroyer of the true principles of church music, also 'burdening the parish in many cases with a stipend equal to, or greater than, that of the curate'. Finally, if an organ must be had, it should be placed 'at the west end, either of the nave or of an aisle, *and on the ground*. Then, the singers being rightly placed in the chancel, it will not drown the voices nor make them dependent on itself' (*Ecclesiologist* III, 1843: 1–5). This article resulted in many letters and much discussion, but the editors stuck to their point:

> We do not believe that its distance from the choir in the chancel will be a great inconvenience in the case of a church of moderate size: besides, in a parish church much figured musick, to be performed by a choir alone, is surely to be deprecated. We must express our dislike, as a general rule, to what are called 'services'; which turn the hymns and canticles ... into a kind of difficult anthem, in which the great body of worshippers cannot possibly take a part. (IV, 1845: 6–7)

We find here a total rejection of the type of 'fully choral service' instituted by Dr Hook at Leeds, where, indeed, 'the great body of worshippers could not possibly take a part' in the carefully rehearsed singing of the trained choir. On the other hand we find support for the placing of the choir in the chancel, a move which might be thought to discourage congregational participation.

This was another dilemma that faced the early theorists of Tractarian worship. The Gothic plan for a parish church, which they were eager to restore, had a definite division between the nave and the chancel, marked by a substantial screen surmounted by a rood-loft. In medieval times, the people sat or stood in the nave looking eastward, while the clergy conducted the devotions in the chancel. The long chancels were built to house the clergy, and their grandeur was an outward sign of the importance of the clergy in medieval life (Addleshaw & Etchells: 16). They were not meant for the lay singers, who occupied the rood-loft. The Cambridge Camden Society at first disapproved of seating laymen in the chancel (*A few words*, 1st edn: 10). But Neale himself soon afterwards published an authoritative pamphlet in which he said, 'None ought to be in the chancel but they who are taking part in the performance of the Divine Office, *and they ought*' (1843: 16). From then on the official policy was to encourage the placing of the choir in the chancel, and to build parallel choir stalls facing inwards for its accommodation (Hewett: 8). The screen was removed, or a screen of light tracery was erected; the priest was now placed in a stall just inside the chancel, and moved to the nave when he went into the pulpit to preach, or into the newly provided lectern to read the lessons. With the choir in the chancel, the moving of the organ to the north or south chancel followed as a practical corollary. In a medieval church or a new church built in close imitation of the medieval plan, the choir stalls occupied most of the narrow chancel, and the object of making the altar the focus of worship was largely defeated. The more creative Victorian architects modified the medieval plan by widening the chancel (Pl. 27, 34).

Some commentators have seen the separation of the clergy and choir from the people as an expression of the Tractarians' ideal, which is 'not so much that the services should be a corporate offering of priest and people but that they should be offered by clergy and a choir in such a way as to call out from the people an attitude of awe and adoration' (Addleshaw & Etchells: 209; paraphrased Davies: III, 278). This was certainly the attitude of Jebb, Hook, and other conservative high churchmen. As a summary of

Tractarian views, however, this interpretation relies too much on architectural evidence. The Tractarians took over the Decorated church, lock, stock and barrel, for a number of reasons, none of them practical; and they were then faced with a feature (the deep chancels with parallel stalls) which may have suited the conditions of the fourteenth century, but had little to do with those of the nineteenth. The clergy of a parish church were not numerous enough to fill a chancel; nor did they wish to separate themselves from the congregation. After some hesitation, therefore, the ecclesiologists decided to install a choir in the chancel. F. F. White may be near the mark when he suggests that 'the surpliced choir in the chancel caught on and won the battle for deep chancels by giving them a practical purpose' (:96). It is certain that the Tractarians did not want the choir to take the singing away from the congregation. On the contrary, we find them constantly attempting, in face of great difficulties, to induce congregations to sing the liturgy, led by the choir.

At St Peter-in-the-East, Oxford (Pl. 6), Walter Kerr Hamilton, as curate and then (from 1838) as incumbent, encouraged congregational chanting of the canticles, for which purpose he published a pointed version with Anglican chants in 1838 (PC 364). The next year he promoted *A collection of psalm and hymn tunes, chants, and other music* (PC 366) which was prepared by the organist at St Peter's, Alexander Reinagle. This time the chants were Gregorian (ex. 60), arranged by G. V. Cox (Rainbow: 14–15). Hamilton had not given up the congregational ideal in 1860, when, as Bishop of Salisbury, he preached a sermon on church music to the first meeting of the diocesan choral association: 'Congregational singing is the great end to be aimed at, and ... a choir should be so used as to help to bring about this blessed result; ... the music of the Church should be as our reformers intended it to be, plain, melody rather than harmony; ... the music of the Church should be cut off as much as possible from all bad, meretricious associations', and the melodies of St Ambrose, modified by St Gregory, were the best for the purpose (W. K. Hamilton: 9–10).

In London a small district chapel in Margaret Street, near Oxford Circus, became the focus of Tractarian innovation. It was an unlikely building for such a role: designed as a dissenting meeting house, a large low room with a flat whitewashed ceiling, box pews covering the floor, and a gallery for the charity children. In 1829 William Dodsworth became minister, and he began to give the services a Tractarian slant when the new ideas began to emanate from Oxford. In 1837 he published *A selection of psalms, to which are added hymns chiefly ancient*, for the use of the chapel (L. Benson: 500). In the same year he became the first incumbent at the newly built Christ Church, Albany Street, St Pancras. In 1839 Frederick Oakeley, who had been chaplain of Balliol College, Oxford, and was a disciple of a leading Oxford Tractarian, W. G. Ward, became minister at Margaret Chapel, and quickly made it a centre for the new ideals of worship. He removed the three-decker pulpit, decked the altar in imitation of Littlemore, and introduced daily services (as Dodsworth had at Christ Church) with regular observation of feasts and fasts. Fifty years later his services were 'still remembered by some as having realised for them, in a way never since surpassed, the secrets and consolations of the worship of the Church': one of the early attenders was William Gladstone, the future prime minister (Rainbow: 16).

The music at the daily services included antiphonal chanting of the psalms. Only a few boys were available: one verse was sung by Oakeley and one boy, the next by the other boys in the gallery, who were supposed to lead the congregation. The boys, who wore surplices, were trained by Oakeley himself, who was a gifted musician. The congregation could not really be expected to join in the chanting without a pointed psalter, and at first, no doubt, they did not do so. Richard Redhead, the organist, published a selection of chants, responses, and Sanctus settings, with 26 hymn tunes, in 1840 (PC 369); the chants were Anglican ones, single and double, at this stage. Later, in 1843, Oakeley and Redhead produced *Laudes diurnae* (PC 372), a fully pointed psalter set out with unharmonised Gregorian chants. They were now in a position to invite the congregation to join in the chanting. Whether they actually did so, and with what success, is not recorded. From about this time Oakeley's efforts were more and more restricted by episcopal injunctions, and in 1845 he followed Newman into the Roman Church (Rainbow: 15–25). Redhead stayed on as organist, throughout the period (1850–9) when the chapel was closed in preparation for the building of a new church. Choral services were continued in a temporary building. Redhead's own edition of Marbeck was used. His *Hymns and canticles used at morning and evening prayer* (1849: PC 382) has the Gregorian tones harmonised in four parts, with dominant sevenths and even chromatic harmonies, suggesting that Oakeley's successor, Upton Richards, was somewhat less radical in his ideal of church music. The new church, All Saints, Margaret Street, was opened in 1859. It was a model church of the Cambridge Ecclesiological Society and an important centre of Anglo-Catholic worship. It was equipped with a deep and high chancel, culminating in an elevated altar surmounted by a richly ornate reredos, and furnished with choir stalls. For the first time the surpliced choir could take its appropriate place in a church that worthily expressed the Tractarian ideal. However, the music of the services hardly continued the tradition established by Oakeley, as we shall see.

The issue of the placing of the choir caused a dispute in 1845 at Ruardean, where the Tractarian incumbent, Henry Formby, had followed ecclesiological fashion by erecting choir stalls in the chancel. A group of parishioners presented a petition asking him to return the choir to the west gallery, because the chancel was damp, its acoustics poor, and the attendance of both singers and parishioners had dropped as a result of the innovation. Formby stuck to his principles. Sacred music, he said, was a 'high employment'. There were two kinds of psalmody 'wholly distinct and separate from each other', that of trained choirs in cathedrals and colleges, and that of congregations; a gallery choir in a parish church silenced the congregation. Moreover, he said, the gallery had been the scene of 'exceedingly profane behaviour'. Acoustics were subordinate; dampness could be remedied. 'The hope that many parishioners who have absented themselves from our church would return to it, both as singers, and as members of the congregation' was dismissed, since if they returned only because of the proposed change, their return would not be genuine.

This exchange was published, with approval, in *The English Churchman*, and then as a separate pamphlet (Formby). A few months later Formby defected into the Roman Church. Although one can admire his strength of principle in the face of unpopularity and a declining congregation, his stand was too idealistic to win ultimate success, and contained a contradiction within itself. The policy of placing the choir in the chancel, however appropriate it might be from a visual or symbolic point of view, was acoustically unsatisfactory, as the Ruardean parishioners pointed out; and it 'silenced the congregation' quite as much as a west-gallery choir. More, the placing of organ and choir in an enclosed chancel, and the robing of the choir, increased the physical and psychological separation of the music from the congregation. It hindered the Tractarian ideal of congregational singing.

The plan of placing the choir in the chancel, with the organ to one side of it, originated at Leeds parish church, where it was based on the traditional high-church principles of John Jebb. In 1843 Jebb wrote that this was the only proper place for the choir: 'The gallery, the modern place of the performance, is altogether an innovation of later times, and . . . POPISH in origin.' The choir must be regarded as assisting the clergy, and the organ should be as close to it as possible, preferably on the north side, and should be small. But William Spark, who had been Wesley's deputy organist at Leeds, and returned in 1850 as organist of St George's church, Leeds, disagreed with Jebb's view. In a lecture to the Yorkshire Architectural Society on 26 May 1852, with Dr Hook in the chair, he denied that there was any uniform position for choir or organ, or that large organs were to be condemned: the question depended on whether the service was congregational. He gave four cardinal rules. An organ should not play over one choir to another choir (as at the Temple Church and St Andrew, Wells Street); the people should not be between the choir and the organ (as at St Paul, Knightsbridge); the singers in the choir should not have their backs to the people; and a choir should never be placed in a gallery (1852: 8–14).

An important influence in the spreading of Tractarian ideas about church music was the College of St Mark, Chelsea, which was opened in 1841 as the first training college for teachers in the National Schools (Church of England schools). Music played a prominent part in the college curriculum, since it was realised that here was an opportunity to spread a knowledge of church music into the towns and villages of the nation. John Hullah, whose sight-singing methods were just beginning to spread a knowledge of vocal music to the lower classes of London society, was appointed to provide the basic musical training to the students, who were not selected for their musical talent; and Thomas Helmore, the vice-principal, was charged with teaching them to sing the choral service (Rainbow: 48). The men were joined by boys from the model school which was part of the foundation, and performed unaccompanied choral services daily – there was no organ in the college chapel until 1861. Their repertory included an ambitious range of sixteenth- and seventeenth-century works, both English and Italian, by way of anthems and settings of the canticles. Tallis's responses and litany were used, and the psalms were chanted to either Anglican or Gregorian chants. The 'congregational' parts of the service were sung by all, while the most proficient students sang the anthems and services. As the principal, Derwent Coleridge, pointed out in his report to the National Society in 1844, all the students leaving the college would be able to teach elementary music in parochial schools, and 'make themselves more or less useful in a parochial choir' (Rainbow: 51, 54). The activities of St Mark's college were commended in an article in *The Ecclesiologist*, which pointed out that it was 'now beginning to be recognised that church musick is almost exclusively *vocal*' (III, 1843: 2). An indefatigable worker in spreading the methods of St Mark's to churches all over the country was Frederick Helmore, younger brother of Thomas, known as the 'musical missionary' (Rainbow: 115–39).

Another important influence in the spread of Tractarian ideals of worship was the Society for Promoting Church Music,* with its journal, *The Parish Choir*. It was founded by an enterprising physician and amateur musician, Robert Druitt, who began by publishing his manifesto, *A popular tract on church music, with remarks on its moral and political importance* (1845). He pointed out that music in parish churches was in a deplorable state; and that attempts at reform had been misconceived, concentrating on psalms or hymns in 'the intervals of the service', while the people's part of the service itself had been left to the clerk and charity children. After a sweeping condemnation of Tate and Brady's metrical psalms, he laid down some first principles about church music. It should be as good as possible, and should wear well. In its 'phrases and modes of expression – in what may be called its common-places', it should 'have little or no affinity with the secular or theatrical music of the day'. 'Old music, as a rule, is better than new', as proved by its long survival (so Druitt speciously argued): and it is 'free from any resemblance to the conventional prettinesses of the day'. Church music should be 'chaste, severe, and simple in its style'. Adaptations of secular music were to be condemned. Gregorian chants were best; some Anglican were acceptable. Metrical hymns and psalms were all right in their place, but good old tunes should be used. The music of modern tunes 'never rises above the level of the dullest mannerism; the same whining cadences; the same crawling minor to represent contrition, and the jig-like dotted quavers for praise'. As to texts, the early Christian hymns were better than new original ones. 'The worship of the Infinite and Eternal is surely not a thing to be varied by place, time, or circumstances. They who hope to join the saints above ... would rather cling to the words which their forefathers in the faith sung before them' (Druitt: 34–44).

These principles provide a religious justification for the revival of old music, which the Romantic movement had already stimulated on other grounds. They were widely adopted by Tractarians. Despite the relative obscurity of Druitt, he gained influence through his persistent advocacy and administrative ability. He proposed that every parish should form a 'parochial association for the promotion of church music', to consist of 'as many persons as possible belonging to any respectable class of society'; the costs to be borne by the wealthier members. The organist or a choirmaster would be paid to conduct choir practices. The choir would begin by

---

* A similar plan had been proposed by the Reverend Rann Kennedy in 1821 (:26–32).

improving music already known, then learn a harmonised Amen, Tallis's responses and Litany – always to be sung unaccompanied, then psalm chanting with Gregorian or other old single chants, then the canticles, first to chants and then to 'some of the simpler compositions of Boyce, Tallis, &c.'. The choir should not be separate; the singers should disperse over the whole church. 'It would be desirable, nevertheless, to have some boys who can sing well, and a few singers placed on opposite sides, near the clergyman, so as to lead the rest of the congregation.' (This illustrates the persistent dilemma about the role and place of the choir.) Druitt condemned the organ, which 'has contributed as much as anything to the decay of congregational singing ... But the surest method of all, to extinguish anything like singing, is to set up a grinding organ.' This was much worse than the old village choir and band, which 'with patience, and encouragement, and instruction, ... might be made the nucleus of a true congregational choir' (:46–52).

Many such parochial societies were actually formed, and their efforts to develop 'a true congregational choir' were encouraged by the central society through its monthly journal, *The Parish Choir*, beginning in February 1846. The society quickly gained the support of influential Tractarian clergymen, who contributed articles to the journal. The opening article judiciously pointed to the prayer book as the ultimate source of all rules for the conduct of worship. As a first step it advised that all children be taught to sing: 'not only in the National and charity schools' for the poor, 'but also in the private schools to which people in good circumstances send their children' (I, 1846: 1–2). Another article in the first issue, called 'How to begin', advised that no real improvement could be achieved until the congregation as a whole became 'a singing, as well as a praying, body', and that this would only happen when the people had been taught the rudiments of music. An account of Hullah's method of teaching singing was to appear in the second issue (:6). There was also some advice about learning to chant.

Each subsequent issue contained lively correspondence from readers and reports from various parts of the country about progress in the desired reforms. Each issue also included some music useful for parish choirs. The second issue was accompanied by a complete set of Anglican chants, one for each morning and evening of the month (thus covering the whole psalter) and others for the canticles (ex. 59a). All were single chants – that is, taking in one verse rather than two – for, as was rightly pointed out, none of the psalms have their verses arranged in pairs, so that a double chant is inappropriate. The decision to recommend Anglican rather than Gregorian chants produced a good deal of criticism from some readers, and in June 1846 the editor justified it in a leading article. While agreeing that Gregorian chants were ideally the best, he said that recent attempts to introduce them had been unfortunate, and he had decided that Anglican chants must be used until people had got accustomed to some of the other changes advocated (:37; cited Rainbow: 101–3). The Gregorian tones appeared in the second volume (1847–8), with various harmonisations. Advice on their use had already been provided: they could be sung antiphonally (two halves of the choir and congregation singing alternate verses) or responsorially (the minister or another man singing one verse the whole choir and congregation the next). 'They should be sung in unison, with an organ accompaniment. If sung in harmony, the harmonies should be sung by a few skilled voices only, whilst the mass of the people should still sing the melody' (I, 1846: 87).

There were formidable problems, indeed, in inducing congregations to sing either Anglican or Gregorian chants. Chanting of any sort needs practice, and even though pointed psalters were now abundant, it was too much to expect an ordinary unskilled churchgoer to be able to chant from them correctly. Hence the canticles, which were regularly repeated, were easier to chant than the psalms, as Evangelicals had already found out. Most Anglican chants had been designed for cathedral choirs; they were essentially harmonised tunes, often with a range of over an octave, and the tune was carried by the high treble voices of the choirboys (ex. 59a). When parish congregations tried to sing them, they were generally much too high, and in particular the strain of chanting a long verse on a high reciting note was too much for an untrained adult singer. This problem did not exist with Gregorian chants, because they consisted of only a few notes of melody in a small compass, and could be pitched in a medium or low register (ex. 59b). The great difficulty with the Gregorian chants was their rhythm. Anglicans had a uniform number of notes in a well-understood rhythm in common time, upon which the words of the psalm could be hung. Gregorians were fluid; some had more notes than others, and the natural urge to treat some of their notes as strong or stressed tended to distort their character.

The experts of the day felt that in the middle ages the words had been chanted without any musical rhythm, but in the same rhythm in which one would naturally read the words in prose. The monks of Solesmes would later reach the same conclusion. There is little evidence either to support or contradict it. But it was certainly followed by those who laid down the guidelines of Tractarian church music. 'We ... entirely repudiate *measured time* in chanting', announced *The Parish Choir* (I, 1846: 15). But to sing a melody without measured time, without any sense of a periodic beat, was something entirely outside the experience of the ordinary person in the 1840s: the nearest thing to it in the music of the day was recitative, which was sung in Italian by professional *solo* singers to wealthy audiences. Moreover, English is a language of strong contrast between stressed and unstressed syllables, in this respect differing from both Latin and Italian. It is not surprising that most of the early attempts to adapt the Gregorian psalm tones to English words tended to supply a metrical accent.

In the first collection for Anglican use, Reinagle's of 1840 for St Peter-in-the-East, Oxford (PC 366), the melodies of the chants were inaccurate (ex. 60); this was also true of James Burns's version of 1842, which was used at St Mark's college, Chelsea (Rainbow: 50). Redhead's *Laudes diurnae* for Margaret Chapel (PC 372) was better in this respect, being based on Novello's *Cantica vespera* prepared for the use of Roman Catholic churches, which were also engaged in reviving Gregorian chant. All three of these early efforts used barlines, which inevitably suggested that the note following the barline bore a metrical accent. Oakeley in *Laudes diurnae* made no attempt to correlate the verbal stresses of the English prose to these implied musical stresses; he simply set one syllable to each note of the mediation and ending of the chant, and the rest to the reciting note, a method equivalent to the old 'rule of 3 and 5' in Anglican chanting (ex. 61). The result was neither faithful to the accepted character of the chant nor satisfactory to an uninformed singer.

A more subtle method of adapting the chants to English prose was put forward by William Dyce in the appendix to his *Order of daily service* (PC 371), which was an adaptation of Marbeck to the current liturgy. Briefly, he proposed that the treatment of *quantity* in the chanting of Latin should be applied to *stress* in the chanting of English, and that this should determine both the distribution of syllables to the notes following the reciting note and the durations allotted to these notes. This method was adopted by Thomas Helmore (Pl. 29) in his *Psalter noted* (1849: PC 379), which was the result of several years' experiment at St Mark's (Rainbow: 85–6). In the following year it was enlarged to form *A manual of plainsong* which also contained the canticles and other texts, and a 'brief directory' giving instructions for users of the book.

Helmore's publication has a distinctly archaic air, using the old form of musical note (black longs, breves and semibreves), the four-line stave, with old clefs, and even the old-fashioned form of lower-case 's', similar to an 'f'. These features may have expressed the Tractarian passion for antiquity, but they can only have added to the difficulties of those who used the psalter. From a practical point of view, five-line staves, G clefs, and minims, crotchets and quavers would have served better. Helmore also used the word 'noted' in an obsolete sense in his title, but it did describe a novel feature of the psalter, which was that every word of every psalm was supplied with its own note. Thus pointing was unnecessary. For the reciting notes Helmore supplied a breve or semibreve for each syllable, according to whether in his judgment it should be sung to a longer or shorter note. For the mediations and endings he distributed the syllables according to Dyce's principles. The intonation, for the first verse of each psalm, was directed 'to be used on festivals' only, following medieval tradition as recently discovered (ex. 62).

Helmore's manual immediately attained an authoritative position, which it kept throughout the Victorian period. It was revised by H. B. Briggs and W. H. Frere in 1902, and again by J. H. Arnold; each time, alterations were made in light of recent scholarship, and a more practical form of notation adopted, but the preface acknowledged the editors' debt to Helmore's pioneering work. The ideal of congregational chanting of the psalms, as set out in the psalter, had been achieved at St Mark's, where a group of dedicated and committed young men could be daily rehearsed by Helmore himself. But in the very different conditions of an ordinary parish church it is doubtful how successfully such music could be introduced. The very fluidity and subtlety that made its word setting acceptable to sensitive ears also removed the chief bulwark which the common man needed to grasp an unfamiliar piece of music – a strong periodic accent. Despite the idealism and determination of the new generation of Tractarian clergy that had come out of Oxford and Cambridge, few churches, even in London, permanently adopted Gregorian tones.

For the other parts of the liturgy, Cranmer's Litany and Marbeck's *Book of common praier noted*, as revived in several editions, were recommended for congregational use, and adapted where necessary to subsequent changes in the liturgy. For the responses to the commandments (introduced in the 1552 prayer book) Dyce adapted Marbeck's setting of the 1549 Kyrie eleison which it replaced, and this adaptation has survived in the modern revisions of Helmore. For harmonised responses, Tallis's harmonisations, which had been reprinted by Crotch, were now adopted in Tractarian parish churches.

Another great contribution of the Tractarians to public worship was the liturgical hymn, which rapidly completed the transformation of 'psalmody' into 'hymnody' in the Church of England. This development was stimulated by their discovery of the Latin hymns of the Roman Breviary, which brought home the fact that hymns were Catholic as well as Evangelical. In translating these, and reviving the tunes that went with them, they not only enriched the store of English hymns, but changed the status of the hymn itself from an unauthorised addition to an integral part of the service of public worship.

Anglican hymnody

Before the nineteenth century, hymns, while never totally excluded from the Church, had been only just permitted. The Evangelicals found them an important vehicle of religious expression, and, since nobody could show that they were illegal, introduced them with growing confidence, ultimately winning a legal victory in 1820. The Archbishop of York's selection of psalm and hymns that emerged from that episode seemed to confer at least indirect authority on hymn singing. Nevertheless, traditional high churchmen stuck to metrical psalms, perhaps because hymns were so closely connected with Evangelicals and, above all, Nonconformists. For instance Charles Wollaston, the high-church rector of East Dereham depicted in *Lavengro* (Borrow: chap. 3; Boston & Puddy: 129), published *A collection of psalms* (2nd edn 1813) in which he provided selections from the New Version, the only hymns being Ken's morning and evening hymns and special hymns for Christmas and Easter. In his preface he condemned modern hymns, 'many of them, from an improper warmth of expression, justly offensive to sober thinking Christians' (Wollaston).

A different view was taken by another high churchman, Reginald Heber, rector of Hodnet from 1807 to 1822, and then Bishop of Calcutta. He had certain affinities with the Evangelicals, and soon after his installation at Hodnet he wrote to ask a friend where he could purchase 'Cowper's Olney hymns, with the music, and in a smaller size without the music, to put in the seats? Some of them I admire much, and any novelty is likely to become a favourite, and draw more people to join in the singing' (A. Heber: 352). Soon afterwards he published some hymns of his own in *The Christian Observer*, clearly stating that he intended them to be sung 'between the Nicene creed and the sermon': each was suited to a particular Sunday or holy day, and was related to the Gospel or Epistle for the day. But he pointed out that he had avoided all 'fulsome or indecorous language ... erotic addresses to him whom no unclean lips can approach'. He refused to let near-dissenter Rowland Hill preach in his parish, and other statements in his letters make it clear that he was a strict high churchman (A. Heber: 336, 359, 371, 407–16, 423).

Heber contributed some of the best hymns in the English language, including 'Holy, holy, holy', 'From Greenland's icy mountains' and 'Ride on, ride on in majesty'. His collection was designed to cover the whole Church year and other miscellaneous occasions, and drew on many sources. He included some metrical psalms, but he boldly put them in their appropriate place in the scheme, instead of in a separate section, as was customary in the many 'Psalms and hymns' selections published at about this time. Before his departure for India (where he died) he tried unsuccessfully to have the collection adopted officially by the church authorities. It was published by his widow in 1827 as *Hymns written and adapted to the weekly church service of the year*, and the Archbishop of Canterbury accepted the dedication. The importance of the collection was partly in its evident high-church slant, its emphasis on liturgical propriety rather than individual feeling, and its acceptance by the highest prelate in the church. It also lay in the literary distinction of the hymns, which were really a collection of sacred poetry: L. Benson calls it 'Reginald Heber's romantic hymnal' (:437). It prepared the minds of high churchmen for the recognition that hymns were not exclusively the property of 'ranting dissenters'.

John Keble, regarded as the founder of the Oxford movement, published *The Christian year* (also in 1827) which similarly followed the feasts and fasts of the liturgical year, and contributed several hymns to the permanent repertory. But the real turning-point was the rediscovery of the hymns of the Roman breviary, omitted by Cranmer from the prayer book. The Oxford leaders were at first reluctant to believe that medieval hymns could be anything but 'barbarous in their latinity as defective in their doctrine', as John Chandler put it in the preface to *Hymns of the primitive Church* (1837). Isaac Williams hesitated to introduce unauthorised texts in public worship, and couched some of his earliest translations in 'unrhythmical harsh metres to prevent this' (L. Benson: 495). Richard Mant's *Ancient hymns, from the Roman breviary* (1837) was explicitly 'for domestic use'. But as more of the Latin hymns became known through translation, 'they at once commended themselves to the thoughtful mind who would repair the breaches of the Reformation' (so Newman, in his preface to *Hymni ecclesiae* (1838)).

The Tractarians' choice of Latin hymns for translation was uncritical in these early years. Anything Latin was regarded as 'primitive', but in fact many of those included had been written in the seventeenth and eighteenth centuries. Such hymns now form a substantial proportion of those in use in the Church of England. For example, *Hymns ancient and modern revised* (1950) contains nineteen post-Tridentine hymns, eleven of them from a single source, the Paris Breviary of 1736 (Frere & Frost: 20–1). These include such favourites as 'The advent of our King' and 'On Jordan's bank the Baptist's cry', both translated by Chandler. L. Benson suggests that 'to men educated in the classical atmosphere of Oxford the language of the later hymnals, in its approach to classical models, appealed more than the early hymns could have done, even if they had known them' (:497).

These discoveries, however misguided from a scholarly point of view, completely altered the status of the hymn in the minds of the Tractarian party. It was suddenly found to be an integral part of the daily office (and hence of morning and evening prayer) and even of the mass (and hence of the communion service). Moreover, although the liturgy itself could not legally be altered in a Catholic direction, there was nothing to prevent the singing of translated Catholic hymns in public worship. The battle for hymns had already been won by the Evangelicals: here was an unforeseen chance to capitalise on their victory in a way that would restore a lost tradition of the ancient Church.

It was left to Neale, the real founder of the Cambridge Camden Society, to undertake a more thorough scholarly investigation and revival of the truly ancient hymns of the Church. At first, in 1840, he declared his 'general dislike of hymns', but he soon changed his opinion on becoming familiar with the Tractarian translations, and embarked on patient research in early sources, both English and continental, until he had mastered the history and liturgiology of the medieval hymn. In a series of articles he shared his knowledge with sympathetic churchmen, and prepared the ground for an authoritative collection of pre-Reformation hymns. In a paper on 'English hymnology, its history and prospects', he criticised not only the current Evangelical hymnody, but also the Oxford translators in their misplaced zeal for the Paris breviary and their careless treatment of the Latin texts (Neale, 1850). His *Mediaeval hymns and sequences* (1851) was the first fruit of his labours, and gave the Church one of the most popular of all its hymns, 'Jerusalem the golden'.

But Neale's most important venture was the *Hymnal noted*, in two parts (1851, 1854). It was an attempt to provide an official hymn book for public use, which would supply all the needs of the Church, and would be made up exclusively of translations of Latin hymns that had been used *in England* before the Reformation, set to their original melodies. So stated the prospectus issued in advance of publication (Rainbow: 92). It thus represented an extreme and idealistic statement of the newly formed Tractarian view of hymnody. It was officially sponsored by the Ecclesiological Society: Neale had the primary responsibility for translating and editing the texts, while Helmore deciphered and transcribed the melodies, often from sources brought to him by Neale from the libraries in which he had conducted his research. In the end continental as well as English sources were tapped, as in the case of one of the best known hymns in the collection, now called 'O come, O come, Emmanuel'.

The *Hymnal noted* was far too narrow and extreme to be widely adopted. Only three London churches (St Alban, Holborn; All Saints, Lambeth; and St Columba, Haggerston) used it exclusively throughout the period 1866–94 (Mackeson, 1866–95). It became best known through its use at St Alban, Holborn, a new church built in 1862, but it was supplemented there by an Appendix of conventional hymns and tunes, mostly modern (L. Benson: 504n.). The Sarum plainsong hymn melodies, which Helmore gave in the same archaic notation he had used in the *Psalter noted*, were difficult for the average organist and singer. They lacked the square rhythm expected of a hymn tune, they were often in unfamiliar modes, and the festal hymns had long melismas on certain syllables. As in the case of the Gregorian psalm tones, the uncompromising austerity of the music made unlikely the widespread congregational adoption desired by the compilers of the book. Nevertheless its influence on Anglican hymnody was very great, and most hymn books except those of the extreme low church have included some of the translations and tunes first printed there.

The use of hymns in Tractarian worship at first differed little from the traditional use of metrical psalms. They were sung in the places legally permitted: before, after, or between services. An additional place for them was instead of the anthem, as Bisse had first suggested, after the third collect. Later, Helmore would encourage interpolations, especially in the communion service.

As far as hymn tunes were concerned, the distinctive contribution of the period from 1830 to 1850 was the recovery of the treasures of the past: first the traditional psalm tunes, then the Sarum melodies and other plainsong tunes, finally the German chorales. At the same time there was a tendency to curb the effusions of the late Georgian ornate melodies. The favourite 'Evening Hymn' (ex. 57) was an obvious candidate for the axe. Charles Hackett's *National psalmist* printed the popular version in editions of 1839 and 1840, but in 1842 reversed itself, printing an inaccurate transcription of Ravenscroft's version of Tallis's original canon, headed by an un-necessarily violent comment: 'The outrageous corruption which this fine melody has undergone, renders the immediate adoption of the *original*, indispensably necessary.' In a surprisingly short time 'Evening Hymn' had disappeared from the hymn books, though it lived on in folk tradition (Temperley, 1971: 376). Other ornate tunes were pruned, for example 'Mount Ephraim' (Frere & Frost: 412), and the reaction against them was so swift that in a short time even low-church writers were condemning them (Pears: 23–4).

The new tunes of the period are generally dull and undistinguished. Their qualities are mainly negative, as if composers were cowed by the fierce criticisms of Georgian tunes for their triviality, secularity and sentimen-tality. They eschew triple time, extended melismas, and repeated lines of text; the result is almost inevitably a four-square type of tune, innocuous but uninspiring, like Turle's 'Westminster' (1836), Steggall's 'St Edmund' (1849) or the anonymous 'Innocents', published in *The Parish Choir* in 1850. Two of the most successful tunes of the period won their fame through association with children's hymns by Mrs Cecil Alexander, 'There is a green hill far away' (tune 'Hofsley' by W. Horsley, 1844) and 'Once in royal David's city' (tune 'Irby' by H. Gauntlett, 1849). Though they partake of the characteristic sweetness of Victorian hymn tunes, they are still chaste enough to have evaded the strictures of Dr Crotch. Signs of the boldness and freedom, largely harmonic, that would lead to the great Victorian development of hymn tunes are found in one or two early tunes of Samuel Sebastian Wesley, such as 'Wesley' (1839), sung to 'Christ is our corner-stone', which is Chandler's translation of part of the *Urbs beata Jerusalem*, one of the oldest hymns of the Christian church.

The rediscovery of tradition (1800–50)

The adoption of hymnody by the Tractarians, who eventually carried with them the more reluctant traditional high churchmen, meant that hymns were now an established part of Anglican worship, accepted with enthusiasm by all parties within the Church. Whatever difficulties there might be in persuading congregations to chant the psalms or sing the responses, there was no doubt that they could sing the hymns. The time would soon be ripe for an official Church hymn book, which *Hymns ancient and modern* was in all but name, and hymn singing would become the most characteristic and universal part of Anglican parish church music.

Summary and evaluation

The period discussed in this chapter and the last is perhaps the most important one in the history of parish church music, with the exception of the Reformation itself. It was in these years that the modern concept of Anglican worship was evolved, as were many other aspects of modern English life. The Oxford movement, though its contribution was important and distinctive, was not in the end the decisive factor in the evolution of the new style of Anglican church music.

Fuller-Maitland summed up the 'musical results of the Anglican revival' as 'threefold: the restoration of Gregorian music to a place of honour; the encouragement of the practice of making adaptations from sacred music written for the Roman Church; and the creation of a school of composers whose education was not sound enough to keep them from outside influences, men who perpetrated weak imitations of Spohr and Gounod' (1910: 9). The Oxford movement was certainly not responsible for the third of these, and only partially for the second. But it undoubtedly earned the principal credit for the revival of Gregorian chant and much other early music. The Romantic movement may have produced a few antiquarian scholars, but it was the Tractarians' belief in the unique authority of the traditions of the early Church that brought plainsong out of the libraries into the churches.

The new veneration for traditional psalm tunes was followed by a search for still more ancient music, and the rediscovery of Marbeck, Tallis, and plainsong provided material for the Tractarians in the ultimate reform, the introduction of congregational singing in the prayers and responses of the liturgy. The Gregorian psalm tones, which they revived, were in some respects more suitable for congregational chanting than Anglican chants, but posed formidable problems of word setting and rhythm which were not resolved until the first phase of the Oxford movement was over. Although Gregorian chant failed to win acceptance from more than a minority in the Church, that minority has used it continuously since that time.

The Oxford movement brought about a period of turmoil and excitement in the Church such as had not been known for two centuries, and helped to generate needed thought and action, though the resulting changes did not all meet with the approval of the Oxford party. The Tractarians were not in favour of elaborate choir music, nor of secular influences on the music of the Church. They cultivated a special style for religious music that was restrained, archaic, and holy. Their greatest musical achievements were in the revival of old music; for living composers their principles had at first a largely negative effect. But their discovery of the medieval hymn, and consequent change of attitude towards hymn singing in general, paved the way for a fruitful synthesis of Evangelical and Tractarian ideals in the Victorian hymn tune.

9 The Victorian settlement (1850–1900)

The ritualist controversy

The patterns of Anglican worship in the Victorian age seem extraordinarily complex, more so than in any preceding period. No doubt one of the main reasons for this is the abundance of information that is available. Not only are the archives and records more complete than those of earlier times, but there was far more discussion in print of every aspect of religion and worship, as well as a great deal of systematic study of the subject by government commissions, church authorities, and independent investigators. It was partly a matter of more activity in general, more administrative enquiry, more writing, more printing. But in addition, religion had once more become an object of passionate interest to a large portion of the educated community, including many who doubted its teachings and attacked its influence.

The complexity of the evidence has allowed for varying interpretations. Some have seen the period as one of Anglican revival, led by the Oxford movement: the term 'Anglican Revival' has indeed become accepted as a description of the early Victorian period. Others have seen it as the time when Anglicans lost the faith of their fathers, through pressure from scientific and materialistic advances, and by attrition to Catholicism and dissent. Again, it was certainly a time of internal strife within the Church: and yet many now look back with envy on the Victorians for, among other things, their comfortable security of religious belief and worship.

All these judgments clearly have some truth in them. To choose among them would be far beyond the scope of this book or the capacity of its author. But if we are to deal with music and its place in worship, it is necessary to disentangle and distinguish two main patterns. There was, certainly, a prolonged battle between high and low church parties about doctrine and worship. At the same time, however, there was a gradual evolution of a new style of worship, which would come to be accepted by almost everybody in the Church. The two trends could exist at the same time because the controversy between high and low was carried on by a small articulate minority at both ends of the scale. The majority, which included most of the clergy, almost all professional musicians, and (we can safely say) all parochial congregations, did not belong to either extreme. They moved more slowly, not without the influence of the radicals on both sides, to evolve the mode of worship that is now everyone's idea of traditional Anglicanism.

The ritualist controversy of the mid-Victorian period was part of that hardening of opposition and division into camps that unfortunately followed the Oxford movement. Evangelicals and low churchmen were united by their deep fear of any Romeward tendencies, and formed a new low-church party which for a while seemed to concentrate most of its energies on the prosecution and persecution of its opponents. Tractarians joined traditional high churchmen in a new high-church party, whose radical wing sometimes seemed exclusively preoccupied with trivial details of ceremonial. A third, far less united group, which came to be called the 'broad church party', found a spokesman in F. D. Maurice. It was motivated partly by abhorrence of the squabbles between the other parties, and pressed for a broadly comprehensive liturgy and a national Church on liberal principles. The term 'broad church' is sometimes used as if it included everyone who was not high church or low church. But there was no compulsion to belong to any party at all. 'Broad church' actually represented a cogent set of opinions held by a small, specific group of church leaders, however unorganised (Davies: IV, 283–315). A realistic classification must include a fourth or 'central' group, 'to which in the nineteenth century the great mass of English churchmen belonged' (Kinloch: 54).

Some of the great *causes célèbres* of the ritualistic controversy involved clear theological issues. The Gorham case (1847–50) was about the meaning of the sacrament of baptism, while the Denison case (1853–8) was concerned with the doctrine of real presence in the communion. Others turned on more superficial, though symbolic, matters, such as the decoration of altars, the use of the cross, vestments, processions, liturgical colours, candles, incense, and Gregorian chants (Pl. 28). These were the issues that caused rioting at St Barnabas, Pimlico in 1850, and at St George-in-the-East in 1856, and were the subject of litigation later on. In all cases it may be said that the strength of emotional involvement was in great part due to differing conceptions of the identity and character of the Church of England, which had been, from the beginning, a Church of compromise. High churchmen valued its catholicity and stressed its independence from secular authority: their innovations inevitably brought Anglican worship closer to that of Rome. Low churchmen emphasised its protestantism, and felt a close kinship with the nonconformist bodies in England and the Reformed churches abroad: they reacted with horror to anything that made the Church of England look more like the Roman Catholic Church. In ritualistic matters the high-church party always had the initiative in this period, so that low churchmen found themselves in the role of defenders of tradition – but of recent tradition only, against their opponents' policy of reviving ancient ceremonial customs that had fallen into disuse, or, in some cases, of bringing in practices more recently developed in continental Catholic churches.

The ritualists advanced by stages. The restoration of chancels and altars, the establishment of surpliced choirs in facing choir stalls, candles and coloured altar cloths had all been revolutionary in the 1840s, but were becoming commonplace in the 1850s. Next eucharistic vestments, incense, and perpetual reservation of the sacraments were brought in; and with the publication of John Purchas's *Directorium anglicanum* in 1858, specifically Roman Catholic practices were introduced (P. T. Marsh: 113; Thureau-Dangin: II, 443–4).

At first public opinion tended to ignore the activities of the ritualists, but the re-establishment of the Roman hierarchy in 1850 led directly to the Pimlico riots, as the age-old fear of Rome was aroused. Opponents within the Church saw that ritualism was spreading fast, and was gaining many adherents, especially in the slums of London where the fearlessness and self-denial of Anglo-Catholic priests won widespread admiration. In such districts many people who had scarcely before been aware of Christianity were now invited to witness colourful spectacles of ritual and music. It did not offend their religious traditions, since they had none. Moreover the high-church party was growing bolder in its methods. The earlier ritualists, guided by the Cambridge Camden Society, had made a point of adhering to the letter of the *Book of common prayer*; after 1850 their more advanced followers openly departed from the rubric, interpolating matter of all kinds from Roman sources. What is more, they had scored a legal victory.

In 1833 parliament had abolished the old High Court of Delegates, and had made the Judicial Committee of the Privy Council the supreme court of appeal in matters of ecclesiastical law (Flindall: 32–4). The Clergy Discipline Act (1840) safeguarded the position of the bishop in complaints against clergy within his diocese, but allowed for appeals to the provincial court, and thence to the Judicial Committee, which was composed chiefly of lay judges (:78–80). In the first ritual case to come before it, *Westerton* v. *Liddell* (1857), the Committee upheld the legality of some moderate ritualistic practices that had been disallowed by the lower courts, such as coloured altar cloths, candles, and crosses behind the altar (:159–62). In 1860 the high-church party went on the legal offensive by forming the English Church Union, and tried to use the courts to prevent Evangelicals from holding mission services in unconsecrated buildings such as theatres (P. Marsh: 124).

Alarmed by these developments, the low-church party in 1865 founded its own body, the Church Association, which besides issuing tracts and pamphlets attacking ritualism began a series of prosecutions of ritualistic clergymen, who were generally defended by the English Church Union. In 1867 the Association started its first case, the prosecution of A. H. Mackonochie, vicar of St Alban, Holborn, under the Act of 1840. He was charged with kneeling or prostrating himself before the consecrated elements, using lighted candles on the altar other than for the purpose of giving light, using incense during communion, and mixing water with the wine used at communion. In the Court of Arches Sir Robert Phillimore allowed the candles and the kneeling but not the other practices, but on appeal the Judicial Committee ruled all four practices illegal (*Martin* v. *Mackonochie*; Flindall: 202–5). A similar result was obtained against John Purchas, vicar of St James, Brighton, in 1871: again the Judicial Committee reversed the judgments of the lower courts in a low-church direction (*Elphinstone* v. *Purchas*, later *Hebbert* v. *Purchas*; Flindall: 213–17). This time the condemned practices included the eastward position at the altar during communion, which was no ritualistic innovation, but a high-church practice of long standing.

Pressing forward to what it believed was to be a resounding victory, the Church Association announced that it would harry the bishops until they enforced the decision throughout the Church, and continued its prosecutions. In 1874, after the electoral defeat of Gladstone, who was always sympathetic to the high-church position, Disraeli and Archbishop Tait secured the passage of the Public Worship Regulation Act (1874), which gave the courts much stronger powers against recalcitrant clergymen. After due monition, a disobedient incumbent could be suspended from his office and even committed to prison for contempt of court. But a prosecution under the Act could be vetoed by the bishop, and it is estimated that seventeen out of twenty-three representations under the Act were vetoed (Flindall: 231–2). Nevertheless, five clergymen were imprisoned between 1877 and 1887 for refusal to obey judgments under the Act.

But the heavy legal reinforcements brought against the ritualists were of little avail. Although the judgments could be enforced against individual priests, they had no direct effect on the growing numbers of others who were following the same practices, and prosecution was expensive and invidious. Moreover the ritualists were seen to be persecuted and began to take on the guise of martyrs in the eyes of the public. Their determination to do what they thought right, their impressive demeanour in the face of harassment, and their self-denying ministries in some of the most unattractive parishes in the country, won widespread admiration, including that of bishops and clergy who did not share their views about worship. Fortified by the support of their parishioners and of like-minded colleagues, they generally succeeded in defying the law (P. Marsh: 230–3). Eventually even the legal tide turned in the high-church direction, when Edward King, bishop of Lincoln, was tried by the Archbishop of Canterbury with assessors, who in 1890 upheld his right to continue certain moderate ritualistic practices, including the singing of the Agnus dei in English after the prayer of consecration. The judgment was largely upheld on appeal to the Privy Council (*Read & others* v. *The Bishop of Lincoln*; Flindall: 256–60; *Law Times* LXIV n.s., 1891: 149–80). This judgment marked the decisive proof of 'the moderate acceptance of the Tractarian ideals as a permissible Anglican alternative' (Davies: IV, 126).

On the whole music played only an incidental part in these disputes. Although music, as much as any visual phenomenon, can bear symbolic meanings, these are not universally or readily appreciated: no music would so immediately suggest 'popery' to the prejudiced as would the sudden appearance of a cross on an altar. Moreover, although parties in the Church certainly disagreed about how music should be used in worship, all accepted that it had its place there. Nobody now was against organs, choirs, anthems, and counterpoint, as the Puritans had been in the sixteenth century; both chanting and hymn singing were practised by high and low churchmen alike.

It is instructive, however, to see what the musical arrangements were in the churches that were in the forefront of the battle. At St Barnabas, Pimlico, splendid choral services were planned for its consecration on 11 June 1850 and the week following. At the service of consecration, the choir processed into the church chanting a psalm from Helmore's *Psalter noted*, Tallis's responses were sung with organ accompaniment, and the anthem and service settings were also by Tallis; Aldrich's 'O give thanks' was sung at the offertory. The only hymn admitted was an English version of *Coelestis urbs Jerusalem* with its authentic tune, which was repeated at every evening service throughout the week. Gregorian tones were used daily for the psalms, and later in the week there were anthems by Byrd, Farrant, Gibbons, Batten, Rogers, Aldrich, and adaptations from Lassus and Palestrina. Service settings included Gibbons in F, Rogers in D, Ouseley in A, and Marbeck's communion service (*Parish Choir* III, 1850: 116–19; cited Rainbow: 156).

The choir, clad of course in cassocks and surplices, consisted of twelve boys, who were educated in the choir school attached to the church, and twelve men. It was trained by Thomas Helmore. The splendid organ was presented by Frederick Ouseley, who was one of the curates in the parish, but who, as Rainbow has pointed out, did not approve of the selection of music, particularly the Gregorian chants (Rainbow: 158). A sympathetic observer noted that a large and varied congregation attended the services, and that many of them had joined in the chanting of the psalms (:157).

Helmore, more than any other individual, represented the musical ideal which the extreme Anglo-Catholic party strove to attain. It was he who had corrected the blunders of the early attempts to adapt Gregorian chant to the English service, and had shown how both choirs and congregations could be trained to sing this unfamiliar music both devoutly and artistically. His mature thoughts on the subject were expressed in a lecture delivered to the Church Congress at Wolverhampton in 1867. 'A distinction has grown up in the minds of English Christians between cathedral service, and parochial service, which ought never to have existed; and the continuance of which ought no longer to be tolerated.' But he did not mean by this that in parish churches, as in cathedrals, all the music should be performed by the choir alone. On the contrary: 'both the clergy and the people must learn to sing'. He considered the reasons for the present lack of musical skill in the clergy and upper and middle classes, and proposed remedies. 'One of the first things to teach the people is, *the music of the entire communion service*.' He recommended several settings, and even approved the adaptation of Gounod's Mass in B flat with harp accompaniment which 'has lately been introduced with charming effect in St. Andrew's, Wells Street. At All Saints', Margaret Street, they have for very many years used more questionable adaptations from the masses of Haydn and Mozart, part, I believe, of the service being taken from one, and another from the other of these great composers: an objectionable practice, in my opinion.' For plainer singing he recommended Marbeck for the choir and people together, or 'another plainsong service [adapted] from the famous *Missa de Angelis*' as used at St Alban, Holborn. He also suggested

prefixes, affixes, and additional music introduced into the body of the service, such as the 'Agnus Dei' ... eucharistic hymns ... and sequences between the Epistle and Gospel, peculiarly suitable in high celebrations during the preparation for the reading of the holy Gospel. ... The interspersing other hymns than those already provided in the body of the service, if a license, as I suppose we must allow, is yet so justified on grounds of convenience, edification, spiritual comfort, and above all, of Catholic usage, that we may claim allowance for the practice, above all from those who themselves break the continuity of the services according to the present prayer-book order, by the introduction of a metrical psalm or hymn before the morning sermon, immediately after the Nicene Creed, or between the second lesson of the evening prayer and the 'Nunc dimittis'. (T. Helmore: 4–6, 17–19)

Helmore, it is clear, was still fighting the battle for what he considered true church music, sung by choir and people. The Gregorian psalm tones, which had become the musical badge of the Anglo-Catholics, won a limited acceptance, especially in London. They were used in 8.4 per cent of London churches in 1869; by 1875 the proportion had climbed to 19.6 per cent; but after that it dropped off, reaching 13.6 per cent in 1882 (see Table 15, p. 279). Charles Mackeson, in a survey of London church music compiled in 1876 for visitors to the Church Congress, found that a service consisting entirely or even largely of ancient music was becoming rare. At All Saints, Margaret Street, St Mary Magdalene, Paddington, and St Alban, Holborn, Gregorian psalm tones were used, but hymn tunes and anthems were mainly of recent date, and the communion service was frequently sung to adapted masses of modern composers (Mackeson, 1876: 40). The hymn book in use at St Alban, Holborn, was introduced as an 'Appendix' to Helmore's *Hymnal noted* (PC 398), but contained tunes 'of the most florid character'. The editor, the Reverend H. A. Walker, who was 'precentor' at the church (where Mackonochie was vicar), said in his preface that 'many persons having made application for the tunes to which the hymns were sung ... as being so eminently congregational, it has been thought advisable to publish the collection'. A critic, John Heywood, complained that many of the tunes were of the 'music-hall' type, far too secular, and included many derived from the Roman Catholic *Crown of Jesus*, 'which has been the means of importing much rubbish and more unblushingly secular matter into our services than the 18th century dissenters would ever have used. If only the book be Roman it must be good ...' Ex. 68 is one of the worst examples, 'a specimen of what our ecclesiastical-acrobat friends call "go"', often sung during the communion of the celebrant (Heywood, 1881: 20–2).

Such a glaring contrast between the austerity of Gregorian tones and the triviality of modern hymn tunes was approved by Mackonochie, one of the most uncompromising of the ritualist clergy. 'Mackonochie was no aesthete; he appreciated forms only as they were moving demonstrations of Catholic truth' (Davies: IV, 124). However painful the musical incongruities must have been to such as Helmore, who was an aesthete and a sensitive musician, they were not inconsistent with the *religious* aims of Anglo-Catholicism, which included the full and genuine participation of the congregation in the service of praise. What was incompatible with Mackonochie's views was the performance by the choir of parts of the liturgy in elaborate music in which the congregation could not join: and this he did not allow.

It is interesting to turn from this to the other extreme in the Church. Steuart Pears, an assistant master at Harrow School, stated the low-church position cogently in *Remarks on the protestant theory of church music* (1852), which was addressed 'especially' to 'the Evangelical clergy':

> There are two theories of church music – the one scriptural, primitive, and protestant, the other opposed to the spirit of scripture, having its origin in a corrupt age of the Church, and peculiarly characteristic of the Church of Rome. (Pears: 2)

According to the 'true' theory, all the people sing from their hearts; according to the 'false' theory, a small portion 'is deputed to perform this service on behalf of the rest' (:3). Even in many Evangelical churches, he pointed out, the choir and organ monopolised the singing. But 'English men and women *can* sing together in good time and tune, without preparation or training' (:20).

Pears proposed, as a first step, to 'abolish the red curtain, and disband the choir'. More skilful singers should sit in their ordinary places, and lead the singing of the congregation. (One is reminded of the vain efforts of clergy in the early eighteenth century to secure the same object.) People must be encouraged to get over the 'outer crust of reserve in all English churchmen, and among highly educated persons especially'. The organist must be genuinely religious. Chanting is more suited to a choir than a congregation; 'therefore, if not entirely discontinued, it should be strictly limited to one psalm or canticle in each service ... The singing of prayers, such as the earnest ejaculations in the communion service after each commandment, appears to me so absolutely inconsistent with serious devotion, as to require no remark here' (:21–2). The choice of hymn tunes was important. 'Pretty' tunes were to be avoided, especially those with secular associations such as 'Drink to me only'. A good psalm tune was the work of a master, but it must be suitable for the simplest of Christians. 'Mozart composed his masses for the most accomplished singers of the day: the Protestant psalm tune is for the peasant and the mechanic.' Hence the really good ones were few: 'Dr. Crotch's selection, (the best,) contains, of all measures, only 78.' (:23–4.) He summed up his position thus:

> It must, however, be borne in mind, that our great object is not the revival of a pure taste, but the encouragement of a popular psalmody. And if there are tunes of a lower standard than the very best, yet so well-known and well-liked, as to be acceptable to the people, we must be contented, and thankful to have it so. (:25)

One of the few churches in which this ideal was satisfactorily realised was St Pancras. When Henry Smart, one of the most prominent organists of the day, was appointed organist there in 1864, he discussed the musical situation with the low-church vicar, Weldon Champneys.* Smart offered a choice between a 'strictly choral' and a 'strictly congregational' form of service. Champneys said that he could not approve of the congregation listening in silence to the choir singing the liturgy. Smart replied that in that case the only way was 'the old way, the way of the Germans and the Dutch ... to make them sing in unison, or in octaves, which is musically the same thing. This, again, is not enough. In a hymn of six or eight verses the same harmony repeated gets tiresome, and if the organist is what he should be, he will vary the harmonies according to the verbal expression, keeping them ecclesiastical in style' (Curwen, 1880: 167–8). Smart had already published samples of this type of organ accompaniment (PC 391: see ex. 82).

---

* In 1880 Champneys still changed his surplice for a black 'Geneva gown' for the sermon (Curwen, 1880: 169).

They set to work on these principles: Smart 'encouraged the timid by playing out boldly, and in a short time nine-tenths of the congregation sang ... I do as I like now; there is no need to play loudly unless the sentiment requires it. ... When I vary the quantity of tone, the congregation imitate perfectly ... We never had any congregational practices. What the people do they have picked up. I don't know any congregational singing in London so good as ours at St. Pancras' (:168). The canticles were evidently chanted by the congregation (:171). Others confirmed Smart's enthusiasm. William Spark attended matins on Whitsunday, 1873. He was impressed by the responses spoken by a congregation of over two thousand, led by a parish clerk '(a character that I thought had long ago vanished)'. There was no choir; the Venite was chanted by the schoolchildren and congregation. 'No one seems to "put in a second" or attempts to do a bit of harmony on his own account – but all sing the melody – and a grand unison it is!' The psalms were read, the canticles chanted to double chants. 'The rest of the music was confined to hymns and organ voluntaries' (Spark, 1892: 47). Charles Box, visiting the church on Palm Sunday, 1884, commented on the remarkable singing of the hymns and canticles, but noticed 'a few children in charity attire placed beside the organ, and tolerably well-trained', who 'keep the melody prominent enough to guide the congregation'. Efforts to introduce a surpliced choir had been defeated (Box: 190).

The success of this conservative and uncompromisingly low-church style of musical service was undoubtedly due to the talent and personality of the organist, and the co-operation of the vicar. The descriptions show that it was a rarity, and even Smart acknowledged that the St Pancras service would not 'do everywhere. Good taste is a quality not so universally distributed that we may rely on finding it in every church, and my plan leaves much to the judgment of the organist' (Curwen, 1880: 170). In the majority of 'low' churches, the principle adopted was the negative one of refusing to follow the innovations of the ritualists, or following the more moderate ones only grudgingly and many years later. In 1881 it was estimated that probably fifty London churches still had a service sung by charity children, who would chant the canticles and Glorias, sing 'a couple of hymns of antique flavour, which after having been introduced by the presiding clergyman in a roundabout harangue, are played over on the organ, then partly read out, and finally rendered by those present', and a setting of the responses to the commandments (Crowest: 85–7). At St George, Hanover Square, 'the most fashionable in the Metropolis, especially for marriages', the services were said to 'partake in no degree of the fashionable and ambiguous character of too many in that locality and elsewhere. The ceremonials at St. George differ but slightly from those of the last generation.' A small choir, accompanied on the organ, chanted the canticles, responses and amens, and sang the hymns; the psalms were read. The situation was similar at the nearby St James, Piccadilly (Box: 179–80, 183–4).

The striking fact about the two extremes is that they had so much in common, though in the heat of the battle they never knew it. Both had as their ideal the full and hearty participation of the congregation in all parts of the singing, including chanting if this was possible. Both were prepared to sacrifice aesthetic matters to this higher aim. In a few model churches where exceptional talent could be called upon for the direction of the music, this ideal could be achieved in a way that also satisfied the canons of good taste. But in ordinary circumstances this was unattainable. Musicians at this date were entranced by harmony. Few shared Helmore's or Smart's enthusiasm for simple congregational melody, and in a church where the incumbent insisted on congregational singing, he would normally have to settle for an organist of second-rate ability and taste. If, on the other hand, a professional musician was given a free hand, he would generally introduce a 'fully choral service' of more and more ambitious proportions, and the congregation would return to its long-established role of audience.

It is particularly significant that both the high-church Helmore and the low-church Pears objected to the adapted masses of Haydn and Mozart, which were being more and more widely used in choral communion services. Again, both Mackonochie and Pears were willing to admit hymn tunes of secular origin and inferior musical quality, if these would induce the congregation to sing.

The middle ground: choral service

Despite the alliances between Tractarians and high churchmen on one side, and between Evangelicals and low churchmen on the other – alliances which were defensive and partly political in character – there was yet a majority, on each side, that would not go all the way with the advance guard. The traditional high churchmen had succeeded in establishing a cathedral model for parish church worship at Leeds in 1841, and this was widely imitated elsewhere. Low churchmen, too, had for different reasons encouraged professionalism in church choirs. At first they had wanted choirs to sing metrical psalms, hymns, set pieces and anthems, but as the chanting of the psalms and liturgy gradually became common it won the acceptance of moderate low churchmen, who came to see it as the ultimate 'improvement' of psalmody. And the bulk of ordinary Anglicans, neither high nor low, went along with any gradual and moderate change that made the services more interesting and attractive. Finally, broad churchmen encouraged anything that they perceived as tending to unite the national Church.

So it was that the middle ground of parish church music was won by an originally high-church form of service that was nominally congregational, but in which the choir and organ tended in practice to monopolise most of the music. In the new arrangement of churches the choir was set apart from the people by its physical position, its apparel and formal appearance, and in many cases by its processional entry and exit. All these features tended to associate the choir with the clergy and to separate it from the people. To the congregation the service was increasingly perceived as a performance provided for its benefit, in a separate part of the church set before it like a stage. Even the organ was now in the chancel. The organist, often robed like the choir and in later Victorian times wearing an academic hood, had become an impressive figure, whose professional standing must be deferred to in musical matters. His efforts to improve and enrich the musical offering were received by most congregations with approval and even excitement. Congregations grew where music flourished.

It is important to recognise in the Victorians' acceptance of 'fully choral' services the same desire for decorum, elegance and propriety that had activated their Georgian ancestors. Added to it was a love of grandeur, which expressed in part their conviction of superiority to all preceding ages, induced by the rapid material progress they saw all around them. Factories, bridges, town halls, railway stations were getting bigger, more imposing, and more efficient year by year; improvements and reforms of all kinds were heightening the quality of secular life. A commensurate change might be looked for, not only in the architecture of the parish church, but in its services. More and more did the old psalmody, of both the town and the country varieties, seem a relic of an unenlightened past ('hymns of antique flavour', in Crowest's words).

In a period of great social mobility, the new and growing middle-class public was anxiously looking for symbols of its new status. It turned its back on both rural traditions and the industrial society that supported it. Hence there was great appeal in the paid, semi-professional, robed parish church choir, singing cultivated liturgical music which was in sharp contrast with the congregational hymnody of dissenting chapels, and which approached the aristocratic dignity of cathedrals (Reader: 136–7; cited Rainbow: 266). The urban poor, made acutely conscious of class divisions, found the activities of most Anglican churches irrelevant to their lives (Meacham).

Even the dissenters felt the lure and glamour of the cathedral service. The Anglican liturgical renewal, including the revival of Gothic architecture and of choral chanting, was followed about a generation later by a move in the same direction in nonconformist worship. 'It was too much to expect of human nature that the nonconformists who had suffered so long from political and legal disabilities should not attempt to emulate the splendour of Anglican worship, in its architectural setting and its praise, however inappropriate this was for the more oracular type of worship that was their own tradition' (Davies: IV, 70). Chanting was already to be heard in several dissenting chapels before 1850 (*Parish Choir* I, 1847: 145–6).

So the Victorian establishment of the surpliced choir can be traced back, not only to the traditional high-church ideal of 'the beauty of holiness', but eventually also to the low-church aspiration to 'improved psalmody'. For the first, the cathedral service had always been the model; for the second, liturgical music took its place side by side with elaborate metrical psalmody and hymnody. Both parties preferred a cultivated choir to an uncouth congregation, and in this they differed sharply from both extremes in the Church.

An eminent high churchman who was influential in promoting the new ideal was Sir Frederick Ouseley, baronet, clergyman, and (from 1855) professor of music at Oxford. We have already seen how he acquiesced in the musical arrangements at St Barnabas, Pimlico with reservations: he was never wholly able to accept Gregorian chants. When the choir of St Barnabas was disbanded on the resignation of the vicar, W. J. E. Bennett, in 1851, Ouseley kept the boys together at his own expense, and they ultimately became the nucleus of his foundation of St Michael's College, Tenbury, which was opened in 1856. Here he set up a model for the proper performance of the choral service, exclusively based on cathedral practice, but intended for imitation in parish churches as well (Alderson & Colles; Rainbow: 161–8).

Ouseley never went to the lengths of Jebb and Joule in categorically denying the right of the congregation to sing the liturgy at all. But in a sermon at Derby in 1861 he called on 'those who have been blessed by God with voices, and ears, and musical susceptibility' to 'devote their whole powers to the praise of God', while the unmusical were to pray for musical enlightenment and meanwhile ask God to 'accept their good-will, in default of power', and to support choral services with their monetary offerings (Ouseley & Dykes: 14). In addressing the Church Congress at Leeds in 1872 he remarked that it was no longer possible to maintain Jebb's distinction between cathedral and parochial music (*Church Congress*, 1872: 326), and two years later he congratulated the congress on still further advance, which he attributed to the sight-singing movement of John Hullah, the introduction of organs and harmoniums, the removal of the choir to the chancel, and the rise of choral unions taking advantage of railway travel. But there was still much to be done. 'Why should not *every* parish join in the movement?' he asked. 'Why should not every chancel be filled with devout and earnest singers . . . men and boys arrayed in white robes, as an outward sign of the purity and holiness of the work they are come to do?' (*Church Congress*, 1874: 96–101).

Ouseley's sense of a great change in parochial music in the decade between 1863 and 1872 (or 1874) is well supported by other evidence. It was just at that time that the movement in the direction of choral services swelled to a tide. The Leeds model was at first imitated in only a few churches. In 1847 *The Parish Choir* reported that St Peter, Newcastle was 'the only parish church in the diocese [of Durham] in which any part of the choir are properly robed, the boys being in surplices. Here too the choir are correctly placed.' The whole service was sung, except the priest's parts and the litany, though there was no organ (*Parish Choir* I, 1846–7: 136). At St James, Morpeth, though the choir was not in surplices, the entire service including the priest's part was sung, with Tallis's harmonised responses on festivals, and anthems by 'old Church composers' (:136). *The Parish Choir*'s local correspondents were unable to find any properly conducted choral services in the parish churches of Bristol, Sheffield, Worcester, or Dover (II, 1847–8: 12–13, 62, 100–1, 118). At Birmingham, the church of Holy Trinity, Bordesley had a fully choral service with a surpliced choir of men and boys, but no intoning by the priest, while SS. Peter & Paul, Aston had had fully choral services 'for some years', using the Leeds service book (PC 370); two or three others had partially choral services (II: 83–4, 171; Heywood, 1905: 23n.8). At Liverpool only St John Evangelist was fully choral (*Parish Choir* III, 1849–51: 168).

The first reliable guide to the situation in London churches was compiled by the indefatigable Charles Mackeson, and published in 1858. Out of 264 churches listed in London (which still implied approximately the same

area as that covered by the old 'Bills of Mortality'), only 14 had fully
choral services, with a further 6 out of 151 suburban churches, making
about 4.8 per cent in all. By 1869 the proportion had jumped to 21.5 per
cent, and it continued to rise steadily until 1882 at least (see Table 15).
Similarly, in Birmingham in the 1870s 'just over half' the 46 Anglican
churches had surpliced choirs; Ouseley and Monk's psalter (PC 390) was
'almost universally used', and 'for versicles and litany the Tallis and Barnby
compilations' were 'fairly general' (Sutcliffe Smith: 93). As the short-lived
Concordia pointed out in 1875, 'not long ago, the only well conducted
musical services' were 'Roman Catholic or High Anglican'; but 'a due
regard for the artistic element in worship is no longer regarded as
symptomatic of advanced opinions' (I, 1875: 9). The organist William
Spark, who made his low-church standpoint abundantly clear in his
description of services at Leeds in 1885, nevertheless strongly approved of
choral services, including choral communion: 'Our English communion
office, until within these few years, was a sober, secret, and almost
somniferous celebration, without choir, and almost without communicants. And so it is now in too many of our local churches' (Spark,
1892: 67). Thus the spread of choral services indicated the acceptance by
central and low-church opinion of what had been a moderate high-church
practice.

Mackeson's London statistics provide a clear distinction between the
ritualist movement and the more broadly based liturgical and choral
renewal that was taking place at the same time. The first five items in Table
15 show a steady and indeed remarkably rapid growth in the thirteen-year
period 1869 to 1882 (extended backwards to 1858 in two cases). It can be
said that these became normal features of the late Victorian service, while in
early Victorian times they had been rare. Although they had all been
associated with high churchmanship, they came to be accepted by all except
the extreme low-church sector of the Church. The next item (choral

Table 15. *Characteristics of services in London and suburban parish
churches (1858–82) in percentages*

Year	1858	1869	1872	1875	1878	1882
No. of churches in sample	415	588	705	775	854	903
Weekly communion	6.3	26.5	32.3	38.2	45.6	54.0
Weekly offertory	...	18.2	30.4	45.0	47.3	56.1
Surplice in pulpit	...	...	38.9	50.1	54.1	72.5
Surpliced choir	...	19.6	26.0	36.1	41.5	52.6
Choral service	4.8	21.5	23.1	24.5	30.5	38.7
Choral communion	...	7.1	12.1	12.6	14.0	16.6
Gregorian tones	...	8.4	10.8	19.6	13.5	13.6
Eucharistic vestments	...	2.4	3.3	4.6	4.1	4.1
Incense	...	1.4	1.0	2.2	1.6	1.1

Sources: Mackeson, 1858; Mackeson, 1866–95: XVI (1882), 172.

communion) also grew steadily, though naturally it was not adopted in so large a number of churches. The last three are more exclusively associated with extreme ritualism. They reached a peak in the mid 1870s, though not a very high one. Then they tended to fall off as the zeal of the ritualists diminished.

The first practical steps in organising parish church choirs had been taken by the Society for Promoting Church Music, of which *The Parish Choir* was the official journal; and during those early years many local societies were formed, sometimes consisting of a single church choir, more often of a number of them in one locality. Such societies continued to be active, but it was undoubtedly a great step upward in their prestige when in 1856 the first diocesan choral festival was held at Lichfield cathedral. It was attended by choirs from many parts of Staffordshire and Derbyshire, an area already noted for its choral music. The choirs sang chanted psalms and responses (Marbeck and Tallis), a few hymns, and some simple anthems. Two years later similar festivals were held at Southwell and Ely, and within a few years they had spread to most dioceses (*Ecclesiologist* XVIII, 1858: 360–3; Rainbow: 273–4). The music quickly became more ambitious, and new music introduced at the annual festival was at once added to the repertoires of the member choirs. There grew up a natural rivalry between the choirs in a diocese, and local pride was a potent addition to the motives, religious and otherwise, that made up the choral movement. 'Every little church now has, or wants to have, its choir' (*Musical Standard* III, 1864: 57). In 1884 the Reverend C. H. Hylton Stewart, precentor of Chester cathedral, pointed out (with more force than logic) that 'a church without its full choral matins and evensong, and in many cases without its choral celebration [of communion], is difficult to find' (*Church Congress*, 1884: 326). The new standards hastened the demise of the few remaining gallery choirs and bands, which were replaced by organs: by 1886 it was said that 'the cases are so very rare in which even the smallest country church is without either an organ or [a] harmonium' (*Church Congress*, 1886: 225). 'In some of the most rural villages in England,' said a writer in 1882, 'where it is quite impossible to find even one boy with a really musical voice, we find ten or twelve in surplices in "the choir" on Sunday; they look well, but to hear them sing is to hear discord to perfection' (*Church music in town and country*: 7).

The difficulties of forming a competent choir in a small village were still great, but had been lessened somewhat by improved prosperity and communications. The high-church Benjamin Armstrong, who became vicar of East Dereham in 1850, began daily services at 7 a.m. in 1853, but did not 'feel strong enough' to form a choir for the Sunday services until 1858, when he 'took the opportunity of inserting a choir of men and boys into the chancel, the boys being clad in surplices'; the men were also robed from 1865. In 1867 he suggested that the psalms be chanted instead of read, but yielded to objections; but the following year, on the occasion of a visit from a colonial bishop, he brought in chanted psalms and responses, and 'was delighted to find that everyone joined in the singing' (Armstrong: 11).

In 1856 the Reverend George Newbolt became rector of the conjoined parishes of Knotting and Souldrop, which had a combined population of

461 in 1861. 'The music at both the churches ... was of the ordinary village style. At Souldrop a bass viol [i.e., cello] led the singers. Mr. Newbolt as soon as possible after his arrival, endeavoured to make an improvement in the style.' A harmonium was substituted for the cello, a hymn book replaced the metrical psalm collection; 'a master from Bedford was found necessary to teach singing once a week, and also to instruct a boy to play the harmonium ... Mr. N ... gives a supper to his singers at Christmas time.' The Souldrop church was restored and reopened in 1861, with an organ bought for £142 6s 0d 'by subscriptions from the parishioners and friends'. Choral services were introduced on Sundays and festivals. In 1864 Marbeck's music was tried for the Nicene creed: 'we purpose to chant it for the future on Sundays', Newbolt wrote in his diary. In 1870: 'On Easter Day ... I put my choir into cassocks and surplices, the boys violet cassocks, the men black' (Bell: 206–13).

In many villages the difficulty of finding enough singers was eased by admitting girls and women, who had often been part of the old gallery choirs. Though high churchmen such as Ouseley tended to disapprove of this development, it gained growing support. It was advocated by Hullah at a lecture delivered in 1856 to the Durham and Northumberland Association for the Promotion of Church Music. He admitted that the proposition would come with 'a sort of shock' to many, but pointed out that a similar shock had been experienced the year before when young women were sent to the Crimea to bind the soldiers' wounds. 'The fact is, that the objections to women singing in church *avowedly* (for nobody objects to their singing *un*avowedly) belong to and apply to a state of things entirely different [from the chancel choir now recommended] ... involving ... meretricious music and self-contemplative performers; in fact, the "gallery" system in all its glory.' (Hullah, 1856: 24.) Sometimes the girls were not admitted to the chancel, but were placed in a front pew or at the side (*Church music in town and country*: 34–5; *Church Congress*, 1886: 225; 1895: 528). In 1874 the Diocesan Inspector of Schools for the Archdeaconry of Surrey said:

I do not know whether any one has ever seen what I have, viz., young girls in a village choir put – I was going to say into surplices, but not exactly surplices – all the boys being ranged on one side of the chancel, and the maidens ranged on the other side vested in white capes, which, at a distance, had practically much the same effect as the white surplices of the boys. This, certainly, tended to inculcate in these village maidens a modesty and sobriety of demeanour in the divine service which I do not think the bonnets and flowers of the present day would have done. (*Church Congress*, 1874: 114)

R. B. Daniel in 1894 considered that further improvement in village choirs could only be made if women were allowed to replace boys (:147–59).

In town churches, few practical difficulties stood in the way of the development of elaborate choral services. A period of unprecedented opulence had begun, and there was wealth to spare for the music of the Church as there was for countless other public and private objects. Labour was still cheap; a good organist could be had for less than £100 a year, and there was an abundance of well-printed church music available at very little cost. The College (later Royal College) of Organists and other musical academies were springing up to ensure professional musical standards, while a large number of periodicals, pamphlets, books and societies provided ample advice to the clergy, choir, and choir trainer.

The expenditure of time and money on choral music in town churches during the later Victorian period is astonishing by any standard. At the parish church of Holy Trinity, Hull, for example, the organ was enlarged no less than six times between 1845 and 1900. Fully choral services were started as early as 1845, and were continued with growing elaboration. From 1868 the organists were generally graduates in music from Oxford or Cambridge (G. H. Smith: 28–43). At an unspecified London church in 1864 a silent congregation listened to a choir which cost £266 per year ('Psalmody': 607). At All Souls, Leeds (a church built in memory of Dr Walter Hook), the fully choral services in 1885 were performed by a choir of 30 boys and 17 men (Spark, 1892: 68), while there were several other large church choirs in the same city (:64–85). The size of London church choirs averaged nearly 30 at this date (Mackeson, 1866–95), a larger number than the average cathedral choir.

At St John, Torquay, a growing resort town, a new church building was opened in 1864. When in 1870 a high-church vicar, Canon Robinson, was installed, although he was not himself a musical man, he wished to increase the number of choirboys to 24 or 30, so that fully choral services could be well maintained. But he insisted on principle that the choir should be voluntary, a usual high-church position. In order to attract boys of good quality on these terms, it was found necessary to build a day school for them, and this was promptly done by some wealthy parishioners. Robinson greatly increased the number of services, as did Prebendary Airy, who became vicar in 1886. The height of musical elaboration at St John was during the organistship of Thomas Noble (1887–1905), who was an Associate of the College of Organists. The Sunday services consisted of choral matins and evensong at 10.30 and 6.30, holy communion at 7, 8, and (choral) 11.45, and children's service at 3.30. On holy days there were celebrations at 7, 8, and (choral) 10.45, and choral matins and evensong at 10 and 5. On ordinary weekdays there was communion at 7.45 and matins at 8.30; litany (choral) on Wednesdays and Fridays at 12; and choral evensong at 5. This astonishing programme, in an ordinary church (not the main parish church) in a town of moderate size and importance, equalled that of many cathedrals in extent. The funds collected to support it amounted to £1029 in 1887, but steadily declined after that year; after 1900, the number of services was gradually reduced, and in 1920 it was found necessary to close the choir school (Boggis).

The larger churches in the late Victorian period were able to support a substantial staff. The incumbent was often assisted by two or three curates, one of whom, in some cases, was named 'precentor' (in imitation of the cathedral office) and was placed in overall charge of the music. There would be, of course, the parish clerk, who had lost most of his importance in the services but who had plenty of menial tasks to perform, and might be assisted by a sexton and verger. Some churches had a choirmaster as well as an organist, and there might even be assistants to each, as well as a secretary and librarian for the choir. Dr John Troutbeck recommended three officers to run the music of a parish church: a precentor (the superior officer, 'one of the parochial clergy'), a choirmaster, and an organist (R. B. Daniel: 172). So normal had this become by 1887 that churches maintaining only one professional musician often called him 'organist and choirmaster'.

To help in the formation of parish choirs, a large number of books of advice appeared. In a list of 29 English books of all periods dealing with the training of choirboys, 20 appeared between 1870 and 1910 (8 of the remainder between 1910 and 1940) (Yeats-Edwards: 168–72). Some were written by cathedral choirmasters who passed on their knowledge to parochial colleagues, others by parish clergy or organists who shared their own experience with others.

The parish churches in old cathedral cities, still too numerous for their populations, tended to lag behind in the choral revival. But many larger cities were now able to offer their Anglican citizens a choice among several churches, with different shades of churchmanship and varying degrees of choral music. Improved communications had largely done away with the older notion that everyone attended his own parish church. Such a rule was pronounced 'obsolete' in 1924 (*The choral foundations*: 10), but it had begun to weaken nearly a hundred years before that date, particularly in growing towns where new churches were constantly springing up. (See 'Sunday morning services in Leeds', Spark, 1892: 64–109; *Church music in town and country*: 43–7.)

The breakdown of the older parochial ordering of society, in which each parish was a microcosm of the larger social order, was nowhere more evident than in central London. The nineteenth century saw 'the systematic sorting-out of London into single-purpose, homogeneous, specialized neighbourhoods' (Olsen: 267). The development of the omnibus made it unnecessary for the new districts to have stables and mews, and strict segregation resulted; one district might be entirely upper middle class, another entirely working class. But the higher classes were free to choose their church from any respectable neighbourhood. The City of London had experienced 'rapid depopulation ... with its curious consequence, the regeneration of church choirs' (Pearce, 1909: 44). City churches gradually gave up all pretence of serving the needs of resident parishioners, and set out to attract congregations from other parts of London. At St Mary-le-Bow, 'the charity children became fewer and fewer, and their "psalmody" eventually so intolerable that in 1864 a committee of the vestry "resolved to try the experiment" of appointing a lady at a salary of £15 as leader. Mrs. Parsons was assisted by several friends (members of her bible class) and "the improvement thus effected gave general satisfaction".' In 1869 'the rector and churchwardens were empowered to select choirboys elsewhere than from the charity school, provided they had sufficient musical attainments'. In 1870 £50 was voted 'for the purposes of the choir during the next year'. In 1871 the organist's salary was 'raised to sixty guineas' (Pearce, 1909: 44). In 1882, Box recorded that the prayers and psalms were chanted at this church, and an anthem and setting of the canticles was sung by a choir of nine voices (:154).

At St Sepulchre, Newgate, the introduction of choral services, with chanted psalms and responses and service settings, met with protest on the part of some parishioners, and a discussion was held in the vestry on 29 August 1864, which was fully reported by *The Musical Standard* (III, 1864: 78–80). The chief complainant, Thomas Wright, saw 'no reason why he should be annoyed with one hour's music out of a two hours' service'. A Mr Lardner replied that 'the introduction of the choir was a very great improvement. Anyone who used to attend the church before the introduction of the choir must remember that the congregations were very small as compared with the present. It was all very well to talk about twenty-four years ago; then the people dwelt in the parish, now it was impossible for them to do so. Cleanliness would bring people. Singing would attract them, and might be the means of bringing them to a good condition.' Another speaker 'never recollected that the church was so well filled as now, and the congregation universally admired the singing of the choir'. He felt the present service 'commended itself to the conscience of every right thinking person. It was alike removed from the antics of the Puseyite and the slovenliness of the Puritan.' There was some dispute as to whether the singing of the choir allowed the congregation and the 'children' (probably the charity children) to join in. A Mr Wooltorton asked 'why should they be deprived of the privilege of joining in the whole service? . . . The choral service was only a step towards the wearing of the white surplice in the pulpit . . . It was no fair argument to say that they must have singing to fill the church.' But the debate was settled by an amendment approving the present services, carried by a majority of fifteen to four.

At some of the fashionable churches of the West End musical elaboration was taken to extremes.

There was a certain *cachet* about S. Andrew's, Wells Street . . . This church set a fashion of perfectly conducted Anglican worship which was high church without being in the least Anglo-Catholic. The music was as ornate as the furnishings. Twice daily . . . the finest Anglican psalmody [chanted psalms] as well as the most elaborate anthems were rendered by the choir school. On Sundays and every 'red letter day' in the *Book of common prayer* there was a solemn celebration of the holy communion, sung frequently to English adaptations of the masses of Beethoven, Cherubini, Schubert, Haydn, Mozart, Hummel, and other continental composers. During the early 'seventies Charles Gounod used to attend the services when he was staying in London. Several of his Passiontide motets, adapted from the Latin by [the vicar,] Mr. [Benjamin] Webb, were first sung in this country at S. Andrew's. (Anson, 1960: 204)

Benjamin Webb, a founder of the Cambridge Camden Society, was vicar at St Andrew from 1862 to 1885. The organist and choirmaster from 1863 to 1871 was Joseph Barnby, and at the dedication festival of the new church building in 1866 he introduced a harp. The entire service, including the opening sentences and exhortation, was sung, the general confession being accompanied 'with certain harmonised inflections' on the organ. Tallis's responses were used, with accompaniment; the psalms were sung to single Anglican chants, the canticles to Attwood's setting in C major; the creed was monotoned, but the harp entered at the reference to the Incarnation, and also in the anthem 'O strengthen, Lord' (adapted from a mass by Cherubini) and in the communion service (from a mass by Gounod)

(*Church Choirmaster* I, 1867: 2). Later, Barnby moved to St Anne, Soho, where he introduced choral services on similar lines, with a choir of 36 boys and 28 men, surpliced of course. A detailed description and commentary on the services there was given by Curwen (1880: 179–83), who pointed out that they hardly conformed with Barnby's own statement of ideals for a congregational parish service expressed at the Church Congress (in 1873). Even the hymns, Curwen found, were 'sung in harmony by the choir ... A quiet hum of treble, both men and women, may be heard in the well-known hymns, but the congregational voice is not in any sense a musical force at St. Anne's. The service is, in short, an illustration of the saying that the better the choir the worse the congregational singing' (:182). Barnby was a noted choral conductor of the time: his own interests and ambitions were obviously in the direction of choral performance. In 1873 he introduced no less a work than Bach's *St John Passion* at a communion service in St Anne's church.

There was no lack of opposition to the ever advancing choral movement, and it was generally led by the clergy. At St Mary, Lowgate, Hull, efforts to 'improve' the music after 1849 were resisted by the low-church vicar, John Scott, who 'engaged in a newspaper war on the work and office of choirs' and preached a sermon on the text 'And let all the people *say* Amen'. However, when his son, Canon Scott, succeeded him in 1864, the services speedily became 'choral' (G. H. Smith: 54–63). The meetings of the Church Congress, founded in 1861, were the scene of reiterated complaints by the clergy about the silencing of congregations by choirs. These were often voiced from the floor of the meeting after a lecture on church music by a leading professional (*Church Congress*: 1864: 303–11; 1872: 340–5; 1873: 452–5; 1874: 108–21; 1884: 317–29; 1886: 236–40; 1891: 272–3; 1898: 170–6). Some musicians wholeheartedly favoured congregational music, such as E. G. Monk, Helmore and Smart; others, such as Ouseley and Barnby, gave lip service to the idea, but in practice indulged their love of choir music; most had no scruples in letting the choir take over completely. Laymen frequently deplored the development, and contrasted it adversely with the position in nonconformist churches. Some tried to use financial pressure to restrain the proliferation of choir music. 'A society which helps to provide churches with curates requires, whenever its aid is asked for a church, to know how much that church expends on its music. This must often have an injurious effect on church music' (R. B. Daniel: 13n.). In 1891, Edward Griffith, Fellow of the College of Organists, reported to the Church Congress as 'hon. editorial secretary of the Church Congregational Music Association, Chislehurst'. He pointed to the 'painful' fact that 'responding and singing in our churches is now *not* congregational', and said he knew of 'but one church in London where the whole service is joined in by the congregation without even the lead of a choir.* An organist ... leads a congregation of 2,000 earnest worshippers.' The result was most inspiring. (Almost certainly this church was St Pancras.) 'At another neighbouring church [St Andrew, Wells Street?], principally attended by a

* Unfortunately this remark is ambiguous. Are we to understand that there was no other church in which the whole service was joined in by the congregation, or that there was no other church in which the congregation sang without the lead of a choir?

fashionable congregation of some 1200 people, the whole of the service was "performed" by a large and efficient choir.' He cited authorities from the three principal parties in the Church – Archdeacon Howell, Archdeacon Farrar and Canon Body – as being united in support of the conclusion that 'choirs' professionalism has ruined congregational devotion' (*Church Congress*, 1891: 272–3; see also Elstob: 53–6).

We may conclude that the advance of choralism was in no sense a victory for the Oxford movement, or, indeed, for any idealistic group of churchmen. Rather, it was an expression of secular middle-class values and tastes, a part of the immense growth in appreciation of professional musical performance that marked the age. As we might predict, the music that these choirs performed was, for the most part, neither the austere Gregorian chant revered by the Tractarians, nor the heartfelt melody beloved of the Evangelicals. It was a music primarily harmonic in conception, with as much variety of colour as circumstances allowed, echoing the rich orchestral and operatic sonorities of Spohr, Meyerbeer, and Mendelssohn, or later of Gounod, Liszt, Brahms, and Wagner. The popularity of continental mass music was due less to the fact that it was Roman Catholic than to the fact that it was a model of religious music frankly secular and theatrical in idiom. It was at least equalled by the liking for excerpts from oratorios. In providing new choral music, composers tried to produce similar effects with the limited resources of a parish choir.

Music for choral worship

In the provision of anthems and service settings for parish use, *The Parish Choir* had drawn mostly on music of the sixteenth and seventeenth centuries (Rainbow: 312–18), partly because of its simplicity and suitability for unaccompanied singing, but also out of a conviction that the style of that period was specially appropriate for religious music. *The Musical Times* also, in its first decade (1844–53), concentrated chiefly on the treasures of the past, though including the eighteenth century. Of the fifty-odd anthems published in its supplements, there were examples by Tallis, Farrant, Creyghton, Croft, Greene, Nares, and Clarke-Whitfeld. There were also adaptations from Handel, Haydn, Mozart, Beethoven and Winter; and no fewer than thirteen anthems by Vincent Novello, the proprietor of the journal (Scholes, 1947: 556).

But early music turned out to have little appeal to the ordinary Victorian organist, choir singer, or churchgoer, however much it might be valued by religious leaders, or by sophisticated musicians from Crotch to Stainer. The time was one of aggressive commercial enterprise, and it did not take long for music publishers to find out what kind of music would sell. Foremost among them was the firm of Novello & Co. The octavo supplements to *The Musical Times* were found to be an ideal medium for large-scale distribution of easy choral music, both sacred and secular. Those of its second decade were transitional in character. By the third (1864–73), a new pattern had strongly asserted itself, to remain for the rest of the century. Contemporary English composers dominated the 1864–73 selection:

Elvey, Ouseley, S.S. Wesley, Barnby and Sullivan. There were three anthems by Gounod, and one by Berthold Tours, a Dutch organist settled in London, who in 1878 was to become musical adviser to Novello & Co.: other foreign composers were Mozart, Spohr and Hauptmann. 'The older English composers are now almost dropped by *MT* [*The Musical Times*]', as Scholes pointed out. His explanation was 'not that their works have gone out of use but rather that . . . . they are now sufficiently brought into general use for *MT*'s help in popularising them to be no longer necessary' (1947: 556). But there is no evidence that early English cathedral anthems had been 'brought into general use' in parish churches or cathedrals on any large scale, and all indications point to a contrary conclusion.

Table 16 summarises samples of choral repertories of parish churches at various dates in the nineteenth and twentieth centuries. The sources are not all of the same kind: some record music actually used, others music recommended for use. Nevertheless the general trend is unmistakable. At each period the repertory tends to be dominated by the music of the preceding era, so that the main effect is that music of the nineteenth century gradually replaced that of the eighteenth in popularity. There is a very slight revival of interest in the sixteenth and seventeenth centuries, but this made little real headway until the twentieth century was well advanced. Baden Powell's recommendations of 1901 included only 4 pre-1800 anthems out of 47. In 1910 there were still complaints of the infrequent performance of early cathedral music (Fuller-Maitland, 1910: 12–13). A

Table 16. *Parish choir repertories from various sources* (c. 1815–1951)

The body of the table gives the percentage of services or anthems, in each source, that derives from each century from the 16th to the 20th.

	Services		Anthems					
Source	(4)	(6)	(1)	(2)	(3)	(4)	(5)	(6)
Source date	1881–3	1951	c. 1815	c. 1850	1859	1881–3	1901	1951
16th century	...	5.7	...	1.7	0.8	5.3	8.5	17.9
17th century	...	5.7	...	1.7	4.6	5.3	...	7.1
18th century	22.2	2.9	68.8	70.0	59.2	42.1	19.1	10.7
19th century	77.8	34.3	6.2	25.0	33.1	37.4	72.3	34.5
20th century	...	48.6	...	...	...	...	...	28.6
Unidentified	...	2.9	25.0	1.7	2.3	...	...	1.2

Sources:
(1) *Anthems and hymns used in Gateshead church* (word book, c. 1815).
(2) *Words of the anthems used at the parish church of St. John the Evangelist, Preston* (1859). The first part, evidently reprinted from an earlier edition of c. 1850.
(3) The second part of the same book.
(4) Service settings and anthems mentioned by Charles Box in a survey of London parish churches at Sunday services in 1881–3 (Box).
(5) Anthems recommended for parish choirs in 1901 by James Baden Powell, precentor of St Paul, Knightsbridge (Baden Powell).
(6) Music sung by 116 visiting parish choirs at St John, Waterloo Road, London, during the Festival of Britain, 1951 (*English Church Music* xxi, 1951: 30–1).

partial explanation is implicit in Box's comment that choirs were now found 'not only in the metropolis but in comparatively obscure towns and villages throughout England . . . To meet this state of things, compositions of a much simpler character than those used at cathedrals must be resorted to. This want has not eluded the notice of musicians eminent in the modern school of church music' (:234–5).

Perhaps the most important publication that catered to this need was Novello's Parish Choir Book, an octavo series begun in 1866, one of the many that this enterprising firm initiated in the format that had been found so successful for the *Musical Times* supplements. The series was subtitled 'A collection of music for the service of the Church, by modern composers'. Initially it was 'published under the patronage of the Ely Diocesan Church Music Society'. The society had found that 'one of the principal desiderata amongst parish choirs was an arrangement, or rather several arrangements, of the *Te deum laudamus*'. Novello & Co. accordingly commissioned and published for the first volume in the series no fewer than forty-six new settings of the Te deum for choir and organ, with four other canticle settings to make a book of fifty pieces.

The composers responded to this challenge in a variety of ways, and the results make an interesting study. Some, such as Ouseley and W. C. Macfarren, wrote very austere Te deums, little more than varied chants alternating unison and plain diatonic harmony. Barnby, among others, also wrote a chant setting, but with all manner of chromatic harmonies, mostly on the organ. Henry Smart's setting gives a full, cathedral-like effect, with big climaxes which would have stretched the vocal but not the musical powers of an average parish choir. Sullivan's is boldly original, demanding, and dissonant. One of the most appropriate settings (ex. 64) was by Robert Stewart, who held all the principal Anglican musical posts in Dublin at this time. It is notable for making the most of the modest resources available. Much of the music is homophonic, and is made up of the simple, rather square phrases of which contemporary hymn tunes were composed. Variety is attained through simple key contrasts between sections, and changes of time and tempo. Stewart is very cautious in varying the texture, but he introduces unison phrases in bars 26–41, and takes the opportunity to provide a fourfold sequence. The rising key changes produce an effect of growing excitement, but they are made easy for the choir by the intervening unison phrases. Each harmonised phrase begins with the major triad built on the note that has just been sung in unison. The only counterpoint is in bars 129–45, and it is in two parts only, well assisted by the organ; here also a more remote key-change is attempted. Difficult entries are anticipated by the organ (119, 156). The limitations of parish organists are also kept well in mind. The essential pedal part is restricted to a few long notes (111–15, 129–44). Though directions for alternation between *decani* and *cantoris* sides are given, these are quite clearly optional: the music can easily be performed by one four-part choir.

The series has continued to this day, with over 1,600 numbers in all. It has concentrated chiefly on canticle settings, responses, and hymns; anthems have tended to appear in other series. Novello & Co. published large numbers of anthems by most of the leading Victorian composers, including Barnby, Elvey, Garrett, Goss, E. J. Hopkins, J. L. Hopkins, G. A. Macfarren, E. G. Monk, W. A. Monk, Ouseley, H. T. Smart, Stainer, Sullivan, T. A. Walmisley, and S. S. Wesley, as well as the foreign-born Benedict, Costa, Gounod, and Tours, and countless other composers now forgotten (Foster: 161–96). There is no doubt that many of these anthems were specially commissioned and designed for average parish choirs, which constituted a far more promising market than cathedral choirs. Diocesan and local festivals often assured the initial sales of newly commissioned works.

There were other early efforts to provide for the new parish choirs. J. F. Forster's *Parochial choir book* (PC 383) attempted a complete range of music – chants, psalm tunes, responses, 12 anthems along simple lines (some old, some new), and four voluntaries. Thomas Fowle, an amateur organist, was more ambitious in his collection, *Parochial anthems by the cathedral composers of 1863* (PC 396), for he commissioned 24 anthems from the principal cathedral composers of the day (but Wesley is conspicuously absent), adding two of his own. As in the Novello series, some of the composers took great pains to create the maximum effect with limited resources: William Spark's 'All we like sheep' and Steggall's 'Hear ye, and give ear' contain effective passages for unison choir with organ harmony. J. Powell Metcalfe, vicar of Bilbrough, tried a new departure with his *Fifty metrical anthems for the use of small choirs*. He adapted various cathedral anthems and other pieces, including some by Handel and Mozart, to metrical psalms in the S.P.C.K. version, 'firstly, to make a short piece, by repetition, according to the verses, long enough for use – secondly, to render anthem-music available without the introduction of a separate anthem-book [of words]' (PC 393: preface). These were set pieces, or merely elaborate psalm tunes, designed to satisfy easily and cheaply the ambitious village choir's yearning to sing 'anthems'. Later Metcalfe said it would be 'a great boon to us country-folk' if more leading composers would publish simple anthems 'in not very high treble and not very low bass . . . adding the enrichment of a separate accompaniment' (Metcalfe: 51).

It is clear, then, that the preference of Victorian parish choirmasters for music of their own day was not simply a matter of taste. Contemporary composers, strongly stimulated by publishers, were producing quantities of music that catered exactly to their needs, in ways that earlier music did not. These simple anthems and services not only took care to keep within the technical capacities of a modest choir and a half-trained organist, and to make the most of those capacities. They also stayed close to the idiom which parish musicians understood best: the idiom of the hymn tune. Example 67, by Varley Roberts, organist of Halifax parish church, is an unpretentious specimen of the type, somewhat resembling Cecil's 'I will arise' (ex. 48).

As the choral movement advanced by giant strides, the leading town parish churches soon had choirs that were at least the equal of cathedral choirs in their size, capacity, and training. A large number of others were not much below this standard. Such choirs had no need to seek specially simple music, but could select from the full range of cathedral music then available. They provided, in fact, an immense new market for cathedral music, and allowed publishers to produce cheap editions of kinds of music that at one time had been printed only in large expensive folios, to be copied by hand into cathedral part-books. This new market would eventually make possible the reprinting of many of the important anthems and services of the sixteenth and seventeenth centuries. For the time being, however, the great bulk of the music that flowed from the press every year was contemporary. One has only to study the library catalogue of a large parish choir such as that of Halifax to see how eagerly it adopted the latest cathedral music (MS 20). Perhaps there has been no time when choirs were so uncompromisingly up-to-date in their choice of music. Again, one suspects that a mutually profitable alliance between composers and publishers was the explanation, rather than any deliberate choice by parish choirmasters.

In the matter of chants for the psalms and canticles, there was no need for any special provision for parish churches. The chants used in cathedrals could be taken over unchanged, even though many of them were much more difficult to sing than choirmasters realised. In the early nineteenth century, parish choirs had used a relatively small number of well-known chants. Now, especially if they aspired to daily choral services, a much larger range of chants was desirable. Manuscript chants in cathedrals and colleges were collected and printed in chant books. John Goss, organist of St Paul's cathedral, made use of the extensive manuscript collection there in the preparation of his *Collection of chants* (1841), while Thomas Attwood Walmisley produced in 1845 *A collection of chants with the responses in use at the chapels of King's, Trinity, and St. John's colleges, Cambridge*, at two of which he was organist. Edward Rimbault prepared a more scholarly collection, *Cathedral chants of the 16th, 17th, and 18th centuries* (1844). It goes without saying that the sudden appearance of many printed collections of chants was not occasioned by an increase in chanting in cathedrals. In the same period a large number of pointed psalters appeared. The same principle was adopted for chanted psalms as for metrical psalms or hymns: that is to say, the choice of the chant was independent of the psalm being chanted, and was probably, in most cases, left to the organist or choirmaster.

In the 1850s it began to appear that there were advantages in a book which combined the music and the words on the same page, so that the choice of hymn tune or chant would be made by the editor of the book rather than the local clergyman or organist. William Mercer, incumbent of St George, Sheffield, whose *Church psalter and hymn book* (1854) was one of the first to be planned in this way, found it necessary to explain and justify this proceeding in the preface (PC 389).

In a later edition (1860) Mercer added the music for the choral singing of the daily services, thus completing a comprehensive musical companion to Anglican worship which was a prototype for several others of the kind. In 1864 Mercer was able to point out with pride that 'its distinguishing feature, the invariable allocation of the music to the words', had been 'adopted by many of the recent hymn-books', among which he might have mentioned *Hymns ancient and modern*. The book was a considerable success, and was published in at least 22 different forms, which contained various combinations of the daily services, canticles, psalms, epistles and gospels (without music) and hymns; eight of the forms had no music, and one had the hymns in tonic solfa notation (PC 389/1864: 286, advertisement). Several other psalters set out in Mercer's format soon appeared. Elvey's (1856), Monk and Ouseley's (1862), and Turle's *SPCK psalter* (1865) were among the most popular.

The pointing of the psalms in Mercer's *Psalter* was distinguished from 1864 onwards by a feature that was characteristic of Victorian chanting: the accented syllable near the end of the recitation. For instance the first verse of the *Venite* appeared in the following form:

> O come, let us sîng un ᵛ to the Lord: let us heartily
> rejôice in the ᵛ strength of ᵛ our salvation.

Mercer explained this notation at the end of the book:

To rectify a habit which prevails in some places, of invariably dwelling on the syllable which immediately precedes the first accent [i.e., barline] in each division of the verse, whether emphatic or otherwise, a circumflex accent has been introduced into the present form of the work, to mark the syllable which is properly entitled to the emphasis. (PC 389/1864: 285)

He cautioned against dwelling too long on this accented syllable, but laid down that the time of the reciting note, though it could be lengthened for a long verse, must never be reduced to less than a semibreve. This principle had been first described by Stephen Elvey in his psalter of 1856. It was clearly foreshadowed by Jacob in 1819 (ex. 49).

The same system was more explicitly described in *The cathedral psalter*, which eventually supplanted Elvey's, Mercer's and all the other early Victorian psalters. The instructions in the edition with chants (PC 405/1878) called the portion of the words 'from the commencement of each verse and half-verse up to the accented syllable' the Recitation.

On reaching the accented syllable, and beginning with it, the *music* of the chant commences, in strict time (*a tempo*), the upright strokes corresponding to the bars. The Recitation must therefore be considered as *outside* the chant, and may be of any length ... If there is no syllable after that which is accented, the accented syllable must be held for one whole bar [as in the first half-verse of the *Venite*] ... If other syllables follow the one accented, the first ... bar of the chant will have to be divided into *parts of a semibreve*.

Elaborate instructions followed to show exactly how this was to be done. The first verse of the *Venite* appeared thus:

> O come let us sîng | unto.the | Lord: let us heartily
> rejôice in the | strength of | our sal-|-vation.

A new form of compromise had been found between the tradition of chanting prose and the strong metrical rhythm which was a feature of classical art music. Where the Georgians had played the chant slowly enough to allow the whole of the recitation to be fitted into the first semibreve, the Victorians abandoned this attempt, chopped off the last few syllables of the recitation, used them to begin 'the *music* of the chant' which they sang in strict time and quite fast, and left the remainder of the recitation to take care of itself. The preface to *The cathedral psalter* gave no assistance in the singing of the words preceding the 'accented syllable', other than to say that 'the words should be deliberately recited'.

The cathedral psalter had first been published without music, in 1875: three years later the edition with music appeared, set out with one or more chants printed at the head of each psalm in the fashion introduced by Mercer; the musical editors were Stainer, organist of St Paul's; Turle, organist of Westminster Abbey; and Barnby, organist of St Anne, Soho. One of the editors of the texts was John Troutbeck, precentor of Westminster Abbey. Rainbow has pointed out (:297) the significance of the title of a book that primarily catered for the parish church. Whether because of its title, the air of authority conferred by the editorial committee, or its method of pointing, the book was an immediate success, and was soon adopted by the great majority of parish churches throughout the country. In 1895 it was in use at over 65 per cent of the churches in the diocese of Truro (Donaldson: 407). It is still widely used. There can be little question that its method of pointing helped to bring chanting within reach of the parish choir. For it turned the psalms into something very like hymns. The general effect was that of a strictly metrical hymn-like tune repeated many times over, only occasionally delayed by an unusually long recitation. Unsophisticated singers immediately felt more at ease, for they found that this chanting was not, after all, so very different from the kind of music they already knew how to sing. Choirmasters found that one of their most intractable problems had been solved for them.

The music for the daily services was naturally based on that used in cathedrals. In the early nineteenth century, however, there was great variety in the music in use from one cathedral to another (Jebb, 1847–57: II, preface, 13–15). In the course of centuries of oral transmission, the adapted plainsong of Marbeck had undergone various transformations. Until relatively recent times the responses had been sung in unaccompanied unison at many cathedrals (:13). Harmony was introduced from about 1780 onwards, and it was often of a rich five-part variety, with the melody in the treble, dominant sevenths at the cadences, and a good deal of dissonance and movement of inner parts. One arrangement used at Lichfield Cathedral was adopted at Bridport parish church (ex. 65b). Another was prepared by Peter Penson for the use of Durham cathedral, where he was a minor canon from 1815 and precentor from 1834 to 1848. It was this version that was adopted at Leeds parish church when the daily choral services were instituted in 1841, and it was published in that year by one James Hill (PC 370), and later revised by the organist, Robert Burton, assisted by Vincent Novello (ex. 65c).

During the next twenty or thirty years the trend was towards standardisation in the cathedrals, and the 'use' of St Paul's and Westminster Abbey seems to have prevailed. In the 1860 edition of Mercer's *Church psalter and hymn book*, a setting was printed in which the original sources (Cranmer's Litany of 1544 and Marbeck's publication of 1550) were 'scrupulously adhered to, even if it involved an occasional deviation from the modern uses of our metropolitan cathedrals'. The melodies were harmonised in a plain style by John Goss, organist of St Paul's (ex. 65d). For the preces and responses before the psalms, however, there was evidently some opposition to this return to Marbeck, for in some copies of his 1864 edition Mercer inserted a printed half sheet headed 'As sung at St. Paul's' and giving a different version of these responses (see ex. 65e). It was this second and more familiar version that prevailed in the typical 'fully choral service' of the late Victorian parish church. In *The cathedral prayer book* (1891), edited by John Stainer and William Russell, the whole of the prayer book was printed 'with the music necessary for the use of choirs'. The versicles and responses were 'from the arrangement used in St. Paul's cathedral (Stainer and Martin, founded on Goss). They follow Marbeck, although with one or two slight variations which have become traditional in the cathedral of the metropolis, and, more recently, in many other churches.' These differed from ex. 65b in only minor, though significant, details: a dominant seventh was substituted for the plain dominant on the word 'name' in 'The Lord's name be praised'; for the last of the responses after the creed, a special harmonisation was provided, ending on D major instead of the dominant of E minor, and marked '[Soft and slow]'. This practice was certainly adopted in many parish churches, and survives in some to this day. The Church Music Society's anonymous paper *Music in village churches* in 1917 specifically warned against dragging the final response (:11). In such a simple way had Stainer (if it was he) subtly turned the daily responses into a musical work of art, with a romantic coda. In an appendix he gave an arrangement, with considerable alteration, of one of Tallis's two choral services, which he called (though with little apparent historical justification) 'Tallis's festival responses and litany' (elsewhere 'festal responses and litany').*

The practice of singing the opening and closing prayers of morning and evening prayer appears to be a custom of Victorian origin: it certainly was not normal in cathedrals in the seventeenth century (Clifford). It may have originated at Leeds. By 1864 it was certainly becoming common. Mercer included monotones for these prayers, with harmonised amens. Crowdy reported five ways in which the General Confession was sung: (1) the minister recited in monotone, followed closely by the choir in each sentence after he had uttered its first few words; (2) the minister completed each sentence, which the choir then repeated; (3) a monotone by the choir alone; (4) one or two of the sentences harmonised; (5) all the sentences harmonised, sometimes deviating from a monotone in the treble part: the 'Leeds use' had a harmonised perfect cadence at the end of each sentence (Crowdy: 13–17). Provided that the minister was capable of singing, he would intone the opening sentences, Exhortation, Absolution, prayers, and

---

* A number of sixteenth- and early seventeenth-century harmonised settings of preces and responses, including both of Tallis's, were associated with simple settings of proper psalms for Christmas and other major feasts, and were probably used on such occasions, while the unharmonised Marbeck responses were used on ordinary days (see le Huray: 161–3). But there is no justification for calling one *harmonised* setting 'festal' and another 'ferial', a practice that appears to derive from Stainer. Many parish churches reserved the Tallis settings for great festivals, and used the 'Victorian' harmonised responses on ordinary days.

blessing; if not, he would read these, but the amens would be sung by the choir (Box, *passim*). In a setting called the 'Ely Confession', the general confession was selectively harmonised to underline the meaning of certain words: George Macfarren complained in 1867 of 'the breaking forth into symphonic song at the words "like lost sheep"' (*Church Choirmaster* I, 1867: 142). On St Andrew's Day, 1866, when Barnby introduced a harp to accompany the service at St Andrew, Wells Street, it entered at the reference to the Incarnation in the creed. In many other churches, the creed and prayers were monotoned, but the 'monotony' was relieved by improvised harmonies on the organ: this practice will be considered in a later section.

The singing of the litany was also based on plainsong, harmonised in a similar way that was partly traditional, and was revised by Goss and Stainer. Tallis's setting was also used on occasion. The choral use of the litany in parish churches declined sharply after 1872, when the Act of Uniformity Amendment Act allowed it to be separated from matins (Blunt: 93–5).

Before the mid-Victorian period, music in the communion service was very restricted in extent, even in cathedrals. The first part, or ante-communion, which included the sermon, was an obligatory part of the daily service; the second part was used only when there was to be an actual celebration of communion, which was seldom. The custom was for the choir and organ, if any, to sing only in the ante-communion service. Liturgical music was restricted to the responses to the ten commandments (sometimes called 'the Kyrie' because of their superficial resemblance to the *Kyrie eleison* of the Roman mass) and the short phrase 'Glory be to thee, O Lord' which was traditionally sung after the naming of the gospel, though it had been omitted from the prayer book from 1552 onwards. There was also a metrical psalm or hymn before and after the sermon, and the Sanctus was often sung as an introductory anthem, separating the ante-communion from the matins and litany that had preceded it. Even when the second part of the service was performed, the choir played no part in it. The inclusion of the Gloria in excelsis in cathedral service settings was very rare between 1660 and 1850 (Fellowes: 29). In those parish churches where choirs attempted to sing parts of the liturgy, they would often sing the responses to the commandments, several settings of which were included in early nineteenth-century collections for parish church use (see PC 333, 338, 349 etc.).

Under the influence of the Oxford movement, choral settings of the entire communion service were revived, and Margaret Chapel was probably ahead of any cathedral in this innovation (Fellowes: 31). As ritualists became bolder they not only restored music to those parts of the old mass that survived in the prayer-book communion service, but interpolated parts that did not. The additions that were most clearly unauthorised were the Benedictus after the Sanctus, and the Agnus dei during the communion of the clergy. There were many, indeed, who objected to 'that latest novelty in church music, the "choral celebration"': R. B. Daniel thought its introduction was 'probably more often due to the Romanizers in the Church than to musical enthusiasts', but he added: 'The fact that a number of people of fashion (chiefly of the gentler sex) and musical enthusiasts like the choral service, does not justify us in using a kind of service which the humbler class cannot understand' (:41, 51).

The choral celebration was a Victorian creation: an amalgam of authorised, revived, and newly interpolated elements. It is not surprising, therefore, that it presented a challenge to composers. No complete traditional settings existed: those whose preference was for old music were compelled to select and adapt parts of various compositions of earlier centuries. Others adapted masses by continental composers from Palestrina to Gounod, but of course the texts had not only to be translated but considerably altered, rearranged, or shortened. The result was generally a musical travesty. The only hope of a solution that was artistically satisfying was to compose an entirely new setting of the required texts. In the music for choral celebrations, therefore, the late Victorians·showed an even greater bias for contemporary music than in other parts of the service. Baden Powell in 1901 recommended 25 'concerted' services: 7 were adaptations of continental masses, the rest were by modern English composers, all published during the previous thirty years. (Five of these eighteen, mostly published in the 1870s, he marked with a symbol which meant 'without *Benedictus* and *Agnus Dei*'.) For unison services Baden Powell recommended two English settings (by Garrett and Armes) and adaptations of plainsong by J. B. Croft, A. King and H. Walker.

There were those, however, who would not go along with the interpolations of the 'Romanisers', but who still could approve the fully choral performance of the communion service as it was printed in the prayer book. The cathedrals, indeed, were gradually adopting it, though there was prejudice against it. When E. G. Monk tried to introduce choral communion at York Minster in 1866, the Archbishop protested strongly, and it had to be discontinued (MS 106: I, 336a). At St Paul's the choir left after the sermon until choral communions were instituted in about 1875 (W. Frost: 21). Conservative parish churches naturally followed in the wake of cathedrals, as they did for every aspect of choral services. Mercer, it is true, provided music for the whole service in 1864. For the responses to the commandments, he gave a harmonised monotone, with 14 alternative composed and adapted settings. For the Nicene creed he gave two settings: one Marbeck's, with harmonies presumably by Goss; the other attributed to Goss, 'partly founded upon Tallis', a very simple chant setting reminiscent of the harmonised Litany. For the Sanctus, Marbeck and five alternative settings; for the Gloria, Marbeck (harmonised Goss), and a quadruple chant. It is doubtful whether Mercer's choral arrangement was ever much used in either cathedrals or parish churches. Stainer followed a similar principle in *The cathedral prayer book*, but without alternative composed settings of the Responses and Sanctus. His version of Marbeck altered the rhythms considerably, fitting them into common time, and also modernised harmonies and added dynamics and changes of tempo. After the consecration prayer, Stainer provided, as an alternative to the plain Amen, a 'Sevenfold Amen' of his own composition (ex. 66), which became hugely popular for parochial use. Stainer's model was adopted for choral communion in many churches that did not go in for advanced ritualism.

The deluge of hymns

All sectors of the Victorian Church, even the extremists at both ends, were united in their interest in hymns. As the successors to metrical psalms, hymns were the most traditional form of parochial church music; they were congregational, but could also be choral; they were Evangelical, but could also be liturgical.

The Victorians produced a torrent of hymns and hymn tunes unequalled before or since. The tide appears to have reached its height in the 1860s. Nor was the phenomenon merely one of quantity. If one may judge by the staying power of hymns, those of the Victorian age must have been of a quality at least equal to any others. Many have survived the reaction against almost everything Victorian that dominated taste in the earlier twentieth century. The most widely used hymn book in the Church of England to-day is *Hymns ancient and modern revised*: Table 19 (p. 340) shows that for both words and tunes the Victorian period is the prevailing source of its hymns. It might be argued that the history of this particular book gives it a Victorian bias. On the other hand the fact that a book with a Victorian bias is still the leading hymnal in the Church tells its own story. And even such a book as *Songs of praise*, though its principles were explicitly anti-Victorian, could not do without a large component of Victorian hymns.

A combination of circumstances made the mid-Victorian period a great one for hymn production. (There was a sharp falling-off after 1880, as Table 19 shows.) The legality, propriety, and value of hymns had been universally accepted; there was a vigorous drive to improve the quality of parish church music in general; methods of printing, promotion and distribution had become more efficient and less expensive; new sight-singing methods had been introduced in the nation's schools. All these factors combined to provide an unparalleled opportunity to have one's hymns sung. It was not merely the profit motive that stimulated hymn production, though this should certainly not be discounted. More important was the simple encouragement of having one's artifacts accepted and used. Many a clergyman and organist must have felt surprised and exhilarated to find his own hymns or tunes appearing in books that were selling by the millions. And, on a higher level, this was a time of great intensity in English religious life. Hymns were one expression of this intensity, which glows through the best examples of the period, regardless of questions of taste. The editors of *Songs of praise*, in the preface to the enlarged edition of 1931, did not shrink from calling the hymnody of the Victorian era 'debased', a word echoed by Erik Routley in 1957 (:134). If it was so, then the stigma must be attached to millions of people of every generation since that time, of all classes and educational backgrounds, of many nations, languages and religions, who have found emotional and spiritual sustenance in Victorian hymns.

Local collections of psalms and hymns had proliferated since the later eighteenth century, but now it was easier to promote hymn books nationwide. They could be advertised in religious and musical journals and local newspapers, and such organisations as the Church Congress (from

1861) and the diocesan festivals also helped to disseminate knowledge of the latest books. The consequence was that hymn books went into mass production. Bickersteth's *Christian psalmody* (1833) had sold 248,000 copies by 1867; Kemble's *Selection of psalms and hymns* (1853) had sold 500,000 by 1869; the S.P.C.K. *Psalms and hymns* (1853) had sold two million by 1869; Mercer's *Church psalter and hymn book* in 1869 boasted an annual sale of 100,000, while *Hymns ancient and modern* was selling half a million copies a year (J. Miller: xi–xii). There was sharp commercial rivalry between the publishers of the various books; bishops and prominent clergy 'allowed' their recommendations to be quoted in advertisements; compilers tried to attract the prestige of well-known names and therefore commissioned authors and composers to produce hymns. This was a boon for unpaid poets (or ill-paid clergymen), and for ill-paid musicians, and they responded eagerly. The huge and growing demand made it possible, and even commercially desirable, for publishers to adopt a bold policy of innovation, and to bring out books in which a substantial portion of the hymns and tunes were new.

In the 1850s the rivalry was unrestrained, and involved not only the strife between parties in the Church but competition within each party. The Evangelical succession was chiefly maintained by Bickersteth's *Christian psalmody*, which was revised and augmented by the original compiler's son in a book entitled *Psalms and hymns, based on the Christian psalmody* (1858), which in turn developed into the *Hymnal companion* of 1870 (PC 400). Kemble's *Selection* perhaps represented a more traditional kind of low churchmanship, as did the S.P.C.K. collection, which was to blossom into the *Church hymns* of 1871 (see PC 403); Mercer's *Church psalter and hymn book* (PC 389) took a middle position. The extreme high-church wing was shared by Neale and Helmore's *Hymnal noted* (PC 385) and William Blew's *Church hymn and tune book* (PC 385a/1852), both of which drew almost exclusively on medieval Latin hymns. Several more moderate high-church books appeared, most notably *The Salisbury hymn book* (1857), edited by Keble and Earl Nelson, which later became *The Sarum hymnal* (L. Benson: 506–9).

The most representative, as well as one of the most successful, of these books was Mercer's, which was central in its churchmanship and also catered to the growing wish for choir-led congregational music. As already pointed out, Mercer printed the music along with the words. This was not an absolute novelty: it had been done by Helmore in 1851 and by Blew in 1852, but their books were specialised collections, destined to circulate only in a small sector of the Church, whereas Mercer's had a broader appeal. It included many traditional metrical psalms, and identified them as such, but still placed them among the other hymns, arranged partly by the Church year and partly by phases of Christian experience – thus catching both high and low in its net. The tunes and harmonies were generally simple; favourite eighteenth-century tunes of the Methodist type, when included, were frequently ironed out into plainer musical language. The music was printed in four-part harmony on two staves, serving the organ as well as the voices, another new departure which was becoming standard practice. The musical editor, Goss, introduced the book at St Paul's cathedral, where it was used in the popular nave services begun in 1858 (Bumpus: 513). The success of these services undoubtedly enhanced the reputation of the hymn book, which was soon adopted in several other cathedrals (PC 389/1864: preface). In view of the widespread acceptance of the cathedral as the model for parochial worship, this was an important boost to the book's popularity. It continued in use at St Paul's until 1871, ten years after the appearance of *Hymns ancient and modern* (L. Benson: 508). In a crowded field it was used in about eight per cent of London churches in 1867, by which time its use was already on the decline.

But the future belonged with the moderate high-church party, if they could unite their efforts. F. H. Murray, rector of Chislehurst, and W. Denton, vicar of St Bartholomew, Cripplegate, were each the compiler of a moderately successful high-church hymnal. Meeting in a railway carriage in the summer of 1858, they decided to give up their rivalry and amalgamate their books. Murray then secured the collaboration of other high churchmen who were also planning to publish hymn books, the most important of whom was Sir Henry Baker, vicar of Monkland. A committee was formed, meeting at the vicarage of St Barnabas, Pimlico. Baker advertised its intentions in *The Guardian* and secured the cooperation of over two hundred clergymen. The committee, now greatly enlarged, went ahead with the preparation of the hymn book, and it appeared in completed form in 1861 under the happily chosen title *Hymns ancient and modern* (PC 395). The 'ancient' was strongly emphasised in this first edition, for of its 273 hymns nearly half were translations from Latin and other languages, and most of the tunes were old. The appendix of 1868 redressed the balance, with only 26 translations out of 114 hymns, and most of the English hymns by contemporary writers: half its tunes were newly published, and many of the others were from recent publications (Frere & Frost: 119–21). Just as with the *Hymnal noted* and its appendix, a compromise with the taste of the majority had been found expedient.

John Keble, the elder statesman of the Oxford movement, gave the following advice to the committee: 'If you wish to make a hymn book for the use of the Church make it comprehensive' (Frere & Frost: 120). His counsel was followed, for while the majority of hymns were either ancient or the work of high churchmen, space was also found for traditional English metrical psalms and hymns, including those of Watts, the Wesleys, and later Evangelicals; Lutheran hymns and (from 1868) translations from the Eastern Orthodox church were set beside medieval and modern Latin hymns. The arrangement followed the Church year, with ample provision for occasional services. In this way the book contained enough of everybody's favourites to become widely acceptable, while at the same time its prevailing high churchmanship was clearly asserted.

The musical editing was entrusted to W. H. Monk, organist of King's College, London, who had the assistance of Ouseley for everything except the unbarred plainsong melodies. (Many of these were taken from Helmore's *Hymnal noted*.) The chief contributors of new tunes were Monk (17), Dykes (7), Ouseley (5) and Gauntlett (5). In the 1868 appendix the largest number of new tunes was contributed by Dykes. The tunes were printed in the same style, and indeed very similar type, to those of Mercer's

Psalter and hymn book. A new edition appeared in 1875, to be known later on as the 'standard edition', and another supplement in 1889: each added new texts and tunes, so that the balance of the book was increasingly modern rather than ancient. An important innovation in the 1875 edition was the use of expression marks in the words of the hymns, anticipated in Barnby's *The hymnary* (PC 401). (They appeared in the editions without music as well as those with, presupposing that the ordinary churchgoer would be able to interpret such musical abbreviations as *pp, mf, dim.*)

The success of *Hymns ancient and modern* was startling. The proportion of London churches using it had reached one in four as early as 1867, when it had already overtaken its nearest rival, the S.P.C.K. *Psalms and hymns*. In subsequent years its share rose steadily, until by 1894 it was used in three out of every five London churches, and in three out of four of those less than twenty years old (statistics compiled from Mackeson, 1866–95). The provincial city of Sheffield showed greater resistance, with only 38 per cent by 1915, rising to 55 per cent in 1928. But in rural areas its dominance was almost total, as Table 17 clearly shows.

Table 17. *Hymn books used in the dioceses of Truro (1895) and Sheffield (1915–28) in percentages*

Region	(1) Diocese of Truro	(2) Sheffield deanery		(3) Remainder of Sheffield diocese	
Year	1895	1915	1928	1915	1928
No. of churches replying	222	47	47	115	126
Church hymns	*3.6*	*31.9*	*21.3*	*1.7*	*2.4*
Ancient & modern (1861–89)	*94.1*	*38.3*	*55.3*	*88.7*	*91.3*
Hymnal companion	*1.8*	*25.5*	*19.1*	*7.0*	*1.6*
English hymnal	*...*	*...**	*4.3*	*...**	*4.0*
Other	*0.5*	*4.3**	*...*	*2.6**	*0.8*

Sources:
(1) Questionnaire sent by the precentor of Truro cathedral to all incumbents in the diocese of Truro (Donaldson: 407).
(2) and (3) Questionnaire sent by W. Odom, vicar of Heeley, to all incumbents in the diocese of Sheffield (*Sheffield diocesan calendar* I (1915): 72–103; XIV (1928): 53–83). Sheffield deanery consisted of the city and suburbs.

* The 'other' hymn book listed in 1915 was probably the *English hymnal*.

The inevitable decline of books such as Mercer's that had been popular before, and the total eclipse of the remaining tune books and local parish collections, underline the completeness of *Ancient and modern*'s victory. By about 1880 its only formidable rivals were Bickersteth's *Hymnal companion to the Book of Common Prayer* and the S.P.C.K. *Church hymns*. These three books covered 'nearly all the ground', as the chairman of *Hymns ancient and modern* put it (*Church Congress*, 1879: 342). The *Hymnal companion* superseded most other Evangelical books, and had also captured some of the 'centre' by including many popular hymns of ancient or high-church origin, in addition to those inherited from Bickersteth's *Psalms and hymns*. Its literary taste was more distinguished than that of *Hymns ancient and modern*, but it borrowed much from that book not only in its form and arrangement, but in its music, particularly in the editions of 1876 and 1890. Its independent musical contribution was slight. *Church hymns* occupied a somewhat similar position. Less pronouncedly Evangelical than the *Hymnal companion*, it was still low-church by comparison with *Hymns ancient and modern*: and, free from the necessity of supplying hymns for every saint's day and season of the Church, it was able to pay greater attention to literary values and to be more scrupulous in its treatment of authors' texts (L. Benson: 568). Its musical editor in 1874 was Arthur Sullivan. It contributed one of the greatest of Victorian tunes, Scholefield's 'St. Clement' (ex. 69). Two distinguished tunes by Sullivan himself appeared in this book: 'Lux eoi' and 'Noel', the latter associated with the Christmas carol 'It came upon a midnight clear' and skilfully based on a traditional carol melody.

The rivalry between the various hymn books was exactly like that of other commercial concerns, in a time of rapidly expanding, unfettered capitalism. *Hymns ancient and modern* first 'took over' the smaller high-church hymnals, while two large competitors absorbed the low-church and left-of-centre markets; it then modified its policies so as to cater for as much of the central and uncommitted market as possible; in the end, it succeeded in capturing the bulk of its rivals' adherents, though it never achieved a complete monopoly, as had *The whole book of psalms* with state protection. To tell the story in these terms does not necessarily reflect on the sincerity of the clergymen and musicians who compiled and promoted the books. From their point of view, the success of their efforts was a triumph of the forces of virtue and true religion; the fame and fortune that attended it were incidental rewards. As the compilers of *Hymns ancient and modern* put it in their 1875 preface, 'the very fact of its large circulation is their best apology for revision. It is a simple debt they owe to the Church.' Their work had been done 'with the sole view of the glory of God, and the good of his Church' (*Church Congress*, 1879: 243). In 1891–2 the possibility of *Hymns ancient and modern* becoming the official book of the Church was put forward by a committee of the Convocation of the province of Canterbury. The proprietors declined, on the grounds that they felt an obligation to complete and perfect what they had begun, by further revision of their work. No more was heard of the proposal, which was not mentioned at the time of the 1904 revision (Frere & Frost: 122).

There were still, however, groups in the Church that would not accept *Hymns ancient and modern* or any book based on its principles. The advanced ritualists went on using Neale and Helmore's *Hymnal noted*, though more often than not with a much more popular appendix; or, if their tastes were less austere, they chose *The hymnary*, with music compiled by Barnby from 1872 onwards: it carried to extremes the provision of texts and music for every season, day and hour, with a view to daily choral celebrations. Radical Evangelical hymnody was maintained by Charles Snepp's *Songs of grace and glory* (1872), which divided its hymns into three sections, the Trinity, the Book and Church of God, and Man: musically it continued the traditions of Havergal's *Old Church psalmody* (PC 375), and was grounded chiefly on the old psalm tunes and their eighteenth-century successors.

But the degree of success of *Hymns ancient and modern* makes it indisputably the representative book of Victorian hymnody. The extent of its influence reached even beyond its own adherents, for many other books were closely modelled on it and borrowed its texts and tunes wholesale. A very characteristic style of hymnody had emerged from the Anglican revival of the first half of the century. It met with a great deal of criticism and opposition, which has continued to this day, but it prevailed because of its appeal to the ordinary person. In earlier times religious and cultural leaders had often been able to impose their own tastes and views on unwilling congregations. This was hardly possible now. It was not only that the popular will had asserted itself in all spheres of life. A period of declining religious belief and observance had set in, and anything that was popular must be encouraged for fear of speeding the decline on its way. We shall see to what lengths this policy would be taken in more recent times.

An excellent contemporary survey of hymns and hymn tunes was made by John Heywood, organist of St Paul, Balsall Heath, near Coventry. His articles were originally printed in *The Choir and Musical Record* in the 1870s, and were collected into a book in 1881. Heywood felt there had been a 'gradual declension in purity of style as exemplified in the popular hymn tune ... We have nearly reached a very *bathos* of degradation.' The Methodist hymn tune, 'outrageously boisterous and vulgar ... under Evangelical auspices' had 'soon found its way into the Church'. The Oxford revivalists had revived old tunes and added German chorales and many new tunes; but the selection was dictated by unmusical clergy, who chose 'popular' rather than good tunes (Heywood, 1881:7–9). Their choice was generally eclectic: in country churches, where the vicar's wife or daughter was often in charge, it was even more so, though he admitted that in some country churches 'the exertions of the clergyman's wife have raised the style of the music' to a higher level than that in many town churches with professional organists (:12–13).

Too many hymns, Heywood felt, were of 'an *ultra*-subjective cast', and this stricture was by no means limited to Evangelical examples. Newman's 'Lead, kindly light' was certainly one, however fine its poetry, as was F. W. Faber's 'O Paradise', with its 'slangy air of the ordinary music-hall species': this could apply to Henry Smart's tune to the hymn, but is more apt as a description of John Dykes's (ex. 70). (Both appeared in the 1868 appendix to *Hymns ancient and modern*, but neither survived the revisions after 1900.) The 'music-hall' type of tune Heywood found particularly objectionable in the 'St. Alban's Appendix' to the *Hymnal noted*, as already pointed out. He found *Hymns ancient and modern* thoroughly eclectic in character. It had far too many 'pretty tunes', as for example Henry Lahee's 'Nativity' (still found in the 1950 revision: its second half is identical to that of the nursery song 'Mary, Mary, quite contrary'). In some metres, notably those of 6 and 5 syllables alternating, only tunes of what Heywood called 'the "tum-tum" class' were available: 'why do almost all tunes of this metre so rejoice in repeated chords?': 'Caswall' and 'Eudoxia' were examples. Some tunes were there 'that ought not to be admitted into any hymnal that seeks to elevate popular taste'. Heywood's examples here were two eighteenth-century tunes that became and have remained great favourites ('Hursley'and 'Miles Lane') and a Victorian immortal, 'Ewing' ('From Greenland's icy mountains'). Heywood quoted with approval George Macfarren's remark about 'Hursley': 'An execrable spoliation of the lively, piquant, and sarcastic melody of *Se vuol ballare* ... [from Mozart's *Le nozze di Figaro*], in its almost blasphemous misapplication to Keble's exquisite poem, "Sun of my soul"'. He wished that some of the worst tunes could be omitted from the next edition, since 'this hymnal will, probably, exercise more influence upon the hymnody of the future than any other publication of the kind at present known' (:22–4).

Hymns ancient and modern was indeed eclectic, as Heywood put it, or comprehensive, as Keble had advised. Its original high-church impulse had been greatly modified as early as the first appendix of 1868, and was still more so by 1875. The plainsong melodies which had been so prominent a part of the first edition were still there; but they had become a much smaller proportion of the whole, and were now (1875) provided with barlines and more modern harmonies, so that they approached closer to what was acceptable to the majority (see ex. 63). Alongside these were many traditional English tunes, but subtly altered to conform with the times, and many selections from continental sources, similarly disguised. Among the new tunes, many had characteristics that had been unknown a generation earlier. Heywood, reviewing a new batch of hymn books (including the 1875 *Ancient and modern*), observed that 'the majority of new tunes that are perpetually springing up around us ... are written for ideal congregations of part-singers, and are, as vehicles of common song, under our present circumstances, all but useless' (1881: 64). Yet many of the very tunes he criticised did, in fact, become 'vehicles of common song' throughout the Church – and, indeed, in many nonconformist and Roman Catholic churches, to say nothing of the Empire and the United States.

Many of Heywood's criticisms were well taken. The proprietors did try to remove the 'worst' tunes in the revised edition of 1904, and to purge those that remained of 'bad' Victorian features (ex. 74, 75). A musical committee was appointed in 1896, including Parratt, Stanford and Wood, under the chairmanship of W. H. Frere, later bishop of Truro. The standard of scholarship was much higher than before, particularly in the accuracy and harmonic treatment of the plainsong melodies. But the edition, though commended by some critics, was a failure, and the proprietors were compelled by popular demand to go on reissuing the 1875–89 edition, which continued in use in thousands of churches (Frere & Frost: 122). The Supplement of 1916 built on the 1889, not the 1904, edition. The truth is that the original compilers, and the clergymen who were ultimately responsible for the decision to adopt the book in their churches, had little desire to 'elevate popular taste'; and the fate of the 1904 revision showed how unpractical any such policy would be. The consumers knew what they wanted, and if they did not find it in *Hymns ancient and modern* they would seek it elsewhere.

There is no doubt that the Victorian hymn tune has been a lasting success. It has spread far and wide, enhancing the emotional and religious experience of untold millions, and has outlived the almost complete disappearance of most other serious music of its time and place. At the same time it has been almost universally condemned by music critics from its own times to the present. Music historians are uncomfortable about its staying power, which they feel unable to attribute to its own qualities and must try to explain in some other way (Long: 359–60).

The attacks on Victorian hymn tunes have usually been in quite general terms. They have been accused of 'insincerity' (Long: 360), 'debasement' (Routley, 1957: 134), 'effeminacy', 'cheaply sugary harmony' (Walker: 308), 'unctuous optimism' (C. Phillips: 157), and, almost universally, of 'sentimentality'. One of the most violent outbursts came from the pen of Sir Charles Stanford: he said that these tunes 'degrade religion and its services with slimy and sticky appeals to the senses, instead of ennobling and strengthening the higher instincts ... They are flashy enough to seduce the untutored listener and to spoil his palate for wholesome and simple fare; much as the latest comic song will temporarily extinguish the best folk-song' (:310). Ralph Vaughan Williams claimed that 'it is indeed a moral rather than a musical issue. No doubt it requires a certain effort to tune oneself to the moral atmosphere implied by a fine melody; and it is far easier to dwell in the miasma of the languishing and sentimental hymn tunes which so often disfigure our services' (PC 411: xi).

When critics have attempted to attack Victorian hymn tunes in more technical terms, they have been revealingly unconvincing. One has pointed to the tendency to 'rigid four-bar phrases' and the 'complete disregard for the rhythms ... of the words' (Long: 360). But these criticisms are mutually contradictory. The vast majority of hymns are in metres that alternate strong and weak syllables, in a pattern of repeating or alternating lines. If the 'rhythms of the words' are to be observed in a strophically repeated tune, the result will inevitably be a series of phrases of equal length, generally two or four bars. This is just as true of psalm tunes of the seventeenth and eighteenth centuries as it is of hymn tunes of the nineteenth and twentieth. To avoid such regularity will distort the 'rhythms of the words', unless the text has been specially designed to accommodate variety of rhythm.

Much has been made, also, of the 'chromaticism' of the tunes, their frequent use of unprepared dissonances, their modulations, and their reliance on harmonic progressions at the expense of interesting movement of the parts, even to the extent of pedal basses or inverted pedals in the upper parts. These characteristics, however, were shared by much of the greatest music of the period: the symphonies of Brahms, the operas of Wagner and Verdi, the piano music of Chopin and Liszt. It is not easy to see why hymn tunes should be debarred from using the most productive features of contemporary musical style. But several writers have explicitly objected to the Victorians' imitation of leading continental composers, as if such influences were in some way pernicious. Fuller-Maitland (1902: 101) was inclined to attribute all the faults of Victorian church music to 'the various foreign elements which have been introduced': once they had been eliminated, he looked forward to the restoration of English church music to 'its high place in the world'. In flat contradiction Davies has called Victorian church music 'insular' (:v, 119). Another favourite scapegoat has been the influence of 'secular music'. But this cannot possibly be sustained. Secular influences have affected church music in all periods, and Vaughan Williams himself successfully adapted a number of secular folk songs as hymn tunes for *The English hymnal*.

A related criticism, often repeated, is that the hymn tunes are too much like 'partsongs' (Heywood, 1881: 64; Rainbow: 294). To a certain extent this is simply to say that they are Victorian in their harmonic language, for the partsong was another typical product of the period. But it also suggests that the lower voice parts, instead of being merely accompaniments to a basically congregational melody, were frequently given the dominant melodic interest at the expense of the 'tune'. This is indeed true of many Victorian hymn tunes, as Erik Routley has pointed out in detail (1957: 123, 265). Dykes's tune 'St. Andrew of Crete' begins with eleven repetitions of the same note, while the 'melody' is carried by the lower parts; in his 'Stabat mater no. 2' melodies in the alto and tenor are actually marked with accents (PC 395/1875: no. 117). But another frequent objection is that the inner parts of Victorian hymn tunes are *lacking* in melodic interest: Gardner points to the alto part of 'Abide with me' (Monk's 'Eventide') as 'surely the *nadir* of dull part writing' (1918: 63). Here the melodic interest is concentrated in the treble part. Surely both criticisms cannot be valid. If all four parts of a tune were to share equally in the melodic interest, one would have something verging on polyphony – hardly appropriate for congregational singing.

Clearly it is no longer necessary for a writer on English church music to find adjectives to denigrate the Victorians. Let us therefore try to characterise the Victorian hymn tune in more dispassionate language. We may well begin by recalling the conditions for which it was designed. In most churches the music of the service was dominated by a large choir, prominently placed, and accompanied by a substantial organ. The congregation, if it took part, took only one part in an experience that could be aptly described as a musical performance. This was quite a different matter from truly congregational singing, in which the tune was the essential music, and any other, whether choral or instrumental, was merely an accompaniment.

Hymn singing, therefore, had become an artistic form of expression, comparable to the performances at concerts which were now experienced by so large a part of the population. The concert hall as well as the cathedral was a possible model for imitation. Accomplished professional musicians of wide experience were providing new kinds of hymn tune in which these models were followed; their tunes were not simply aids to congregational worship, they aspired to be works of art in their own right.

The congregation, as an untrained, intractable element in the performance, must either be silent, or must be made to appear artistic by adroit management of the music it was asked to sing. Here the skills of the new generation of composers were brought into play. The people would sing in much the same way as before. But the notes that they sang were not treated simply as a tune, but as an element in a more complex musical texture. A perceptive contemporary writer was aware of this trend. The new tunes, he said (writing in 1867), were based on an altogether new principle, which he ascribed to the invention of Dykes (Pl. 30).

Their difference from the old style of hymn and psalm tune may be described roughly as consisting in a tendency to treat the short musical phrases of which the sections of tunes consist as connected sentences, rather than as made up of a succession of isolated chords. Hence the frequent occurrence of quasi-pedal phrases, and an indifference to passing dissonances so long as the musical passage brings itself well home at its close. (*Church Choirmaster* I, 1867: 182).

For hundreds of years, through all the changes in the style of metrical psalm and hymn singing, one principle had remained: each syllable in the text, whether sung to one note or several, had been harmonised by a single chord. All manner of ornamentation and passing dissonance might decorate the basic harmony, but the harmony itself belonged to the syllable to which it was sung. (Where this norm was departed from, as in the fuging tune, the congregation was altogether excluded from the result.) In the 'old way', each note of the tune had been an event in itself; when this style gradually lapsed, the series of events was still recognised in the succession of chords. It is difficult to find any significant exceptions to this in congregational psalm or hymn tunes before the Victorian period.

But the Victorian composers discovered that they could abandon this principle, and could design a tune which had a harmonic motion independent of the succession of syllables in the text. The people would still sing normally one note to a syllable, sometimes a brief melisma of two or three notes; but the composer was free to treat any of these as passing notes if he wished, or, conversely, to change harmonies while one syllable was being sung. Furthermore, there was no reason why the congregation should not be robbed of the melody in places, and sing a repeated note or other form of 'accompaniment' while other parts in the harmony carried the melodic flow. The people singing the tune would not detect anything unusual, unless they were musically accomplished; yet their 'tune' would actually have become merely one part in a musical composition. The 'tune' was no longer, by definition as it were, the foremost element in the musical texture.

Such cleverness in the manipulation of limited musical resources paralleled the developing art of orchestration. When Beethoven tuned the timpani in the scherzo of the Ninth Symphony to sound an octave apart on the minor third of the key, the timpanist played them exactly as before, yet their effect was totally new: instead of merely reinforcing the dominant and tonic chords of the home key, they could be used in all sorts of new ways, and could even play the theme all by themselves. Berlioz, Wagner and a long succession of later composers constantly found new ways of using old tools. The congregation in the parish church found itself being used in the same way, though, of course, to a less spectacular degree. Instead of a body of assembled worshippers whose expression of praise was the paramount purpose of the music, it had turned almost insensibly into a section of the church 'orchestra'. Clergymen might complain that 'choirs' professionalism had ruined congregational devotion': they did not always perceive how this process had been subtly aided by a change in the character of the hymn tune, which they themselves had often encouraged. Congregations, it is clear, enjoyed their new status. Singing hymns was now almost like singing in an oratorio chorus – the summit of many Victorians' musical ambitions. Thanks to the skill of a Dykes, Barnby or Stainer, they could sing a tune that was no more difficult than one of the traditional psalm tunes, but in doing so could feel the thrill of participation in something that sounded like great art music. The resemblance was, in reality, superficial: but the average singer was very far from the position of a music critic listening judicially to a new symphony or opera.

Symbolic of the new approach were the innovations in notation and format made in several hymn books. Crotchets replaced minims as the basic unit, marking the general speeding up of hymn singing: one of the first books to make this change was the 'St. Alban's Appendix' to the *Hymnal noted* (PC 398). Barnby's *The hymnary* (1872) also abolished the double bars that had traditionally divided the musical phrases corresponding to the lines of the text. Metronome speeds were added, and expression marks, sometimes in the music as well as in the text. Rests were used, not to divide each line from the next, but for specific musical effect. The result was to transform the appearance of the tunes into a continuous musical composition. In the example given (ex. 71) it is not at all obvious where the breaks between lines of text occur in the tune. This is not merely a matter of notation: musically, too, every effort has been made to play down these breaks. The music is tailored to the sense and verbal rhythms of the first verse: the phrase in bars 4–6 fits 'Awake, Jerusalem, arise!' like a glove, but is less happy in the third verse to the words 'With harp and lute and psaltery'. (Moreover, in verse 3, line 5, the *ff* in the text is hardly consistent with the *diminuendo* marked in the music.) The congregation, led by the choir trebles and organ, is made to perform two sustained *crescendos* in each verse, coupled with a gradual rise in pitch, that would make some demands on the breathing capacities of even a trained singer (bars 10–14, 18–21). Several syllables are set to chords that have no independent status but are merely passing dissonances, for instance in bars 18–19.

Two of Dykes's best known tunes may be cited for early examples of this kind of writing.* 'Hollingside' (1861), associated with Charles Wesley's 'Jesu, lover of my soul', has two clear examples of syllables treated purely as passing chords (marked 'X' in ex. 72). The opening phrase is extremely easy to sing as a melody, but when congregations first learned to sing it, they may have been surprised to find that on their fifth note they were singing a rather pronounced dissonance, which was resolved in an irregular manner, and then only to the short sixth note. When this phrase is repeated, the same note is part of a chord that sounds like a plain dominant triad in second inversion, but turns out to be a supertonic seventh with three accented passing notes. The emotional tension produced by these chords is

---

* For an appreciation of Dykes see Hutchings, 1973.

considerable, but all the strain is borne by the harmonies: the melody remains quite conventional. Similarly in 'The king of love my shepherd is' (ex. 73) the marked chords, and the dominant pedal in the last phrase, are not implied by the melody, which is of a simple, traditional kind; but they add enormously to the richness of the whole. Dykes did the same kind of thing in many other tunes. In 'Strength and stay' (ex. 74a) his harmonies proved too much for the revisers of 1904, who printed the tune with 'original harmonies slightly altered'; but it is noticeable that the main effect of the alterations was to remove chromaticisms and extreme dissonances, leaving Dykes's 'passing chord' effects unchanged (ex. 74b). A more drastic revision of James Armstrong's 'Newland' (1889) was made for the 1904 edition, removing all passing chords, chromatic or otherwise, and, for better or worse, taking away most of the tune's character (ex. 75). Also removed is the 'join' between the second and third phrases provided by the bass part, which was another example of the conversion of a hymn tune into a 'work of art'. Exactly the same had been done by Monk in his famous tune to 'All things bright and beautiful' (1887). (This time the revisers left it alone.) It was particularly charming, perhaps, to apply such artistry in accompanying the simple voices of children. The Victorians specialised in an attitude to children which set off their innocence against the observer's sophistication. In their hymn tunes they treated adult congregations in the same way.

An astute contemporary commentator, John Spencer Curwen, noticed the fundamental change that had come over the harmonisation of hymn tunes. By way of illustration he provided three settings of 'Old Hundredth', which he labelled 'Past', 'Present' and 'Future'. The 'Past' setting is simply the standard harmonisation, with a separate chord (generally in root position) for each note. The 'Future' setting is a grotesque caricature of chromaticism. But in the 'Present' setting (ex. 76) Curwen hit off exactly the change that had taken place: the rate of harmonic change is no longer one chord to a syllable: several notes in the tune are provided with passing harmonies only. The tune gains considerable onward momentum as a result, but loses its dignity and integrity as a grand specimen of congregational melody (Curwen, 1880: 130–2).

Dykes and others attempted some more radical experiments in what might be called the acculturation of the hymn tune. Dykes's 'Christus consolator' (ex. 77) is largely in one key, G minor, until the last phrase ('Be at rest!') which is in F: the organ supplies the necessary modulating link for the next verse, and the whole is turned into a continuous composition. Miniature 'cantatas' were also attempted by Monk ('Melton Mowbray' and 'Litany of the four last things', the latter a set of linked tunes in C major and E minor and major, with the organ holding an E to connect the tunes). Dykes's 'Dies irae' and Barnby's 'The foe' amount to set pieces. Nearly all these and similar tunes were rejected in 1904, but lived on in the old edition as revised in 1916. Stainer's 'Rest' (1873) survived to the 1950 edition, almost unaltered (ex. 78). The construction of its melody is entirely based on descending scales of varying lengths, and in two cases these overlap the verbal phrases. The singers have reached the end of the eight-syllable line and may think they are also at the end of a musical phrase, but they are mistaken. The incompleteness of the melodic phrase is in each case accentuated by the harmony. An additional twist is provided by the displacing of the dotted-note motive in the fourth phrase. In this ingenious tune the melody is, once again, entirely diatonic and easy to sing.*

In some tunes modulations were a feature, often to the mediant minor as in Barnby's much scorned but ever popular 'Cloisters' (1868), or the more remote mediant major as in Herbert Oakeley's 'Edina' (1889). Chromaticism reached almost Wagnerian levels in Dykes's 'Sanctuary' (1871). But a contrasting type of tune cultivated a deliberate austerity, using only plain triadic harmony and a melody that avoided leaps or emotional curves. Monk's 'Miserere' (1861) is 'Hollingside' drained of emotional exuberance. It is inspired no doubt by the early harmonisations of the old psalm tunes, but its archaism is unconvincing (ex. 79). It conveys instead a strong aura of self-abasement, drawn from the text for which it was written. The singers, again presented with no problem in the melody they are asked to sing, find themselves taking part in a romantic musical representation of prayer. A similar atmosphere prevails in Redhead's 'Petra', a much more famous tune sung to Toplady's 'Rock of ages, cleft for me', and even more in the same composer's 'St. Prisca'. Monk and Redhead were both advanced high churchmen. Their cult of severity was obviously beside the mainstream of the Victorian hymn tune, but still illustrates its manipulation of congregational melody for artistic effect.

In the revised arrangements of plainsong melodies that appeared in the 1875 edition of *Hymns ancient and modern*, there was a similar effort to make the ancient melodies sound like a 'piece of music' in the contemporary sense. The compilers knew enough to avoid chromatic harmonies, modulations or unprepared dissonances in their harmonisations. But the tune *Aeterna Christi munera*, for instance (ex. 63d), was now fitted into $\frac{3}{2}$ time, and its harmony included a second inversion triad (bar 5), dominant sevenths (8, 11), expressive dissonance (6), and harmonised anticipation (3, 11). Partly, no doubt, this was done to persuade congregations to sing tunes which would have been entirely beyond them if left in their pure form.

One more type of 'tune' found in *Hymns ancient and modern* and other Victorian hymnals was the metrical chant – a succession of chords, similar to a Gregorian or Anglican chant, including periodic reciting notes to which several syllables could be sung. The lines of the hymn were 'pointed' to indicate the first syllable after the reciting note (ex. 80). Some tunes mixed chanting with measured music. It is not known exactly when, or by whom, this practice was revived in the Victorian period; an early precedent existed in Crowley's *Psalter* of 1549. Curwen remarked that the custom had 'become general of late' (1880: 125).

In sum, many of the characteristics of the Victorian hymn tune that have caused both its enormous popularity and its low reputation among musicians can be traced to the desire to make church music more artistic – the same motivation that had caused the mushrooming of fully choral services. The point must be made that this change, carried out with

* Routley, however, has called this a tune of 'abysmal bathos' (1957: 128).

considerable technical skill by such musicians as Dykes, Stainer, Barnby and Monk, was not in itself a disgraceful one. Nor was it in any way a failure. Congregations evidently enjoyed this kind of hymn singing. They were not (in most churches) merely listening to the choir, as in the anthems, services, and responses; and they were not left on their own to sing the rough music of pre-Tractarian times. Instead, they were part of a performance that had some of the qualities of good music.

The greatest Victorian hymn tunes were those that combined the artistry of the partsong with inspiring melody of a truly congregational kind, so that both elements in the performance – the choir and organ on one side, the people on the other – could play a significant and appropriate part in the whole. In such a case the music could touch true greatness in a way that can be claimed for very little English parish church music. A churchful of people singing with vigour and spirit can be, as John Brown had put it years before, 'one of the grandest scenes of unaffected piety that human nature can afford'. When reinforced by all the resources of nineteenth-century harmony and the almost orchestral quality of the romantic organ, it could be overwhelming. The greatest Victorian tunes have these qualities. Monk's 'Eventide', E. J. Hopkins's 'Ellers', Scholefield's 'St. Clement', J. Parry's 'Aberystwyth', Sullivan's 'Lux eoi' and 'St. Gertrude', Dykes's 'Nicaea', 'Gerontius', 'Dominus regit me' and 'Melita', Stainer's 'Love divine', Barnby's 'Cloisters', S. S. Wesley's 'Aurelia', Harwood's 'Thornbury', Goss's 'Praise, my soul', Martin's 'St. Helen' – all these have joined the immortals. And it may be pointed out in passing that no later generation has been able to equal them; whatever the 'English Renaissance' may have done for English music in general, it did not reform the Victorian hymn tune out of existence, nor produce an alternative 'school' of tunes that would be a serious rival, however excellent some individual twentieth-century tunes may be.

Standing almost outside the general history of Victorian hymn tunes was the towering figure of Samuel Sebastian Wesley. A remarkable analysis of his style has been published by Erik Routley (1968: 195–232), who was concerned to explain the fact that so few of Wesley's tunes ever attained much popularity in Victorian times, 'Aurelia' being the chief exception. Routley concluded that Wesley, 'as nobody before him but as so many after him, usually packed too much music into his tunes' (:222–3). They were not fully appreciated until some time after his death, when Basil Harwood printed a large number of them in *The Oxford hymn book* (1908).

Wesley spent a fair proportion of his creative energy on hymn tunes. *The European psalmist*, his tune collection published in 1872, was the culmination of a life's work (PC 402). It contains no less than 615 tunes, 143 of which are his own compositions, and a much larger number harmonised by him. It is distinctly old-fashioned in its plan and format: one of the last of the older 'tunebooks' printed separately from the words, published by subscription, and with the tunes set out for organ with the alto and tenor parts on separate staves above in the eighteenth-century manner. Aggressively Wesley turned his back on the new trends in hymn tune writing, and Routley suggests that he was 'making a dead set at Dykes' by pointedly omitting any of his tunes, and by providing alternative tunes to some of the texts for which Dykes's most successful tunes had been written (:217). On the other hand Wesley carried his own methods of harmony to extremes that were unacceptable to his contemporaries: harsh rather than sweet, intellectually challenging rather than smooth, responding to the fullest implications of the melody. He had absorbed the modality of the early tunes and harmonies far more profoundly than most of the antiquarians who had revived them, and had also, from early childhood, mastered the style of J. S. Bach. Some of his reharmonisations of early tunes (ex. 81a) dwell on the ambiguities of the modal scale to the point of asperity. A very remarkable case, discussed at length by Routley (:228–32), is his version of 'Eltham'. Among his original tunes, 'Kerry' is another instance of the gulf separating him from his contemporaries (ex. 81b). It was written for Keble's 'Sun of my soul', and one could hardly imagine a greater contrast between the spikiness of Wesley's tune, with a harmonic surprise in almost every bar, and the smooth gracefulness of the popular tune, 'Hursley', so much scorned by Macfarren. Wesley was working against the grain: only a few musicians appreciated his hymn tunes.

Organ accompaniment

By the mid-Victorian period, almost every church in London and other towns had a pipe organ; the larger churches possessed instruments of considerable power, with several manuals, a complete set of pedals, and a variety of stops, many of them voiced to imitate orchestral instruments. 'Pedal organs are now indispensable', it was said in 1873 (Shepherdson: 10). English organs had been reformed in design, compass and tuning so that they were now capable of playing music of the great continental schools, above all that of Bach (Long: 335–6). Towards the end of the century, electropneumatic action was coming in, allowing for the possibility of a detached console. The only church in the City of London to have this in 1884 was St Michael, Cornhill (Box: 158).

For smaller churches, many cheap organs of poor quality were being manufactured, and for those that could not afford an organ at all, the harmonium was a cheap substitute, and had generally replaced the church band or barrel organ by about 1880. At the end of the century a church without an organ or harmonium was an extreme rarity. Less than a century before, a court had declared, as a proposition that none could doubt, that an organ was not 'necessary' for parochial worship.

The change had come about through the spread of choral singing. In the smaller churches, even more than the larger, it would be impossible to sing choral music with any semblance of decency without the support of a keyboard instrument. But the function of the organ in accompanying the choir was far more than that of regulating the pitch and providing harmony for solo passages. It was the indispensable agent in turning parish worship into an 'artistic' experience. As Curwen put it, 'the real value of the organ, when properly used, is that it floods the building with sound ... The musical effect ... is improved ...; harsh and loud voices are levelled; the interstices are as it were filled up, and the congregational voice is rounded into harmonious unity' (1880: 93). Instead of drowning or silencing the people altogether, as some had hoped the organ would do in Georgian times, it was now to draw them into a more gratifying musical performance. The prevailing attitude was expressed in a journalist's comment, written in 1891:

Among the London churches, happily every year becoming more numerous, that do the best music in the best way, St. Peter's Eaton Square, stands in the foremost rank ... Given an adequate and sufficiently orchestral organ ... the most intricate music can be perfectly negociated without the aid of a conductor.

As an example, Gounod's *Redemption* had been performed three times during Lent that year: 'the organ was supplemented by trumpets and harps' (*Musical News* I, 1891:95).

Curwen in 1880 estimated that 'five or more harmoniums and American organs' were in use for every 'legitimate organ', but he was including nonconformist places of worship in the reckoning (:109). The distinction between the harmonium and the American organ was that in one the air was blown outwards through the metal reeds, and in the other sucked inwards. The harmonium was the more expressive of the two, because by increasing pressure on the pedals that blew the bellows the player could vary the volume of sound, much more sensitively than with the swellbox pedal of a pipe organ. This gave obvious opportunities for abuse, but also, properly used, was an asset in the grand object of making church music more artistic. The greatest disadvantage of either instrument, compared with a pipe organ, was its weakness of rhythmic attack. It could not invigorate and marshal the singing of a large congregation, but could only 'accompany' (:111). Hence it gave still further encouragement to the replacement of the congregation by the choir, especially in the smaller village churches which were the very ones that frequently could not afford a pipe organ.

The conservative use of the organ or harmonium merely required the duplication of the harmony of the voices in hymns and chants, and the playing of independent accompaniments as written for anthems or other more elaborate pieces. The custom of playing interludes between the verses of hymns was dying out, although the improvised prelude before the anthem was still common. Beyond this, the organ had for some time been encouraged to 'fill out' harmonies by doubling some of the voice parts in another octave, and to provide for greater smoothness by tying over all repeated notes in the lower parts, though this was considered inadvisable in the melody. These two points were made in almost identical terms by Joshua Done in 1830 (PC 357a: 1–2), by Edward Hopkins in 1879 (Grove, 1879–89: I, 25), and by Henry Richards in 1911 (H. W. Richards: 18, 49–50). In the last twenty years of the nineteenth century, however, a growing number of articles and books on organ accompaniment proposed a greatly extended role for the organ in accompanying choir and congregation. At least nine full-length books on the subject were published between 1880 and 1920 (Yeats-Edwards: 280–7). The ideas and methods set down in these books no doubt embodied the results of experiments that had begun to be made some years before. We have already noted Henry Smart's varied accompaniments for hymn tunes (ex. 82).

Curwen wrote: 'There is an ambition among some players to use greater freedom in accompanying than a mere doubling of the voice-parts allows; to employ the organ, in fact, as Handel and Mendelssohn employ the orchestra to accompany their choruses. These "free-parts" are especially in demand for chanting, where, with twenty or thirty repetitions of the same short phrases, variety is felt to be welcome.' He recommended as a model for free accompaniment Sullivan's arrangement of the tune 'St Anne' in *Church hymns* (ex. 83) (1880: 101). In this setting Sullivan had used simple, unaccompanied harmony for the quieter verses, as interludes between the unison verses dominated by the organ: he reserved a dramatic stroke for the ending. Curwen also provided his own examples, which included occasionally leaving the voices unaccompanied, inverting the soprano, alto and tenor parts, bringing a lower part into prominence by use of a solo stop, inserting scales or arpeggios to fill in the gap between lines of a hymn tune, and adding 'free parts' in quicker notes to the given harmonies of hymns and chants. He condemned, however, 'the habit of accompanying chants and Gregorian tones by running up and down the chromatic or diatonic scales, as is the custom of some organists' (:103). The Gregorian tones were often regarded as especially suitable for varied harmonic treatment, simply because they had no harmonies of their own: this was the attitude of both Hopkins (Grove, 1879–89: I, 25) and Bridge (:13).

When Curwen wrote this survey, he 'was not aware that anything was in print elsewhere upon this subject of extemporising additional parts on the organ'. By the time he published a second edition of his work in 1888, several others on the subject had appeared. He quoted at length from a series of articles by C. J. Frost in *Musical Opinion* (1887), which included a 'specimen of contrapuntal treatment of the *tenor*' in a single chant by E. G. Monk (ex. 84). It is not entirely clear how this would be played during the recitation of a long verse of the psalm. Frost, who was organist of Christ Church, Newgate Street, and St Peter, Brockley (Brown & Stratton: 153), confessed his diffidence in expounding these ideas, because of the danger of their abuse by inexperienced organists, 'although it is perhaps not quite so bad as placing loaded firearms within reach of a child' (Curwen, 1888: 210–11).

Frederick Bridge, organist of Westminster Abbey, published an authoritative manual, *Organ accompaniment of the choral service*, in 1885. His recommendations were still fairly moderate, being confined largely to amplification of the harmony by doublings and inversion of parts, and changes of registration. He provided an example of the use of such variety in the accompaniment of an entire psalm. An appendix by W. S. Hoyte, organist of All Saints, Margaret Street, gave advice on the accompaniment of Gregorian chants. He suggested not only varying the harmonies between one verse and another, but within one verse: 'When there is a long sentence to be recited, a good effect is produced by giving to the recitation note a *series* of chords, taking care, however, that that note should always form part of each chord.' For examples of varied harmonies he recommended Warwick Jordan's *One hundred and fifty harmonies for the Gregorian tones* and Arthur Brown's *Organ harmonies for the Gregorian tones* (PC 407). (Jordan and Brown were both organists of London parish churches.)

This principle could obviously be applied with still greater freedom to the accompaniment of extended monotones, for example during the singing of the Creed, Lord's prayer or General Confession. We have already seen that as early as the 1860s varied choral harmonies had been provided in some churches, and there can be little question that musicians such as Barnby improvised similar harmonies on the organ, though no printed examples from before 1900 have been found. Examples were printed by H. Richards (:81–7), some giving simple chords only, others working out a modest theme (ex. 85).

The extreme in this type of accompaniment is represented in *Modern organ accompaniment* (1907) by Madeley Richardson, organist of Southwark cathedral, whose general principle was uncompromising: 'Many an organist hardly realises the fact that the notes he sees before him of a hymn tune or chant should not to-day be regarded as written for "organ or voices", but should be taken as *for voices only*, his accompaniment being left for his own construction' (A. M. Richardson: 21). As models for the kind of thing that could be done, he quoted orchestral accompaniments to chorales from Mendelssohn's oratorios, and went on: 'When the organ is used for the same purpose it should be employed on the same lines, not slavishly following the voices, but giving an artistic and appropriate version of their music' (:24). These ideas Richardson then proceeded to work out to their logical extremity. Taking the first line of Samuel Webbe's tune 'Melcombe' as a base, he took the student step by step through an incredible array of accompaniments. The accompaniment of monotones, he continued, 'is, before all things, the mark of an accomplished organist. In it he shows his own individuality more than in any other branch of his work ... It is often thought sufficient to play a succession of chords indiscriminately ... Monotone accompaniment should be genuine music, with unmistakable evidence of design of its own ... It should include the elements of musical form – rhythm, melodic outline, and recurrence' ·(:101–2). The rhythm of the prose should be ignored, and music played that had its own strict rhythm, whether in duple or triple time. Of the almost limitless possibilities that this method allowed, Richardson gave several instances, one of which is reproduced in ex. 86.

Although Richardson's book was eccentric, and was firmly denounced in *The Musical Times* (XLVIII, 1907: 386), it was only carrying to the limit a principle which had been widely adopted. The organist, as the only professional musician in many churches, had the duty of turning the amateurish efforts of the parish choir and congregation into something worthy of the name of music, and the organ was by far the most powerful agency at his disposal. Varied harmonies, often rising or descending chromatically against a persistent monotone, were an old device of classical and romantic opera: they can be found as far back as Mozart's *Idomeneo* (1780), in the chorus 'Accogli, O re del mar', and in many a dramatic work of Spohr, Meyerbeer, Verdi, and Gounod. To bring them in during a monotoned prayer was entirely consistent with the predominant trends in parish church music of the time.

Summary and evaluation

From the point of view taken in this chapter, the rivalries between high- and low-church parties, and between supporters of Anglican and Gregorian chants, are seen to be a side issue in the parish church music of the Victorian period. Instead, the most significant changes were of a kind that neither Evangelicals nor Tractarians had sought. They amounted to a victory for the forces of 'reform' over an older tradition of popular psalmody.

The kind of reform that now prevailed was not primarily religious in nature, but cultural. It had begun two centuries earlier when persons who had been exposed to the art music of the day sought to introduce its styles and forms into the parish church, and to silence the uncouth singing of the congregations by means of an organ, or failing that, a choir of singers trained to read musical notes. The effective fulfilment of these ambitions had been delayed by popular resistance, apathy of clergy and gentry, lack of financial resources, and the intervention of the country psalmody tradition which the new choirs had generated of their own accord. Now, in the Victorian period, social and economic change accelerated to a point where the conclusion of this reform was inevitable.

Organs and choirs were established in almost every church, and provided music that was emphatically of the professional variety. Efforts were made, sometimes genuine, sometimes perfunctory, to draw the congregation into the performance, and the music was composed or adapted in such a way that the congregational singing would not detract from the artistic standards now to be maintained. But in many churches the music was in reality a performance by robed choir and organ in the chancel.

The cathedral service was the principal model for the new style of parish church music, and hence we can see that it was the traditional high-church view that had ultimately prevailed. In some respects this party was allied with the Tractarians, whose conflicting ideal of an austerely congregational music was established in a relatively small number of churches. The religious idealism of the Tractarians, and of other groups in the Victorian Church, was one of the motivating factors in carrying through the large-scale practical reforms that were needed. But the more secular, materialistic inclinations of the majority were decisive in establishing the character of Victorian parish church music.

A great deal of service music, including chants and anthems, was successfully composed or adapted for the use of parish choirs. But the greatest musical achievement of the period was the Victorian hymn tune, which brought together all parties in the Church and gave congregations a genuine and appropriate part to play in a joint performance with choir and organ. The best Victorian hymns are among the monuments of English church music, and have ample strength to survive the ferocious criticism they have received. They transcended all the anxieties and ambitions about gentility and good taste, and, paradoxically, gave the people once more a popular church music. As a minority of the Committee on Church Worship would put it in 1918, 'In hymns there is a really living and popular interest in British Christianity' (*The Worship of the Church*: 36).

10   The twentieth century

For Christian churches in advanced countries, the twentieth century has been a time of inexorable decline. The accelerating growth of materialism and secularism has been halted only in times of crisis, such as the two world wars. The Church of England has declined with the rest. With each decade its importance in the life of the nation and of the English people has diminished.

Leaders in the Church have responded to this permanent crisis with more and more urgent efforts to show the continuing significance of Christianity in a world in which many have found it irrelevant. There has been growing pressure for change: not merely for a bringing up to date of the institutions and outward forms of the Church, but for a return to the first principles of the Christian religion and a building of new forms on these. An agonising question for Church leaders has been how far to resist these pressures for the sake of maintaining permanent values.

In the earlier part of the century resistance to change was still predominant. But two shocks were in store: the War of 1914–18, and the rejection by the House of Commons in 1928 of the bill to reform the liturgy, prepared after more than two decades of discussion. A period of relentless self-examination followed. Antagonism between the different parties in the Church was stilled: Anglo-Catholics and Evangelicals learned to appreciate each other's particular strengths, and the ecumenical movement shamed Anglicans of all parties out of their insularity and chauvinism. Old theological issues yielded to fresh approaches; old modes of worship were brought to life by new inspirations. Since 1965 radical experiments in liturgical change have been made with full ecclesiastical and legal authority.

Because of the profundity of these changes, and the uncertainty of their outcome, this chapter must be more tentative and probably more superficial than its predecessors. To a greater extent than before, we must often be content with describing what has actually happened in parish church music, and must sidestep the questions of why certain changes have taken place, or which of them are truly significant and appropriate to the times.

Before 1914 the Victorian patterns of worship continued, with intensified contrasts between the extreme sections of the Church. The situation, in the words of Horton Davies, was one of 'ceremonial chaos' which it is 'hardly possible to exaggerate', in which an uninitiated observer 'might readily suppose that there were three Churches of England, not one' (:v, 284). But the extreme developments, though prominent and colourful, were insignificant in the number of their supporters. The broad mass of the Church continued in the central Victorian tradition of choral worship.

The extreme Evangelical party remained principally conservative in its modes of worship. Of the Victorian innovations, it had accepted only the surplice for officiating clergy and the placing of the communion table against the east wall of the chancel. The choir, if it existed, was unrobed, often unstalled, and composed of both men and women: its chief function was to lead the congregation in the singing of hymns. The emphasis of the service was placed upon the sermon. The interior and furnishing of the church building were stark and unadorned; the Lord's prayer, creed and commandments were still painted on panels over the altar or on the railings of the galleries (Pl. 33). The conduct and atmosphere of the services differed as little as possible from those of the nonconformists. The music emphasised hymns of the traditional kind, with psalms spoken or chanted to Anglican chants and an occasional anthem.

The Anglo-Catholic side had divided into two competing streams, both bent on further change and innovation, but on differing principles. One section, led by Percy Dearmer (Pl. 31), concentrated on a pedantically accurate restoration of the modes of worship of the time of Edward VI, which it had found to be not only permitted but even required by the current rubrics in the Book of Common Prayer. The Alcuin Club, in a series of publications beginning in 1897, established the strict legality of a number of ornaments and practices that had fallen into disuse, and these were publicised by Dearmer in his popular *Parson's handbook* and put into practice at his church of St Mary-the-Virgin, Primrose Hill from 1901 onwards. Visitors were astonished by what they saw and heard there (Pl. 34), but all Dearmer's novelties were legally defensible, and they were taken up with enthusiasm by other Anglo-Catholics. The 'English Use' which Dearmer advocated paralleled the imperialism and protectionism of the day, for it rigidly excluded all innovations that were not English in origin or long use. 'The substitution of foreign ornaments is mischievous from the countenance it gives to those who profess to see in the present revival in the Church of England only an imitation of the Church of Rome. And we do not want the things, our own are better' (Micklethwaite: 62; cited Davies: v, 285). The most important musical product of this school was *The English hymnal*, and we shall be discussing its musical characteristics in detail at a later stage.

The opposite point of view was taken by another Anglo-Catholic group, which modelled its worship on recent continental Roman Catholic practice. A typical church of this persuasion at the turn of the century was St Cuthbert, Philbeach Gardens, consecrated in 1887. Its first vicar, Henry St Leger Westall, had furnished it with costly *objets d'art* in imitation of current Italian churches; he wore a biretta and green chasuble, and was accompanied by acolytes wearing scarlet cassocks and cottas. At the communion 'the altar was a blaze of light ... The young men held their candles aloft, and the priest immediately held up high above his head a wafer, whereupon the people bowed as low as they could' (Anson, 1968: 182). Other churches following variants of the 'Roman Use' were St Michael, North Kensington; St Augustine, Kilburn; and St Alban,

Holborn. The excesses in these and other churches were described in great detail in the Evangelical *Record*, and reprinted in 1899 in *The celebration of Mass in city, town, and village churches*. Later, the 'ultramontane' school had its own association, the Society of SS Peter and Paul, founded in 1911 by Samuel Gurney, and including among its followers the brothers Ronald and Wilfred Knox and the architect Martin Travers. They openly denied the value of Anglican tradition, both before and after the Reformation, and sought to introduce the Catholic practices of the baroque and rococo periods, with the avowed ultimate object of corporate reunion with the Roman Church. They brought in such recent Roman devotions as Benediction and the Rosary, and such ornaments as votive candles, monstrances, thuribles, tabernacles, and crucifixes. In their services the 'ultramontane' clergy freely altered the established liturgy of the prayer book by the substitution of parts of the Roman missal and breviary, sometimes even in Latin. On their neo-baroque altars pride of place was frequently given to a crowned and richly robed statue of the Virgin. As Anson remarks, 'the Reformation might never have taken place' (1960: 326).

The 'ceremonial chaos' that permitted such excesses was the subject of growing concern among moderates. In 1904 a Royal Commission on Ecclesiastical Discipline was appointed to investigate 'breaches or neglect of the law relating to the conduct of divine service in the Church of England and to the ornament and fittings of churches' and to make recommendations for dealing with them. The commission heard complaints of irregularities in 687 separate services in 559 churches, and reported its findings in 1906 (*Royal Commission Report*: 1). Setting aside deviations from the law due to convenience or inadvertence, the commission found a large number of 'breaches having significance', mostly connected with the communion service, but also with the adoration of the Virgin and saints, and prayers for the dead. Invariably these practices were in the direction of Rome. They had been shown to exist in 'considerable numbers' but 'cannot accurately be described as prevalent; and some of them seem to be very rare'. Interestingly enough, they had been found mostly 'in the metropolitan area (especially in the poorer districts), or in seaside towns; but they exist also in other places, including some rural parishes ..'. They were 'far more numerous in the south than in the north of England' (:54–5).

But, as in the Victorian period, it must be emphasised that the objectionable practices described were taking place in only a small minority of churches. The commission itself was at pains to point out that 'the evidence gives no justification for any doubt that in the large majority of parishes the work of the Church is being quietly and diligently performed by clergy who are entirely loyal to the principles of the English Reformation as expressed in the Book of Common Prayer' (:76). Although the commission had listed no less than 21 types of deviation from the strict law which had become 'widespread' (:12–15), these were not felt to present any real threat to the spirit of Anglican religion, and for the most part the commission simply recommended legalising them.

Parliament did not act on these recommendations. Before long, however, there was in existence a movement for much greater reform than a merely minimal adjustment to permit existing breaches. The War of 1914–18 shook up the complacency of those who survived it, and many venerable institutions and traditions were suddenly called into question, not excluding the Church of England and the Book of Common Prayer. The experience of army chaplains, in particular, suggested a need for change. They had found the orders for morning and evening prayer were 'too penitential in their approach to worship, the prolix exhortations too dull, and many of the prayers out of touch with the practical needs of their charges' (Davies: v, 291). They found that the communion service served their spiritual needs more effectively, and so gave it a more central position in worship. Many of them admired features of the Scottish and American prayer books and of the services of other denominations into which they had come into contact in the course of their army duties.

The two archbishops set up five committees of inquiry to investigate the state of the Church in wartime, and the report of one of these in 1918 demanded a thorough reconsideration of worship. It recognised how antagonistic the contemporary society had become to the ideals of Christian worship: competitive materialism, aggressive individualism, and class warfare militated against fellowship, simplicity, and sacrifice, and had alienated the poor from the Church, so that 'the idea of the Church as an institution governed by and administered for comparatively small circles of the well-to-do classes steadily took root in the mind of the people' (*The worship of the Church*: 14). The committee proposed not only reform of the prayer book, but a change in the conventional priorities of Sunday services that would give communion the central place at present occupied by morning and evening prayer. A more radical appendix was added by the three serving army chaplains on the committee, who found the prayer book services 'uninstructive and misleading to some, irritating and alienating to others'. They proposed sweeping revision and simplification of the prayer book, and the provision of new acts of devotion of a more popular kind, including the use of bidding prayers, in which 'the picture of Christ ... must be brought before the mind, and interwoven with the whole devotion'; silence should be used to 'grasp and realize the presence and picture of God'; services should be more congregational in character, by avoiding intonation and chanting and introducing more hymns, for 'in hymns there is a really living and popular interest in British Christianity'; and 'services and acts of devotion should end with an act of dedication in which all join – should end on a note of faith rather than of need' (:35–9).

Measures to test these ideas in practice were soon taken. The Convocations of Canterbury and York in 1919 presented identical addresses to the King asking for the establishment of a church assembly which could legislate for the Church subject to the overriding control of parliament (Flindall: 337–41), and on 23 December 1919 the Church of England Assembly (Powers) Act, setting up the Church Assembly and defining its powers and relationship to parliament, received the royal assent. During the next eight years the Assembly undertook the huge task of considering and agreeing upon detailed recommendations that would give effect to some of the ideas of the archbishops' committee. In the long process of discussion, the old party lines were formed again, and in particular the vociferous opposition of the minorities at both extremes gave the impression of far greater strife than was actually present in the Church at large. Not until 1927 did the Assembly agree on a revised prayer book, known as the 'Deposited Book', which contained the whole of the 1662 Book of Common Prayer intact but provided for additions and alternatives at many points. The three houses of the Assembly all passed the Prayer Book Measure by a total vote of 517 to 133, but the minority was formidable and articulate. It could not be said that the Church was unanimously in favour of the new prayer book, and perhaps for this reason it was twice rejected by the House of Commons, though approved by the Lords. In the long process of discussion the momentum generated by the war and the archbishops' committee had been dissipated, and old rivalries had come to the fore. The defeat left the Church in disarray and bewilderment. Morale was low, authority was diminished. The bishops fell back on the inalienable right of the Church, independent of secular government, to formulate its own orders of worship, and let it be known that they would allow the use of the revised prayer book in the parishes of their dioceses. In practice, the result of the parliamentary rebuff was that many clergymen felt free not only to use the revised prayer book of 1928, but to introduce other variations as they saw fit. The ideal of a common worship practice, never perhaps attained to the full, was now seen to be openly abandoned. But the unofficial licence to experiment with the liturgy would allow some important trends to develop, which would eventually lead to the radical and officially recognised changes of recent years.

Aesthetes and populists

Ultimately, parish church music would become congregational. The people's desire to sing the liturgy could not, in the end, be resisted in a period of declining church attendance. But there was great opposition to the change, above all from professional musicians and the amateur choirs they taught, which by the beginning of the twentieth century had become thoroughly entrenched in churches large and small. Protests against choralism and professionalism have been noted throughout the eighteenth and nineteenth centuries, but they were ineffective until after the First World War. 'We should like to see experiments made in the suppression of choirs', said the three army chaplains on the archbishops' committee in 1917 (*The worship of the Church*: 37). After the war, the difficulty of recruiting and maintaining choirs made it easier for such ideas to be put into practice.

The situation just before the war is described in detail in a report on church choirs in the diocese of Wakefield. The committee, appointed by the bishop, included the cathedral precentor, the organists of Halifax, Huddersfield and Dewsbury parish churches, and a number of local clergy and laity. Out of 180 questionnaires sent to parishes, 135 were returned. All reported the existence of choirs, varying in size from 7 at St John, Bradshaw to 72 at St Paul, Huddersfield, with an average size of 31.6. Only 65 of the 4,268 choir members were paid (8 of them at Halifax). Women were numerous in some regions, rare in others: if present, they sat behind the men in the choir stalls, or in the front pews. Choir attendance at services was pronounced good, but not (at least on the part of adults) at choir practices, which were usually held once a week. It was found difficult to persuade adult choir members to practise psalms and hymns, 'on the ground that they know them quite well already', so these were often rehearsed by the boys alone: the responses and litany were rarely practised ('Church choirs': 104–7).

The priest's part was usually sung, sometimes monotoned; 'in a very few instances' it was said. Communion was generally said. The organist was usually appointed by the incumbent: organists' salaries varied from £5 to £120, the average falling between £15 and £20. Hymns were usually chosen by the incumbent, anthems and services by the choirmaster, who might or might not be the same person as the organist. The old edition of *Hymns ancient and modern* and the *Cathedral psalter* were generally in use. Tallis's responses were sung in various editions; few churches distinguished 'festal and ferial uses'. Anthems were sung in 'most churches'. New anthems were constantly being added to choir libraries, often too heavy and difficult, or 'worthless'. Canticles were mostly chanted. Choral celebrations of communion, though on the increase, were still not found in many churches. 'Unaccompanied singing ... does not seem to be receiving that attention which it deserves, and but little is done by means of practices to encourage congregational singing.' The clergy often hindered musical progress, partly from 'musical inefficiency, which a short course of lessons from a competent teacher would do much to remedy in many cases'. The psalms and canticles were 'usually too hurried, the words on the reciting note being too often a mere jumble of sounds'. Voluntaries were often spoilt by 'prolonged bell ringing' (:100–11).

The committee suggested abandoning all music for the opening and closing prayers, and provided a short list of recommended anthems and services. These are almost exclusively Victorian or post-Victorian, the only exceptions being Marbeck's communion service, one anthem each by Farrant and Gibbons, and two by Crotch (:118–20).

Such was the ordinary conservative ideal, directly descended from the traditional high-church view of earlier times. A moderate concern is expressed for the lack of congregational participation, but the main attention is directed towards maintaining and improving the standard of choral singing. There is no hint of any dissatisfaction with Victorian taste, either in choir music or in hymn tunes; it would be a long time before any such change in taste was felt in provincial centres.

But two movements for reform and change were growing in force. Their purposes were different, though they were often simultaneously present in the same institution or even the same individual. In the higher academic circles of the musical profession, and among aristocratic connoisseurs of church music, there was a demand for changes in the choral repertory that would favour Elizabethan rather than Victorian music; for a more perfect performance of choral music, especially chanted psalms; and for hymns of a more elevated taste, both literary and musical. Among the clergy and many devout laymen, there was a move towards simpler and more congregational music, especially after the experiences of the War.

In cathedrals, in the chapels of religious orders, and in college and school chapels, there was little conflict between the two aims, and it was in such places that the revival of early Anglican choir music was carried on, and speech-rhythm chanting successfully introduced. In the great majority of parish churches the two movements, if both present, tended to conflict. Elizabethan music, apart from the psalm tunes, was not congregational, nor within the reach of the average parish choir; nor did it appeal to the average priest or layman. A possible class of music that satisfied both ideals was folk song – but it must be rural folk song, archaic in idiom, not the present-day urban folk song, which aesthetes regarded with horror, though it had been used by the Moody and Sankey revivalists and the Salvation Army.

A strong advance-guard of this aesthetic movement was led by Robert Bridges, a distinguished poet (later poet laureate) and amateur musician. As 'precentor' of the choir in the village of Yattendon, where he had settled in 1882, he took charge of the hymnody by reviving many old tunes and writing new hymn texts to go with them. The result was *The Yattendon hymnal*, which he edited with H. E. Wooldridge and published, sumptuously printed, in 1899 (PC 410). Routley considers this book 'typical of the unashamed and even aggressive championship of high culture which was characteristic of Bridges' (1957: 138). The tunes, many unfamiliar, were printed in four parts for unaccompanied choral singing: the congregation was to join in if it could. 'Congregational singing of hymns is much to be desired; but, though difficult to obtain, it is not permissible to provoke it by undignified music' (PC 410: Appendix, 5). Bridges set out this argument at greater length in an article on hymns, published also in 1899. He pointed out that 'the ecstasy of listening to music, and the enthusiasm of a crowd who are all singing or shouting the same hymn or song are emotions of quite different value and nature'. In the latter case, the emotion was that of 'the average man, or one rather below the average, the uneducated, as St. Augustin says the weaker, mind; and that in England is, at least artistically, a narrow mind and a vulgar being' (Bridges, 1899–1900: 43, 47). The answer, he felt, was to find music that was 'at once dignified, sacred, and popular'; and in a brief historical conspectus of hymn tunes, he rejected all tunes later than the Restoration period as unfit for the purpose. He had compiled *The Yattendon hymnal* on these principles, though adding seven new tunes composed in archaic style by Wooldridge. But the new tunes and texts did not catch on in a popular sense. As Benson pointed out in 1915, 'the decision in such a matter lies with the people, who have not hitherto responded heartily to the elevated appeal of Bridges' verse' (:448–9).

Bridges continued to attack current standards. In a letter to the Church Music Society in 1911, which they printed as an 'occasional paper', he wrote:

It seems to me that the clergy are responsible. If they say that the hymns (words and music) which keep me away from the church draw others thither, and excite useful religious emotions ... all I can urge is that they should have at least *one* service a week where people like myself can attend without being moved to laughter.

A book such as *Hymns ancient and modern*, he said, 'fills the sensitive worshipper with dismay so that there are persons who would rather not go inside a church than subject themselves to the trial' (Bridges, 1911; quoted Routley, 1957: 138). On similar grounds he also led a reform in the chanting of psalms, which will be discussed later.

Although Bridges gave nominal support to congregational hymn singing, his distinction between 'sensitive' and 'vulgar' worshippers lent credence to those who complained that the worship of the Church of England had become an exclusive preserve of the upper classes. Quite simply, it was impossible for a congregation in an ordinary parish church to achieve standards of musicianship that would satisfy his aesthetic sensibilities.

Certain exceptional parishes in the London suburbs, with determined leadership, were able to attract a congregation, chiefly resident outside the parish boundaries, that would support and even take part in an uncompromisingly artistic, perfectionist form of worship. Such churches were invariably Anglo-Catholic. One of them was St Mary-the-Virgin, Primrose Hill, Hampstead, where Percy Dearmer was inducted in 1901. The congregation was already accustomed to Gregorian psalm tones and plainsong hymns. Dearmer, a purist among ritualists, appointed G. H. Palmer as choirmaster to teach the choir to sing Gregorian chant 'properly' (N. Dearmer: 118). He began weekly congregational practices, at which (in contrast to the situation in the diocese of Wakefield) *only* the psalms were practised. New hymns and tunes were tried out at services, with the help and advice of Ralph Vaughan Williams, and these became the nucleus of *The English hymnal* (1906) which Dearmer and Vaughan Williams edited together. In 1909 Martin Shaw was appointed organist. 'I really believe', he wrote, 'that S. Mary's, Primrose Hill, was the only church in London where, for instance, the popular weak Victorian hymn-tune was never heard' (N. Dearmer: 164). He and Dearmer published *The English carol book* in 1913, and, with Vaughan Williams, *Songs of praise* in 1925 and *The Oxford book of carols* in 1928. These books between them certainly add up to the greatest contribution to parish church music in the twentieth century, despite the fact that they have never been adopted for regular use in more than a small proportion of Anglican churches.

The English hymnal took a very strong line in its selection of hymns and tunes and in its advice about singing them. It was a refreshing reaction to Victorian attitudes which was eagerly welcomed by the sophisticated. In the preface, both Dearmer and Vaughan Williams clearly set out their aim of improving popular taste. 'The English Hymnal is a collection of the best hymns in the English language', began Dearmer. 'It is not a party-book, expressing this or that phase of negation or excess ... We therefore offer the book to all broad-minded men, in the hope that every one will find within these pages the hymns which he rightly wants' (PC 411: iii). The qualification 'rightly' was necessary. This was a book of the 'best', not the most popular hymns; 'we have attempted to redress those defects in popular hymnody which are deeply felt by thoughtful men; for the best hymns of Christendom are as free as the Bible from the self-centred sentimentalism, the weakness and unreality which mark inferior productions' (:v).

But it was obviously easier to introduce new texts than new tunes. In the section of the preface dealing with the music, Vaughan Williams asserted that the tunes were 'intended to be essentially congregational in character ... Where there is congregational singing it is important that familiar melodies should be employed.' But, he went on, 'the task of providing congregations with familiar tunes is difficult; for, unfortunately, many of the tunes of the present day which have become familiar and, probably merely from association, popular with congregations are quite unsuitable to their purpose. More often than not they are positively harmful to those who sing and hear them' (:x). He therefore had taken upon himself the duty of providing better tunes than those that were popular, in the hope that 'many clergymen and organists are now realizing their responsibility in this matter, and will welcome a tune-book in which enervating tunes are reduced to a minimum ... It is indeed a moral rather than a musical issue.' He conceded that 'it is not by any means necessarily bad music that is popular. The average congregation likes fine melody when it can get it, but it is apt to be undiscriminating' (:vi).

Dearmer and Vaughan Williams did not, like Bridges, pointedly dissociate themselves from the common man. But they were sure that their taste was better than the common man's, and that once he had been made familiar with the superior texts and tunes now offered him, he would prefer them to his 'old favourites'; so that the new popular taste would also be good taste. At its best their ideal was shown in such a tune as 'Sine nomine', by Vaughan Williams himself (ex. 87). It was a genuinely congregational tune if ever there was one. But it treated the congregation in the way they had become used to being treated – as an element in a musical performance. In this case the organ, not the choir, was the essential element that turned their singing into great music – for it is no less – and supplied the rhythmic drive they needed to support them; the famous 'bump' on the first beat prevented the delayed or ragged start that sensitive musicians so often complained of in hymn singing. Vaughan Williams included another setting of the tune for unaccompanied choir. A 'simpler alternative tune' by Fuller-Maitland for the same hymn was added, while Barnby's tune went into the Appendix, Part II, for 'additional tunes which do not enter into the general scheme of this book' – in other words, Victorian tunes too popular to be ignored.* But 'Sine nomine' overshadowed the other tunes and soon replaced them as the accepted melody for 'For all the saints'.

The tunes were drawn from far and wide. Many unknown old tunes, from the continent as well as Britain, were revived; a lot of plainsong melodies were included. Vaughan Williams found a fertile source of new tunes in English folk song. Although folk songs have been turned into hymn tunes at every period of our history, the motive in this case was new: it was not so much to take advantage of familiar tunes by allying them to religious words, as to bring in unfamiliar tunes from a fresh and native stock. Old folk tunes that were still popular, for instance as nursery rhymes, were avoided, because of their associations. Two of the most successful matchings of this kind were 'Forest Green' with 'O little town of

---

* Vaughan Williams called this appendix the Chamber of Horrors (Hutchings, 1973: 41).

Bethlehem', and 'Kingsfold' with 'I heard the voice of Jesus say'. These tunes had been popular only in the distant past, but they have become popular once again.

A very different matter was to admit tunes of contemporary popular style. The editors included some from American or Welsh Methodist sources used in the Moody and Sankey revival meetings, but they confined them to a section for 'mission services', where, in the revised edition of 1933, they were marked 'not for ordinary use' (Routley, 1964: 201). Such tunes were more strongly rhythmical, frankly cheerful, and low-brow than had been thought seemly in the average Victorian church, though there were high-church precedents for them, for instance in the 'St. Alban's Appendix' to the *Hymnal noted* (ex. 68).

The editors, following *The Yattendon hymnal*, were scrupulous in preserving the original forms of both texts and tunes wherever possible; few other hymn books have imitated this practice, and the editors of *Hymns ancient and modern revised* gave a reasoned defence of their policy of revising texts and tunes (PC 417: vii, ix). This admirable standard in *The English hymnal* often proved an obstacle to the use of the book, for the recovered 'correct' version of a tune was difficult to impose on a congregation that already knew the tune in an altered form.

Vaughan Williams made several important suggestions about 'the manner of performance' (this phrase showed an unconscious acceptance of the Victorian transformation in the nature of hymn singing). The pitch was kept low to encourage the congregation, who were advised to sing invariably in unison. Expression marks were omitted, 'as it is considered that subtleties of expression are entirely unsuitable for congregational singing' (:xv). Metronome tempo marks were provided, as it was felt that hymns were generally sung 'much too fast' in English churches (:xiv).

The editors must have recognised that their plea for primarily congregational singing would meet with opposition from choirs, and from the musical profession generally. When Dearmer said to the organist of St Mary-the-Virgin (Shaw's predecessor) 'I think at last the people are beginning to join in that hymn', it is said that the organist replied 'Oh, then I'll change it' (F. Stephens: 41). They accordingly provided various compromises between choral and congregational singing. Some verses were marked for 'unison singing' – that is, with the accompaniment on the organ only; while in tunes designed primarily for unison, such as 'Sine nomine', a choral setting was provided for certain verses (ex. 87). Antiphonal singing between choir and congregation was suggested in the preface. But the most fruitful invention was what would later be known as the 'faburden' or 'faux-bourdon' setting – an old word revived with a new meaning. The tune, marked 'people's part', was sung in unison, while the choir sang (or the organ played) a four-part version with the same tune in the tenor part. This allowed many of the early harmonisations of psalm tunes in East and Ravenscroft to be restored in their original form. It also brought into prominence a treble part which was not the tune, and which began to be thought of as a 'descant'. During the First World War, when male voices were scarce, this type of setting was especially convenient. All the men present, whether in the choir or not, combined with higher voices to sing the tune, while the women and children who formed the only numerous part of the choir sang an upper part. This simplified form reduced the setting to two voice parts, the 'tune' and the 'descant', the latter sung by the choir trebles and generally higher than the tune, while the rest of the harmony was supplied by the organ. More prominent, even spectacular descant parts were written. Hymn tune descants became popular in about 1916, according to Scholes (1947: 548): they were also useful in boys' public schools, where most of the voices tended to be either baritones of unstable quality, or trebles. Special collections of descants began to appear, and many hymn books provided descants with the tunes (ex. 88).

The English hymnal really represents a compromise between the two goals of reform, both of which it pursued with unashamed vigour. The Moody–Sankey tunes would hardly have appealed to Vaughan Williams: they surely stand for a principle of Percy Dearmer's, in the Mackonochie tradition, from which he would not budge for any merely musical consideration: as he said, the book was to 'suit the needs of learned and simple alike' (PC 411: iii). In return he was willing to allow austere tunes by Tallis and Lawes, and such patently choral settings as Bach's chorale harmonisations or that ideal partsong, Vaughan Williams's 'Down Ampney'. The editors would not admit any incompatibility. 'It is a great mistake to suppose that the result [of the choir giving way to the congregation] will be inartistic', wrote Vaughan Williams. 'A large body of voices singing together makes a distinctly artistic effect, though that of each individual voice might be the opposite' (PC 411: xii). And indeed the two goals were both served by some tunes, most triumphantly by 'Sine nomine'.

Although Dearmer might say *The English hymnal* was 'not a party-book', it seemed to many Anglicans so extremely Anglo-Catholic as to be unusable. Five hymns in particular were objected to because they contained words of 'direct invocation of saints', and Charles Gore, bishop of Birmingham, though a high churchman, actually banned the use of the book in his diocese. A special edition was issued without the offending hymns, but the original edition remained the standard one (N. Dearmer: 182–5). There is no doubt that the book's theological stance was a bar to its widespread use. Many of its new texts and tunes have become popular largely through their adoption in other, more moderate hymn books, sometimes with altered words. But its influence on twentieth-century hymnody, though often indirect, has been enormous.

In the year of publication of *The English hymnal*, 1906, came the foundation of the Church Music Society, after an abortive attempt in 1897–1900. The chairman was Henry Hadow, a prominent academic musician. Its avowed object was to facilitate 'the selection and performance of the music which is most suitable for different occasions of divine worship, and for choirs of varying powers'. Of course, the question of what music was 'most suitable' was precisely the issue that would impede its efforts. But since the Society was concerned with cathedrals quite as much as with parish churches, it is perhaps not surprising that its goals were at first mainly for higher artistic standards rather than for congregational participation. Its most successful and important work, in fact, was the publication and dissemination of cathedral music of the sixteenth and early seventeenth centuries, including a correct edition of Tallis's responses.

The changing objectives of the society are shown in its series of occasional papers. The first of these, by J. A. Fuller-Maitland, was called 'The need for reform in church music', and dwelt primarily on the superior quality of the music of the sixteenth and seventeenth centuries and the desirability of reviving it, both in cathedrals and in parish churches. Much of the music currently in use, Fuller-Maitland wrote, appeared to be designed for 'the lower class of domestic servant' (1910: 13). He had perhaps forgotten that domestic servants outnumbered their masters and mistresses in most parishes, and that even these ladies and gentlemen were not, as a rule, noted for their appreciation of early English church music. Bridges's letter *About hymns* came next. Walford Davies, in a paper published in 1913, offered a different ideal of excellence, suggesting greater use of the music of German composers from Bach to Brahms. Hadow followed with a paper on 'Hymn tunes', in which he not only stated 'the characteristics by which we may distinguish the better from the worse' (:6), but provided a list of recommended hymn tunes and versions of hymn tunes. Of 328 approved tunes and versions, 267 were to be found in the *English hymnal*, 134 in the *Oxford hymn book* (1907), 168 in the unsuccessful 1904 revision of *Hymns ancient and modern*, and only 94 in the old edition of *Hymns ancient and modern*, which was the one actually used in the great majority of churches (:14–24). We have here an unequivocal effort to tell people what they should like. Hadow, like Vaughan Williams, 'firmly believed' that 'the noblest tunes become also the most widely beloved', and he had no doubt about his ability to identify the 'noblest' tunes, which in practice excluded most of those composed in the Victorian era.

The World War brought the winds of change to the Church Music Society as to many other institutions. A series of shorter, more practical papers was begun in 1917, with much greater emphasis on the people's part in church music. The first, 'Music in village churches', was anonymous; the second, 'Music in larger country and in smaller town churches', was by George Gardner; the third, 'Music in parish churches: a plea for the simple', was by Harvey Grace. All conveyed a similar message. 'Let us at once divest ourselves of the deep-rooted idea that all village services must be modelled upon those of cathedrals: it is the pit into which many fall, and it is the main cause of failure to inspire the worshippers' (*Music in village churches*: 3). 'There is likely to be a demand for a much more congregational type of service' (Grace, 1917: 9): the difficulties experienced during the war were likely to continue thereafter. Hymns should be sung generally in unison. A few 'simple faux-bourdons in two parts' (in other words, tunes with descants) were recommended for village churches. The lists of recommended choir music showed few signs of the revival of Elizabethan music. Apart from Marbeck and plainsong, most of the suggested music was of recent composition. A good deal of criticism was now heaped on the Victorian choral revival. 'As regards the majority of English churches, it cannot be said that, in the opinion of competent and up-to-date musicians, the results achieved have been commensurate with the labour expended' (Gardner, 1917: 11).

In the same year, 1917, that saw the publication of these pamphlets, a new movement began in the Cirencester neighbourhood: the hymn festival. Nine hundred people assembled on a Sunday evening after practising twenty hymns in their parishes, and sang them *en masse*. As a kind of rival to the regional choir festival the hymn festival flourished in the interwar period (*Hymn festivals*).

The report on *The worship of the Church* in the following year articulated the desire for a style of worship that was a simple expression of popular devotion. Meanwhile another of the archbishops' committees was preparing a report on church music. Many of this committee were leading members of the Church Music Society. The report, which appeared in 1922 with the title *Music in worship*, stated unequivocally that 'the ideal in all parish churches is congregational singing', and set out a number of practical proposals to bring about this object.

Much of this report was the work of Sydney Nicholson (Pl. 32), organist of Westminster Abbey since 1918, and it was he who took the lead in its implementation. Two parallel organisations were founded. The School of English Church Music, inaugurated in 1927 and registered as a limited company in 1930, was to provide information and guidance to church choirs all over the country, which could become affiliated to the school for an annual fee of £1. By the end of 1928, 105 choirs had joined: the number had risen to over 700 by 1932, to 1,500 in 1939, and to 3,000 in 1955. From January 1931 a periodical, *English Church Music*, was issued (its predecessor had been a newsletter sent to member choirs), and in March 1931 the first choir music book was published. From 1930 there was a triennial series of festivals at the Albert Hall or the Crystal Palace, when member choirs combined under Nicholson's direction. Cosmo Lang, Archbishop of York, was the first president, and continued in office when he became Archbishop of Canterbury. In 1936 he decided to institute a new diploma in church music, called the Archbishop of Canterbury's Diploma in Church Music, which was to be administered by the school: it was available only to qualified organists and choir trainers. In 1945 the school became the Royal School of Church Music (B. Simpson: 52, 88, 122–33, 298; Grove, 1954: vii, 525).

Nicholson's second foundation, to which he devoted much of his private fortune, was the College of St Nicholas, Chislehurst, which was opened in 1929 as a training school for church music. A boys' choir school was formed; students resided in the college, and there were also courses for ordinands. Daily services were held at the college at 7.30 a.m. and 7.00 p.m., using all types of music, including plainsong two days a week. The college choir also sang the services at St Sepulchre, Holborn. The Chislehurst buildings were closed in 1939, and the college merged with the school. In 1954 the joint institutions moved to Addington Palace, Croydon, a former residence of the archbishops of Canterbury, and there the R.S.C.M. continues to flourish (the separate name 'College of St Nicholas' was dropped in 1953). A prominent and important part of its work is a series of residential and non-residential courses offered throughout the year (B. Simpson: 89–100, 341; Grove, 1954: vii, 526; Castle: 7–8).

327

Nicholson's foundations had, from the beginning, the full support of the highest Church authorities as well as of the Church Music Society and the leading church musicians of the day. The R.S.C.M. differs from Ouseley's foundation at Tenbury in the fact that from the first its emphasis had been on the parish church rather than the cathedral. It owed its origins chiefly to the impetus for reform of parish church music that had arisen during the First World War, with its concern for services in which everybody could take a meaningful part. Nevertheless the activities of the school, especially in its earlier years, were in practice largely devoted to the improvement of *choral* music. This was perhaps inevitable, because the affiliated members of the school were not parish churches or their congregations, but parish choirs, who were of course more interested in enhancing their own activities than in learning how to subordinate their singing to that of the congregation. Moreover the leading musicians of the day, who were invited to advise and instruct the member choirs, had all been trained as cathedral musicians, including Nicholson himself, despite the fact that he resigned his post at Westminster Abbey in order to devote all his time to his foundations. These professional musicians travelled the country advising, coaching and judging local choirs. Regional chapters were formed, and local festivals organised, carrying on the tradition of the diocesan choral meetings (Pl. 35).

So it came about that the work of the school and college tended to reinforce the Victorian ideal of the fully choral service, though with some modifications. A clear statement of Nicholson's policy is contained in a pamphlet, *Principles and recommendations*, which he prepared in 1941. The 'principles' dealt with technical standards of choir singing; clearness and correct emphasis of words; 'proper rendering of the simpler parts of the service' (responses, amens, and so on) by the choir: care in the choice of choir music; and leadership of the congregation, whether in singing or saying. The 'recommendations' mainly dealt with which portions of the service should be said, sung in monotone or unison, or sung in harmony. These marked a substantial reduction in the amount of music by comparison with the typical Victorian practice. Nevertheless, the central part of the service was still choral in conception: this was no return to eighteenth-century tradition. The only one of the 18 'recommendations' to mention hymns was one discouraging the use of processional hymns before and after communion.

Choirs were, indeed, reluctant to give up the standing that they had gained in Victorian times, nor were most congregations eager to replace them. Despite all the pressure for more congregational music, 'the average organist is still tempted to take as his model the services to be heard in a neighbouring cathedral', as Edith Stewart wrote in 1933 (:3). 'One often finds the erroneous idea that where there is good "choir-singing" there cannot be good congregational singing, but it would be extremely difficult to find a satisfactory reason', wrote Clifford Roberts in 1931 (:42). He himself put forward one reason: 'An old-fashioned respectability seems to demand that people should sing in church, if at all, in something less than a quarter voice.' A more comprehensive discussion of the problem was provided by Stuart Morgan in *Music in the village church* (1939), with a foreword by Nicholson. Morgan, who was rector of West Chelborough, attacked the cathedral model for country churches, which he felt was still predominant. The standard service music, as set out (for example) in *The cathedral prayer book* (PC 408), 'is the only one that they have ever sung [in country churches]. It is for them the "proper" music for divine service. I don't suppose that an organist could even vary one of the chords which inevitably accompany the creed when it is sung on G without the people feeling that something not quite sacred had been introduced into the service.' This music was 'founded on the mistaken notion that what was right for cathedral choirs must be right for country congregations, and it has fixed on us – for all time unless we do something about it – the mannerisms and fashions of' the Victorian age (S. Morgan: 15–16).

The anthem and the canticle setting are another area in which parish churches have continued to imitate cathedrals. Large numbers of works for four-part choir with or without organ have continued to be printed by Novello, Boosey & Hawkes and other publishers. The *Musical Times* supplements, until very recent years, consisted in the main of anthems for SATB unaccompanied, generally of moderate difficulty so that many parish choirs could sing them. Anthems for unison voices have appeared from time to time, but until about 1953 they were a rarity.

In the year of the Festival of Britain, 1951, the R.S.C.M. organised a scheme by which affiliated parish choirs sang the services at the Festival church, St John, Waterloo Road, London. Each choir was asked to send in a short list of music ordinarily in use, from which a committee of the R.S.C.M. made a selection. The resulting list of anthems and services, summarised in Table 16 (see p. 287), is thus more varied than the average parochial repertory of the time, since the committee wished to avoid too much repetition of the same music. The choice also no doubt reflects the policy of the R.S.C.M.: for example, it includes two services and four anthems by Sir Sydney Nicholson. In spite of this, the proportion of sixteenth- and seventeenth-century works is still much smaller than of the nineteenth and twentieth centuries. More than one third of the 116 choirs sang the canticles to chants only: this was attributed to 'the desire in parishes for congregations to join in the canticles' (*English Church Music* XXI, 1951: 30).

A significant attempt at a compromise between choir and congregation in the twentieth century has been the hymn–anthem, or anthem based on a well known hymn tune in which the congregation can join. There were precedents for this form in the elaborate psalm tune settings of the sixteenth century, in William Lawes's unique 'Psalmes to the common tunes' (MS 87), and in occasional later examples, such as Sterndale Bennett's 'Lord, who shall dwell?', introducing the psalm tune 'St. Mary'. But a more immediate model was probably certain cantatas of Bach. Stanford composed two, both in *Hymns ancient and modern revised* (nos. 162, 527); his pupil Charles Wood produced a whole series of compositions based on the Genevan and English psalm tunes (Long: 378), and Edward Bairstow also explored the possibilities of the form (:415–16). Some hymn–anthems have been written for grand occasions with massed voices, such as Vaughan Williams's setting of 'Old Hundredth', written for the coronation of Queen Elizabeth

329

II in 1953. Others, like Holst's 'Turn back, O man' and Harris's 'O what their joy', have been effective in parochial use.

In 1976, only one in three of the Sussex churches canvassed had anthems 'regularly'; others had them only on special occasions such as Christmas and Easter (Appendix 2, Table 4). The Alternative Services, Series 2 and 3, provide for hymns or anthems to be sung by the choir during the communion of the people. Parish choirs tend to choose anthems from the cathedral repertory that are within their technical capability, in preference to simple anthems specially composed for parochial use.

After the Seond World War, the archbishops once again set up a committee to consider the use of music in worship. Its report appeared in 1951 under the title *Music in church*, and was in effect a revision of the 1922 report. It gave still greater emphasis to congregational participation, and the R.S.C.M., responding to its demands, issued in 1953 a new statement of policy. 'In future encouragement and advice ... will no longer be offered solely, or even mainly to organists and choirs but also to clergy and congregations' (B. Simpson: 284). But Nicholson's *Principles and recommendations* were still being issued to affiliated choirs in 1976, with only minor revisions. In practice the scheme of courses offered, for example, in 1974–5 shows that the R.S.C.M. has continued to be, in the main, an organisation for the training and guidance of choirs, choirmasters, and organists.

Chanting the psalms

The twentieth century inherited from the nineteenth the vexed question of Gregorian versus Anglican chants, which unfortunately has continued to be a highly charged political issue in the Church (*Music in church*: 34; Routley, 1964: 108). But it has been overtaken by larger issues. A second revolution in the principles of chanting has taken place, and the value of congregational chanting has been called into question. The Victorians had abandoned the pretence that the whole of a chant could be sung in strict tempo, and had divided it into reciting sections in free rhythm (which they had tended to gabble through as quickly as possible) and 'strict tempo' sections which began with an 'accented syllable' near the end of the recitation. The method was fully explained in *The cathedral psalter*. But the new form of distortion that this produced soon had its critics, particularly among those for whom the language meant more than the music. Several attempts were made, even before 1900, to find a way of chanting that would not distort the natural rhythms of speech: for example Francis Pott's *Free rhythm psalter* (PC 409). The free-rhythm chanting that was prevailing in Roman Catholic churches, and was made official by papal edict in 1903, was probably an influencing factor. The spearhead of the reform of Anglican chanting was Robert Bridges. He conducted a thorough historical study of chanting, both to Latin and English texts, and an analysis of the poetic structure of the psalms in Hebrew and in the prayer book translation. His conclusion was that the chant must be regarded as a flexible series of musical notes or chords, in which the duration of each chord is strictly dependent on the rhythm of the syllable or syllables to which it is sung. The words themselves must be chanted with the natural rhythm of slow reading; there must be no difference between the speed of recitation and that of the 'measured' part of the chant. The arbitrary 'accented syllable' disappeared. The musical accents remained, and the psalms must be pointed so that verbal accents corresponded with them; but they played no part whatever in determining the lengths of time actually taken up by the successive notes or chords of the chant (Bridges, 1910–12).

These theories were tried out at New College, Oxford, under Hugh Allen, and at the Temple Church, London, under Walford Davies. A number of psalters appeared later, based on these principles, of which the most important were *The Oxford psalter* (1929), edited by Henry Ley, Stanley Roper and C. Hylton Stewart, and *The parish psalter* (1928) edited by Sydney Nicholson. *The parish psalter* had sold over 30,000 copies by 1939 (S. Morgan: 45), and has continued to make headway (see Appendix 2, Table 12). Of course, the changes concerned cathedrals quite as much as parish churches; indeed it is arguable that speech-rhythm chanting can only be attempted with advantage by choirs of trained singers who are able to devote a great deal of time to its rehearsal. As sung by the choir of King's College Chapel, Cambridge, for example, it is exquisite, in spite of the inherent contradiction between the square-cut tunes and harmonies of eighteenth- and nineteenth-century Anglican chants and the lack of regularly recurring accents in their performance.

When speech-rhythm chanting is applied to parish churches, there is a more serious conflict. Even if a parish choir can, with skilful direction and great expenditure of effort, achieve a good effect, it is almost impossible for a congregation to do so, even if it is prepared to rehearse the psalms at a congregational practice. In 1939 *The parish psalter* was introduced at a country parish church, 'with the usual results – some people complained that they could not sing, others claimed that they had been driven away from church' (*English Church Music* IX, 1939: 120). 'The countryman is not going to believe readily that there was anything wrong with the old way, to which he has been accustomed all his life' (S. Morgan: 57). But there was more involved than mere conservatism and obstinacy. Speech-rhythm chanting was not only unfamiliar; it was totally unlike anything that the ordinary person had ever sung, or recognised as music. Without an underlying, unvarying beat to guide him, he was lost.

The movement towards speech-rhythm chanting thus produced, in many parish churches, a head-on collision between the two principles which we have so often seen in conflict: the principle of artistic perfection in the offering of praise, and the principle that all have a right to take part in that offering. A large number of churches went on using the old *Cathedral psalter*, and have continued to do so to this day (see Appendix 2, Table 12). An alternative was the *New cathedral psalter* (PC 412), which had appeared in 1910, edited by C. H. Lloyd, precentor of Eton College. Its method of pointing was similar to its predecessor's – 'even worse' in Long's opinion (:397) – and it offered a number of alternative typographical methods of showing the pointing, of which one using bold type proved the most popular. There were editions for 'cathedral', 'parish church', and 'village church' use, but they differed only in the choice and pitch of the chants. The 'parish church' edition had reciting notes up to D, the 'village church' edition only up to C. Other psalters on conservative principles have continued to appear. However one may deplore the distortions they produce in English prose, they are based on a compromise which does enable congregations to chant. According to an observer in 1960, the congregation joined in only where *The cathedral psalter* was used (Luff: 70–1). If the compromise is rejected, one is forced to the conclusion reached by the archbishops' committee on church music in 1951: 'It may be a regrettable fact, but it has to be admitted that the psalms, whether they be sung to plainsong tunes or to Anglican chants, do not lend themselves readily to singing by the average congregation' (*Music in church*: 34). The same opinion had been formed a hundred years earlier by an impartial observer, at a time when the movement for congregational chanting was making some headway in the face of growing choral professionalism (Engel: 47).

A possible compromise has emerged in the psalm settings of Joseph Gélineau, a French catholic priest, which have been translated into English psalm versions in the same rhythm by Dom Gregory Murray (ex. 89). The congregational part is limited to a short antiphon, repeated after every verse to a unison phrase accompanied by the organ. The choir chant the actual psalm, either in harmony or in unison, and although the chant does contain reciting notes of indefinite length, the number of syllables to be sung to them does not vary as much as in the ordinary prose psalms, and the rhythm of the words is carefully chosen to make chanting easy. The Gélineau psalms have been widely used, and some have been reprinted in more than one Anglican hymn book.

Parish communion

For a number of reasons (Davies: v, 309–19), the twentieth century has tended to restore the communion service to the central place in worship, a position which had been occupied by morning prayer during most of the history of the Church of England after the Reformation. As in the case of other changes discussed, a strong impetus in this direction was given by the experiences of the First World War, both on the front and at home. Recognising this, the Church Music Society's paper on *Music in village churches* said, in 1917, 'Holy communion ... is becoming the chief service in an increasing number of churches' (:6). There were few settings available that were simple enough for village church use. Apart from the inimitable Marbeck, several recent adaptations from plainsong were recommended, together with Martin Shaw's *Modal setting* and ordinary settings by Arthur Somervell and Sydney Nicholson.

The centrality of the communion was more and more often expressed in a new type of service called 'parish communion', which was first tried out by A. G. Hebert in the rural parish of Temple Balsall in 1913 (Hebert: 261). Hebert defined 'parish communion' as 'the celebration of the Holy Eucharist, with the communion of the people, in a parish church as the chief service of the day, or better, as the assembly of the Christian community for the worship of God . . . On Sundays the most suitable hour will generally be not long before or after 9.0 a.m.' (:3). It allowed the congregation to communicate fasting. It was frequently followed by a 'parish breakfast', conceived as an equivalent of the love-feast or *agape* of the early Church, which happily connected a social function with worship and tended to bring the Church closer to the life of the people. In several ways, the service itself was altered, generally within the limits laid down in the prayer book, so as to involve the people more. At the offertory, representatives of the people, or even each member of the congregation, brought their offerings of bread and wine to the altar for consecration; the epistle was often read by a layman; the entire congregation sang in the responses; 'often babies in arms or small children accompany their parents to the communion rail, to be blessed perhaps by the priest as he moves along administering the sacrament' (Pierce: 4; quoted Davies: v, 320). Parish communion at first spread slowly, but after the publication of Hebert's book in 1937 it was much more widely adopted, and by 1965 had become 'almost the normative celebration of the Eucharist in the Church of England'. It had great practical advantages for families, and has been an important element in lessening tension between parties in the Church, since it is approved by both high and low churchmen (Davies: v, 321). (See Appendix 2, Table 8.)

The spread of parish communion drew attention to the inappropriate character of the elaborate music used in the late Victorian 'choral celebration', often adapted from a mass by a continental composer. In some Anglo-Catholic churches congregational settings based on plainsong, such as the *Missa de Angelis*, had been in use, and Marbeck's music had also been sung congregationally. J. H. Arnold addressed himself to the problem in a paper published by the Church Music Society in 1946, when evidently few congregations were as yet in the habit of singing the liturgy of the communion service. Besides plainsong and Marbeck, he named a few other unison settings, some with optional four-part harmony for the Sanctus and Agnus dei. 'The wise omission of special music for the creed (assuming the use of the ancient traditional melody, or Marbeck's tune) is becoming common practice' (:9): the traditional creed was embodied in all numbers of the Oxford Liturgical Series, which included settings by Byrd, Vaughan Williams, and Shaw. Arnold pointed out that there was no reason why choirmasters should not choose items from several different settings for one service; and this, increasingly, has been done.

The most successful of all modern settings has been Martin Shaw's *Anglican folk mass* (PC 413), which, according to David Lumsden, 'is almost as familiar as Marbeck's setting and just as effective for congregational use' (PC 423: v, xiii). Despite its name it has little relation to folk music, ancient or modern. It is an apparently simple but actually extremely subtle and artful work, carefully constructed to satisfy both the fastidious critic on the look-out for false accents and the parish choirmaster looking for an easy tune to learn. (The year of its composition, 1917, was a critical one in our story.) Its style is based not so much on Marbeck as on the accompaniments to Marbeck composed by Shaw himself, and by others or the accompaniments to plainsong hymns in *The English hymnal*. In these the notes of the unbarred modal melody are treated as equal units. Two or three of them (sometimes more) are grouped over a single chord, often by treating one as a passing note. This suggests momentarily a conventional tune in duple or triple time; it is soon interrupted, however, by the next grouping, sounding like part of another conventional tune. The chords vary in length, never in any constant pattern, so 'squareness' is avoided; at the same time they are so arranged that the first note of any group harmonised with a single chord is assigned to a stressed syllable. The result is 'flowing' and vaguely 'tuneful', but these characteristics are spurious in that they come not from the original melodies but from their modern interpretation and accompaniment. In Shaw's *Folk mass*, on the other hand (ex. 90), they are part of the music as originally conceived. An added quality making for ease of comprehension is the economic use of melodic materials. In the creed, for example, the entire melodic line is derived from bars 2–6 (bar 1 is traditional plainsong, but is well integrated into the rest). This style became, and still remains, the bread-and-butter of many high-church parochial services, where plainsong is extensively used. It is a trademark of Anglo-Catholic church music of the twentieth century. But few examples as distinguished as Shaw's *Folk mass* can be found. (See also ex. 63e, f.)

The relative novelty of congregational singing of the communion may have eased the acceptance, in this department, of music in the pop idiom. Geoffrey Beaumont's *Folk mass*, published in 1956 but attracting little attention until it was televised in October 1957 (le Huray, 1967b: 16), opened a new era in Anglican liturgical music. Its pop idiom was mild and somewhat old-fashioned, but still unmistakably crossed a stylistic boundary that had never been crossed before (ex. 91). The melodies were no more tuneful, no more repetitive, than those in Shaw's *Folk mass*; but instead of Shaw's studied avoidance of periodic rhythms, Beaumont provided an insistent bass, relentlessly pounding out the beats, generally repeating in a two-bar pattern, just as the double-bass did in small-band pop music of 1930 to 1950. This left the melody free to engage in mild syncopation from time to time, with no danger of the singers losing their way rhythmically. To make sure that the people would catch the tunes, Beaumont set almost the entire mass in the form of 'dictation', each phrase of two or three bars being sung by a cantor and immediately repeated note-for-note by the congregation. The priest's part is sung to Marbeck's music. It is a strange irony that lining out, used in the seventeenth century to help people sing the right text, should have been revived in the twentieth to help them sing the right music.

Soon after the appearance of Beaumont's *Mass*, he founded a group of composers and authors known as the Twentieth Century Church Light Music Group. One of its members, Patrick Appleford, produced in 1961 a *Mass of five melodies* 'in response to many requests for a setting in the idiom of modern light music which would not require the repetition by the people of phrases first sung by a cantor' (PC 422: preface). This, too, is made up of simple and commonplace tunes, which repeat themselves as much as Beaumont's, though not in a set dictation pattern.

Both Beaumont's and Appleford's settings of the communion have become part of the normal parish communion repertory, though still probably in a minority of churches. They have had few successors. The pop church music movement has flourished, but it has been found that hymnody is its natural place in the scheme of things. Even Beaumont's and Appleford's masses were constructed around tunes, which could easily be separated from their contexts and sung as hymn tunes; and, after all, the pop idiom has a far more natural affinity with the strophic, always popular form of the hymn than with the sacerdotal prose of the liturgy.

Liturgical experiment

After the débâcle of the 1928 prayer book, a number of experimental changes in the liturgy were tried out, despite the fact that they had no legal authority. 'After thirty years of increasing liturgical diversity in the Church of England conditions are favourable for the production of completely new forms', said *The Church of England Newspaper* on 5 July 1963. In 1965 a momentous step was taken by the Church Assembly, in the passing of the Prayer Book (Alternative and Other Services) Measure. Parliament had given the Assembly the authority to pass measures regulating the affairs of the Church, including the conduct of worship; any such measure was to be laid before parliament, and, on address from each house asking that it be presented to the king, would, on receiving the royal assent, have the force and effect of an act of parliament (Flindall: 344). The Prayer Book Measure was passed on 23 March 1965. It authorised the experimental use of services approved by the convocations of both provinces for stated terms not exceeding seven years, which could be extended for further terms, not exceeding fourteen years in all. Thus the Church had at last achieved the full sanction of the law for at least temporary changes in its liturgy. Under the terms of the measure, no form of service could be introduced in a parish church or in any church in a parish without the approval of the parochial church council, the body which had replaced the old parish vestry in most ecclesiastical matters. The services of the 1662 prayer book always remained as a lawful alternative to any new form of service.

The convocations of Canterbury and York lost little time in appointing a Liturgical Commission, which devised a series of alternative services, known as 'Series 1', which was authorised for use for seven years from 7 November 1966. During the next few years, two further series were published, generally with shorter periods of authorisation. Each series was more radical in its departures from the old liturgy than its predecessor. Some parish churches have accepted each new series soon after its appearance; others have chosen some services from one series, some from another; many have remained loyal to the 1662 or 1928 prayer book (see Appendix 2, Table 7.) A great many parishes, after discussion in the parochial church council, have tried to cater for strongly held differences of opinion by alternating two or more types of service from one Sunday to the next, or between two churches in the same parish.

Other types of experimentation, outside those officially authorised, have also continued. In some parishes the incumbent and parochial church council have together devised their own service to meet the local needs. Generally these services have little that is entirely new, but are eclectic combinations of passages from the various authorised alternatives. A popular type of service is called a 'family service', derived from the Sunday School meeting of earlier times. It is generally a simplified matins, designed for children as well as adults to appreciate, and the music will often be entirely restricted to hymns. It is in this type of service that pop music has made the greatest inroads (Pl. 37).

The new services have created an immediate problem for church musicians. For Series 1 and 2 the changes were sufficiently small to allow the adaptation of existing music, at least as an adequate temporary solution to the problem. But Series 3 offered virtually a new text, both for the communion service and for morning and evening prayer, in which new translations of the canticles were provided. Many composers eagerly responded to the challenge of setting the new texts to music, and the Royal School of Church Music provided an excellent clearing-house to inform choirmasters of what was available. The difficulties facing church musicians have been comparable to those at the time of the Reformation.

We are thus in the middle of a period of flux, both in the liturgy and in the music that accompanies it. Presumably the experiments will be followed by a new settlement, in which one or more forms of service will be permanently approved, and musicians will be able to begin building a body of music to go with them. Until that time, it would be not only wrong, but virtually impossible, to judge the long-term significance of current developments in liturgical music.

Changing the physical setting

The popularity of parish communion and the other liturgical experiments has brought out clearly the unsuitability of the traditional arrangement of churches for contemporary needs. The Victorian adaptation of the medieval plan had placed the altar, where the priest celebrated communion, at a great distance from the people, separated from them by choir and organ. The new need was for a plan in which priest, choir and people were intimately linked in a joint act of worship. A common solution in old churches was to set up an altar, temporary or permanent, at the east end of the nave and in front of the chancel screen: the chancel was then used only for weekday or early morning services at which few worshippers attended. Many new churches presented an opportunity for more radical experiments, in which the architectural design was based from the first on the assumption that parish communion would be the principal service (Addleshaw & Etchells: 237–42; see also Pl. 38).

The tradition of placing the choir in chancel stalls (although only a century old) has resisted many efforts to dislodge it, especially in medieval or Victorian churches where it so obviously suited the physical plan of the building (Pl. 36). In new churches, even those that have no separate chancel, choir stalls have sometimes been placed in the old position, between the congregation and the altar; but other schemes have been tried, including the eighteenth-century plan of putting the singers in a gallery. The Victorian preference for an enclosed organ in the north or south chancel has had few defenders in recent times, and many new churches have reverted to an organ in the west gallery. Electropneumatic or electronic organ actions have allowed the convenience of a remote console, so that the player can sit in a position where he has the best contact with the priest and the choir, while the sound can come from a different place chosen on acoustical principles. Since about 1970, however, the fashion in organ building has favoured mechanical action, which requires the console to be placed close to the pipes. There is great variety in the placing of choirs and organs, and there are many considerations to be taken into account in deciding such a complex question.

In many smaller churches the cost of keeping a pipe organ in repair has been found prohibitive: some, indeed, have never had a pipe organ. Nevertheless, two out of three churches in a rural area of Sussex had pipe organs in 1976 (Appendix 2, Table 1). Harmoniums are still used in some churches; Hammond or other electronic instruments are also frequently found. Pianos are becoming more common. In churches where pop music styles have been cultivated, the guitar is a natural accompaniment, especially at a 'family service'. Occasionally it is joined by other instruments (Appendix 2, Table 10 and 'Extracts from comments').

The Victorian ideal of a choir of some ten men and twenty boys in surplices has been eroded, but it is still there as an ideal, nurtured by the Royal School of Church Music. Only two parish churches still had choir schools in 1970: St James, Grimsby and St Mary, Reigate (Mould: 11). Another source of choirboys, the church school, is virtually extinct (*Music in church*: 10). Many less tangible reasons, some of them moral, have been put forward to explain the decline (Dakers: 98–111). But choirs continue to sing, especially in village churches. The decline in numbers was steepest just after the First World War. In rural Sussex the average choir was actually larger in 1976 than it was in 1922 (Appendix 2, Table 3). Of 25 churches in 1976, 2 had a choir of children only, 3 of men and women only, 1 of men and boys only, and 15 of men, women and children; the other 4 had no choir. In all there were slightly more women than men, by contrast with the situation in about 1950 (see Table 18).

Table 18. *Size and make-up of choirs in about 1950*

	Choirs	Boys	Girls	Men	Women	Total
Number in sample	244	2689	133	1429	665	4916
Percentage		*54.7*	*2.7*	*29.1*	*13.5*	*100.0*

Average size of choir: 20.1.

Source: Reports of the S.E.C.M. chief commissioner in *English Church Music*, for the periods Sept.–Nov. 1949 (:xx, 14), Dec. 1949–Feb. 1950 (:xx, 35), June–Nov. 1951 (:xxII, 10), Dec. 1951–Feb. 1952 (:xxII, 63). The choirs reported on included a small proportion (less than 10%) that were not in parish churches. The chief commissioner pointed out that choirs were not necessarily at full strength at the time of his visit, but there is no reason to suppose that their numbers were less than normal.

Most of these changes have tended to reinforce the move towards informality and congregational singing. A mixed choir without surplices is visibly closer to the people in character than a surpliced choir of boys and men. The congregation will be more inclined to sing with the choir, rather than listen to it, when it is placed behind them. They can add their own voices to the chorus of praise moving, so to speak, in an easterly direction, and the theatrical aspect of the robed choir appearing in the chancel is no longer present.

The problems have certainly been more severe in large towns, where the parish is no longer a viable or even recognisable unit in ordinary life. Clergy have often had to undertake strenuous publicity campaigns simply to inform their parishioners of the existence and activity of the parish church. With the declining number of churchgoers, many town parishes have been amalgamated and churches declared redundant: naturally this has happened most frequently in the older cities. In the City of London, many special uses have been found for parish churches that are no longer needed for parochial purposes. The Guild Churches Act (1952) set aside 16 City churches to provide for the needs of daily workers in the City by means of lunch-time services, and to serve as national centres for special religious causes. Most of the music heard in these churches is not of the 'parochial' type, but consists of concerts and organ recitals (see *English Church Music* XXVII (1959), 88–9).

The continuing practice of hymnody

In the seventeenth century, we found that the abolition of the *Book of common prayer* and its restoration sixteen years later had little effect on the practice of parish church music: people simply went on singing metrical psalms in the Old Version. In the twentieth century, changes more peaceful but hardly less drastic have been tried out in the liturgy, and they have affected liturgical music: but the oldest form of Anglican parish church music, hymn singing, has again continued without a break (Appendix 2, Table 5). In the alternative services, Series 2 and 3, points are indicated for the singing of hymns.

An undoubted trend in hymns, beginning with *The English hymnal* and greatly accelerating in recent years, has been towards informality of text and tune. In the effort to engage the minds and hearts, as well as the voices, of ordinary people, the majestic periods, the elaborate metaphors, the obscure references, and the archaic diction of the Victorian hymn have been jettisoned.

> Father eternal
>   Lord of the ages,
> You who have made us,
>   You who have called us,
> Look on your children
>   Gathered before you,

Worship they bring you,
Father of all.

(1st verse of a hymn by G. B. Timms.
PC 429: no. 45)

As in the Series 3 alternative liturgy, God is often addressed as 'you' rather than 'thou', and the whole effect is of a conversation with a neighbourly adviser rather than a deferential approach to a distant Almighty. It is not surprising that a more conversational tone has also been sought in the music.

Songs of praise (1925), the second hymn book prepared by Dearmer, Vaughan Williams and Shaw, drew on a wide range of religious poetry of a kind that the Victorians would not have considered solemn enough for church: and this was the reaction of many. For the music further recourse was had to English folk songs, and other tunes of homely, cheerful rhythm were provided. *The Oxford book of carols* (1928), by the same editors, was a further step in removing pomposity from hymn singing. 'Carols are songs with a religious impulse that are simple, hilarious, popular, and modern', began the preface. Carols, as opposed to Christmas hymns, had not been sung in church until the first carol service was presented at Truro cathedral in 1880. The point now made was that carols are indeed secular (some of those included had little direct connection with Christianity), but that they are suitable for use in church as well as in door-to-door singing, in private houses, in schools, or in concert halls. 'Groups of carols, both during and after a service, are a good way of marking Easter and other festivals, as well as Christmas', wrote the editors. 'On ordinary Sundays appropriate carols would form a sound and very popular substitute for anthems in many churches' (PC 415: 482). They even suggested a 'carol service' to be held every Sunday in the year. In practice carols have continued to be associated chiefly with Christmas, but the special tradition of Christmas carols allowed popular, informal verse to be sung for the first time in many parish churches, for instance, 'Tomorrow shall be my dancing day' (PC 415: no. 71). It was a precedent that would make it easier to accept more general informality in hymnody later on.

Hymns ancient and modern revised appeared in 1950. It had been largely edited by Sir Sydney Nicholson, who, however, had died in 1947. It was an excellent, but thoroughly conservative book: copyright difficulties prevented the incorporation of successful material from *The English hymnal* or other recent collections, even if the editors had been minded to include any. There were a number of new hymns and tunes, Nicholson himself being represented by one text and fifteen tunes, but they were only mildly advanced in idiom, and the bulk of the contents of the book remained Victorian, as Table 19 clearly shows. Yet in 1972 it was probably the most widely used Anglican hymn book (Long: 400; see also Appendix 2, Table 11). This fact serves as a reminder that the bulk of the Church has quietly continued in its old ways, leaving more spectacular developments to the eager minority. *Hymns ancient and modern revised* was purged of the more obviously 'Victorian' features: chromatic harmonies (in some tunes: see ex. 75), frequent *crescendos* and *diminuendos* (though some dynamic marks

Table 19. *Sources of hymn texts and tunes in* Hymns ancient and modern revised *(1950), arranged by decade*

| Period | Texts | | | Tunes | | |
| | English | Foreign | | British | Foreign | |
		Original	Translation		Original	Adaptation
Before 1541	1	118	1	1	60	2
1541–1550	...	...	...	...	4	....
1551–1560	...	...	...	1	9	3
1561–1570	2	1	...	5	1	6
1571–1580	...	...	...	1	...	...
1581–1590	...	...	...	1	2	...
1591–1600	1	1	...	3	3	...
1601–1610	...	...	...	...	7	...
1611–1620	...	...	...	5	1	1
1621–1630	...	...	1	12	6	...
1631–1640	5	2	1	4	1	...
1641–1650	3	2	...	...	7	...
1651–1660	2	3	...	...	5	...
1661–1670	3	2	...	...	6	...
1671–1680	5	3	...	...	7	...
1681–1690	3	5	...	1	7	...
1691–1700	3	3	...	1	6	...
1701–1710	9	2	...	13	5	...
1711–1720	12	2	...	3	1	...
1721–1730	1	1	...	3	3	4
1731–1740	8	12	2	4	8	...
1741–1750	18	3	1	6	6	5
1751–1760	12	1	...	3	2	...
1761–1770	4	1	...	11	2	1
1771–1780	17	2	...	6	2	1
1781–1790	6	3	...	13	6	2
1791–1800	2	...	...	8	4	...
1801–1810	8	2	...	2	2	1
1811–1820	9	1	...	1	3	...
1821–1830	39	2	...	4	2	...
1831–1840	22	...	21	10	6	...
1841–1850	35	...	23	9	5	6
1851–1860	34	2	51	23	4	33
1861–1870	69	...	28	79	1	40
1871–1880	45	...	7	67	...	13
1881–1890	11	...	6	20	1	9
1891–1900	13	...	8	8	...	4
1901–1910	13	1	5	24	...	19
1911–1920	9	...	1	20	...	5
1921–1930	12	...	...	13	...	5
1931–1940	10	...	16	12	...	12
1941–1950	21	...	5	32	...	23
Totals	457	175	175	429	195	195

For each hymn text, the earliest known published source was ascertained, and the hymn was counted in the decade of its publication in column 1 or 2, unless the date of its authorship was known to be much before its first publication. If the original hymn was in a foreign language it is counted in column 2, and also in column 3 by the date of the translation used in *Hymns ancient and modern revised*. Similarly with the tunes, except that column 6 counts the earliest known adaptation of the foreign tune to *any* English hymn text. The information is largely based on the notes in Frere & Frost (1962) except in the case of column 6. The total number of hymn texts, 632 (457 plus 175), is less by four than the numbered hymns in the book, because four hymns appear there twice (in longer and shorter versions). There are 624 tunes (429 plus 195): many are repeated with different hymns, but many hymns have alternative tunes.

---

were retained). The editors were 'concerned to provide a setting which should not be too elaborate to be rendered by a congregation supported by a choir of average ability' (PC 417: ix), an unexceptionable policy. The revolution in the treatment of plainsong hymns, begun in the 1904 edition (ex. 63e), was completed (ex. 63f). They had already been shorn of all regular accent, and of inappropriate tonal harmony, and a few notes in them had been treated as passing. Now, larger groups of notes were clustered together over a single chord, giving a smooth, supple effect quite different from the solemnity of the Victorian treatment.

In recent years the proprietors of *Hymns ancient and modern* and *The English hymnal* have both published supplements containing some of the most successful recent hymns not included in their collections (PC 426, 429).

The pop hymn movement in the Church of England was fairly launched with the broadcasting of Geoffrey Beaumont's tune 'Chesterton' from Martock parish church in October 1955 (Routley, 1964: 169). This and two other tunes were then incorporated in the *Folk mass*; collections of tunes by Beaumont and other members of the Twentieth Century Church Light Music Group appeared later on (PC 421, etc.). Routley shrewdly points out that the source of these tunes' effective style is the 'big tune' of the musical comedy (:170).

Beaumont and his followers set their pop tunes to traditional hymn texts. As Routley observed, 'invention in religious verse has lagged behind invention in music' (1964: 184). By contrast, Sydney Carter began to write religious lyrics that were in the ordinary, secular language of today, and when these were set to popular tunes the transformation of the hymn was complete. The best known of Carter's hymns is 'Lord of the dance' (ex. 92) which he set to an old American Shaker tune. It succeeds in dealing with a central religious theme with striking imagery, biblical reference, theological message, and yet without any of that remoteness from everyday modes of expression that had seemed an inevitable part of 'religion', especially Anglican religion.

It is astonishing how quickly these new styles have spread through the Church in the wake of the liturgical experiments, which have perhaps eased their passage. People can accept a wholly new worship experience where they would resist a jarring contrast between old and new. In little more than a decade many rural parish churches have taken pop music in their stride (see Appendix 2, Table 9). Some of the clergy have no doubt accepted it against their personal inclinations because of its probable appeal to the younger generation. Some professional musicians, brought up in the strictly conservative tradition symbolised by the Royal College of Organists, have still been anxious to remain open-minded. Allan Wicks, organist of Canterbury Cathedral, wrote in 1964:

A great step has been made in recent years on the use of pop music in church, and again I would not be exclusive about this; all I would say is that if you are going to have pop music, then let it be really pop and not a sort of sentimentalized and watered down concept of pop. The idea of the Church as something which continually takes the edge off things, spoils the fun of things, makes mediocre, is still very strong. (Wicks: 83)

Peter le Huray has drawn a distinction between pop liturgical music and the use of pop idioms in parts of the service that are designed for congregational singing. He disputes the prevailing notion that the congregation has the right to join in all parts of the service, and on these grounds rejects the masses of Beaumont and Appleford. But he does believe 'that there is room for experiment in two particular directions – the hymn and the psalm', and approves both Gélineau psalms (or other attempts along similar lines by Peter Tranchell) and the use of pop idiom in hymn tunes, where he favours the efforts of Malcolm Williamson (1967b: 17–18, 22–4).

Lionel Dakers, organist of Exeter cathedral, writing in 1970, drew a distinction between the music of Carter, Williamson, and Gélineau, which he treated as derivatives of 'the folk music style', and the work of Beaumont and his followers, which he classified as 'a thoroughly alien importation and a self-conscious parasite ... "Pop", together with the incidental noise and ironmongery which seems to be a necessary part of its presentation, can be quickly dismissed as an irrelevant and mercifully transient stunt' (:133). The foreword to Dakers's book was written by Gerald Knight, Nicholson's successor as director of the Royal School of Church Music, whom Dakers shortly afterwards succeeded in the same office. The School has had a difficult decision in drawing a line between the acceptable and the unacceptable, in its publications and in the advice it gives to member choirs, many of which still perform only traditional church music. It appears that the line has been drawn approximately where Dakers drew it in 1970.

The dilemma of the R.S.C.M., and of individual musicians and clergy, over its attitude to pop music is only one aspect of the present dilemma of the Church, which is forever caught between the need to be relevant and the need to preserve what is permanently valuable. But it also reflects that other old dilemma, peculiar to the realm of parish church music: should people be listening to the best possible music, or singing as best they can?

Summary and evaluation

In the earlier years of the twentieth century, efforts to improve church music generally took the form of improving the artistic quality of choral performance, both by changing the repertory (reviving the cathedral music of the Elizabethan and Jacobean periods) and by more sensitive singing, particularly of chanted psalms. These changes were exactly what was required for cathedral music, but they seemed less and less relevant for parish church music as the dominance of upper-middle-class and professional values receded. In retrospect it seems that the First World War was the turning point.

Most parish churches could no longer afford to be miniature cathedrals; most congregations, especially in towns, were no longer willing to defer to their social superiors; most people wanted to take part in the music, and in music which suited their own tastes and capacities. It is clear that the efforts of leading musicians to banish the Victorian hymn tune were misdirected, since this had been one of the few elements in the parish church service which the ordinary churchgoer could readily understand and take part in, and which the amateur local choir could lead with confidence. A similar mistake was the introduction of speech-rhythm pointing in the psalms. *Hymns ancient and modern* (*revised* or otherwise) and *The cathedral psalter* have survived in many parish churches through all the bewildering experiments of the last two generations; the standard Victorian setting of the responses has remained in most places where the prayer book service is still in use.

Between 1917 and 1965, then, in a context of increasing liturgical diversity, the main trend in parish church music was a decline in choralism with, on the whole, a survival of the Victorian repertory and style. Older and newer music were available, to be sure, but they made only modest inroads on the habits of most parish churches. It is significant that Erik Routley, the most knowledgeable and perceptive commentator on modern hymnody, said in 1964 that Cyril Taylor's 'Abbots Leigh', from the *BBC hymn book* (1951), was 'easily the most successful "new tune" since Vaughan Williams's "For all the saints" [1906]' (1964: 104). 'Abbots Leigh' (ex. 93a) is an entirely traditional tune with a fine melodic sweep, needing organ accompaniment. It would be unjust to call it Victorian, as it consciously avoids characteristics that have been perceived as faults in the typical Victorian tune. Yet it has nothing in it that would have surprised or dismayed the Victorians, and it does, in fact, bear an astonishingly close resemblance to an actual Victorian hymn tune, the anonymous 'St. Philip' from *Church hymns* (ex. 93b),* though it is surely an improvement on its model.

In 1949 A. S. Duncan-Jones, dean of Chichester, who was a veteran of the first archbishops' committee on church music, said to a meeting of the Church Assembly: 'The whole of the movement for the improvement of church music [in the twentieth century] was dominated by the idea that music in church is primarily an offering presented to God, and only secondarily for the edification of the congregation,' and must above all be 'good of its kind' (*English Church Music* xx, 1950: 11). This was a classic restatement of the traditional high-church point of view. But it was already out of tune with the times. The prevailing view is that of Canon H. M. Waddams: 'neither priest not organist nor choir has, nor can have, any other function than to help God's people to do the liturgy, to do their service.'

---

* As well as the opening phrases, compare bars 25–32 of ex. 93a with 9–16 of ex. 93b.

11   Past and present

The Church of England rejoices in two separate and distinct musical traditions. The older, the cathedral tradition, has provided for cultivation of the highest art, continuing a practice that has lasted a thousand years. Its growth has been, on the whole, slow and steady. The younger, the parochial tradition, took independent root only at the Reformation. It has flourished more fitfully, throwing off many shoots of curious shape, and has been grafted with alien matter. Its healthiest growths have survived to the present day.

In the middle ages parish church music, if any, was choral, and as close to cathedral music as resources permitted. The master stroke of the English reformation settlement was to allow for active congregational worship, but yet to retain a liturgical form. The same liturgy could be sung in cathedrals and spoken in parish churches. A new kind of singing was admitted, outside the liturgy, designed for the voices of the people. For more than two centuries parochial music largely consisted of the development of popular, metrical, strophic song; and, after many vicissitudes, this is again its chief resource.

But the division of benefits evolved in the Elizabethan settlement – high art music in the cathedrals, people's participation in the parishes – has never satisfied everybody. Some, in earlier times, wanted to abolish the cathedral service and make all worship popular: for a time they succeeded. Others, more prevalent in later times, wanted to go in the opposite direction, to make the parochial service, too, a form of art. They were prepared to silence the congregation, purchase an organ, and train a choir to provide singing of the desired standard. Beginning in the early eighteenth century, and culminating in the late nineteenth, there was a strong move to make the parish service once more resemble that of the cathedral.

Neither extreme has been acceptable in the long run. At the centre of efforts to find a compromise has been the parish priest. Though art and music have not typically been an important part of his make-up, he is an educated man, familiar with cathedral worship, and he knows that the parish church has a certain prestige not enjoyed by its nonconformist rivals. He has not generally been happy with untamed congregational singing. In the seventeenth century he treated it as something to be tolerated, but beneath his own dignity to support or take part in. In the eighteenth and nineteenth centuries he supported various plans to improve it, especially when the Methodists drew large numbers away from the established Church by the attraction of their singing.

On the other hand, the parish priest is not as a rule disposed to accept a totally vicarious service, where the choir sings everything on the people's behalf. In his pastoral work he is constantly made aware of the spiritual needs of his flock, and he sees that these can be partly satisfied by a service in which all can join. Singing can be a powerful release and expression of religious feeling, and he does not want his people to be deprived of it.

So the clergy have initiated or supported a continual series of efforts to improve the quality of congregational singing. These efforts have been motivated by simple practical needs. They have been to a great extent independent of theological positions taken by the leaders of parties within the Church. The conflicts about singing have not, in reality, arisen from theological issues, but from the inescapable fact that most people are not very musical. Critical standards have continued to rise with each generation, and have stayed far ahead of the slowly rising musical capacities of congregations. The standards set by cathedral music, and, even more, by secular music, have stood as a constant rebuke to the modest efforts of the country choir. In the age of long-playing records the contrast has become intolerable to many.

The sixteenth-century reformers never thought for one moment that parish congregations could sing artistically – still less that they could sing the liturgy. They let them sing popular tunes, not because they thought them beautiful, but entirely because they were popular. However, when well-known folk tunes were used, people thought of or actually sang the original words, defeating the Puritan objective of putting down lewd ballads. New tunes were therefore provided by unknown hands, and some of them quickly entered the popular domain.

For over a hundred years metrical psalmody was allowed to develop as a purely popular tradition. It diverged in style from the secular folk song that had been its model, probably because it was separated from dancing and mime. The 'old way of singing', coupled with lining out, was a totally inartistic phenomenon, but it had complete integrity as a folk music, as do the traditions that have descended from it to this day.

Towards the end of the seventeenth century came the first move to make psalmody more artistic. High-church clergy formed religious societies of young men, who learned to sing from notes. They sang, at first, the old tunes, but in 'correct' and harmonised forms provided by professional musicians. Where possible, organs were erected, and charity children taught to sing. The congregations could join in the new singing up to a point, which varied from place to place. But as the choirs or organists advanced, there came a time when they left the people behind. When it was clear that they were singing alone and the people were listening, they could choose music with no pretence that it was popular. In town churches, cathedral anthems or glee-like set pieces were sung: in the country, an interesting development took place that was midway between art and folk music, and is now beginning to be appreciated in its own right, especially in its American offshoot.

At this point the reaction of the clergy varied, as they began to see the dilemma they had got themselves into. Some turned against the country choirs and their teachers and demanded a return to the old way or an improved version of it, regulated if possible by an organ. Others encouraged the choirs to ever more ambitious efforts in the direction of

345

secular art music, or of cathedral music. The Methodists and Evangelicals brought in a new wave of popular music, taking over tunes from the theatre, concert hall, and tavern, and getting all the people to sing them to new hymn texts. By this time many congregations were sufficiently in touch with art music to be able to do this. Evangelicals, and later Tractarians, now introduced an entirely new conception: the congregation was to learn to sing its part in the liturgy itself – first the canticles, then the psalms, then the responses and prayers. But as before, the choir appointed to lead eventually outstripped its followers, with encouragement from many who wanted a cathedral style of worship. The Victorian 'fully choral' service was the result. With modifications it would persist until quite recent times, and even at this day is probably most people's idea of traditional Anglican parochial worship.

About 1800 a complicating factor entered the conflict: romantic antiquarianism. The old psalm tunes, originally chosen or written because they were humble and popular, were now exalted as sublime, the highest form of art. Still older music was sought out and revived – Gregorian psalm tones, medieval hymns, the plainsong of the pre-Reformation liturgy and its derivative, Marbeck's *Booke of common praier noted*. Of course, these revivals appealed to more than a merely aesthetic sensibility. When an Anglican is told (even if falsely) that a certain text or music was part of English worship centuries ago, he responds with an emotion part patriotic, part nostalgic, but also part religious. He wishes to preserve a link through time with Christ made human, not merely with Christ as a disembodied ideal; and this was a central message of the Oxford movement.

Such feelings are strong in a devout and educated minority, but rarely affect the majority of a congregation, whose religious and emotional associations are ineradicably bound up with the music they knew in their youth. However suitable Gregorian tones may be for congregational chanting, few congregations have taken to them with enthusiasm. The old psalm tunes may have been popular when they were composed, but most of them were no longer so when they were revived.

If William Crotch, William Havergal, or Robert Bridges could have heard how the early psalm tunes were really sung in the sixteenth or seventeenth century, they would have rejected them with indignant amazement. Instead they took the tunes in printed form, or in harmonised versions composed for cultivated amateurs, and built an idealised conception on these which they wished to 'revive' in contemporary use. Similarly the folk tunes collected by Vaughan Williams had to undergo a fairly drastic transformation to meet the accepted criteria for a hymn tune. The freely flowing speech rhythms of revived plainsong probably bear little resemblance to the way these melodies were sung in the middle ages. Nobody questioned the scholarly authenticity of these 'revivals'. A few of them eventually reached the popular domain, but they have made a relatively small dent in it. It has taken several generations for congregations to become thoroughly at home with the standards of art music that were imposed by the leaders of the early Victorian period – a time of great religious zeal and strong motivation for reform. The rapid changes of taste in the twentieth century have proved far above most people's heads.

We live in an age when a large public is not only familiar with classical music performed by the greatest artists, but even knows something of musical history and authenticity of style. Amateur musicologists abound. For a parish choir to perform an anthem to a congregation that includes sophisticated music-lovers is a daunting prospect, and it is not surprising that this side of parish church music is on the way out, especially in towns. Nobody to-day needs the parish church services as an opportunity to hear 'good music'. So the real function of parish church music, as an opportunity for people to sing in worship, has re-emerged from a long torpor.

But the idea of 'performance' is so strong that even congregational singing is often thought of in this way. To whom are we performing? As Kenneth Long remarked, God is not a music critic (:34). The criteria for acceptability are not the same for a participant as for a listener. The singer must feel satisfied with his own singing. In the seventeenth century, perhaps that was all. Today, he must also feel that his own singing is part of a larger musical offering that is impressive in itself.

A congregation led by a choir can sing elementary settings of a liturgy, hardly more than articulated speech. (Such are the plainsong and Marbeck settings, or the new music for the Series 3 communion service composed by Christopher Dearnley and Allan Wicks (PC 427).) It can chant, but the experience will hardly be satisfying if long stretches of prose are left to be sung without a clear rhythmic framework. Above all, it can sing hymns (or metrical psalms). Hymns have proved themselves the most enduring musical possession of Protestant Christianity. They allow all the people to share in an expression that is effective but also genuine, musical but also religious. They are independent of the liturgy and have survived when the liturgy has been undergoing radical change. The tunes have lived longer than the words. Only two hymns* in *Hymns ancient and modern revised* have words that were sung in Anglican parish churches before 1696; more than forty have tunes that were. Words became obsolete through changes in theology, in views and fashions concerning worship, in aesthetic taste, and in the language itself. Tunes are subject only to changes in musical language and taste. These have certainly in the past caused the eclipse of hundreds formerly popular. But many have resisted the attempts of reformers to get rid of them, while others have come back through the efforts of antiquarians. We now possess a heritage of perhaps two hundred tunes that are a distillation of all previous eras, and are well rooted in popular knowledge and affection.

It is pointless to ask whether those that have survived are the 'best'. By what standard can they be judged? Not that of aesthetic excellence, for as we have seen, hymns exist for the singers, not for an audience, still less for a critic. If a hymn tune gives pleasure to a musical connoisseur, this must be a merely incidental benefit. Attempts to replace the established tunes suddenly by promoting or publishing 'better' ones have always failed, and in any case have no valid purpose. Of course, there is a gradual process of

---

* Nos. 93, 166. No. 157 appears in the 1662 prayer book, but in the ordination service, which is not a parochial service.

change, and from time to time a new or revived tune enters the 'core repertory'. I see no need to resist new tunes; nor any reason to seek them out self-consciously. Very few tunes composed in the last generation have so far become widely popular, though some have. Certainly the Church does not owe composers a living. It has no duty to 'support modern music' unless such music is found to meet its needs. There is no pressing need for new hymn tunes at the present time.

The same arguments apply to church music in the pop idiom. At the Reformation, folk tunes or tunes like them had to be used, as there was (in England) little tradition of secular hymn singing. Now, this is unnecessary, as a rich and strong popular hymn-singing tradition does exist. It is possible that modern popular tunes, from films, musical comedies, or pop records, will be successfully adapted for use with hymns, though I know of no case so far.

The incomparable liturgy of the Church of England no longer serves to unify the worship of the Church in cathedral and parish church alike. Perhaps it will again. Meanwhile the greatest unity, the greatest continuity seems to lie in hymnody. The same words and tunes, from all periods of the Church's history, including the middle ages, supplemented from post-Tridentine Catholic, Lutheran, Methodist, Nonconformist, and humanist sources, are sung in churches everywhere. The music represents many styles and tastes; it can be satisfying at various levels, and to people of all kinds. It is a strong emotional bond for those who remain in the Church, and even between them and those outside.

Appendix 1 Collegiate parish churches and others endowed for choral music

A certain number of collegiate parish churches managed to retain their musical endowments after the Reformation, and a few others have in one way or another received permanent endowment for their music. Some information about these is given below. The list may not be exhaustive, but it includes most of the parish churches in which endowment had a noticeable effect on the character of the music. Some of the great medieval abbeys, such as Bath, Beverley, Hexham, Romsey, St Albans, Selby, Sherborne, Southwark, and Tewkesbury, survived as parish churches, but lacked any endowment for music. The same was true of many other medieval collegiate churches (see Cook).

The 1801 population of each parish, where relevant, is given in parentheses.

London: St Katherine-by-the-Tower (2,652). The collegiate foundation consisted of a master, three brethren in orders, three sisters, a chapter clerk and an organist. An organ must have existed in 1710, when James Heseltine retained his position as organist after appointment to Durham cathedral, and put in a deputy to perform his duties. A new 3-manual instrument was built in 1778. The medieval church was demolished in 1824, and the parish reduced to a 'precinct'. A new church was built in Regent's Park, where the organ was re-erected and the collegiate foundation retained. (*The Organ* 8, 1922: 118–20; Pearce, 1909: 193)

Ludlow (3,897). As the seat of the Lord President of the Welsh Marches this became in Elizabethan times a kind of miniature chapel royal. The choir was paid by the municipal corporation, which took over this responsibility on the suppression of the Guild of Palmers in 1547: the churchwardens paid only for paper and music copying. The choir consisted of six men and six boys. The master of the choristers chose the music and played the organ. Latin polyphony was sometimes sung as well as English anthems and services, which have survived in a set of partbooks dating from *c.* 1570 to *c.* 1625. Choral service was sung on Sundays, and then, after the sermon (as in many cathedrals), the choir moved to the nave to sing the metrical psalms with the congregation, accompanied by the organ. Weekday service was 'said or sung in plainsong'. As far as is known, these special conditions were not revived after the Restoration, but cathedral music may have been sung in the eighteenth century. Mr Valentine, organist of Ludlow, subscribed to two copies of *Harmonia sacra Glocestriensis* [London, 1731], a collection of anthems and a morning service by William Hine, organist of Gloucester cathedral. The organist was still being paid by the corporation in 1832. (Parl. Papers, 1835: XXVI, 2801; A. Smith: 306–13: A. Smith, 1968; MS 94)

Manchester (120,929). The medieval collegiate foundation of St Mary was suppressed in 1547, but it was restored by Mary I in 1553, and refounded by Elizabeth I in 1578 as 'Christ's College'. The college buildings became Chetham's Hospital and School, but the church retained a warden, four fellows, two chaplains or vicars, four clerks (singing men), and four choristers. New statutes confirming the foundation were granted in 1635, giving the warden and fellows the discretion to appoint an organist and master of the choristers. Apart from the interval of the Commonwealth this establishment remained intact until the church became a cathedral in 1847.

A small choir organ was built in 1684. Bishop Gastrell in 1717 found that the warden and fellows took preaching in turn, the two chaplains read prayers, and 'cathedral service' was performed by the four singing men, four choristers and organist. A large 'parish organ' was built in 1742. In 1816 it was noted that 'on Sundays, the service is read in the place commonly used in parish churches; but on other days, every morning at ten, and every evening at four, it is performed, cathedral fashion, in the choir, in weekly rotation, by the two chaplains, assisted by the singing-men and boys, who wear white surplices'. At the 'parochial' services on Sundays, the psalms were sung by the boys of Chetham's Hospital, assisted by the lay-clerks and choir boys, all sitting in the organ loft.

Edward Betts, an organist of Manchester collegiate church, published a collection of psalmody in 1724 (PC 84). John Wainwright, singing man and later organist, composed the tune for the well-known Christmas hymn 'Christians, awake', whose words are by John Byrom, also of Manchester. He did not include it in his *Collection of psalm tunes, anthems, hymns, and chants* (1767?: PC 196), which gives a good idea of the music then in use at the church. His son Robert, who succeeded him as organist, also contributed a hymn tune of lasting popularity, 'Manchester New'. Torrington, on a Tuesday afternoon in 1790, found the singing 'too bad to tempt my continuance'. (Aston: 65–6; Boutflower: 7; Hackett: 41; Hibbert: 152–67; Gastrell: 19, 57; Torrington: II, 206)

Middleham (728). The church nominally retained its collegiate status, with a dean, 'minister for divine service', and six chaplains. Torrington in 1792 described an ordinary parochial service there, with a dozen singers, two bassoons, and no organ. As a distinguished visitor he sat in the pew of the non-resident dean. No appointments to the chaplaincies were made until about 1830 when the dean, Dr P. S. Wood, appointed six chaplains and instituted a 'cathedral service' in the church. On Wood's death in 1856 the decanal office and collegiate foundation were suppressed. (*Victoria history of the county of York*: III, 366; Torrington: III, 58)

Newark (6,730). There was no collegiate foundation, but Thomas Magnus in the sixteenth century founded a song school (as well as a grammar school), to provide choirboys for the church. The master of the song school was also organist, and was appointed by the trustees, of whom the vicar was only one: thus the music had an unusual degree of independence of the incumbent. Edward Manesty, master in 1595, made an inventory of goods belonging to the school, which included part-books of anthems and services. There were organists in the eighteenth century: one, Thomas Jackson, published *Twelve psalm tunes and eighteen double and single chants for four voices* (PC 244) which may have been used at Newark. After his death in 1781, singing was apparently discontinued for a time (Torrington: IV, 139). But by 1815 the six singing boys had been joined by six 'low boys' or probationers. A singing boy got 4 guineas a year and a surplice, a low boy got 2 guineas and a cloak. There is no evidence of singing men at this stage. Two nineteenth-century organists, Edward Dearle (1835–64) and Samuel Reay (1864–1905), were involved in prolonged disputes with successive vicars, who complained of their incompetence and insubordination, but failed to get them removed. (A. Smith: 315–16; N. G. Jackson)

Ripon (10,413). The medieval foundation was suppressed in 1547. It was restored in 1604 with a dean, subdean, six prebendaries, two vicars-choral, six singing men, six choristers, an organist and a verger – an establishment comparable to that of many cathedrals. After the Restoration the collegiate foundation was maintained until the church was made a cathedral in 1836.

Detailed orders were made by the chapter in 1637, as in many cathedrals at about the same time, for the more 'decent' conduct of the choral service. The full choir and organ were back in place by 1663. Thomas Preston, organist, was paid for copying anthems into part-books from 1696 to 1708. During the later eighteenth century the chapter was in financial difficulties, and there was no increase in the salaries of the singing men (£40 a year shared among the six) between 1677 and 1835. The choristers received £2 each. There was no choir school, but the organist 'instructs the boys and the choir occasionally in the minster and at his own residence'. In 1835 cathedral service was sung on Sundays and holy days in the morning and evening; and on Monday, Tuesday and Saturday mornings and Saturday evenings except in Lent. On other days prayers were read in the chapter house. (MS 91; Hackett: 46; Hallett.)

Southwell (2,305). The medieval foundation was suppressed in 1547, and refounded under Queen Elizabeth I, with a song school. The new statutes (1586) provided for singing men, and six choristers to be instructed by a skilled 'rector chori'. It is not known whether there was an organ in Elizabethan times, but in 1635 the archbishop was told at his visitation: 'We have all things for singing and saying divine service and sacraments saving a pair of good organs.' An organ was opened in 1663, and daily services appear to have been maintained continuously from then until 1839. The choristers were instructed for an hour every morning in the song school, and attended choral service twice each day. Copying of part-books continued until 1819 at least, and several printed collections of cathedral music were purchased between 1757 and 1824.

It is remarkable that Lord Torrington, who toured England in the late eighteenth century making generally unfavourable comments in his journal about the music in most of the cathedrals, was highly impressed by the service he attended at Southwell on the afternoon of Monday, 8 June 1789. The prayers were read slowly and decently; the organ was 'excellently played'; four men and eleven boys 'sang as carefully as if at the Ancient Concert' (the aristocratic Concerts of Ancient Music held every year in London); the anthem, Kent's 'Sing, O heavens' (chosen by Torrington himself), was 'capitally performed'.

In 1835 the Church Commissioners recommended the dissolution of the collegiate foundation, and this was carried into effect. No new canons were appointed, the last dying in 1873. Choral services were reduced in 1839 to five mornings and three evenings a week, and the church was gradually transformed into an ordinary parish church. So it remained until it was made a cathedral in 1884. (*The Organ*, 203 (1972): 89; W. A. James; Hackett: 52; Torrington: IV, 141–2)

Tenbury. St Michael's College, founded and endowed by Sir Frederick Ouseley, was dedicated in 1856, and was attached to a newly built parish church of which Ouseley himself was the first vicar. The college was residential, and its purpose was to provide 'a model for the choral service of the church in these realms'. The choir of men and boys performed daily services of cathedral type in the college chapel, but also Sunday services in the parish church. St Michael's was the first new collegiate foundation since the Reformation. (Alderson & Colles: 1-32; Rainbow: 164–8)

Wimborne (3,039). The ancient foundation was suppressed in 1547, and the church became a royal peculiar, served by three priest–vicars, each to do duty for one month in turn. This foundation remained until 1876, renewed by charters of James I and Charles I. An organist, singing men and choristers were added to the staff at the discretion of the governors. In 1600 service was sung on Sundays and holy days at 8 a.m. and 2 p.m. by 4 boys and 6 men, with organ accompaniment. Choir stalls were built in 1610 to accommodate the newly established choir; they remain in place to-day. The organ of 1533 was in use until 1643. A new one was installed in 1664 at a cost of £180. Hutchins in 1773 wrote: 'The only cathedral service in this county is kept up in this church on Sundays and holy days.' (Score; Hutchins: III, 207; Fletcher)

Wolverhampton (24,536). A foundation of seven vicars-choral survived the Reformation. By the end of the seventeenth century these 'had evolved into an establishment of three curates or readers, who presumably had some ministerial qualifications, three lay "singing men", and an organist. The parochial duties of St. Peter's fell on the sacrist.' The dean was always, by custom, also dean of St George's chapel, Windsor, and was therefore almost invariably absent. It is unlikely that this tiny foundation was able to maintain choral services. However, in about 1750 James Lyndon, organist of Wolverhampton, published a verse anthem for tenor, bass and four-part choir (PC 140) which may possibly have been sung there. A long series of legal battles failed to regain for the college its lost lands, so the income was small, and most of it went to the dean. An Act of 1811 suppressed the three readerships, and in 1848 the college was dissolved. (*Victoria history of the county of Stafford*: III, 326–9)

Appendix 2 Changing conditions in Sussex rural churches (1853–1976)

In 1853 the Reverend Edward Boys Ellman, rector of Berwick, sent a questionnaire to the incumbents of all parishes in the rural deanery of Seaford asking questions about their music, chiefly to discover whether they had organs and what psalm or hymn books were in use. He followed it up with another questionnaire, asking somewhat different questions, in 1864. In his recollections, published in 1912, he gave a vague and somewhat garbled account of the episode, but fortunately the returns were preserved by Canon K. H. Macdermott and the details were copied by him and remain among his papers at the Sussex Archaeological Society, Lewes. Macdermott himself sent a questionnaire to the organists and choirmasters of his own rural deanery (Selsey) in 1922, and tabulated the results of this, too. (Ellman: 155–6; MS 23: I, 36–7, 296–7)

In 1976, with the co-operation and active assistance of Mrs S. E. Graney, of the Chichester Diocesan Fund and Board of Finance, I sent a questionnaire to the incumbents of all parishes formerly in the rural deaneries of Seaford and Selsey which still survived as separate entities, and received replies from 26 of them. On the basis of these replies some comparative statistics have been drawn up. The questions asked for information about the services both before and after the introduction (if any) of alternative services authorised by the Prayer Book (Alternative Services) Measure, 1965. Where the answers were not clear the church was excluded from the sample, which thus varies in size. Respondents were invited to add comments, and extracts from some of these are given after the tables.

Parishes included in the survey

Area A: Rural deanery of Seaford in 1853

Churches replying in 1853 and 1864	Churches in use in 1976 (united livings and pluralities are bracketed together)	Replies (1976)
Berwick	⎰Berwick	...
Alciston	⎱Selmeston with Alciston	...
Arlington	Arlington	...
Glynde	⎧Glynde	X
Firle	⎨West Firle	X
Beddingham	⎩Beddingham	X
Bishopstone	Bishopstone	X

Denton	Denton	X
Tarring Neville	Tarring Neville with South Heighton	X
Blatchington	East Blatchington	X
Laughton	Laughton	X
Ripe		
Chalvington	Ripe with Chalvington	X
Seaford	Sutton-cum-Seaford (Chapel of ease: Chington)	X
Upper Dicker	Upper Dicker	...
Chiddingly	Chiddingly	X

Area B: Rural deanery of Selsey in 1922

Churches canvassed in 1922	Churches in use in 1976 (united livings and pluralities are bracketed together)	Replies (1976)
Apuldram	Apuldram	X
Barnham	Barnham	X
Birdham (no return)	Birdham	...
Itchenor	Itchenor	...
South Bersted	South Bersted with North Bersted (Chapels of ease: Holy Cross, North Bersted; St Peter)	X
Bognor: St John	...	
Bognor: St Wilfrid (no return)	Bognor: St Wilfrid	...
Donnington	Donnington	X
Earnley	Earnley with East Wittering	X
East Wittering	(Chapel of ease: The Assumption, East Wittering)	
Felpham		
Middleton	Felpham with Middleton	X
Eastergate	Eastergate	...
Hunston	Hunston	X
Mundham	Mundham North	X
Merston	Oving with Merston	X
Pagham (no return)	Pagham	...
Selsey	Selsey (Chapel of ease: St Wilfrid)	X
West Wittering	West Wittering	X

Table 1. *Type of organ or other keyboard instruments*

Year	Area	Sample	Pipe organ	Barrel organ	Harmonium	Electronic organ	Piano	None
1853	A	13	23.1	7.7	...	...	...	69.2
1922	B	16	62.5	...	37.5	...	...	...
1976	AB	25	68.0	...	12.0	12.0	8.0	...

Table 2. *Make-up of choir*

Year	Area	Sample	Adults and children	Adults only	Children only	None
1922	B	16	75.0	...	18.7	6.3
1976	AB	25	64.0	12.0	8.0	16.0

Of the adult choir members, 45.7 % were men in 1976 (no data for 1922).

Table 3. *Size of choir*

Year	Area	Sample	Average size of choir	Smallest choir	Largest choir
1922	B	15	15.3	1 (Merston)	34 (St John, Bognor)
1976	AB	21	17.1	6 (Apuldram)	30 (Felpham; Sutton-cum-Seaford)

Table 4. *Music sung by choir alone*

Year	Area	Sample	Canticle settings	Anthems Regularly	Anthems Occasionally	Chanted psalms	Responses	None*
1976	AB	21	19.0	33.3	28.6	9.5	14.3	9.5

* This answer implies that the choir's sole function is to lead the congregation.

Table 5. *Music sung by congregation*

Year	Area	Sample	Hymns	Chanted canticles	Chanted psalms	Responses
1976	AB	25	100.0	96.0	88.0	56.0

Table 6. *Whether psalms chanted*

Year	Area	Sample	Chanted	Not chanted
1864	A	16	56.3	43.7
1922	B	16	93.7	6.3
1965	AB	26	88.5	11.5
1976	AB	26	88.5	11.5

Table 7. *Most recent liturgy in use in 1976*

Year	Area	Sample	1662	1928	Series 1	Series 2	Series 3
1976	AB	26	23.1	3.8	3.8	34.6	34.6

The pattern of use of the various liturgies at different churches was too complex to show in a table: over half the churches used a combination of two or more liturgies. The above indicates the latest liturgy in use at each church.

Table 8. *Types of service held on Sundays*

Year	Area	Sample	Matins	Family service*	Traditional communion	Parish communion	Evensong
1965	AB	22	77.3	...	45.5	50.0	81.8
1976	AB	25	52.0	28.0	24.0	76.0	68.0

* It is likely that more churches offered 'family services' than the table indicates, as the questionnaire did not list this as a separate class of service.

Table 9. *Introduction of pop music*

Answers to the question 'Has any rock, folk music, or other popular music been introduced?'

Year	Area	Sample	No	Family services only	Hymn tunes only	Yes
1976	AB	26	50.0	11.5	7.7	30.8

Table 10. *Use of non-keyboard instruments*

Year	Area	Sample	None	Guitar	Flute	Violin	Recorder
1853	A	13	84.6	...	15.4	...	...
1976	AB	26	73.1	23.1	3.8	3.8	3.8

One church in 1853 (Berwick) used a pitchpipe.

Table 11. *Hymn books in use*

Year	Area	Sample	Tate & Brady	Double cottage	Church hymns	A & M (1861–89)	English hymnal	A & M rev. (1950)	Other	None
1853	A	17	41.2	17.6	23.5	...	...	...	5.9	11.8
1864	A	17	14.8	8.8	35.3	29.4	...	...	5.9	5.9
1922	B	16	...	...	...	93.7	6.3	...	...	...
1976	AB	26	...	...	...	23.1	9.0	47.4	20.5	...

Table 12. *Psalters in use*

Year	Area	Sample	Prayer book*	Helmore	Cathedral	New Cathedral	Parish	Other
1864	A	9	55.6	11.1	...	...	...	33.3
1922	B	15	...	...	80.0	13.3	...	6.7
1965	AB	21	4.8	...	38.1	28.6	19.1	9.6
1976	AB	21	9.6	...	38.1	19.1	23.8	9.6

* Includes churches replying 'don't know'. The proportion of churches that did not chant the psalms at all is shown in Table 6 above.

Extracts from comments written on questionnaires

Laughton (Rev. Hugh Robinson, vicar). 'In the last hundred years the population of the village has declined (700 in 1974). In 1864 practically the whole village was part of the estate of the Earls of Chichester, the population was largely employed in farming, the children were educated at the all-age village school. Today, whilst Laughton is still a farming village, only a small proportion are farm workers. There is a high proportion of elderly and retired people, commuters to London or elsewhere, and weekenders, who have bought up and converted farm cottages. The village school, now a primary school, serves three villages, children over 11 go to secondary school in Ringmer or Lewes.

These changes have of course meant a decline in church-going, and the church is no longer the focal point of the social and cultural life of the village. This of course means that our church music is of a far more basic character than it was a hundred years ago, when singing in the church choir and bell-ringing were prominent among the few social activities available in the village.

Oddly enough, there has been some very good music performed in the parish church during the last year, but it has been imported. Once every couple of months in place of Evensong we have what our Victorian ancestors would call a "sacred concert". These have included a performance of the St John Passion by an Eastbourne school, visits from neighbouring choirs, both church and school, and organ recitals. These have drawn large congregations.

There is a tendency at the present time to use country churches, as well as urban churches, as quasi-concert halls, often in connection with "flower festivals" and for church restoration funds. Laughton's musical activities raised about £500 in the last year to restore the organ.' (No choir; pipe organ; Series 1 parish communion.)

Chiddingly (Rev. Hugh Robinson, vicar). 'Compared to Laughton, Chiddingly (population 850) is a more integrated village with a younger population and a strong social life. This bears favourably on church life, worship, and music. The choir is R.S.C.M. affiliated. It lapsed for a couple of years, and was reformed two years ago. It is composed of girls only, as the boys preferred to become bell-ringers.' (Choir of 7 women and 12

357

children; pipe organ; 1928 evensong and family matins; Series 2 communion.)

Apuldram (Mrs. M. E. Gostling, organist). 'Apuldram is a small rural parish of 200 inhabitants, until recently [held] in plurality with another parish. Our music is "enthusiastic" rather than "professional". Our young people are encouraged to contribute with their own instruments.' (Choir of 6 children; pipe organ; Series 2 matins and parish communion; family service once a month.)

Earnley (Rev. J. H. Richardson, rector). 'This is a small, very small church, seating 60 people in a very small village [of] 300 inhabitants without shop or inn. It has 3 services a month, 9 a.m. Holy Communion Series 2 on the first Sunday of the month, evensong on the second and fourth Sunday at 6.30. The average attendance is around 20. The village is on the fringe of a coastal strip/holiday area, but largely unaffected by it. Liturgically it is rather traditional, not really representative, not really like St Anne's, East Wittering for which I am also responsible where we have Series 3, choir, and [are] generally much more up to date.

'It is probably not important than Earnley tends to be like this as most things are done in a joint way between the 2 parishes so that Earnley can be more traditional without holding back church life in general.' (No choir; harmonium; 1662 services with Series 2 communion.)

Ripe (Rev. G. H. Paton, rector). 'At Parish Communion we use Patrick Appleford's "Mass of Five Melodies" ... A category not included on your list is the Family Service which has taken hold at Ripe and is held about once a month, on days chosen for general appropriateness rather than strictly by the calendar. We include one hymn from the book "Someone's Singing, Lord" in use at the school, and some of these would come into these [Table 9] categories. We actually had everyone, ancient as well as young, clapping in the course of one hymn where indicated.' (No choir; harmonium; Series 3 parish communion.)

Chalvington (Rev. G. H. Paton, rector). 'About 1918 ... the church of Chalvington lost its status as a parish church ... There is now an early said service of Holy Communion on all Sundays except the last in the month when it is held at Ripe. The two churches are less than $\frac{1}{2}$ mile apart. Chalvington church is distinctly smaller than Ripe; there are fewer people, more scattered. In the winter we use only one church on any Sunday, to economise with heating (55° F would be regarded as reasonable in the coldest weather).' (No choir; piano; 1662 matins; Series 3 traditional communion.)

Bibliography

1 MANUSCRIPT SOURCES

These are arranged alphabetically according to the town and library in which each manuscript is now located. After the reference number used in the text of this book (in such citations as 'MS 1', etc.) there follows, in italics, the number or other identification (if any) assigned to the manuscript at the library concerned, and then, in roman type, a brief description of the relevant contents.

Bradford (West Yorks): *Cathedral Library.*
    1 Bradford parish vestry minutes and churchwardens' accounts.
Bradford (West Yorks): *Central Library.*
    2 *Case 4, Box 1, Item 20.* Extracts from a book of memoranda formerly in Bradford parish church, *c.* 1800.
Cambridge: *Pepys Library, Magdalene College.*
    2a *1236.* Book of choral polyphony probably emanating from Kent, *c.* 1460–5.
Cambridge: *Rowe Music Library, King's College.*
    3 A. H. Mann. Notes on musical events in Cambridge and Cambridgeshire. Compiled *c.* 1860–1925.
Chicago (Illinois): *Newberry Library.*
    4 Printed book *VM2136/T16c/1738.* (PC 113/1738.) Choir music added by John Jones, 1742.
Doncaster (South Yorks): *Public Library.*
    5 *LOC/R885, R4743, R5064.* Accounts of Doncaster Corporation, 1772–1835.
Dorchester (Dorset): *Dorset County Museum.*
    6 *Box File, Folk-Music, Church Music. L.1957/53/1–3.* Six oblong books of choir music used in various Dorset parish churches, *c.* 1760–1870.
    7 *Box Files, Places: Bere Regis.* 'Bere Regis church', by Nesta M. Howard. Typescript, *c.* 1950.
    8 *P7: Bartlett MS.* Music sung at Wareham, in the hand of Thomas Oldfield Bartlett, Rector of Swanage; *c.* 1801–41.
Dorchester (Dorset): *Dorset Record Office.*
    9 *P5/CW3.* Wyke Regis churchwardens' accounts.
  10 *P63/VE2.* Lady St Mary, Wareham, vestry minutes.
  10a *P68/CW1.* Winterborne Whitchurch churchwardens' accounts.
  11 *P70/CW22.* Blandford Forum: faculty for erecting an organ.
  12 *P87/CW2.* St Peter, Dorchester, churchwardens' accounts.
  13 *P167/CW1.* Subscription list for a bass viol at East Stoke.
  14 *P173/CW4.* Holy Trinity, Dorchester, churchwardens' accounts.
  15 *P196/CW11.* Organ book, treble partbook, and bass partbook used at Bridport parish church, 1823 and after.
  16 *P204/CW42.* Wimborne Minster churchwardens' accounts.
  16a *P220/CW1.* Charmouth churchwardens' accounts.

17   *P227/CW3*. Poole churchwardens' accounts.

Durham (Co. Durham): *Cathedral Library*.

17a   *C.20.v*. Alto partbook for the use of the cathedral choir, containing (pp. 56–70) the preces, responses and litany as arranged by the Rev. Peter Penson, transcribed 1819–20.

Halifax (West Yorks): *Central Library*.

18   'A short history of the choir and choirmasters of Halifax parish church', by A. T. Pinder. Typescript, 1941.

Halifax (West Yorks): *Parish Church*.

19   Halifax parish vestry minutes (1816–) and churchwardens' accounts (1726–1832).

20   'Catalogue of the music library of the choir', by A. T. Pinder. Typescript, 1941.

Huddersfield (West Yorks): *Parish Church*.

21   Huddersfield parish churchwardens' accounts and minutes, 1817–1942.

Leeds (West Yorks): *Parish Church*.

22   Leeds parish churchwardens' accounts.

Lewes (East Sussex): *Sussex Archaeological Society, Barbican House*.

23   *Mis 6 (1–2)*. 'Sussex church music in the past'. 2 vol. scrapbook compiled by Canon K. H. Macdermott, *c*. 1910–30.

London: *Battersea Public Library*.

24   Mackness, R. C. Narrative of his career as an organist. Holograph, 1919.

London: *British Library, Department of Manuscripts*.

25   *Add. 5665*. Sacred and secular vocal music, copied *c*. 1510.

26   *Add. 15166*. Treble partbook containing settings of psalm tunes, anthems, and hymns, *c*. 1559–65.

26a   *Add. 15177*. Songs with lute accompaniment, *c*. 1600.

27   *Add. 30513*. The 'Mulliner Book', containing organ pieces and organ reductions of anthems and partsongs, *c*. 1550–60.

28   *Add. 34191*. Partbook, bass and tenor, *c*. 1545.

29   *Add. 36661, fol. 66–67v*. Organ settings of psalm tunes, 17th century.

30   *Add. 47775*. Notes on 18th- and 19th-century parish church music by Canon K. H. Macdermott, including letters to him, *c*. 1925–45.

31   *Add. 50888*. Chants, psalms, anthems. Owner's inscription dated 1718.

32   *Add. 50889*. Anthems, chants, psalms, canons. Owner's inscription dated 1758.

33   *Add. 50891*. Two books of psalm tunes composed by J. Darwall, vicar of Walsall. Autograph, 1783.

34   *Egerton 2836*. Order of service, discipline, and catechism for the English congregation at Frankfurt, [1555].

34a   *Harl. 7337–42*. The 'Tudway manuscripts'. Scores of anthems and services copied by Thomas Tudway, *c*. 1715–20.

34b   *Harl. 7578*. Tenor partbook of sacred and secular works, mid-16th century.

35   *Lansdowne 213, fol. 315*. 'A relation of a short survey of twenty-six counties, describing their citties and their scytuations in 1634, by a captain, a lieutenant, and an ancient.' *c*. 1634.

36   *Royal 18.B.xix*. 'The praise of musick.' Anon, *c*. 1605–10.

37   *Roy. App. 74–6*. The 'Lumley partbooks'. Triplex, contratenor, and tenor partbooks (bass missing) of anthems, canticles, and settings of metrical psalms, *c*. 1550.

London: *British Library, Department of Music*.

38   *A.1231.rr*. (PC 249.) pp. 81–[162]. Anthems and psalm tunes in two-voice score, added by Francis Bell Jackson, *c*. 1783.

39   *C.73.b.* (PC 123.) Psalm tunes and anthems probably added by Henry Howitt, *c.* 1752.

London: *British Library, Department of Printed Books.*

40   *C.36.g.3.* (*Book of common prayer*, 1702.) Interleaved annotations by Bishop White Kennet, early 18th century.

41   *C.130.bb.3.(3).* Old Romney (Kent) Religious Society. Minutes of meeting, 1701.

42   *796.g.31.* ('The report of the committee appointed by a general vestry of the Parish of St. Botolph without Aldersgate, London: February 22. 1732', London, 1733.) Interleaved notes by the Rev. William Freeman, *c.* 1733–5.

43   *3433.bb.11.* (Sternhold *et al.*, 1753.) Interleaved psalm tunes. In same hand as MS 44, *c.* 1760.

44   *3435.cc.12.* (Sternhold *et al.*, 1759.) Interleaved psalm tunes. In same hand as MS 43, *c.* 1760.

London: *Finsbury Library.*

45   St James, Clerkenwell, vestry minutes.

London: *Greater London Record Office, County Hall.*

46   *P76/JNB/24.* St John, Clerkenwell, vestry minutes, 1723–1828.

47   *P79/JN1/138–44.* St John, Hackney, vestry minutes, 1657–.

48   *P92/S/452.* St Saviour, Southwark, vestry minutes, 1704–38.

London: *Guildhall Library.*

48a *635.* St Augustine [and St Faith] vestry minutes, 1601–1800.

49   *858 (1).* List of subscribers to an organ at St Olave, Hart Street, 1781.

50   *1568A.* St Bennet Gracechurch churchwardens' accounts, 1835–90.

51   *1704.* All Hallows, Staining, churchwardens' accounts, 1814–1911.

52   *3016 (2).* St Dunstan-in-the-West vestry minutes, 1664–1701.

53   *3146 (2).* St Sepulchre, Holborn, churchwardens' accounts, 1664–83.

54   *3149 (2).* St Sepulchre, Holborn, vestry minutes, 1662–83.

55   *3570 (4).* St Mary Aldermanbury vestry minutes, 1815–49.

56   *3863 (1).* St Botolph, Aldersgate, vestry minutes, 1756–1812.

57   *4049 (2).* All Hallows, Lombard Street, vestry minutes.

58   *4241 (5).* St Ethelburga, Bishopsgate Street, churchwardens' accounts, 1809–25.

59   *4410 (2).* St Olave, Old Jewry, churchwardens' accounts and vestry minutes, 1762–1827.

60   *4526 (4).* St Botolph, Bishopsgate, vestry minutes, 1754–87.

61   *4894.* Scrapbooks of documents connected with the Company of Parish Clerks of London, compiled by E. A. Ebblewhite, 6 vol. *c.* 1900–30.

62   *5714 (4).* St Mary Somerset churchwardens' accounts, 1826–1900.

London: *Islington Central Library.*

63   St Mary, Islington, vestry minutes.

London: *Lambeth Palace Library.*

64   *Cartae Miscellanae VII.* Answers to the Court of Star Chamber's questionnaire about the type of vestry in each London parish. 1635–6.

London: *Minet Library, Lambeth.*

65   *P3/2.* St Mary, Lambeth, vestry minutes and churchwardens' accounts, 1652–1703.

London: *Newington District Library.*

66   St George, Southwark, churchwardens' accounts.

67   St Mary Magdalen, Bermondsey, vestry minutes.

68   St Olave, Southwark, vestry minutes.

London: *Parry Library, Royal College of Music.*

69   *674–5.* Two organ books used at St Margaret's chapel, Bath, compiled by the organist, J. W. Windsor, *c.* 1798–1814.

70 *2042.* Bass partbook containing anthems and hymns in several hands. Inscribed 'Abraham Whorly His Book 1729'.

London: *St Dunstan's Church, Stepney.*

71 St Dunstan, Stepney, vestry minutes.

London: *Stationers' Hall.*

72 *Copyright Register.* Register of books deposited for copyright, 1554–.

73 *Court Books.* Record of proceedings of the court of the Company. Book C, 1602–54; D, 1654–79; E, 1674–83; F, 1683–97; G, 1697–1717; etc.

74 *English Stock Books.* Records of the warehouse-keeper listing books delivered by the stock-keeper of the English Stock of the Company, 1663–1774.

London: *Westminster Public Library.*

75 *B14/CA.* St Clement Danes churchwardens' accounts, 1685–1706.

76 *D1756.* St James [Piccadilly], Westminster, vestry minutes, 1685–94.

76a *F2005.* St Martin-in-the-Fields vestry minutes, 1684–1716.

76b *G1003.* St Mary-le-Strand vestry minutes, 1776–.

Manchester: *Public Library.*

77 Printed book *BR.f537.Kj21.* (PC 229.) Arrangement of Handel's 'I know that my redeemer liveth' as an 'Introduction' to an anthem in the printed book, Key's 'Now is Christ risen'. *c.* 1780.

Manchester: *University of Manchester, John Rylands Library.*

78 *English MS. 97.* Christ Church, Manchester, churchwardens' accounts, 1664–1711.

New Haven (Connecticut): *Yale University Music Library.*

79 *Ma21/Y11/C47.* Book of church music, containing also laundry lists, addresses in South London, and other memoranda, and a transcript of the Introduction to PC 83. In the hand of Charles Pudge, *c.* 1793.

Norwich (Norf.): *Norfolk and Norwich Record Office.*

80 *427–52.* A. H. Mann. Notes on musical events and musicians in East Anglia. Compiled *c.* 1860–1925.

81 *11200–13.* A. H. Mann. Notes on the life and works of William Crotch, compiled in preparation for his biography.

82 *11214–26.* Letters of William Crotch, with notes by A. H. Mann.

83 *PD39/69–73.* St Margaret, King's Lynn, churchwardens' accounts.

Oxford: *Bodleian Library.*

84 *Mus.f.38.* 'A booke of psalme tunes with directions by the rull how to sing them taken out of the works of John Playford' by Edmund Dirrick, parish clerk of Ubley, 1696.

85 *Mus.Sch.e.420–2.* The 'Wanley partbooks'. 1st alto, 2nd alto, and bass partbooks (tenor missing), containing anthems, service music, and metrical psalm settings. *c.* 1550.

Oxford: *Christ Church.*

86 *437.* Organ book containing choir music, including (at fol. 2v, 4v, 9, 16, 29, 50v) chants written out to the first verse of the Venite, for four voices. *c.* 1680.

87 *768–70.* Three partbooks (alto, tenor, bass) containing 12 settings of metrical psalms by William Lawes, designed to alternate with the 'common tunes'. *c.* 1670.

Oxford: *St John's College.*

88 *315.* Organ book containing choir music, including (pp. 234–5) chants for four voices. *c.* 1660.

Poole (Dorset): *Parish Church.*

89 Poole parish churchwardens' accounts and vestry minutes.

Reading (Berks): *Public Library*.
  90   *q/R/RJ*. 'Reading's musical history', by S. T. Chamberlain. Typescript, 1929.

Ripon (North Yorks): *Minster Library*.
  91   *Registrum A-E*. Records of the proceedings of the chapter of Ripon collegiate church, 1604–1840.

Selby (North Yorks): *Abbey Library*.
  92   Selby parish churchwardens' accounts.

Sheffield (South Yorks): *City Library*.
  93   *PR 19/3–4, 19/38–40*. Records of Doncaster parish church, 1691–1915.

Shrewsbury (Salop): *Shropshire Record Office*.
  94   *356 Mus. 1–5*. Five partbooks used at Ludlow parish church, c. 1570–1625.

Trent (Italy): *Castello del Buonconsiglio*.
  95   *Codex 90*. Book of 15th-century choral polyphony.

Urbana (Illinois): Nicholas Temperley.
  96   Returns to a questionnaire sent to Sussex incumbents, 1976.
  97   'Part of the reminiscences of the 50 years from 1837 to 1887', by Lucy Chater. Typescript, c. 1930.

Urbana (Illinois): *University of Illinois Rare Book Room*.
  97a *E79–10*. Psalm tunes and parochial anthems in score, copied c. 1760. Cover embossed with owner's name 'William Marriott'.

Wakefield (West Yorks): *City Library*.
  98   St John, Wakefield, parish records, 1791–1832.

Winterbourne Abbas (Dorset): *Rectory*
  99   Winterbourne Abbas churchwardens' accounts.

York (North Yorks): *Borthwick Institute of Historical Research*.
  100 *PR/RUF/8*. Rufforth churchwardens' accounts.
  101 *PR/TAD/1*. Tadcaster churchwardens' accounts.
  101a *PR/WAL/10*. Walton in Ainsty churchwardens' accounts.
  102 *PR/Y/ASN/12*. All Saints, North Street, York, churchwardens' accounts.
  102a *PR/Y/M.Bp.S/16*. St Mary Bishophill Senior, York, churchwardens' accounts.
  103 *PR/Y/MCS/18*. St Martin, Coney Street, York, churchwardens' accounts.
  104 *PR/Y/MCS/25*. List of music used at the services at St Martin, Coney Street, York, 1832–3 and 1835–6.
  105 *PR/Y/SAV/15*. St Saviour, York, churchwardens' accounts.

York (North Yorks): *City Library*.
  106 *Y942/7411*. 'Notes on the organs organists clerks and quires in York churches since the Reformation', by J. W. Knowles. 1924.

York (North Yorks): *Minster Library*.
  107 St Michael-le-Belfry, York, vestry minutes and churchwardens' accounts.

2 PRINTED COLLECTIONS OF MUSIC

This section of the bibliography serves also as a representative list of collections of music designed wholly or partly for use in English parish churches. It is comprehensive for collections designed *principally* for parochial use and printed before 1801 (PC 1–326). A selective list of parochial collections after 1800 is given, and lists of collections for London hospitals, proprietary chapels, English congregations abroad, and the Anglican Church in Wales, where these have some relation to English parish church music. Collections for use in cathedrals, college chapels and dissenting places of worship, or for domestic or secular use, are not listed unless there is evidence that they were, in part at least, designed principally for use in parish churches. In many cases the decision to include or exclude a collection has been a matter of discretion, but doubtful cases have generally been included (e.g., PC 13, 24, 112).

The subsections are as follows:

2A	*Collections primarily for parish church use*	PC 1–429
2B	*Collections for London hospitals*	PC 501–550
2C	*Collections for proprietary chapels associated with the Church of England*	PC 601–661
2D	*Collections for English congregations abroad*	PC 701–715
2E	*Collection in Welsh for the Anglican Church in Wales*	PC 801

Reference in the text is by means of the numbers in the lefthand margin (e.g., 'PC 1'). After the reference number in the list comes the name of the *musical* editor or compiler, where this is known or can be inferred, using standardised modern spelling; the title (in italics), shortened as necessary, using the original spelling; and the place and date of publication (if no place is given, the place is London). Information in parentheses () is taken from the book, but not from the title page; information in backets [] is from external sources. For conjectural dates of publication, – (before date) means 'not later than', – (after date) means 'not earlier than'. The STC number, for imprints up to 1640, refers to the *Short Title Catalogue*; the Wing number, for imprints from 1641 to 1700, refers to the first edition of Wing. Details of any facsimile reprint or scholarly edition of the book follow.

Where only part of the book contains parish church music, this is next identified. Finally, information is given in parentheses about secondary sources describing the book in detail, the source of the music if it is largely taken from another collection, and other relevant information. Details of later editions are then given. Where a later edition is sufficiently revised to change the title, or the coded information at the right of the page, it is given a separate entry and cross-reference.

Coded information

In the columns at the right of the page will be found coded information about the book's designed use, provenance, musical contents, and musical forces. This is arranged as follows.

Designed use (first line, left)   *Subsections 2A, D, E only*

1   For a particular church or congregation
2   For town parish churches
3   For country parish churches
4   For parish churches
5   For cathedrals or collegiate churches
6   For dissenting places of worship
7   For domestic or school use

Provenance (first line, centre)   *Subsections 2A, D, E only*

The place or region for which the book was designed or in which it was used, where this can be determined.

Musical contents by genre (second line, left)

P   Psalm tunes (for strophic performance of metrical psalms or canticles)
P   The same, with the metrical psalms complete
H   Hymn tunes (for strophic performance of hymns)
T   Set pieces (continuous or 'through-composed' settings of metrical texts)
R   Settings of the responses to the ten commandments
L   Intoned or chanted settings of other parts of the liturgy
S   Services (continuous settings of the prose canticles)
A   Anthems (continuous settings of other prose texts)
C   Chants or chant settings for prose psalms or canticles

Secular music is disregarded. Instrumental settings of psalm and hymn tunes are listed but not independent instrumental music such as voluntaries.

Musical forces: vocal (second line, centre)

s   soprano/treble, or mean/medius of soprano range
a   alto/contra/counter, or mean/medius of alto range
t   tenor, or contra/counter of tenor range
b   bass or baritone
g   part in the G clef that could either be sung as written, or an octave lower by men's voices
c   congregational melody

Boldface letter: This part carries the tune in some multi-voice settings of psalm or hymn tunes in this collection.

A part in the G clef will be listed as s, a, t, g, or c according to circumstances; a part in the C clef (unless congregational) according to compass; a part in the F clef as b.

Musical forces: instrumental (second line, right)

o   optional organ part: either figures over the vocal bass, or a written-out part that merely doubles the voices
O   independent organ part (fully written out or figured bass)
i   optional instrumental parts
I   independent instrumental parts
BO   transcription of barrel organ setting

Other abbreviations and symbols

Italics: information inferred, or based on external evidence
()   instrumental or vocal part occurring in a substantial minority of pieces
/   alternative part or combination of parts
*   The first edition of this work contains a list of subscribers.

Coded information pertains only to the majority or a substantial minority of the pieces making up each collection. For example, two hymns in a collection of 100 metrical psalms, or a single 4-part anthem in a book of 3-part pieces, will generally have been left out of consideration.

Bibliography

2A   Collections primarily for parish church use

PC

1	[Cranmer, Thomas.] *An exhortation unto prayer. A letanie with suffrages.* 1544. STC 10619. Facs. (ed. J. E. Hunt), 1939.	45 L	t
2	Crowley, Robert. *The psalter of David newely translated into Englysh metre.* 1549. STC 2725. (1 chant.)	45 P	s a t b
3	Marbeck, John. *The booke of common praier noted.* 1550. STC 16441. Facs. (ed. J. E. Hunt), 1939.	45 L	t
4	S[eager], F[rancis]. *Certayne psalmes.* 1553. STC 2728. (Frost: 339–42.)	457 P	s a t b
5	[Day, John. *Psalms of David.* 1559.] (No copy survives. See Arber: I, 124.)	457 P	c
6	[Day, John ?] *Psalmes of David in English metre, by T. Sternholde and others.* 1560. STC 2427. (Frost: 5–8. An extension of PC 701.) See PC 7.	457 PH	c
7	Day, John. *Psalmes of David in English metre, by Thomas Sternholde and others.* 1560 (1561). STC 2429. (Frost: 11–13. An extension of PC 6.) Later edns. (as *The first parte of the psalmes*) 1564, 1569; see also PC 9.	457 PH	c
8	Day, John. *The residue of all Davids psalmes in metre, made by J. Hopkins and others.* 1562. STC 2429.5. (A supplement to PC 7.)	457 PH	c
9	Day, John. *The whole booke of psalmes, collected into English metre by T. Starnhold I. Hopkins & others.* 1562. STC 2430. (Frost: 13–15. A combination of PC 7, 8.) About 450 later edns 1563–1687; see also PC 13, 16, 29, 33, 702.	457 PH	c
10	[Day, John or Parsons, William ?] *Tenor (Contra tenor – Medius – Bassus) of the whole psalmes in foure partes.* 1563. STC 2431. (Frost: 15–17.)	457 PHA	**s a t b**
11	Day, John. (*Certaine notes set forth in foure and three parts.* 1560.) *Mornyng and evenyng prayer and communion, set forthe in foure partes.* 1565. STC 6418–19. (le Huray: 182–3.)	45 PHSAC	s a t b a a t b
12	Barker, Christopher. *The order of prayer ... to be used throughout the realme by order aforesaide, to avert Gods wrath from us, threatned by the late terrible earthquake.* (1580.) STC 16513. (1 tune.)	45 P	c
13	East, Thomas. *The whole booke of psalmes: with their wonted tunes.* 1592. STC 2482. Ed. E. Rimbault, 1844. (Frost: 24–5; Illing, 1969. Text from PC 9.) Later edns 1594, 1604, 1611; see also PC 14.	457 PH	s a t b
14	Barley, William. *The whole booke of psalmes with their woonted tunes.* [1599?] STC 2495. (Frost: 30–1; Illing, 1968. Based on PC 13.)	457 PH	a a t b
15	*The whole booke of Davids psalms, both in prose and metre.* 1601. STC 2505. (Temperley, 1976. Based on PC 702.) 21 later edns 1603–43,	46 PH	c
16	Ravenscroft, Thomas. *The whole booke of psalmes ... Composed into 4. parts by sundry authors.* 1621. STC 2575. Ed. W. Havergal, 1847. (Frost: 36–8, 271–90; Illing, 1969. Text from PC 9.) Later edn 1633; see also PC 95.	457 PH	s a t b

17	Wither, George. *The songs of the old testament.* 1621. STC 25923. (Frost: 408–20.)	*457* P		s b a b t b	*o/i* *o/i* *o/i*
18	W[ither], G[eorge]. *The hymnes and songs of the church.* 1623. STC 25908–10a. Ed. E. Farr, 1856; facs. 1881. (Frost: 420–33.)	*457* PH		s b t b	*o/i* *o/i*
19	[Harper, Thomas ?] *Al the French psalm tunes with English words.* 1632. STC 2734. Later edn 1650.	*45* P	c		
20	Barton, William. *The book of psalms in metre.* 1644. Wing B2401. (Frost: 453–9.) 7 later edns, 1645–96.	*47* P	c		
22	[King, Henry or Griffin, Edward]. *The psalmes of David, from the new translation of the bible.* 1651. Wing B2446. Later edn 1654.	*4* P	c		
23	Playford, John. *A brief introduction to the skill of music.* 1658. Wing P2448. (sig. Elr ff:) The tunes of the psalms as they are commonly sung in parish-churches. (Temperley, 1972a: 344–6.) 5 later edns 1660–70; see also PC 27, 28.	*23* P	c		*o/i*
24	Tomkins, Thomas. *Musica deo sacra.* 1668. Wing T1837. (p. 308:) Tunes of psalms. (4 tunes.)	*45* P			O
25	Playford, John. *Musicks hand-maid.* 1678. Wing P2493. (Double sheet, printed *c.* 1669, set in some copies.) The tunes of psalms to the virginal or the organ. (4 tunes.)	*47* P			O
26	Playford, John. *Psalms & hymns in solemn musick of foure parts.* 1671. Wing P2498. (Frost: 44–7; Temperley, 1972a: 353–60.)	*47* PH	a a t b t		O
27	Playford, John. *An introduction to the skill of music.* 6th edn 1672. Wing P2479. (pp. 73 ff.:) The tunes of psalms used in parish-churches. (Temperley, 1972a: 360–3. Based on PC 23.)	*23* P	c		
28	Playford, John. *A brief introduction to the skill of music.* 7th edn 1674. Wing P2454A. Facs. edn 1966. (pp. 73ff:) The most usual common tunes sung in parish-churches. (Temperley, 1972a: 360–3. Based on PC 23.) Many later edns 1679–.	*23* P	c		*o/i*
29	Playford, John. *The whole book of psalms . . . compos'd in three parts, cantus, medius, & bassus.* 1677. Wing B2527. (Frost: 47–50; Temperley, 1972a: 363–72. Text from PC 9.) 18 later edns 1694–1738; see also PC 165.	*237* PH	g g b		*o/i*
30	Goodridge, Richard. *The psalter or psalms of David set to new tunes.* Oxford, 2nd edn, 1684. Wing B2554. (2 tunes.)	*4* P	c		
31	[Rogers, William ?] *A new and easie method to learn to sing by book.* 1686. Wing N540. (Entered at Stationers' Hall, 20 April 1686.)	*47* PH	g g b		
32	Barber, Abraham. *A book of psalme tunes in four parts.* York, 1687. Not in Wing. Copy: Royal College of Music, Frost Collection. (Largely based on PC 10. Entered at Stationers' Hall, 17 February 1687.) See PC 40.	*14* P	W. Yorks **s a t b**		
33	M[athew], T[homas]. *The whole booke of psalmes, as they are now sung in the churches.* 1688. Wing B2565. (Text from PC 9. Tunes largely from PC 16.)	*4* P	c		
34	[King, Robert ?] *The psalms and hymns, usually sung in the churches and tabernacles of St. Martins in the Fields, and*	*1* P	Westminster **g g b**		

Bibliography

St. *James's Westminster*. 1688. Not in Wing. Copy: Euing Library, Glasgow University. See also PC 36.

35 Warner, Daniel. *A collection of some verses out of the psalms*. 1694. Not in Wing. Copy: Bodleian Library, Oxford. Later edns (rev. H. Hunt) 1698, 1700.
    4
    PH   g b

36 [Courteville, Raphael ?] *Select psalms and hymns for the use of the parish-church and tabernacle of St. James's Westminster*. 1697. Not in Wing. (Partly based on PC 34.) 3rd–6th edns 1699–1704; see also PC 58.
    1   Westminster
    P   s b

37 Brady, Nicholas & Tate, Nahum. *A new version of the psalms of David*. 2nd edn 1698. Wing B2606. (Part II:) The tunes of the psalms.
    47
    P   s a t b

38 Patrick, John. *The psalms of David in metre: fitted to the tunes used in parish-churches*. 1698. Wing B2608. (Part II:) The tunes of the psalms. 5 later edns 1701–42.
    46
    P   g b

39 Milbourne, Luke. *The psalms of David in English metre . . . suited to all the tunes sung in churches*. 1698. Wing B2609.
    4
    P

40 Barber, Abraham. *Psalm tunes in four parts, in two books*. 3rd edn York, 1698. Not in Wing. Copy: Manchester Public Library. (Revision of PC 32.) 4th edn York, 1700; see also PC 60.
    4   W. Yorks
    P   (s a) t b

41 [Hayes, John ?] *Some of the psalms of David in metre. Done by J. Patrick, D.D. and by Mr Brady and Mr Tate*. Cambridge, 1698. Wing B2611.
    46
    P   g b

42 (Smith, Thomas.) [*Selected psalms. c.* 1698.] (Title page missing on only known copy.) Not in Wing. Copy: British Library, A.1233.x. (Texts from PC 9, 37.)
    4
    P   c

43 Ireland, Edmund. *The tunes of the psalms in two parts*. York, 1699. Not in Wing. Copy: New York Public Library. 2nd edn 1713; see also PC 76.
    12   Hull
    P   g b

44 [Hely, Benjamin.] *The compleat violist . . . with a collection of the psalm tunes set to the viol, as they are now in use in the churches where there are organs*. [1699.] Wing C5660. Copy: Bodleian Library, Oxford.
    47
    P   I

45 [Playford, Henry. *The psalmody, or . . . Directions to play the psalm tunes by letters instead of notes*. 1699.] (No copy known. Advertised *The post boy*, 27 June 1699.)
    47
    P   I

46 [Webb, William. *An introduction to the singing of psalms, viz. treble and bass, with a collection of tunes now in use*.] (No copy known. Advertised *The post man*, 28 March 1699.)
    4
    P   g b

47 [Hall, Elias ?] *The psalm-singer's necessary companion*. 1700. Wing P4147. 2nd edn, 1700. See also PC 56.
    3   Lancs
    P   s a t b

48 [Brady, Nicholas & Tate, Nahum.] *A supplement to the new version of psalms by Dr. Brady and Mr. Tate*. 1700. Wing B2624. (Part II:) The usual tunes to the psalms. 4 later edns 1700–4; see also PC 57.
    47
    PH   c

49 Porter, Samuel. *Plaine and easie directions for psalm-singing: with a collection of the best tunes (now in use) in two parts; bass and treble*. 1700. Not in Wing. Copy: Cambridge University Library.
    4
    P   g b

50 S[henton], S[amuel] & H[all], J[ohn]. *Tunes to the psalms of David in four parts*. 1700. Not in Wing. Copy: Euing Library, Glasgow University. (Based on PC 26.)
    46
    P   a a t b

No.	Description					
51	Playford, Henry. *The divine companion.* 1701. 4 later edns 1707–22.	237	PHA		g (g) b	
52	Wanless, Thomas. *The metre psalm-tunes, in four parts. Composed for the use of the parish-church of St. Michael's of Belfrey's in York.* 1702.	1 / PHC		York	s a t b	
53	*The Christians daily manual of prayers and praises. In two parts ... The second containing a course of select psalms and hymns, with their proper tunes.* 1703. (Second part missing in the only surviving copy.) See also PC 87.	147 / PH		Old Romney	c	
54	Darby, C. *The book of psalms in English metre.* 1704.	46	P		c	
55	Hawes, William. *A collection of psalms, proper to be sung at churches.* 1704. Later edn 1707.	4 / P			g b	
56	Hall, Elias. *The psalm-singer's compleat companion.* 1706. Later edn 1708. (A revised version of PC 47?)	3 / PHA		Lancs	(g) a g b	
57	Brady, Nicholas & Tate, Nahum. *A supplement to the new version of psalms by Dr. Brady and Mr. Tate.* 6th edn 1708. (An enlarged version of PC 48.) 4 later edns 1712–40.	4 / PH			g b	
58	*Select psalms and hymns for the use of ... St. James's Westminster.* 1709. (Based on PC 36.) 5 later edns 1712–c. 1750.	1 / PH		Westminster	g g b	
59	Bishop, John. *A set of new psalm tunes.* [1710.] (Advertised *The post man*, 16–19 November 1710.) Later edns [1722], [1730].	1 / PA		Reading	s a t b	
59a	Reading, John. *A book of new anthems.* [c. 1710.]	2 / A		London	g (b)	O
60	Barber, Abraham. *A book of psalm-tunes; in four parts.* 6th edn York & Wakefield, 1711. (Revision of PC 40.) See also PC 66.	3 / PHA		W. Yorks	(a) a t b	
61	*A collection of psalm tunes in four parts ... With five anthems in four parts.* 1711.	3 / PA			s a t b	
62	S[henton], S[amuel]. *The devout singer's guide.* 1711. 4th edn 1719.	4 / P			g b	
63	Greene, John & James. *A book of psalm-tunes.* 2nd edn 1713. Copy: Leeds University Library. See also PC 67.	3 / PA		W. Yorks	((s)a) t b	
64	Bennet, Robert. *A collection of the choicest and best psalm tunes with a necessary introduction to singing.* Nottingham, 1714. (No copy survives; described by A. H. Mann in a manuscript note inside a copy of PC 70.)	3 / P		Nottingham	g (b)	
65	Stansfield, Ely. *Psalmody epitomiz'd.* York, 1714. 2nd edn. London, 1731.	4 / P		Yorkshire	a t t b	
66	Barber, Abraham. *A book of psalm-tunes in four parts.* 7th edn Wakefield, 1715. (Revision of PC 60.)	3 / PHA		W. Yorks	a a t b	
67	Green, John & James. *A collection of choice psalm-tunes.* 3rd edn Nottingham, Sheffield, & London, 1715. (Revision of PC 63.) See also PC 72.	3 / PHA		W. Yorks/N. Mid.	((s) a) t b	
68	Robinson, David. *An essay upon vocal musick.* Nottingham, 1715.	47 / PHA		N. Midlands	g g b	
69	[Hart, Philip.] *Melodies proper to be sung to any of the versions of yᵉ psalms of David, figur'd for the organ; ... the treble of each melody transpos'd for the flute.* [1716] (Advertised *The post man*, 17–19 July, 1716) Later edn [1720].	27 / P				O i

70	Bennet, Robert. *The psalm-singer's necessary companion.* 1718. (Revision of PC 64.)	3 P	Nottingham g (b)	
71	Chetham, John. *A book of psalmody.* 1718. (Advertised in *Nottingham Weekly Courant*, 27 February 1717.) 2nd edn 1722. See also PC 86 and p. 183.	3 PAC	W. Yorks/N. Mid. s a t b	
72	Green, James. *A collection of psalm-tunes.* 4th edn 1718. (Advertised in *Nottingham Weekly Courant*, 24 July 1718. Revision of PC 67.) See also PC 98.	3 PHA	W. Yorks/N. Mid. (s) a t b	
73	Purcell, Daniel. *The psalms set full for the organ or harpsichord.* 1718.	12 P	London	O
74	[Warner, Daniel. *An intire guide to parish-clarks; being the treble and bass of the singing-psalms, ... with rules for singing or playing.*] [–1719.] (Advertised in PC 78. A copy lacking title page, presumably of this work, is in the British Library, K.4.e.17(2).)	4 P	Oxon g b	
75	Warner, Daniel. *A further guide to parish clarks ... Being a full account of all the psalm tunes, and what psalms are sung to each of them.* [–1719.] (In two vols., one with the treble part, one with the bass. The bass vol. has not survived, but both are advertised in PC 78.)	4 P	Oxon g *b*	
76	Ireland, Edmund. *The psalm singer's guide.* 3rd edn London & York, 1719. 4th edn York, 1720.	3 P	Yorkshire ((g) a) g b	
77	Marsden, Joshua. *The psalm-singer's instructor.* Liverpool, 1719.	46 PH	(s) a t b g (g) b	
78	Warner, Daniel. *The singing-master's guide to his scholars.* 1719.	4 PH	Oxon c (b)	
79	Baker, George. *A collection of the best and most musical psalms taken from Mr. Playford's last edition.* 1720.	4 PH	g b	
80	Timbrell, Francis. *The divine musick scholar's guide.* [c. 1720–35.] (Various unique copies.)	3 PHAC	Northants (s) a t b g b	
81	Barber, Robert & John. *A book of psalmody.* 1723. See also PC 106.	3 PHAC	N. Derbys. s a t b	
82	Langhorne, William. *A book of the choicest and most select psalm-tunes.* 2nd edn 1723.	3 PHA	S. Lincs ((s) a) t b	
83	Church, John. *An introduction to psalmody.* [c. 1723.] Later edn [c. 1740].	2 PHA	s (s) (t) b	(O)
84	Betts, Edward. *An introduction to the skill of musick.* 1724.	125 AC	Manchester s a t b	(O)
85	Bridges, George. *A new book of psalmody.* 1724.	4 P	g b	
86	Chetham, John. *A book of psalmody.* 3rd edn 1724. 4th edn 1731. See also PC 111a.	3 PASC	W. Yorks/N. Mid. s a t b	
87	*The Christian sacrifice of praises, consisting of select psalms and hymns ... collected by the author of the Christians daily manual.* 1724. (Revision of PC 53.)	147 PH	Old Romney t t b	
88	Holdroyd, Israel. *The spiritual man's companion.* [c. 1724.] 4 later edns [c. 1730]–1753.	3 PHASC	W. Yorks s a t b	
89	Broom[e], Michael (and John). *Michael Broom's collection of church musick.* [Collection I. 68 leaves.] [n.p., –1725.] See also PC 107.	3 PHAC	s a t b g (g) b	
90	Bishop, John. *A supplement to the new psalm-book.* 1725.	3 PA	s a t b	

91	S[herwin?], W. *An help to the singing [of] p[s]alm-tunes by the book ... with directions for making an instrument with one string ... as also a large collection of tunes.* 1725.	47 P	g b	
92	[Anchors, William ?] *A choice collection of psalm-tunes, hymns and anthems. Taught by William Anchors.* [1726?]	3 PHAC	(a) g b	
93	Barber, Robert. *The psalm singer's choice companion.* 1727.	3 PHA	N. Midlands s a t b	
94	Birch, John. *A choice collection of psalm-tunes.* 1728.	3 PHASC	*Notts.* s a t b	
95	Ravenscroft, Thomas (rev. by William Turner.) *The whole book of psalm-tunes.* 1728. (Based on PC 16). Later edn 1746.	3 P	s a t b	
96	Leman, James. *A new method of learning psalm-tunes, with an instrument ... call'd the psalterer.* 1729.	46 P	s s b	I
97	Richardson, William. *The pious recreation.* 1729.	12 HA	London suburbs s(s)b	O
98	Green, James. *A book of psalmody.* 6th edn [1729–]. (Advertises PC 97. A revision of PC 72.) 8th, 9th edns 1734, 1738. See also PC 123.	3 PAC	N. Lincs s a t b	
99	Barrow, John. *A new book of psalmody.* 1730. See also PC 131.	3 PHAC	*Here.* s a t b	
100	Street, Josiah. *A book containing great variety of anthems, ... likewise, a sett of psalm-tunes.* [c. 1730.] See also PC 129.	3 PA	W. Yorks s a t b	
101	Wilkins, Matthew. *A book of psalmody.* Great Milton, Oxfordshire, [c. 1730]. (British Library, A.992.a.) Later edn (as *A second book of psalmody*, British Library A.992.b) London, [c. 1750]. See also PC 182a.	3 PHA	Oxon s a t b g b	
102	Broom[e], Michael. *A choice collection of psalm-tunes, hymns and anthems.* n.p., [–1731]. Later edn [c. 1740].	3 PHASC	Middx s a t b	
103	*The psalms by Dr. Blow set full for the organ or harpsichord.* [c. 1731.]	2 P		O
104	Pearson, William. *The second book of the Divine Companion.* [1731–.] (A sequel to PC 51.) Later reissued as *The divine companion*, printed and sold by J. Robinson. [c. 1745.]	237 PHA	London (s) s a t b g b	(O) (O) (I)
105	Smith, B[enjamin]. *The harmonious companion; or, the psalm-singer's magazine ... corrected by Mr. Prelluer.* 1732. (See Brown & Stratton: 379.)	3 PHA	s a t b	o
106	Barber, Robert. *A book of psalmody.* 2nd edn 1733. (Revision of PC 93.) 3rd edn (as *David's harp well tuned*) 1753.	3 PHASCL	N. Midlands s a t b	
107	Broom[e], Michael. *Michael Broom's collection of church music.* [Collection II. 79 leaves.] [Birmingham, c. 1733.] (Entirely different from PC 89. Copy: Birmingham Public Library.)	3 PASC	Birmingham s a t b	
108	Broome, Michael. *A choice collection of sixteen excellent psalm-tunes.* Birmingham, [1733–].	2 P	Birmingham s a t b	o
109	W(illis), R(ichard). *The excellent use of psalmody.* Nottingham, 1734.	4 PH	Nottingham g b	
110	Tans'ur, William. *A compleat melody.* (1734.) 2nd edn 1735. See also PC 113.	3 PHASC	Surrey g(a) t b	o
111	Tans'ur, William. *The melody of the heart.* 1735. Later edns 1737, 1751.	3 PHA	Surrey g(a)t b	o

Bibliography

111a	Chetham, John. *A book of psalmody*. 5th edn 1736. (Revision of PC 86.) 6th–11th edns Wakefield, 1741–Leeds, 1787. See also PC 338.	*23* PASC		W. Yorks s a t b		o
112	[Bedford, Arthur ?] *Divine recreations, being a collection of psalms, hymns, and canons. ... To be continued quarterly.* [3 numbers.] 1736–7. (PC 107 contains a prospectus of this work.)	*47* PH		s a t b		
113	Tans'ur, William. *A compleat melody.* 3rd edn 1736. (Based on PC 110.) Later edns 1738, 1743. (See MS 4.)	*3* PHASC		Surrey g(a) t b		o
114	*An introduction to psalmody ... with a collection of various, easy, and pleasant tunes in two parts.* 1737.	*467* PH		**g** b		
*115	Knapp, William. *A sett of new psalm-tunes and anthems.* 1738. 7 later edns 1741–70.	*3* PHA		Dorset **g** a **g** b		
116	Tans'ur, William. *Sacred mirth: or the pious soul's daily delight.* 1739.	*347* PHA		Surrey g(a) **g** b s a t b		o o
117	Arnold, John. *The compleat psalmodist.* 1741 (1740). 2nd–7th edns 1750–79.	*3* PASCL		Essex s a t b		
118	Sreeve, John. *The divine music scholar's guide.* 1740. Later edn 1741.	*3* PH: A:		*S. England* g(a) **g** b (s) a t b		o o
119	Needham, Joseph. [Collection of church music. –1741.] (No copy known; mentioned in Prefaces to PC 117/5 and 120.)	*3* PA		*Suffolk*		
*120	Buckenham, John. *The psalm-singer's devout exercise.* 1741.	*3* PHAC		Suffolk s a t b		(O)
121	Sreeve, John. *The Oxfordshire harmony.* 1741. Vol. III. (No copy known of vol. II, which contained psalms.	*3* PHAS		S.and W. England g(a) **g** b		o
121a	Tans'ur, William. [?*The royal psalmist; or Tans'ur's harmony compleat.* Rugby, 1742.] (British Library, A.1237.x. Likely title and imprint supplied from a MS. note in PC 125a/1750, British Library copy, A.1232.j.) See also PC 125a.	*3* PAS		*Midlands* s a t b		
122	Broome, Michael. *A choice collection of twenty-four psalm-tunes ... and fifteen anthems.* Birmingham, [–1744]. (Owner's inscription dated 1744 in Bodleian Library copy, Mus. 54.f.28.)	*2* P A		Midlands s a t b **g g** b		o
123	Green, James. *A book of psalmody.* 10th edn 1744. (A revision of PC 98.) 11th edn 1751.	*3* PHASC		N. Lincs s a t b		
124	Bellamy, John. *A system of divine musick.* 1745.	*3* PASC		Notts s a t b		
125	Broderip, John. *A new set of anthems and psalm tunes.* Wells, [1745]. Later issue, London, [c. 1750]. See also PC 136.	*25* PAS		Somerset s a t b		
125a	Tans'ur, William. *The royal psalmodist compleat.* [n.p.], 1745. (Many sheets printed from plates of PC 121a. Copy: Clark Memorial Library, Los Angeles.) Later edns [1747?], 1748, [1750?]. '2nd edn' 1753 (title page only, British Library, A.479.b.)	*3* PAS		Midlands s a t b		
126	Alcock, Dr John (the elder). *Psalmody: or a collection of psalm tunes.* Reading, [c. 1745].	*3* PH		Reading **g** b		O
128	(Woodmason, Charles.) *A collection of psalm tunes with basses fitted for the voice and figured for the organ, for the use of Gosport in Hampshire.* [c. 1745]. Later edn (Portsmouth, 1748).	*1* P		Gosport **g** b		o

372

No.				
129	Street, Josiah. *A book containing great variety of anthems ... Likewise a set of psalm-tunes.* 2nd edn 1746. Later edn (as *A collection of anthems*) Carlisle, 1785.	*3* PHAC	W. Yorks s a t b	
130	Evison, James. *A compleat book of psalmody.* 1747. Later edns 1751–69.	*3* PHAS	Sussex s a t b	
131	Barrow, John. *The psalm-singer's choice companion.* 2nd edn [*c.* 1747] (Possibly 2nd edn of PC 99). 3rd edn [1755] (Advertised *Whitehall Evening Post*, 2 Jan. 1755).	*3* PHAC	Midlands s a t b	
*133	Smith, John. *A set of services, anthems and psalm tunes.* [1748.] Later edn (as *A 1st set ...*) [*c.* 1760]. See also PC 143a.	*3* PAS	Hants g a g b	
134	East, William. *The voice of melody.* Waltham, [*c.* 1748]. 2nd edn (as 'Book I') Waltham, 1750. See also PC 137.	*3* PHA	N. Midlands s a t b (g a) g b	
135	Watts, Joseph. *A choice collection of church music.* Fennycompton & Banbury, 1749.	*3* PHASC	S. Midlands (g) a g b s a t b	
136	Broderip, John. *A second book of new anthems and psalm tunes.* [–1750.] (A sequel to PC 125.) Later issue [1764].	*25* PHA	Somerset s a t b	
137	East, William. *The voice of melody.* Book II. Waltham, 1750. (Sequel to PC 134.)	*3* PHAS	N. Midlands s a t b g a g b	
138	Moore, Thomas. *The psalm singer's compleat tutor and divine companion.* 2nd edn Manchester, 1750.	*367* [I]: PHA [II]: PHAC	Lancs ((s)a) t b(b) (s) a t b g b	
139	Adams, Abraham. *A choice collection of psalm tunes and anthems.* [*c.* 1750.] (No copy known; advertised in PC 145. May have been 1st edn of PC 146.)	*3* *PA*		
139a	Barker, John. *A select number of the best psalm tunes, extant.* Birmingham, [*c.* 1750].	*12* [I]: PA [II]: HT	Coventry s a t b **s** (s) b	o O
140	Lyndon, James. *My God, my God, look upon me. A single anthem for a tenor-bass.* [n.p., *c.* 1750.]	*25* A	*Wolverhampton* s a t b	O
141	Milner, Abraham. *Sacred melody.* [*c.* 1750.]	*4* A	s(a(t))b	
142	(Tans'ur, William.) [*A collection of church music.*] [*c.* 1750.] (Copy, lacking title page: British Library, A.1232.f.)	*3* PA	g a g b	
143	Hinton, Simon. *A collection of church musick.* [n.p., –1751.]	*3* PHA	g a g b	
*143a	Smith, John. *Book the second. Containing twelve anthems and twelve psalm tunes.* Lavington, 1751. (A sequel to PC 133.) Later edn (as *A set of services ...*) London, [*c.* 1760]. See also PC 154.	*3* PA	Hants g a g b	
144	Milner, Abraham. *The psalm singers companion.* 1751. 4th edn [*c.* 1765].	*36* PHA	London (s) (a) t b	
145	*The organist's pocket companion, being a collection of all the psalm tunes that are generally used in parish churches and chapels.* [*c.* 1751.] Later edn [*c.* 1767].	2 P		O
146	Adams, Abraham. *The psalmist's new companion.* 2nd edn 1752. (No copy known; advertised Dec. 1752. 5th edn advertised March 1756. See PC 174.)	*3* *PHA*	Kent	

147	[Fox, Joseph. *The parish clerk's vade mecum: being a collection of singing psalms.* London?, 1752.] (No copy survives; deposited at Stationer's Hall 4 July 1752.)	4 P		
148	Knapp, William. *New church melody.* [c. 1752.] 4 later edns 1754–64.	3 PHA	Dorset g a g b	
149	Broome, Michael. *A collection of twenty eight psalm tunes* [I]: in four parts. [Birmingham], 1753.	2 P	Midlands s a t b	o
		[II]: 3 P	Midlands s a t b	o
150	Broome, Michael. *A choice collection of eleven anthem's.* [Birmingham], 1754.	3 A	Midlands s a t b	
151	East, William. *The sacred melody.* Waltham, 1754.	3 PHAS	N. Midlands g a g b	
152	Crisp, William. *Divine harmony,* 1755.	3 PASC	Norfolk, Suffolk s a t b	(o)
153	Davenport, Uriah. *The psalm-singer's pocket companion.* 1755. 2nd, 3rd edns 1758, 1785.	3 PHASC	s a t b	
154	Smith, John. *Book the third, containing twelve anthems and twelve psalm tunes.* Lavington, 1755. (A sequel to PC 143a.) Later edn (as *A third set of services ...*) London, [c. 1760].	3 PAS	Hants g a g b	
155	Tans'ur, William. *The royal melody compleat.* 1754–5. 2nd, 3rd edns 1759–60, 1764–6. Also '3rd' edn, Boston II: [Mass.], 1767; '4th' edn, Newburyport [Mass.], 1768; III: [5th–9th edns, as *The American harmony; or, Royal melody complete,* Newburyport, 1769–74. See R. T. Daniel: 169–70.]	23 P HRASC	Cambs; Hants s a t b g a g b	o o(O)
156	Broome, Michael. *A choice collection of twenty four psalm tunes ... and fifteen anthems ... With the addition of nine psalm tunes ... one anthem ... and a full Te Deum.* Birmingham, [c. 1755]. (Copy lacking additional matter, British Library, A.902; copy lacking title page, with additional matter including some not mentioned on title page, Birmingham Public Library.)	2 PAS	Midlands s a t b g g b	o o
157	East, William. *Collection of church musick.* Waltham, [c. 1755].	3 PRAS	N. Midlands s a t b g a g b	
158	Pratt, Jonas. *A set of anthems and psalm tunes in four, five, and six parts.* [c. 1755.]	3 PA	N. Mid./Lincs. s a t b	o(I)
159	Bremner, Robert. *The rudiments of music.* [Part II:] A collection of the best church tunes, canons and anthems. Edinburgh [& London], 1756. (Entered at Stationer's Hall, 27 November 1757). 2nd edn, Edinburgh [& London], 1762. See also PC 187.	2 PA	g g b	(O)
160	Hutchinson, John. *A select set of psalms and hymns ... sung in the parish church of Grantham.* [Grantham], 1756. Later edn 1792.	13 PH	Grantham g b	
*161	Alcock, Dr John (the elder). *The pious soul's heavenly exercise.* Lichfield, (1756).	23 PHC	Midlands s a t b	o
163	Arnold, John. *The psalmist's recreation.* 1757.	3 PA	*Essex* s a t b	O i
164	Everet, John. *The divine concert.* Waltham, 1757.	3 PAS	N. Mid./Lincs. g a g b	o

No.					
165	Playford, John (rev. by Joseph Fox). *The whole book of*	[I]: 14	Westminster		
	psalms ... *Composed in three parts.* 20th edn 1757. (Based	PH	g g b		
	on PC 29.)	[II]: 12			
		A		s a t b	O
166	Hill, John. *A new book of psalmody.* [c. 1757.]	3	Kent; Northants		
		PHA		s a t b	
				g(g a)b	
167	Broome, Michael. *Divine Harmony: being a collection of*	4	*Birmingham*		
	... twelve anthems. Birmingham, 1758.	A		s a t b	
168	Stephenson, Joseph. *An anthem taken out of the 44 chap.*	3			
	of Isaiah. [c. 1758.]	PA		s a t b	OI
169	Arnold, John. *The Leicestershire harmony.* 1759. Later	3	Leics		
	edn 1767.	PAS		s a t b	
170	French, J. *The young psalm singer's complete guide.* 1759.	3	*Wilts*		
		PAS		g a g b	
171	Stephenson, Joseph. *Church harmony sacred to devotion.*	34	Dorset		
	3rd edn 1760. 4th edn [c. 1775].	PHAS		g a g b	
172	Tans'ur, William. *The psalm-singer's jewel.* 1760.	37	Lincs		
	Reissued as *The psalmist's jewel,* 1766.	P		(s) a t b	
173	West, Benjamin. *Sacra concerto.* 1760. 2nd edn 1769.	3	S. Midlands		
		PA		g a g b	
174	Adams, Abraham. *The psalmist's new companion.* 6th edn	3	Kent		
	[c. 1760]. 10th–12th edns [c. 1775] – [c. 1795]. See also PC	PHA		g a g b	
	139, 146.				
175	Ashworth, Caleb. *A collection of tunes.* [Part I.] [c. 1760.]	36			
	2nd edn 1765, 3rd edn 1766, 4th edn 1775. See also PC 185.	PH		(g)a g b	
176	Beesly, Michael. *A book of psalmody.* [Oxford?, c. 1760.]	3	Oxon, Berks		
	Another edn (as *An introduction to psalmody*) Oxford,	PAC		s a t b	
	[c. 1760].			g a g b	
177	Beesly, Michael. *A collection of 20 new psalm tunes.*	3	Oxon, Berks		
	Oxford & Newbury, [c. 1760].	P		g a g b	
*179	Catchpole, Robert. *A coronation anthem ... for the use of*	3	*E. Anglia*		
	country choirs. [1760?]	A		s a t b	O
180	*A collection of psalm tunes with a thorough bass for the*	27	*London*		
	harpsichord or organ. [c. 1760.]	PHA		(g) g b	o
181	Johnson, J. *Ten full anthems ... for the use of country*	3			
	churches. [c. 1760]. Later edn [c. 1770].	A		g a g b	
182	Milner, Abraham. *The psalm singers pocket amusement.*	46	London		
	[c. 1760.]	PH		t b	
182a	Wilkins, Matthew. *A book of psalmody.* Great Milton,	3	Oxon		
	Oxfordshire, [c. 1760]. (British Library, A.992. Entirely	PHA		g a g b	
	different from PC 101.)				
183	Catchpole, Robert. *A choice collection of church music.*	3	E. Anglia		
	Bury St Edmunds, 1761.	PA		s a t b	(o)
184	*A small collection of psalms to the old tunes, sung by the*	2	Chichester		
	charity children of the city of Chichester. 1761.	P		s b	o
185	Ashworth, Caleb. *A collection of tunes.* Part II. 2nd edn	36			
	1762. (A sequel to PC 175.) 3rd edn 1763.	PHA		(g) a g b	
186	Riley, William. *Parochial music corrected ... A collection*	4	London		
	of psalm tunes. 1762. Later edns [c. 1770], [c. 1771].	P		s a (t) b	o
187	Bremner, Robert. *The rudiments of music.* [Part II:] A	2			
	collection of the best church tunes, canons and anthems.	P		s a t b	o
	3rd edn 1763. (Revision of PC 159.) Later edn 1790.	A		s(a)t b	
		C		g g b	o

188	Thompson, W. *Several select portions of the psalms.* Newcastle, 1763.	2 P	Northumb. g b	
189	Williams, Aaron. *The universal psalmodist.* 1763. 2nd–4th edns 1764–70. [Also republished as *The American harmony, or Universal psalmodist*, '5th'–'9th' edns, Newburyport [Mass.], 1769–74. See R. T. Daniel: 170.]	236 PHA	gagb	
190	Arnold, John. *Church music reformed.* 1765.	2 PH	s b	o
191	*A collection of melodies to the psalms ... according to the version of Christopher Smart.* 1765.	47 P	s (a) b	o
192	Hewett, James. *An introduction to singing.* 1765.	3 PHA	s a t b g a g b	
193	Williams, Aaron. *Royal harmony.* [c. 1765.]	3 A	(g) a g b	
194	Cole, William. *The psalmodist's exercise.* London & [I]: Ipswich, [c. 1766]. [II]:	3 P 3 A	E. Anglia g g b s a t b	
195	Clark, Edward. *Six easy hymns or anthems.* [1767.]	247 T	London g	o
196	Wainwright, John. *A collection of psalm tunes, anthems, hymns, and chants.* [1767?]	12 PHAC	Manchester s a t b	o/O
*197	Bond, Capel. *Six anthems in score.* 1769. 5 later edns 1769–77.	235 A	Coventry s a t b	O
198	Harrott, John. *The Rutland-harmony or sacred-concert.* Stamford, 1769.	3 P	Rutland, Leics g a g b	
199	Williams, Aaron. *Psalmody in miniature.* 1769. See also PC 236.	46 P	*London* g b	
200	Harrott, John. *The divine vocal and instrumental harmony.* Great Bowden, 1770.	3 PA H	Rutland, Leics g a g b g b	(I)
201	[Kempson, James.] *Collection of 21 psalm tunes.* Birmingham, 1770.	46 P	Birmingham s a t b	
202	Williams, Aaron. *The new universal psalmodist.* 1770. '5th edn' (1770). '6th edn' [c. 1775].	236 PHA	gagb	
203	Clark, Edward. *New anthem.* [c. 1770.]	2 A	London g	O
204	Cook, Richard. *Kentish psalmodist's companion.* [c. 1770.]	3 PAS	Kent g a g b	
205	Harwood, Edward. *A set of hymns and psalm tunes.* [c. 1770.] (See also PC 259.)	246 PHT	Lancs; Ches. g (a) g b	
*207	Alcock, Dr John (the elder). *Six and twenty select anthems in score.* 1771.	45 A	s a t b	O
208	Wise, Samuel. *Three anthems ... for the use of parochial churches.* [1771.]	14 A	Nottingham s a t b	O I
210	Tans'ur, William. *Melodia sacra.* 2nd edn 1772.	3 PCSA	g a g b	
211	*A course of singing psalms.* 1773.	4 P	g b	o
212	Ivery, John. *The Hertfordshire melody.* London & Hertford, 1773.	3 PHA	Herts g a g b	

214	Langdon, Richard. *Divine harmony, being a collection in score of psalms and anthems.* 1774.	25	Exeter		
		PHAC	s a t b		O
215	*Twenty psalm tunes in three parts . . . composed by the late Mr. Coombes and other eminent masters.* London and Bristol, [–1775].	256	Bristol		
		P	g g b		
216	Williams, Aaron. *An ode or anthem for the New Year.* [–1775.]	2	London		
		A	s a t b		
217	Williams, Aaron. *Two new anthems for Christmas-Day.* [–1775.] (Advertised in PC 216.)	47	*London*		
		HT	g g b		I
218	Chapman, T. *The organist's universal companion.* 1775.	12	Westminster		
		P	g		O
219	Newton, James Williams. *Psalmody improved.* Ipswich, 1775.	3	Suffolk		
		PAS	s(a) t b		o
			a t b		o
			t b		o
220	Cook, Richard. *The psalmodist's companion.* [c. 1775.] (Title page derived from that of PC 204 by alteration of plate; contents different.)	3	S.E. England		
		PA	g g g b		
221	Goodwin, S[tarling]. *The complete organist's pocket companion.* [c. 1775.]	2			
		P			O
222	[*Harmody divine, being a collection of psalm and hymn tunes, anthems, &c.* London?, c. 1775.] (No copy found; advertised in PC 202/6.)	4			
		PHA			
223	Hayes, William. *Sixteen psalms . . . set to music for the use of Magd: Coll: Chapel in Oxford . . . To which is added a score, without the organ part, for . . . country churches.* [c. 1775.] See also PC 278.	3			
		P	s a t b		
			g g b		
224	Kempson, James. *A collection of psalm tunes in four parts.* Birmingham, [c. 1775].	46	Birmingham		
		P	s a t b		
225	Kempson, James. *Eight anthems in score.* Birmingham, [c. 1775].	2	Birmingham		
		A	s a t b		O
226	Senior, D. *The food of devotion.* [c. 1775.]	3	Kent		
		P	g a g b		o
227	Stephenson, Joseph. *The musical companion.* [c. 1775.]	3			
		PHAS	s a t b		I
228	Wilkins, Elizabeth. *A collection of church music.* Great Milton, [c. 1775].	3	Oxon		
		PHA	g a g b		
229	Key, Joseph. *Eight anthems.* 2nd edn Nuneaton, 1776. 3rd edn ('Book First') Nuneaton, [c. 1795].	3	Midlands		
		AS	g a g b		I
230	Bond, Hugh. *Twelve hymns and four anthems for four voices.* [c. 1776.]	257	Exeter		
		PT	s a t b		O
			g		O
231	Pearce, Samuel. *Sacred music.* [c. 1776.]	46			
		PH	g (a) b		
			g a g b		
232	Alcock, John (the younger). *Parochial harmony.* 1777.	3	N. Midlands		
		PHAS	s a t b		O I
233	Arnold, John. *A supplement to the complete psalmodist.* [1777.] (A sequel to PC 117.)	37	Essex		
		PA	g a g b		O
234	Alcock, John (the younger). *A collection of anthems.* [c. 1777.] (Seven anthems, also published separately, [c. 1773–6].)	23	N. Midlands		
		A	s a t b		o I

Bibliography

No.	Entry				
*235	Crompton, John. *The psalm singer's assistant*. 1778.	3	Suffolk		
		PHAS	((s) a) t b		
236	Williams, Aaron. *Psalmody in miniature*. In III books. (An enlargement of PC 199.) 2nd edn 1778. Supplement, 1778; 2nd supplement, 1780. 3rd edn [in v books], 1783.	46	London		
		PH	g b		o
237	Roome, Francis [& Dr John Alcock]. *The harmony of Sion*. [1779.] (Contents partly taken from PC 126.)	23			
		PHC	s a t b		o
238	Williams, Aaron. *A new Christmas anthem*. [–1780.] (Advertised in PC 241.)	23			
		A	s a t b		O I
239	Addington, Stephen. *A collection of approved anthems*. Market Harborough, 1780. 2nd edn 1795.	3	Leics		
		AT	g a g b		
240	Kempson, James. *A choice collection of ... thirteen anthems*. Birmingham, 1780.	4	Birmingham		
		A	s a t b		
241	Williams, Thomas. *Harmonia coelestis*. 1780.	23	London		
		A	s a t b		O
			(g) g b		O/I
242	Beatson, John. *A complete collection of all the tunes sung by the different congregations in Hull*. [Hull?, c. 1780.]	26	Hull		
		P	(g) g b		
243	Ganthony, Joseph. *An anthem for Christmas Day ... Also two favorite psalm tunes and a canon*. [c. 1780.]	12	London		
		PA	s a t b		O
244	Jackson, Thomas. *Twelve psalm tunes and eighteen ... chants*. [c. 1780.]	12345	Newark		
		PC	s a t b		o
245	*Select portions of the psalms of David, for the use of parish churches*. [c. 1780.] 2nd edn 1786.	4			
		P	g g b		
246	Smith, Isaac. *A collection of psalm tunes*. [c. 1780.] A new edn with supplement [c. 1782]. 4th edn [c. 1784]. 5th edn with additions by S. Major [c. 1790].	26	London		
		PA	g g b		
*248	Gawler, William. *Harmonia sacra*. 1781.	2	London		
		PHTA	s		O
			s a t b		O
249	*Musica sacra: or, a collection of easy tunes, ... with a psalm or hymn adapted to each*. [n.p., –1783.]	46			
		PH	g (g) b		
250	Barwick, John. *Harmonia Cantica divina, or the Kentish divine harmonist*. [c. 1783.]	3	Kent		
		P	s a t b		o
		A	s a t b		
251	Billington, Thomas. *The Te Deum, Jubilate, Magnificat and Nunc Dimittis*. Opera XI. (1784.)	3			
		S	a t b		i
253	Harrison, Ralph. *Sacred Harmony*. Vol. I. [1784.] Later edns [1786], [1793], [c. 1795]. See PC 258.	36	Manchester		
		PHT	g a g b		o
254	Ganthony, Joseph. *An anthem for Easter-day*. [c. 1785.]	12	London		
		A	s a t b		
255	Marsh, John. *A verse anthem ... ten new psalm tunes*. [c. 1785.]	45			
		PHAC	s(a t) b		O
256	Tremain, Thomas. *Twenty psalms, set to music*. [c. 1785.]	2			
		PT	s a t b		O
*257	Valentine, John. *Thirty psalm tunes*, Op. 7. [c. 1785.]	23	Leics		
		PT	s a t b		O
258	Harrison, Ralph. *Sacred harmony*. Vol. II. [1786.] (A sequel to PC 253.)	36	Manchester		
		PHTC	g a g b		o
259	Harwood, Edward. *A second set of hymns and psalm tunes*. Chester, (1786). (A sequel to PC 205.)	246	Lancs; Ches.		
		PHA	s a t b		o
			g g b		o
260	*Select psalms and hymns for the use of the parish church of Cardington*. 1786. Later edn, 1787.	13	Cardington		
		PH	g b		

261	Cuzens, Benjamin. *Divine harmony*. 1787. Later edn [*c*. 1800].	3 TAS	Portsmouth s a t b	I
262	[Firth, Thomas. *Sun's harmony, consisting of psalms, hymns, anthems, &c*. Leeds? 1787.] (No copy known; entered at Stationer's Hall, 13 January 1787.)	*3 PHA*	*Leeds*	
262a	Webbe, Samuel. *Eight anthems in score, for the use of cathedrals and country choirs*. [1788.] (Reviewed, *Analytical Review* 2 (1788), 359.)	35 A	s a t b	O
263	Dalmer, William. *Twenty psalms and hymns*. [*c*. 1788.]	2 PH	Bath s a (t) b	O
*264	Hill, John. *Hill's church music*. [1788–91.]	*2* PAS	Midlands s a t b	O/o
265	Cuzens, Benjamin. *Five anthems and five collects*. [1789.] (Only the title page is extant.) Later edn [*c*. 1800].	A	s a t b s a t b	I o
266	Dixon, William. *Psalmodia Christiana*. Guildford, 1789.	36 PHT	Surrey t a s b	O(i)
267	Harrod, W. *Select psalms of David in the Old Version*. Stamford, 1789.	4 PH	E. Midlands t b	o
*268	Jones, William [of Nayland]. *Ten church pieces for the organ with four anthems in score*. Opera II. (1789.)	123 A	E. Anglia s s b s(s) a t b	O O
269	Williams, Thomas. *Psalmodia evangelica*. 2 vol. 1789. Later edns 1790, 1792.	*36* PH	g g b	
270	Heron, Henry. *Parochial music corrected: ...for the use of the charity-schools in London, Westminster, &c*. 1790.	27 PHAC	London s (s) (b)	O
*271	Miller, Edward. *The psalms of David for the use of parish churches*. (1790.) Later edns [*c*. 1790]–[*c*. 1818].	2 P	N. and E. Eng. s b s a/t b	O o
272	Bland, John. *Bland's collection of divine music*. [*c*. 1790.] (See also PC 308.)	27 PHT	(s) s a(t) s b	O O
*273	Collins, Thomas. *A collection of anthems and psalms*. Nuneaton, [*c*. 1790].	3 PHTA	Midlands s a t b	I/i
274	Cooke, Matthew. *Twelve psalm tunes ...for the use of the church at North Mims*. [*c*. 1790.]	13 P	Herts s a t b	(I)
275	Dixon, William. *Six anthems in score*. [*c*. 1790.]	3 A	s a t b	O/I
276	Dixon, William. *Four services in score*. [*c*. 1790.]	3 S	s a t b	O/I
277	Filewood, Thomas R. *Six anthems*. [*c*. 1790.]	3 A	Surrey s a t b	O
278	Hayes, Philip. *Sixteen psalms ... Selected from Merrick's version*. [*c*. 1790.] (Revision of PC 223.)	235 P	Oxford g g b s a t b	O
279	Key, Joseph. *Eleven anthems*. Book II. Nuneaton, [*c*. 1790]. (Book I unknown.) See PC 323.	3 A	Midlands g a g b	I
280	Riley, William. *The divine harmonist's assistant*. [*c*. 1790.]	2 P	London g b	O
281	Burdett, Henry. *An anthem for Christmas Day* [etc.] *by James Rodgers*. [*c*. 1790.]	125 PRAS T	Peterborough s a t b ss a t b	O O
289	Wainwright, Robert. *The Lord is risen. A favorite anthem, or hymn for Easter Day*. [*c*. 1790.]	*12* T	*Manchester* s a t b	I o

Entry					
290 Wright, John. *The Essex melody.* [c. 1790.]	3			Essex	
		PHA	g a g b		O/I
291 Arnold, Dr Samuel & Callcott, John W. *The psalms of David, for the use of parish churches.* 1791.	4				
		PH	s a t b		o
			a t b		o
			s/t s/t b		o
			g b		o
292 Tattersall, William D. *Psalms selected from the version of ... Merrick.* [1791.]	3			Glos	
		P	g g b		
293 Beaumont, John. *Four anthems adapted for public worship.* (1793.)	46				
		PHTA	g a g b		O
		C			O
*294 Hellendaal, Peter (the elder). *A collection of psalms and hymns for the use of parish churches.* Cambridge, [1793]. Later edn [c. 1795].	2			Cambridge	
		PH	s a t b		O
295 Monzani, Tebaldo. *A selection of twelve psalms and hymns.* (1793.)	245				
		PH	s a (t) b		O
		A	s a t b		I o
295a Alcock, John jun. *Six new anthems* [by the compiler and Dr John Alcock (the elder)]. [1794.]	25				
		A	s a t b		O/I
296 Randall, John. *A collection of psalm & hymn tunes.* Cambridge, 1794. Later edn Cambridge, [c. 1800].	46			Cambridge	
		PHC	g b		O
*297 Tattersall, William D. *Improved psalmody.* Vol. I. The psalms of David [psalms 1–75]. 3 parts and appendix. In score, 1794. In parts, 1795. (Vol. II did not appear.)	13			S. England	
		P	g g b		
298 Addington, Stephen. *A collection of approved anthems.* 2nd edn Miles End, 1795.	46				
		A	s a t b		
299 Smart, George T. *Divine amusement; being a selection of the most admired psalms, hymns, and anthems.* 2nd edn [1795].	457				
		PHT	g b		O
300 Cooke, Matthew. *Select portions of the psalms of David.* [c. 1795.]	456				
		PC	g b		O
301 Figg, W. *A first collection of four anthems and eight psalms.* [c. 1795.]	3			Sussex	
		PA	s a t b		(o)
302 Friend, John. *Parochial harmony, consisting of a collection of old psalm tunes.* [c. 1795.]	3			Durham	
		P	s a t b		O
303 Major, S. *Sacred melody.* 9th edn [c. 1795]. Later edns [c. 1796], [c. 1800].	236				
		PHT	a g b		
304 *Select portions of psalms and hymns ... as sung at Oxford, Welbeck, and Portland chapels [-of-ease in the parish of]* St. Mary Le-Bone. 2nd edn [1795?].	1			London suburb	
		PH	g		O
305 (Charlesworth, J.) *Fifty select tunes ... adapted to the ... first ninety-six psalms.* (1796.)	4				
		P	g g b		o
306 Bond, Hugh. *The psalms of David in metre.* [c. 1796.]	4				
		PH	g b		O
307 Gresham, William. *Psalmody improved.* [–1797.] Later edn [c. 1800].	14			S. Midlands	
		PS	g b		O
308 Linley, Francis. *Linley's continuation of Bland's collection of divine music.* Nos. 17–20. [c. 1797.] Sequel to PC 272.)	367				
		PHA	g(g) b		O
309 Broderip, John & Robert. *Portions of psalms.* Bath, (1798).	2			W. England	
		P	a t s b		o
			s/t b		o

*310	Loder, A. *A collection of church musick ... as performed ... at St. James's church and the Countess of Huntingdon's chapel in the city of Bath.* Bath, 1798.	26 PHS	Bath s a t b		(o)
311	Page, John. *Divine harmony ... a collection of psalm & hymn tunes ... composed ... by the late ... Phocion Henley ... [and] Thos. Sharp.* 1798.	2 PH	London a t(t) s b		o
312	Peck, James. *Two hundred and fifty psalm tunes.* (1798.)	46 P	a g b		o
*313	FFitch, George. *The country chorister.* London & Chelmsford, [1799]. Later edn 1801.	3 PAS	Essex s a t b		
314	Willoughby, Robert. *Sacred harmony in parts.* (1799.)	46 PASC	London s a t b		O i
315	Sampson, Richard. *Ancient church-music.* [c. 1799.]	123 P	Wakefield g g b		
316	Page, John. *Harmonia sacra.* (1800.)	45 A	s a t b		O
317	Camidge, Matthew. *A musical companion to the psalms used in the church of St. Michael le Belfrey, York.* [York, c. 1800.] Later edn [c. 1808]. See also PC 355.	12 P	York		O
318	[*The choir, a collection of anthems. c.* 1800.] (No copy survives; advertised on PC 303/c. 1800.)	45 A			
319	*The chorister's companion.* [c. 1800.]	3 TRAS	a t s b a t s b		I O/o
321	Harvey, William. *The Melksham harmony.* [c. 1800.]	36 PHAT	Wilts g (a) g b		(O/I)
322	Howgill, William. *An original anthem ... with ... 38 psalm tunes.* [c. 1800.]	37 P A	Cumb. g b s t b		O O
323	Key, Joseph. *Five anthems, four collects, twenty psalm tunes ...* Book III. [c. 1800.] Later edn [c. 1807]. See PC 279, 334b.	3 PHAS	Midlands g a g b		I
324	Linley, Francis. *A practical introduction to the organ,* Op. 6 ('9th edn'). [c. 1800.]	45 P			O
325	Marsh, John. *Fourteen new psalm tunes ... two hymns for charity children.* [c. 1800.]	2 PHC	London s		O
326	Shoel, Thomas. *Thirty psalm tunes, first sett.* [1st edn ?Montacute, c. 1800.] (No copy known. Listed in Brown & Stratton.) 2nd edn (enlarged) [c. 1805].	3 P	W. England g a g b		O/I

After 1800 this list is selective.

327	Shoel, Thomas. *Twenty-four psalm tunes, two hymns,* [etc.] *Second set.* Montacute, [1801]. Reissued London, [1801]. (A sequel to PC 326. Five more sets published, 1802–[c. 1825].)	3 PHTA	W. England t a s b		i
328	Wyvill, Zerubbabel. *Anthem, two hymns and two dismissions selected & composed for the general thanksgiving June 1st, 1802.* (1802.)	13 HA	Middx s a t b		I/o
329	*A collection of the psalm-tunes most commonly used in parish-churches.* (Printed by C. & W. Galabin, London.) 1803.	3 P	s a t b		

Bibliography

330	Crotch, William. *Tallis's Litany, adapted to the Latin words with additions by Dr. Aldrich; a collection of old psalm tunes ... and Tallis's Come Holy Ghost.* 1803. Later edn 1807.	1 PH L	Oxford s a t b s a t b b		o
331	FFitch, George. *Nine psalm tunes, six anthems, and a hymn.* Chelmsford, 1803.	3 PHA	Essex s a t b		
332	Porter, Samuel jun. *Four anthems and two psalm tunes.* [1803.]	3 PA	Kent a t (t) b		I
*333	Page, John. *A collection of hymns, dedicated ... to the Society of Patrons of the Anniversary of the Charity Schools in London and its Environs.* 1804.	2 PTR	London s (s) b		O/o
*334	Bloomfield, Isaac W. *Six anthems for the use of choirs where there is no organ.* [c. 1805.]	3 A	Suffolk s a t b		
334a	Guest, George. *A morning and evening hymn, as performed by the children of the charity schools ... in the parish church of Wisbeach.* [1806.] (Reviewed in *The Monthly Magazine*, 1 October 1806.)	12 H	Cambs s(t) b		O
334b	Key, Joseph. *Five anthems ... ten psalm tunes.* Book IV. [1807?] See PC 323.	3 PA	Midlands g a g b		I
335	Guest, Ralph. *The psalms of David ... for the use of parish churches.* [1808 or 1809.]	14 P	E. Anglia c		O
336	*A selection of psalms & hymns, as set on the organ, in the parish church of Sutton on the Forest in Yorkshire.* 1809.	1 PH	N. Yorks		BO
337	Bennet, Saunders. *A selection of sacred music for three voices, composed for the use of Woodstock church.* (1810.)	14 PS	Oxon. s t b		O
338	Stopford, [Thomas]. *Sacred music: consisting of a new book of psalmody.* Halifax, 1811. (A revision of PC 111a.) See also PC 359 and p. 183.	12 PHTRAC	W. Yorks t a s b		o
339	Gardiner, William. *Sacred melodies.* 6 vol. 1812–15.	45 PHA	 s a t b		O
340	Barber, Thomas. *Sacred harmony.* Woodbridge, [1814].	3 PHTA	E. Anglia s a t b s s b		(I)
340a	Simms, Bishop. *Addison's version, of the 19th psalm, the music arranged from Haydn's grand chorus in the Creation.* 2nd edn [1815].	12 P	Birmingham s a t b		O i
341	Dixon, J. *Canto recitativo, or a system of English chant.* (1816.)	45 C	 g		O
342	Knapton, Philip. *A collection of tunes for psalms and hymns, ... supplement to those now used in several churches in York.* York, [1816]. (A supplement to PC 317.)	2 PH	York c		O
343	Lolhurst, H. *Four New Version of the psalm, ... four hymns, ... and four anthems.* [1817.] (Copy: Dorset County Museum, Dorchester.)	3 PHA	Dorset s a t b		I o
344	Philo, James. *A selection of psalms and hymns for the use of country congregations.* [1817.]	3 PHA	Norfolk c		O
*344a	Jacob, Benjamin. *National psalmody.* [1817.] Later edns c. 1830, c. 1855. (Reviewed in *The Monthly Magazine*, 1 January 1818.)	4 PLSC	London a t s b		O
345	Cross, William. *A collection of psalm tunes.* (1818.)	123 P	Oxford s a t b		O

No.	Description	Qty	Libs	Place	Voices	Avail.
346	Coombs, James M. *Coombs's Divine Amusement . . . sacred pieces selected from the works of Marcello, Handel, Haydn, Luther, Mason, Boyce &c.* [1819.] Later edn [1825].	467	PHTA	Wilts	g (g)	O
348	Brown, John. *Sacred music.* [Book 1: no copy known.] Books 2, 3: [1820]. (Copies: Dorset County Museum, Dorchester.)	4	PHLAS	Dorset	s a t b	O
349	Greatorex, Thomas. *Parochial psalmody.* [1820.]	14	PRC	London	s a t b	o
350	Luppino, Thomas W. *Psalms and hymns for Ware church.* [Hertford, *c.* 1821.] 2 later edns *c.* 1825, 1845.	12	PHT	Herts.	g	o
351	*The music and words of a select portion of psalms and hymns used in Portland Chapel* [*St. Marylebone*.] 1822. Later edn [1833].	1	PH	London	g g b a t s b	o o
351a	Camidge, Matthew. *24 original psalm and hymn tunes.* York, 1823. (An 'appendix' to PC 317 and 342.)	2	PH	Yorks	c	O
352	Knyvett, Charles jun. *A selection of psalm tunes sung at St. George's Hanover Square.* 1823. 3 later edns 1825–50.	1	P	Westminster	g	O
353	*A selection of psalms, as set on the organ, in the parish church, of Stokesley.* Stokesley, 1824.	13	P	N. Yorks		BO
*354	Greenwood, John. *A selection of ancient and modern psalm tunes, chants, and responses.* Leeds, [1825].	12	PHLC	Leeds	a t s b	o
355	Camidge, Matthew. *A musical companion to the psalms used in the church of St. Michael le Belfry.* 3rd edn [*c.* 1825]. (Enlargement of PC 317.)	12	PRC	York		O
*356	Major, Joseph. *A collection of sacred music for churches and chapels.* [*c.* 1825.]	46	PH		s a t b	o
357	Goss, John. *Parochial psalmody.* (1827.)	12	PHRC	Chelsea	g	O
357a	Done, Joshua. *A selection of the most popular, with many original, psalm and hymn tunes, etc.* [1830.] 2nd edn (augmented) [1835].	47	PHC	London	g	O
*358	Mather, Samuel & Cotterill, Thomas. *Christian psalmody.* 1831.	147	PHTRSC	W. Yorks	g	O
359	Houldsworth, John. *A new and enlarged edition of Cheetham's Psalmody.* Halifax, 1832. (A revision and enlargement of PC 338.) 2nd–20th edns 1834–68. See also PC 389a, 404, 406 and p. 183.	12	PHRC	W. Yorks	t a s b	o/O
360	Gray, Jonathan. *Twenty-four chants: to which are prefixed, remarks on chanting.* London & York, 1834.	45	C	York	s a t b	o
361	Crotch, William. *Psalm tunes selected for the use of cathedrals and parish churches.* 1836.	45	P			O
362	Sale, John B. *Psalms and hymns for the service of the Church.* 1837.	12	PHRC	Westminster	a t s b	O
*363	Chapman, Shadrach. *Sacred music . . . designed for public or family worship.* 1838.	37	PHTA	Somerset	g g b	I
364	(Hamilton, Walter K.) *The psalms and hymns taken from the morning and evening services.* Oxford, 1838.	1	RC	Oxford		O
365	Hackett, Charles D. *The national psalmist.* 1839. 5 later edns 1840–61.	4	PHRAC		s a t b s	O/I O
366	Reinagle, Alexander R. *A collection of psalm and hymn tunes, chants, and other music.* 1839. Later edn Oxford, 1840.	14	PHC	Oxford		O

367 Baxter, John A., (& Baldwyn, Charles.) *Harmonia sacra*. Rev. V. Novello. 1840.

147 Kidderminster
PHRC a t s b   O

368 Head, F. A. *Choral psalmody, a collection of tunes to be sung in three parts, without instruments, by all village choirs*. [1840.]

13 Devon
P   g g (g) b

369 Redhead, Richard, [& Oakeley, Frederick]. *Church music*. 1840.

14 London
PLC s(s) a t b   O

370 Hill, James. *The choral service as used in the parish church of Leeds*. 1841. 4th edn (rev. R. S. Burton & V. Novello) 1848.

12 Leeds
LC s a a t b

371 Dyce, William. *The order of daily service ... with plain tune*. 1843. (Based on PC 3.)

45
LC c

372 Redhead, Richard. *Laudes diurnae*. 1843.

14 London
C c

372a Cecil, William. *The church choir*. 1845.

3 Cambs
PH g(g) b   o/i

373 Gauntlett, Henry J. & Kearns, William H. *The comprehensive tune book*. 1846.

457
PRAC a t s b   o

374 *The Parish Choir or Church Music Book*. 3 supplements 1846–50.

4
P s a t b   O
H c   O
C s a t b   o
L s a t b
A s a t b   O/o

376 Parr, Henry. *Church of England psalmody*. (1847.) 2nd–8th edns 1855–80. Revised edn 1889.

4 *Taunton*
PHRC s a t b   O

377 Spark, William. *A collection of fifty tunes and chants*. 1847.

14 Northants
PC s a t b   o

378 Spencer, Charles C. *Short anthems, or introits ... The music derived from ancient sources*. 1847.

4
A c   O
   s a t b

378a Havergal, William H. *Old Church psalmody. A manual of good and useful tunes either old or in old style*. [1849.] 4 later edns 1855–64.

4
P s a t b   O

379 Helmore, Thomas. *The psalter noted*. 1849. Enlarged edn: *A manual of plainsong*. 1850. See also PC 410a. *Accompanying harmonies*. 1849.

45
C c
C c   O

*380 Joule, Benjamin St J. B. *Directorium chori anglicanum. The choral service of the United Church of England and Ireland*. 1849. 8th edn 1880.

145 Manchester
LC s a t b   o

*381 Steggall, Charles. *Church psalmody. A manual of the most sterling psalm & hymn tunes, chiefly in the old Church style*. 1849. 3rd edn 1855.

4 W. London
PH s a t b   o

382 Redhead, Richard. *Hymns and canticles used at morning and evening prayer*. 1849.

45 *London*
CS s a t b

383 Forster, J. F. *The parochial choir book*. [c. 1850.]

4
PCLA s a t b   O/o

384 Gauntlett, Henry J. & Kearns, William H. *The comprehensive tune book*. Series 2. 1851. (Sequal to PC 373.)

457
PCSA a t s b   o/O

385 Helmore, Thomas. *The hymnal noted*. 1851–4.

45
H c

Accompanying harmonies. 1852–8.

H s a t b   o

No.	Description					
385a	Blew, William J. & Gauntlett, Henry J. *The Church hymn and tune book*. London, 1852. 2nd edn 1854.	4 H	c			O
386	Gauntlett, Henry J. *The choral use of the Book of Common Prayer, for choirs and places where they sing*. [1852.] Later edns 1854, 1855.	45 CL	s a t b			o
387	Maurice, Peter. *Choral harmony, a collection of tunes in short score*. 1854. 5th edn 1860.	4 PH	s a t b			o
389	Mercer, William. *The church psalter and hymn book*. 1854. 'Re-arranged' ('Oxford edition'), 1864.	467 PHCR	s a t b			o
*389a	Frobisher, Joseph H. *Supplement to Cheetham's Psalmody, consisting of a selection of psalm tunes, chants, responses, &c*. Halifax, 1855. (Sequel to PC 359.)	12 PHCRA	W. Yorks t a s b			o/O
390	Ouseley, Frederick A. G. & Monk, Edwin G. *The psalter, with the canticles . . . set to appropriate chants*. [1855.]	45 C	s a t b			o
391	Smart, Henry. *A choral book, containing a selection of tunes employed in the English Church*. [c. 1855.]	14 PH	s a t b			O O
393	Metcalfe, J. Powell. *Fifty metrical anthems for the use of small choirs*. (1858.)	3 T	s a t b			O
394	Joule, Benjamin St J.B. *A collection of chants for the daily and proper psalms*. [1860.] 17 later edns.	45 C	Manchester s a t b			o
395	Monk, William H. *Hymns ancient and modern*. 1861. Appendix, 1868. Revised edn 1875. Supplement, 1889. Revised edn 1904. 2nd Supplement, 1916. Standard edn 1922. See also PC 417.	45 H	s a t b			o
396	Fowle, Thomas L. *Parochial anthems by the cathedral composers of 1863*. Winchester, [1863].	4 A	s a t b			O/o
397	Wesley, Samuel Sebastian. *A selection of psalms and hymns . . . by C. Kemble . . . The music . . . selected, arranged, and partly composed by S.S. Wesley*. 1864. Later edns 1865, 1866.	4 PH	s a t b			o
398	[Walker, Henry A.]. *Appendix to the Hymnal Noted as used at St. Alban's, Holborn*. 1866. (Supplement to PC 385.)	14 H	London s a t b			o
399	*Novello's Parish Choir Book. A collection of music for the Church, by modern composers*. 1866–. (In progress.)	4 SLH	s a t b			O
400	*Hymnal companion to the Book of Common Prayer with tunes*. 1870. Later edns 1876, 1890.	4 PH	s a t b			o
401	Barnby, Joseph. *The hymnary: a book of church songs*. 2nd edn, with music, 1872.	4 H	s a t b			o
*402	Wesley, Samuel Sebastian. *The European psalmist*. 1872.	4 PHCSA	a t s b			o
403	Sullivan, Arthur. *Church hymns*. 1874. (Previous edn, without music, 1871, based on *Psalms and hymns*, 1853.) Published by the S.P.C.K. Later edns 1875, 1888, 1903.	45 H	s a t b			o
404	Roberts, J. Varley. *Houldsworth's Cheetham's Psalmody. A new and enlarged edition, with an appendix*. [1875.] (A revision of PC 359.) Later edns [1879], [1885].	4 PHCRA	W. Yorks t a s b s a t b			o/O o
405	*The cathedral psalter containing the psalms of David together with the canticles and proper psalms pointed for chanting*. [1878.] Later edns [1886], 1890.	45 C	s a t b			o
406	Gauntlett, Henry J. *Pohlmann's National Psalmody, or new appendix to Houldsworth's Cheetham's Psalmody, for home and congregational use*. Halifax, 1878. (Sequel to PC 359.) See also PC 404.	147 HCRA	W. Yorks s a t b			o

Bibliography

No.	Reference			Place	Voices	Acc.
407	Brown, Arthur H. *Organ harmonies for the Gregorian tones*. 1880.	45	CL	London	c	O
408	Stainer, John, & Russell, William. *The cathedral prayer book, being the Book of Common Prayer with the music necessary for the use of choirs*. London & New York, 1891.	45	CL		s a t b	
409	Pott, Francis. *The free rhythm psalter*. 1896.	45	C			c
410	Bridges, Robert & Wooldridge, Harry E. *Hymns: The Yattendon hymnal*. 1899.	145	H	Berks	s a t b	
410a	Briggs, Henry B. & Frere, Walter H. *A manual of plainsong*. 1902. (Based on PC 379.) Later edn (rev. J. H. Arnold), 1951.	45	CL		c	
411	Dearmer, Percy & Vaughan Williams, Ralph. *The English hymnal*. 1906. Later edn 1933. See also PC 429.	45	H		s a t b	o
					c	O
					c s a t b	O
412	Lloyd, C. Harford. (a) *The new cathedral psalter containing the psalms of David ... set to appropriate chants (for parish church use)*. [1910.]	24	C		s a t b	o
	(b) *The new cathedral psalter containing the psalms of David ... set to appropriate chants (for village church use)*. [1910.]	3	C		s a t b	o
413	Shaw, Martin. *An Anglican folk mass*. 1917.	145	L	London	c	O
414	Dearmer, Percy, Vaughan Williams, Ralph & Shaw, Martin. *Songs of praise*. 1925. Enlarged edn 1931.	45	H		s a t b	o
					c s a t b	o
					c	O
415	Dearmer, Percy, Vaughan Williams, Ralph & Shaw, Martin. *The Oxford book of carols*. 1928. 2nd edn 1964.	47	H		s a t b	o
					c	O
416	Nicholson, Sydney H. *The parish psalter with chants*. 1932.	4	C		s a t b	o
417	[Nicholson, Sydney H. & others.] *Hymns ancient and modern revised*. 1950. (Revision of PC 395. See also PC 426.)	45	H		s a t b	o
					c	O
418	*The BBC hymn book with music*. 1951.	4567	PH		s a t b	o
419	Beaumont, Geoffrey. *Folk mass*. 1956.	245	L		t/b c	O/I
420	[Murray, A. Gregory.] *Twenty four psalms and a canticle. Translated from the Hebrew and arranged for singing to the psalmody of J. Gélineau*. [1956.]	467	C		c	O
					s a t b	o
421	*Thirty 20th century hymn tunes*. Published by the Twentieth Century Church Light Music Group. 1960.	467	H		c	I
422	Appleford, Patrick. *Mass of five melodies*. 1961.	45	L		c	O/I
423	Knight, Gerald H. & Reed, William L. *The treasury of English church music*. 5 vol. 1965.	45	ASL	various		
424	Holbrook, David & Poston, Elizabeth. *The Cambridge hymnal*. Cambridge, 1967.	4567	HT		s a t b	o(i)
					c	O(i)

386

425	Carter, Sydney. *Nine carols or ballads*. 1968.	47			
		H	c		I
426	*100 hymns for today*. 1969. (A supplement to PC 417.)	45			
		H	s a t b		o
			c		O
427	Dearnley, Christopher & Wicks, Allan. *An order for holy communion with music for the congregation*. Alternative Services, Series 3. 1973.	4			
		L	c		
428	Mayhew, Kevin. *20th century folk hymnal*. Vol. I. 1974.	47			
		H	c		I
429	[Dearnley, Christopher.] *English praise: A supplement to the English hymnal*. 1975. (A supplement to PC 411.)	47			
		HC	s a t b		o
			c		O

2B For London hospitals

There are arranged alphabetically by the name of the hospital (date of foundation in parentheses), and, for each hospital, chronologically by date of publication. For background information see p. 207, and Frost & Frere: 100–3. In the tabulated information at the right, only the musical contents and forces are listed.

Asylum or House of Refuge for Female Orphans (1758)

PC				
501	Riley, William. *Psalms and hymns for the use of the chapel of the Asylum or House of Refuge for Female Orphans.* [1767.] Later edns (rev. W. Gawler) *c.* 1776–90. Supplement, *c.* 1785.	P HT	s s(s)	O O
502	Callcott, John W. *The anthems, hymns, psalms, and sentences, sung at the Asylum Chapel.* [1800.]	TA	s(s)	O
503	Horsley, William. *A collection of hymns & psalm tunes, sung in the chapel of the Asylum for Female Orphans.* (1820.)	PHT	s(s)	O

City of London Lying-in Hospital (1770)

511	*The hymns used at the City of London Lying In Hospital set for the organ, harpsichord voice and German flute.* [1777.]	H	s	O i

Hospital for the Maintenance and Education of Exposed and Deserted Young Children (1741) (The Foundling Hospital)

521 (541)	*A collection of psalm and hymn-tunes as they are performed at the Magdalen and Foundling Chapels. Properly set for the organ, harpsichord and guittar.* [1762?] (See PC 542.)	PH	s	O i
522	*Psalms, hymns and anthems for the use of the children of the Hospital for the Maintenance and Education of Exposed and Deserted Young Children.* [1774.] Later edn [c. 1760].	PHA	s(s)	O
523	*Psalms, hymns and anthems for the Foundling Chapel.* 1796. Revised edn (by William Russell), 1809.	PHAR	s(s)	O

Lock Hospital (1746)

531	[Madan, Martin.] *A collection of psalm and hymn tunes never published before ... To be had at the Lock Hospital.* [1769.]	H	ss	O

532	[Madan, Martin.] *A collection of psalm and hymn tunes never published before ... To be had at the Lock Hospital.* [*c.* 1775.] (An enlarged edition of PC 531.)	HT	ss	O
533	[Madan, Martin & Lockhart, Charles.] *A new, and improved edition of the collection of psalm and hymn tunes sung at the Chapel of the Lock Hospital.* (1792.)	HT	ss	O

Magdalen Hospital (1758)

541	See PC 521.			
542	Call, Thomas. *The tunes & hymns as they are used at the Magdalen Chapel, properly set for the organ, harpsichord and guittar.* [1762.] (Largely the same as PC 521. A prefatory note warns against a pirated edition, probably PC 521. Entered at Stationers' Hall 12 June 1762.)	PH	s	O i
543	*The hymns anthems and tunes with the ode used at the Magdalen Chapel.* Book I. [1765?] (An enlarged edition of PC 521.) See also PC 548.	PHT	s	O
544	*An appendix to the Magdalen hymns &c.* [1768?] (Reissued as:) *A second collection of psalms and hymns used at the Magdalen Chapel.* [1772.] See also PC 548.	PH	s(s)	O
545	*A third collection of hymns for the use of the Magdalen Chapel.* [1770?] See also PC 548.	H	s(s)	O
546	Smith, Adam. *The new musical pocket companion to the Magdalen Chapel.* [1770?] (Selections from PC 543–5.)	PHT	s(s)	O
547	*A fourth collection of hymns for the use of the Magdalen Chapel.* [1772?] See also PC 548.	H	s(s)	O
548	*A companion to the Magdalen-Chapel containing the hymns psalms ode and anthems used there.* [1772?] (A reissue of PC 543, 545, 547, and 544, in that order.) See also PC 550.	PHT	s(s)	O
549	*A fifth sett of psalms and hymns used at the Magdalen Chapel.* [1785?] See also PC 550.	PHT	s	O i
550	*The music performed at the Magdalen Chapel consisting of anthems hymns and psalm tunes, composed by Handel and other great masters.* [1810?] (A reissue of PC 548 and 549.)	PHT	s(s)	O

2C For proprietary chapels

Conventions as for section 2B.

Bedford Chapel (Bloomsbury Street, London)

PC

601 (611)	(Johnson, Thomas.) *An abridgement of the New Version of the psalms, for the use of Charlotte-Street and Bedford Chapels: with proper tunes adapted to each psalm.* (1777.)	P	c	O
602	*The psalm tunes and hymns used, and taught by the editor, in Bedford Chapel.* [1791.]	P	g(g)(b)	
603	(Costellow, Thomas.) *A selection of psalms and hymns with favorite and approved tunes for the use of Bedford Chapel.* (1791.)	PHC	g(g)	O

604	Costellow, Thomas. *Sunday's amusement. A selection of sacred music as sung at Bedford Chapel.* [1801.]	HTAS	g(g)	O

Charlotte Street Chapel (London)

611   See PC 601.

The Countess of Huntingdon's Chapel (Bath)

621	Milgrove, Benjamin. *Sixteen hymns as they are sung at ... the Countess of Huntingdon's Chappel in Bath.* [Bath?, 1768.]	HT	(s)(a)**c** b
622	Milgrove, Benjamin. *Twelve hymns as they are sung at ... the Countess of Huntingdon's Chappel in Bath.* Book 2nd. [Bath?], 1772.	HT	(s)(a)**c** b
623	See PC 310.		

Ebury Chapel (Ebury Street, Chelsea, Middlesex)

631	Smith, Theodore. *Eight tunes, selected, composed for, and adapted to the selection of psalms, hymns, and anthems, of Ebury Chapel.* [1795?]	PH	g(g)	O

Portman Chapel (Portman Square, St Marylebone, Middlesex)

641	*Select psalms for the use of Portman-Chapel.* 1780. (Reissued 1801.)	P	g(g)b	O
642	Beale, William G. F. *Congregational psalmody. A collection of psalm and hymn tunes sung at Portman Chapel.* [1852.]	PHC	s a t b	O

Surrey Chapel (Blackfriars Road, Southwark, Surrey)

651	(Jacob, Benjamin.) *A collection of hymn tunes ... composed for the use of Surry Chapel ... dedicated ... to the Revd. Rowland Hill.* [1797.]	HT	s s b a t s b	O o
652	Novello, Vincent. *Surrey Chapel music.* 1847.	PHCRA	s(s)	O

St John's Chapel (Bedford Row, St Marylebone, Middlesex)

661	Cecil, Theophania. *The psalm and hymn tunes, used at St. John's Chapel, Bedford Row.* 1815.	PHA	s a t b	o

2D   For English congregations abroad

This list is highly selective, and excludes Scotland. It is arranged chronologically by date of publication. Conventions are as for section 2A.

PC

701	[Whittingham, William.] *The forme of prayers and ministration of the sacraments.* (Part II:) *One and fiftie psalmes of David in Englishe metre, whereof 37 were made by Thomas Sterneholde.* (Geneva, 1556.) STC 16561. (Frost: 3.) Later edns 1558, 1560, 1561, 1569. See also PC 5, 6, and Church of Scotland. Book of Common Order.	P	Geneva c	

702 Schilders, Richard. *The psalmes of Dauid in meeter, with the prose. For the use of the English church in Middleburgh.* Middleburgh, 1599. STC 2499.9. (Temperley, 1976.) Later edn 1602: see also PC 15.
    P   Middleburg (Holland) c

703 Ainsworth, Henry. *The book of psalmes englished both in prose and metre.* Amsterdam, 1612. STC 2407. (Frost: 394–405.) 3 later edns, 1617–44.
    P   *Amsterdam* c

704 *The psalms hymns, and spiritual songs, of the old & new-testament: faithfully translated into English meetre.* [The 'Bay Psalm Book'.] 9th edn, Boston [Mass.], 1698. (Part II:) *The tunes of the psalms.* (Lowens: 25–38.) [For later American psalmody books, see Hixon.]
    P   New England g b

705 Bradley, A. *The psalms of David in metre. Collected out of the principal versions now in use.* Dublin, 1740.
    4 PH *Ireland* c(b)

706 *Select psalms, for the use of the parish-church of New St. Michan's in Dublin.* Dublin, 1752.
    1 P Dublin c

707 Triemer, Johann Z. *A new version of the psalms of David, by N. Tate & N. Brady. And set to music by J. Z. Triemer.* Amsterdam, 1753. 2 later edns 1765, 1772.
    PH *Holland* c

708 de la Main, Henry. *Six new psalm tunes in score.* 1781.
    12 P Cork s a t b O

709 Thomson, Michael. *Six anthems performed in Hillsborough Church* [county Down, Ireland]. Hillsborough, 1786.
    1 A Hillsborough s a t b O

710 McVity, J. *Select psalms and hymn tunes.* Dublin, 1787.
    4 PH Ireland **g** (g) b o

711 Rooyen, G. van. *A selection of hymns for the use of the English Presbyterian Church in Rotterdam.* Rotterdam, [c. 1790].
    P Rotterdam

712 Weyman, David. *Melodia sacra; or the psalms of David ... with hymns, anthems and chorusses.* 2 vol. Dublin, 1814, 1816. Later edn (rev. John Smith) Dublin, [1864].
    PHTA Ireland (s)s a t b O

713 Weyman, David. *The hymns and psalms &c. &c. as sung in the Magdalen Asylum Leeson Street* [Dublin]. Revised by R. W. Beaty. Dublin, (1825).
    PHRC Dublin s a t b O

714 Stewart, Robert P. *The Church hymnal.* Dublin, 1864. (Authorised hymn book for the Church of Ireland.) Later edns 1873, 1891.
    45 H Ireland s a t b O

715 Martin, George C. *The book of common praise.* Oxford, 1909. (Authorised hymn book for the Church of England in Canada.) Later edns 1910–62.
    45 H Canada s a t b O

2E Collection in Welsh for the Anglican Church in Wales

Conventions as for section 2A.

PC

801 Prys, Edmund. *Llyfr y psalmau, wedi eu cyfiethu, a'i cyfansoddi ar fesur cerdd, yn Gymraeg.* 1621. STC 2745. (Frost: 405–8.) Later edns 1630–1770.
    457 P Merioneth c

3 OTHER SOURCES

When the date of a book or monograph is placed in parentheses ( ), this is the date of the first edition, but a later edition, specified immediately afterwards, has been used for page citations. In a few cases of rare publications, the library location of the copy consulted is given. Printed collections of music are included where they do not qualify for the second section of the bibliography (PC). Dissertations and gramophone records are included.

Abbey, C. J. & Overton, J. H. *The English church in the 18th century.* 2 vol. London, 1878.

Abbot, H. *The use and benefit of church-musick, towards quickening our devotion. A sermon preach'd in the cathedral-church of Gloucester.* London, 1724.

An account of the rise and progress of the Religious Societies. See Woodward, J.

An account of the Societies for the Reformation of Manners. London, 1701.

[Adams, T.] *A history of the ancient town of Shaftesbury.* Shaftesbury, [1808].

Addington, S. *A collection of psalm tunes for public worship.* Market Harborough, 1780. (See also PC 239.)

Addison, W. *The English country parson.* London, 1947.

Addleshaw, G. W. O. *The early parochial system and the divine office.* Alcuin Club, Prayer Book Revision Pamphlets, no. 15. London, 1957.

Addleshaw, G. W. O. & Etchells, F. *The architectural setting of Anglican worship.* London, 1948.

Addy, J. *The archdeacon and ecclesiastical discipline in Yorkshire 1598–1714: clergy and the churchwardens.* Borthwick Institute of Historical Research: St Anthony's Hall Publications, no. 24. York, 1963.

Advice to the readers of the common-prayer. See Seymour, T.

Ahier, P. *The story of the three parish churches of St. Peter the Apostle, Huddersfield.* Huddersfield, 1948.

A[insworth], H. *The book of psalmes englished both in prose and metre.* Amsterdam, 1612. (STC 2407.)

Alderson, M. F. & Colles, H. C. *History of St. Michael's College, Tenbury.* London, 1943.

Allen, G. *Shaw church in by-gone days.* York, 1907.

Allen, W. D. B. & McClure, E. *Two hundred years: the history of the Society for Promoting Christian Knowledge, 1698–1898.* London, 1898.

Allison, R. *The psalmes of David in meter, the plaine song beeing the common tunne to be sung and plaide upon the lute, orpharyon, citterne or base violl.* London, 1599. (STC 2497.) Repr. Menston, 1968.

Anson, P. F. *Fashions in church furnishings, 1840–1940.* London, 1960.

Anson, P. F. 'Confusion and lawlessness.' *The Church Quarterly Review* CLXIX (1968), 178–91.

Anthems and hymns used in Gateshead church. [Newcastle-upon-Tyne, c. 1815.] (Copy: Yale University Library, WB 32707 (2), with owner's inscription dated 1818.)

Arber, E. ed. *A transcript of the registers of the Company of Stationers of London: 1554–1640 A.D.* (1875–7). 5 vol. Birmingham, 1894.

Arber, E. ed. *A brief discourse of the troubles at Frankfort 1554–1558 A.D. Attributed to William Whittingham, dean of Durham.* London, 1907.

Archbishops' Committee. See *Music in church, Music in worship.*

Armstrong, B. J. *A Norfolk diary.* ed. H. B. J. Armstrong. London, 1949.

Arnold, J. H. *The music of the holy communion.* Church Music Society Occasional Papers, no. 16. London, 1946.

Ashton, C. ed. *Services of the Church ... consisting of the preces, responses, etc. as sung in Durham cathedral*. London, 1844.

Aston, J. *A picture of Manchester*. Manchester, 1816. Facs. edn Manchester, 1969.

Atchley, C. *The parish clerk, and his right to read the liturgical epistle*. London and Oxford, 1924.

Atkins, I. *The early occupants of the office of organist at Worcester*. London, 1918.

Atterbury, F. 'The usefulness of church musick.' (Sermon preached on St Cecilia's Day, 1698.) Atterbury, *Sermons and discourses* IV (London, 1737), 235–63.

Avison, C. *An essay on musical expression* (1752). 2nd edn London, 1753. Facs. edn 1967.

Bacon, F. *Resuscitatio*. London, 1657.

Baden Powell, J. *Choralia: A handy book for parochial precentors and choirmasters*. London, 1901.

Baigent, F. J. *A history of the ancient town and manor of Basingstoke, South Hampton*. Basingstoke, 1889.

Baillie, H. 'A London church in early Tudor times.' [St Mary-at-Hill.] *Music and Letters*, XXXVI (1955), 55–64.

Baillie, H. *London churches, their music and musicians, 1485–1560*. Ph.D. diss., University of Cambridge, 1957.

Baker, G. *The history and antiquities of the county of Northampton*. 2 vol. London, 1822, 1830.

Baldwin, W. *The canticles or balades of Salomon, phraselyke declared in Englyshe metres*. London, 1549.

Balleine, G. R. *A history of the Evangelical party in the Church of England* (1908). New edn London, 1951.

Banner, R. *The use and antiquity of musick in the services of God. A sermon preached in the cathedral church at Worcester*. Oxford, 1737.

Barbour, J. M. *The church music of William Billings*. East Lansing (Michigan), 1960.

Barmby, J. *Churchwardens' accounts of Pittington and other parishes in the diocese of Durham*. Surtees Society Publications, no. 84. Durham, 1888.

'Barr-Brown' (pseud.). 'Gigantic singing trumpets.' *The Crown*, 20 April 1907.

Baskervill, C. R. *The Elizabethan jig and related song drama*. Chicago, 1929. Repr. New York, 1965.

Battell, R. *The lawfulness and expediency of church music asserted, in a sermon preached at St. Brides-church, upon the 22d of November, 1693*. London, 1694.

Baumgarten, C. F. *Martin Luther's hymn. Sung by Mr. Incledon, with the greatest applause in the Oratorios at the Theatre Royal, Covent Garden*. London, [1805?].

Bax, A. R. 'The church registers and parish account books of Ockley, Co. Surrey.' *Surrey Archaeological Collections* x (1891), 20–78.

'Bay Psalm Book.' See Cotton, J. *et al*.

Beacon, T. 'Jewel of Joy.' *The seconde parte of the bokes which Thomas Beacon hath made* (London, 1560), II, ii.

Beckwith, J. C. *The first verse of every psalm of David, with an ancient or modern chant in score*. London, 1808.

Bedford, A. *The great abuse of musick*. London, 1711. Facs. edn 1965.

Bedford, A. *The excellency of divine music*. London, 1733.

Bell, P. 'The Rev. G. D. Newbolt of Souldrop, 1856–95.' *Bedfordshire Historical Record Society Publications* XL (1960), 200–25.

Bell-Irving, E. M. *Mayfield: the story of an old Wealden village*. London, 1903.

Benham, E. *The prayer-book of Queen Elizabeth*. Edinburgh, 1909.

Bennett, J. 'Some recollections. IV. On "supply" duty.' *The Musical Times* XXXIX (1898), 654–6.

Benson, C. *Rubricks and canons of the church of England considered.* London, 1845.

Benson, L. F. *The English hymn: its development and use in worship.* Richmond (Virginia), 1915. Repr. 1962.

Beresford-Hope, A. J. B. *Worship in the Church of England.* London, 1874.

Beveridge, W. *A defence of the Book of Psalms collected into English metre by T. Sternhold.* London, 1710.

Bickersteth, E. ed. *Christian psalmody.* London, 1833. (Revised and enlarged, 1841.)

Bickersteth, E. H. ed. *Psalms and hymns based on the Christian Psalmody.* London, 1858. (Partly based on E. Bickersteth.)

Bishop, E. & Gasquet, F. A. *Edward VI and the Book of Common Prayer.* London, 1890.

Bishop, J. *Remarks on the causes of the present generally degraded state of music in our churches.* Cheltenham, 1860.

Bisse, T. *The beauty of holiness in the Common Prayer.* (4 sermons.) London, 1716.

Bisse, T. *Decency and order in publick worship recommended in three discourses.* London, 1723.

Blagden, C. *The Stationers' Company: a history, 1403–1959.* London, 1960.

Blankenburg, W., translated H. Heinsheimer. 'Church music in Reformed Europe.' Blume, 507–90.

Blume, F. *Protestant church music: a history.* New York, 1974.

Blunt, J. H. *The annotated Book of Common Prayer.* London, 1907.

Boggis, R. J. E. *History of St. John's Torquay.* Torquay, 1930.

Book of Common Prayer. See Church of England. Book of Common Prayer.

Borrow, G. *Lavengro.* London, 1851. (References are by chapter.)

Bostock, C. & Hapgood, E. *Notes on the parish church, Lymington, and the daughter church of All Saints.* Lymington, 1912.

Boston, N. & Langwill, L. G. *Church and chamber barrel-organs.* Edinburgh, 1967.

Boston, N. & Puddy, E. *Dereham. The biography of a country town.* Dereham, 1952.

Bourgeois, L. *Pseaulmes LXXXIII. de David ... Le tout a quatre parties.* (4 part-books.) Lyon, 1554.

Boutflower, A. *Personal reminiscences of Manchester, 1854–1912.* Leighton Buzzard, [1913].

Bowles, W. L. 'Our parochial psalmody.' Bowles, *The parochial history of Bremhill ... Wiltshire* (London, 1828), 203–27.

Bowley, A. L. *Wages in the United Kingdom in the nineteenth century.* Cambridge, 1900.

Box, C. *Church music in the metropolis: its past and present condition.* London, 1884.

Boyce, W. ed. *Cathedral music.* 3 vol. London, 1760–73.

Brady, N. *Church music vindicated: a sermon preached at St. Bride's church on Monday, November 22nd, 1697.* London, 1697. Facs. edn 1955.

Bray, T. *A short discourse upon the doctrine of our baptismal covenant.* London, 1697.

Brekell, J. *A discourse on musick, chiefly church musick; occasioned by the opening of the new organ in St. Peter's church in Liverpool.* London, 1766.

Brewster, S. [the younger]. *Collectanea ecclesiastica.* London, 1752.

Bridge, J. F. *Organ accompaniment of the choral service.* London, [1885].

Bridgeman, G. T. O. *The history of the church and manor of Wigan.* 4 vol. Chetham Society Publications, n.s., nos. 15–18. Manchester, 1888–90.

Bridges, R. 'A practical discourse on some principles of hymn-singing.' *Journal of Theological Studies* I (1899–1900), 40–63.

Bridges, R. *About hymns.* Church Music Society Occasional Papers, no. 2. London, [1911].

Bridges, R. 'English chanting.' *Musical Antiquary* II (1910–11), 125–41: III

(1911–12), 74–86.

A brieff discours off the troubles begonne at Franckford. See Whittingham.

Brightman, F. E. *The English rite.* 2 vol. London, 1915. Facs. edn 1970.

Brilioth, Y. *Three lectures on Evangelicalism and the Oxford Movement.* London, 1934.

British Museum [British Library]. *Catalogue of manuscript music.* See Hughes-Hughes, A.

British Museum general catalogue of printed books. 263 vol. London, 1959–66. *Ten-year supplement 1956–1965.* 50 vol. 1968. *Five-year supplement 1966–1970.* 26 vol. 1971–2.

The British union-catalogue of early music. See Schnapper.

Britton, A. P. *Theoretical introductions in American tunebooks to 1800.* Ph.D. diss., University of Michigan (Ann Arbor), 1949.

Bronson, B. H. *The ballad as song.* Berkeley & Los Angeles, 1969.

Brooke, J. M. S. & Hallen, A. W. C. eds. *The transcript of the registers of the united parishes of S. Mary Woolnoth and S. Mary Woolchurch Haw, in the City of London.* London, 1886.

Brown, J. *A dissertation on . . . poetry and music.* London, 1763.

Brown, E. H. P. & Hopkins, S. V. 'Seven centuries of building wages.' *Economica* XXII, n.s. (1955), 195–206.

Brown, J. D. & Stratton, S. S. *British musical biography.* Birmingham, 1897.

Broxap, E. *Extracts from the Manchester church-wardens' accounts.* Chetham Society Publications, no. 80. Manchester, 1921.

Buechner, A. *Yankee singing schools and the golden age of choral music in New England, 1760–1800.* Ph. D. diss., Harvard University, 1960.

Bullinger, H. *The decades of Henry Bullinger,* ed. T. Harding. 5 'decades' in 4 vol. Parker Society Publications, nos. 7–10. Cambridge, 1852.

Bumpus, J. S. *A history of English cathedral music 1549–1889.* London, 1908. Facs, edn 1972.

Burch, B. 'The parish of St. Anne's Blackfriars, London, to 1665.' *Guildhall Miscellany* III, no. 1 (1969).

[Burges, C.] *Reasons shewing the necessity of reformation of the publick 1. doctrine, 2. worship, 3. rites and ceremonies, 4. church-government, and discipline.* 2nd edn London, 1660.

Burgess, R. *The faithful steward. A sermon occasioned by the death of the Rev. John Graham, rector of St. Saviour . . . York.* London, 1844.

Burnet, G. 'On church musick. [Sermon] occasioned by the opening [of] the organ at St. James's, Clerkenwell, 1734.' Burnet, *Practical sermons on various subjects* (2 vol. London, 1747): I, 265–84.

Burney,.C. *A general history of music.* 4 vol. London, 1776–89.

Burroughs, J. *The devout psalmodist.* Two sermons. London, 1712. Repr. 1765.

Burrow, J. *Reports of cases argued and adjudged in the Court of King's Bench, during the time Lord Mansfield presided in that court; . . . 1756 to . . . 1772.* 5 vol. London, 1812. Vol. I–III repr. *The English Reports,* 97 (1909). (References are to the 1812 edn.)

Buszin, W. E. 'Luther on music.' *Musical Quarterly* XXXII (1946), 80–97.

Butler, C. *The principles of musick.* London, 1636. Facs. edn 1970.

Buttrey, J. 'William Smith of Durham.' *Music & Letters* XLIII (1962), 248–54.

Byng, John. See Torrington, John Byng, 5th Viscount.

Byrne, M. 'The church band at Swalcliffe.' *Galpin Society Journal* XVII (1964), 89–98.

Calvin, J. 'La forme des prieres et chants ecclesiastiques.' In *Pseaumes octantetrois de David mis en rime françoise par Clement Marot et Theodore de Besze* (Geneva, 1551: facs. edn 1973).

Campbell, L. B. *Divine poetry and drama in sixteenth-century England.* Cambridge, 1959.

[Cameron, Lucy L.] *The singing gallery.* London, 1823.

Campion, T. *A new way of making fowre parts in counterpoint* (1613?). Repr. in Campion, *Works,* ed. W. R. Davis (New York, 1967), 319–56.

Canons. See Church of England. Canons.

Capes, W. W. *The English Church in the 14th and 15th centuries.* London, 1900. Facs. repr. 1968.

Cardwell, J. H., Freeman, H. B. & Wilton, G. C. *Two centuries of Soho.* London, 1898.

Carr, B. *Vital Spark, or the Dying Christian: A study of the musical settings of Pope's ode as they appeared in selected early American tunebooks.* M.A. thesis, State University of New York at Buffalo, 1967.

Carter, P. C. *The history of the church and parish of St. Mary the Virgin, Aldermanbury.* London, 1913.

[Case, J.] *The praise of musicke.* Oxford, 1586.

Castle, L. 'The School of English Church Music.' *Church Music Review* I (1931), 7–8.

Cecil, R. *Remains.* See Pratt, J.

Chadwick, O. *The Victorian Church.* Part I. London, 1966.

Chancellor, E. B. *Memorials of St. James's Street.* London, 1922.

Chandler, J. *Hymns of the primitive Church.* London, 1837.

Chanter, J. R. & Wainwright, T. *Reprint of the Barnstaple records.* 2 vol. Barnstaple, 1900.

Chappell, P. *Music and worship in the Anglican Church.* London, 1968. (Referred to as 'P. Chappell'.)

Chappell, W. *The ballad literature and popular music of the olden time.* 2 vol. London, 1855–9. Facs. edn 1965. (Referred to as 'Chappell'.)

Charles, S. R. 'The provenance and date of the Pepys MS 1236.' *Musica disciplina* XVI (1962), 55–71.

Chase, G. *America's music from the pilgrims to the present.* New York, 1955.

Chauncey, N. *Regular singing defended.* New London (Connecticut), 1728.

The Choir and Musical Journal. Monthly journal. 1910–.

The Choir and Musical Record. Weekly journal. 23 vol. 1863–78.

The choral foundations in the Church of England. Church Music Society Occasional Papers, no. 8. London, 1924.

The Christian Observer. Monthly journal. 76 vol. 1802–77.

The Christian Remembrancer. Quarterly journal. 78 nos. 1819–68.

Christie, J. *Some account of parish clerks.* London, 1893.

Church Association. Papers, 1867–9. Lectures, 1867–72.

The Church Choirmaster. See *The Organist.*

'Church choirs in the diocese of Wakefield. The report of the Bishop's committee (October, 1914).' *Wakefield Diocesan Gazette* XX (1914–15), 103–24.

The Church Congress: Reports of Proceedings. Annual publication, 1861–1925. (Subsequent vols. have separate titles.)

The church-goer. Being a series of Sunday visits to the various churches of Bristol. 3rd edn Bristol, 1850.

The church-goer: rural rides. 2 series. I: 3rd edn Bristol, 1851. II: 2nd edn Bristol, 1850.

Church music in town and country. By 'the stranger within thy gates'. London, 1882.

The Church Music Review. Quarterly journal. 5 nos. 1931–2.

The Church Music Society, past and present. Church Music Society Occasional Papers, no. 15. London, [1944].

The Church Musician. Monthly journal of the Church Choir Guild. 5 vol. 1891–5.

Church of England. Book of Common Prayer, 1549 version. *The booke of the common prayer and administracion of the sacramentes, and other rites and ceremonies of the churche after the use of the Churche of England.* London, 1549. Repr. in E. C. S. Gibson. (See also PC 3.)

Church of England. Book of Common Prayer, 1552 version. *The boke of common prayer and administracion of the sacramentes, and other rites and ceremonies in the Churche of England.* London, 1552. Partially repr. in E. C. S. Gibson.

Church of England. Book of Common Prayer, 1559 version. *The boke of common praier, and administration of the sacramentes, and other rites and ceremonies in the Churche of Englande.* London, 1559. Repr. in Benham.

Church of England. Book of Common Prayer, 1662 version. *The book of common-prayer, and administration of the Sacraments, and other rites and ceremonies of the church, according to the use of the Church of England, together with the psalter or psalms of David, pointed as they are to be sung or said in churches.* London, 1662. Repr. in standard modern editions. (See also Reeves, J.; Stephens, A. J.; Warner, R.; PC 370, 371, 380, 386, 408.)

Church of England. Book of Common Prayer (proposed), 1928 version. *The Book of Common Prayer. With the additions and deviations proposed in 1928.* London, 1928.

Church of England. Canons of 1603. *Constitutions and canons ecclesiasticall treated upon by the Bishop of London, President of the Convocation for the Province of Canterbury, and the rest of the bishops and clergy of the said province.* London, 1604. Repr. in E. Gibson (1713).

Church of England. Homilies. *Certayne sermons, or homilies.* [Book I.] London, 1547. 1623 edn repr. in facs. Gainesville (Florida), 1968.

Church of England. Homilies. *The second tome of homilies.* London, 1563. 1623 edn repr. in facs. Gainesville (Florida), 1968.

Church of England. Injunctions of 1547. *Injunctions geven by ... Edwarde the VI.* London, 1547. Repr. in Frere & Kennedy.

Church of England. Injunctions of 1559. *Injunctions geven by the Queenes Maiestie.* London, 1559. Repr. in Frere & Kennedy.

Church of Scotland. Book of Common Order. *The forme of prayers and ministration of the sacraments &c. used in the English Church at Geneva, approved and received by the Churche of Scotland ... with the whole Psalmes of David in English meter.* Edinburgh, 1564. (See Cowan.)

Clark, K. *The Gothic revival* (1928). 2nd edn London, 1950.

Clay, W. K. ed. *Liturgies in the reign of Queen Elisabeth.* Parker Society Publications, no. 30. Cambridge, 1847.

[Clemens, J. (called Clemens non Papa), ed.] *Souter Liedekens ghemaect ter eeren Gods, op alle die Psalmen vā David.* Antwerp, 1540.

C[lifford], J. *The divine services and anthems usually sung in his majesty's chappell and in all collegiate choirs of England and Ireland.* London, 1663.

Clutton, C. & Niland, A. *The British organ.* London, 1963.

Cobbe, H. *Luton church.* London, 1899.

Cole, W. *A view of modern psalmody.* Colchester, 1819.

Coleire, R. *The antiquity and usefulness of instrumental musick in the service of God, a sermon on erecting an organ at Isleworth.* London, 1738.

Coleridge, A. D. *Reminiscences.* London, 1921.

Collier, J. *An ecclesiastical history of Great Britain,* ed. F. Barnham. 9 vol. London, 1841.

Collier, J. P. ed. *Trevelyan papers.* Part II. Camden Society Publications, no. 84. Westminster, 1863.

Collins, J. A. *St. Mary's church, Bridport.* Bridport, 1906.

Collinson, P. 'The authorship of *A brieff discours off the troubles begonne at*

Franckford.' Journal of Ecclesiastical History x (1958), 188–208.

Common Prayer, Book of. See Church of England. Book of Common Prayer.

Concordia. Fortnightly journal. 2 vol. (52 nos.) 1875–6.

'Congregational psalmody.' *British Quarterly Review* LXX (April 1862), 366–94.

Considerations on select vestries. London, 1829.

Cook, G. H. *English collegiate churches of the Middle Ages.* London, 1959.

Cooke, P. ed. 'Gaelic Psalms from Lewis.' Scottish Tradition no. 6. Tangent Records, TNGM 120.

Cosyn, J. *Musike of six, and five partes. Made upon the common tunes used in singing of the psalmes.* (6 partbooks.) London, 1585.

Cotterill, T. *A selection of psalms and hymns for public and private use, adapted to the services of the Church of England* (Newcastle, 1810). 8th edn (enlarged), Sheffield, 1819.

[Cotterill, T. rev. Harcourt, V., Archbishop of York.] *A selection of psalms and hymns for public worship.* (The 'Archbishop's Selection'.) London, 1820. (See also PC 359.)

Cotton, J. *Singing of psalms a gospel-ordinance.* London, 1650.

[Cotton, J. *et al.*] *The whole booke of psalmes faithfully translated into English metre.* (The 'Bay Psalm Book'.) Cambridge (Massachusetts), 1640. Facs. edn 1903. (See also PC 704.)

Cowan, W. 'A bibliography of the Book of Common Order and psalm book of the Church of Scotland: 1556–1644.' *Edinburgh Bibliographical Society Papers*, x (1913), 53–100.

Cowell, H. J. 'The church of the strangers.' *Proceedings of the Huguenot Society of London* XIII (1929), 483–515.

Cox, J. C. *Churchwardens' accounts.* London, 1913.

Crabtree, J. *A concise history of the parish and vicarage of Halifax.* Halifax, 1836.

Cresswell, B. F. *The Edwardian inventories for the city and county of Exeter.* Alcuin Club Collections, no. 20. London, 1916.

Crosse, J. *An account of the grand musical festival, held in September, 1823, in the cathedral church of York.* York, 1825.

Crotch, W. *The substance of several courses of lectures on music.* London, 1831.

Crowdy, J. *The church choirmaster: a critical guide to the musical illustration of the order for daily prayer.* London, 1864.

Crowest, F. J. *Phases of musical England.* London, 1881.

Crowley, R. *An apologie, or defence, of those Englishe writers & preachers which Cerberus the three headed dog of Hell, chargeth with false doctrine, under the name of Predestination.* London, 1566.

Cudworth, W. *Musical reminiscences of Bradford.* Bradford, [1885].

Cuming, G. J. *A history of the Anglican liturgy.* London, 1969.

Curwen, J. S. *Studies in worship music.* [1st ser.] London, 1880. 2nd edn London, 1888.

Curwen, J. S. *Studies in worship music.* 2nd ser. London, 1885.

Curwen, J. S. 'The old village musicians.' *The Strand Musical Magazine* III (1897), 137–9.

Dakers, L. *Church music at the crossroads.* London, 1970.

Damon, W. *The psalmes of David in English meter, with notes of foure partes set unto them.* (4 partbooks.) London, 1579. (STC 6219.)

Damon, W. *The former booke of the musicke of M. William Damon.* London, 1591. (STC 6220.) *The second booke ...* London, 1591. (STC 6221.)

Daniel, R. B. *Chapters on church music.* London, 1894.

Daniel, R. T. *The anthem in New England before 1800.* Evanston (Illinois), 1966.

Daniel, R. T. & le Huray, P. comp. *The sources of English church music 1549–1660.* London, 1972.

Davey, H. *A history of English music.* London, 1895.

Davies, H. *Worship and theology in England,* 5 vols. Princeton (New Jersey), 1961–75. (Referred to as 'Davies'.)

Davies, W. *Music in Christian worship.* Church Music Society Occasional Papers, no. 3. London, [1913].

Davies, W. & Grace, H. *Music and worship.* London, 1936.

Dearmer, N. K. *The life of Percy Dearmer.* London, 1940.

Dearmer, P. *The parson's handbook.* London, 1899.

Dearnley, C. *English church music 1650–1750.* London, 1970.

DeVos, B. R. *The emergence of Tudor church music in the vernacular.* Ph.D. diss., University of Boston, 1971.

Dexter, H. M. *The Congregationalism of the last 300 years.* New York, 1880.

Dibb, J. E. *Key to chanting. The psalter ... and portions of the morning and evening services of the Church, appointed to be sung or chanted, with a peculiar arrangement to facilitate the practice.* London, 1831.

Dibb, J. E. *The sub-diaconate.* London, 1866.

Dickson, W. E. *A letter to the Lord Bishop of Salisbury, on congregational singing.* Oxford, 1857.

Dickson, W. E. *Fifty years of church music.* Ely, 1895.

The Dictionary of National Biography. 22 vol. London, 1908–9. (Referred to as *DNB*.)

A directory for the publique worship of God throughout the three kingdoms of England, Scotland, and Ireland (London, 1644). 2nd edn London, 1645. (Wing D1547.) Repr. in P. Hall, III.

D'Israeli, I. 'On psalm-singing.' D'Israeli, *A second series of curiosities of literature* (London, 1823).

Ditchfield, P. H. *The parish clerk.* New York, 1907.

D[od], H. *Al the psalmes of David, with certene songes and canticles of Moses, Debora, and others, not formerly extant for song.* London, 1620.

Dodsworth, W. *A selection of psalms, to which are added hymns chiefly ancient.* London, 1837.

Dodwell, H. *A treatise on instrumental music in holy offices.* London, 1700.

Doe, P. 'Latin polyphony under Henry VIII.' *Proceedings of the Royal Musical Association* XCV (1968–9), 81–96.

Donahue, Sister B. J. *From Latin to English: Plainsong in Tudor England.* Ph.D. diss., Catholic University (Washington, D.C.), 1966

Donaldson, A. B. *The bishopric of Truro: the first twenty-five years, 1877–1902.* London, 1902.

Doncaster Report. See *Report of the committee.*

Douen, O. *Clément Marot et la psautier huguenot.* 2 vol. Paris, 1877–8. Facs. edn Nieuwkoop, 1967.

Doughtie, E. ed. *Lyrics from English airs 1596–1622.* Cambridge (Massachusetts), 1970.

Draper, J. W. *William Mason: a study in eighteenth-century culture.* New York, 1924.

Druitt, R. *A popular tract on church music, with remarks on its moral and political importance, and a practical scheme for its reformation.* London, 1845.

Dryden, H. E. L. *On church music, and the fitting of churches for music.* London, 1854. (Copy: New York Public Library, Drexel 3810.)

[Dunster, C.] *Psalms and hymns ... for the use of a parochial church.* London, 1807.

Durel, J. *A view of the government and worship of God in the Reformed Churches beyond the seas.* London, 1662.

Ebblewhite, E. A. *The parish clerks' company.* London, 1932.

The Ecclesiologist. Journal of the Cambridge Camden Society (4 vol., Cambridge, 1841–5), later the Ecclesiological Society (25 vol., London, 1846–68).

Eden, J. B. D. *Church music: a sermon preached at the opening of the new organ in the parish church of St. Nicholas. . . . Bristol.* Bristol and London, 1822.

Eliot, G. *Scenes of clerical life.* 2 vol. Edinburgh, 1858. (Reference is by chapters.)

Eliot, G. *Adam Bede.* 3 vol. Edinburgh, 1859. (Reference is by chapters.)

Elliott-Binns, L. E. *The early Evangelicals.* London, 1953.

Ellman, E. B. *Recollections of a Sussex parson* (1912). New edn London, 1925.

Elstob, J. G. *The Church, her music and service.* Chester, 1906.

Elvey, S. *The psalter, or canticles and psalms, pointed for chanting, upon a new principle.* London, 1856.

Engel, C. *Reflections on church music.* London, 1856.

The English Churchman. Weekly journal, 22 vol. 1843–64.

English Church Music. Journal of the School of English Church Music, later the Royal School of Church Music. Quarterly, 32 vols., 1931–62; annual, new series, 1963–.

Erasmus. See Froude, J. A.

Erk, J. & Böhme, F. W. *Deutscher Liederhort.* 2 vol. Leipzig, 1893.

An essay on psalmody. See Romaine, W.

Estwick, S. *The usefulness of church music: a sermon preached at Christ Church* [Newgate Street, London] *November 27, 1696.* London, 1696. Facs. edn 1955.

The Eton College hymn book. Oxford, 1937.

Evans, W. 'Old hymns lined and led by Elder Walter Evans.' Sovereign Grace Recordings 6057 and 6444.

Evelyn, J. *Diary.* ed. W. Bray. 4 vol. London, 1850–52. (References are by date of entry.)

Every, G. *The high church party, 1688–1718.* London, 1956.

Farr, E. ed. George Wither, *Hymns and songs of the Church.* London, 1856. (See also PC 18.)

Faulkner, T. *An historical and topographical description of Chelsea, and its environs.* 2 vol. London, 1829.

Fawcett, J. *A memorial . . . of the parish church of St. Peter's, Bradford.* Bradford, 1845.

Fellowes, E. H. *English cathedral music from Edward VI to Edward VII* (1941). 5th edn (rev. J. A. Westrup) London, 1969.

A few words to church builders. Cambridge Camden Society Publications. 1st edn Cambridge, 1841. 2nd edn Cambridge, 1842.

Fish, J. L. *On the application of plain song to the services of the Church.* Oxford, [1845?].

Fishwick, H. *The history of the parish of Poulton-le-Fylde.* Chetham Society Publications, n.s. no. 8. Manchester, 1885.

Flagg, J. *A collection of the best psalm tunes.* Boston (Massachusetts), 1764.

Fletcher, J. M. J. [List of the organists at Wimborne Minster.] *Somerset and Dorset Notes and Queries* XX (1931), 165–6.

Flindall, R. P. *The Church of England 1815–1948: a documentary history.* London, 1972.

Flower, W. B. *The prayers to be said or sung. A plea for musical services.* London, 1851.

Flower, W. B. *Choral service. The sacrifice of praise: a sermon preached at St. John's, Bovey Tracey.* London, 1853. Repr. in Flower (1856).

Flower, W. B. *Choral services, and ritual observances. Two sermons.* London, 1856.

[Ford, D. E.] *Observations on psalmody. By a composer.* London, 1827.

Ford, T. *Singing of psalms the duty of Christians under the New Testament; or, a vindication of that gospel ordinance.* London, 1653.

A form of publick devotions, to be used by a religious society, within the Bills of Mortality. (London, 1713). Repr. Boston (Massachusetts), 1728.

Formby, H. *Parochial psalmody considered.* (Repr. from *The English Churchman.*) London, 1845.

Forster, W. R. *The choir school* [of All Saints, Margaret Street, London]. All Saints' Church Booklet Series, no. 2. London, 1954.

Foster, M. B. *Anthems and anthem composers.* London, 1901.

Fowler, J. T. ed. *The life and letters of John Bacchus Dykes.* London, 1897.

Fowler, M. *History of All Hallows Church, London Wall.* London, 1909.

Frere, W. H. 'Edwardine vernacular services before the first prayer book.' *Journal of Theological Studies* I (1899–1900), 229–46.

Frere, W. H. *The English Church in the reigns of Elizabeth and James I.* London, 1904. Facs. repr. 1968.

Frere, W. H. & Frost, M. *Historical companion to Hymns ancient and modern.* ed. Frost. (Revision of Frere's *Historical edition of Hymns ancient and modern,* 1909.) London, 1962.

Frere, W. H. & Kennedy, W. M., eds. *Visitation articles and injunctions of the period of the Reformation.* 3 vol. Alcuin Club Collections, nos. 14–16. London, 1910.

Frost, M. ed. *English and Scottish psalm and hymn tunes, c. 1543–1677.* London, 1953. (Referred to as 'Frost'.)

Frost, W. A. *Early recollections of St. Paul's Cathedral.* London, [1926]. (Referred to as 'W. Frost'.)

Froude, J. A. *The life and letters of Erasmus.* London, 1894.

Fuller-Maitland, J. A. *English music in the XIXth century.* London, 1902.

Fuller-Maitland, J. A. *The need for reform in church music.* Church Music Society Occasional Papers, no. 1. London, [1910].

Galpin, F. W. 'The village church band: an interesting survival.' *Musical News* V (1893), 31–2, 56–8.

Galpin, F. W. 'Notes on the old church bands and village choirs of the past century.' *The Antiquary* XLII (1906), 101–6.

Galpin, F. W. *Old English instruments of musick* (1910). 4th edn (rev. R. T. Dart), London, 1965.

Gardiner, W. *The music of nature.* London, 1832.

Gardner, G. *Music in larger country and in smaller town churches.* Church Music Society Shorter Papers, no. 2. [London], 1917.

Gardner, G. *Worship & music: suggestions for clergy and choirmasters.* London, 1918.

Garrett, C. H. *The Marian exiles.* Cambridge, 1938.

Gasquet, F. A. *Parish life in mediaeval England.* London, 1906.

Gastrell, F. *Notitiae cestrienses.* Chetham Society Publications, nos. 8, 19, 21, 22. Manchester, 1845–50.

Gateshead. See *Anthems and hymns.*

The Gentleman's Magazine. Monthly journal. 303 vol. 1731–1907.

George, M. D. *London life in the XVIIIth century.* London, 1925.

Gepp, E. 'High Easter churchwardens' books, 1814–1877.' *Essex Review* XXVI (1917), 101–15.

Gibson, E. *Codex juris Ecclesiastici Anglicani.* London, 1713.

Gibson, E. ['The excellent use of psalmody, with a course of singing-psalms for half a year.'] In *Directions given by Edmund Lord Bishop of London to the clergy of his diocese, in ... 1724.* London, 1724. Repr. separately as Gibson, *The excellent use of psalmody* [London, 1725?]. (Also repr. in preface to PC 109.)

Gibson, E. C. S. ed. *The first and second prayer books of King Edward the Sixth.* London, 1910.

Gill, H. *The village church in the olden time.* Nottingham, 1903.

Goodwin, P. *Religio domestica rediviva.* London, 1655.

Grace, H. *Music in parish churches. A plea for the simple.* Church Music Society

Shorter Papers, no. 3. [London], 1917.

Grace, H. *The complete organist*. London, 1920.

Graham, J. *A sermon preached in St. Saviour's church, York, ... on the occasion of the death of Jonathan Gray, Alderman*. York, 1838.

Gray, [Almyra], Mrs E. *Papers and diaries of a York family, 1764–1839*. London, 1927.

[Gray, J.] *Hymns, selected as a supplement to a collection of psalms used in several churches*. York, 1817. (See also *The York psalm and hymn book* and PC 342.)

Gray, J. *An inquiry into the historical facts relative to parochial psalmody*. York, 1821.

The Gregorian Quarterly Magazine. 4 nos. 1879.

Gresley, W. *A sermon on church music, preached in St. Paul's church, Brighton, September 12, 1852*. London, 1852.

Grove, G. *A dictionary of music and musicians*. [1st edn] 4 vol. London, 1879–89. 5th edn 9 vol. London, 1954. 6th edn (as *The New Grove dictionary of music and musicians*) London, 1979.

Hackett, M. *A brief account of cathedral and collegiate schools*. [London], 1827.

Hadow, M. W. H. *Hymn tunes*. Church Music Society Occasional Papers, no. 5. London, [1914].

Haggard, J. *Reports of cases argued and determined in the Consistory Court of London: containing the judgments of Sir William Scott*. London, 1832. Repr. *The English Reports*, 161 (1917). (References are to the 1832 edn, cited as 'Haggard, 1832a'.)

Haggard, J. *Reports of cases argued and determined in the ecclesiastical courts at Doctors' Commons and in the High Court of Delegates*, III (1829–32). London, 1832. Repr. *The English Reports,* 162 (1917). (References are to the 1829–32 edn, cited as 'Haggard, 1832b'.)

Hall, J. *The courte of vertu*. London, 1565. (STC 12632.)

Hall, P. *Reliquiae liturgicae*. 5 vol. Bath, 1847.

Hallett, C. W. C. *The cathedral of Ripon*. London, 1901.

Hamilton, J. A. *Catechism of the organ*. 3rd edn London, 1851.

[Hamilton], W. K., Bishop of Salisbury. *Church music: A sermon, preached at the church of St. Mary, Sturminster Newton ... on Thursday, April 12, 1860*. Salisbury, [1860].

[Hanway, T.] *Thoughts on the use and advantages of music*. London, 1765.

Hardy, T. *Under the greenwood tree*. London, 1872. (Reference is by chapter.)

Hargrave, E. 'Musical Leeds in the 18th century.' *Thoresby Society Publications* XXVIII (1928), 320–55.

Harley, J. *Music in Purcell's London: the social background*. London, 1968.

The Harmonicon. Monthly journal. 11 vol. 1823–33.

Harrison, F. Ll. *Music in medieval Britain* (1958). 2nd edn London, 1963.

Harwood, B. ed. *The Oxford hymn book*. Oxford, 1908.

Haslewood, F. 'Notes from the records of Smarden church.' *Archaeologia Cantiana* IX (1974), 226–34.

[Hatton, E.] *A new view of London*. London, 1708.

Hawkes, W. [Letter relating to the competition for the post of organist at Whitchurch parish church, Shropshire.] *Aris's Birmingham Gazette*, 15 April 1805.

Hawkins, J. *A general history of the science and practice of music*. 5 vol. London, 1776.

Hayes, W. *The 100 psalm as performed at St. Paul's*. London, [1790].

Heales, A. 'Early history of the church of Kingston-upon-Thames, Surrey.' *Surrey Archaeological Collections* VIII (1883), 13–156.

[Heber, A.] *The life of Reginald Heber, Lord Bishop of Calcutta, by his widow*. 2 vol.

London, 1830.

Heber, R. *Hymns, written and adapted to the weekly church services of the year.* London, 1827.

Hebert, A. G. ed. *The parish communion: a book of essays.* London, 1937.

Helmore, F. *Church choirs.* London, 1865.

Helmore, T. *On church music.* London, 1868.

Helps, A. *A guide to the ancient church of St. Mary's, Puddletown.* Revised edn Dorchester, 1955.

Hemy, H. F. *Crown of Jesus music.* London, 1864.

Herrmann-Bengen, I. *Tempobezeichnungen.* Münchner Veröffentlichungen zur Musikgeschichte, Band 1. Tutzing, 1959.

Hewett, J. W. *The arrangement of parish churches considered.* Cambridge, 1848.

Hewlett, J. T. J. *The parish clerk.* [A novel] ed. T. E. Hook. 3 vol. London, 1841.

Heylyn, P. *Examen historicum: or a discovery and examination of the mistakes, falsities and defects in some modern histories* ... 2 vol. London, 1659.

Heywood, J. *Our church hymnody.* (Repr. from *The Choir and Musical Record.*) London, 1881.

Heywood, J. *The art of chanting.* London, 1893.

Heywood, J. *Music in churches, and the part of the laity therein, past – present – future.* Birmingham, 1905.

Hibbert, S. *The history of the college and collegiate church, Manchester.* (1830.) Vol I of *History of the foundations in Manchester.* 4 vol. Manchester, 1828–48.

Hickman, C. *A sermon preached at St. Bride's church, on St. Caecilia's Day, ... 1695.* London, 1696.

Hierurgia Anglicana, rev. V. Stanley. London, 1902.

Hiley, R. W. *Memories of half a century.* London, 1899.

Hine, R. *The history of Beaminster.* Taunton, 1914.

Historical Manuscripts Commission. *Report on MSS. in various collections.* 8 vol. London, 1901–14.

The history and antiquities of the parish church of St. Michael Crooked Lane, London. London, 1833.

Hixon, D. J. *Music in early America: a bibliography of music in Evans.* Metuchen (New Jersey), 1970.

Hodges, E. *An apology for church music and music festivals.* London, 1834.

Hodson, L. J. *Ticehurst: the story of a Sussex parish.* Tunbridge Wells, 1925.

Holden, G. *On psalmody: a sermon preached on the opening of a new organ, in the chapel of Maghull, July 30th, 1846.* Ormskirk, 1846.

Holinshed, R. *The ... chronicles of England, Scotlande, and Irlande.* 2 vol. (1577). As Vol. I of *Holinshed's Chronicles.* London, 1807. Facs. edn 1965.

Holmes, N. *Gospel musick. Or, the singing of Davids psalms.* London, 1644.

Homilies. See Church of England. Homilies.

Hooker, R. *The laws of ecclesiastical polity.* Vol. 5, London, 1597.

Hooper, J. C. *A survey of music in Bristol with special reference to the eighteenth century.* M.A. thesis, Unversity of Bristol, 1963.

Houblon, Lady A. F. A. *The Houblon family.* 2 vol. London, 1907.

Houseman, J. W. 'History of the Halifax parish church organs.' *Halifax Antiquarian Society: Papers, Reports, &c.* (1928), 77–112.

Hudson, F. 'The New Bedford manuscript part-books of Handel's setting of "L'Allegro".' *Notes* XXXIII (1976–7), 531–52.

Hughes-Hughes, A. *Catalogue of manuscript music in the British Museum.* 3 vol. London, 1906–9. Vol. I. Sacred vocal music.

Hullah, J. P. *Music in the parish church: a lecture.* London, 1856.

Hullah, J. P. [Paper on parish church music read to the Church Congress at Bristol, October 1864.] *Church Congress: Reports of Proceedings, 1864* (Bristol, 1865),

296–302.

Hunt, J. E. ed. *Cranmer's first Litany, 1544 and Merbecke's Book of Common Prayer Noted, 1550*. London, 1939.

Hunter, J. *South Yorkshire: The history and topography of the deanery of Doncaster*. 2 vol. London, 1828–31.

Hutchings. A. *Church music in the nineteenth century*. London, 1967.

Hutchings, A. 'Dr. John Dykes, 1823–1876.' *English Church Music* XI, n.s. (1973), 41–56.

Hutchins, J. *The history and antiquities of the county of Dorset* (1773). 3rd edn ed. W. Shipp & J. W. Hodson. 4 vol. London, 1861–70.

Huttar, C. A. *English metrical paraphrases of the psalms, 1500–1640*. Ph.D. diss., Northwestern University, 1956.

Hutton, W. H. *The English Church from the accession of Charles I to the death of Anne*. London, 1903. Facs. repr. 1968.

Hymns and anthems for the use of Ramsgate Chapel. 3rd edn Ramsgate, 1813.

Illing, R. 'Barley's pocket edition of Est's metrical psalter.' *Music and Letters* XLIX (1968), 219–23.

Illing, R. *Est-Barley-Ravenscroft and the English metrical psalter*. Adelaide, 1969.

Injunctions. See Church of England. Injunctions.

Irving, W. *Sketch book of Geoffrey Crayon, gent*. London, 1820.

Jackson, A. G. *The history of St. Thomas's church, Regent Street*. London, 1881.

Jackson, G. P. 'The strange music of the Old Order Amish.' *Musical Quarterly* XXXI (1945), 275–88.

Jackson, N. G. 'A nineteenth century Newark Song School master.' *Transactions of the Thoroton Society of Nottinghamshire* LXVI (1962), 83–95.

Jackson, T. *The life of the Rev. Charles Wesley*. 2 vol. London, 1841.

Jacobson, W. *Fragmentary illustrations of the history of the Book of Common Prayer*. London, 1874.

James, J. *The history of Bradford and its parish*. London, 1866.

James, W. A. *An account of the grammar and song schools of the collegiate church of ... Southwell*. Southwell, 1927.

Jebb, J. *The choral responses and litanies of the United Church of England and Ireland*. 2 vol. London, 1847, 1857.

Jebb, J. *The choral service of the United Church of England and Ireland*. London, 1843.

Johnson, J. *The clergyman's vade-mecum* (1706). 6th edn London, 1731.

Jones, W. (vicar of Nayland). 'The nature and excellence of music'. Jones, *Theological and miscellaneous works*, new edn. (London, 1810), IV, 74–90.

Jones, W. (vicar of Nayland). *The diary of the Reverend William Jones*, ed. O. F. Christie. London, 1929.

Joule, B. St J. B. *A collection of words of 2,270 anthems*. London, 1859.

Julian, J. *A dictionary of hymnology*. 2nd edn London, 1907. Facs, edn 1957.

Keble, J. *The Christian year*. Oxford, 1827.

Kemble, C. ed. *A selection of psalms and hymns arranged for the public services of the Church of England*. London, 1853.

Kempthorne, J. L. *Falmouth parish church*. Falmouth, 1928.

Kennedy, R. *Thoughts on the music and words of psalmody as at present in use among members of the Church of England*. London, 1821.

Kerley-Miller, C. ed. *Memoirs of ... Martinus Scriblerus*. New Haven (Connecticut), 1950.

Kilner, T. *Congregational responding*. London, 1848.

Kinlock, T. F. *An historical account of the Church Hymnary: Revised Edition*. Cambridge, 1928.

Kitto, J. V. *St. Martin-in-the-Fields: the accounts of the churchwardens 1525–1603*.

London, 1901.

Knappen, M. M. *Tudor Puritanism*. Chicago and London, 1939.

Knights, E. S. 'West gallery choirs.' *Essex Review* XLIII (1934), 144–9.

Krummel, D. W. *English music printing 1553–1700*. London, 1975.

L., W. 'A short account of the several sorts of organs used for church services.' *Gentleman's Magazine* XLII (1772), 562–5. Repr. *The Gentleman's Magazine Library* XVI (1894), 159–64.

[Lampe, J. F. and Wesley, C.] *Hymns on the great festivals, and other occasions*. London, 1746.

Landon, E. H. *A manual of councils of the holy catholick Church*. London, 1846.

Langwill, L. 'The bassoon: its origin and evolution.' *Proceedings of the Royal Musical Association* LXVI (1939–40), 1–21.

Lasco, J. à [Laski, J.]. *Opera*, ed. A. Kuyper, 2 vol. Amsterdam, 1866.

Latrobe, J. A. *The music of the Church considered in its various branches, congregational and choral*. London, 1831.

Lavington, G. *The influence of church-music. A sermon preach'd in the cathedral-church of Worcester. . . . September 8th, 1725*. London, 1725.

Lawton, G. *Collectio rerum ecclesiasticarum de diocesi eboracensi*. 2 vol. London, 1840.

Leadman, A. D. M. 'Alborough church, near Boroughbridge.' *Yorkshire Archaeological and Topographical Journal* IX (1886), 163–96.

[Leather, F. S.] *Some account of Lyme Regis*. London, 1882.

Legg, J. W. ed. *The Clerk's Book of 1549*. Henry Bradshaw Society Publications, no. 25. London, 1903.

Legg, J. W. 'London church services in and about the reign of Queen Anne.' Transactions of the St Paul's Ecclesiological Society VI (1906–10), 1–34.

Legg, J. W. *English church life from the Reformation to the Tractarian movement*. London, 1914.

le Huray, P. *Music and the Reformation in England, 1549–1660*. London, 1967. (Referred to as 'le Huray'.)

le Huray, P. 'Popular elements in church music.' *English Church Music*, IV, n.s. (1967), 15–24. (Referred to as 'le Huray, 1967b'.)

Lely, J. M. *The statutes of practical utility . . . being the fifth edition of 'Chitty's Statutes'*. London, 1894.

Lightwood, J. T. *Methodist music of the eighteenth century*. London, 1927.

Lilly, J. *A collection of seventy nine black-letter ballads and broadsides, printed in the reign of Queen Elizabeth*. London, 1867.

Lindeboom, J. *Austin Friars: History of the Dutch Reformed Church in London*. The Hague, 1950.

Linley, Francis. *A practical introduction to the organ, Op. 6*. 9th edn London, [1800?].

Livingston, N. *The Scottish psalter of 1635*. Glasgow, 1864.

Locke, M. *The present practice of musick vindicated*. London, 1673.

London County Council. *Survey of London*. 38 vol. London, 1900–75.

The London Guide. London, 1782.

London parishes: An account of the churches, vicars, vestries. London, 1824.

Long, K. R. *The music of the English Church*. London, 1972.

Lorenz, E. S. *The singing church: the hymns it wrote and sang*. Nashville (Tennessee), 1938.

L[owe], E. *A short direction for the performance of cathedrall service*. London, 1664.

Lowens, I. 'The origins of the American fuging tune.' *Journal of the American Musicological Society* VI (1953), 43–52. Repr. in Lowens, *Music and musicians in early America* (New York, 1964), 237–48.

Luff, A. H. F. 'Gélineau in England.' *English Church Music* XXX (1960), 70–1.

Lupson, E. J. *St. Nicholas' church, Great Yarmouth: its history*. Yarmouth, 1881.

Lyra davidica: or, a collection of divine songs and hymns. London, 1708.

McCutchan, R. G. *Hymn tune names*. New York and Nashville, 1957.

Macdermott, K. H. *Sussex church music in the past*. Chichester, 1922.

Macdermott, K. H. *The old church gallery minstrels*. London, 1948.

Macdougall, H. C. *Early New England psalmody*. Brattleboro (Vermont), 1940.

Mace, T. *Musick's monument*. London, 1676. Facs. edns Paris, 1958; New York, 1966.

Machyn, H. *The diary of Henry Machyn*, ed. J. G. Nichols. Camden Society Publications, no. 42. London, 1848.

Mackeson, C. *Guide to the church services of London and its suburbs*. London, 1858.

Mackeson, C. *A guide to the churches of London and its suburbs*. 20 nos. London, 1866–95.

Mackeson, C. 'Notes on London churches.' *The Church Congress handbook* (London, 1876), 30–46.

Mc Kinnon, J. W. 'Representations of the Mass in medieval and Renaissance art.' *Journal of the American Musicological Society* XXXI (1978), 21–52.

McMaster, J. *A short history of the royal parish of St. Martin-in-the-Fields*. London, 1916.

McMurray, W. *The records of two City parishes* [St Anne and St Agnes, Aldersgate.] London, 1925.

Macnutt, F. B. & Slater, G. *Leicester cathedral organ*. Leicester, 1930.

Macro, T. *The melody of the heart: a sermon preached at the opening of an organ in St. Nicholas's church, in Great Yarmouth, December the 20th, 1733*. London, 1734.

Madan, M. *Thelyphthora*. London, 1780.

Mainzer, J. *The Gaelic psalm tunes of Ross-shire, and the neighbouring counties*. Edinburgh, 1844.

Mant, R. *Ancient hymns, from the Roman breviary, for domestic use*. London, 1837.

Marot, C. & de Bèze, T. *Pseaumes de David mis en rime francaise*. Paris, 1562.

Marrocco, W. T. & Gleason, H. *Music in America*. New York, 1964.

Marsh, J. *The cathedral chant book*. London, 1804.

Marsh, P. T. *The Victorian Church in decline: Archbishop Tait and the Church of England 1868–1882*. London, 1969.

Mason, W. *Essays on English church music*. York, 1795. Repr. in *The Works of William Mason* (4 vol. in 2, London, 1811), III. (References are to the 1795 edn.)

Matthews, J. H. *A history of the parishes of St. Ives, Lelant, Towednack and Zennor in the county of Cornwall*. London, 1892.

Maurice, P. *The popery of Oxford confronted, disavowed, and repudiated*. London, 1837.

Maxwell, W. D. *John Knox's Genevan service book 1556*. Edinburgh and London, 1931.

Mayo, C. H. *The official guide to Sherborne Abbey church*. Sherborne, 1925.

Meacham, S. 'The Church in the Victorian city.' *Victorian Studies* XI (1967–8), 359–78.

Mee, J. H. *Bourne in the past: being a history of the parish of Westbourne*. Hove, 1913.

Merrick, J. *The psalms of David translated or paraphrased in English verse*. Reading, 1765. (See also PC 292, 297.)

Metcalfe, J. P. 'Our parish church singing: how to improve it.' *The Church Choirmaster and Organist* I (1867), 34–5, 142–4; II (1868), 51–2.

Micklethwaite, J. T. *The ornaments of the rubrics*. Alcuin Club Tracts, no. 1. London, 1897.

Milbourne, L. *Psalmody recommended in a sermon preach'd to the Company of the*

Parish Clerks. London, 1713.

Mildon, W. H. *Puritanism in Hampshire and the Isle of Wight.* Ph.D. diss., University of London, 1934.

Miller, E. *Thoughts on the present performance of psalmody in the Established Church in England.* London, 1791.

Miller, E. *The history and antiquities of Doncaster.* Doncaster, 1804.

Miller, J. *Singers and songs of the Church.* London, 1869.

Millington, W. *Sketches of local musicians and musical societies.* Pendlebury, 1884.

The Modern Churchman. Monthly journal, 1911–.

Moorman, J. R. H. *A history of the Church of England.* London, 1954.

Morgan, D. *The Church in transition: reform in the Church of England.* London, 1970.

Morgan, S. M. *Music in the village church.* London, 1939.

Morgan, W. *The parish priest: pourtrayed in the life, character, and ministry, of the Rev. John Crosse, A.M., late vicar of Bradford.* London, 1841.

Mould, A. 'Choir schools in a changing education system.' *English Church Music* XI, n.s. (1973), 10–17.

Mullins, E. L. C. *Texts and calendars.* Royal Historical Society Guides and Handbooks, no. 7, London, 1958.

Munkhouse, R. *Occasional discourses.* 3 vol. London, 1805.

Music in church. Report of the Committee appointed in 1948 by the Archbishops of Canterbury and York. Westminster, 1951. Revised edn Westminster, 1957.

Music in village churches. Church Music Society Shorter Papers, no. 1. [London], 1917. Repr. 1922, 1931, 1950.

Music in worship. Report of the Archbishops' Committee appointed in May, 1922 (1922). Revised edn London, 1932.

The Musical Herald. Weekly journal. 2 vol. 1846–7.

The Musical Standard. Weekly journal, 135 vol. (in 4 series) 1862–1933.

The Musical Times. Monthly journal. 1844–.

The Musical World. Weekly journal. 71 vol. 1836–91.

The Musician, Organist and Choirmaster. See *The Organist.*

Neale, J. M. *Church enlargement and church arrangement.* Cambridge Camden Society Publications. Cambridge, 1843.

Neale, J. M. 'English hymnology, its history and prospects.' *Christian Remembrancer* XVIII (1850), 302–43.

Neale, J. M. *Mediaeval hymns and sequences.* London, 1851.

Nelson, R. *The life of Bishop Bull* (1713). Repr. G. Bull, *Works*, ed. E. Burton (Oxford, 1827), VIII.

Nettl, B. 'The hymns of the Amish: an example of marginal survival.' *Journal of American folklore* LXX (1957), 323–8.

A newe ballade of a lover extollinge his ladye. To the tune of Damon and Pithias. London, 1568. (STC 18876. Copy: British Library, Huth 50/27.) Repr. Ward, 1957: facing p. 168.

New remarks of London: or, a survey of the cities of London and Westminster, of Southwark, and part of Middlesex and Surry. London, 1732.

Newbolt, G. D. Diary. See Bell, P.

Newes from Pauls ... A contention about the lawfulness of organs and other ceremonies. London, 1642.

Newman, J. H. *Hymni ecclesiae.* Oxford, 1838.

Newman, J. H. et al. *Tracts for the times.* Collected reissue, 6 vol. London and Oxford, 1838–41.

Newte, J. *The lawfulness and use of organs in the Christian Church asserted, in a sermon preached at Tiverton, in Devon, on the occasion of the organs being erected in that parish church.* London, 1696. Repr. 1701.

Newton, J. *The diary of John Newton, Rector of Wath, 1816–1818*, ed. C. P. Fendall & E. A. Crutchley. Cambridge, 1933.

[Newton, J. & Cowper, W.] *Olney hymns.* 3 vol. London, 1779.

Nicholas, J. *The progress and public procession of Queen Elizabeth.* 3 vol. London, 1823.

Nicholas, J. F. & Taylor, J. *Bristol past and present.* 2 vol. Bristol, 1881.

Nicholls, W. *A comment on the Book of Common Prayer.* London, 1710.

Nicholson, S. H. *The organ voluntary.* Church Music Society Occasional Papers, no. 6. [London, 1915.]

[Nicholson, S. H.] *The School of English Church Music: Principles and recommendations.* S.E.C.M. Publications, no. 12. Tenbury Wells, [1941].

Northbrooke, J. *A treatise wherein dicing, dancing, etc. are reproved.* London, 1577. Repr. 1843.

Notes and Queries. Weekly journal, 1849–1952; monthly, 1953–.

Oakeley, F. *Historical notes on the Tractarian movement (A.D. 1833–1845).* London, 1865.

Odom, W. *Memorials of Sheffield: its cathedral and parish churches.* Sheffield, 1922.

Ollard, S. L. & Walker, P. C. eds. *Archbishop Herring's visitation returns, 1743.* 5 vol. Yorkshire Archaeological Society Record Series, nos. 71, 72, 75, 77, 79. Leeds, 1928–31.

Olsen, D. J. 'Victorian London.' *Victorian Studies* XVII (1974), 265–78.

The Organ. Quarterly journal. 1921–.

The Organist. Monthly journal, nos. 1–9, April–December 1866; followed by *The Church Choirmaster*, nos. 1–24 (2 vol.), 1867–8; *The Choirmaster*, nos. 25–8, January–April 1869; *The Musician, Organist and Choirmaster*, nos. 29–36, May–December 1869; *The Musician*, nos. 37–41, January–May 1870.

The Organist and Choirmaster. Monthly journal, 28 vol. 1893–1920.

Ouseley, F. A. G. & Dykes, J. B. *The choral worship of the church. Two sermons preached at St. Peter's Church, Derby, . . . Dec. 9, 1860.* Derby, 1861.

Outhwaite, J. ed. *Documents relative to Bradford church.* Bradford, 1827.

Ouvry, F. 'Extracts from the churchwardens' accounts of the parish of Wing.' *Archaeologia* XXXVI (1855), 220–37.

Overall, W. H. ed. *The accounts of the churchwardens of the parish of St. Michael, Cornhill in the City of London, from 1456 to 1608.* London, [1871].

Owen, E. *Sermon preached at the opening of the organ in the parish church of St. Neot's, Huntingdon, Sep. 26, 1749.* London, 1749.

The Oxford psalter . . . newly pointed for chanting. Ed. H.G. Ley, E. S. Roper and C. Hylton Stewart. London, 1929.

Page, W. *The inventories of church goods for the counties of York, Durham, and Northumberland.* Surtees Society Publications, no. 97. Durham, 1897.

The Parish Choir or Church Music Book. Monthly journal. 3 vol. 1846–51. (See also PC 374.)

Parker, M. *The whole psalter translated into English metre.* London, [c. 1565]. (STC 2729. With nine tunes by Thomas Tallis.)

Parker, W. *The pleasures of gratitude and benevolence improved by church-musick, Sermon.* London, 1753.

Parks, E. D. *The hymns and hymn tunes found in the English metrical psalters.* New York, 1966.

Parks, E. D. *Early English hymns: an index.* Metuchen (New Jersey), 1972.

Parliamentary Papers, Session 1831: XVIII. *Census Reports 1801–1831.* Facs. edn, *British Parliamentary Papers. Population I.* Shannon (Ireland), 1968.

Parliamentary Papers, Session 1835: XXIII–XXVI. *Reports from commissioners on municipal corporations in England and Wales.* Appendix to the first report, 30 March 1835.

Paterson, J. *Pietas Londinensis*. London, 1714.

Patrick, J. *A century of select psalms*. London, 1679. (Later expanded to become PC 38.)

Patrick, M. *Four centuries of Scottish psalmody*. London, 1949.

P[ayne], B. *The parish-clerk's guide: or, the singing psalms used in the parish-churches suited to the feasts and fasts of the Church of England*. London, 1709.

Pearce, C. W. *Old London city churches, their organs, organists and musical associations*. London, 1909.

Pearce, C. W. *Notes on English organs of the period 1800–1810 ... taken chiefly from the MS. of Henry Leffler*. London, 1911.

Pearce, C. W. 'English sacred folk song of the west gallery period (circa 1695–1820).' *Proceedings of the Musical Association* XLVIII (1921–2), 1–27.

Pears, S. A. *Remarks on the Protestant theory of church music*. London, 1852.

Pepys, S. Diary. London, 1905. (References are by date of entry.)

Peter, R. & Peter, O. B. *The histories of Launceston and Dunheved*. Plymouth, 1885.

Pevsner, N. *Yorkshire: the West Riding*. The Buildings of England, no. 17. Harmondsworth, 1959.

Peyton, S. A. ed. *Kettering vestry minutes*. Northamptonshire Record Society Publications, no. 6. Kettering, 1933.

Phelps Brown, E. H. See Brown, E. H. P.

Philipps, E. 'A list of printed churchwardens' accounts.' *English Historical Review* XV (1900), 335–41.

Phillimore, J. *Reports of cases argued and determined in the Arches and Prerogative Courts of Canterbury, and in the High Court of Delegates: containing the judgments of the Right Hon. Sir George Lee*. II (1754–8), London, 1832. Repr. *English Reports*, 161 (1917). (References are to the 1832 edn.)

Phillips, C. H. *The singing Church*. London, 1946.

Phillips, H. L. *Poole church and its rectors*. Poole, 1915.

Pierce, M. *The parish communion*. Alcuin Club Pamphlet. [London, n.d.]

Pittman, J. *The people in the church, their rights and duties in connection with the poetry and music of the Book of Common Prayer*. London, 1858.

Playford, J. *A booke of new lessons for the cithern & gittern: containing many new and excellent tunes*. London, 1652. (Copy: Euing Musical Library, Glasgow.)

Playford, J. *A breefe introduction to the skill of musick*. London, 1654. Later edns 1655–1730. (See PC 23, 27, 28.)

Playford's Brief Introduction to the Skill of Musick. An account, with bibliographical notes. London, 1926.

Plumstead, W. *Observations on the present state of congregational singing*. London, 1846.

Pococke, R. *The travels through England of Dr. Richard Pococke*, ed. J. J. Cartwright. Camden Society Publications, n.s. nos. 42, 44. London, 1888–9.

Poole, G. A. *The use and excellence of church music; a sermon, preached at the opening of an organ, in the parish church of Kenilworth May 25, 1834*. Bristol, [1834].

[Poole, G. A.] *Dialogue on the choral service*. Leeds, 1842.

Pope, A. 'Memoirs of P. P., clerk of this parish.' Pope, *Works*, ed. J. W. Croker, W. Elwin & W. J. Courthorpe (London, 1886, repr. New York, 1967), x, 435–44.

Popham, F. S. *A history of Christianity in Yorkshire*. Wallington, 1954.

Porter, W. S. *Notes from a Peakland parish* [Hope]. Sheffield, 1923.

Porteus, B. *A charge delivered to the clergy of the diocese of London ... in 1790*. Porteus, *Works* (London, 1811), VI, 239–46.

Portus, G. V. *Caritas Anglicana, or, an historical inquiry into those religious and philanthropical societies that flourished in England between the years 1678 and 1740*. London, 1912.

Pott, F. & Brown, A. H. *An introduction to the principles and practice of chanting in free rhythm and true antiphony.* London, 1896. (Originally the preface to PC 409.)

Pratt, J. *The life, character, and remains of the Reverend Richard Cecil.* London, 1816.

Pratt, W. S. *The Music of the French psalter of 1562.* Columbia University Studies in Musicology, no. 3. New York, 1939.

Preston, Lancs. See *Words of the anthems.*

Procter, F. *A new history of the Book of Common Prayer*, rev. W. H. Frere. London, 1901.

Psalmi aliquot Davidici in metrum Latini traducti. Oxford, 1681. (A later edition of Wing B2769, the only one with music. Not in Wing or Schnapper. Copy: University of Illinois, Urbana, Illinois.)

'Psalmody of the Reformation.' *Eclectic and Congregational Review* VI (1864), 601–19.

Psalms and hymns for public and private devotion. Sheffield, 1802.

Purchas, J. *Directorium Anglicanum, according to the ancient uses of the Church of England.* London, 1858.

Purvis, J. S. *Tudor parish documents of the diocese of York.* Cambridge, 1948.

Puttenham, G. *The arte of English poesie.* (*c.* 1570?) Repr. Cambridge, 1936.

The Quarterly Musical Magazine and Review. 10 vol. 1818–28.

Rainbow, B. *The choral revival in the Anglican Church 1839–1872.* London, 1970.

Ramsgate chapel. See *Hymns and anthems.*

[Ravenscroft, T.] *Pammelia. Musicks miscellanie, or mixed varietie of pleasant roundelayes, and delightfull catches.* London, 1609. Repr. Philadelphia, 1961.

Reader, W. J. *Life in Victorian England.* London, 1964.

Reading, J. *A sermon . . . concerning church music.* London, 1663.

The Record. Weekly journal. 1828–.

[Reeves, J.] *The Book of Common Prayer* [with an introduction by John Reeves]. London, 1801.

Rennert, J. *William Crotch (1775–1847): composer, artist, teacher.* Lavenham, 1975.

Report of the committee appointed at a meeting of parishioners of Doncaster, held at the parish church the 4th of October 1832. [Doncaster], 1832. (Copy: Sheffield City Library, PR 19/40.)

Report of the Royal Commission on Ecclesiastical Discipline. See Royal Commission . . .

Richards, H. W. *The organ accompaniment of the church services: a practical guide for the student.* London, 1911.

Richards, R. *Old Cheshire churches.* London, 1947.

Richardson, A. M. *Modern organ accompaniment.* London, 1907.

Richardson, C. F. *English preachers and preaching 1640–70.* London, 1928.

[Richardson, W.] *A collection of psalms.* York, 1788. (See also *The York psalm and hymn book* and PC 317.)

Riley, H. T. 'The parish documents of Hartland, N. Devon.' *Royal Commission on Historical Manuscripts, Fifth Report* (1876), 571–5.

Roberts, C. 'The attitudes of the musical and unmusical towards congregational singing.' *Church Music Review* I (1931), 41–2.

Roberts, F. *Clavis Bibliorum.* London, 1648. Later edns 1649, 1665, 1673.

Robin Hood. An opera. As it is perform'd at . . . Bartholomew-Fair. London, 1730.

Robinson, H. ed. *Zurich letters.* Parker Society Publications, nos. 50–1. Cambridge, 1842–5.

Robinson, H. ed. *Original letters of the Reformation.* 2 vol. Parker Society Publications, no. 53. Cambridge, 1846–7.

Rodgers, B. *Cloak of charity*. London, 1949.

[Romaine, W.] *An essay on psalmody*. London, 1775.

The Roman Catholic Question. 2 series. London, 1850–1.

Roper, W. O. ed. 'Materials for the history of the church of Lancaster.' *Chetham Society Publications* n.s. nos. 26, 31, 58, 59. Manchester, 1892–1906.

Routh, F. *Early English organ music from the middle ages to 1837*. London, 1973.

Routley, E. *The music of Christian hymnody*. London, 1957.

Routley, E. *The English carol*. London, 1958.

Routley, E. *Twentieth century church music*. London, 1964.

Routley, E. *The musical Wesleys*. London, 1968.

The Roxburghe ballads, ed. W. Chappell & J. W. Ebsworth. 8 vol. Hertford, 1871–99.

Royal Commission on Ecclesiastical Discipline: Report. London, 1906.

Sabol, A. J. 'Two unpublished stage songs for the "Aery of Children".' *Renaissance News* XIII (1960), 222–32.

Sadler, E. A. *A guide to the Ashburne (St. Oswald's) parish church. Derbyshire*. Ashburne, 1934.

St. Dorothy's Home: A tale for the times. London, 1866. (Copy: Dr Bernarr Rainbow, Richmond, Surrey.)

St John the Evangelist, Preston. See *Words of the anthems*.

The Salisbury hymn book, ed. Earl Nelson. Salisbury, 1857.

Schickler, Baron F. de. *Les Eglises de refuge en Angleterre*. 3 vol. Paris, 1892.

Schnapper, E. B. ed. *The British union-catalogue of early music printed before the year 1801*. 2 vol. London, 1957.

Scholes, P. A. *The mirror of music*. London, 1947.

Scholes, P. A. *The Oxford companion to music* (1938). 9th edn. London, 1955.

The School of English Church Music: principles and recommendations. See Nicholson, S. H.

Score, G. F. *Guide to Wimborne Minster*. London, 1903.

Secker, T. 'A charge delivered to the clergy of the diocese of Oxford, in the year 1741.' In Secker, *Eight charges* (London, 1769). Repr. in Secker, *Works* (London, 1811), v, 332–54. (Reference is to the 1811 edn)

[Seymour, T.] *Advice to the readers of the common-prayer, and to the people attending the same*. London, 1682.

Sharp, H. B. 'Church band, dumb organist, and organ.' *Galpin Society Journal* XIV (1961), 37–40.

Shaw, H. W. 'Church music in England from the Reformation to the present day.' Blume, 693–732.

Shaw, M. F. & Dearmer, P. *The English carol book*. London, 1913.

Shaw, W. A. *History of the English Church . . . 1640–1660*. 2 vol. London, 1900.

Shearme, J. *Lively recollections*. London, 1917.

Shepherdson, W. *The organ: hints on its construction, purchase, and preservation*. London, 1873.

Sherlock, W. *A sermon preach'd at St. Paul's cathedral, November 22, 1699* (London, 1699). Repr. Sherlock, *Sermons* (London, 1719), I, 345–66.

Shore, S. Royle. 'The choral eucharist since the Reformation.' *Cathedral Quarterly* I (1913), ii, 9–19.

A short title catalogue of books printed in England, Scotland, and Ireland and of English books printed abroad, 1475–1640. Compiled by A. W. Pollard, G. R. Redgrave and others. London, 1926. (Referred to as 'STC'.)

Shuttleworth, J. *A sermon preached at Bridgwater in Somersetshire, . . . at the opening of the organ lately erected there*. London, 1700.

Simpson, B. N. *The Royal School of Church Music*. M.A. thesis, University of Sheffield, 1971.

Simpson, C. M. *The British broadside ballad and its music.* New Brunswick, 1966.

Skinner, J. *Journal of a Somerset rector,* ed. H. Coombs & A. N. Bax. London, 1930.

S[latyer], W[illiam]. *Psalmes, or songs of Sion: turned into the language, and set to the tunes of a strange land.* London, [1631]. (STC 22635. Complete copy: Cambridge University Library, Syn.8.63.193.)

Smith, A. *The practice of music in English cathedrals and churches, and at the court, during the reign of Elizabeth I.* Ph.D. diss., University of Birmingham, 1967. (Referred to as 'A. Smith'.)

Smith, A. 'Elizabethan church music at Ludlow'. *Music and Letters* XLIX (1968), 108–21.

Smith, G. G. *Elizabethan critical essays.* 2 vol. Oxford, 1904.

Smith, G. H. *A history of Hull organs and organists.* London, [c. 1910].

Smith, H. 'English metrical psalms in the sixteenth century and their literary significance.' *Huntington Library Quarterly* IX (1946), 249–71.

Smith, H. P. 'William Knapp, the Dorset composer.' *Proceedings of the Dorset Natural History and Antiquarian Field Club* XLVII (1926), 159–67.

Smith, P. *Blandford.* Blandford, 1968.

Smith, T. C. & Shortt, J. *The history of the parish of Ribchester, in the county of Lancashire.* London, 1890.

Snepp, C. B. *Songs of grace and glory for private, family, and public worship.* London, 1872.

Society for Promoting Christian Knowledge. *Psalms and hymns.* London, 1855. (Englarged to become PC 403.)

Somers, J. *A collection of scarce tracts.* 16 vol. London, 1748.

Spark, W. *Lecture on church music, more particularly the choral service of the Church of England as applied to parochial worship.* Leeds and London, 1851.

Spark, W. *Choirs and organs: their proper position in churches.* London, 1852. Repr. in Spark, 1892.

Spark, W. *Musical memories.* London, 1888.

Spark, W. *Musical reminiscences.* London and Leeds, 1892.

The Spectator. Daily broadsheet. 1711–14. Repr. 4 vol. 1919–26.

Stainer, J. 'On the musical introductions found in certain metrical psalters.' *Proceedings of the Musical Association* XXVII (1900–1), 1–50.

Stanford, C. V. *Pages from an unwritten diary.* London, 1914.

Steele, R. *The earliest English music printing.* London, 1903.

Stephens, A. J. *The Book of Common Prayer: with notes, legal and historical.* 2 vol. London, 1849.

Stephens, F. *St Mary's Primrose Hill: A guide & history.* London, 1972.

Stephens, W. R. W. *The life and letters of Walter Farquhar Hook.* 2 vol. 2nd edn London, 1879.

Sternhold, T. *Certayne psalmes, chosē out of the psalter of David and drawē into Englishe metre.* London. [1549]. (STC 2419. Without music.)

[Sternhold, T. & Hopkins, J.] *Al such psalmes of David as Thomas Sternholde, late grome of the Kynge's Maiestie's roobes did in his lyfe tyme drawe into English metre.* London, 1549. (STC 2420. Without music.) Repr. in various edns 1550–4. (See also PC 7–9, 701.)

Sternhold, T., Hopkins, J. and others. *The whole book of psalms.* Many editions without music, 1590–1861. (For editions with music see PC 9, etc.)

[Sternhold, T. *et al.*] *Psalmes of David in metre.* [Wesel, 1556?]. (STC 2426.8. Without music.)

Stevens, D. ed. *The Mulliner Book.* Musica Britannica I. London, 1951.

Stevens, D. ed. *Music at the court of Henry VIII.* Musica Britannica XVIII. London, 1962.

Stevenson, R. *Protestant church music in America.* New York, 1966.

Stewart, E. *Points of view*. Church Music Society Shorter Papers, no. 7. [London], 1933.

Stockdale, J. *Annales Caermoelenses: or annals of Cartmel*. Ulverston and London, 1872.

Stockwell, J. *A sermon preach'd . . . in Abingdon, April 2d, 1726*. Oxford, [1727].

Stow, J. *The annales of England*. London, [1592]. Later edn London, [1605]. (See also Stow & Howes.)

Stow, J. & Howes, E. *Annales, or, A generall chronicle of England. Begun by John Stow: continued . . . by Edmund Howes*. London, 1615. Later edn (revised) 1631.

Strype, J. *Annals of the Reformation* (1709–25). A new edn (4 vol. in 7) in Strype, *Works* (Oxford, 1824), I–VII.

Stubbs, G. E. *How to sing the choral service. A manual of intoning for clergymen*. London, 1899.

Style, A. J. [Report of benefactions to the parish of Little Bookham.] *Surrey Archaeological Collections* x (1891), xxvii–xxx.

Survey of London. See London County Council.

Sutcliffe Smith, J. *The story of music in Birmingham*. Birmingham, 1945.

Sutton, F. H. *Church organs: their position and construction*. 3rd edn London, 1883.

Swanson, J. P. *The use of the organ in the Church of England (1660–1800)*. Ph.D. dissertation, University of Minnesota, 1969.

Sydenham, C. *A christian, sober and plain exercitation on the two grand practical controversies of these times; infant-baptism, and singing of psalms*. London, 1653.

Sydenham, H. *The well-tuned cymball . . . A sermon, occasionally preached at the dedication of an organ lately set up at Bruton in Somerset*. London, 1637.

Sykes, N. *Church and state in England in the XVIIIth century*. Cambridge, 1934.

Sylvester, D. W. *Educational documents 800–1816*. London, 1970.

Taas, W. *The elements of music*. Aberdeen, 1787.

Tallmadge, W. H. 'Baptist monophonic and heterophonic hymnody in southern Appalachia.' *Yearbook for Inter-American Musical Research* XI (1975), 106–36.

Tans'ur, W. *A new musical grammar*. London, 1746.

Tate, N. *An essay for promoting of psalmody*. London, 1710.

Tate, N. & Brady, N. *A new version of the psalms of David, fitted to the tunes used in churches*. London, 1696. (See also PC 37, 48, 57.)

Tate, W. E. *The parish chest: a study of the records of parochial administration in England*. 2nd edn Cambridge, 1951.

Taylor, R. V. *The ecclesiae Leodienses*. London, 1875.

Taylor, T. F. *Thematic catalog of the works of Jeremiah Clarke*. Detroit Studies in Music Bibliography, no. 35. Detroit, 1977.

Telford, J. ed. *Letters of John Wesley*. 8 vol. London, 1931.

Temperley, N. 'The adventures of a hymn tune'. *The Musical Times* CXII (1971), 375–6, 488–9.

Temperley, N. 'John Playford and the metrical psalms'. *Journal of the American Musicological Society* XXV (1972), 331–78. (Referred to as 'Temperley, 1972a'.)

Temperley, N. 'Kindred and affinity in hymn tunes'. *The Musical Times* CXIII (1972), 905–9. (Referred to as 'Temperley, 1972b'.)

Temperley, N. 'Tuning and temperament'. *Encyclopedia Britannica*, 15th edn (1974), XIII, 741–3.

Temperley, N. 'Middleburg psalms'. *Studies in Bibliography* XXX (1976), 162–70.

Temperley, N. *Jonathan Gray and church music in York*. Borthwick Institute of Historical Research: St Anthony's Hall Publications, no. 51. York, 1977.

Temperley, N. 'Croft and the charity hymn.' *The Musical Times* CXIX (1978),

539–41.

Temperley, N. 'Organs in English parish churches.' *The Organ Yearbook* (forthcoming).

Temperley, N. 'Psalms, Metrical'. In Grove (forthcoming).

Thiselton-Dyer, T. F. *Church-lore gleanings*. London, 1891.

Thomas, J. H. 'Parish registers in the Uxbridge deanery.' *The Antiquary* XVIII (1888), 17–20.

Thompson, A. H. *Parish history and records*. Historical Association Pamphlet, no. 66, revised edn London, 1926.

Thompson, A. H. *Song-schools in the Middle Ages*. Church Music Society Occasional Papers, no. 14. [London], 1942.

Thompson, E. M. & Frere, W. H. eds. *Registrum Matthei Parker*. Canterbury and York Society Publications, no. 63. [London], 1928.

Thompson, W. *The history and antiquities of the collegiate church of St. Saviour, Southwark*. London, 1894.

Thoresby, R. *The diary of Ralph Thoresby*, ed. J. Hunter. 2 vol. London, 1830.

Thorp, C. *The churchman's song of praise. A sermon preached upon the opening of the organ in Gateshead church*. Newcastle[-upon-Tyne], 1824.

Thoughts on the use and advantages of music. See Hanway, T.

Thureau-Dangin, P. (translated W. Wilberforce) *The English Catholic revival in the nineteenth century*. (Paris, 1899–1906). Revised edn 3 vol. London, 1914.

Tilmouth, M. 'A calendar of references to music in newspapers published in London and the provinces.' *Royal Musical Association Research Chronicle* I (1961), ii–vii, 1–107.

Torrington, John Byng, 5th Viscount. *The Torrington diaries (1781–1794)*, ed. C. B. Andrews. 4 vol. London, 1934–8.

Tottel, R. *Songes and sonettes*. London, 1557.

Toulmin, J. *The history of Taunton*. New edn enlarged by J. Savage. Taunton, 1822.

Towerson, G. *A sermon concerning vocal and instrumental musick in the church, as it was delivered in the parish church of St. Andrew, Undershaft, May 31st, 1696 . . . the day wherein the organ there erected was first made use of*. London, 1696.

A transcript of the register of the Worshipful Company of Stationers from 1640–1708 A.D. 3 vol. London, 1913–14.

Trask, H. E. 'The last of the church bands.' *Dorset Year Book 1945/6*, 126–9.

Trumble, E. *Fauxbourdon: an historical survey. Vol. I*. Institute of Mediaeval Music Musicological Studies, no. 3. Brooklyn (New York), 1959.

Twining, T. *Recreations and studies of a country clergyman of the 18th century*. London, 1882.

Tye, C. *The actes of the apostles, translated into Englyshe metre*. [London], 1553. (STC 2984.)

Vaux, J. E. *Church folk-lore: a record of some post-Reformation usages in the English Church now mostly obsolete*. 2nd edn London, 1902.

Victoria history of the county of Lancashire. Vol. IV. London, 1911.

Victoria history of the county of Leicester. Vol. V. London, 1964.

Victoria history of the county of Stafford. Vol. III. London, 1970.

Victoria history of the county of York. Vol. III. London, 1913.

Views of the parish churches in York. York, 1831.

Vincent, W. *Considerations on parochial music*. London, 1787. 2nd edn London, 1790.

Waddams, H. M. 'Liturgy and music.' *English Church Music* III, n.s. (1965), 18–22.

Wakefield, Bishop of. Committee on Church Choirs. See 'Church choirs in the diocese of Wakefield.'

Walker, E. *A history of music in England*. Oxford, 1907.

Wallcott, M. E. C. *The history of the parish church of St. Margaret in Westminster*.

Westminster, 1847.

Wallcott, M. E. C., Coates, R. P. & Scott Robertson, W. A. 'Inventories of parish church goods in Kent, A.D. 1552.' *Archeologia Cantiana,* VIII (1972), 74–163; IX (1874), 266–84; X (1876), 282–97; XI (1877), 409–16.

Walter, T. *The grounds and rules of musick explained, or an introduction to the art of singing by note.* Boston (Massachusetts), 1721.

Walters, H. B. *London churches at the Reformation.* London, 1939.

Ward, J. 'Music for *A handefull of pleasant delites.*' *Journal of the American Musicological Society* X (1957), 151–80.

Ward, J. 'The lute music of MS Royal Appendix 58.' *Journal of the American Musicological Society* XIII (1960), 117–25.

Warner, R. *The Book of Common Prayer* [annotated]. London, 1806.

Warton, T. *The history of English poetry.* 4 vol. London, 1774–81.

Watson, F. *The English grammar school to 1660.* Cambridge, 1908.

Watts, Isaac. *Hymns and spiritual songs.* 3 vol. London, 1707–9.

Watts, Isaac. *The psalms of David imitated in the language of the New Testament.* London, 1719.

Webb, S. & B. *English local government.* Vol. I, 'The parish and the county'. London, 1906.

[Webbe, S.] *An essay or instruction for learning the church plain chant.* London, 1782.

Wesley, C. *The journal of the Rev. Charles Wesley,* ed. T. Jackson, rev. J. Telford. 2 vol. London, 1909.

[Wesley, J.] *A collection of tunes, set to music, as they are commonly sung at the Foundery.* London, 1742.

[Wesley, J.] *Select hymns with tunes annext.* London, 1761. The musical portion repr. as *Sacred melody,* [1765].

[Wesley, J.] *Sacred harmony.* [London, 1780.]

Wesley, J. *The journal of John Wesley,* ed. N. Curnock. 8 vol. London, 1909–16.

Wesley, J. Letters. See Telford, J.

Wharton, R. *An essay on psalmody, considered as part of the public worship.* 2nd edn London, 1791.

What can be done for church music? being a critique on the 'Parish Choir'. Repr. from *The Oxford and Cambridge Review.* London, 1846.

Wheatly, C. *The Church of England man's companion: A rational illustration of the book of common prayer,* 2nd edn, Oxford, 1714.

White, J. F. *The Cambridge Movement.* Cambridge, 1962.

[Whitefield, G.] *The divine musical miscellany.* London, [1754].

Whitefield, G. *The works of the Rev. George Whitefield.* 6 vol. London, 1771–2.

Whitley, W. T. *Congregational hymn singing.* London, 1933.

[Whittingham, William ?] *A brieff discours off the troubles begonne at Franckford in Germany Anno Domini 1554.* [Zurich?], 1575. See Arber (1907); Collinson.

Wickham Legg, J. See Legg, J. W.

Wicks, A. 'Towards the relevant – in church music.' *The Modern Churchman* VIII n.s. (1964–5), 80–3.

Wienandt, E. A. & Young, R. H. *The anthem in England and America.* New York, 1970.

Williams, C. F. A. *The story of the organ.* London, 1916.

Williams, N. P. & Harris, C. *Northern Catholicism.* London, 1933.

Williams, P. F. *English organ music and the English organ under the first four Georges.* Ph.D. dissertation, University of Cambridge, 1962.

Williams, T. *A treatise on singing.* London, 1834.

Wilson, F. W. *The importance of the reign of Queen Anne in English Church history.* Oxford, 1911.

Wing, D. G. comp. *Short-title catalogue . . . 1641–1700*. New York, 1945.

Wither, G. *A preparation to the psalter*. London, 1619.

Wither, G. *Psalmes of David translated as lyricke verse*. London, 1632. (STC 2735.)

[Wollaston, C.] *A collection of psalms from the New Version*. 2nd edn East Dereham, 1813.

Woodforde, J. *The diary of a country parson*, ed. J. Beresford. 5 vol. London, 1924–31.

Wood, A. à. *Athenae Oxonienses*. 4 vol. London, 1813–20.

Wood-Legh, K. L. *Perpetual chantries in Britain*. Cambridge, 1965.

[Woodward, J.] *An account of the rise and progress of the religious societies* (1697). [2nd edn] London, 1698. 3rd edn, enlarged. London, 1701.

Words of the anthems used at the parish church of St. John the Evangelist, Preston. Preston, 1859. (Copy: Cambridge University Library, MR230.e.85.3.)

Worley, G. *Southwark cathedral*. London, 1905.

The worship of the Church, being the report of the Archbishop's second committee of inquiry. London, 1918.

Wren Society [Publications]. 20 vol. Oxford, 1924–43.

Yates, R. *The Church in danger*. London, 1816.

Yeats-Edwards, P. *English church music: a bibliography*. London, 1975.

The York psalm and hymn book. [A combined revised edition of W. Richardson, *A collection of psalms*, and J. Gray, *Hymns*.] York, 1839.

Zahn, J. *Die Melodien der deutschen evangelischen Kirchenlieder*. 6 vol. Hildesheim, 1963.

Zurich letters. See Robinson, H.

Index

a cappella ideal 241, 248–9, 253–4, 257–9, 321
Aarau (Switzerland) 27
Aachen, Council of (816–17) 7
Accession service 47–8, 165
Act against Conventicles (1664) 84
Act for Regulating Select Vestries (1663) 84, 113–15
Act of Uniformity (1549) 14, 46; (1552) 16, 26, 46; (1559) 39, 46, 57; (1662) 84, 105
Act of Uniformity Amendment Act (1872) 48, 294
Adams, Abraham (pst of Shoreham, Kent, c. 1752–90) 164n., 176, 190, PC 139, 146, 174
Addington, Stephen (1729–96, Independent minister and pst) 190, 212–13, 240, PC 239, 298
Addison, Joseph (1672–1719, writer) 57, 145,156; metrical psalm versions 123, 232; see also Spectator
'Adeste fideles' 212, 236, 245
advowson (the right to present the incumbency of a parish on its next falling vacant) 206, 207
aesthetes 273, 320
Agnus Dei 271, 272, 294, 295, 333
Ainsworth, Henry (1571–1622, pastor of an English Separatist community at Amsterdam) 56, PC 703
Airy, Basil R. (1845–1924, v. St John, Torquay, 1886–1924) 282
Akeroyde, Samuel (fl. 1685–1700, composer) 164n., 166
Alcock, Dr John (1715–1806, composer; o. St Andrew, Plymouth, 1737–41; St Lawrence, Reading, 1741–9; Lichfield cathedral, 1749–60; Sutton Coldfield, 1761–86; Tamworth, 1766–90) 134, 136, 160; PC 126, 161, 207, 295a
Alcock, John jun. (c. 1740–91, o. Newark, 1756–68; Walsall, 1773–91) 136, 150; PC 232, 234, 295a
Aldborough (Yorks, E.R.) 51
Aldingbourne (Sussex) 157
Aldrich, Henry (1647–1710, dean

of Christ Church, Oxford; composer) 88, 177, 272, PC 330
Alexander, Mrs Cecil Frances, née Humphreys (1818–95, hymn writer) 265, ex. 75
Allegri, Gregorio (1582–1652, Italian composer) 249
Allen, Sir Hugh P. (1869–1946, o. New College, Oxford, 1901–18) 331
Allison, Richard (fl. 1592–1606, composer) 37, 61, 68, 71
Almondbury (Yorks, W.R.) 142
altars 153, 251–2, 254, 256, 316, 317
Alternative Services (services differing from the prayer book, permitted after 1965, called Series 1, 2, 3) 335–6, 357; provision for music 330, 338; music for 336, 347, 357–8
alto voice 187, 189–90, 198
amens, sung 15, 293–4, 295, 328, ex. 66
American organ (type of metal-reed organ similar to harmonium) 311
American psalmody see psalmody: American
Amersham (Bucks) PC 35
Amish singing 96
Amsterdam (Holland) 56, PC 703
Anchors, William (fl. 1726, pst) PC 92
'Ancient Concerts' (Concerts of Ancient Music, London) 245, 247, 352
Andrewes, Lancelot (1555–1626, bishop of Winchester, 1618–26) 50, 127
'Anglican' party (16th c.) (moderate reformers and humanists) 39–42, 50; among Marian exiles 27, 28, 30–3, 43; influence on p.c.m. 32, 55; see also 'high church' party
Anglican revival (1800–50) 204, 246, 268
Anglicans, under Mary Tudor 27, 28, 30–3; under the Commonwealth 77–8
Anglo-Catholic party (alliance of

Tractarians and conservative high churchmen after c. 1850) 269–73; strife with Evangelicals 270, 319; divides into two camps 316: ritual innovations 269–70, 294, 316–17, 325
effect on p.c.m. 271–3, 294–5, 308, 325, 333; views resemble Evangelicals' 275–6, 286
Anne, reign of (1702–14) 103, 110–11, 123, 127, Pl. 5
ante-communion (the first part of the communion service, used alone when there is no sacrament) 44, 48, 153, 294
anthems (through-composed settings of English sacred texts, usually prose, for use by church choirs) 49; authorised by Elizabeth I 40; disapproved of 79, 213–14, 254; performed before or after service 39, 49, 163, 165; after the collects 49; during communion 165, 330; for special occasions 102, 111, 160, 165, 339–40
cathedral type, sung in parish churches 102, 160, 165, 167, 177, 200, 224, 225, 250, 289–90; adapted for parochial use 288–9; models for parochial anthems 165, 167, 195
parochial type, before 1570 15, 24, 53, ex. 6a; 1700–1840 in town churches 111, 126, 230, 287, ex. 25; 1700–1840 in country churches 161, 163–7, 169, 190–6, 235–6, 287, exx. 28–35
parochial/cathedral type (1840 to the present) 239, 287, 288–9, 320, 329–30
with metrical text 47, 165–7, 289, see also 'set pieces'
Anthony, Christopher (15th c. composer) ex. 1
antiphon (verse added to prose psalms as refrain) 332
antiquarianism 244–9, 346, see also revival of early music
ap Rhys, Philip (early 16th c.

416

Index

Index

Index

Index

Index

tunes, English (*continued*)
Glassenburie (F. 109) 68, 70n., ex. 14; Hanover 124, 236, 237, 245; Helmsley 212, 236, ex. 46; Hollingside 306, ex. 72; Hotham 212, ex. 45; Hursley 302, 310; Innocents 265; Irby 265; Irish 236; Kentish (F. 111) 74, 83, ex. 14; Kerry 310, ex. 81b; Kingsfold 324; Litany of the Last Four Things 307; Litchfield *see* London (ii); London (i) (F. 45) 67, 68, 69n., 71, *see also* Southwell; London (ii) (F. 25) 74, 75, 83; London Long (F. 392) 83; London New (F. 222) 125, 236, exx. 52, 82; London Old *see* London (ii); Love Divine 309; Low Dutch (F. 19) 68, 70n., 73, 74, 75, 83, ex. 15b; Lux Eoi 300, 309; Magdalen (i) *see* London New; Magdalen (ii) *see* Evening Hymn; Manchester (F. 246a) 125, 131, ex. 81a; Mariners *see* Sicilian Mariners; Martyrs (F. 209) 49, 70, 71, 83, 96; Meer 125; Melcombe 313; Melita 309; Melton Mowbray 307; Mere 125; Miles Lane 302; Miserere 308, ex. 79; Morning Hymn 236, 237; Mount Ephraim 236, 265; Nativity 301; Nayland *see* St Stephen's; New Town *see* London New; New Verse (F. 394) 83; Newland 307, ex. 75; Nicaea 309; Noel 300; Norwich 170, ex. 36; Oakingham 125; Oxford 49, 67, 68, 69–70, 70n., 75, 83, ex. 14 descants to 74, ex. 14; Paradise 301, ex. 70; Pause (F. 391) 83; Petra 308; Portuguese Hymn (Portugal New, Adeste fideles) 212, 236, 237, 245; Praise my soul 309; Rest 307, ex. 78; Rockingham 176; St Albans 125; St Andrew of Crete 304; St Anne's 124, 125, 310, ex. 83; St Clement 300, 309, ex. 69; St David's (F. 234) 70, 124, 125, 130, exx. 19–22; St Edmund 265; St Francis ex. 80; St Gertrude 309; St

Helen 309; St Helena *see* Mount Ephraim; St James('s) 125, 132, ex. 23; St Mary (F. 333) 125, 329; St Matthew 124, 245; St Peter (F. 154b) 125; St Philip 343, ex. 93b; St Prisca 308; St Stephen('s) 236; St Thomas 176; Salisbury (F. 143 b) 71; Sanctuary 308; Savoy 236; Scot(t)ish 69; Shirland 236, 237; Sicilian Mariners 236, 237; Sicily *see* Sicilian Mariners; Sine nomine (ii) 323, 324, 325, ex. 87; Southwell (F. 45) 71, 94, 142, ex. 16; Southwell New 125; Stabat Mater No. 2 304; Sterling 168; Strength and Stay 307, ex. 74; Suffolk *see* Evening Hymn; Tallis *see* Evening Hymn; The Foe 307; Thornbury 309; Upminster ex. 41; Wareham 176, 236, exx. 44, 55; Warrington 176; Watford ex. 43; Wesley 265; Westminster (i) (F. 362c) 71, 125, 142; Westminster (ii) 265; Winchester (F. 103) 59, 68, 71, 83; Windsor (or Eton) (F. 129) 67, 68, 69, 70n., 74, 83, 96, 125, exx. 15a, 18; York (F. 205) 70, 83, 94, 96, 124, 125, ex. 17
Turle, James (1802–82, o. Westminster Abbey, 1831–75) 265, 291, 292
Turner, William (1651–1740, composer) 163, 168, ex. 31a
twentieth century 315–43, 347–8, 353–8, exx. 85–93
Twentieth Century Church Light Music Group 334, 341
Twining, Thomas (1734–1804, r. St Mary, Colchester, 1770–1804) 74
Twydall (Kent) Holy Trinity Pl. 38
Tye, Christopher (*c.* 1500 – *c.* 1573, composer) 12, 247
Actes of the Apostles (1553) 54, 60, 70

Ubley (Som.) 90, 143, 145, MS 84
ultramontane party 316–17
unreformed church music (18th–19th c.) 138–9, 238–42
Urbs beata Jerusalem (hymn) 265

Valentine (*fl.* 1731, o. Ludlow) 349

Valentine, Henry (*fl.* 1710, organ builder) 102
Valentine, John (*fl.* 1765–85, composer of Leicester) PC 257
vamphorn (plain horn to amplify voice) 198
Vaughan Williams, Ralph (1872–1958) 322; editor of hymn books 322–5, 339, PC 411, 414, 415; critic of Victorian hymn tunes 303, 323, 323n.; views on hymn singing 323, 324, 325; use of folk songs as hymn tunes 304, 323–4, 346
liturgical music 333; hymn tunes 323, 325, 343, ex. 87; orchestral setting of 'Old Hundredth' 329
Veni creator spiritus 55, 219, 246
Venite (Ps. 95) 12, 220, 275, 291, exx. 2, 62; metrical 32, 55
Venn, Henry (1725–97, Evangelical v. Huddersfield, 1759–71) 215, 223
Verdi, Giuseppe (1813–1901) 303, 313
Vermigli, Pietro Martire ('Peter Martyr') (1500–62, Italian protestant, in England 1547–53) 16, 43
Vernon (after 1813, Harcourt), Edward (1757–1847, archbishop of York, 1807–47) 209
Vernon, G. V. (chancellor of York diocese, 1820) 208
vespers 7
vestiarian controversy (1563–8) 40–1, 252
vestments 16, 28, 39, 41, 251–2, 279
vestries (governing bodies of parishes) 84, 90, 106, 109–18, 283–4, 335; corruption in 115, 116–17; vote money for music 109, 110, 115, 225–6, 228; reluctant to spend money on music 52, 109, 225–6, 283–4; *see also* general vestries, select vestries
vestries (robing rooms) 152, 153
vicars *see* incumbent
Victoria, Tomás L. de (*c.* 1535–1611, Spanish composer) 248
Victoria, Queen (1819–1901), reign of (1837–1901) 244–314; Victorian desire for progress 277; religious zeal 250, 268, 346; love of grandeur 277; complexity of patterns of worship 268; evolution of new mode of worship 268–9, 276–7

Index